# The Lotus Guide

*LOTUS BOOKS* Pathways to Mastery

## Who Should Read This Book

For novice to advanced-intermediate users. This book helps you quickly master LotusWorks for immediate business results. Here you'll find countless new ways to be productive with the powerful wordprocessing, spreadsheet, database, and communications services in LotusWorks.

## What's Inside:

- Accessible, incisive tutorials covering all the new features in LotusWorks 3.0 and a wealth of shortcuts, good ideas, and tips to extend your computing skills
- Special work-saving techniques for automating office tasks
- Practical examples that you can use right out of the book
- Suggestions and strategies for creating custom applications that suit your business needs

## About *LOTUS BOOKS*

*LOTUS BOOKS*, written in collaboration with Lotus Development Corporation, help you derive the most from Lotus software. These books comprise four series:

**Start Here** books introduce beginning users to Lotus software with simple step-by-step instructions.

**Pathways to Mastery** titles provide the authoritative perspective and expertise from Lotus. Each book is a fast-paced, clear, and concise guide that helps you build on what you know and teaches new product features quickly.

**Business Solutions** books concentrate on using software to meet your specific business and professional needs; they provide essential tools for working faster and smarter.

**Technical Reference** titles provide advanced information for experts, programmers, and applications developers.

# The Lotus Guide to LotusWorks

Bill Harrison, Jr.

Brady Publishing

*LOTUS BOOKS*

New York   London   Toronto   Sydney   Tokyo   Singapore

Copyright © 1992 Bill Harrison, Jr.
All rights reserved,
including the right of reproduction
in whole or in part in any form.

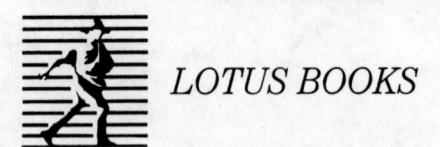

*LOTUS BOOKS*

Published by Brady Publishing
A division of Prentice Hall Computer Publishing
in association with Lotus Publishing Corporation.

Manufactured in the United States of America

10 9 8 7 6 5 4 3 2 1

ISBN: 0-13-539396-5

## Limits of Liability and Disclaimer of Warranty

The authors and publisher of this book have used their best efforts in preparing this book and the programs contained in it. These efforts include the development, research, and testing of the theories and programs to determine their effectiveness. The authors and publisher make no warranty, expressed or implied, with regard to these programs or the documentation contained in this book. The authors and publisher shall not be liable in any event for incidental or consequential damages in connection with, or arising out of, the furnishing, performance, or use of these programs.

## Trademarks

LotusWorks is a registered trademark of Lotus Development Corporation.

# Contents

| | | |
|---|---|---|
| **Foreword** | | xv |
| **Preface** | | xvii |
| **Chapter 1:** | **Putting LotusWorks to Work for You** | 1 |
| | A Launchpad for Personal Productivity | 1 |
| | What LotusWorks 3.0 Can Do for You | 2 |
| | Limits of LotusWorks 3.0 | 3 |
| | How to Upgrade from Previous Versions | 5 |
| | Maximizing Your Personal Productivity | 5 |
| |     Set Work-saving as a Goal | 6 |
| |     Make LotusWorks Your Silent Partner | 7 |
| |     Analyze Your Paperwork | 7 |
| |     Organize Your Files | 8 |
| |     Use the Same Data Over and Over | 12 |
| |     Save Your Setups | 13 |
| |     Automate Everything You Can | 13 |
| |     Create Your Own Tools and Menus | 13 |
| |     Keep Everything Clear and Simple | 14 |
| |     Take It Easy | 14 |
| | How to Use This Guide | 14 |
| **Chapter 2:** | **Getting Going Quickly** | 17 |
| | Equipment Considerations | 17 |
| |     Computers, Computer Memory, and Disk Storage | 18 |
| |     Monitors | 19 |
| |     Printers | 19 |
| |     Pointing Devices | 19 |
| |     Modems | 20 |
| |     Local Area Networks | 21 |
| | Installing LotusWorks 3.0 | 21 |

| | |
|---|---|
| Starting LotusWorks 3.0 | 23 |
| The Start-up and LotusWorks Screens | 23 |
| The LotusWorks 3.0 Window Design | 24 |
| Using Combination Keys | 26 |
| Using a Mouse or Other Pointing Device | 26 |
| Moving Around in LotusWorks | 27 |
| Issuing Commands | 27 |
|     Menus, Submenus, and Dialog Boxes | 28 |
|     Selecting Menu and Submenu Items | 29 |
|     Using Accelerator Keys | 30 |
|     Dimmed Menu Items | 30 |
|     Using Dialog Boxes | 31 |
|     Accelerator Key Cues | 36 |
|     Exiting Submenus and Dialog Boxes | 36 |
|     Command Sequences | 37 |
| Opening a Service | 37 |
| Entering Data | 37 |
| Correcting Typing Mistakes | 38 |
| Saving Your Work | 38 |
| Retrieving a Saved File | 39 |
| Scrolling the Window Contents | 40 |
|     Scrolling from the Keyboard | 40 |
|     Scrolling with a Mouse | 41 |
| Working with Multiple LotusWorks Windows | 42 |
|     Opening a New Task Window | 43 |
|     Switching Windows | 43 |
|     Sizing and Moving Windows | 43 |
|     Closing Windows | 45 |
| Getting Help On-Screen | 45 |
| Using DOS Access | 47 |
| A Brief Tour of the Menus | 48 |
|     The LotusWorks Menu Item | 48 |
|     The Common Menus | 49 |
|     The Service-Specific Menus | 51 |
| Changing the Default Setup | 51 |
| Safeguarding Your Data | 53 |
| Exiting from LotusWorks | 54 |

| Chapter 3: | **Writing Well with Word Processing** | **57** |
|---|---|---|
| | Working Smart with Word Processing | 57 |
| | Elements of Economical Writing | 59 |
| |     Putting Thoughts into Writing | 59 |
| |     Putting Writing into Good Form | 61 |
| | Techniques for Sharing the Workload | 62 |
| | Creating and Printing a Word Document | 64 |
| | Starting a Word Document | 64 |
| | Setting Up and Saving Document Formats | 67 |
| | Saving Word Documents | 71 |
| | Previewing Documents | 72 |
| | Working with Text Blocks | 73 |
| |     Selecting Blocks of Text | 73 |
| |     Canceling a Text Selection | 73 |
| | Revising Your Writing: Copying, Cutting, and Pasting Text | 74 |
| |     Deleting Text | 74 |
| |     Restoring Text Deletions | 75 |
| | Assigning Type Attributes: Bold, Italic, and Underlining | 75 |
| | Creating Headers and Footers | 76 |
| |     Entering a Header or Footer | 76 |
| |     Specifying a Starting Page for a Header or Footer | 78 |
| |     Editing a Header or Footer | 78 |
| |     Deleting a Header or Footer | 78 |
| | Automatically Printing Dates and Times | 78 |
| | Automatically Numbering Pages, Figures, and Tables | 79 |
| | Setting Initial Numbers | 80 |
| | Hyphenating and Keeping Words Together | 81 |
| | Controlling Page Breaks | 82 |
| | "Intelligent" Editing | 82 |
| |     Checking Your Spelling | 82 |
| |     Finding Synonyms | 85 |
| |     Searching for and Replacing Text | 87 |
| |     Combining Word Documents | 89 |
| |     Including Graphs and Spreadsheet Data in Word Documents | 90 |
| | Printing Word Documents | 92 |

|  |  |
|---|---|
| Mail-Merge | 95 |
|     Creating a Master Document | 96 |
|     Printing Envelopes and Mailing Labels | 99 |
| Creating and Using Boilerplate | 100 |
| Creating and Using "Styles" | 101 |
| Using Multiple Windows | 102 |
| Example Documents | 102 |
|     Memo | 102 |
|     Letters | 103 |
|     Reports | 104 |
| Launching Documents with Macros | 107 |
| A Final Word About Word processing | 107 |

## Chapter 4: Managing Your Necessary Data — 109

|  |  |
|---|---|
| Working Smart with Databases | 109 |
| Four Steps to Efficient Data Use | 111 |
| When to Use a Database | 112 |
| Designing Databases | 113 |
|     Five Types of Data Fields | 114 |
| Setting Up and Testing Databases | 116 |
|     Creating the Database File and Fields | 116 |
|     Entering Data and Testing the Database | 117 |
|     Modifying Fields | 121 |
|     Adding Fields | 122 |
|     Renaming Fields | 122 |
|     Deleting Fields | 122 |
| Using Rules to Ease Data Entry | 123 |
|     Types of Field Rules | 124 |
| Using Forms for Data Entry | 129 |
|     Advantages of Data Entry Forms | 129 |
| Viewing Data | 130 |
|     Viewing Data in Tables | 133 |
|     Viewing Data in Forms | 133 |
| Finding the Records You Want | 134 |
|     Conducting a Search | 134 |
|     Writing Search Expressions | 137 |
|     Compound Search Expressions | 138 |
|     Operators | 139 |

| | |
|---|---|
| Searching for Strings of Characters | 139 |
| Searching for Dates | 140 |
| Saving, Retrieving, and Deleting Search Criteria | 140 |
| Restoring Inactive Records | 141 |
| Deleting Records | 141 |
| Clearing Flagged Records | 143 |
| Creating a Sort Order | 143 |
| Sort Expressions | 143 |
| Creating a New Sort Order | 145 |
| Saving and Retrieving a Sort Order | 147 |
| Modifying a Sort Order | 147 |
| Deleting a Sort Order | 148 |
| Creating Custom Tables | 148 |
| Creating the Table | 149 |
| Retrieving a Custom Table | 151 |
| Modifying A Custom Table | 152 |
| Deleting a Custom Table | 152 |
| Creating a Print Layout for a Table | 153 |
| Creating a Summary Report Table | 155 |
| Creating Custom Forms | 162 |
| Using the Forms Editor | 166 |
| Retrieving a Form | 172 |
| Creating a Print Layout for a Form | 172 |
| Printing from Databases | 175 |
| Printing Tables | 175 |
| Printing Forms | 177 |
| Printing Labels | 179 |
| Merge Printing (Mail-Merge) | 181 |
| Copying Data from One Database to Another | 181 |
| Appending Records from Another Database | 182 |
| Extracting Records to a New Database | 182 |
| Using Data from External Databases | 183 |
| Using Macros with Databases | 185 |
| Dialing and Logging Telephone Calls from a Database | 187 |
| Modifying the Address Example Database | 188 |
| Accessing the Q_ADDRS Database | 189 |
| Adding a Field | 189 |
| Deleting a Field | 191 |
| Creating a Telephone Log Table | 192 |
| Composing with Database Functions | 194 |

|  |  |  |
|---|---|---|
| | Syntax | 194 |
| | The IF Function | 195 |
| | A Final Word About Databases | 196 |

## Chapter 5: Saving Work With Numbers — 197

|  |  |
|---|---|
| Working Smart with Spreadsheets | 197 |
| When to Use a Spreadsheet | 199 |
| Spreadsheet Terms | 200 |
| Designing Spreadsheets | 203 |
| Setting Up and Saving Spreadsheets | 204 |
|     Building a Practice Spreadsheet | 205 |
|     Entering Text and Numbers into Cells | 207 |
|     Selecting Cells and Ranges for Further Action | 208 |
|     Editing Data | 209 |
|     Erasing the Contents of a Cell or Range | 210 |
|     Creating, Viewing, and Deleting Range Names | 211 |
|     Changing Number Formats | 213 |
|     Adjusting Column Widths | 217 |
|     Inserting Rows and Columns | 218 |
|     Deleting Rows and Columns | 219 |
|     Copying Data | 220 |
|     Moving Data | 222 |
| Creating Spreadsheet Formulas | 224 |
|     Writing Spreadsheet Formulas | 224 |
|     Entering Formulas | 225 |
|     Using Cell Pointing | 226 |
|     Operators | 226 |
|     Order of Precedence in Spreadsheet Formula Calculations | 228 |
|     Copying and Moving Formulas | 229 |
|     Saving Work with Relative, Absolute, and Mixed Cell References | 229 |
|     Converting Formulas to Values | 231 |
|     Finding Cells by Value or Formula | 232 |
|     Recalculating Spreadsheets | 233 |
|     Using Spreadsheet @Functions | 235 |
|     The @IF Function | 236 |
|     Entering Dates and Times | 237 |
|     Performing Data and Time Math | 239 |
| Tailoring the Appearance of Spreadsheets | 240 |

| | |
|---|---|
| Setting Titles | 240 |
| Hiding and Unhiding Columns and Cells | 241 |
| Aligning Labels within Columns | 242 |
| Creating a Line in a Cell or Row | 242 |
| Sorting Rows Based on Data | 243 |
| Protecting and Unprotecting Cells and Spreadsheets | 246 |
| Printing Reports from Spreadsheets | 247 |
| Using Multiple Ranges within a Spreadsheet | 251 |
| Viewing Through Window Panes | 251 |
| Using Lookup Tables | 253 |
| Combining Data from Other Spreadsheets | 255 |
| Using Macros with Spreadsheets | 257 |
| Creating and Running Spreadsheet Macros | 257 |
| Editing Spreadsheet Macros | 261 |
| Importing and Exporting Spreadsheet Data | 261 |
| Importing Spreadsheet Data | 261 |
| Exporting Spreadsheet Data to a DIF File | 262 |
| Copying Data To and From the Word Processing Service | 263 |
| Modifying the LotusWorks Quickstart Spreadsheets | 264 |
| Example Spreadsheets | 265 |
| A Daily Appointment Schedule and To-Do List | 265 |
| A Loan Amortization Schedule | 269 |
| A Calculator for Business Financial Ratios | 273 |
| An Interactive Financial Statement | 280 |
| Spreadsheet Ideas | 289 |
| A Final Word About Spreadsheets | 290 |

## Chapter 6: Making Numbers Graphic    291

| | |
|---|---|
| Saying It with Graphs | 292 |
| Choosing the Right Graph | 293 |
| Data Ranges for Graphs | 299 |
| Line, Bar, and Stacked Bar Graphs | 299 |
| XY Graphs | 299 |
| Pie Charts | 300 |
| Generating Graphs | 301 |
| Specifying the Graph Type | 301 |
| Specifying the Data Ranges | 303 |

| | | |
|---|---|---|
| Selecting and Deselecting Symbols and Lines | | 304 |
| Previewing the Basic Graph | | 304 |
| Adding Titles, Data Labels, Legends, and Grids | | 305 |
|     Legends | | 305 |
|     Titles | | 306 |
|     Data labels | | 306 |
| Scale | | 310 |
|     Adjusting the Scale | | 310 |
|     Suppressing the Scale Unit Indicator | | 311 |
|     Using a Skip Factor to Reduce Crowding on the X-Axis | | 312 |
|     Formatting Numbers on the X- and Y-Axes | | 312 |
|     Quitting the Graph Options Submenu and Reviewing Your Work | | 313 |
|     Grid Lines | | 313 |
|     Naming and Saving Graphs | | 314 |
|     Retrieving Graphs | | 315 |
| Printing Graphs | | 315 |
| Bringing Graphs into Word Processing Documents | | 316 |
| Examples | | 317 |
|     Where Our $$ Come From, Where Our $$ Go | | 317 |
|     Break-Even Calculator | | 320 |
| Graphic Ideas | | 324 |
| A Final Word About Graphs | | 325 |

## Chapter 7: Telecommunicating — 327

| | |
|---|---|
| Using PC Communications to Work Smart | 327 |
|     Resources | 327 |
|     Accessing the Resources | 331 |
| A Brief Introduction to Data Communications | 331 |
| Setting Up to Telecommunicate | 333 |
| Getting Connected | 335 |
|     Before You Begin... | 335 |
|     Preparing to Communicate | 336 |
|     Setting and Saving the Communications Parameters | 336 |
|     Dialing | 338 |
|     Answering | 341 |
| Disconnecting | 341 |

Contents **xiii**

| | |
|---|---|
| Interrupting a Data Transfer | 342 |
| Viewing and Capturing the Communications Dialog | 342 |
|     Viewing the Communications History On-screen | 342 |
|     Capturing the Communications History in a File | 343 |
|     Viewing Communications Full-Screen | 344 |
| Sending and Receiving Data Files | 344 |
|     Sending | 345 |
|     Receiving | 346 |
|     A Note About Using Binary Protocols | 347 |
| Using Accelerator Keys in Communications | 347 |
| PC-to-PC Telecommunications | 348 |
| Composing and Sending E-Mail | 349 |
| Automating Dialups and Logins | 350 |
|     Recording a Login Script | 350 |
|     Using a Login Script | 352 |
|     Editing a Login Script | 352 |
|     Launching the Login Script with a Macro | 353 |
| Automating File and Text Transfers | 354 |
| Using Your PC as a Terminal | 355 |
| Examples | 356 |
|     A login script for PC-to-PC communications | 356 |
|     A login script and launching macro | 358 |
| Ideas for Telecommunications | 360 |
| A Final Word About Telecommunications | 363 |

**Chapter 8: Building Applications**   **365**

| | |
|---|---|
| Using Macros to Assemble Your Own Applications | 365 |
| Building a Custom Desktop Environment | 365 |
| Building an Automated Telephone Dialer and Log | 371 |
| Ideas for Other Custom Applications | 373 |
| A Final Word About Custom Applications | 373 |

**Appendices**

| | |
|---|---|
| A. Upgrading to LotusWorks 3.0 | 375 |
| B. Database Functions | 379 |
| C. Spreadsheet @ Functions | 409 |
| D. Macro Keynames | 449 |

# Foreword

## The *Lotus* Guide to LotusWorks Release 3.0

Thank you for your interest in LotusWorks Release 3.0. A team of Loti, as we call ourselves, has worked diligently for 18 months to bring you this product, which we believe represents the state-of-the-art in DOS applications software. We hope that you enjoy the fruits of our labors.

If you are just getting started, The Lotus Guide to LotusWorks Release 3.0, along with the advanced learning aids we supplied with the software, should have you up and running in no time.

If you are already familiar with LotusWorks, we're sure you'll agree that Release 3.0 is not "just another upgrade." It is more like, as my Scottish mother would say, "A new head and a new handle, but still the same old broom." For this major new release, we completely overhauled the LotusWorks user interface, adding pull down menus, dialog boxes, and an advanced windowing system, all without requiring megabytes of memory or hard disk capacity of monumental (and expensive) proportions. This new interface gives you much simpler access to the rich functionality of LotusWorks. We also added a superb electronic tutorial and greatly improved the word processing and printing aspects of the product. Finally, for those of you who know Lotus 1-2-3 or work with people who do, we made the LotusWorks spreadsheet much more like 1-2-3.

Our enhancements were based not on our own flights of fancy, but on interviews and focus groups involving roughly 350 people. We made a point of listening not only to experienced computer and LotusWorks users, but to people who swore they'd never use a PC because it's just too difficult. After hours of reviewing videotape, we let our creativity flow. The team came up with simple but innovative learning tools like selectable "Novice" and "Expert" menu options, which we affectionately call "training wheels." We also invented some useful features, such as movable dialog boxes, that are unavailable even in today's most powerful PC applications. The result is one of the best software values in the marketplace. LotusWorks delivers an impressive array of functionality via an intuitive interface, surrounded by an outstanding collection of learning tools, and does so at an extremely attractive price.

Lest you wonder why a large, global enterprise like Lotus would offer you such a compelling value, I'll tell you. It's not that our pencil sharpeners have lost their edge. The reason is that LotusWorks is among the first PC software products that many people, in fact well over one million so far, try to learn and use. We sincerely hope that each of our customers enjoys LotusWorks, and finds it to be productive, fun, and well worth the price paid. If that's the case for you, we hope you'll buy more Lotus products in the future. We also hope that we'll have helped you discover that personal computing can be a rewarding part of your professional or personal life. For those of us who devote most of our waking hours to staring at compiler messages, test scripts, bug reports, documentation files, and project schedules, that's what the late nights and weekends away from home are all about.

Bruce Johnston
General Manager
Lotus Development Corporation

# Preface

Welcome to *The Lotus Guide to LotusWorks*. This guide is dedicated to helping you save work. It helps you:

- learn the LotusWorks 3.0 functions and features
- analyze your work
- apply the powers of LotusWorks imaginatively to your work

This guide is for anyone who uses or is considering using LotusWorks 3.0. It complements the LotusWorks electronic tutorial and the written *User's Guide.* Whereas the tutorial and user guide emphasize individual functions, features, and procedures of LotusWorks 3.0, this guide focuses on how to apply the various LotusWorks powers to the work typically found in small-business, professional, and home offices.

You do not need to have any previous knowledge of LotusWorks or computers to use this guide.

Because there is much more to LotusWorks than anyone can learn at one sitting, this guide is designed to help you start performing useful work immediately and to add to your repertoire as you learn more about LotusWorks. It shows how to use LotusWorks and also how to organize workoads to get the most benefit from Lotus-Works 3.0.

You are encouraged to try the examples in this guide as you read about them. That practice will make the explanations more meaningful and help you learn faster.

It takes many hands to produce a useful book. I owe special thanks to Khan Lowe and Gene Thornton and their staffs at LotusWorks Development Corporation for their generous technical assistance and good ideas, to Jennifer Hooper for extraordinary technical editing, and to Susan Hunt of Brady Books for good ideas, unflagging good cheer, and exceptional patience.

I hope you have much pleasure using the new LotusWorks.

# 1

# Putting LotusWorks to Work for You

Welcome to LotusWorks 3.0! This guide is designed to help you get the most out of LotusWorks 3.0 in the shortest possible time. It shows how to operate and use LotusWorks 3.0, how to organize your work to get the most benefit from LotusWorks, and how to adapt many ready-made examples to your own needs.

## A Launchpad for Personal Productivity

You will find that LotusWorks 3.0 is an excellent multi-purpose computer tool for small business, professional, and home offices. It is flexible and easy to use, and it includes the software tools that these offices need most. You probably know already that LotusWorks 3.0 encompasses four common software systems: a word processor, an electronic spreadsheet and graphing system, a database management system, and a data communications system. Some people say LotusWorks is like a Swiss Army knife for PCs.

But LotusWorks 3.0 is much more than four separate tools. As you will see, it is a closely integrated system—a personal productivity environment—that lets you view and work on several projects with different tools (services) at once. You get the most out of LotusWorks 3.0 when you use the various services in combination with one another and when you use LotusWorks' powers to automate as many tasks as possible.

*In this chapter, you'll learn:*

- *The powers and limits of LotusWorks 3.0*
- *How to upgrade from earlier versions*
- *Ten principles for getting the most from LotusWorks 3.0*
- *How to use this guide*

> ### A Word to Computer Novices
>
> Many first-time computer users feel uneasy about learning computer terms and procedures. It is a natural feeling. Fortunately, it doesn't have to last long. This guide is designed to help you move quickly from novice to confident user. Once you get started, learning the jargon and procedures gets easier as you go along. Three things to remember:
>
> 1. **The computer is very literal.** It can only understand what you actually type, not what you intended to type. Take care to be precise in entering commands and data into the computer. If something doesn't work, check your typing first.
>
> 2. **Everyone makes mistakes, especially at first.** Don't worry, your mistakes won't harm the computer, and with some reasonable precautions that are explained in this guide, they won't harm either LotusWorks or your own data.
>
> 3. **Procedures that are hard to remember at first soon become second nature to you.** Once you start using them regularly, and especially when you start getting good results, you'll probably be surprised at how quickly the LotusWorks procedures become familiar to you.

# What LotusWorks 3.0 Can Do for You

Until you learn to use a tool, it's hard to know what it can do for you. LotusWorks 3.0 is no exception. The range of possible uses is hard to imagine at first. Here are some of the many things LotusWorks 3.0 can do for you.

- Store information (numbers and text) and let you use them over and over.
- Make calculations (add, subtract, multiply, divide, raise to a power, etc.) based on numbers, dates, and times of day.
- Update stored information with automatic calculations.
- Enable you to select stored items of information that meet certain criteria that you specify, such as "all the customers in New York" or "all invoices more than 30 days overdue," and then perform actions on these items.

- Format, store, and print documents that you write. Depending on the printer you install, you can use a variety of printers, type faces, type styles, and type sizes.
- Check your spelling.
- Help you find the right word to use (Thesaurus).
- Search for words and phrases and replace them with others that you specify.
- Copy or move parts of a document from one place to another or to another document entirely.
- Show on the screen how your documents will look when they're printed.
- Automatically address and insert stored information into form letters.
- Insert into documents automatically calculated information, such as dates and financial amounts.
- Create forms for entering and displaying data, such as a name-and-address card file or an employee data form.
- Display numbers in tables and graphs.
- Print labels and lists from stored information.
- Write simple formulas to perform complex statistical and financial calculations.
- Automatically number pages, tables, and figures in word processing documents. (LotusWorks will also count the words in a document for you.)
- Print one or more lines of text (including the date and page number) that appear as a "header" or "footer" at the top or bottom of successive pages of a document.
- Record a sequence of keystrokes or operations in a "macro" that LotusWorks performs automatically when you issue a single keystroke command.
- Automatically dial the telephone using a modem and connect to an on-line information service or another PC.
- Enable you to create a menu or series of menus to hold boilerplate, document formats, spreadsheets, databases, and applications you have created and then access these items from the menu(s).

## Limits of LotusWorks 3.0

As all things do, LotusWorks 3.0 has some limits. It is designed to be a general-purpose system for small businesses and home office use. Its functions and features are more than adequate for these purposes. The word processor, database management system, and electronic spreadsheet are quite powerful and flexible. Databases and worksheets are limited in size only by the amount of available file storage space you have on a hard disk or floppy disk. The system supports a wide range of printers and enough type styles and sizes to fit most business needs.

Word processing files can always contain at least 64,000 characters. In most business formats this amounts to approximately 20 to 30 pages. The maximum size of word processing files depends on the amount of available random access memory in your computer. The available RAM, in turn, depends on the amount of conventional computer memory being used by other application programs running at the same time as LotusWorks. The more you can devote the full 640K of conventional memory to LotusWorks, the larger the word processing files can be.

> If you ever come close to filling the available memory with a large word processing document, LotusWorks gives a low-memory warning and advises you to save the file.

Even with limited RAM, it is easy to have much larger documents by creating each document in parts, saving the parts in separate files, and having LotusWorks print them sequentially. For example, you can create a lengthy report in sections, save each section as a separate document, start each section's page numbers and table numbers where the previous section left off, and then print the sections to form a single report.

You might want to supplement LotusWorks 3.0 with other software if you have unusual or highly specialized needs. For instance, if you frequently need to publish highly complicated word processing documents involving footnotes, graphics, indexes, and/or tables of contents, you might want to consider a more specialized word processor such as Lotus's Ami Pro. You could still use LotusWorks 3.0 for database, spreadsheet, graphing, and communications purposes.

Similarly, if your small business requires unusually extensive spreadsheet functions or programming capabilities, you might need to use 1-2-3 for those purposes. (LotusWorks 3.0 can read 1-2-3 Version 2.3 spreadsheets, and vice versa. However, LotusWorks 3.0 cannot process 1-2-3 macros.) If you require multiple and linked databases or database applications requiring professional-level programming, you might need to consider a stand-alone database management system. If you need to make extensive high-style presentations, you might want to consider a stand-alone business graphics package, such as Lotus Freelance Plus. You can still use LotusWorks 3.0 for the tasks the stand-alone systems don't perform.

Most small businesses do not require such specialized systems. You will probably be surprised at how many tasks you can perform with LotusWorks 3.0 and how easily you can learn to perform them, especially considering the low price and modest computer requirements of 3.0.

## How to Upgrade from Previous Versions

LotusWorks 3.0 uses a different file structure for word processing documents from that used in previous versions. LotusWorks 3.0 can convert word processing files created in the previous versions, but the previous programs cannot read files created by LotusWorks 3.0.

There is no need to remove a previous version of LotusWorks before installing Version 3.0 unless you need the space on your hard disk. The installation program puts Version 3.0 into a separate directory (named \LWORKS3) unless you tell it to do otherwise. Once Version 3.0 is installed, you can upgrade any word processing files that are in your old directories and then delete the old programs and files. *If you decide to delete an old version before installing Version 3.0, be sure not to delete any word processing files that you want to upgrade.*

To convert word processing documents from previous versions for use with LotusWorks 3.0, run the Upgrade program and specify the files to be converted. See Appendix A of this guide for directions.

If you own an earlier version of LotusWorks or AlphaWorks, you can upgrade to LotusWorks 3.0 for substantially less than the cost of buying LotusWorks 3.0 outright. Contact Lotus sales for the latest prices.

# Maximizing Your Personal Productivity

Many PC users make the mistake of learning one or two tools and then using only those. That's okay as far as it goes, but it's settling for half the loaf. The more important objective is to increase your productivity as much as possible. LotusWorks enables you to do this in a variety of ways.

The key to using LotusWorks for maximum personal productivity is to plan for it. In principle, there are three steps that have to take place:

1. Learn the LotusWorks 3.0 features and functions.
2. Analyze your workload.
3. Apply the LotusWorks features and functions to your work.

In practice, you may do the steps in different orders or even do all three at once. As you learn LotusWorks, you will no doubt see some work-saving features you can apply immediately. Others may not occur to you until you gain more skill and familiarity with LotusWorks. In some cases you may have to modify your work procedure to take advantage of LotusWorks. In other cases you may first decide that you want to automate a particular aspect of your work and then study LotusWorks to find a way to do it.

How you analyze your workload and polish your procedures is mostly a matter of personal work style. If you want to maximize your productivity and get the most out of LotusWorks, what matters is to get in the habit of thinking about how to do it as you go along.

Productivity is a journey . . . not a destination. Here are 10 specific things you can—and should—do to start the journey. They will help you become a sophisticated user as soon as you begin using LotusWorks 3.0.

## 1. Set Work-saving as a Goal

Once you see some of the things LotusWorks 3.0 can do for you, the next step is to set work-saving as an ongoing goal.

Have you ever been in a hurry and thought, "It's easier just to do it by hand"? This is a common feeling, especially among people just learning to use a PC. Sometimes it may even be easier and quicker to do a task manually than to take the time to learn to set it up on the computer, especially if you're not sure about how to do it on the computer, anyway. If you keep this up, of course, you never get around to computerizing things. Understandable as it is, this attitude robs you of some of the PC's power to perform recurring tasks. These are the very tasks where the PC can help you the most.

A work-saving goal simply means an attitude of getting the PC to do as much work for you as possible. The way to acquire this attitude is to practice it. Set yourself the goal of working smart and getting the PC to do as much work for you as possible, then consciously focus on this goal as you learn to use LotusWorks 3.0. Pretty soon a work-saving attitude will become a good habit and part of your standard way of working with LotusWorks.

## 2. Make LotusWorks Your Silent Partner

Another way to get the most out of LotusWorks 3.0 is to make it your silent partner. You can view LotusWorks not just as an adjunct to your business or work but as an integral part of it. You can build it right into your standard procedures. Just as you design LotusWorks applications to fit your work, you can design your business and office practices to take advantage of the powers of LotusWorks.

If this seems daunting, don't let it be. You are the one who stands to benefit by being able to work smarter. It's mostly a matter of organizing your work in your own mind to enable LotusWorks to help you. The remaining numbered items below will help you integrate LotusWorks into your work.

## 3. Analyze Your Paperwork

The purpose of analyzing your paperwork is to identify work items that can benefit from LotusWorks automation. Don't be put off by the word "analyze." You don't have to get fancy. Just review the kind of paperwork you normally do—letters, memos, reports, etc.—and list on a sheet of paper the items to which LotusWorks might be applied. Here are some things to look for:

   a. **Formats.** Each type of document has a format that can be stored and used over and over. The documents may include memos, letters, form letters, forms, reports, product or service descriptions, fee schedules, price lists, brochures, or some such. You may find that you use more than one type of memo, letter, or report format. Don't worry about describing them at this point. Just list each separate document format that you can identify.

b. **Boilerplate.** Look for standard words, phrases, sentences, and paragraphs that you use repeatedly. LotusWorks can store these for you and let you use them without having to retype them each time. Add these to your list of candidates for LotusWorks automation. Examples might include your company name, a product name, a service, standard wording for proposals and agreements, standard greetings and closings in letters, and even entire form letters.

c. **Form Letters.** LotusWorks can individually address and merge variable information into standard form letters. If you have not already listed them, add to your list any individually addressed standard letters you send. Examples are sales letters, sales notices, requests for payment (dunning letters), teacher's letters to parents, and confirmations of doctor or dentist appointments.

d. **Lists.** LotusWorks can enable you to draw on lists of things in a variety of automated ways. If you have lists, these are candidates for inclusion. Examples are address lists, customer lists, lists of people who owe you money (accounts receivable), prospect lists, mailing lists, vendor lists, parts lists, class lists, and lists of your equipment, furniture, belongings, and other assets. Even your record of bank checks and deposits is a candidate.

e. **Financial Reports.** Financial reports that you prepare for others or for yourself are good candidates for your list. LotusWorks can store the setups and automate the calculations. Examples are profit-and-loss statements, fee calculations, office-expense journals, payment schedules, amortization schedules, break-even calculations, and lease-or-buy calculations.

f. **Things You're Not Doing.** Besides the items in your ordinary paperwork, look for things that you don't do currently (perhaps because of the amount of time and work involved) but you would like to. Examples could be any of the items above.

The list will help you get started. You will probably be able to add to it as you get more familiar with LotusWorks 3.0.

## 4. Organize Your Files

It is important for you and LotusWorks to be able to find your computer files easily. As with paper files, having your computer files organized in a coherent manner can save a lot of time and confusion. It can also save precious disk space. You won't actually build any computer files until you start using Lotus-

Works, but it's good to plan your file organization before you start building it. Here are 6 principles to follow:

a. **Keep the LotusWorks programs and your documents in separate subdirectories.** It's a good practice to store your document files and the LotusWorks program files in separate subdirectories on your hard disk. That way, when you need to remove data files from the disk, you're not likely to remove any program files by mistake. Toward this end, the LotusWorks 3.0 installation program automatically puts program files in a subdirectory called LWORKS3 and the document files in a subdirectory called LWORKS3\LWDATA, unless you tell it otherwise. It is possible to create further subdirectories of LWDATA.

---

### About MS-DOS Directories and Commands

If you are unfamiliar with MS-DOS directories and commands, you should learn them from your MS-DOS manual before going further. MS-DOS designates each disk drive in your computer system with a letter: A, B, C, D, E, etc. Typically, the first floppy disk drive is labeled Drive A; if you have a second floppy disk drive, it is labeled Drive B; the hard disk drive is usually labeled Drive C. If you have a local area network or a hard disk divided into separate virtual drives, you may have additional letters in your system. The disk drive is indicated on the screen with the "DOS Prompt," which looks like this: A> or C>.

Each floppy disk and hard disk has a directory that lists the names of the files contained on the disk. Each directory may also be divided into one or more subdirectories which, in turn, may be divided into further subdirectories. The disk is like a filing cabinet, and the subdirectories are like drawers and folders in the filling cabinet.

You can display the contents of a disk by typing the DIR command followed by the drive indicator at the DOS prompt (for example *DIR A:* or *Dir C:*) and pressing the Enter or Return key. You can create a new subdirectory with the MKDIR command (MD for short). Be sure to specify all the disk and subdirectory names in the path to the new subdirectory you are creating. For example, to create a subdirectory called DOCS within the LWORKS3 directory on Drive C, you would type *MD C:\LWORKS3\DOCS* and press the Enter key.

See your MS-DOS manual for more about DOS commands. See, especially, the instructions for the DIR (directory), COPY (copy), DEL (delete), FORMAT, MKDIR (make a directory), RMDIR (remove a directory), and XCOPY (copy a directory) commands and the instructions for using the * and ? wildcard characters in DOS commands.

---

b. **Keep setups and document formats in a subdirectory by themselves.** You will want to use "empty" letters, spreadsheets, and databases as templates for new documents. It's a good practice to keep these in a separate subdirectory so that they don't become confused with actual documents.

c. **Keep related information in the same subdirectory.** Keeping files of things that are alike or that belong to each other in the same subdirectory makes it easier to create distinctive DOS filenames for them because the subdirectory name can help distinguish the files within the subdirectory. It also is easier to copy backup files onto floppy disks and keep track of them if you keep related things grouped in the same subdirectory. What kinds of items you group together depends on your own work. If you have a small business or professional practice with several documents for each client, it may make sense to keep the files for each client in a separate subdirectory. On the other hand, if you have a large number of customers and only one or two documents for each, it may be best to keep each type of document in a separate subdirectory. If you are a teacher, it may be best to have a separate subdirectory for each class. You need to look at your own work to determine which files belong together.

d. **Build a family tree of subdirectories.** Group your files that belong to each other into layers of subdirectories in family (parent-child-grandchild) relationships. This makes it easier to keep track of documents and to keep your subdirectories small.

```
                    C:\LWORKS3\LWDATA\
        ┌───────────┬──────┴──────┬───────────┐
    ABCCORP\     WEZ&CO\      AFFASSN\     NSGINC\
```

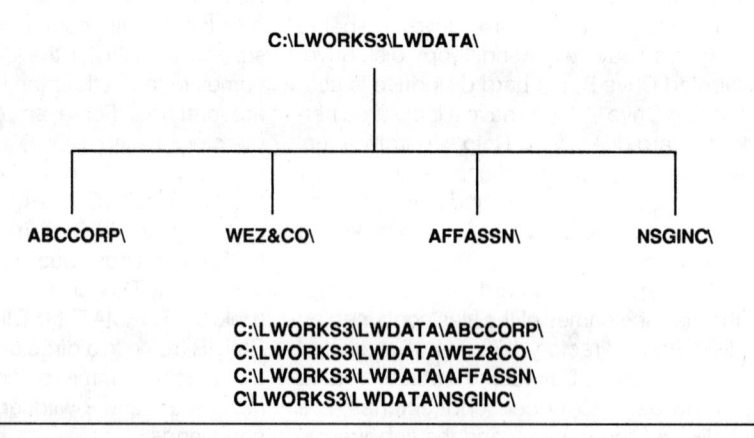

C:\LWORKS3\LWDATA\ABCCORP\
C:\LWORKS3\LWDATA\WEZ&CO\
C:\LWORKS3\LWDATA\AFFASSN\
C\LWORKS3\LWDATA\NSGINC\

**FIGURE 1.1:** Subdirectories based on clients

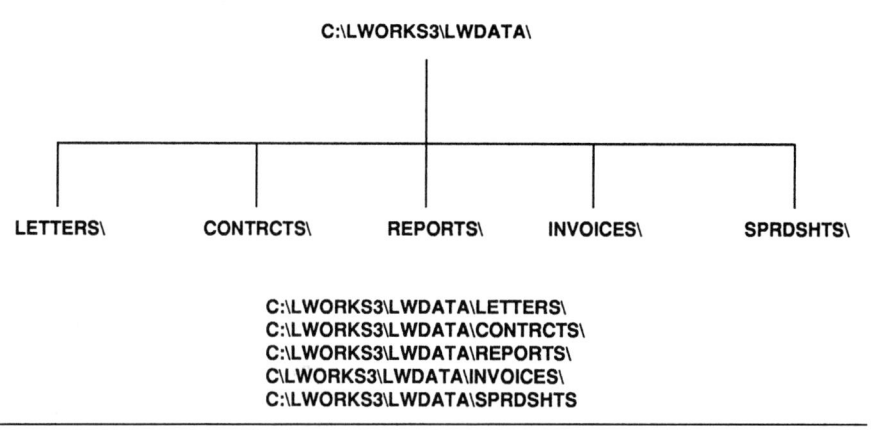

```
                        C:\LWORKS3\LWDATA\
                               |
    ┌──────────┬───────────────┼───────────────┬──────────┐
 LETTERS\  CONTRCTS\        REPORTS\        INVOICES\  SPRDSHTS\

              C:\LWORKS3\LWDATA\LETTERS\
              C:\LWORKS3\LWDATA\CONTRCTS\
              C:\LWORKS3\LWDATA\REPORTS\
              C\LWORKS3\LWDATA\INVOICES\
              C:\LWORKS3\LWDATA\SPRDSHTS
```

**FIGURE 1.2:** Subdirectories based on type of document

**Is it better to have more or fewer subdirectories?** There is a trade-off here. Each subdirectory you create eats up a small amount of disk space just for the subdirectory alone. That leaves less room for files. On the other hand, if you keep all your documents in only one or two directories or subdirectories, then it is more difficult to create distinctive and descriptive filenames within the constraints of DOS's eight-character filenames and three-character filename extensions. You can't use the subdirectory name to help designate the files inside. It also is more difficult to select related files for removal to a floppy disk for backup and archiving. On balance, it seems more useful in most cases to have a large number of subdirectories.

Here are some examples of family-tree subdirectory structures.

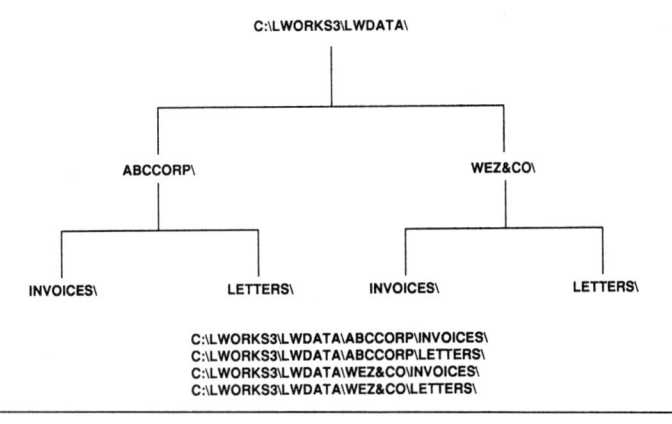

```
                        C:\LWORKS3\LWDATA\
                               |
              ┌────────────────┴────────────────┐
           ABCCORP\                           WEZ&CO\
              |                                  |
       ┌──────┴──────┐                   ┌───────┴───────┐
   INVOICES\     LETTERS\             INVOICES\      LETTERS\

              C:\LWORKS3\LWDATA\ABCCORP\INVOICES\
              C:\LWORKS3\LWDATA\ABCCORP\LETTERS\
              C:\LWORKS3\LWDATA\WEZ&CO\INVOICES\
              C:\LWORKS3\LWDATA\WEZ&CO\LETTERS\
```

**FIGURE 1.3:** A directory structure based on client names

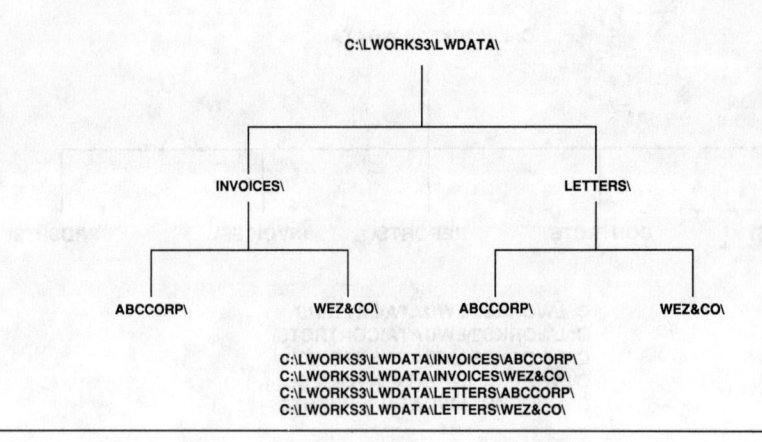

```
                        C:\LWORKS3\LWDATA\
                    ┌───────────┴───────────┐
                 INVOICES\                LETTERS\
              ┌─────┴─────┐           ┌─────┴─────┐
           ABCCORP\    WEZ&CO\     ABCCORP\    WEZ&CO\

                    C:\LWORKS3\LWDATA\INVOICES\ABCCORP\
                    C:\LWORKS3\LWDATA\INVOICES\WEZ&CO\
                    C:\LWORKS3\LWDATA\LETTERS\ABCCORP\
                    C:\LWORKS3\LWDATA\LETTERS\WEZ&CO\
```

**FIGURE 1.4:** A directory structure based on type of document

e. **Employ a consistent (and coherent) file-naming scheme.** The file-naming scheme you set up should depend on the nature of your work and your own taste. The challenge is to make a large number of file names distinct and descriptive within the eight characters that MS-DOS allows. (LotusWorks reserves the three-character file name extension to distinguish among types of documents.) There are no firm rules for document file names. Just be consistent and remember that you may need to be able to decipher a file name a year or more after you create it.

One useful convention is to put the addressee's initials, the month and year, and a character designating the type of document into the file name. For example, L could designate a letter; M, a memo; R a report, S a spreadsheet, etc. Thus TAS1091L would indicate an October 1991 letter to a person or company with initials T.A.S.; TAS1091M would indicate a memo to the same addressee. This kind of file name is less cryptic if the client name is indicated by the subdirectory name.

If you have any employees who create LotusWorks documents, be sure they are fully instructed in using your directory structure and file-naming scheme.

f. **Divide your files into active files, research files, and archive files; remove the research and archive files from your hard disk.** Just as with paper files, it's a good idea to reorganize your files from time to time. Group the files you use frequently into an "active" category, those you use infrequently into a "research" category, and those you are keeping for record purposes into an "archive" category. (If you're not keeping files for one of these purposes, you should purge them.) Put your research files and archive files on floppy disks and store them in a safe place. That will leave more space on your hard disk for active files.

## 5. Use the Same Data Over and Over

For efficient computing, strive to enter data into the computer only once. This means putting as much information as possible into a few databases and spreadsheets, where it can be accessed for other documents. Because you work from only one database at a time, it also means keeping the number of databases to a minimum. When special needs arise, you can copy data from one database to another, rather than re-entering it. This strategy may require a bit of planning and organizing in the short run, but it saves many keystrokes and chances for error in the long run. When you see how much easier it is to use names and addresses over and over instead of retyping them each time you need to use them, you'll catch on to this principle fast.

## 6. Save Your Setups

When you format a word document or set up a database or spreadsheet that you expect to use again, before you enter any data into it be sure to save the document to a disk, give it a generic name, and make it accessible by menu. (More about this later.) The next time you need to create a similar document, you can simply copy the saved document, rename it, and begin entering data immediately. This saves time, ensures that your formats will be consistent, and guards against errors in databases and spreadsheets.

## 7. Automate Everything You Can

LotusWorks 3.0 has many features to enable you to automate various aspects of the production of documents. Three basic principles to keep in mind:

- Let LotusWorks do the calculating for you.
- Let LotusWorks enter dates and the time of day.
- Use boilerplate whenever possible. Put it in a macro or menu.

Be sure to take advantage of these features to automate everything you can. Chapters 3 through 8 describe ideas for automation in more detail.

## 8. Create Your Own Tools and Menus

It may not occur to you at first to think of your document creations as "tools" or to design custom menus for them. When you set up and save an empty document with your own specifications, however, you have created a tool that can be used repeatedly. As you become more proficient with LotusWorks 3.0, you will be able to create more powerful tools. LotusWorks' macro feature makes it possible to create pseudo-menus of your own. When you want to select or activate a tool, you simply call up the menu and execute the launching macro of your choice. This saves time, makes it easier for other people to use your creations, and keeps your creations from getting lost or forgotten. Here are three principles to keep in mind:

- If you plan to use a document format or setup again, it's a tool.
- Put everything you can into menus. (That way, you won't forget them.)
- Build a family-tree structure for your menus.

## 9. Keep Everything Clear and Simple

The ninth principle for getting the most out of LotusWorks 3.0 is to keep everything clear and simple. The objective is to avoid confusion. It's amazing how much we can forget if we set work aside for a while! This principle means that you should design databases and spreadsheets to be as simple as possible; you should label files and directories clearly and consistently; and you should document your work so that it will be clear if you have to revise it in the future. Chapters 3 through 8 give more suggestions for designing, labeling, and documenting your work.

## 10. Take It Easy

The final principle is "take it easy." Don't try to do everything at once. Whether you are learning LotusWorks or implementing an automated solution to a problem, things can get complicated fast. If the task looks too complicated at first (which is often the case with computers), use the "sausage" approach to problem-solving: start at the top and slice off one piece at a time. Solve it before tackling the next piece. Then slice off another piece, and so on. Pretty soon you'll have the whole problem solved.

With these few principles in mind, you are ready to install LotusWorks 3.0 and begin putting it to work for you.

## How to Use This Guide

Learning to use LotusWorks is a bit like learning to swim: you learn best when you get your feet wet. If you have LotusWorks 3.0 and a PC at your disposal, by all means try out the examples as you read about them in this guide.

This guide is designed to help you integrate LotusWorks into your work and, in the process, learn about the various LotusWorks 3.0 features and functions. The chapters are not necessarily organized in the order that you might first use the four LotusWorks services. Rather, the chapters are organized to help you organize your work to get the most from LotusWorks.

The first two chapters, "Putting LotusWorks 3.0 to Work for You" and "Getting Going Quickly," give you the basics for operating LotusWorks and the foundation for using LotusWorks most effectively. You should read these first.

Chapters 3 through 7 address each LotusWorks service separately. They are organized in the order needed to analyze and plan your overall use of information, starting with word processing. But if you need to use one of the other services, such as the spreadsheet or database service before using the others, by all means feel free to jump ahead and read the chapter covering that topic.

The last chapter addresses building more complex applications. It is probably best to read this one after you have read the others.

The appendices contain reference information that you may wish to consult as you read the other chapters.

# 2

# Getting Going Quickly

Installing LotusWorks 3.0 is a simple process. You run the Install program, answer a few questions about your computer equipment and the parts of LotusWorks you want to install, and then let the Install program do the rest. Once LotusWorks is installed, you can begin using it immediately with the factory-set default settings.

Selecting computer equipment, however, is not so simple. Before you set up and run LotusWorks, it's a good idea to be sure that your computer equipment will produce the results you want and to take some steps to protect your equipment, software, and data from loss or damage.

## Equipment Considerations

There is such a great variety of PC equipment available that choosing can be difficult. Fortunately, LotusWorks 3.0 runs well on a wide variety of IBM PC and compatible computers. If you already own an IBM-compatible PC with at least 640K of RAM, LotusWorks 3.0 will probably run just fine on the equipment you have. If you are considering the purchase of new equipment to run with LotusWorks 3.0, or if you have plans to add or change equipment in the future, it is useful to know about the different options available and the effects they can have on LotusWorks 3.0.

The rest of this section reviews the major current equipment options and their implications for LotusWorks 3.0.

---

*In this chapter, you'll learn how to:*

- *Check your computer equipment for suitability with LotusWorks 3.0*
- *Install LotusWorks 3.0*
- *Move around in LotusWorks 3.0*
- *Issue commands*
- *Use dialog boxes*
- *Use LotusWorks windows*
- *Change the default setup*
- *Safeguard your data*

## Computers, Computer Memory, and Disk Storage

At the heart of any personal computer system are three elements:

- a central processing unit (CPU)
- Random Access Memory (RAM) for running programs
- disk storage devices for storing data and programs when they are not running in RAM

Each of these elements has some effect on how LotusWorks 3.0 performs.

### Central Processing Units (CPUs)

LotusWorks 3.0 runs on a variety of central processing units, including IBM PC, IBM PC XT, IBM PC AT, IBM Personal System/2, COMPAQ, and any 100 percent-compatible machines. If most of your use is word processing, the type of CPU makes little difference because they all run fast enough for word processing. However, if you need to create very large databases or large spreadsheets with numerous formulas, the slower machines (IBM-PC, /XT, and compatibles) will take longer to process the databases and spreadsheets than the faster machines (AT, PS/2, and compatibles). Still, for most people the computer performs these tasks so much faster than you could do by hand that the differences in calculation time are hardly noticeable.

### Computer Memory

LotusWorks 3.0 requires a minimum of 640 kilobytes (640K) of random access memory (RAM) to run. Even more is better. With more memory you can have more different LotusWorks services and windows open at a time. For instance, you can have a combination of word processing, database, spreadsheet, and communications services all open at the same time.

### Disk Storage

The amount of disk storage is important for two reasons: it determines how many documents you can store and how large they can be. In some setups it determines how many services and windows you can have open at a time.

Make sure you have at least 640K of RAM and, if you can afford it, a 40-megabyte or larger hard disk. You may be surprised at how quickly even a small business operation can fill a 40-megabyte hard disk.

## Monitors

LotusWorks 3.0 runs very satisfactorily on a monochrome monitor or any of the IBM-compatible color formats: CGA, EGA, or VGA. The graphical user interface of LotusWorks 3.0 is actually text-based, so LotusWorks does not require a high-resolution graphics or color monitor.

If you have a color monitor, you can choose among two different color setups to suit your personal taste. For the most part, however, whether to use a color monitor or not is a matter of personal preference and pocketbook.

## Printers

Your printer is one piece of equipment that can make a big difference in the appearance of LotusWorks documents. It is not essential to have a printer in order to run LotusWorks 3.0, but a printer is highly desirable for most uses. For business purposes, it's mandatory, and you should probably invest in the best printer you can afford—one that produces attractive type, in the type styles you need, at an efficient rate.

LotusWorks 3.0 can run on most IBM-compatible printers, including H-P LaserJet and PostScript laser printers. Laser printers offer the advantage of being able to produce high-quality text and graphics and multiple type styles, sizes, and faces on the same machine. They can produce such popular proportionally spaced type fonts as Helvetica and Times Roman, as well as "typewriter-style" fixed-space type fonts such as Courier. Laser printers are marginally more expensive than other types of printer, but for business uses their quality and versatility may be worth the extra cost. Because they offer so many options, laser printers are more complicated to operate than other types of printer, but LotusWorks 3.0 helps you here.

These days it is also possible to get quite high-quality print and graphics from many dot-matrix printers, especially 24-pin dot-matrix printers. These are slower than laser printers, and they offer fewer type sizes and fonts, but they also cost less.

## Pointing Devices

Pointing devices provide an alternative to the keyboard for accessing screen menus and issuing commands to the computer. The most common are the "mouse" and the "trackball." The mouse is a hand-held device that moves the cursor on the screen as you move the device across a flat service; it issues commands when you press one or more of its buttons. The trackball is a stationary device that moves the cursor on the screen when you rotate a ball on the device with the palm of your hand. Like the mouse, it issues commands when you press one or more buttons on the device.

You can use LotusWorks with a pointing device or with the keyboard alone. Whether or not to use a pointing device and which one to use are matters of personal preference. Many people find it quicker and easier to use a mouse or other pointing device rather than the keyboard when they are first learning LotusWorks and for certain LotusWorks actions, such as scrolling the screen, marking a block of text for further action, and selecting menu items. Others prefer to use the keyboard or a combination of a pointing device and the keyboard. Some people find a mouse easiest to use; others find a trackball easier to control or more convenient to keep on the desk.

LotusWorks 3.0 supports all types of IBM-compatible pointing device. You must properly connect the pointing device to the computer and install its driver software, then simply select the LotusWorks Setup program and switch the mouse option on.

## Modems

Modems are the devices that enable computers to communicate over telephone lines. They convert the digital "on-off" signals of computers into the wave-like analog signals used by telephones, and back again. When two computers communicate, each must have a modem connecting it to the telephone line.

LotusWorks 3.0 can use any type of Hayes or 100-percent Hayes-compatible modem that IBM-compatible PCs can use. If you are considering the purchase of a modem to use with LotusWorks, be sure that it is 100-percent Hayes-compatible.

Most inexpensive modems today communicate at rates of 1200 or 2400 bits per second (bps), but rates of 9600 bps or more are possible over dial-up telephone lines. Even faster rates are possible with data compression or special dedicated data lines. In order to squeeze more data across the telephone line at a time, most high-speed modems use some programming scheme to "compress" the data or a combination of data-compression and error-checking schemes. Because most data-compression schemes are proprietary rather than standard, if you want to communicate between two PCs, be sure that both modems use the same type of data compression.

Most modems will adjust or "roll back" to a slower speed if they detect noisy telephone lines or a slower modem at the other end of the line; however, they cannot adjust to different forms of data compression.

## Local Area Networks

A local area network (LAN) makes it possible to connect a group of PCs via cabling to enable them to communicate with each other and to share certain resources, such as programs, data files, and printers.

One reason to use LotusWorks 3.0 on a LAN is to take advantage of a network printer or to transfer data files to another PC. You can use LotusWorks 3.0 on a local area network (LAN), but you must follow some precautions.

LotusWorks 3.0 is a single-user rather than multi-user software system. It is designed for only one user to access its files at a time. If you wish to use LotusWorks 3.0 on a LAN, be sure to install and run LotusWorks on your own workstation rather than on another workstation or the network server. That will eliminate the chance of collisions between LotusWorks and other programs running on the LAN. Only one workstation at a time can use LotusWorks on the LAN. Use the LAN only to print or transfer your LotusWorks files.

> CAUTION: Do not use more than one copy of LotusWorks 3.0 at a time on a local area network. If you run more than one copy of LotusWorks 3.0 on a LAN at the same time, you risk corrupting your data files.

# Installing LotusWorks 3.0

Before you can run LotusWorks 3.0, you have to install it. This involves telling LotusWorks the type of CPU, monitor, and printer you have, so that LotusWorks uses the appropriate driver programs for these devices. It also involves telling the Install program where to copy certain program files to your hard disk.

The installation procedures are detailed clearly in the "Getting Started" section of the LotusWorks 3.0 User's Guide. In brief, the steps are as follows:

## How To Install LotusWorks 3.0

1. Identify your CPU, monitor, and printer in advance.

    The installation program will ask you to specify the type of CPU, monitor, and printer in your computer configuration. If you know this information in advance, you'll be ready to answer. Consult your equipment manuals, if necessary.

2. Make a backup copy of the LotusWorks program disks.

    This is a safety measure. You should always keep a backup copy of your software disks. You can use the command **COPY A:*.* B:** to copy all the files from the disk in drive A to the disk in drive B. Be sure to label the backup copies clearly. When you have finished copying the disks, store the original program disks in a safe, well-ventilated place, and perform the rest of the installation from the backup copies.

3. Run the installation program.

    Insert the disk labeled Disk 1 Install into drive A and enter *A:* to make the A drive the current drive (that is, type *A:* and press the Enter key to bring the A> prompt to the screen). If you are installing to a hard disk and have a drive B, you may insert the Installation Disk into drive B, if you wish, and make that drive current by typing *B:* and pressing Enter. Type *Install* and press Enter to start the program, then respond to the instructions and requests for equipment configuration information that appear on the screen.

    The installation program lets you choose whether or not to install each of the various elements of LotusWorks. If you are upgrading from an earlier version of LotusWorks, you should check the Upgrade item. Unless you have a need to run LotusWorks under Windows, you can leave the Windows item unchecked. It's a good idea to install all the other options. You'll find the Help, Tutorial, and Quickstart Files very helpful, especially when you are learning LotusWorks. Later, when you know how you use LotusWorks, if you absolutely need to free up space on your hard disk, you may want to consider deleting the Tutorial and Quickstart files.

    When the installation program is ready to generate type fonts, it asks whether to generate a Basic, Medium, or Extended set of fonts. These are screen display fonts to match your printer. If you have a PostScript printer, select Extended. Otherwise, make a choice based on the kind of printing you intend to do and the amount of disk space you want to devote to fonts.

    When you have finished installing LotusWorks, remove the last disk from the disk drive and store all the backup program disks in a safe place.

If you ever change computers, monitors, or printers, or if you add more type fonts, you should run the Install program again to tell LotusWorks which things have changed.

The first time you run LotusWorks, you should set the Setup options to match your printer connections, screen color preferences, and modem. See "Changing the Default Setup" later in this chapter.

# Starting LotusWorks 3.0

To start LotusWorks, turn on the computer, type the name of the disk drive containing LotusWorks (such as C: or D:) and press Enter. Type *cd\lworks* and press Enter to make LWORKS3 the current subdirectory. When the screen prompt appears, type *lw* and press Enter.

# The Start-up and LotusWorks Screens

The first screen that appears is the Start-up screen. After a brief pause, it changes into the LotusWorks Screen:

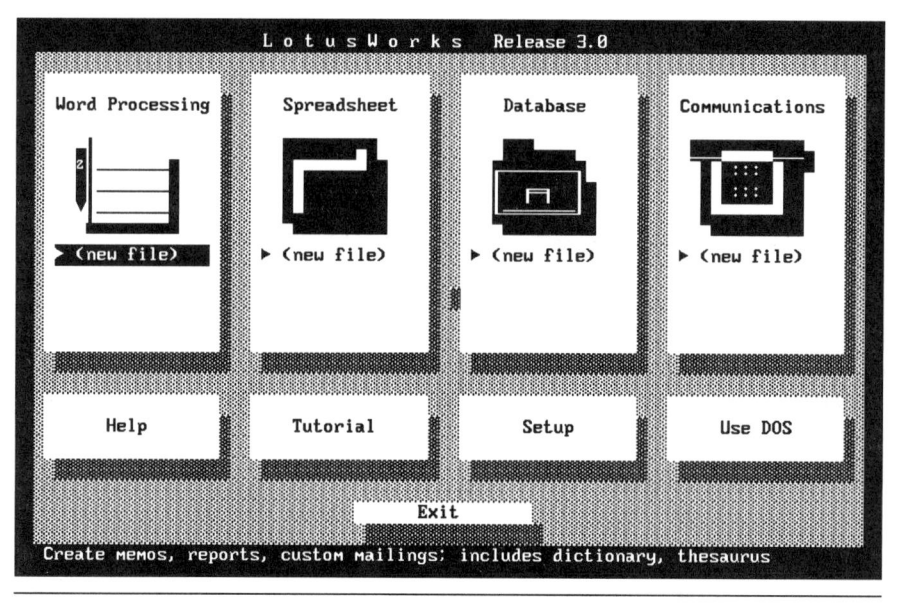

**FIGURE 2.1:** The LotusWorks Screen

The LotusWorks Screen is the main menu in LotusWorks 3.0. It enables you to select and launch LotusWorks services (WordProcessing, Spreadsheet, Database, and Communications) and LotusWorks' special-purpose accessories (Help, Tutorial, Setup, and DOS access). It also shows which services and files are open in the current LotusWorks session, enables you to choose among them, and enables you to exit LotusWorks when you are finished. You can return to the LotusWorks Screen from anywhere in LotusWorks by holding down the Ctrl key and pressing the F6 key or by pressing the F10 key to activate the Menu Line and pressing L (for LotusWorks). In that way you can access any service or task from any other in the system.

If you press the Right and Left Arrow keys repeatedly, you see that the cursor moves from from menu item to menu item, highlighting each in turn.

IMPORTANT: Notice that as you highlight each menu item, a message explaining the item appears on the Prompt line at the bottom of the screen. All LotusWorks 3.0 menus work this way.

## The LotusWorks 3.0 Window Design

A distinguishing mark of LotusWorks 3.0 is its graphical user interface (or "GUI"). The graphical window design provides a set of easily understandable operating conventions that are consistent throughout the LotusWorks services. This makes the system easy to learn and use. Once you know how to use the operating features in one LotusWorks 3.0 window, you know how to use them in all the windows.

Although each LotusWorks service has its own distinctive window design, certain features are common to all the LotusWorks 3.0 windows. The following table lists the common features:

| Feature | Function |
| --- | --- |
| Top Line | Tells you how to get help (press F1) and how to move to the menu bar (press F10). |
| Menu Line | Displays the menu bar. The first three menu names (File, Edit, and Options) are the same in all services, although the contents vary. The remaining menu names vary from service to service. |

| | |
|---|---|
| Edit Line | Varies with the service; does not appear in all services. The edit line for the Spreadsheet service displays the contents of a cell for editing. The edit line for the Database service displays the contents of a field for editing. |
| Title Line | Displays the names of the current service and the current file; enables you to use a mouse to reposition a window on the screen (if the window is not in its full size). |
| Work Space | The central area where you perform work—enter text, data, formulas, etc. |
| Status Line | Displays messages about the current status of the program and certain key settings (such as Insert or Overwrite in the Word Processing service). |
| Prompt Line | Displays a one-line explanation for each menu item. |
| Vertical Scroll Bar | Enables you to use a mouse to move the contents of the screen up or down toward the beginning or end of the document. |
| Horizontal Scroll Bar | Enables you to use a mouse to move the contents of the screen to the right or left. |

Common Features of LotusWorks 3.0 Windows

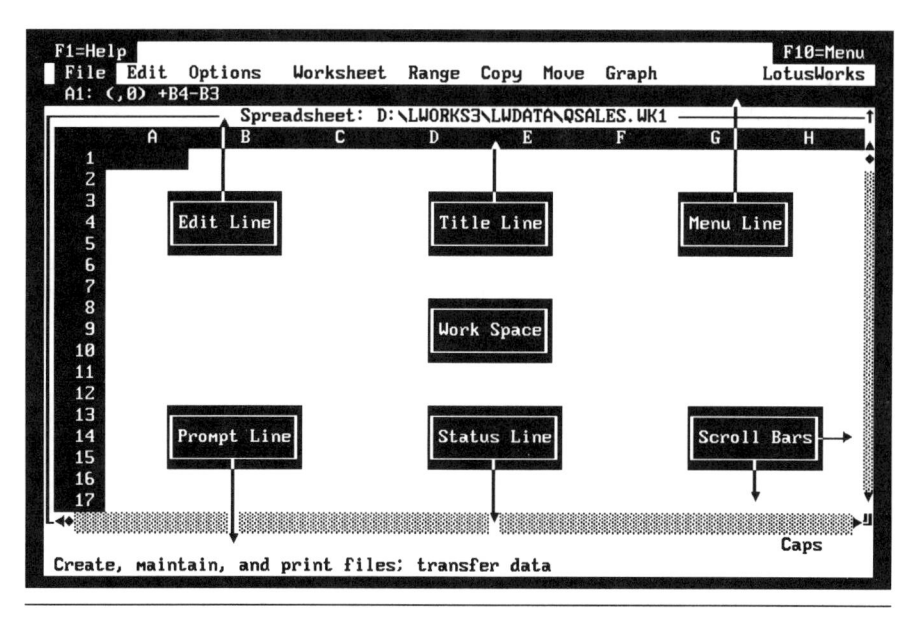

**FIGURE 2.2:** The common features of all LotusWorks 3.0 windows

## Using Combination Keys

Some LotusWorks commands are issued by pressing a combination of two keys. You hold one key down while you press another one, and then you release both keys. Key combinations are indicated by a plus sign between two keynames. For example, Ctrl+F6 means to hold down the Ctrl key ("Control key") and press the F6 key, then release both. Alt+Q means to hold down the Alt key, type Q, and then release both keys. All combination keys in LotusWorks are made with either the Alt key or Ctrl key, plus a letter key or function (F) key.

## Using a Mouse or Other Pointing Device

LotusWorks 3.0 lets you issue many commands with either a mouse or other pointing device, the keyboard, or a combination. Which approach you use is a matter of personal taste. The mouse is easy to learn and is quickest for many operations. On the other hand, some people do not feel comfortable using a mouse. You may wish to try both approaches until you find the approach that is most productive for you.

Because LotusWorks 3.0 responds identically whether you use a mouse or other pointing device, this guide uses the terms "mouse" and "pointing device" interchangeably.

With either type of device, you use the following procedures in LotusWorks 3.0:

- **Click.** Click means to move the mouse until the screen pointer is in the desired position and then press the left button and immediately release it. You can click to move the cursor, open menus and dialog boxes, and select menu items that issue commands.
- **Double-Click.** Double-click means to move the screen pointer to the desired item and press and release the left button twice in quick succession. You can use double-clicking on the LotusWorks screen to choose a service.
- **Drag.** Click-and-drag means to move the pointer to the desired starting point, hold down the left button while you move the screen pointer to the desired ending point, and then release the button. For instance, you can drag in LotusWorks to move windows and other objects, and to select blocks of text in word processing documents or ranges of cells in spreadsheets.

## Moving Around in LotusWorks

To perform work in LotusWorks, you have to move the cursor to the spot where you want to work. This is called "navigating." There two ways to do it: with keyboard commands and with a mouse. Most people seem to find the mouse easiest to learn, but you may want to try both to see which you prefer. The following table summarizes both methods.

| Function | Keyboard Command | Mouse Procedure |
| --- | --- | --- |
| Move up one line | Up Arrow | Click on top scroll arrow |
| Move down one line | Down Arrow | Click on bottom scroll arrow |
| Move up one screen | PgUp | Click on vertical scroll bar above the elevator button |
| Move down one screen | PgDn | Click on vertical scroll bar below the elevator button |
| Move right one column | Right Arrow | |
| Move left one column | Left Arrow | |
| Move right one screen (Spreadsheet and Database only) | Ctrl+Right Arrow | Click on horizontal scroll bar to the right of the elevator button |
| Move left one screen (Spreadsheet and Database only) | Ctrl+Left Arrow | Click on horizontal scroll bar to the left of the elevator button |
| Move to the next window | | |

Moving Around in LotusWorks

## Issuing Commands

To get LotusWorks to do what you want it to do, you have to give it commands. You issue commands by selecting items from menus and submenus and by selecting items and entering information in dialog boxes. You can perform all of these procedures using the keyboard or the keyboard in combination with a mouse. In addition, you can use a mouse to operate the horizontal and vertical scroll bars to scroll large documents past the screen window.

## Menus, Submenus, and Dialog Boxes

Menus pull down from the top of the screen, like this:

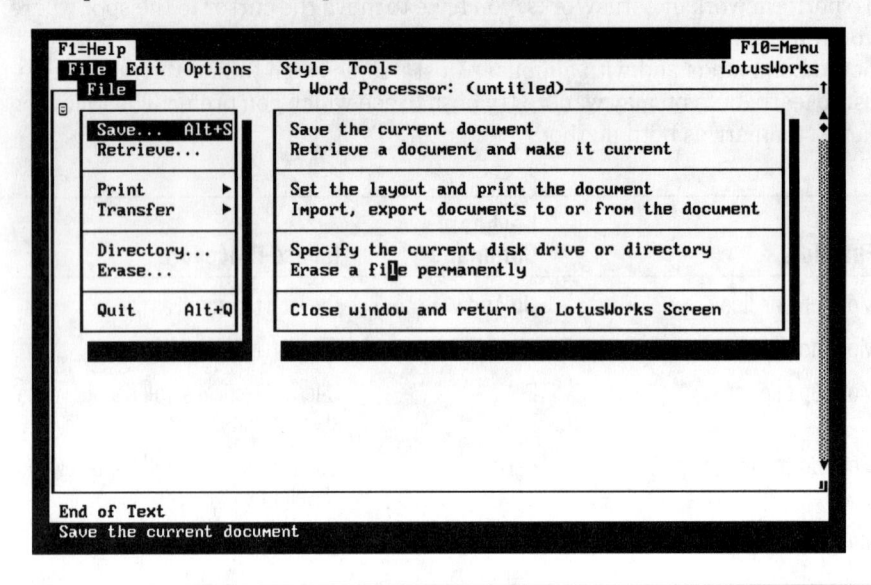

```
F1=Help                                                    F10=Menu
 File  Edit  Options   Style  Tools                       LotusWorks
   File ─────────────── Word Processor: (untitled) ──────────────
   ┌──────────────────┬──────────────────────────────────────────┐
   │ Save...   Alt+S  │ Save the current document                │
   │ Retrieve...      │ Retrieve a document and make it current  │
   │                  │                                          │
   │ Print       ►    │ Set the layout and print the document    │
   │ Transfer    ►    │ Import, export documents to or from the document │
   │                  │                                          │
   │ Directory...     │ Specify the current disk drive or directory │
   │ Erase...         │ Erase a file permanently                 │
   │                  │                                          │
   │ Quit      Alt+Q  │ Close window and return to LotusWorks Screen │
   └──────────────────┴──────────────────────────────────────────┘

End of Text
Save the current document
```

**FIGURE 2.3:** A typical LotusWorks 3.0 menu.

Submenus cascade down from within menus, like this:

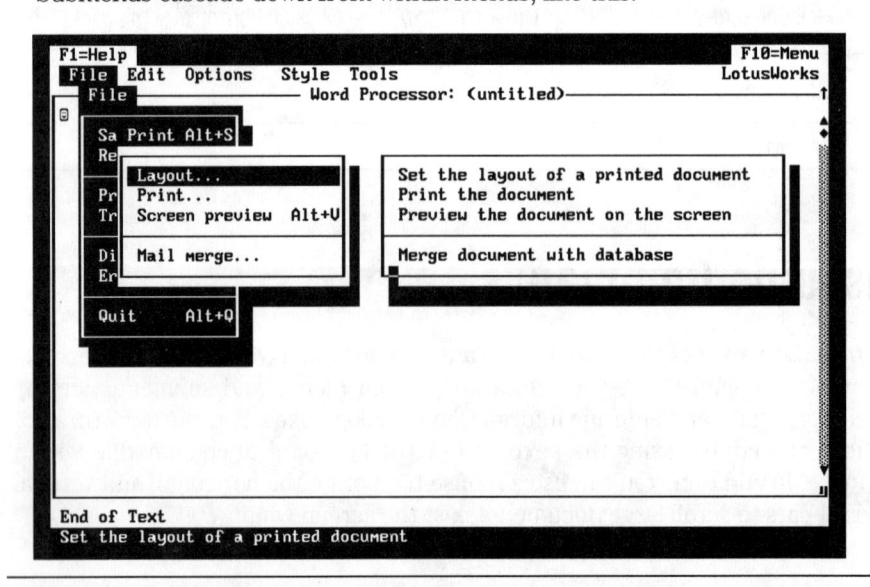

```
F1=Help                                                    F10=Menu
 File  Edit  Options   Style  Tools                       LotusWorks
   File ─────────────── Word Processor: (untitled) ──────────────
   ┌──────────────────┐
   │ Sa  Print  Alt+S │
   │ Re  ┌──────────────────────┐
   │     │ Layout...            │  Set the layout of a printed document
   │ Pr  │ Print...             │  Print the document
   │ Tr  │ Screen preview Alt+V │  Preview the document on the screen
   │     │                      │
   │ Di  │ Mail merge...        │  Merge document with database
   │ Er  └──────────────────────┘
   │                  │
   │ Quit      Alt+Q  │
   └──────────────────┘

End of Text
Set the layout of a printed document
```

**FIGURE 2.4:** A typical LotusWorks 3.0 submenu.

Dialog boxes pop up in the middle of the screen, like this:

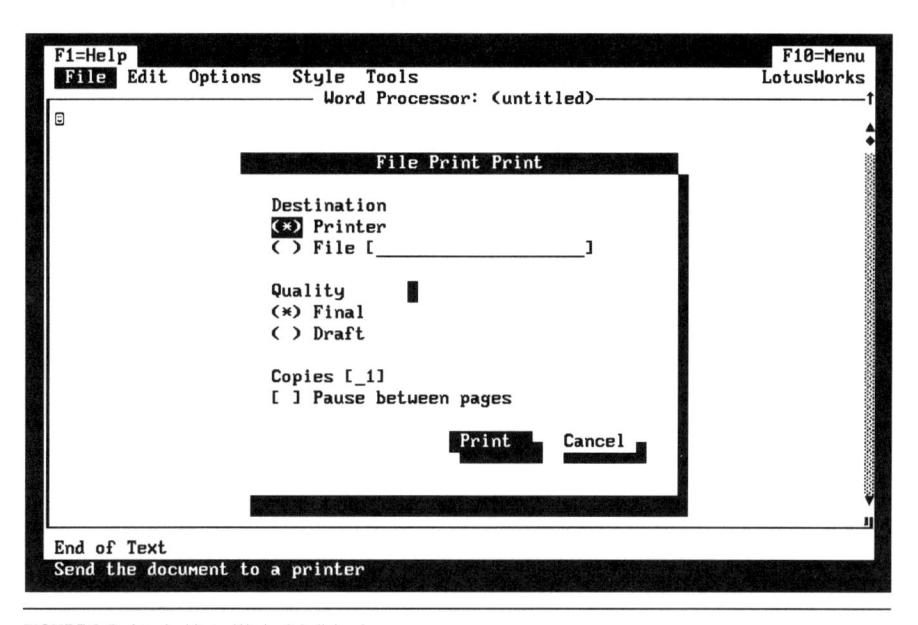

**FIGURE 2.5:** A typical LotusWorks 3.0 dialog box.

Some menu and dialog box items lead to further menus (submenus) or dialog boxes. A solid arrowhead symbol beside a menu item indicates that the item leads to a submenu. When you select the item, a submenu opens. An ellipsis symbol (...) after the menu item indicates that the item leads to a dialog box. When you select it, a dialog box opens.

## Selecting Menu and Submenu Items

LotusWorks gives you a variety of ways to select most menu items. This is not to make your life more complicated but, rather, to make it easy to use the approach that fits your style and level of acquaintance with LotusWorks. Which you use is a matter of personal preference. You should become familiar with all the techniques and then use the ones that feel most comfortable.

## Selecting Menu and Submenu Items

| | |
|---|---|
| With a Mouse | 1. Click on the menu name.<br>2. When the pull-down menu opens, click on the desired command option. Repeat step 2 to select items from submenus. |
| With the Keyboard | 1. Press F10 to move the cursor to the Menu line.<br>2. Type the first letter of the menu you wish to open.<br>OR<br>Press the Right Arrow key until the desired menu name is highlighted, then press Enter. |
| and | 3. When the pull-down menu opens, type the letter that is highlighted in the desired command option (usually the first letter of the command).<br>OR<br>Press the Down Arrow key until the desired command option is highlighted and then press Enter.<br>Repeat step 3 to select items from submenus. |

## Using Accelerator Keys

As a shortcut, you can press a function key or Alt+key combination to issue many frequently used commands. These are called accelerator keys. By pressing the function key or holding down the Alt key while you press another key, you can initiate a command directly. For example, by pressing Alt+C you can copy highlighted data to the clipboard, and by pressing Alt+P you can paste the data from the clipboard to the cursor location. The accelerator keys are listed beside the commands they activate on most of the pull-down menus. Accelerator keys are the quickest method of issuing commands, but they require learning various function keys and Alt+key combinations. Try this method first on the commands you use most often.

## Dimmed Menu Items

Sometimes you'll see menu items that are dimmed. This means that the item is not active at the moment. For example, in the Word Processing service, the Cut, Copy, Paste, and Delete commands are not available until you select some text for them to act upon. Once some text is selected, the commands are undimmed, indicating that the options are active and may be selected.

NOTE: If you get a screen message saying that a command is not available, it does not mean that the command does not work—merely that the command is not appropriate at the moment and therefore is not active.

## Using Dialog Boxes

A dialog box is a special window that opens to give you information or get additional information from you for a LotusWorks command. Each dialog box has a name displayed at the top that shows the sequence of commands leading to the dialog box. If you wish, you can drag the title bar with a mouse to move the dialog box to another area of the window.

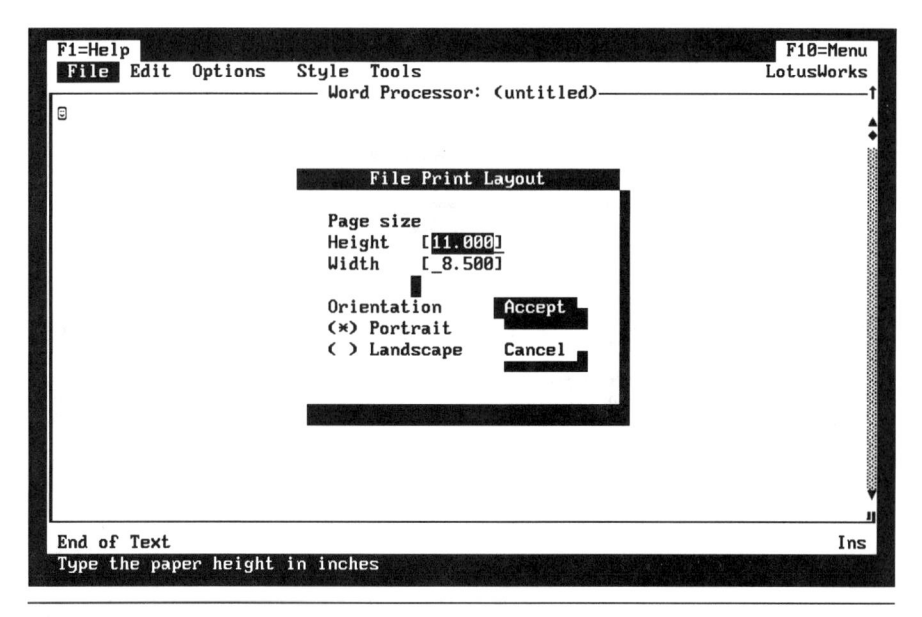

**FIGURE 2.6:** A typical LotusWorks 3.0 dialog box.

Dialog boxes employ several devices to make it easy to give a wide variety of detailed command information to LotusWorks. Once you catch on to how the different devices work, using them is simple. The command devices in dialog boxes take the following forms:

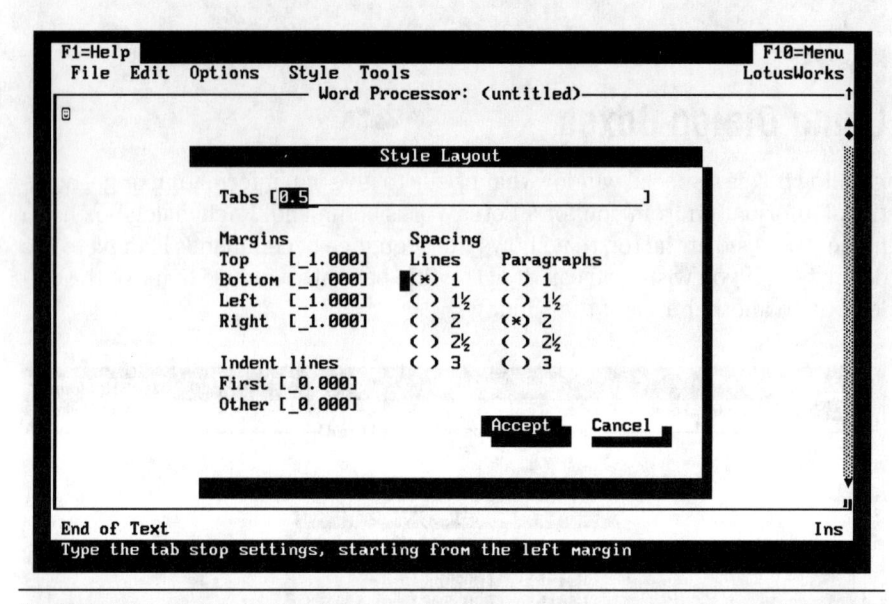

**FIGURE 2.7:** Dialog box features include instructions, check boxes, and action buttons to accept or cancel selections.

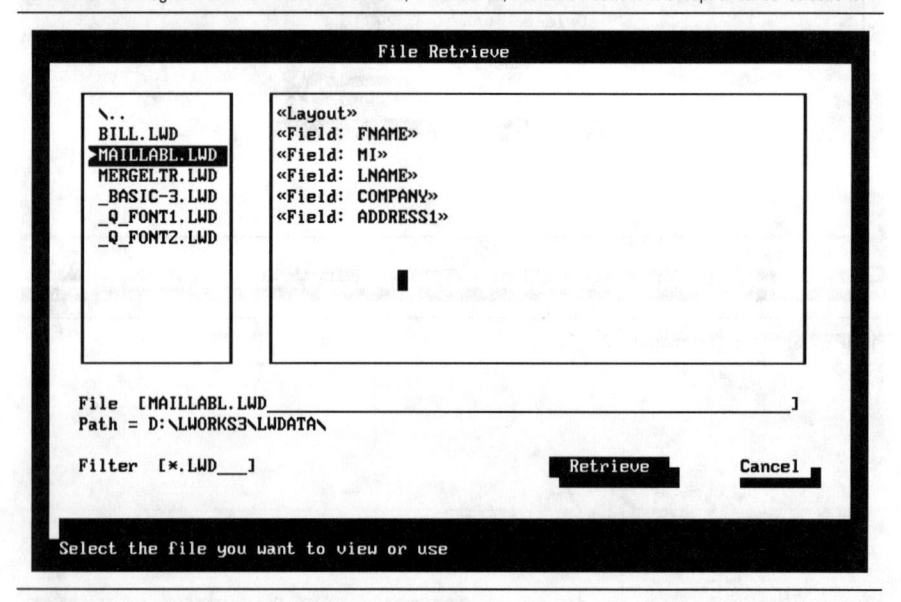

**FIGURE 2.8:** A dialog box with a list box showing available options.

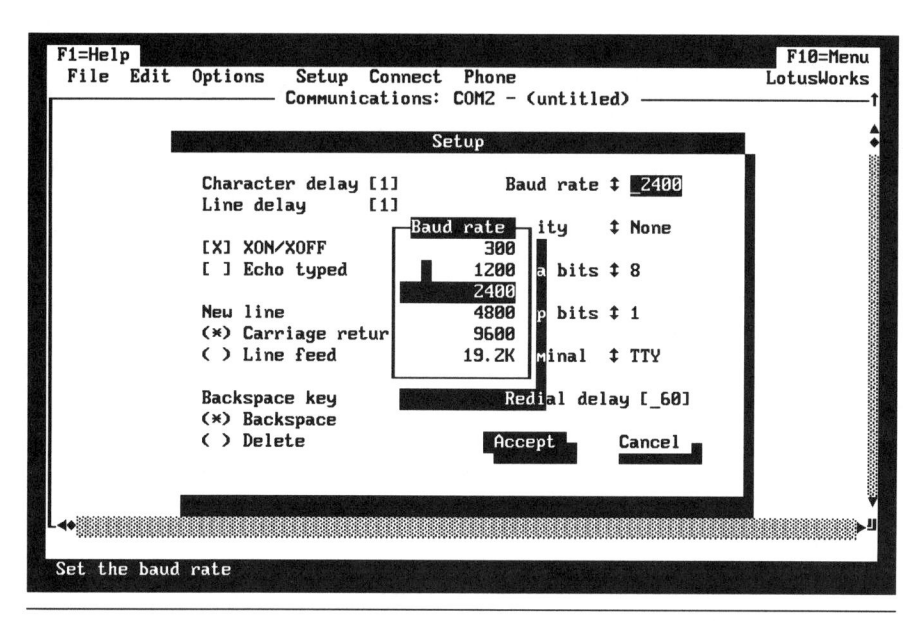

**FIGURE 2.9:** A dialog box with a pop-up menu.

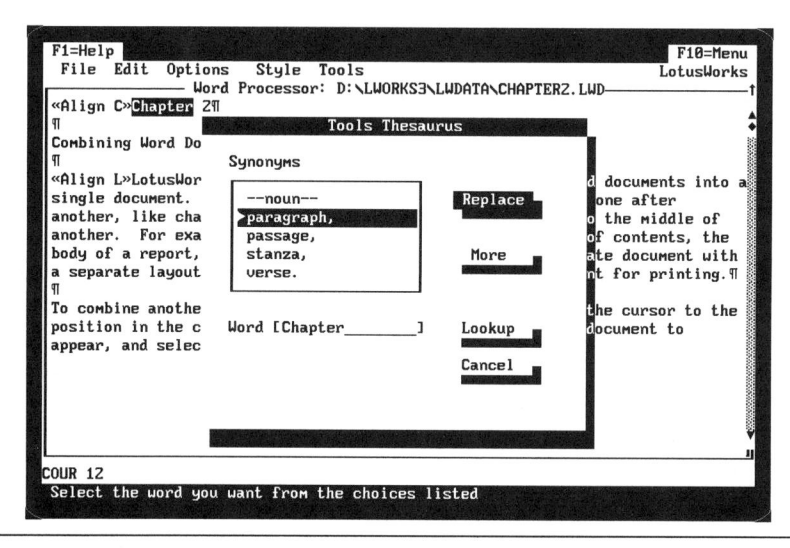

**FIGURE 2.10:** A dialog box containing a text field.

- **Information boxes.** Information boxes display instructions, status information, and error messages from LotusWorks to users. You do not have to enter anything into information boxes.

- **Action buttons.** Action buttons initiate action. Some action buttons open another dialog box. Action buttons usually are located at the bottom right of the dialog box and labeled "Accept" or the name of the dialog box, such as "Retrieve" or "Print." Dialog boxes always include a Cancel button to allow you to cancel your selections and exit the dialog box, if you wish.

- **Check boxes.** Check boxes enable you to turn individual options on or off. An X in a check box indicates the option is turned on. To toggle an option on, click the mouse on the item, or press Tab until the option is highlighted and press the Spacebar. LotusWorks inserts an X in the check box to show that the option is selected. To deselect an option, click on it again, highlight it and press the Spacebar.

- **Radio buttons.** Radio buttons—so named because they resemble buttons on a radio—enable you to select one option from a group. Radio buttons consist of a pair of parentheses. If a button is selected, an asterisk appears between the parentheses, like this (*). Only one button in a group can be selected at a time. To select an option, click the mouse on the item or press Tab until the option is highlighted and then press the Spacebar until an asterisk appears in the desired selection.

*In many dialog boxes you can select an item simply by highlighting the item and pressing Enter. If the action button you want is highlighted. If it is, you can select the item simply by highlighting it and pressing Enter.*

- **List boxes.** List boxes show lists of items and let you select one. The most common ones display the files or macros available in a particular service. To select an item from a list box, click on the item or press Tab to move to the box, press the Up and Down Arrow keys to highlight the desired item, and press Enter.

- **Pop-up boxes.** Pop-up boxes display a currently selected option and, if you wish to change it, let you select an item from a list. Pop-up boxes are indicated by a double-headed vertical arrow beside the menu name. To change the menu option, click on the menu value or press Tab to move the highlight to it. A menu pops up within the dialog box showing the options available for that item. Click on the desired value or move the cursor to it with the arrow keys and press Enter.

- **Text boxes.** Text boxes provide places for you to type text that LotusWorks needs to do your work. For instance, when you save a document, LotusWorks prompts you for a file name. When you want to enter data into a memo field in a database, LotusWorks opens a large text box for your use. In some cases, LotusWorks enters the name of a file for you, which you can either accept or replace.

## Navigating in Dialog Boxes

If you are using the keyboard to navigate, you'll find that moving around in dialog boxes is different from navigating through the rest of the LotusWorks desktop:

- To move the cursor forward, press the Tab key. The cursor moves one item at a time.
- To move the cursor back one item at a time, press Shift+Tab.

> IMPORTANT: Hereafter in this guide, the term "select" is used to mean selecting a command option by any of the techniques described above, whether the option appears on a menu, submenu, or dialog box.

*Most people can save time by using a mouse to select items in dialog boxes. If you have a mouse, try using it and the keyboard to see which you prefer.*

### Using Dialog Boxes

**With a Mouse**

| | |
|---|---|
| To select most items | Click on the item. |
| To select a file name in a file viewer box | Double-click on the file name. |

**With the Keyboard**

| | |
|---|---|
| To move to an option | Press Tab until the option is highlighted. |
| To toggle a check box | Move to the check box and press the Spacebar. |
| To select an item in a list box | Move to the list box and use the Up and Down Arrow keys to highlight the desired item. |
| To select from a pop-up box | Move to the pop-up box, use the Up and Down Arrow keys to highlight the desired item, then press Enter. |
| To select a radio button | Move to the set of radio buttons and use the Up and Down Arrow keys to highlight the desired button. |
| To select an action button | Move to the action button (if it is not already highlighted) and press Enter. |
| To cancel any entries and exit the dialog box | Press Esc or move to the cancel button and press Enter. |

## Accelerator Key Cues

Notice that many items on menus and submenus list keys (such as F4 or F6) or key combinations (such as Alt+S) beside the item names. These are key cues. Pressing the indicated keys produces the same result as selecting the menu item. Key cues are a good way to learn the accelerator keys for commands that you use frequently.

## Exiting Submenus and Dialog Boxes

To exit a submenu without selecting an item, press the Esc key or click the mouse anywhere outside the submenu. To exit a submenu and move all the way to the top of a series of nested menus in one step, press Esc or click the mouse on a blank area in the workspace.

To exit a dialog box without selecting an item, select the Cancel button or press Esc.

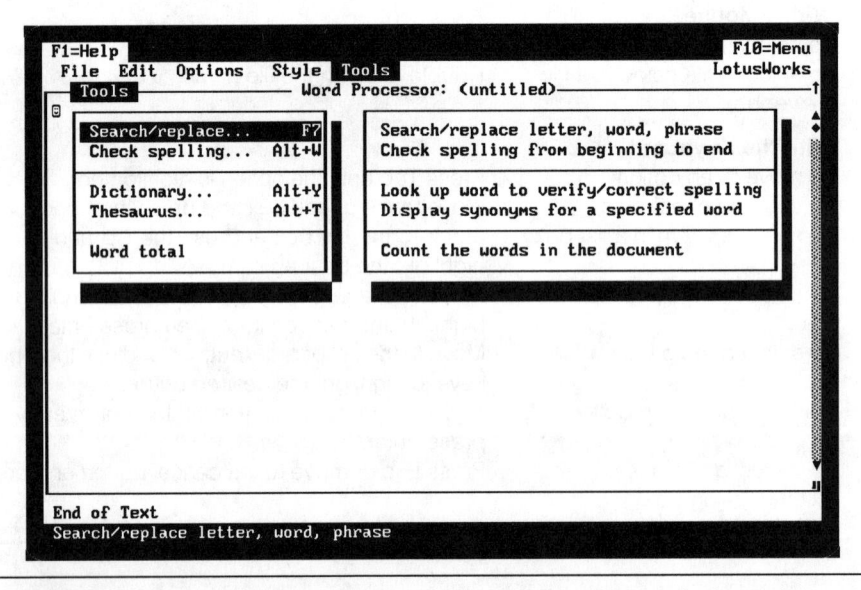

**FIGURE 2.11:** Pressing the accelerator keys cued on a menu item has the same effect as selecting the menu item.

## Command Sequences

Many LotusWorks tasks require selecting options from a succession of menus and dialog boxes to issue a command. In this guide, a sequence of commands is indicated by listing the command options one after another. For example, to retrieve a file in any LotusWorks service, the command sequence is referred to as File Retrieve. This means "select the File menu and then select the Retrieve option." "Select File Print Print" means to select the File menu, then select the Print option, and then select the next Print option.

## Opening a Service

To begin work in LotusWorks, you must open a service (Word Processing, Spreadsheet, Database or Communications). There are two ways to do this.

**From the LotusWorks Screen.** If you are at the LotusWorks Screen, you can open a service by double-clicking on the service or by tabbing to the service and pressing Enter.

**From Another Service.** If you are in one service and you want to open another service, first return to the LotusWorks Screen (press Ctrl+F6, or press F10 and select the LotusWorks option). When the LotusWorks Screen appears, select the desired service option as described above.

The new service appears in a new window overlapping the previous window. Both services are open (although only one window can be active at a time). To move back and forth between them, press F6.

## Entering Data

To do work with LotusWorks, of course, you have to enter some data into the system. Data can be words, numbers, or both.

To enter data into the Word Processing service or into a dialog box, simply type it as you would on a typewriter, but when you reach the end of a line, do not press the Enter or carriage return key. If you keep typing, LotusWorks automatically wraps the words at the end of a line to the next line. Press Enter at the end of a paragraph.

> IMPORTANT: This guide makes a distinction between "typing" data and "entering" it. "Typing" means typing the keys as you would on a typewriter. "Entering" data means typing data and then pressing the Enter key. For example, the phrase "enter *MYFILE1*" means to type the characters MYFILE1 and then press Enter.

## Correcting Typing Mistakes

Don't worry if you make some typing mistakes. Everyone makes them. Fortunately, they are easy to correct.

You can always correct a mistake by pressing the Backspace key until the mistake is erased and then retyping the words correctly. Alternately, you can press the arrow keys or click the mouse to position the cursor just ahead of the mistake and press Backspace to erase the mistake, or you can position the cursor just behind the mistake and press Del to erase the mistake. Retype the deleted material if necessary.

In the Word Processing service, another way to correct a typing mistake is to drag the mouse over the mistake to "paint" (highlight) it and then press Del to erase it. Alternately, you can choose the Select option on the Edit menu and follow the directions on the screen to highlight the mistake and then press Del to erase it.

## Saving Your Work

To save a word processing document, a spreadsheet, or a communications session to a disk, press Alt+S or select the File Save option. LotusWorks prompts you for a name for the file. In the Database service, it is not necessary to select File Save; once you create a database, LotusWorks automatically saves it for you after each modification of the data.

> IMPORTANT: You may enter any eight-character name for the file, following the conventions used by MS-DOS. Do *not* enter an extension to the filename. LotusWorks enters the appropriate filename extension automatically.

If you enter a file name without a disk drive and directory path, Lotus-Works saves the document to the current drive and directory. If you want to save the document to another drive or directory, specify the complete path to the file with the file name. For example, to save the file MYFILE1 to the DOCS subdirectory of the LWORKS3 directory on drive C, enter *C:\LWORKS3\DOCS\MYFILE1*.

For more information on specifying paths and file names, see your MS-DOS manual.

## Retrieving a Saved File

To retrieve a document file into the currently active window, select File Retrieve. If there already is a document in the window, LotusWorks checks to see if you have saved it (except for Databases) and, if necessary, asks whether you wish to save it. Once you respond to the prompt, LotusWorks displays a dialog box containing a list box of available files and a text box for the file name. Select the desired file from the list or type the path and file name in the text box. LotusWorks opens the specified file in the *currently active* window.

*It's a good idea to save your work in progress to disk every 10 or 15 minutes. That way, if there is a power interruption to your computer or the program quits unexpectedly, you will lose at most only 10 or 15 minutes' worth of work.*

```
                       File Retrieve
   \..                         A         B        C        D
  _BASIC-1.WK1      1   Forecast - 1992  Qtr 1    Qtr 2    Qtr 3
  _Q_BUDG2.WK1      2   -                  -        -        -
  _Q_CASH.WK1       3   New York         47,500   60,000   55,500
  _Q_LOAN.WK1       4                                      72,150
                    5   Hartford         23,750   40,000   60,000
                    6       TOTAL SALES: 71,250  100,000  187,650
                    7
                    8   Raw Material     24,000   30,000   42,000
                    9   Labor            12,000   15,000   24,000
                   10   Overhead          9,000   12,000   13,800
                   11       TOTAL COSTS: 45,000   57,000   79,800

  File  [_BASIC-1.WK1_____]
  Path = D:\LWORKS3\LWDATA\

  Filter [*.WK1___]                         Retrieve     Cancel

  Select the file you want to view or use
```

**FIGURE 2.12:** To retrieve a saved file, select File Retrieve, highlight or type the name of the file, and select Retrieve

## Scrolling the Window Contents

Although the computer screen can display only part of a page of data at a time, a LotusWorks document can actually be much larger. For instance, a word processing document may be many pages long; many databases and spreadsheets are both wider and longer than the screen. Therefore, in order to see all of a document that is larger than the screen window, you must move the contents of the document past the window. This is called scrolling the document.

### Scrolling from the Keyboard

You can control scrolling from the keyboard with the Left and Right Arrow keys plus the Page Up (PgUp) and Page Down (PgDn) keys. The following table summarizes the procedures. (Some were described earlier in this chapter under "Moving Around in LotusWorks.")

| To Accomplish This | Do This |
| --- | --- |
| Scroll above the top edge | Hold down Up Arrow |
| Scroll below the bottom edge | Hold down Down Arrow |
| Scroll past the right edge* | Hold down Right Arrow |
| Scroll past the left edge* | Hold down Left Arrow |
| Move up one line | Press Up Arrow |
| Move down one line | Press Down Arrow |
| Move up one screen | Press PgUp |
| Move down one screen | Press PgDn |
| Move up one record (Database) | Press PgUp |
| Move down one record (Database) | Press PgDn |

* Not available in the Word Processing service

Scrolling from the Keyboard

## Scrolling with a Mouse

You can click or drag the vertical and horizontal scroll bars to scroll with a mouse. The vertical scroll bar enables you to scroll the contents of a window up and down, and the horizontal scroll bar enables scrolling sideways. There are three parts to each scroll bar: an arrow, an elevator button, and the space between the arrow and elevator button. Here is how they work:

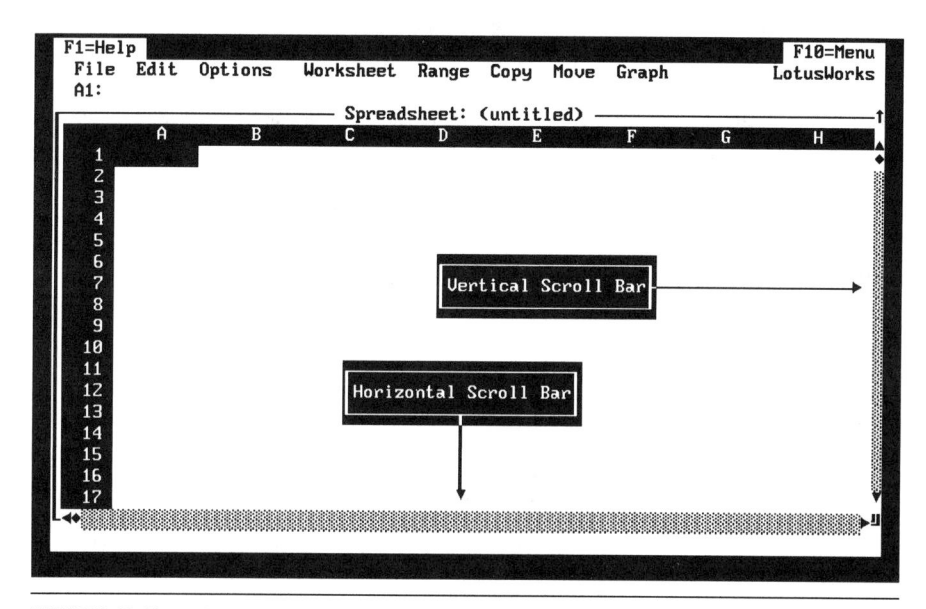

**FIGURE 2.13:** The vertical and horizontal scroll bars

If you click on an arrow, the contents move up or down one line or left or right a few spaces in the direction indicated by the arrow. If you click on the space between the elevator button and the arrow, the contents scroll up or down a screen at a time or left or right one screen-width at a time. You can drag the vertical elevator button up or down to move toward the beginning or end of a document and drag the horizontal elevator button left or right to move toward the left or right edge of a document.

| To Accomplish This | Do This |
| --- | --- |
| Scroll above the top edge | Click and hold on Up scroll arrow |
| Scroll below the bottom edge | Click and hold on Down scroll arrow |
| Scroll past the right edge* | Click and hold on Right scroll arrow |
| Scroll past the left edge* | Click and hold on Left scroll arrow |
| Move up one line | Click on top scroll arrow |
| Move down one line | Click on bottom scroll arrow |
| Move up one screen | Click on vertical scroll bar above the elevator button |
| Move down one screen | Click on vertical scroll bar below the elevator button |
| Move up one or more pages (Word) | Drag elevator button up |
| Move up one or more records (Database in Table view) | Drag elevator button up |
| Move down one or more pages (Word) | Drag elevator button down |
| Move down one or more records (Database in Table view) | Drag elevator button down |

* Not available in the Word Processing service

Scrolling With a Mouse

## Working with Multiple LotusWorks Windows

You can have several LotusWorks task windows open at the same time, and you can display them on the screen together. The number is limited by the sizes of the documents and the amount of memory (RAM) in your computer. This gives you many different ways to work productively with multiple documents. For instance, you can view multiple documents from different services, multiple documents from the same service, and/or multiple views of the same document. You can resize and reposition the windows so that several can be viewed on the screen at once. You can also switch back and forth between viewing each window full-screen or in its sized placement.

By using multiple windows, you can, for example, view an original and edited version of a document alongside each other. You can view widely separated parts of a large spreadsheet simultaneously. You can view documents while you are using the Communications service. You can view part of a spreadsheet while you compose a word document. And you can view a database as you compose a form letter to use with it for mail-merge.

Only one window can be active at a time. The currently active window is indicated by the blinking cursor or highlighted screen pointer, and by a lighter background than the others.

## Opening a New Task Window

To open a new task window, first press Ctrl+F6 or select the LotusWorks menu item to exit the current window and return to the LotusWorks Screen. This leaves the task window open but no longer active. Select the (new file) option under the service that you want to use in the new window. LotusWorks opens a new window with a blank screen for the service you selected. To toggle to the previous task window, press F6. To toggle back to the new window, press F6 again.

## Switching Windows

Whenever you want to switch from one open window to another, simply press F6 (Swap) to go to the last window window you were in, or Alt+F6 (Next) to go forward to another window. If you have several windows open, keep pressing Alt+F6 until you reach the window you want.

If you have trouble remembering F6 and Alt+F6 at first, you may also switch windows by selecting Options Windows Swap or Options Windows Next.

If you are using a mouse, you can switch to another window by clicking on it, provided the window is visible on the screen.

*If you use a mouse, you can switch easily among windows if you adjust their sizes and positioning to make all open windows visible at the same time. To do this, make all the windows slightly smaller than full-screen, and offset each window slightly from the one behind it. To switch, simply click on some part of the window of your choice.*

## Sizing and Moving Windows

Although it is possible to have more than one full-screen window open at a time, it's usually easier to use them if you make the windows smaller and reposition

**44** The Lotus Guide to LotusWorks

them so that you can see all of the open windows at once. If you make a window smaller, you can always view it full-screen by making it active and pressing Alt+Z or selecting Options Window Zoom.

If you use the keyboard, you can move a window and make it larger or smaller as follows:

1. Select Options Windows Placement.

2. The Help line at the bottom of the screen gives directions for sizing and moving the window. To change size, press the arrow keys until the window is the desired size and shape; to move the window, press M and then the arrow keys until the window is in the desired position.

3. Press Enter to accept the changes or Esc to cancel them.

If you use a mouse, you can make a window larger or smaller by dragging the Resize button located in the lower right-hand corner of the window. Drag the button up to make the window shorter and drag it to the left to make the window narrower. To move the window to a new position, drag the top border of the window into the desired position.

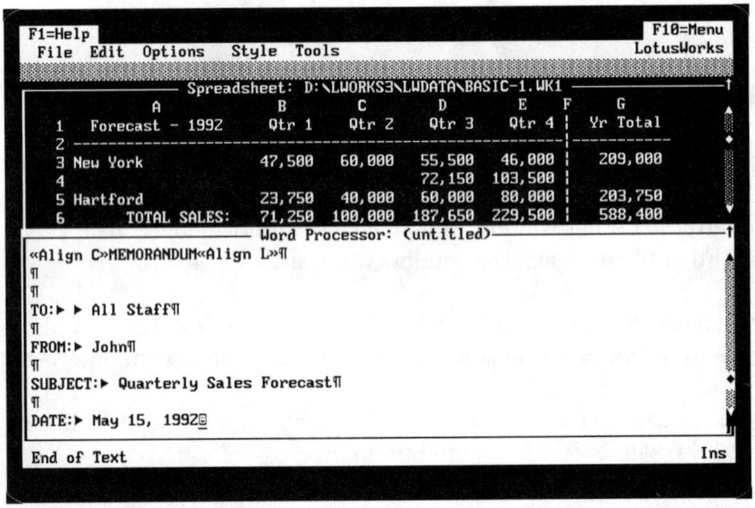

**FIGURE 2.14:** By resizing and repositioning windows, you can view two documents at the same time.

## Closing Windows

When you are ready to close a window, press Alt+Q or select File Quit. Except in the Database service (where LotusWorks saves files automatically), Lotus-Works checks to see if you have saved the current document, prompts you to save it if necessary, then closes the current window and returns you to the previous window. If no other window is open, it returns you to the LotusWorks Screen.

## Getting Help On-screen

LotusWorks 3.0 provides numerous prompts, cues, and messages, but if you're uncertain about how to proceed at any point, there are four ways to get immediate help:

1. **Press F1 for Contextual Help.** You may press F1 from any point in LotusWorks to get contextual help. LotusWorks opens a dialog box containing a help message about the part of LotusWorks where you are. When you finish reading the help message, you may select additional topics or exit the help box to resume at the point where you left.

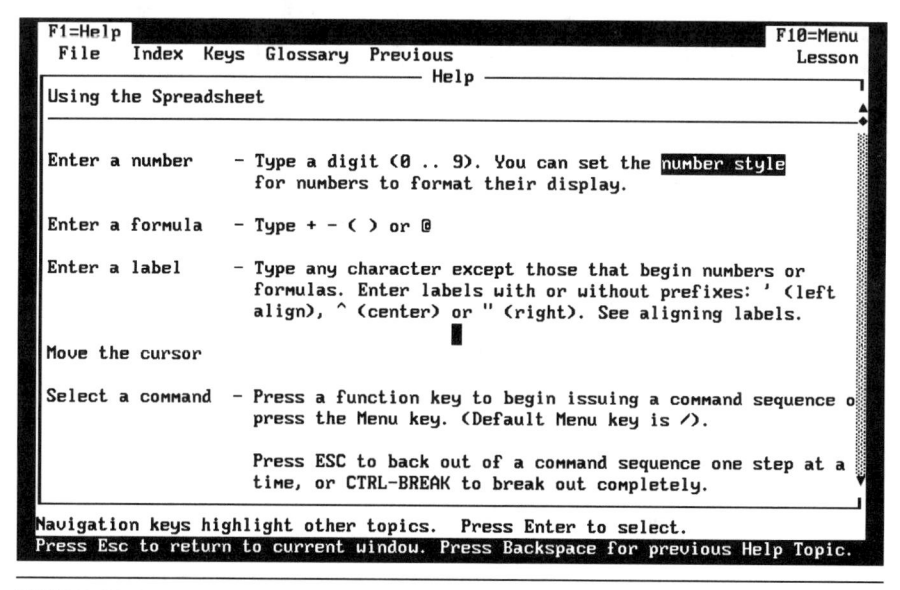

```
F1=Help                                                          F10=Menu
  File    Index  Keys  Glossary  Previous                        Lesson
                                ─ Help ─
 Using the Spreadsheet

 Enter a number    - Type a digit (0 .. 9). You can set the number style
                     for numbers to format their display.

 Enter a formula   - Type + - ( ) or @

 Enter a label     - Type any character except those that begin numbers or
                     formulas. Enter labels with or without prefixes: ' (left
                     align), ^ (center) or " (right). See aligning labels.

 Move the cursor

 Select a command  - Press a function key to begin issuing a command sequence o
                     press the Menu key. (Default Menu key is /).

                     Press ESC to back out of a command sequence one step at a
                     time, or CTRL-BREAK to break out completely.

Navigation keys highlight other topics.  Press Enter to select.
Press Esc to return to current window. Press Backspace for previous Help Topic.
```

**FIGURE 2.15:** A typical Help message

2. **Press Alt+F1 for the on-screen Tutorial.** You may press Alt+F1 from anywhere in LotusWorks to open the on-screen Tutorial. LotusWorks opens the Tutorial to a topic appropriate to the task you are performing. The Tutorial screens contain instructions for operating the tutorial. When you finish doing as much of the tutorial as you want, exit the Tutorial, and LotusWorks returns you to the point where you left.

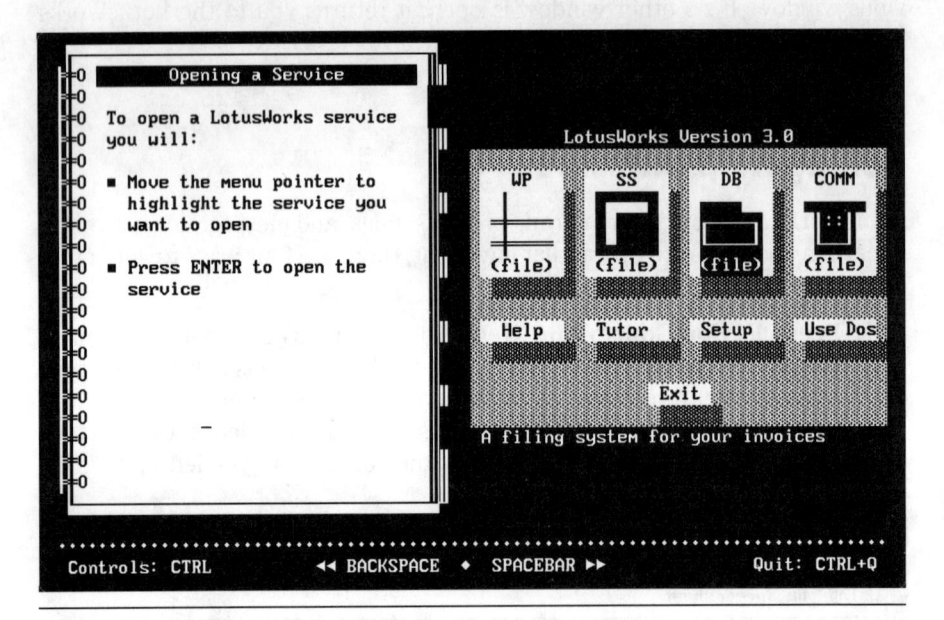

**FIGURE 2.16:** When your press Alt-F1, LotusWorks opens the Tutorial and lets you choose from the table of contents.

3. **Select Tutorial on the LotusWorks Screen.** You may also enter the on-screen Tutorial by selecting it on the LotusWorks Screen. LotusWorks opens the Tutorial to the introductory screen. You may choose to start the Tutorial at the beginning or on any of the topics listed in the table of contents, and you may perform as much of the tutorial exercises as you want. When you exit the Tutorial, LotusWorks returns you to the Lotus-Works Screen.

4. You can also access the Tutorial from the Help menu. To do so, press F1 from any where in LotusWorks to open the Help menu, select the Index option, and then select "Using the LotusWorks Tutorial."

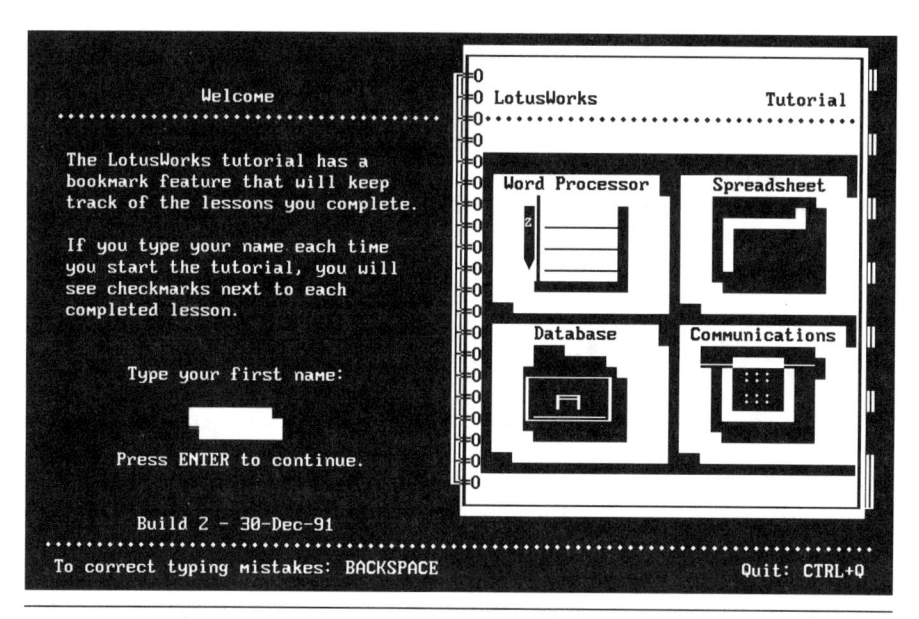

**FIGURE 2.17:** When you select Tutorial from the LotusWorks Screen, LotusWorks displays the introductory screen.

## Using DOS Access

The Use DOS option on the LotusWorks Screen lets you temporarily suspend LotusWorks, access DOS, and give simple DOS commands without exiting from LotusWorks. You can use this feature, for instance, to examine a disk directory with the DIR command, format a new floppy disk for backup files, copy files from one disk to another, or change the access attributes of a file.

To use the DOS Access feature, select the Use DOS option on the Lotus-Works Screen. LotusWorks is temporarily suspended, the LotusWorks Screen temporarily disappears, and the DOS prompt appears. You may then execute DOS commands for as long as you like. When you are finished, type *EXIT* and press Enter to reactivate LotusWorks and bring back the LotusWorks Screen.

## A Brief Tour of the Menus

The menus are the doors to the parts of LotusWorks that can do work for you. Before using LotusWorks, it's good to take a quick tour of the menu bar, to see the variety of functions and menu items in LotusWorks as a whole and in each LotusWorks service.

### The LotusWorks Menu Item

The LotusWorks menu item appears at the right end of the menu bar in all the LotusWorks Services. You can think of it as the express button to the Lotus-Works Screen. It always takes you directly there, from wherever you are in LotusWorks. When you select the LotusWorks item, any services that have been opened remain open.

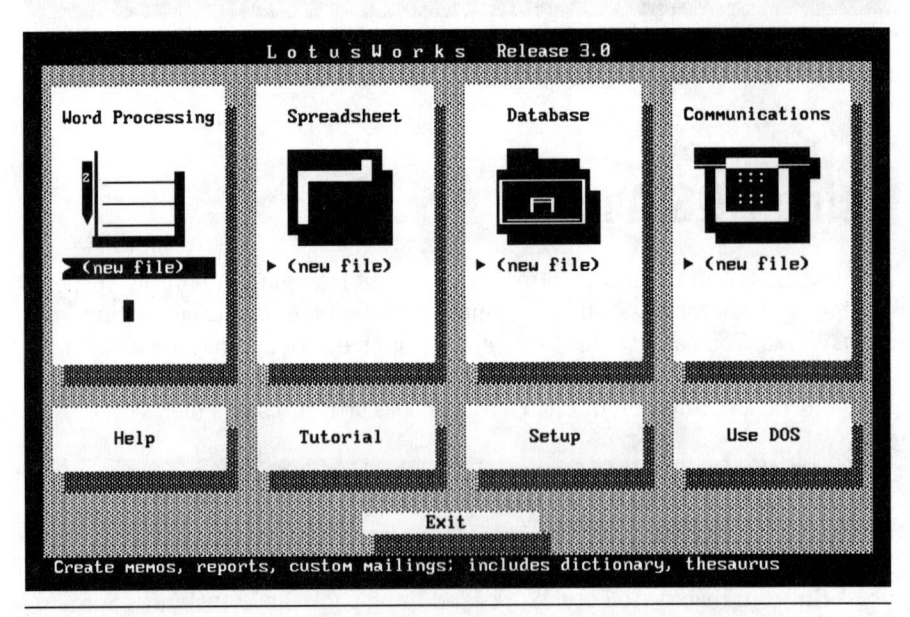

**FIGURE 2.18:** The LotusWorks option (or Ctrl+F6) always takes you directly to the LotusWorks Screen.

## The Common Menus

You can think of the three leftmost menus as the *common* menus. These are the File, Edit, and Options menus. They have the same names and control the same types of function in all LotusWorks services. Although the names are the same, the contents of the menus vary slightly from service to service because some functions are appropriate for one service but not for others.

**File.** The File menu controls various filing functions plus printing, closing windows, and transferring files to and from other system formats. The Print and Transfer options lead to submenus. The menu has additional options in the Database and Communications services that do not appear in the other services. The File menu in the Database service looks like Figure 2.19:

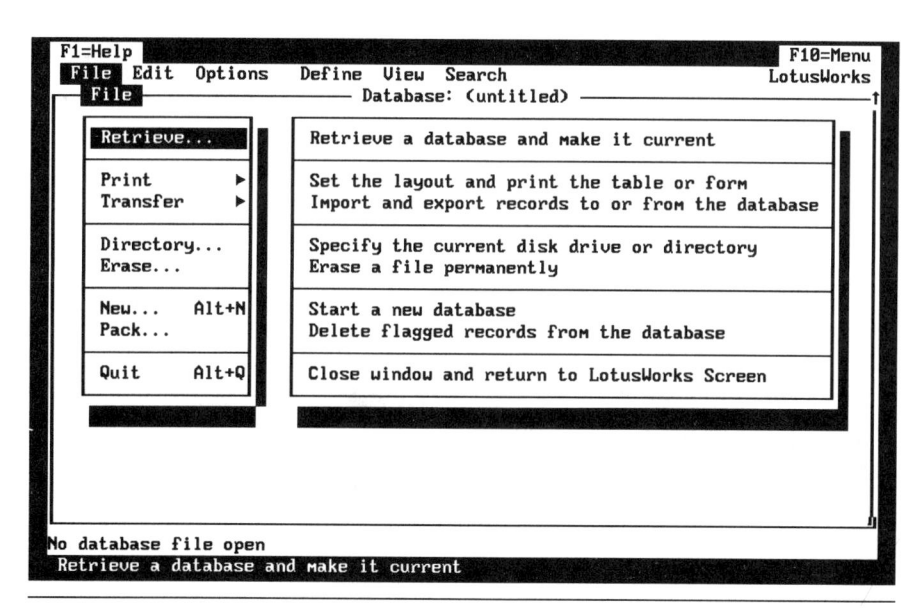

```
F1=Help                                                         F10=Menu
 File  Edit   Options    Define   View   Search          LotusWorks
┌──── File ─────────────── Database: (untitled) ────────────────────┐
│ Retrieve...    │  Retrieve a database and make it current         │
│                │                                                  │
│ Print       ▶  │  Set the layout and print the table or form      │
│ Transfer    ▶  │  Import and export records to or from the database│
│                │                                                  │
│ Directory...   │  Specify the current disk drive or directory     │
│ Erase...       │  Erase a file permanently                        │
│                │                                                  │
│ New...  Alt+N  │  Start a new database                            │
│ Pack...        │  Delete flagged records from the database        │
│                │                                                  │
│ Quit    Alt+Q  │  Close window and return to LotusWorks Screen    │
└────────────────┘                                                  │
│                                                                   │
│                                                                   │
│                                                                   │
No database file open
 Retrieve a database and make it current
```

**FIGURE 2.19:** The File menu in the Database service.

**Edit.** The Edit menu controls various editing functions, such as selecting, deleting, copying, moving, pasting, and restoring data. There are service-specific options in each of the LotusWorks services. The Edit menu in the Spreadsheet service looks like Figure 2.20.

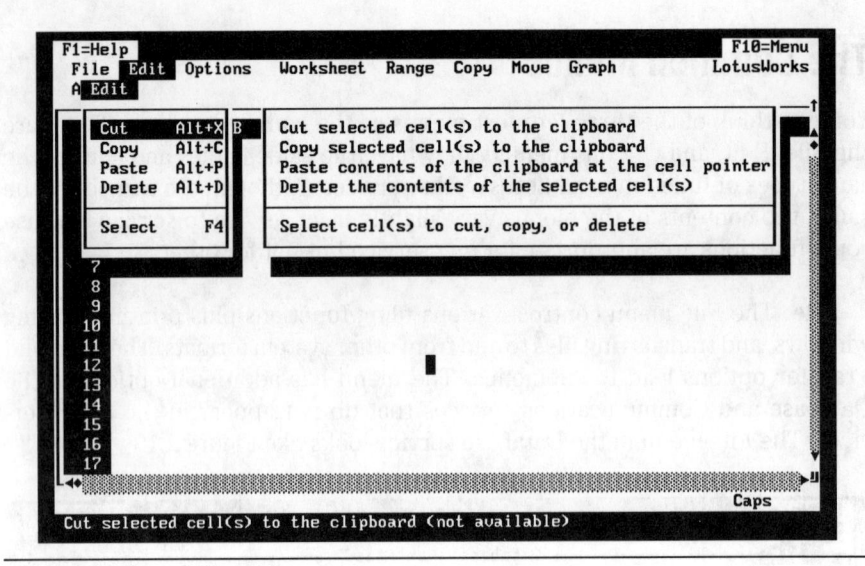

```
F1=Help                                                          F10=Menu
  File Edit Options   Worksheet  Range  Copy  Move  Graph        LotusWorks
A  Edit
   ┌─────────────────┬─────────────────────────────────────────────┐
   │ Cut      Alt+X  │ Cut selected cell(s) to the clipboard       │
   │ Copy     Alt+C  │ Copy selected cell(s) to the clipboard      │
   │ Paste    Alt+P  │ Paste contents of the clipboard at the cell pointer │
   │ Delete   Alt+D  │ Delete the contents of the selected cell(s) │
   │ Select      F4  │ Select cell(s) to cut, copy, or delete      │
   └─────────────────┴─────────────────────────────────────────────┘
   7
   8
   9
  10
  11
  12
  13       ■
  14
  15
  16
  17
                                                                   Caps
  Cut selected cell(s) to the clipboard (not available)
```

**FIGURE 2.20:** The Edit menu in the Spreadsheet service.

**Options.** The Options menu controls certain functions that affect the way LotusWorks operates, such as the size and positioning of windows; the creating and running of macros; and the display of operating statistics about the system. In addition, in most services it contains service-specific options. The Options menu in the Word Processing service looks like Figure 2.21.

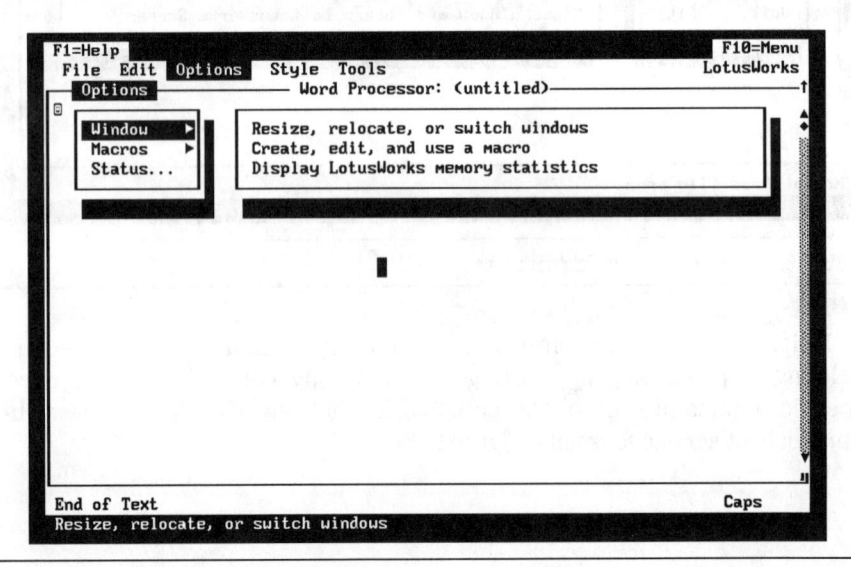

```
F1=Help                                                          F10=Menu
  File Edit Options  Style  Tools                                LotusWorks
   Options ──────── Word Processor: (untitled) ─────────────
   ┌──────────┬────────────────────────────────────────────┐
   │ Window  ▶│ Resize, relocate, or switch windows        │
   │ Macros  ▶│ Create, edit, and use a macro              │
   │ Status...│ Display LotusWorks memory statistics       │
   └──────────┴────────────────────────────────────────────┘




                           ■





  End of Text                                                    Caps
  Resize, relocate, or switch windows
```

**FIGURE 2.21:** The Options menu in the Word Processing service.

## The Service-Specific Menus

Each LotusWorks 3.0 service has some menus that are unique to that service. Rather than try to cover them all here, we'll describe them in the chapters on the services.

## Changing the Default Setup

The first time you use LotusWorks, you should select the Setup program and set the setup options. LotusWorks 3.0 comes with predefined default settings that are appropriate for most users. Unless you change them, LotusWorks always starts up with these default settings. However, you can easily change them to suit your particular equipment and working style. For example, you can have the Communications service automatically default to serial port 2 (COM2) instead of COM1, if that's the one where your modem is connected. You can turn mouse support on or off. If you have a high-resolution screen, you can have LotusWorks operate in Text mode so that type styles appear in different colors or in Graphics mode so that the type on the screen resembles the type that will be printed.

You can change the default settings by going to the LotusWorks Screen and selecting the Setup option. You'll see the following Setup screen:

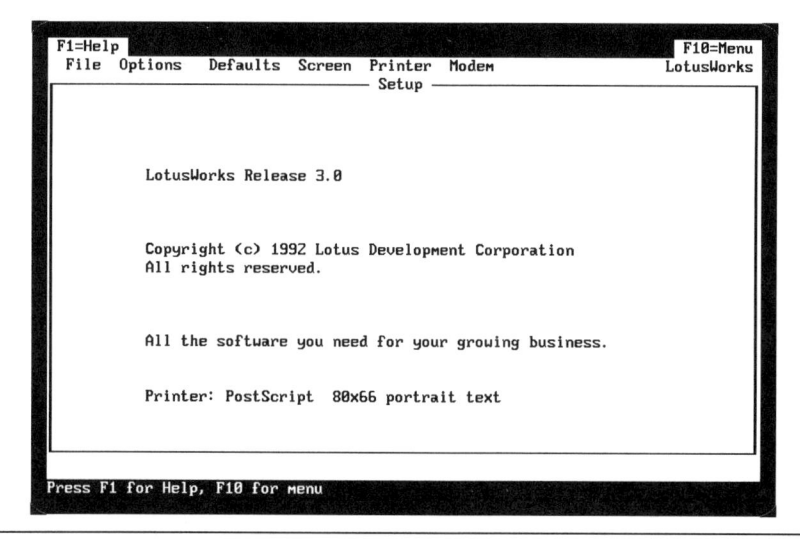

```
F1=Help                                                      F10=Menu
     File  Options   Defaults  Screen  Printer  Modem        LotusWorks
                              ─── Setup ───



            LotusWorks Release 3.0


            Copyright (c) 1992 Lotus Development Corporation
            All rights reserved.



            All the software you need for your growing business.


            Printer: PostScript   80x66 portrait text




 Press F1 for Help, F10 for menu
```

**FIGURE 2.22:** The menu items available on the Setup screen.

You select menu items on this screen just as you do on the screens in the LotusWorks services.

**Defaults.** The Defaults item controls several operating options: whether or not to have a beep sound when an error occurs, whether or not to use a mouse, whether to have menu prompts appear each time you open a menu, whether or not to use expanded memory (EMS) or extended memory (XMS) for temporary file storage, and the drive and subdirectory to use as the working directory. Once you change any of these settings, they remain in effect until you change them again.

Whether or not to have the computer beep on errors is a matter of personal preference. Try it both ways and see which works best for you. Similarly, whether to have menu prompts appear automatically is a matter of preference once you know the system, but in the short run, at least, you should use the prompts to help you learn the system.

If you have a mouse, select the Mouse option, so that you can see how the mouse operates. If your computer has Extended or Expanded memory, select the Use XMS/EMS option for temporary storage. Otherwise, LotusWorks uses disk space for temporary storage, which makes operation a bit slower. You should turn this setting off only if you plan to choose Use DOS from the LotusWorks screen and run a program that uses most of the extended or expanded memory, or if you are running a memory manager program that conflicts with LotusWorks. If you are not sure whether your computer has Extended memory, Expanded memory, or neither, see your computer manual or dealer.

The working directory is the subdirectory where LotusWorks automatically stores document files, unless you direct it to do otherwise. When you install LotusWorks, the installation program automatically creates a subdirectory named \LWDATA for this purpose, unless you specify otherwise. It's a good practice to keep your data files in a separate subdirectory from any program files. Unless you have a compellling reason to change it (such as lack of space on the drive that contains your LotusWorks program files), leave the Working Directory default setting as it is. If you do need to change it, be sure to specify the drive and complete path to the subdirectory you want to use as the working directory.

When all the Default options are set to your liking, select Accept to exit the dialog box.

**Screen.** The Screen item controls the way certain information is displayed on the screen. If you have a high-resolution or color monitor (CGA, EGA, or

VGA), you may choose Text mode (which displays different type styles in different colors) or Graphics mode (which displays type styles on the screen similarly to the way they appear when printed). You may also choose among three color setups: Snowfall, which displays soft colors; Neon, which displays bright colors; and Midnight, which displays LotusWorks in black and white. If you have a low-resolution or monochrome monitor, your choices are more limited. Once you change these settings, they remain in effect until you change them again.

Once you are familiar with the basic LotusWorks operations, you probably should experiment with the Setup defaults a bit to see which settings you like best. Until you are reasonably familiar with LotusWorks, however, it's probably best to leave the default settings as they are. When all the Screen options are set to your liking, select Accept to exit the dialog box.

**Printer.** The Printer item controls the settings needed to coordinate LotusWorks with your printer. This item must be set to fit your particular printer setup. Select the port where your printer is connected (LPT1, LPT2, LPT3, COM1, or COM2). If your printer requires a setup command or setup string each time you print, type the setup string in the text box. (See your printer manual for instructions.) If you are using a serial printer, select the baud rate that LotusWorks should use in communicating with the printer. When all the options have been set, select Accept.

**Modem.** The Modem item controls the settings needed to coordinate LotusWorks with a modem. The settings are explained in Chapter 7.

**Exiting the Setup screen.** When you have finished selecting the Setup options, press Alt+Q or press F10 and select LotusWorks to exit the Setup screen and return to the LotusWorks screen.

# Safeguarding Your Data

Once you have made the effort to create a document, you don't want something to happen to it accidentally. There several things you can do to safeguard your precious work.

- **Save your work frequently.** When you are creating or editing a document, it's a good idea to save it to a disk every ten or fifteen minutes. (In the Database service, LotusWorks does this for you, automatically saving the database immediately whenever you make a change in it.) That way if your computer fails, a disk drive fails, or a power outage occurs, the most you'll lose is only 10 or 15 minutes' work.

- **Keep a backup copy on a floppy.** It's a good idea to save files to a floppy disk as well as to your hard disk. That way, if the hard disk fails you have a backup copy of your data. You might need to save your work to the backup floppy disk only when you exit a document or end a PC session.

- **Back up your entire hard disk.** This, of course, should be a regular practice for anyone with a hard disk. For businesses, it is essential. The frequency depends on the amount of day-to-day data entry you perform and the amount you can afford to lose. If you enter accounting data every day, you probably should back up the hard disk every day. If you enter data only on certain days, a weekly backup is probably sufficient. Even small offices should perform backups weekly.

    You can use a commercial backup program or the DOS Backup command, but it is slow going if you are backing up a 40-megabyte or larger hard disk to floppy disks. That's a principal reason most people don't back up their disks as often as they should. For most businesses, it is well worth the investment to buy an internal or external tape backup unit to ensure a backup copy of valuable business records.

- **Use protection on your spreadsheets.** This is a different kind of protection, but it's important just the same. Once you have built a spreadsheet, select Range Protect and protect the entire spreadsheet from changes. That way you can be sure that neither you nor anyone else can erase data or formulas by accident. You can always purposefully change the spreadsheet by first selecting Range Unprotect, but if you do, be sure to turn protection back on before you put the spreadsheet away.

*Be sure to back up your databases! Because there is no File Save command in the Database service, the easiest way is to return to the LotusWorks Screen, select Use DOS, and use the COPY command to copy the database file to a floppy disk. The file extension for LotusWorks database files is .DBF, so a database named MYDATA has a file name of MYDATA.DBF. When you have finished copying the file, type EXIT and press Enter to return to LotusWorks.*

## Exiting from LotusWorks

To leave LotusWorks from any service and return to DOS, press Ctrl+F6 or select LotusWorks to return to the LotusWorks Screen, then select Exit. LotusWorks checks to see if you have changed any documents since they were last saved and, if necessary, prompts you to see whether you want to save or ignore the changes in each unsaved document. When all the prompts have been answered, the LotusWorks Screen disappears and the DOS prompt appears.

CAUTION: You should always complete the Exit procedure to terminate a LotusWorks session. If you turn off your computer without first exiting LotusWorks, some of your valuable work can be lost.

Now you are ready to begin using the LotusWorks services.

# 3

# Writing Well with Word Processing

Word processing is probably the LotusWorks service that most people use first. Just about everyone needs typewriting, and the word processing service is easy to learn, especially if you already know how to use a typewriter.

This does not mean that everyone uses word processing well. In fact, helpful as word processing is, most users tap only a fraction of its potential for saving work. This chapter shows how to tap much more of that potential.

## Working Smart with Word Processing

The keys to working smart with word processing are to use the word processor as a writing tool as well as a typing tool and to set up your documents to let LotusWorks do as much work as possible. This includes saving and reusing formats and text, maximizing the use of macros, and wherever possible drawing on information that can be stored in the computer. It also means taking advantage of the LotusWorks tools to help you edit and revise your writing.

LotusWorks can automate a number of writing tasks as well as typing tasks. These include:

- **Merge Printing.** As mentioned in the previous chapter, almost everyone can

*In this chapter, you'll learn:*

- *How to work smart with word processing*
- *Intelligent editing and revising*
- *Techniques for sharing the workload*
- *How to set up and save document formats*
- *How to style text*
- *Printing tips*
- *Boilerplate techniques*
- *How to launch documents with macros*

use merge printing to individualize standard documents. Merge printing inserts information from a database into a document created in the Word Processing service. The printing is launched and controlled from the word processing service. Merge printing is ideal for individualized form letters but also can be used to format lists drawn from databases, update information in periodic reports, and automatically address letters and envelopes.

- **Boilerplate.** Boilerplate is text that you save and use over and over again. It can be as short as a few letters (such as an abbreviation or company name) or as long as a few paragraphs (such as standard terms of contracts and agreements). There are several ways to store and use boilerplate with LotusWorks.

- **Launching Documents.** You can design your own document formats, save them, and use macros to call them up automatically whenever you need to start new documents. For example, you can have your own formats for memos, business letters, notes to clients and employees, notices, reports, etc.

- **Copying, Moving, and Pasting.** When you are editing and revising your writing, you can copy and move text from place to place without having to retype it.

- **Spell Checking.** The LotusWorks spell checker can check your documents for misspelled and duplicated words.

- **Word Matching and Thesaurus.** The LotusWorks word-match feature and thesaurus can help you look up words you don't know how to spell, and the thesaurus helps you find synonyms for specified words.

- **Searching and Replacing.** When you decide that a word or phrase needs to be changed, LotusWorks can find every place where it is used in a document and either replace it automatically with your revision or let you decide in each case whether to replace or not.

- **Numbering Pages, Figures, and Tables.** When you need to number pages, figures, or tables in multi-page documents, LotusWorks can number them for you, using the numbering style that you specify.

- **Inserting Dates and Times.** LotusWorks can print the date and time automatically for you.

- **Counting Words.** When you need to count the number of words in a document, LotusWorks can do it for you automatically.

As you can see, there is quite a repertoire of tools in the Word Processing service. The more you can draw on the full repertoire, the more work you can save yourself.

# Elements of Economical Writing

As with any creative act, writing is an intensely personal matter. It is easy for some people and agonizing for others. For many people, however, the improvements that the Word Processing service brings to their writing outweigh the benefits it brings to their typing.

## Putting Thoughts Into Writing

Here are six basic techniques you can use to write economically with LotusWorks:

1. Plan what you have to say.
2. Use a prerecorded format wherever possible.
3. Use stored data where practicable.
4. Edit and revise as you write.
5. Use LotusWorks features to speed editing and revising.
6. Set your work aside, then edit and revise again.

Let's look at each technique in turn.

**Plan what you have to say.** People write in different ways, some putting ideas down in bits and pieces, some working from meticulous outlines, and some writing pretty much in a linear stream as the ideas occur to them. Most people use different techniques for different types of documents. Regardless of writing style, however, most of us (this writer included) find writing difficult because the thoughts in our mind's eye flow faster and more elegantly than the words we put down on the page. Nevertheless, all of us write better when we know what we want to say.

There are a couple of ways to use LotusWorks to help you plan what to say. One way is simply to create an outline or list of topics in a word document and then, in the same document, flesh out each topic with text. This technique works well for short documents.

Another technique is to open two windows on the screen, put an outline or list of topics in one and the document you are composing in the other, and then press the F6 key to switch back and forth between them as you develop and rework the outline and document. This technique is useful for keeping the big picture in mind when you are writing long and detailed documents.

**Use a prerecorded format wherever possible.** Although document formats vary considerably from person to person and from company to company, most people like to use a consistent format in their own documents. For small businesses, it's a must. Using attractive and consistent formats is one of the most effective ways to give your small business a professional image that can compete with larger companies.

To ensure consistent formats and save yourself a lot of time and work, simply create a document format for each type of document you use, give each a name, and save each format without entering any other text. You can think of these as templates for each type of document, whether a memo, business letter, report, or whatever. Whenever you need to write a document, simply retrieve the appropriate template, rename it, enter your text, and save the document under the new name.

**Use stored data wherever practicable.** Stored data can include not only names and addresses but also boilerplate text, pricing information, account balances, and any other information that you can keep in a database.

Here are three basic ways to use stored data in word documents:

- **Macros.** Put the stored data into a macro and run the macro when you want to enter the stored data into a word document. This works well when the stored data is relatively simple and not subject to change. For example, document templates and standard paragraphs for contracts and letters are good candidates for macros. On the other hand, it is usually better to use a storage document to store text containing imbedded commands and a database to store prices that change frequently.

- **Storage documents.** Put the stored data into a separate word document and then copy and paste the desired information into the word document you are composing. For example, you can store a variety of boilerplate paragraphs for business letters in a storage document and then copy and paste only the paragraphs that fit the particular letter you are composing. This approach works well when you have a large number of boilerplate items and when you might like to pick and choose among item.

- **Databases.** Put the stored data into a database and then merge print into a word document. For example, you could put product numbers, descriptions, and prices into a database, and then merge print them into a letter confirming an order. One advantage of this approach is that when data such as prices change, you can update a single database and be assured that the information will be correct in all subsequent documents. Most people think of this approach only when printing form letters to multiple addressees, but if you have applicable data in a database, you can also use the approach for letters, memos, reports, or any other type of word document to an individual addressee.

**Edit and revise as you write.** The best writers are those who can edit and revise their own work. The LotusWorks word processor makes the job much easier. When you finish a sentence or paragraph, read it immediately. If you see that it has errors or does not say what you want it to, revise it immediately.

**Use LotusWorks tools to speed your editing and revising.** The LotusWorks tools that can especially ease your editing and revising are the copy, move, and paste features; search and replace; and the thesaurus, word match, and spell-checking features.

**Put the draft aside, then edit and revise again.** Probably the most important step in putting your thoughts into writing is to set aside the draft document for awhile and then edit and revise it. Looking at a printed draft is a good way to see your work with fresh eyes. Some people call this "putting it in the refrigerator." How long you should set the draft aside depends on your working style and the type of document. For most business memos and letters, you'll probably be doing well to be able to set it aside for any time at all. However, even a few minutes can help. And if you are writing a business plan or a letter to solicit new business, you want to make the document the best you can. You'd probably do well to set it aside for a day or more and to revise it several times, to view it more from the perspective of your readers (and prospective customers).

## Putting Writing into Good Form

The other half of writing economically with the Word Processing service is making your documents look good. Here the trick is to develop good formats for your purposes and stick to them. LotusWorks makes it easy to store and apply formats for consistency. LotusWorks can help you create attractive formats with the following features:

- **Type styles.** If your printer is one that LotusWorks 3.0 supports, LotusWorks can assign as many different typefaces (fonts) as your printer can print. LotusWorks can print each typeface in a variety of sizes (again, depending on what your printer supports and depending on whether you opted for basic, regular, or extended font support when you installed LotusWorks 3.0). LotusWorks can print each typeface in normal, superscript, and subscript positions, and with bold, Italic, or underline attributes.

- **Spacing.** Depending on the settings you specify, LotusWorks can automatically insert up to three vertical spaces between lines of text and between paragraphs, and it can automatically indent the first line and/or subsequent lines of paragraphs. The indents include outdents or hanging indents for numbered paragraphs and paragraphs set off by bullets.

- **Text Alignments.** LotusWorks can automatically center text without your having to count spaces. It can also align text to the right, align it to both the left and right edges (right-justified), and align it to the left (ragged-right).

- **Headers and Footers.** Headers and footers are text that appears at the top and bottom of each page on documents such as letters and reports. They help identify the page and document. LotusWorks lets you enter up to three lines at the top of the page for each header and three lines at the bottom for each footer, and then it prints the lines automatically on every page that you designate.

- **Page Numbers.** LotusWorks numbers pages for you automatically, starting with whatever number you designate and using the type style that you specify. You may include page numbers in headers and footers or place them elsewhere on the page.

- **Figure and Table Numbers.** Just as it numbers pages for you, LotusWorks can also number figures and tables within larger documents.

## Techniques for Sharing the Workload

One way to save work is to share the workload. The most common arrangement is for one person to draft the documents and a second person to put them into final form and print them. You can also have more than one person edit drafts. The same principles can apply to letters, reports, or any other type of word processing document.

If everyone involved has access to a PC, you can simply swap floppy disks to work on the same document or use a local area network. If not everyone has access to a PC, editors can make changes on a printed copy for the finisher to enter into the computer.

Any time that more than one person is involved, however, the chances for miscommunication increase, so it's a good idea to be sure you are organized before you start. Here are some techniques:

- **Agree on how you are going to work together.** Be clear about who is doing what and how. This may seem obvious, but the communication between drafter and finisher should be two-way, with both people contributing ideas and listening to the other.

- **Develop and disseminate a clear file-naming scheme.** Obviously people who are going to be working on a document need to be able to recognize it in a file directory. Also, if one person is away from the office, others need to be able to find the document. See Chapter 2 for suggestions on file-naming schemes.

- **Label and number each draft.** Each draft should be clearly identified. Be sure that the word DRAFT and the number appear at the top of the first page. Incorporate the draft number into your file-naming scheme so that you can recognize each draft in the disk directory.

- **Mark and initial changes.** If someone else is editing a document on-line, have him or her mark word changes to a draft with a distinctive set of symbols that can be easily deleted later. If more than one person is editing the document, have them incorporate their initials into the mark, for example ***WAH***. This way the author can see the original and edited versions.

- **Keep backup copies.** Have everyone keep a backup copy of his or her revisions to the draft document.

- **Proofread before signing.** Even if you have done all the editing yourself, be sure to proofread one last time before signing or releasing a document. It's amazing how many errors can get by you on the screen or a printed draft and show up in the final document.

- **Delete obsolete drafts.** When the document is released in final form, notify everyone involved to delete the drafts from their disks. Obsolete drafts take up valuable disk storage space and can cause confusion. Be careful not to delete the final document, however! That's why you need a clear file-naming scheme that everyone understands.

- **Talk to each other.** Keep communicating with each other about the process of working on documents together. You may not hit the ideal process the first time. The idea is to improve the process each time you use it.

# Creating and Printing a Word Document

The general steps in creating and printing a word document are as follows:

1. Open the Word Processing service.
2. Create a document format, retrieve a format that you have previously created and saved, or use the default format settings.
3. Enter text into the document.
4. Tailor the text with special type treatments.
5. Check the appearance with the Print Preview feature.
6. Check the spelling with the Spell Checker.
7. Print the document.

In practice, you can and probably will vary these steps. For instance, you can tailor the text as you enter it, and you can preview the printed appearance on the screen at any time by simply pressing Alt+V.

# Starting a Word Document

To start a word processing document, you enter the Word Processing service, and simply start typing. When you reach the end of a line, LotusWorks wraps the text around to the next line automatically. When you want to end a paragraph or create a blank line, you press Enter. LotusWorks formats the data as you enter it, according to the Style options set up in the format.

To see how this works, try creating a document with the default Style settings. They are satisfactory for many types of business documents. At the LotusWorks screen, use the mouse or keyboard to select Word Processing. (You can double-click on the Word Processing option or type *W* and press the Enter key.) The following screen appears:

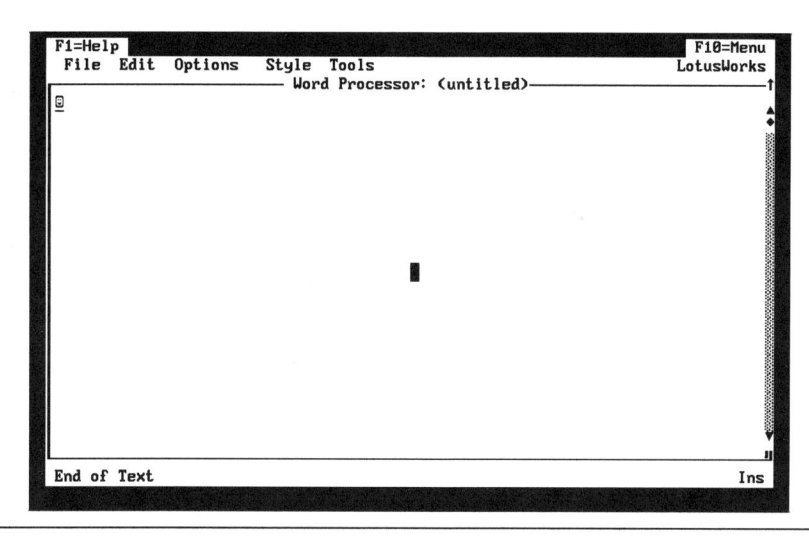

**FIGURE 3.1:** When you select Word Processing, a blank document screen appears.

The screen represents a blank word document. Try typing some text. Type a full line of characters to see how the text wraps at the end of the line. Try pressing Enter to end one paragraph and start another. Use the Tab and Shift keys as you would on a typewriter. When you have become familiar with the default settings, you are ready to start setting up your own document formats and text styles.

To exit from the document, press Alt+Q or select File Quit. LotusWorks displays the following dialog box:

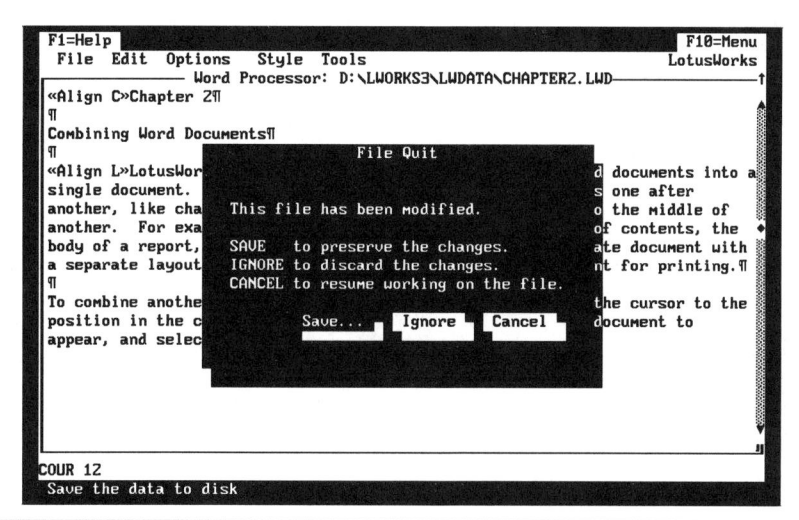

**FIGURE 3.2:** When you select File Quit, LotusWorks lets you save the document, exit without saving, or cancel the command.

LotusWorks gives you the choice of saving the document to a disk file before exiting, exiting without saving the document, or canceling the Quit command and returning to the document. To save the document, click on Save or simply press Enter. LotusWorks displays another dialog box:

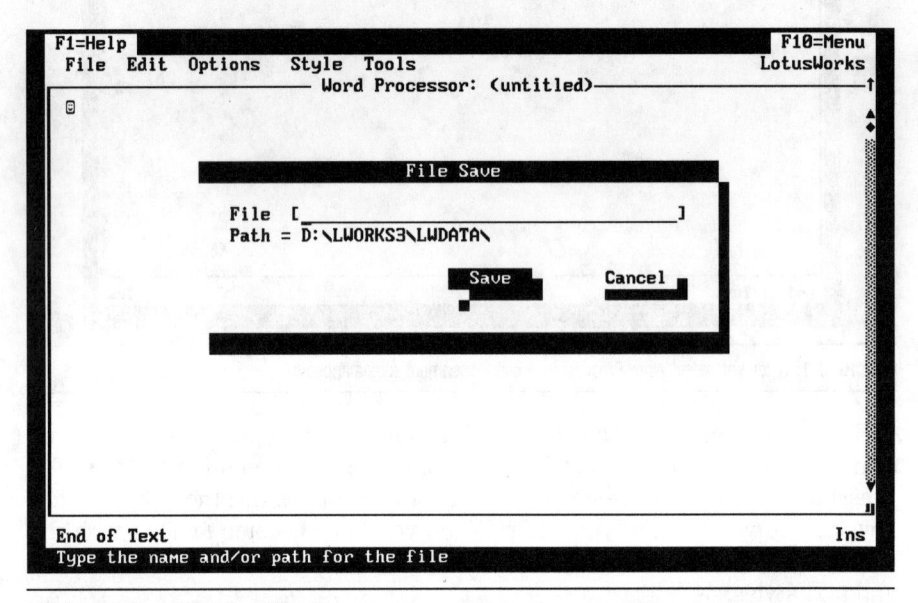

```
F1=Help                                                    F10=Menu
     File  Edit  Options   Style  Tools              LotusWorks
                       Word Processor: (untitled)

                           File Save

              File [_____]
              Path = D:\LWORKS3\LWDATA\
                                Save      Cancel



End of Text                                                     Ins
Type the name and/or path for the file
```

**FIGURE 3.3:** The File Quit Save dialog box

Type a file name for the document in the File text box. LotusWorks proposes a path (the current directory). If you want to use a different directory, type the desired path before the file name. Tab to the Save button and press Enter (or click on Save). For example, to save the document to a file named TEST-FILE.LWD in directory C:\LWORKS3\DOCS, type *c:\lworks3\docs\testfile*. LotusWorks enters the file name extension (.LWD) for you automatically.

> **NOTE:** It is best to let LotusWorks write the file name extension for you. Besides being easier, this method ensures that you can distinguish word processing, database, spreadsheet, and communications files from each other. If you write an extension other than .LWD for a word processing document, the file name will not appear in the directory box with other word files unless you specifically tell LotusWorks to filter for the new extension each and every time you retrieve files.

After you select Save, LotusWorks saves the document in the specified disk file, exits the Word Processing service, and returns you to the LotusWorks screen.

To exit from the Word Processing service without saving the document to a disk file, select Ignore. LotusWorks exits from the Word Processing service and returns you to the LotusWorks screen.

To cancel the Quit command, select Cancel. LotusWorks leaves you in the document where you left off.

# Setting Up and Saving Document Formats

Setting up a document format is quick and easy. You select all the settings from the Style menu. Once you have a custom format set up, you can save it to disk for future use. Here are the steps:

1. In the Word Processing service, select Style Fonts. (If you are using a mouse, click on the Style option and then click on the Fonts option. If you are using the keyboard, you can press F10 to go to the menu line, then type *S F;* or you can use the arrow keys to highlight Style, press Enter, then highlight Fonts and press Enter again.) The following dialog box appears:

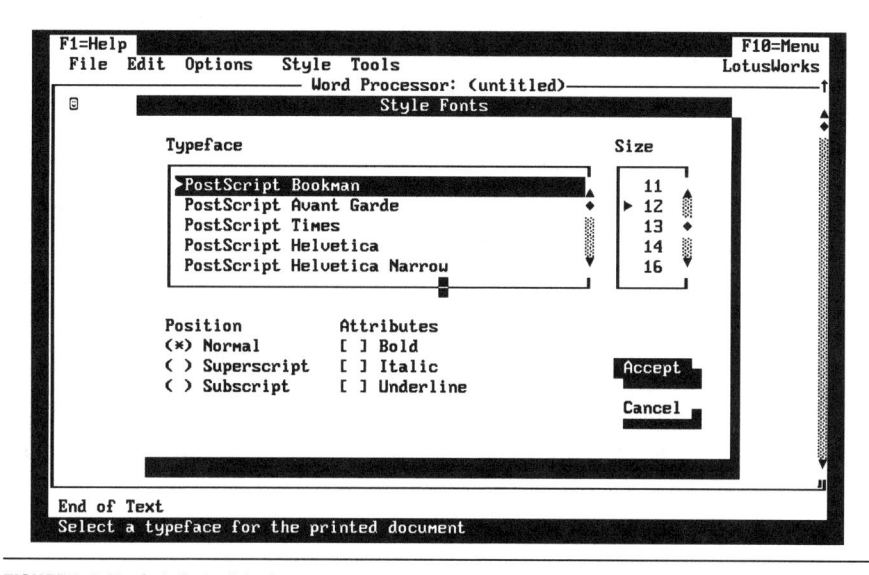

**FIGURE 3.4:** The Style Fonts dialog box

The Style Fonts dialog box controls the type characteristics to be used in the document. You can change these at any point in the document. LotusWorks gives you a choice of typefaces and type sizes, depending on the printer you are using and whether you selected the Basic, Medium, or Extended font set option when you ran the Install program.

To specify the typeface, press the Up or Down arrow keys to highlight the name of the typeface of your choice, or click the mouse on the desired typeface name. The contents of the Typeface text box may differ from the ones shown here.

To specify the type size, click on the desired size or tab to the Size box and use the arrow keys to highlight the desired size.

To specify the type position (normal, superscript, or subscript), click on the desired choice or tab to the Position column and use the arrow keys to highlight the desired choice. (For most purposes you can simply use the default setting, Normal.)

If you want to set a special type attribute (bold, italic, or underline), click on the desired choice or tab to the Attributes column and use the arrow keys to highlight the desired choice.

When all the options are specified as you want them for the beginning of the document, click on Accept or simply press Enter. (If you make a mistake and want to change a selection, you can click on the correct option or press Tab (to move forward) or Shift+Tab (to move backward) until the highlight moves to the desired box and then use the arrow keys to highlight the correct option. If you want to start over entirely, click on Cancel or press Tab until Cancel is highlighted, then press Enter.)

2. Select Style Layout, and check to be sure that the tabs, margins, line and paragraph spacing, and indents are set as you wish. If they are not, enter the settings you want, as follows:

   a. **Tabs.** Tab settings are expressed in inches and decimal fractions of inches. Type the tab stop settings you want. Leave a space after each setting. For example, to set the tabs at one-half inch, one inch, one-and-a-half inches, and two inches, you would type *0.5 1 1.5 2*.

   b. **Margins.** The margins are expressed in inches and decimal fractions of inches. To change the settings, click on or tab to the desired margin (Top, Bottom, Left, or Right) and enter the spacing you want. For one-inch margins you enter *1*. For one-and-a-half-inch margins you enter *1.5*.

c. **Indents.** You can have LotusWorks automatically indent the first line and/or the succeeding lines of paragraphs. Indents are expressed in inches. To indent the first line of each paragraph half an inch, select First line and enter .5.

> NOTE: You can use the indent feature to create a "hanging indent" to offset a paragraph to the right beside a number, letter, or bullet. Set the First line indent to 0 and the Following lines indent to the desired number of spaces for the offset. Usually three or four spaces is good for Arabic numerals, letters, and bullets. Roman numerals require a wider offset.

d. **Spacing.** Click on the options you want for spacing between lines and between paragraphs. If you are not using a mouse, tab to the desired spacing option (Lines or Paragraphs) and use the Up and Down arrow keys to highlight your spacing choice. Repeat the process on the other spacing option, if desired.

When all the Layout options are set, click on Accept or press Enter to accept the settings.

3. Select Style Align. The following menu appears:

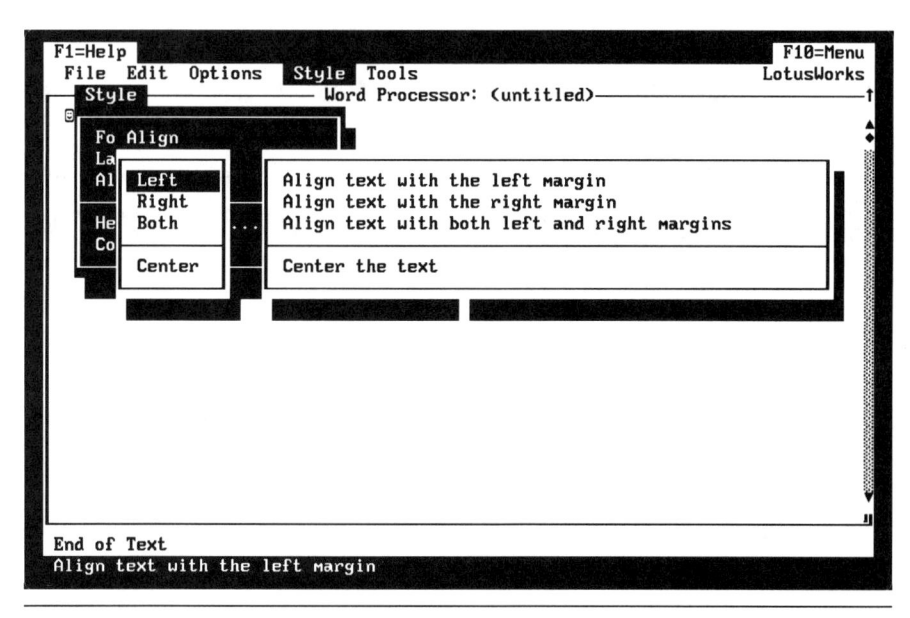

```
F1=Help                                                      F10=Menu
   File  Edit  Options  Style  Tools                        LotusWorks
     Style                   Word Processor: (untitled)
     Fo Align
     La
     Al  Left       Align text with the left margin
         Right      Align text with the right margin
     He  Both  ...  Align text with both left and right margins
     Co
         Center     Center the text




End of Text
Align text with the left margin
```

**FIGURE 3.5:** The Style Align menu lets you align text to the left, right, both, or center.

See if the text alignment is set as you wish. It can be Left (left-justified, or aligned to the left margin), Right (right-justified, or aligned to the right margin), Both (aligned to both margins), or Center (centered between the two margins). Select the alignment you want.

4. If you are creating a standard document format and want to include a header and/or footer (such as a page number or date) on each page, select Style Header/Footer. See "Creating Headers and Footers" later in this chapter.

5. Select Style Configure. The following dialog box appears:

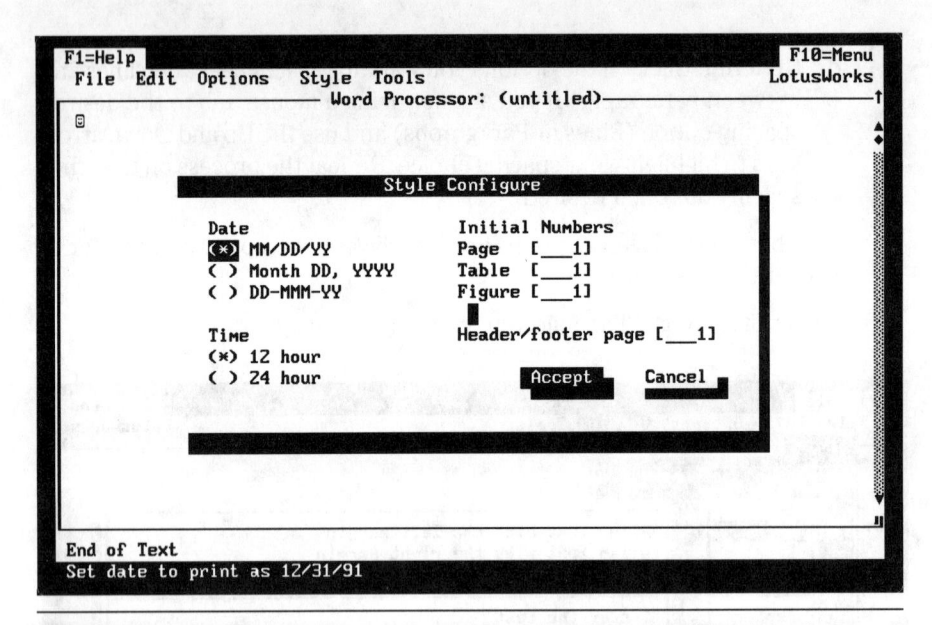

```
F1=Help                                                    F10=Menu
   File  Edit  Options  Style  Tools                   LotusWorks
                ─────── Word Processor: (untitled) ───────

                         Style Configure

          Date                     Initial Numbers
          (*) MM/DD/YY             Page   [___1]
          ( ) Month DD, YYYY       Table  [___1]
          ( ) DD-MMM-YY            Figure [___1]

          Time                     Header/footer page [___1]
          (*) 12 hour
          ( ) 24 hour                 Accept      Cancel




End of Text
Set date to print as 12/31/91
```

**FIGURE 3.6:** The Style Configure dialog box lets you specify date and time formats and initial numbers and header/footer pages for the document.

The Style Configure dialog box lets you specify formats for dates and times created by LotusWorks. It also lets you specify initial numbers for the automatic numbering of pages, tables, and figures and the initial page where headers and footers are to appear.

Check the settings for your document format, enter any changes you wish to make, and select Accept.

6. Save the format. Press Alt+S or select File Save, enter a descriptive file name that you can use to retrieve the format file, and select Save. Do not enter a file name extension. LotusWorks saves the empty document to disk and returns you to the document window.

If you want to use the format immediately, before you enter any data save the empty document a second time and give it a different file name. This way the data you enter into the document is saved to the second file without disturbing the file that holds the format. (If you don't want to save the format for future use, simply enter the text into the document and save the document under a file name that describes the document.)

If you want to save the format or document to a disk drive other than the default drive, be sure to enter the path to the drive as well as the file name when you are saving the document. For example, to save a document to a file named LTRFRMT1 in the subdirectory C:\LWORKS3\DOCS, you enter *C:\LWORKS3\DOCS\LTRFRMT1*.

> NOTE: To change the current default directory, select File, Directory, select or enter the path and subdirectory you want, and then press Enter. The directory remains current until you change it.

*To save a document format for future use, save the document under a file name that describes the format before you enter any text. Then as you enter text, save the document under a different file name.*

Now you are ready to start writing the document. Simply start typing, as described earlier.

## Saving Word Documents

You do not have to exit from a word document to save it to a disk file. You can save a partially completed word document at any time and resume working on the document. To do so, press Alt+S or select File Save. The following dialog box appears:

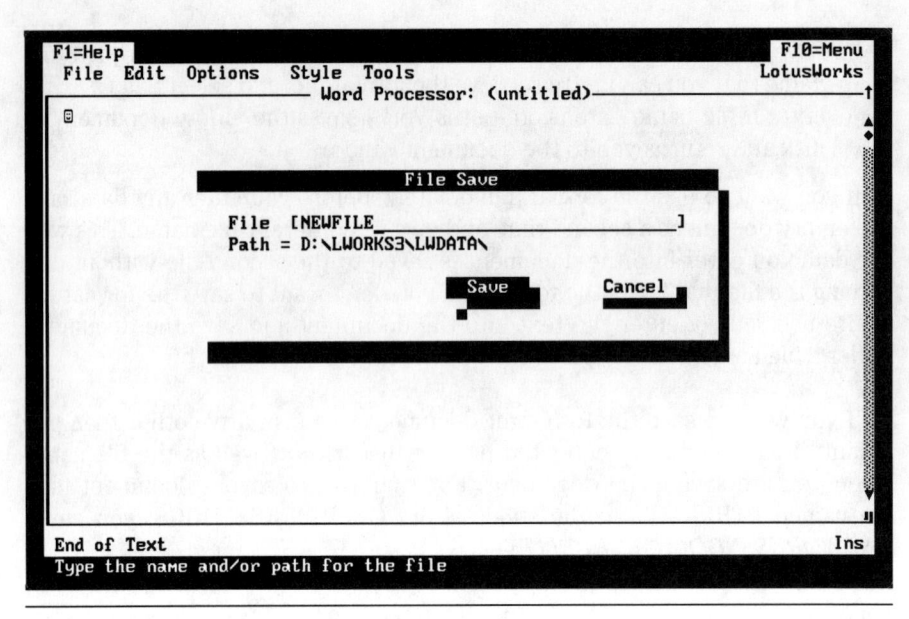

**FIGURE 3.7:** The File Save dialog box

If you wish to save the document under its current file name, simply press Enter. If you wish to save the document under a different file name in the current directory, type the new file name and select Save. If you wish to save the document in a different directory, type the new path and select save. LotusWorks saves the document under the name and in the directory that you have specified and returns you to the document screen.

*To guard against accidental loss of your data, make it a habit to make a backup copy each time you save a document to disk.*

You may save documents as frequently as you like. You are strongly urged to make it a habit to save your work every few minutes to safeguard against losing your work in case of a power or computer failure.

## Previewing Documents

When you have entered some text into a document, you will probably want to see how the text will appear when it's printed. Certainly you should when you have entered all the data, tailored the text, and edited the document. It's a good idea to preview the document before you print it, to be sure the headers, footers, and page numbers appear as you want them to, to check on type attributes and indentations, and to see if the pages start and end where you want them to.

The quickest way to preview the current document is simply to press Alt+V from anywhere in the document. Alternatively, you can select File Print Screen preview. LotusWorks opens the preview screen and displays the document as it will appear when printed, including header, footer, and page numbers.

To page through the document, press PgDn or PgUp, or click the mouse on the vertical scroll bar. To return to the document screen, press Esc.

## Working with Text Blocks

Two of the most important benefits of word processing are the ability to assign multiple type treatments and the ability to revise text easily. LotusWorks lets you work with selected blocks of text to perform these tasks. You can change typefaces (fonts), change the type size, assign special type attributes (bold, italic, and underlining), position the text (normal, superscript, or subscript), copy and move text, and delete and restore text quickly and easily. Each operation is a two-step process. The first step is to select the block of text to receive the special treatment. The second step is to assign the special treatment.

### Selecting Blocks of Text

If you are using the keyboard to select text, use the arrow keys to position the cursor at the top-left edge of the desired text, press F4, use the Arrow, PgUp, and PgDn keys to highlight the desired text, and press Enter. As an alternative to pressing F4, you can select Edit Select to initiate the selection.

If you are using a mouse, position the mouse at the top-left edge of the desired text, hold down the left button and drag to the right and down to highlight the text, then release the button.

### Canceling a Text Selection

If you need to cancel a selection of text, simply press Esc or click the mouse anywhere outside the highlighted block of text.

# Revising Your Writing: Copying, Cutting, and Pasting Text

LotusWorks 3.0 provides three functions to help you revise text: copying, cutting, and pasting. When you tell LotusWorks to *copy* a block of text, LotusWorks copies the block to a section of computer memory called the Clipboard but leaves the original text intact. When you tell LotusWorks to *cut* a block of text, LotusWorks deletes the original block and places it in the Clipboard. Once a block of text is in the Clipboard, you can use the *paste* operation to deposit a copy of it anywhere on the screen. You can paste the block as many times as you like until you copy or cut another block of text to the Clipboard.

> NOTE: When you paste a block of text in the Word Processing service, LotusWorks inserts the block at the cursor location. If there is other text at the point of insertion, LotusWorks pushes it ahead to make room for the pasted block.

To copy a block of text, first select it, then press Alt+C or select Edit Copy. LotusWorks copies the text to the Clipboard.

To cut a block of text, first select it, then press Alt+X or select Edit Cut. LotusWorks cuts (deletes) the original text and places it in the Clipboard.

To paste a block of text, first copy or cut the block to the Clipboard, then move the cursor to the point where you want the text to appear and press Alt+P or select Edit Paste. LotusWorks deposits the text, pushing ahead any other text at the same location.

## Deleting Text

To delete a block of text entirely, first select the block, then press Alt+D or select Edit Delete. LotusWorks deletes the selected block and closes up the remaining text.

> NOTE: Deleting text removes it to the Clipboard. You can paste the deleted text by pressing Alt+P or selecting Edit Paste.

## Restoring Text Deletions

If you make a mistake or change your mind about a deletion, you can restore the most recently deleted block of text by moving the cursor to the point where you want the text to appear and selecting Edit Restore.

> CAUTION: LotusWorks restores only the most recently deleted block of text. If you are about to delete a block of text, be sure that you are satisfied with the previous deletion before proceeding.

# Assigning Type Attributes: Bold, Italic, and Underlining

To assign type attributes, first select the desired text, then select Style Fonts. The following dialog box appears:

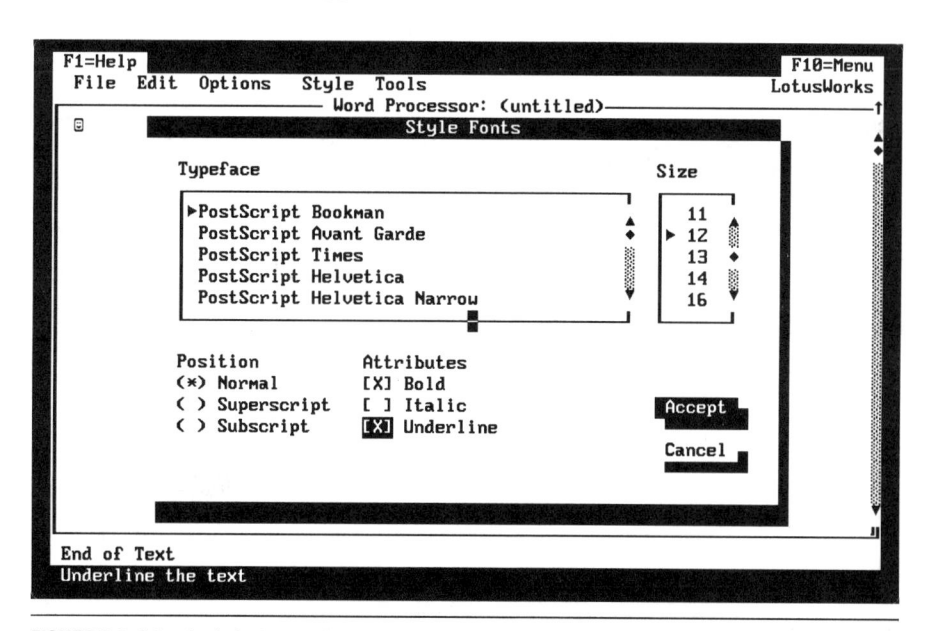

```
F1=Help                                                          F10=Menu
    File   Edit   Options   Style   Tools                       LotusWorks
                        ─ Word Processor: (untitled) ─
                              Style Fonts

        Typeface                                   Size

        ▶PostScript Bookman                          11
         PostScript Avant Garde                    ▶ 12
         PostScript Times                            13
         PostScript Helvetica                        14
         PostScript Helvetica Narrow                 16


         Position              Attributes
         (*) Normal            [X] Bold
         ( ) Superscript       [ ] Italic           Accept
         ( ) Subscript         [X] Underline
                                                    Cancel


    End of Text
    Underline the text
```

**FIGURE 3.8:** Select the desired type attribute from the Style Fonts dialog box.

Tab to the desired attribute (Bold, Italic, or Underline), press the Spacebar to select it, and then select Accept. LotusWorks applies the selected attribute to the selected text.

To assign a combination of attributes—such as Bold and Italic, or Bold, Italic, and Underline—tab to each desired attribute and press the Spacebar to select it. When all of the desired attributes have been selected, select Accept.

## Creating Headers and Footers

A LotusWorks header is one to three lines of fixed text that appear at the top of each page of a document. A footer is one to three lines of fixed text that appear at the bottom of each page.

### Entering a Header or Footer

To create a header or footer, press Alt+H or select Style Header/footer. The following dialog box appears:

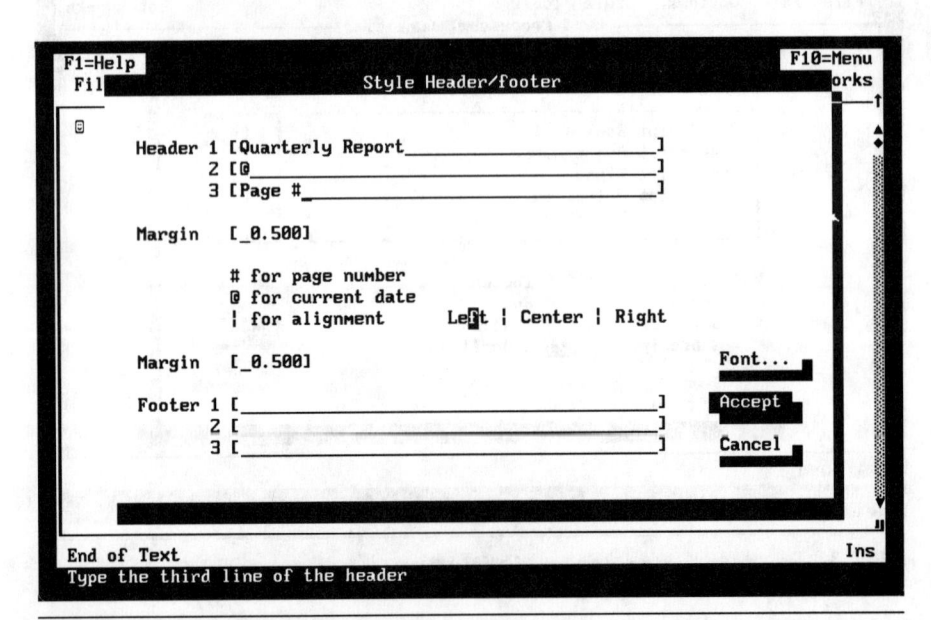

```
F1=Help                                                           F10=Menu
Fil                      Style Header/footer                         orks

        Header 1 [Quarterly Report_____]
               2 [@_____]
               3 [Page #_____]

        Margin   [_0.500]

                 # for page number
                 @ for current date
                 | for alignment        Left | Center | Right

        Margin   [_0.500]
                                                          Font...
        Footer 1 [_____]
               2 [_____]   Accept
               3 [_____]   Cancel


End of Text                                                          Ins
Type the third line of the header
```

**FIGURE 3.9:** To create a header or footer, select Style Header/footer and enter the text that you want to appear on every page.

You can have up to three lines in a header and up to three lines in a footer for each document. On each numbered line of the dialog box, enter the text that you want to appear on each line in the header and/or footer.

The top Margin setting determines the amount of vertical space between the header and the first line of body text. The bottom Margin setting determines the amount of vertical space between the last line of body text and the footer. Enter a number or decimal fraction to specify the number of inches you want for each vertical margin.

You can have LotusWorks automatically print a page number in a header or footer by typing a pound sign (#) where you want the page number to appear in the header or footer.

You can have LotusWorks automatically insert the current date in a header or footer by typing an at sign (@) where you want the date to appear. (The date will be updated each time the document is printed.) The date can be in any of three styles:

| MM/DD/YY | 01/31/92 |
| Month DD, YYYY | January 31, 1992 |
| DD-MMM-YY | 31-JAN-92 |

To configure the date style, select Style Configure, use the Arrow keys to move the cursor to the desired Date style, and select Accept.

You can insert a vertical bar (|) to align all or part of a header or footer to the left, center, or right side of the page. Text entered without a vertical bar is aligned to the left margin. Text entered after one vertical bar is centered. Text entered after two vertical bars is aligned to the right side of the page.

| Enter this text | To print this line in the header or footer |
| --- | --- |
| Sales Report | Sales Report |
| \|Sales Report |                 Sales Report |
| \|\|Sales Report |                               Sales Report |
| Sales Report @ # | Sales Report January 31, 1992 1 |

Aligning Text in a Header or Footer

| Enter this text | To print this line in the header or footer | | |
|---|---|---|---|
| @IDraft 1I# | January 31, 1992 | Draft 1 | 1 |
| @IIPage # | January 31, 1992 | | Page1 |
| I- # - | | - 1 - | |

Aligning Text in a Header or Footer, continued

By combining these elements on different lines, you can create quite attractive and sophisticated documents.

## Specifying a Starting Page for a Header or Footer

*To have more than one header or footer in a document, split the document into multiple documents, create a header or footer for each part, then print the documents in succession. If you have a page number in the header or footer, be sure to change the initial page number for each section of the document. See "Setting Initial Numbers" and "Printing Word Documents" later in this chapter.*

You can have a header or footer start on any page of a document, but there can be only one header and footer in each document. The default is the first page. To specify a different starting page, select Style Configure, tab to the box labeled Header/footer page, type the number of the page where you want the footer and/or header to begin, and select Accept.

## Editing a Header or Footer

To edit a header or footer, press Alt+H or select Style Header/footer, make the desired changes in the text, and select Accept.

## Deleting a Header or Footer

To delete a header or footer, press Alt+H or select Style Header/footer, use the Del key to delete all text from the header or footer, and then select Accept.

# Automatically Printing Dates and Times

LotusWorks enables you to embed the current date and/or time in word documents. When you print the document, LotusWorks automatically reads the date and time from the computer's system clock and prints each in the format that you have specified.

This feature can be especially useful for stored memo and letter formats. When you retrieve and print the stored format, LotusWorks inserts the date and/or time without any effort on your part. The feature can also be used for dating the different drafts of a document, either in a header or footer or in the body of the document. Besides saving time and effort in typing, you are always assured that the spelling and numbers are correct.

To include an embedded date or time in a document, move the cursor to the point where you want the date or time to appear, then select Edit Add and type *D* for the date or *T* for the time.

LotusWorks inserts the word "Date" or "Time" enclosed in double angle brackets («») at the cursor location but does not display the actual date or time on the screen. Instead, LotusWorks inserts the date or time when you print the document. Each time you print or preview the document, LotusWorks inserts the actual date and time at that moment.

> IMPORTANT: If you want the date or time to be updated each time you print a document, use the embedded date or time feature. If you want the date or time to remain fixed regardless of when you print the document, enter the date or time as ordinary text.

*To see how the date or time will appear in the printed version of your document, press Alt+V to preview the document.*

# Automatically Numbering Pages, Figures, and Tables

Another way to save work is to have LotusWorks automatically number pages, figures, and tables for you. This can save you work on any document but is especially effective with long documents and documents that are subject to multiple revisions.

To put a page number in a header or footer, press Alt+H or select Style Header/footer, and type # on the line where you want the page number to appear. When you print or preview the document, LotusWorks inserts the page number in the header or footer.

You can combine the page number with fixed characters to dress up page numbers in headers and footers. For example, to print a page number in the form **- 1 -** at the bottom center of the page, type **|- # -|** on the Footer line where you want the page number to appear. To print a page number in the form **Page 2** at the top right of the page, type **|Page #** on the header line where you want the page number to appear.

If you want page numbers to appear somewhere in the body text rather than in a header or footer, you can use the Edit Add Page Number command. This automatically prints the word "Page" followed by the page number. To use this method, first move the cursor to the point where you want the page number to appear, then select Edit Add Page number. LotusWorks inserts the words "Page Number" enclosed within double angle brackets (« ») at the cursor location on the screen. When you print or preview the document, LotusWorks inserts the word "Page" and the actual page number on each page.

The process for embedding figure and table numbers is similar to embedding page numbers. To embed a figure number or table number, move the cursor to the point where you want the number to appear and select Edit Add Figure number or Edit Add Table number. LotusWorks inserts the words "Figure Number" or "Table Number" enclosed within double angle brackets (« ») at the cursor. When you print or preview the document, LotusWorks inserts the word "Figure" or "Table" and the appropriate numeral at the point you specified.

## Setting Initial Numbers

On letters and many other kinds of documents, it is customary to omit the page number from the first page and start page numbering on the second page. And if you have a long document divided into several small document files (such as sections in a report or chapters in book), you may want the page numbers to run consecutively from the beginning to the end of the entire document rather than starting over with each new section or chapter.

You can accomplish these effects in LotusWorks with the Initial Numbers setting. To have page numbering start on the second page, first put the page number into a header or footer that starts on the second page; then, to get the correct number on each page, select Style Configure and set the initial page number to 2. LotusWorks will begin the page numbering with the number 2 on page 2.

To have page numbering run consecutively from one document to another, set the initial page number for the first document to 1 or 2 (whichever is appropriate) and set the initial page number for each succeeding section or chapter to pick up where the page numbers of the previous section leave off.

You can do the same thing with table numbers and figure numbers. Just select Style Configure and set the Table and Figure options to the appropriate numbers for the document you are about to print.

# Hyphenating and Keeping Words Together

Ordinarily when LotusWorks wraps text from one line to the next, it breaks the line of text between words and after hyphens. This works fine for most purposes. There are times, however, when you may wish to keep a group of words together on the same line, for example, when printing names such as de La Rosa or Smith-Jones. When words are kept together with a space, it is called a non-breaking space; when they are kept together with a hyphen, it is called a non-breaking hyphen or a hard hyphen.

Similarly, there are times when it is desirable to insert an optional hyphen so that a long word will break properly if it extends beyond the end of a line but not break if it fits within the line. If you insert an optional hyphen and the word is too long for the line, LotusWorks breaks the word at the optional hyphen; otherwise, it prints the word without a hyphen. For example, if you inserted an optional hyphen after the third "i" in the word "significance," LotusWorks would print "signifi-" on one line and "cance" on the next if the word extended beyond the end of the line but would print "significance" (without a hyphen) if the entire word could fit on the line.

LotusWorks enables you to set a non-breaking space, a non-breaking hyphen, and an optional hyphen. Here is how they work:

| To Assign This | Do This |
| --- | --- |
| Non-Breaking Space | Move the cursor to the point where you want the hard space to appear and select Edit Add Non-breaking space. |
| Non-Breaking Hyphen | Move the cursor to the point where you want the hard hyphen to appear and select Edit Add Non-breaking hyphen. |
| Optional Hyphen | Move the cursor to the point where you want the discretionary hyphen to appear and select Edit Add Optional hyphen. |

Setting Spaces and Hyphens

## Controlling Page Breaks

Normally LotusWorks flows text automatically from the bottom of one page to the top of the next. Sometimes it is desirable, however, to dictate where one page should end and another begin. An example is when you want to end one section or chapter of a document and begin the next one on a new page. Another example is when the automatic page break occurs at an awkward place, such as between a heading and the following paragraph or in the middle of a table that should be kept together.

To start a new page, simply move the cursor to the point where you want the new page to begin and select Edit Add New page. LotusWorks inserts a nonprinting page-break symbol and dashed line and starts a new page.

## "Intelligent" Editing

"Intelligent" editing does not refer to your intellect (which must be excellent—you're using LotusWorks!). Rather, it refers to using some of LotusWorks' special tools to help you edit and revise your documents.

LotusWorks can help you check your spelling, look up words you're not sure how to spell, find the right word to use, and find and replace specified words and phrases.

### Checking Your Spelling

The LotusWorks spelling checker checks your spelling against words in its dictionary. If it does not find a word, it allows you to accept the current spelling, accept a word that LotusWorks suggests, or correct the spelling. It then allows you to add the word to a temporary dictionary for the duration of the current LotusWorks session or add the word to the permanent dictionary.

LotusWorks gives you two ways to check spelling. You can use Tools Dictionary to check a single word or Tools Check Spelling to check all the words throughout a document.

## Checking a Single Word

If you want to check the spelling of a single word, move the cursor to the word you want to check and press Alt+Y or select Tools Dictionary. The following dialog box appears:

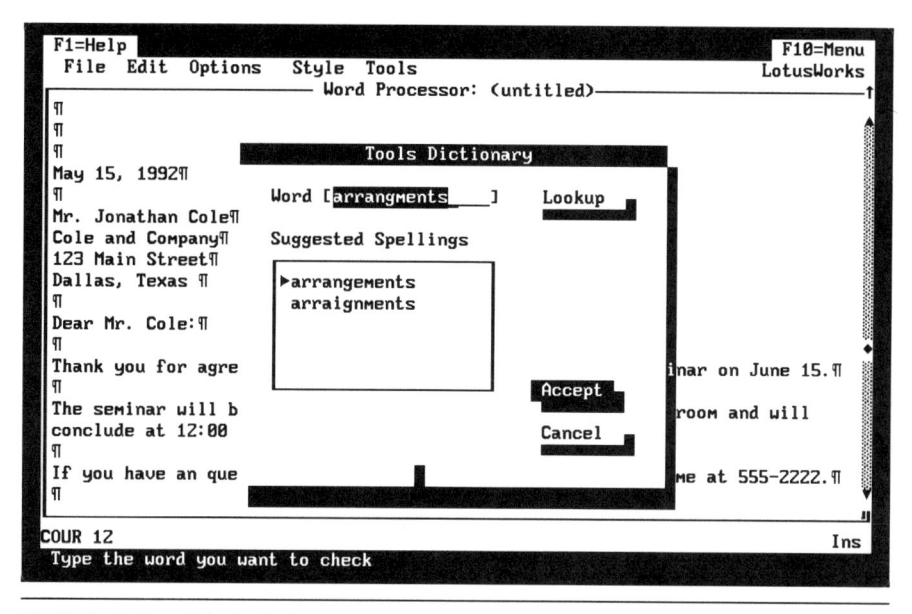

```
F1=Help                                                    F10=Menu
    File   Edit   Options   Style   Tools                LotusWorks
─────────────────── Word Processor: (untitled) ──────────────────┐
¶
¶
¶                      ┌─── Tools Dictionary ───┐
May 15, 1992¶          │                        │
¶                      │ Word [arrangments   ]  Lookup │
Mr. Jonathan Cole¶     │                        │
Cole and Company¶      │ Suggested Spellings    │
123 Main Street¶       │ ┌────────────────────┐ │
Dallas, Texas ¶        │ │ ►arrangements      │ │
¶                      │ │  arraignments      │ │
Dear Mr. Cole:¶        │ │                    │ │
¶                      │ │                    │ │
Thank you for agre     │ │                    │ │ nar on June 15.¶
¶                      │ │                    │ │
The seminar will b     │ │                    │ Accept │ room and will
conclude at 12:00      │ │                    │ │
¶                      │ │                    │ Cancel │
If you have an que     │ │                    │ │ me at 555-2222.¶
¶                      └────────────────────────┘

COUR 12                                                        Ins
Type the word you want to check
```

**FIGURE 3.10:** To spell check a single word, put the cursor on the word and press Alt+Y to display the Tools Dictionary dialog box.

To accept the current spelling of the word, simply press Enter or select Accept.

To review all the suggested spellings, move the cursor to the Suggested Spellings box and press PgDn or use the vertical scroll bar to review additional spellings.

To accept one of the suggested spellings, use the Arrow keys or mouse to highlight the desired spelling, then select Accept. LotusWorks replaces the original spelling with the spelling you have specified.

To look up a different word from the one at the cursor, click the mouse or press Tab or Shift+Tab until the Word text box is highlighted, type the word you want to look up, and select Lookup. LotusWorks displays alternative spellings for the word. To accept one of the alternative spellings, use the Arrow keys or mouse to highlight the desired spelling, then select Accept. LotusWorks replaces the original spelling with the spelling you have specified.

## Checking All Words

If you want to check the spelling of all words throughout a document, press Alt+W or select Tools Check spelling from anywhere in the document. Lotus-Works starts checking the spelling at the beginning of document. If it finds a word that is not in its dictionary, LotusWorks stops, highlights the word, and suggests other possible spellings in the following dialog box:

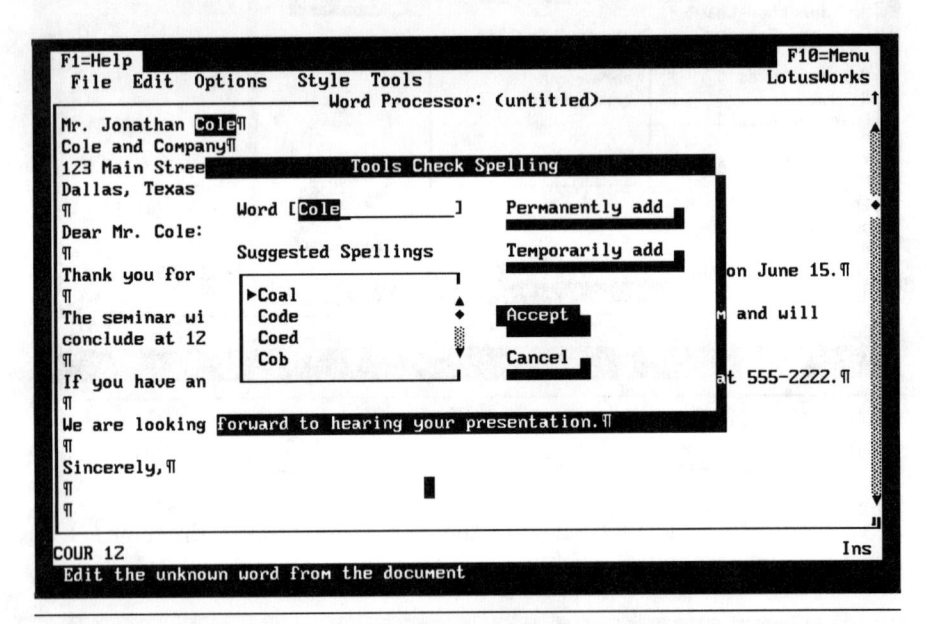

**FIGURE 3.11:** Press Alt+W to display the Tools Check Spelling dialog box and check the spelling of all words in a document.

To accept the current spelling, select Accept. LotusWorks leaves the original word intact and resumes the check for misspelled words.

To accept one of the spellings suggested by LotusWorks, tab to Suggested Spellings, use the mouse or Arrow keys to move the cursor to the desired word, then select Accept. LotusWorks substitutes the selected word for the original word and resumes checking for misspelled words.

In some cases LotusWorks may not be able to suggest the word you want to use. To correct the spelling without accepting one of the suggested spellings, simply type the correct spelling in the text box and select Accept. LotusWorks substitutes the word you have typed for the original word and resumes checking for misspellings.

If a word that you use frequently in your work does not appear in the spell checker (for example, a company name or technical term), you can add it to the permanent dictionary and have LotusWorks include it each time you check your spelling. To do so, first correct the spelling, then select Permanently add. LotusWorks changes the word to the new spelling and enters the new word into its permanent dictionary for inclusion in all subsequent spell checking.

> CAUTION: Once you permanently add a word to the dictionary, you cannot change or remove it. Be absolutely sure you have the correct spelling before you permanently add a word to the dictionary!

If you are creating a document with one or more specialized words in it, you may wish to add the words to the dictionary temporarily so that you can check their spelling throughout the document, even if you don't want to add them to the dictionary permanently. To do so, first correct the spelling, then select Temporarily add. LotusWorks changes the word to the new spelling and keeps the new word in the temporary dictionary and includes it in subsequent spell checking until you exit LotusWorks.

*It is important to remember that the spell checker cannot do all of your editing work for you.* The spell checker can help catch misspelled words, but it can't know when you have accidentally used the wrong word, mistyped a word and formed another word, or duplicated a word (such as "the the") by mistake. You should always use the spell checker to check your work, but always follow it with a visual inspection of your document.

## Finding Synonyms

To help you find just the right words to use in your writing, the LotusWorks thesaurus enables you to look up synonyms for words in a document and then replace the originals, if you wish.

If you want to find a synonym for a word in a document, move the cursor to the beginning of the word and press Alt+T or select Tools Thesaurus. The following dialog box appears:

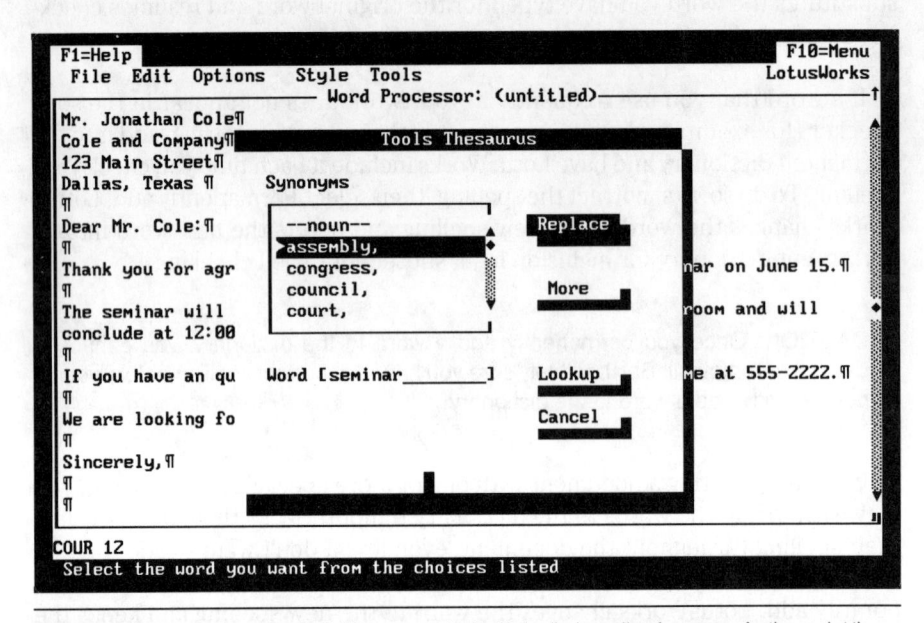

```
F1=Help                                                    F10=Menu
     File  Edit  Options  Style  Tools                   LotusWorks
─────────────────── Word Processor: (untitled) ──────────────────────┬
Mr. Jonathan Cole¶
Cole and Company¶          ┌─── Tools Thesaurus ───┐
123 Main Street¶
Dallas, Texas ¶            Synonyms
¶
Dear Mr. Cole: ¶            --noun--          ┌─ Replace ─┐
¶                          ►assembly,
Thank you for agr           congress,                          ar on June 15. ¶
¶                           council,          ┌─  More   ─┐
The seminar will            court,                             oom and will
conclude at 12:00
¶
If you have an qu          Word [seminar____]  ┌─ Lookup  ─┐  e at 555-2222. ¶
¶
We are looking fo                              ┌─ Cancel  ─┐
¶
Sincerely, ¶
¶
¶
COUR 12
Select the word you want from the choices listed
```

**FIGURE 3.12:** Press Alt+T or select Tools Thesaurus and LotusWorks displays a list of synonyms for the word at the cursor.

The synonyms for the word are listed in the Synonyms box. To see more of the list of synonyms, press the PgDn key or use the mouse to move the elevator box on the vertical scroll bar.

You can also look up synonyms for any of the words listed in the Synonyms box. To do this, move the cursor to the desired word in the Synonyms box and select More. LotusWorks displays a list of synonyms for the selected word. You can use the PgDn key or vertical scroll bar to see more of the list.

If you want to find synonyms for a completely different word, type the new word in the text box and select Lookup. LotusWorks displays any synonyms in its thesaurus for the word you typed.

To replace your original word with one of the synonyms, move the cursor to the desired synonym and select Replace. LotusWorks inserts the synonym in place of the original word in your document.

## Searching For and Replacing Text

The Search and Replace feature is one of the best ways to save work when you're editing. It's a great way to change the spelling or wording of a misused term throughout a document. You can specify a set of characters, a word, or a phrase, and LotusWorks will find every occurrence of the specified text in your document. If you wish, it will replace the text with other text that you specify. You can direct LotusWorks to make the replacements one at a time or to replace all occurrences at once. Here is how it works:

You may conduct a search or a search-and-replace operation either for *part* of a document or for the *entire* document. To conduct the operation for *part* of a document, first select the portion of the document to search: highlight the desired portion with the mouse, or move the cursor to the beginning of the desired portion, press F4, move the cursor to the end of the portion, and press Enter. To have the operation apply to the *entire* document, do not make a selection.

To initiate a search or a search-and-replace operation, press F7 or select Tools Search/replace from anywhere in a document. The following dialog box opens:

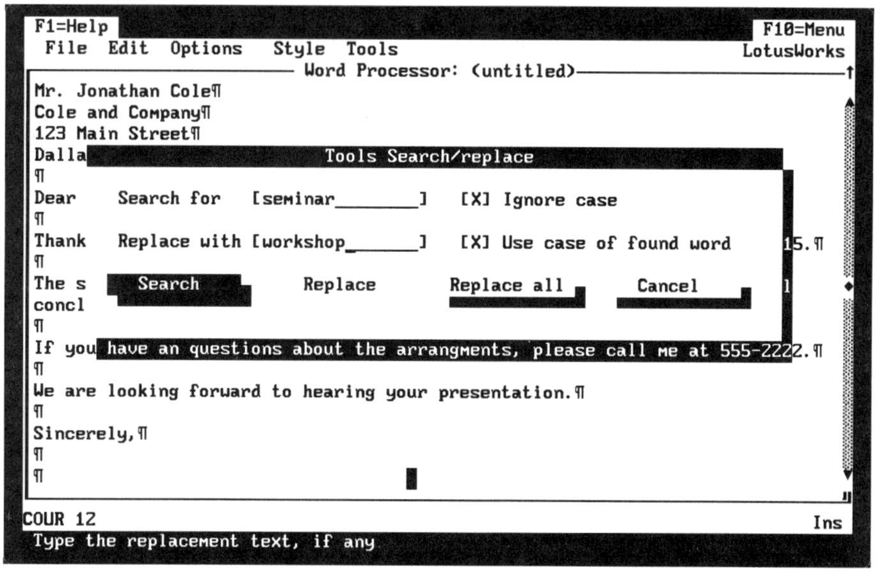

**FIGURE 3.13:** Specify the text to search for and, if appropriate, the replacement text.

Enter the word or phrase to search for. If you want LotusWorks to search for all instances of the specified text without regard to the case (upper or lower) of the characters, leave the "Ignore case" option (the default) selected. If you want LotusWorks to search only for words that exactly match the uppercase and lowercase characters you specify, tab to the Ignore case option and press the Spacebar to deselect it.

If you want to conduct a search without replacing the text, select Search. LotusWorks finds the first occurrence of the specified text and pauses. If you want to find the next occurrence, press Enter to execute the Search option again. You may repeat this process as many times as you wish, until you reach the end of the selection or document. When you reach the end, LotusWorks displays a message telling you how many occurences of the target text were found.

If you want to conduct a search-and-replace operation, enter the replacement text in the Replace with text box. If you want the case of the replacement text to match the case (upper and/or lower) of the found text, leave the option labeled "Use case of found word" (the default) selected. If you want the replacement text to appear exactly as you typed it, regardless of the case of the found text, tab to the "Use case of found word" option and press the Spacebar to deselect it.

If you want to review each occurrence of the specified target text before deciding whether or not to replace it, select Search. LotusWorks finds the first occurrence of the specified text and pauses. If you want to replace that one occurrence of the text, select Replace. If you want to leave the target text intact, simply press Enter to continue the Search option. LotusWorks finds the next occurrence of the target text and pauses again. You may repeat this process as many times as you like until you reach the end of the selection or document. When you reach the end, LotusWorks displays a message telling you how many occurrences of the target text were replaced.

If you want to replace all occurrences of the specified target text without pausing, select Replace all instead of Search after you have entered the replacement text and specified the case option. LotusWorks automatically replaces each occurrence of the target text that it finds and displays a message telling you how many occurrences of the target text were replaced.

## Combining Word Documents

LotusWorks provides a means to combine separate word documents into a single document. You can combine two or more word documents one after another, like chapters in a book, or insert one document into the middle of another. For example, you can format a title page, a table of contents, the body of a report, and one or more appendices each in a separate document with a separate layout and then combine them into a single document for printing.

To combine another word document with the current one, move the cursor to the position in the current document where you want the foreign document to appear, select File Transfer Combine. The following dialog box appears:

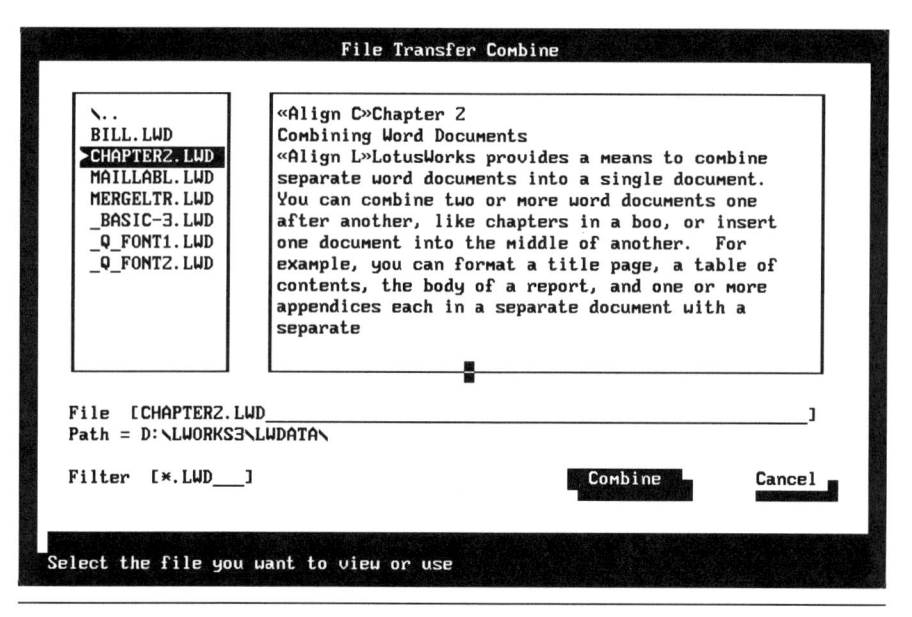

**FIGURE 3.14:** The File Transfer Combine dialog box

Select the document file you want to combine with the current document. If the desired file is in another directory, type the complete path and file name in the text box. When the file name has been entered, select Combine.

LotusWorks makes a copy of the text of the specified document—including styles, fonts, and special Edit Add commands—and inserts it into the current document at the cursor location. LotusWorks uses the header and footer of the current document and does not transfer any header or footer information from the copied document.

> NOTE: When you combine one document with another, LotusWorks inserts the text at the cursor location; it does not write over any existing text.

*To combine text from another document without combining the entire document, open the document in a second window, cut or copy the desired text to the Clipboard, and paste it into the document you are creating.*

Once a document has been combined into another document, the combined document retains no further link to the original document. You can edit the combined document just as you would any other document. If you change text or update a Date or Time command in the original document, it has no effect on the combined document, and vice versa.

## Including Graphs and Spreadsheet Data in Word Documents

You can also bring LotusWorks graphs and spreadsheet data into word documents. For example, you can include a graph and spreadsheet data with text in a word document to create a report.

### Including Data from a Spreadsheet

To include data from a spreadsheet, move the cursor to the point where you want the spreadsheet data to appear and select Edit Include Spreadsheet. The following dialog box appears:

Writing Well with Word Processing  **91**

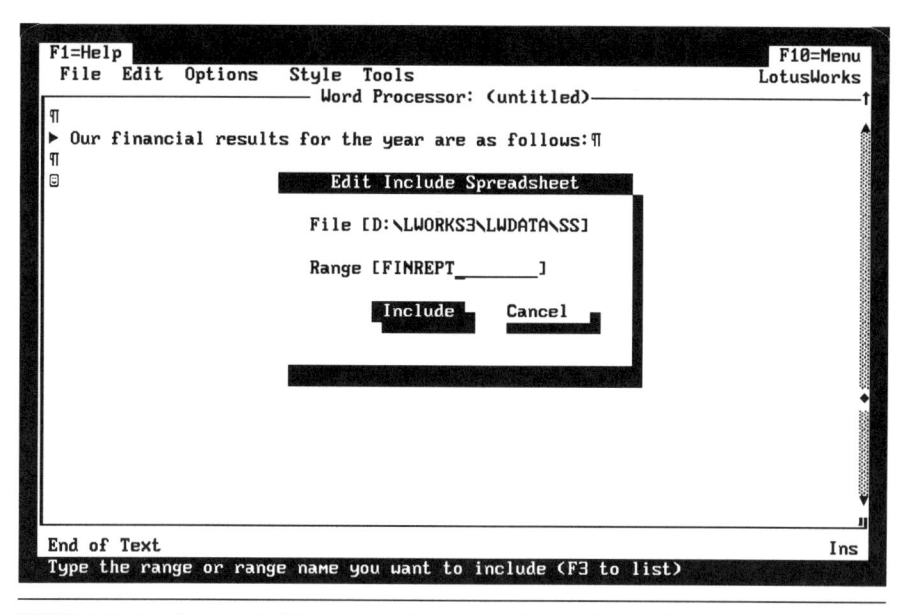

```
F1=Help                                              F10=Menu
   File  Edit  Options  Style  Tools              LotusWorks
   ─────────── Word Processor: (untitled) ───────────
¶
▶ Our financial results for the year are as follows:¶
¶
             ┌──── Edit Include Spreadsheet ────┐
             │                                   │
             │   File [D:\LWORKS3\LWDATA\SS]     │
             │                                   │
             │   Range [FINREPT_____]          │
             │                                   │
             │        Include      Cancel        │
             │                                   │
             └───────────────────────────────────┘


End of Text                                          Ins
Type the range or range name you want to include (F3 to list)
```

**FIGURE 3.15:** Enter the spreadsheet file name and a data range to be included in the word document.

Enter the file name of the spreadsheet and a range address or range name of the data to be included in the word document and select Include. (See Chapter 5 for instructions on writing range addresses and creating range names.) Lotus-Works inserts the word "Range:" and the name and range of the spreadsheet surrounded by double angle brackets (« ») in the document at the cursor location. The actual data does not appear until you print or preview the document.

## Including a Graph

To include a graph, move the cursor to the point where you want the graph to appear and select Edit Include Graph. The following dialog box appears:

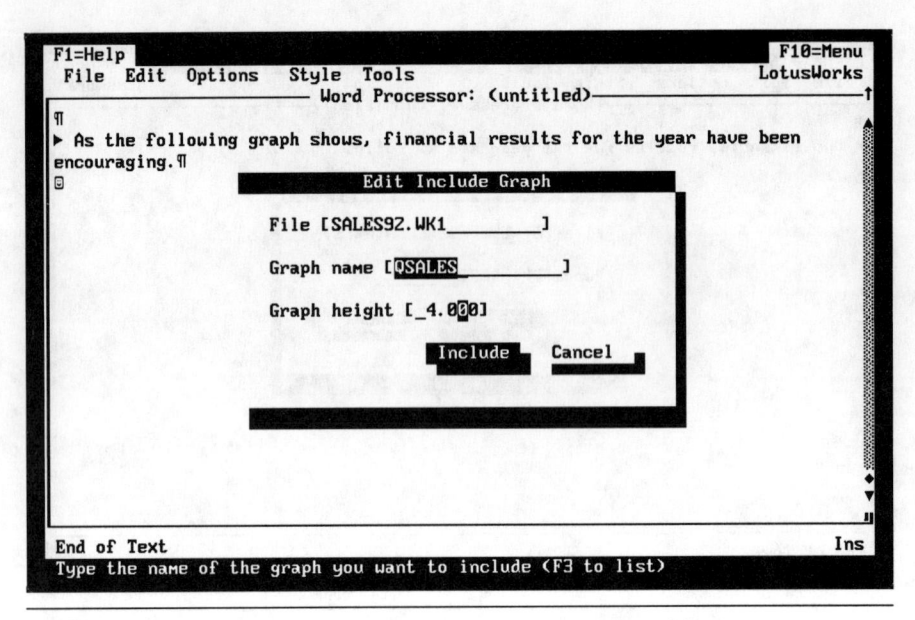

```
F1=Help                                                    F10=Menu
   File  Edit  Options  Style  Tools                       LotusWorks
 ─────────────────────── Word Processor: (untitled) ───────────────────┬
¶
► As the following graph shows, financial results for the year have been
encouraging. ¶
               ┌─────────── Edit Include Graph ───────────┐
               │                                          │
               │    File [SALES92.WK1_____]            │
               │                                          │
               │    Graph name [QSALES_____]            │
               │                                          │
               │    Graph height [_4.000]                 │
               │                                          │
               │               Include   Cancel           │
               │                                          │
               └──────────────────────────────────────────┘

End of Text                                                        Ins
Type the name of the graph you want to include (F3 to list)
```

**FIGURE 3.16:** Enter the file name and graph name of the graph to be included in the word document.

Enter the file name and the graph name of the graph to be included in the word document. Enter the desired height for the graph in inches. This is the height that LotusWorks uses to print the graph. If a graph won't fit at the end of a page, LotusWorks automatically prints it on the next page. When the file name, graph name, and graph height have been specified, select Include. LotusWorks inserts the word "Graph:" and the name of the graph within double angle brackets (« ») in the document where the graph will be printed. The actual graph does not appear until you print or preview the document.

## Printing Word Documents

LotusWorks 3.0 gives you two ways to print word documents: regular printing and mail merge. Mail merge is discussed later in this chapter.

Regular printing entails two simple steps. First, select File Print Layout to check the paper size and printing orientation (landscape or portrait) to be used for the printed document. The following dialog box appears:

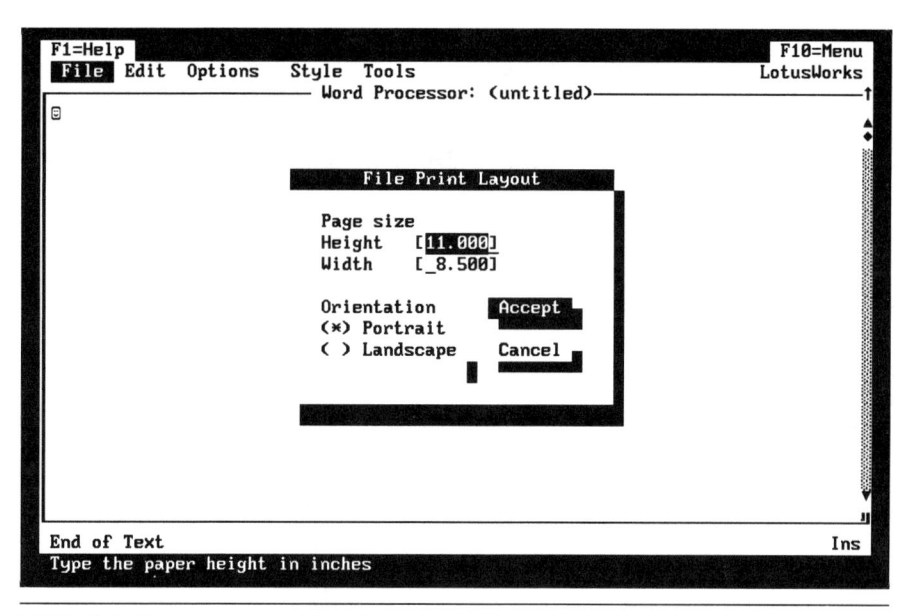

**FIGURE 3.17:** Check the print layout before printing the document.

Enter any changes that you need and select Accept. Unless you are changing the size of paper or the printing orientation, these settings will not need changing. Portrait orientation prints with the narrow edge of the page at the top and landscape orientation prints with the wide edge at the top.

When the layout is set, select Accept and select File Print Print. The following dialog box appears:

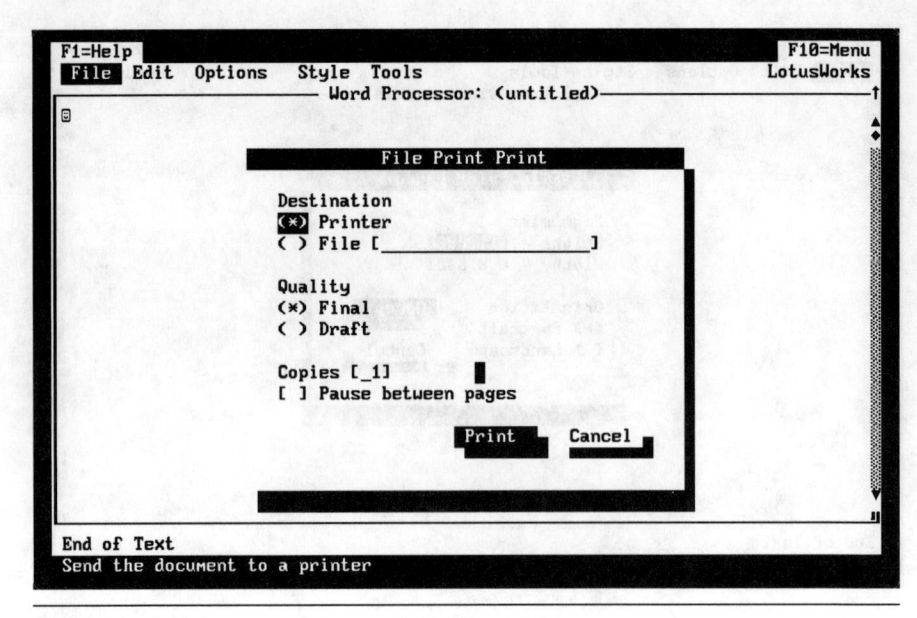

*To print a document sideways on the page, select File Print Layout Landscape, then select File Print Print, and press Enter.*

**FIGURE 3.18:** Check the print options before issuing the print command.

Set the following print options if necessary:

## Print Options

**Destination:** You have the option of sending the document to the printer or a disk file. Normally you will send it to the printer, but if you want to transfer the document to another word processor or send it to another computer via a modem, you may wish to send the document to a disk file. Sending the document to a disk file creates and saves a formatted file of the print output with a .PRN file name extension.

**Quality:** Many dot-matrix printers support a fast draft mode and a slower letter-quality or near-letter-quality mode. If your printer supports these, select the mode of your choice Final or Draft.

**Copies:** Enter the number of copies you want to print.

**Pause between pages:** Select this option if you need the printer to pause after each page while you insert a new sheet of paper into the printer. After each pause, press Alt+G to resume printing.

When all the parameters are set to your liking, select Print. LotusWorks prints the document.

# Mail-Merge

Mail-merge—also known as merge printing—is a powerful tool not only for customizing form letters but also for inserting variable data into individualized word documents, such as employee benefit reports, rental agreements, and student progress reports. Merge printing requires two documents: a master document and a database. The master document contains the fixed text for the printed document and specifies the fields and locations for the variable data. The database contains the variable data to be inserted. When the document is printed, LotusWorks combines the fixed text from the master document with the variable data from the database to produce an individualized document for each active record in the database. Merge printing is launched and controlled from the Word Processing service.

Here is an example of a master document. Notice that the field names are enclosed within double angle brackets. They indicate the positions where different types of variable data are to be inserted.

---

«Field: DATE»

«Field: PREFIX» «Field: FIRSTNAME» «Field: MI» «Field: LASTNAME»
«Field: TITLE»
«Field: COMPANY»
«Field: ADDRESS1»
«Field: ADDRESS2»
«Field: CITY», «Field: STATE» «Field: ZIP.-»

Dear «Field: SALUTATION»:

This is an example of a master document for mail-merge printing. The words between double angle brackets (« ») are field names from the database.

In mail-merge, LotusWorks automatically suppresses blank fields and blank lines. If a field is blank for a particular record, the field is not printed. If a blank field is on a line by itself (for example, the Title field above), the line is not printed.

Good luck in using mail-merge!

Sincerely,

Mary A. Williams

## Creating a Master Document

A master document for merge printing is simply a regular word document that contains field names from a database. LotusWorks helps you look up and write the field names in the proper format.

1. Move the cursor to the point in the master document where you wish the field name to be inserted.

2. Press Alt+F or select Edit Include Mail merge. The following dialog box appears:

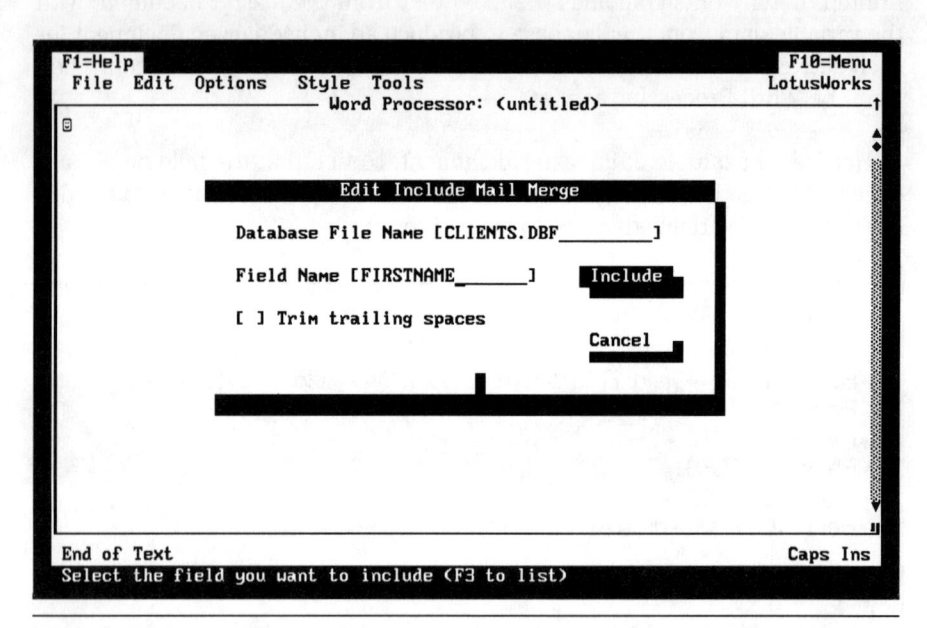

```
F1=Help                                                         F10=Menu
   File   Edit   Options   Style   Tools                       LotusWorks
────────────────────── Word Processor: (untitled) ──────────────────────

              ┌──────────── Edit Include Mail Merge ────────────┐
              │                                                  │
              │  Database File Name [CLIENTS.DBF_____]        │
              │                                                  │
              │  Field Name [FIRSTNAME_____]    Include        │
              │                                                  │
              │  [ ] Trim trailing spaces                        │
              │                                   Cancel         │
              │                                                  │
              └──────────────────────────────────────────────────┘

End of Text                                                  Caps Ins
Select the field you want to include (F3 to list)
```

**FIGURE 3.19:** The Edit Include Mail Merge dialog box enables you to select field names and operators from list boxes.

3. Enter the name of the database that contains the fields to be included in the document. The surest way to get the correct spelling is to tab to the Database File Name text box, press F2 to see a list of database files in the current directory, and then select the database name directly from the list box.

4. Tab to the Field Name text box and enter a field name to insert into the master document, or press F3 to see a list box and select the field name from it.

5. If you don't want the printed document to include trailing blank spaces, check the Trim spaces option. See "Suppressing Unneeded Spaces" below.
6. Select Include. LotusWorks inserts the word "Field" and the field name surrounded by double angle brackets at the cursor position, like this: «Field: COMPANY».
7. Repeat steps 1, 2, and 4 through 6 for each field in the master document.

## Suppressing Unneeded Spaces

Because each field in a database (except memo fields) has a fixed length, LotusWorks inserts blank spaces if the data does not fill an entire field. This is often the case with character fields used in names and addresses. If you print fields such as FIRSTNAME and LASTNAME one after another, the extra blank spaces show up between the fields. For example «Field: FIRSTNAME» «Field: LASTNAME» could look like this when printed: Jack       Jones.

To eliminate the extra spaces (called trailing spaces), check "Trim trailing spaces" in the Edit Include Mail Merge dialog box. In the example above, «Field: FIRSTNAME» «Field: LASTNAME» would look like this when printed: Jack Jones.

## Suppressing Blank Lines

If you are mail-merging an address and an empty data field occurs on a line by itself, you do not have to make any adjustment. LotusWorks 3.0 automatically suppresses the blank line and closes up the subsequent lines so that no gaps occur in the address.

## Printing the Merge Document

Here are the steps to Merge-print a document.

1. Select File Print Mail Merge. The following dialog box appears:

```
F1=Help                                                      F10=Menu
  File  Edit  Options  Style  Tools                          LotusWorks
  ───────────── Word Processor: D:\LWORKS3\LWDATA\MERGELTR.LWD ─────────
«Date»¶
¶
«Field: FNAME» «Field: MI» «Field: LNAME»¶
«Fi┌─────────────────────────────────────────────────────────────┐
«Fi│                     File Print Mail Merge                   │
«Fi│                                                              │
«Fi│    Database [D:\LWORKS3\LWDATA\BILL.DBF_____]   │
¶  │                                                              │
Dea│    Sort order [RECORD NUMBER_____]   Print...    │
¶  │                                                              │
Tha│    Search criteria [------- All Records ---------]  Preview...│
   │                                                              │
   │                                                     Cancel   │
   └─────────────────────────────────────────────────────────────┘


End of Text                                                         Ins
F2 for available sort orders
```

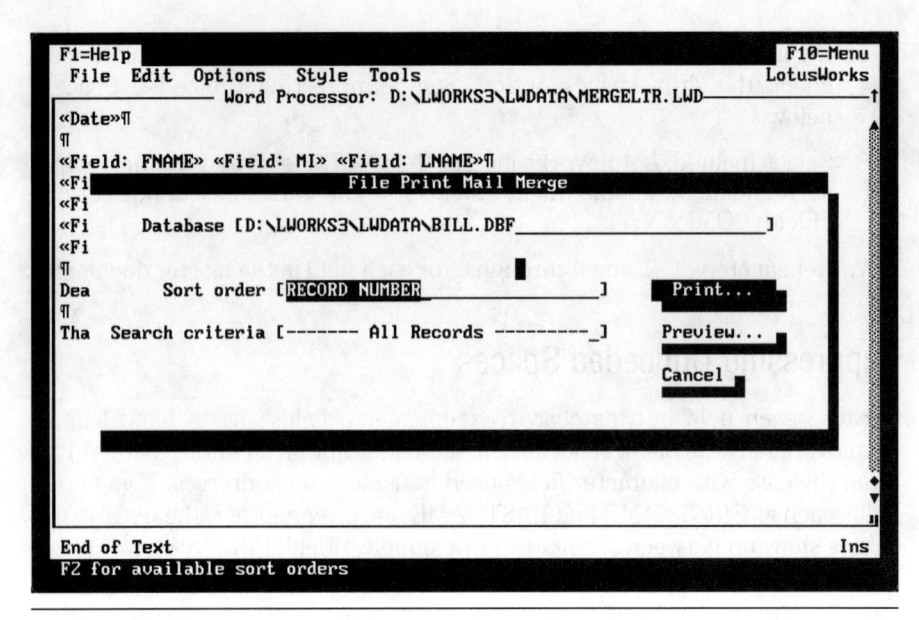

**FIGURE 3.20:** Select File Print Mail Merge and enter the name of the sort order to be used for merge printing.

2. Enter the name of a sort order or press F3 to select from among previously created sort orders. A sort order controls the order in which the records from the database are printed. The default is Record Number order, which means that the records are printed in the order in which they were entered into the database. If you would like the database records to print in some other order (such as ZIP code order or alphabetical order by last name), you can create a sort order in the Database service. See "Creating a Sort Order" in Chapter 4 for information about creating sort orders.

3. Enter the search criteria or press F3 to select from among previously created search criteria. The search criteria determine which records from the database are selected for printing. The default is All Records. You specify search criteria in the Database service. See "Finding the Records You Want" in Chapter 4 for more information about creating search criteria.

4. Select Preview to see how the document will appear when merge-printed. LotusWorks displays the finished document with data from the first active record inserted. Press Ctrl+PgDn to view the document with data from additional records. Check the appearance of several records to be sure the document is laid out as you want it.

5. Select Print. The following dialog box appears:

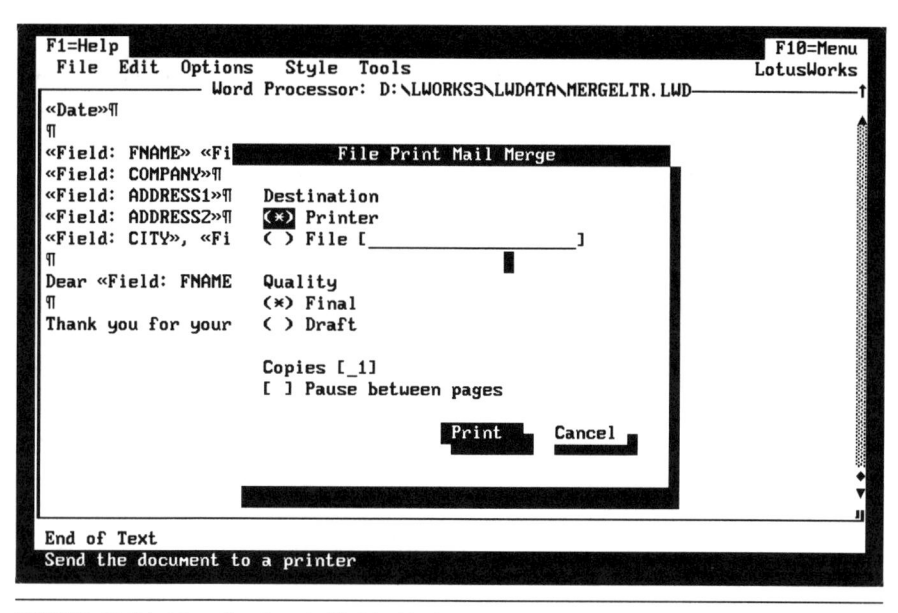

**FIGURE 3.21:** Select the options from the File Print Mail Merge dialog box and then select Print to print the document.

6. Select the options from the File Print Mail Merge dialog box just as you would for printing an ordinary document.

7. When all the options have been set, select Print. LotusWorks prints the number of copies of the finished document you have requested for each record specified in the search criteria. The documents are printed in the sorted order.

# Printing Envelopes and Mailing Labels

Not all computer printers can print envelopes, but if yours can, there are a couple of tricks you can do with LotusWorks to save time.

- **Copy and Paste to a dummy envelope document.** One way to save time is to create and save a word document as a dummy envelope document. Format the dummy document in the style you prefer and in the print orientation (portrait or landscape) that your printer requires for envelopes, and then save the dummy. When you are ready to print an envelope, retrieve the dummy envelope document into a new window, copy the name and address information from your letter document, and paste it into the appropriate location on the envelope document. Before you print the envelope, change the Print Layout settings to a page height and page width equal to the dimensions of your envelope stock.

- **Mail-merge an envelope master document.** Another way to print envelopes is to merge print them from a database. This method is convenient if you are also merge printing letters. Simply format and save a master document containing the field names needed for your envelopes. (They will be the same ones you use for the inside address of business letters.) When you are ready to print envelopes, retrieve the envelope master document, enter the name of the database, specify the record or records to print, change the Print Layout settings to fit the page height and page width of your envelope stock, and print the envelopes. LotusWorks treats each envelope as a separate page.
- **Mailing Labels.** If you have roll-type mailing labels, you can use either of the methods above to print them. Before you print them, change the File Print Layout settings to fit the page height and page width of the mailing labels. LotusWorks treats each label as a separate page. A better way to print roll-type mailing labels is to go to the Database service, create a form the size of the label with the address field positioned to fit within the label, and print the form from the Database service.

If you have a laser printer and sheet-type mailing labels with multiple labels on one page, you must use the Database service to print them. Create a form the size of the label, position the address fields to fit within the label, select File Print Layout, specify the number of labels that appear across each sheet and the number that appear down each sheet, then print the labels. You may have to adjust the top and bottom margins to get the print to position correctly on the page of labels. See "Printing Labels" in Chapter 4 for details.

## Creating and Using Boilerplate

Boilerplate is text that you record and use over and over again without retyping. It can be a major timesaver.

There are two main ways to create boilerplate in LotusWorks:

- **Put boilerplate in a Word Processing macro.** When you are in the Word Processing service, select Options Macros Learn, move the cursor to the Ctrl+key combination of your choice, select Learn, and type the text that you wish to store as boilerplate. (Recall that Ctrl+ [a letter from A to Z] designates a macro.) If you wish, you can change the type style and format of all or part of the boilerplate text. When you finish typing the text, press the Ctrl+key combination you selected for the macro to stop the recording.

To insert the boilerplate into a document, move the cursor to the point in the text where you want the boilerplate to appear and press the Ctrl+key combination of the appropriate macro.

Putting boilerplate in a macro works best for short text with few options. That is because this kind of text is easiest to record without making mistakes and because only 26 service-specific macros can be stored in any one LotusWorks service at a time. In principle, however, you can use a macro for any type of boilerplate.

- **Put boilerplate in a word document and save it.** This approach works better if you have multiple versions of paragraphs or more than 26 pieces of boilerplate.

   The technique is simply to create a separate word document for boilerplate. You can format, style, and record one or more pieces of text within the document, and then save the document under an appropriate file name (such as BOILRPLT). When you want to use the boilerplate, use File Transfer Combine to insert the desired text from the boilerplate document to the appropriate places in the word document you are creating.

   Although this technique requires a bit more time than does a macro, it is much faster—and more accurate—than retyping the text each time you want to use it.

# Creating and Using "Styles"

Another way to save time creating word documents is to use "styles." Just as you can store and retrieve boilerplate text and document formats, you can also store and save combinations of tab, typeface, type attribute, and other settings. A style can be any combination of text styling and formatting commands that you store within a single macro. Styles can be especially useful for format changes in the middle of a document. For example, if you frequently indent paragraphs and use hanging indents for bullets or numbers, you can store all the necessary settings within a single macro. That way you don't have to set tabs and text attributes one-by-one each time. You can also use a style to store settings for standard headers and footers that you use frequently.

To create a style, simply create a macro and record the sequence of keystrokes to set the combination of settings you wish to store. To use a style, move the cursor to the point in the document where you want the new style to appear, and press the key combination that activates the macro. For more information, see "Setting Up and Saving Document Formats" earlier in this chapter.

## Using Multiple Windows

There are several ways to use multiple windows to help in drafting and editing word documents:

- **Comparing drafts.** To facilitate comparing drafts, you can put a draft of a document in one window and another draft in a second window and resize the windows so that the second is directly beneath the first one. Another technique is to put the same draft in both windows, then edit one draft while leaving the first draft intact for comparison. (If you do this, be sure to give the drafts different names, lest you accidentally destroy your original draft when you save the edited draft!)

- **Copying and moving text from other documents.** When you are copying or moving text from one document to another, open both documents in separate windows. That way you can confirm which text has been moved or copied and which remains in the original document. You can also use this technique to verify ranges and graph names when you are transferring information from spreadsheets and graphs.

## Example Documents

*Before you bold the headings, press the Tab key at least once after each heading. Be sure to exclude the tab when you bold the heading. That way the names, subject, and date you enter into the menu will line up neatly beneath each other.*

Here are some sample word document formats that you can adapt for your own use. To save the formats for future use, create the documents without entering text, then save each under a unique file name.

### Memo

This memo has left and right margins of 1.5 inches and top and bottom margins of 1 inch. The headings are in bold type, and the word M E M O R A N D U M is centered and has a blank space after each letter. The page number is centered between hyphens like this (- 2 -) and is placed in a footer that starts on page 2.

To set the margins, press Alt+L or select Style Layout; tab to the margin boxes, enter the desired Top and Bottom margins (1.0) and Left and Right margins (1.5) and select Accept. If you wish to set a type style, select Style Fonts, select the typeface and type size you wish to use, and select Accept.

To center the top heading, select the word MEMORANDUM and select Style Align Center. To bold the headings, select each word separately (MEMORANDUM, TO, FROM, etc.), select Style Fonts, set the attribute to Bold, and select Accept.

---

### How to Create the Footer

1. Press Alt+H or select Style Header/footer.
2. Type the following on the first line of the footer box: I- # - (vertical bar, hyphen, blank space, pound sign, blank space, hyphen).
3. Select Accept.
4. Select Style Configure; enter 2 in the Header/footer page text box and select Accept.

---

MEMORANDUM

TO:

FROM:

RE:

DATE:

## Letters

It is difficult to specify general formats for letters because letterheads and preferences in style vary so much. The following is a common format that allows for top and bottom margins of 2 inches, left and right margins of 1½ inches, and a header identifying the letter, date, and page number on the second and subsequent pages. Although this allows plenty of margin for most letterheads (including ones that have printed second sheets), you should experiment with your own stationery to find the spacing you like.

To set the margins, press Alt+L or select Style Layout, tab to the margin boxes, enter the desired Top and Bottom margins (2.0) and Left and Right margins (1.5), and select Accept. If you wish to set a type style, select Style Fonts, select the typeface and type size you wish to use, and select Accept.

---

### How to Create the Header

1. Press Alt+H or select Style Header/footer.
2. On the first Header line, enter words to identify the sender and addressee (such as "B. Samuels ltr to S.A. Green").
3. On the second Header line, enter @ (at sign) for the current date at printing.
4. On the third Header line, type *Page #*.
5. Set the margin to 1.500
6. Select Accept.
7. Select Style Configure, enter 2 in the Header/footer page text box, and select Accept.

---

The finished header begins on page two and looks like this:

```
B. Samuels to S.A. Green
06/30/92
Page 2
```

## Reports

Reports and proposals are more complicated than letters. They usually entail at least three distinct page formats: a title page, a table of contents, and text pages. The key is to format the title and contents pages without a header or footer and then start the header and footer (including page numbering) on the first page of text. Here is an example.

Title page:

**XYZ Company**


**Proposal for Services**


**Presented to**

**ABC Company**


**November 10, 1991**


Contact:
Susan Q. Brown
Marketing Manager
XYZ Company
123 N. Michigan Avenue, Suite 100
Chicago, Illinois 60602-1234
(312) 555-4444

Contents page:

**Contents**

| | | |
|---|---|---|
| I. | Executive Summary | 1 |
| II. | Description of Customer Needs | 2 |
| III. | Proposed Services | 5 |
| IV. | Schedule | 10 |
| V. | Fee | 12 |

Appendices

    A.   XYZ Company History and Capabilities

    B.   Similar Projects Performed by XYZ Company

    C.   Selected Clients

Header line 1:

XYZ Company||Proposal to ABC Company

Footer line 1:

@||Page #

The text page looks like this:

XYZ Company                          Proposal to ABC Company

    I. Executive Summary

       This is the executive summary of the proposal. Notice that the text is indented, and the first line of the paragraph is indented even further.

       This same page format can be used for the remaining pages of the proposal.

November 15, 1991                              Page 1

## Launching Documents with Macros

A quick way to retrieve a document format that you use frequently is to include the formatting in a macro. When you want to launch a document, you simply trigger the macro.

Rather than try to record all the format settings for the document in a macro, it's easiest to first create, test, and save a format document, then use the macro to retrieve the format document into the current word processing window.

For example, if you created a letter document with the file name of LTRFORM1, you could create a macro to launch it, as follows:

1. Open a new document in the Word Processing service.
2. From the Word Processing service, select Options Macros Learn.
3. Select an unused Ctrl+key combination for the macro.
4. Select Learn. Notice that the letters "Lrn" appear on the status line in the right corner of the screen.
5. Select File Retrieve, enter the file name of the format document, and select Retrieve.
6. Press the Ctrl+key combination again to stop recording.

To launch the document, open the Word Processing service and press the Ctrl+key combination you specified for the macro.

## A Final Word About Word Processing

At first glance, word processing may seem not to offer many opportunities for automation, but in fact it does. Most are variations on the theme of saving your setups and putting frequently used text into boilerplate documents and macros. The key is to use word processing as you would any other LotusWorks tool: look for opportunities to save and reuse your creative handiwork, and let Lotus-Works do as much work for you as possible.

# 4

# Managing Your Necessary Data

For most businesses, the Database service offers the most unexplored work-saving potential of all the LotusWorks services. Although it is not the service most people turn to first, it is an extraordinarily powerful and flexible tool. With a bit of planning, you can use it to automate a wide variety of business tasks. And the sooner you start incorporating it into the organization of your work, the better. Here is what we mean.

## Working Smart with Databases

The term "database" is nothing to be afraid of. A database is simply some information that has been organized in a way that the computer can process. You can visualize a database as a table made up of rows and columns. The rows are called records and the columns are called fields. Each record contains all the information about one particular person or thing. Each field contains the information of a certain type about that person or thing, such as the name, address, or phone number.

The key to working smart with databases is to enter data once and use it many times. Once information is in a database, the computer and LotusWorks can arrange, format, and use it over and over again, for tables,

*In this chapter, you'll learn how to:*

- *Work smart with databases*
- *Determine what databases can do for you*
- *Design and set up databases*
- *Find the data you want*
- *Create forms for data entry and output*
- *Get LotusWorks to calculate some of the data for you*
- *Use data from other databases*
- *Print labels*
- *Create an automatic phone dialer and note log*
- *Modify the LotusWorks example databases for your own use*

forms, calculations, and word processing documents. That's how you save keystrokes: by entering information into the computer only once and then using it many times.

You can use databases for a surprising number of small-business purposes. These include:

**Mail-Merge (Merge Printing).** This is an almost universal use. It enables you to create a series of individualized form letters without having to type each letter separately. You enter the text for a standard letter once into a word processing document and enter the names, addresses and other variable information for each addressee into a database. When you merge-print, LotusWorks prints a letter for each addressee in the database and inserts the database information into the appropriate places in each letter. Merge printing can be used for sales and solicitation letters, notification letters, collection letters, and just about any other kind of document where the same text with minor variations is sent to a number of addressees.

**Lists.** You can use databases to generate and format all sorts of lists. These can include mailing lists, directories, parts lists, membership rosters, class rosters, and inventories.

**Tracking.** You can use databases to keep track of things, such as inventories, equipment purchases, class attendance, and production batches.

**Tables and Forms.** Once you have information in a LotusWorks database, you can output it in a variety of formats that you design yourself. For instance, you can create tables for periodic reports that automatically update themselves from a database. You can create forms and worksheets with certain information pre-printed from a database. You can also create on-screen forms, such as customer-record forms, to ease data entry and lookups.

**Business Contacts.** Perhaps the most powerful use for small businesses, however, is as a sort of computerized card index—a comprehensive database of business contacts. Contacts can include customers, prospects, vendors, and other people with whom you do business. The database can hold all the information you need about each contact. Once you have the information in the database, you can use it in innumerable ways, such as automatic telephone dialing, addressing individual letters and envelopes, looking up order and payment information, and performing other tasks. If you wish, you can even use the database to print labels or cards for an ordinary rotary file or card index.

There's no "one best way" to use databases. How you use them is up to you and the nature of your business. Once you catch on to the principles of databases, you'll probably invent a variety of applications of your own.

## Four Steps to Efficient Data Use

To re-emphasize, the key to working smart with databases is to eliminate repetitious data entry. There are four basic steps to the process.:

- Identify your necessary data.
- Design one or more databases to hold the data.
- Build the necessary databases.
- Build applications based on the databases.

Let's look at each step in turn.

**Identify your necessary data.** Your necessary data are the items of information that you look up and use regularly to conduct your business or work. They may include information about clients, customers, colleagues, accounts, vendors, sales prospects, information sources, or companies with which you do business. The information for each may include addresses and phone numbers; account numbers; parts in inventory; prices for goods and services; records of phone calls; records of orders received, items shipped, services performed, or invoices sent; books and articles; market data; or any of countless other things. The important criteria are that the information be important for your business or work, and that it be organizable into one or more databases.

The idea in identifying your necessary data is to eliminate duplicate and unnecessary data, minimize your keystrokes, and get the computer to do as much work as possible for you. The way to do this is to review all the lists you keep in your business, put as many as possible on the computer, and consolidate as many as possible into one database or a few databases.

To begin identifying your necessary data, make a list. Write down all the types of information you can think of that you regularly use in your work. When your list is as complete as you can make it, look it over and try to identify subjects for which you keep similar items of information, such as clients, prospects, and vendors for whom you keep names, addresses, and phone numbers. Each subject will become a record or row of a database, and each item of information will become a data field in the record.

**Design one or more databases to hold the data.** Before you start building a database, you need to plan it. You must decide on a name for each field, the type of data the field will contain, and, if appropriate, the maximum number of characters and decimal places the field should hold. You also should decide the order in which you want the fields to appear in the database.

If the fields are similar, you can have data for different types of subjects in the same database, provided you have one field that distinguishes the type. For example, you can have information about customers and vendors in the same database if you have one field that tells whether a given record is for a customer or a vendor.

The question of how many databases to have depends on the amount of data, the way you wish to use it, and the size of your computer. These issues are covered in the section on designing databases later in this chapter.

**Build the databases.** To build a database, you need to create a database file, define each field in turn telling LotusWorks the name, type of data, size, etc. of each field in your database design, and then enter the data for each record into the database. The procedures are covered later in this chapter.

**Build applications based on the databases.** Once the database is built, you are ready to use it to save keystrokes. Building applications means creating word documents, tables, and forms that draw on specified portions of the data in the database. The LotusWorks Database service automatically finds the records that match the search criteria that you specify. There are several suggestions for database applications later in this chapter.

## When to Use a Database

Although databases and spreadsheets may appear to be similar in some ways, they are actually quite different. Which to use for storing data depends more on the ways you intend to use the data than on the form of the data. Generally, you should use a database whenever one or more of the following situations apply:

- **Merge Printing**—when you want to use merge printing to insert the data (or some of it) into word documents.
- **Form or Table Layouts**—when you want to view or print data in a form or table layout rather than the format of the database, such as when printing mailing labels.

- **Selecting**—when you want to be able to select certain records for action without acting on all records—for example, when you want to address a letter only to a selected group of recipients. Databases allow you to write statements that select cases that meet the conditions you specify.
- **Calculations Based on Fields**—when you want to perform calculations to transform data for an entire field. Databases enable you to write formulas for data fields, such as formulas that multiply the values in one field by the values in another and put the answer in a third field. Databases do not, however, allow you to write formulas for individual cells, as spreadsheets do (databases do not have cells).
- **Lengthy or Variable-Length Data**—when you want to enter lengthy data or data of varying lengths (rather than of fixed length) into a field. The Memo field type in the Database service is designed specifically for this purpose.
- **Database Functions**—when you want to use one of the special LotusWorks calculation functions designed just for databases. More about these later.

# Designing Databases

There are three steps in designing a database: (1) deciding the number of fields to have, (2) deciding a name for each field, and (3) deciding the type and length of each field. It's a good idea to lay out this information on paper before you start building the database.

Try to consolidate as much information as possible into each database and avoid having the same information in more than one database. That way, if you ever want to send a mailing to all people in your database, you can easily do so. (If you ever need to have information from one database in another, such as for a special merge printing, you can easily copy it. The procedure is explained later in this chapter.)

Once you have decided what to include in a database, make a list of names for the fields you want. Give each field a short, distinctive name (not more than 10 characters) that describes the contents. Beside the field name, write the type of data the field is to hold: Character, Numeric, Date, Logical, or Memo (see below). The order of the fields does not matter as far as LotusWorks is concerned, but if you want certain fields to appear on the screen when you first retrieve the database, you should put them at the beginning of the database.

LotusWorks 3.0 uses different types of fields for different types of data. There are five types. Take a minute to study them if you have not done so already.

## Five Types of Data Field

**Character.** Character fields hold text data—letters and numbers treated as text (such as street addresses, telephone numbers, and ZIP codes). Lotus-Works does not perform math with numbers that are in character fields. Each character field can be up to 254 characters long. When you define a character field, LotusWorks asks you to specify the maximum number of characters the field will hold.

**Numeric.** Numeric fields hold numeric data, which is to say, numbers. LotusWorks can perform math on the data in numeric fields. Each numeric field can be up to 19 digits long, including up to 14 decimal places. When you define a numeric field, LotusWorks asks you to specify the maximum number of digits and the maximum number of decimal places to allow. If you need to perform math on or with the numbers in a field, define it as a numeric field. Otherwise, you can define it as a character field.

**Date.** Date fields are specialized fields that hold dates. The length of the field is fixed by LotusWorks. The data takes the form DD/MM/YYYY, where DD is a two-digit number for the day (such as 01 or 31), MM is a two-digit number for the month (such as 01 or 12), and YYYY is a four-digit number for the year (such as 1992). In entering data into a date field, you don't have to type the / separator; LotusWorks enters it for you automatically. Also, you need enter only the last two digits of the year; LotusWorks enters the first two digits for you. For example, to enter the date for February 29, 1992, you can type 290292; Lotus-Works automatically puts it into the format 29/02/1992. Date fields are useful in two ways: (1) They enable LotusWorks to perform date arithmetic, that is, adding or subtracting a number of days from a date and adding or subtracting one date from another. (2) With date fields, LotusWorks can help you check for mistakes in data entry (such as entering 32 for a day or 13 for a month).

**Logical.** Logical fields hold only one character, either a Y (for Yes), T (for True:), N (for No), or F (for False). For example, in a logical field named

"Billed," an entry of "Y" indicates that the account has been billed; "N" indicates that it has not. Logical fields are useful for indicating conditions to be used in determining whether a given record should be selected or not.

**Memo.** Memo fields are text fields that enable you to add notes and comments to records. A memo field can be very large (at least 64,000 characters and spaces, depending on your computer's configuration), and the length can vary from record to record. Memo fields are useful for all sorts of free-form notes and comments, such as notes on telephone conversations and tickler reminders for future action.

If you were designing a customer database, the beginning of your list might look something like this:

## Customer Database Fields

| Name | Type | Maximum Characters | Decimal Places |
| --- | --- | --- | --- |
| CustNo. | Numeric | 5 | 0 |
| Lastname | Character | 30 | |
| Firstname | Character | 20 | |
| MI | Character | 1 | |
| Salutation | Character | 20 | |
| Phonenum | Character | 14 | |
| Company | Character | 40 | |
| Prefix | Character | 3 | |
| Suffix | Character | 4 | |
| Title | Character | 20 | |
| Lastcontct | Date | | |
| Status | Memo | | |
| Address1 | Character | 30 | |
| Address2 | Character | 30 | |
| City | Character | 30 | |
| State | Character | 2 | |
| ZIPcode | Character | 10 | |

Notice that this database has a Salutation field as well as fields for the customer's first and last names. This is for use in letters or phone calls. The Prefix field is for forms of address (such as Mr., Ms., Dr., or Hon.) that appear before a name, and the Suffix field is for data that comes after a name (such as Jr., III, Ph.D., or Esq.). Be sure to make the Firstname and Lastname fields long enough for double names and hyphenated names (such as Mary Ann Smith-Jones).

As you might guess, there is much variation in people's names, so databases that are to be used for merge printing must be planned carefully to allow for all the possibilities. If you are outside of North America, you may need to provide for variations in names and addresses beyond the ones discussed here.

Notice also that the Phonenum and ZIPcode fields are character fields rather than numeric fields. This is to allow for punctuation to be inserted in phone numbers (1-800-555-2222) and ZIP codes (22222-3333). If these were numeric fields, LotusWorks would interpret the hyphens as subtraction operators (minus signs) and would subtract the numbers each time you entered them. Also, LotusWorks would eliminate any leading zeros in ZIP codes; for example, 04474 would be displayed as 4474.

Outside the United States, you'll probably prefer to name the field "Mailcode" instead of "ZIPcode," and you may need to use different field lengths from the ones shown here.

*If you are designing a database to be used for telephone dialing, put the phone number field near the top of the database so that you will be able to see it on the screen without having to scroll the database or create a special form.*

# Setting Up and Testing Databases

You set up a database according to the specifications recorded on your database design sheet. This involves creating a database file, defining the fields, entering some test data, and testing to see if the database performs as you wish.

## Creating the Database File and Fields

To create a database file and define the data fields, follow these steps.

1. Select the Database service on the LotusWorks Screen.

2. Press Alt+N or select File New (that is, go to the Menu line and select File, then New). The following dialog box appears:

Managing Your Necessary Data **117**

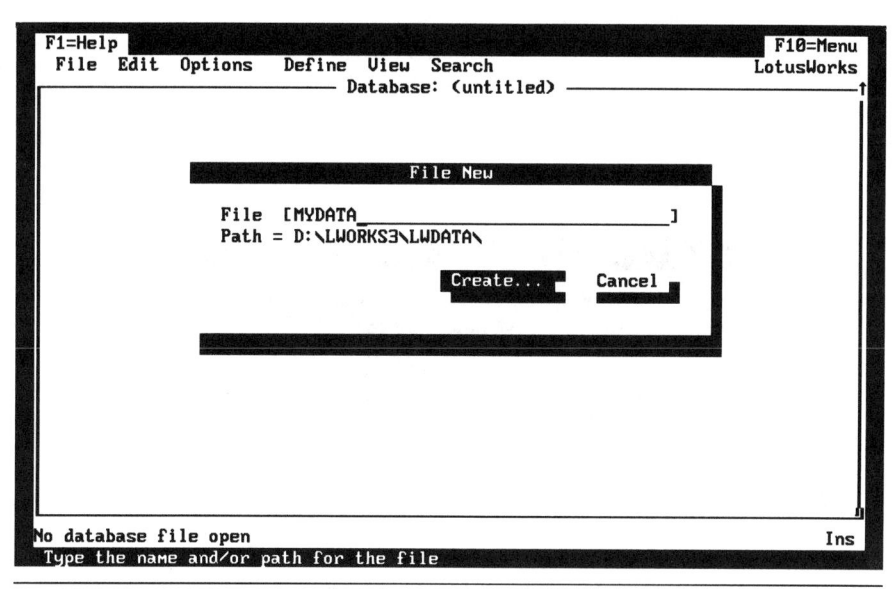

**FIGURE 4.1:** When the File New dialog box appears, enter a DOS path and file name in the File text box.

3. Enter a DOS path and file name of eight characters or less for the database in the File text box. (Do not enter a file name extension.)

4. Select Create: press the Tab key to highlight Create and press Enter to select it or click the mouse on Create. A second File New dialog box appears.

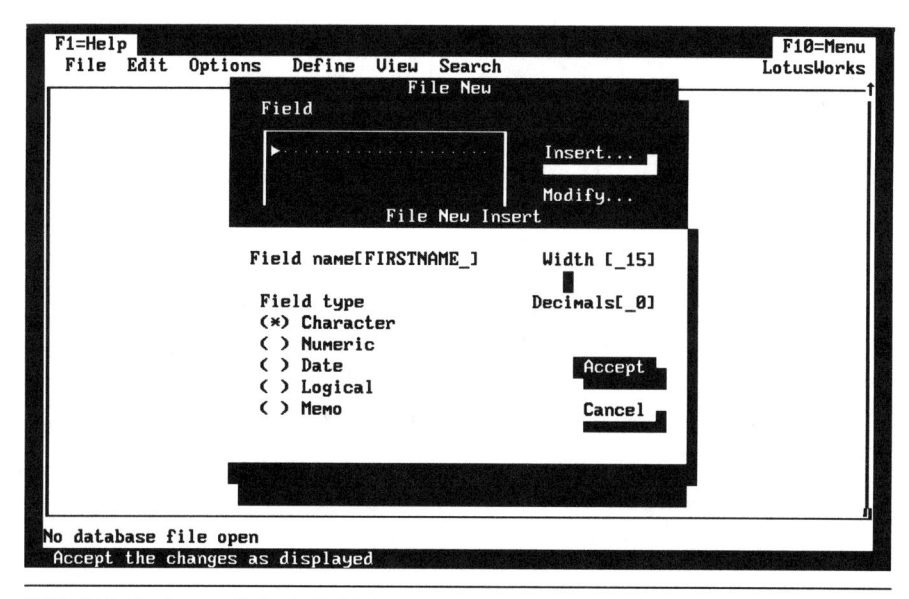

**FIGURE 4.2:** Use the second Define Fields Modify dialog box to insert fields into the database.

**118**  The Lotus Guide to LotusWorks

5. When the second File New dialog box appears, insert fields into the database: press Tab to highlight the Insert option and press Enter or click the mouse to select Accept. The File New Insert dialog box appears:

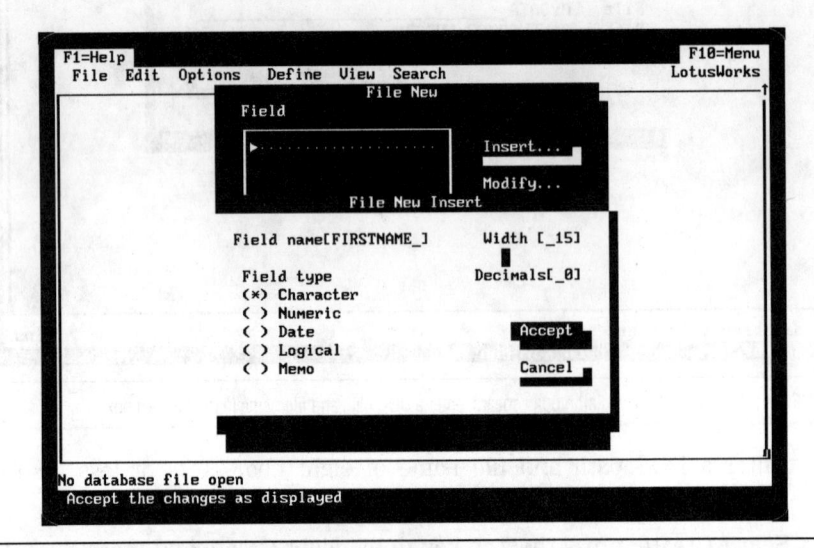

**FIGURE 4.3:** Enter the name, type, and width of each new field.

Enter the name of the first field to be defined. Tab to the Field type option, press the Spacebar until the asterisk appears beside the desired data type, and press the Tab key. The cursor advances to the Width option, if it is appropriate for the field type you have selected. Enter the desired width for the field (number of characters) and, if appropriate, the desired number of decimal places. The maximum field widths are as follows:

- Character fields can be up to 254 characters long.

- Numeric fields can be up to 19 characters long, including a decimal point and a minus sign for negative numbers; a maximum of 14 characters can be on either side of the decimal point.

- Date fields must be eight characters long. LotusWorks sets the length for you.

- Logical fields can hold one character (T, F, Y, or N). LotusWorks sets the length for you.

- Memo fields can be very large. You do not have to specify the length. Memo fields are stored in separate files from the rest of the database.

6. When you have finished entering the first field, select Accept, then select Insert again and enter the name and specifications for the second field. Repeat this process until you have entered names and specifications for all the fields on your list.

7. When you have entered all the field definitions, select Accept to accept the definitions and exit the dialog box.

LotusWorks creates the database you have defined and saves it under the file name you entered.

*Be sure to put Social Security numbers, telephone numbers, and ZIP (mail) codes into Character fields. If you put them into Number fields, LotusWorks interprets the dashes and slash signs as mathematical operators and performs the indicated mathematical operations.*

## Entering Data and Testing the Database

The object of testing the database is to see if you have defined all the fields you need and if all the definitions work as intended. Before you enter data in the database, it's a good idea to try it out with a few sample records. With the database on the screen, press Alt+I or go to the Menu line and select Edit Record insert. (If you have already exited the database, you can retrieve it by selecting File Retrieve and entering the path and name of the database. For example, for a database named CONTACTS saved in the LWDATA subdirectory of the LWORKS3 directory on drive C, you would enter *c:\lworks3\lwdata\contacts.*)

### Entering Data

Type the data for the first field, then press Enter or use the mouse or arrow keys to move the cursor to the next field. (If you fill the field completely, LotusWorks automatically moves the pointer to the next field.) Repeat this process until you have entered data into all the fields. Try to enter sample data that fills up each entire field, so that you can tell whether the fields are long enough.

**Entering Data in a Character Field.** You may enter any characters into a character field, so long as they do not exceed the length you have prescribed for the field.

**Entering Data in a Numeric Field.** You may enter the numerals 0 through 9 into a numeric field, so long as they do not exceed the length and number of decimal places you have prescribed. You may also enter a decimal point but no other punctuation.

**Entering Data in a Date Field.** Date fields must be eight characters long, in the form DD/MM/YYYY, where DD is the number of the day, MM is the month, and YYYY is the year. You do not have to enter the / separator; LotusWorks does that for you. If you enter the last two digits of the year (for example, 92 for 1992), LotusWorks enters the first two digits automatically.

**Entering Data in a Logical Field.** You may enter T for True or F for False; or you may enter Y for Yes or N for No.

**Entering Data in a Memo Field.** Memo fields have a different data entry procedure from other fields. To enter data in a memo field, move the cursor to the field and press F2. The Memo Editor appears:

```
F1=Help                                                          F10=Menu
 File  Edit  Options  Tools
                            ─ Memo Editor ─
¶
¶
¶
You can enter text into the Memo Editor just as you would in the word
processing service.¶
¶
Once text is entered, you can select, cut, copy, paste, delete, and restore
blocks of text from the Edit menu, as you would in the word processing
service.  You can also search for and replace text, check your spelling, and
use the Dictionary, Thesaurus, and Word Total options from the Tools menu.¶
¶
To save an entry and exit the Memo Editor, press Alt+S or select File
Save/Exit.¶
¶
To exit the Memo Editor without saving your entry, press Alt+Q or select File
Quit.¶
¶

New paragraph                                                         Ins
```

**FIGURE 4.4:** Highlight the memo field and press F2 to get to the Memo Editor.

You can enter text into the Memo Editor just as you would enter text in the word processing service. Each memo field can hold at least 64,000 characters.

Once text is entered, you can select, cut, copy, paste, delete, and restore blocks of text from the Edit menu, as you would in the word processing service. You can also search for and replace text, check your spelling, and use the Dictionary, Thesaurus, and Word Total options from the Tools menu.

To save an entry and exit the Memo Editor, press Alt+S or select File Save/Exit. To exit the Memo Edior without saving your entry, press Alt+Q or select File Quit.

> When you enter data into a database, LotusWorks allows you to enter only data of the type you have specified for each field, and only the maximum number of characters that you have specified. This helps you guard against some data entry mistakes.

When you have finished entering or editing data in the last field at the end of a data file, LotusWorks asks if you want to create another record. Go ahead and enter data for two or three more records. When you have finished entering data, you can exit the Record insert mode by selecting Cancel. LotusWorks automatically saves your data.

## Testing the Database

To test the skeleton database, you need to use it as you would use the full-scale one. For example, if you plan to use the database for merge printing, you should create a merge document and try printing single and multiple records. (There are instructions for these operations later in this chapter and in Chapter 3.) Check to be sure that you have fields defined for all the possible needs that you can foresee, and that the fields are long enough to hold your data without being too long for the display or print areas.

If you find that you need to add fields or change some field specifications later, you can easily do so at any time. To save keystrokes, however, it is best to do so before you have entered large amounts of data.

## Modifying Fields

If you find that you need to change the specifications for a field—for instance, to change the data type, field length, or the number of decimal places—you can easily do so by selecting Define Fields Modify. Click the mouse or move the cursor to highlight the field you wish to change, select the Modify option, and enter the new specifications. If you have already entered data into the field, avoid making the following kinds of modification:

1. Decreasing field width.
2. Decreasing the number of decimal places.
3. Changing a character field to a numeric or date field. (You may lose characters that are unacceptable in numeric or date fields)

4. Changing a Memo field to another type. (You may lose data.)

When you finish, select Accept to exit the dialog box. LotusWorks automatically updates and saves the modified database.

## Adding Fields

You can add fields to a database at any time as follows:

1. Select Define Fields Modify.

2. Move the cursor to the point in the list box where you want the new field to appear. LotusWorks inserts new fields just above the line that is highlighted.

3. Select Insert.

4. Enter a name for the new field in the Field name text box, and complete the options to specify the field type, width, and decimals (if appropriate) just as you would for any other new field.

5. Select Accept to exit the dialog box.

To fill a new field with data, you can either enter the data record-by-record, define a rule for the field that will compute data for each record, or copy the data from another database file. See "Using Rules to Ease Data Entry" later in this chapter.

## Renaming Fields

If you want to change the name of a field without changing any other specifications, select Define Fields Rename; move the cursor to the field to be renamed, select Rename, enter the new field name in the Field text box; and select Accept to exit the dialog box.

## Deleting Fields

If you want to delete a field entirely, select Define Fields, select the field to be deleted from the Field list box, and select Delete. LotusWorks prompts you for confirmation before it deletes any data.

> WARNING: When you delete a field, all the data in the field is destroyed. Neither the field nor the data can be recovered. Be very careful in using the Delete option.

## Using Rules to Ease Data Entry

You can have LotusWorks do some of the work of entering data for you by using the Rules feature in the Database service. A rule is a formula that you can define to have LotusWorks enter data into a field automatically or limit the data that can be entered. LotusWorks has nine types of database rules. When you use the Rules feature, LotusWorks computes data by formula from existing fields or copies them from other database files without any additional data entry on your part.

To use the Rules feature, select Define Rules Modify. The following dialog box appears:

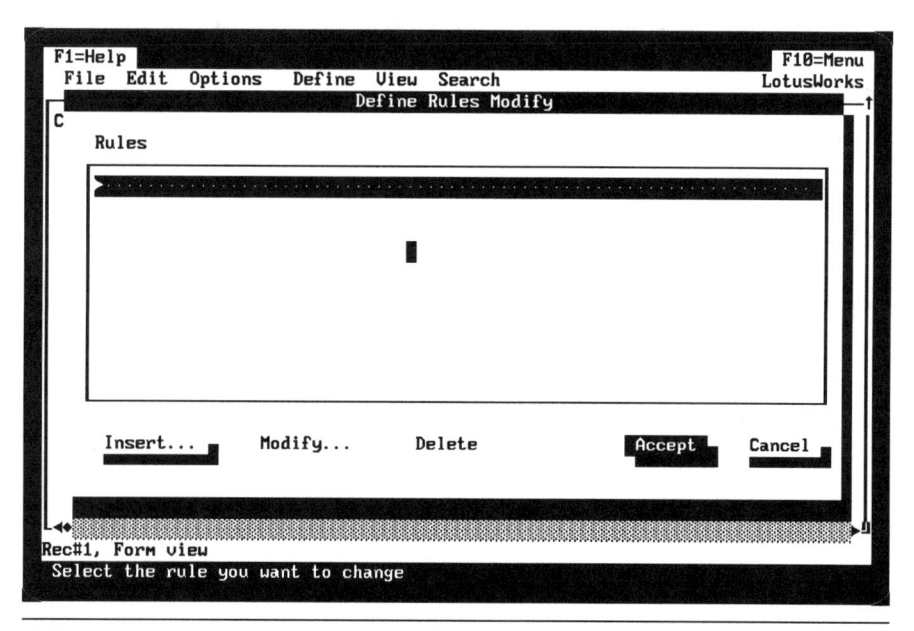

**FIGURE 4.5:** The Define Rules Modify dialog box enables you to select a rule to modify.

Move the cursor to the blank line and select the Insert option or to an existing rule and select Modify. Another dialog box appears, allowing you to specify a type of rule for the change:

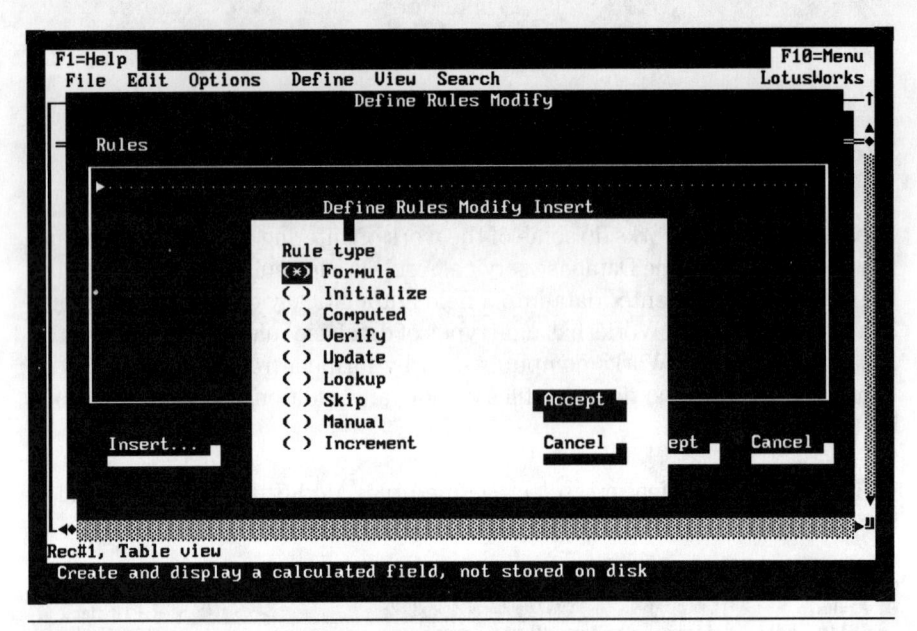

**FIGURE 4.6:** Specify the type of rule that you want to appear in the specified field.

## Types of Field Rules

### Formula Rule

Computes a new value for a "virtual field" based on the values in one or more other fields in the record for use during ongoing operations. It does not actually store the new value in a field. Example: PRINCIPAL * 0.1. This rule multiplies the value in the PRINCIPAL field by 0.1 and uses the resulting value in operations.

## Initialize Rule

Enables you to specify a default value for a field. When you create a new record, the default value is inserted in the field unless you change it. Example: 1000. This rule sets an initial value of 1000 in the field you specify.

## Computed Rule

Computes a value based on the values in one or more other fields in the record and stores the new value in the field. Example: TOTAL/NUMBER. This rule divides the value in the TOTAL field by the value in the NUMBER field and puts the resulting value in the field you specify.

*To prevent writing over a default value created by an Initialize rule, write a Skip rule for the field that is always true.*

## Verify Rule

Checks the validity of the value in a field to see that the value entered meets the conditions that you specify. This is a safety feature to guard against mistakenly entering improper data or data that is out of bounds. Example: MONTH >= 1 .AND. MONTH < 13. With this rule, LotusWorks does not accept a value less than 1 or greater than 12 in the Month field.

You can also have LotusWorks print a message whenever invalid data is entered by typing either ! (single exclamation point) or !! (two exclamation points) and the message immediately after the Verify rule. A single exclamation point means that exceptions to the rule are allowed. For example:

AGE<100!Are you sure the age is correct?

This rule prints the message "Are you sure the age is correct?" if an age greater than 99 is entered.

Two exclamation points mean that no exceptions to the rule are allowed. For example:

MONTH>=1 .AND. MONTH<13 !!Enter a number between 1 and 12.

This rule prints the message "Enter a number between 1 and 12." if invalid data are entered; it will not accept any data that doesn't match the Verify rule.

*With a little planning, you can write error messages to explain how to correct data entry errors.*

## Update Rule

On command, updates (recalculates) the values in all the active records according to a group of one or more field rules you have defined. This type of rule is useful if you change values in fields on which formula or computed values are based or if you wish to update formula or computed values for selected fields only. You may define up to 9 groups of rules for use with the Update command. When you press F9 or select Options Update and specify one of the groups of rules that you have defined, LotusWorks executes the specified group of rules. For example, you can use an update rule to perform a monthly operation that adds the value in a Month-to-Date-Total field to a Year-to-Date-Total field and reinitializes the Month-to-Date-Total field to 0.

## Lookup Rule

Uses the LOOKUP function to find the data for a record in a specified field in an external database file and retrieve the data for use in the current field. The data is not saved in the current database. The two databases must have a field in common (called a key field) that contains a unique value for each record. LotusWorks looks in the key field of the external database, finds the record that matches the current record, then returns the value in the specified field. For example, suppose that you keep customers' names and addresses in a database named "Customer," and you keep account balance information in a database named "Accounts." Suppose each customer has a customer identification number that appears in both databases. You could bring information on each customer's balance into a field in the Customer database with the following lookup formula:

LOOKUP(CUSTID,"BALANCE","ACCOUNTS")

This lookup expression says, "Look up the customer i.d. number for the current record, find the matching number in the CUSTID field of the ACCOUNTS database, and return the value in the BALANCE field for that record.

## Skip Rule

Automatically skips over a field if a condition that you specify in the rule is true. Example: BALANCE < 100. This rule causes LotusWorks to skip over the current field for any record that has a value less than 100 in the BALANCE field.

## Manual Rule

Executes a rule at your request. When you move the cursor into a field for which you have defined a manual rule, you can execute the rule by pressing F2.

## Increment Rule

Assigns a number to the first record and increases each succeeding record by the amount you specify in the rule. For example, entering 1 as an Increment rule increases the value in the current field by 1 for each succeeding record. NOTE: If you write over a value created by an Increment rule, LotusWorks accepts the value you enter but increases the next record as if you had not changed the value.

## Writing Rule Expressions

Expressions are the basic constructs for giving instructions to LotusWorks. An expression is simply one or more values, field names, and/or functions joined by operators to form a logical statement. The following are examples of expressions:

```
2 + 2
BALANCE * 1.10
ORDER > 100
STATE = "IL"
```

Each rule must be defined in an expression that you compose and enter in the appropriate dialog box. As you can see from the examples above, rule expressions can take a variety of forms.

You may have up to 254 characters in a rule expression. You may write rule expressions in all uppercase letters, all lowercase, or a combination of uppercase and lowercase.

It is possible to have rule expressions that are quite complex. For instance, it is possible to have rules that transform data from one type (such as numeric or date) to another (such as character), rules that fetch data from multiple sources, and rules that follow conditional logic (such as "If condition A exists, do this, otherwise do that."). You should try writing simple rules at first, following the examples above and those in the LotusWorks 3.0 documentation. You probably will find this sufficient for quite a while. When you need to write more complex expressions, see the section "Composing with Database Functions" later in this chapter.

The following is a list of operators that can be used in rule expressions.

| Operator | Operation |
| --- | --- |
| **Logical Operators** | |
| < | Less than |
| <= | Less than or equal to |
| > | Greater than |
| >= | Greater than or equal to |
| = | Equal |
| <> | Not equal to |
| .AND. | Logical And |
| .OR. | Logical Or |
| .NOT. | Negation |
| **Numeric Operators** | |
| + | Addition |
| − | Subtraction |
| * | Multiplication |
| / | Division |
| ** | Exponentiation (raise to a power) |
| **String Operators** | |
| + (Database) | Concatenation. Combines two text strings into a new string |
| − (Database) | Concatenation with trim. Strips blank spaces from the first text string and combines it with a second string |
| $ (Database) | Substring Inclusion. Determines if a string of characters is contained within a string |

Operators for LotusWorks Database Expressions

You may use relational operators with numeric data, character data, and dates. For example:

Balance > 500 means a value greater than 500 in the Balance field.

Lastname < "Smith" means last names that come before "Smith" in the alphabet.

Duedate >= 01/01/93 means a value in the Duedate field on or after January 1, 1993.

> **IMPORTANT:** Notice that text in expressions must be enclosed within double-quotation marks. This includes not only letters but also numerals entered in character fields.

To save yourself keystrokes, use the data entry rules wherever you can.

# Using Forms for Data Entry

LotusWorks 3.0 lets you design and use on-screen forms to ease your data entry. A form is simply an alternate display of some or all of the fields of a database. Whereas the database displays the fields one below the other in a single column, Form view enables you to select fields, position them on the screen to appear wherever you like, and add labels, lines, and shading if you wish, like a printed form. When you print from Form view, the data, labels, lines, and shading appear as they do on the screen.

## Advantages of Data Entry Forms

There are two important advantages of using a form for data entry:

- You can arrange the fields into the order that is easiest for data entry. For example, if you often take in information over the telephone, you may wish to arrange the fields into the order that is easiest for people to answer on the phone. This may not be the order in which the fields of the database itself are arranged. You can even have one form for data entry and another for printing and viewing data. For that matter, you can have two different data entry forms for entering data from different departments into the same database.

- You can provide an explicit label or instruction beside each field to indicate the data that should be entered in the field. Full-fledged labels can be clearer and easier to understand than field names, which may be cryptic at times.

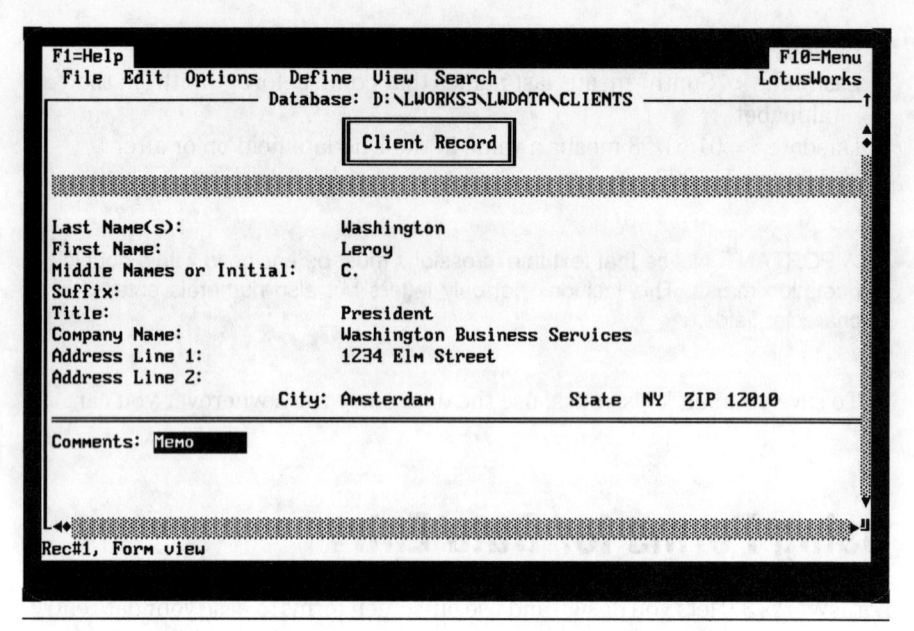

**FIGURE 4.7:** Forms for data entry can contain explicit labels and instructions.

For instructions, see "Creating Custom Forms" later in this chapter.

## Viewing Data

LotusWorks 3.0 gives you two ways to view data: Table view and Form view.

Table view displays multiple records at once. It arrays the records in rows and the fields in columns. Each record occupies one row of the display. To see additional fields, you scroll the screen to the right. To see additional records, you scroll the screen down.

Managing Your Necessary Data **131**

```
F1=Help                                                    F10=Menu
    File  Edit  Options  Define  View  Search              LotusWorks
                    Database: D:\LWORKS3\LWDATA\CLIENTS
    LASTNAME                  FIRSTNAME        MID SUFFIX

    Washington                Leroy            C.
    Walker                    Billie Fay
    Bailey                    Lillian          Ann
    Kyker                     Keith            D.  Jr.
    Muller                    Michael          A.  CPA








Rec#1, Table view
```

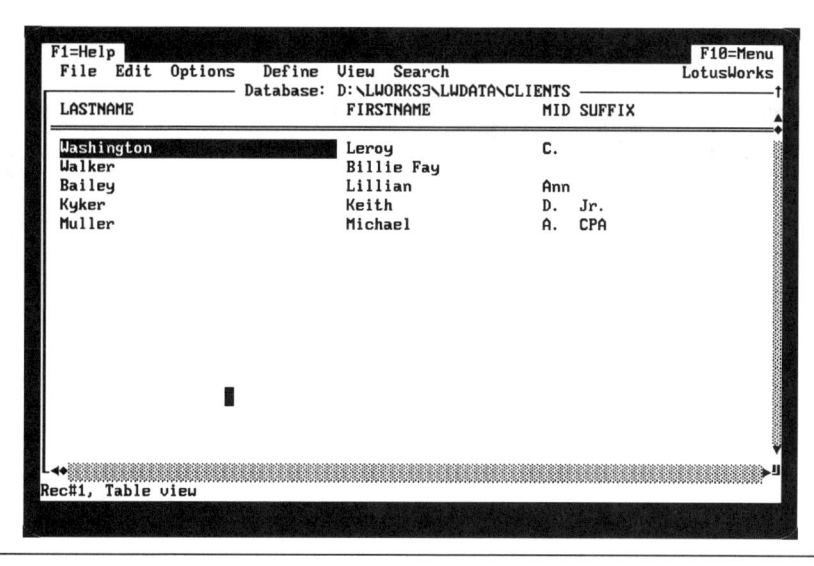

**FIGURE 4.8:** Table view displays field names and data values for multiple records at once.

Form view displays field names and values for a single record at a time. It also enables you to position the fields on the screen wherever you like and to add labels, instructions, lines, boxes, and borders, just as you would on a paper form. To see additional records, you scroll the screen down. The default form looks like this:

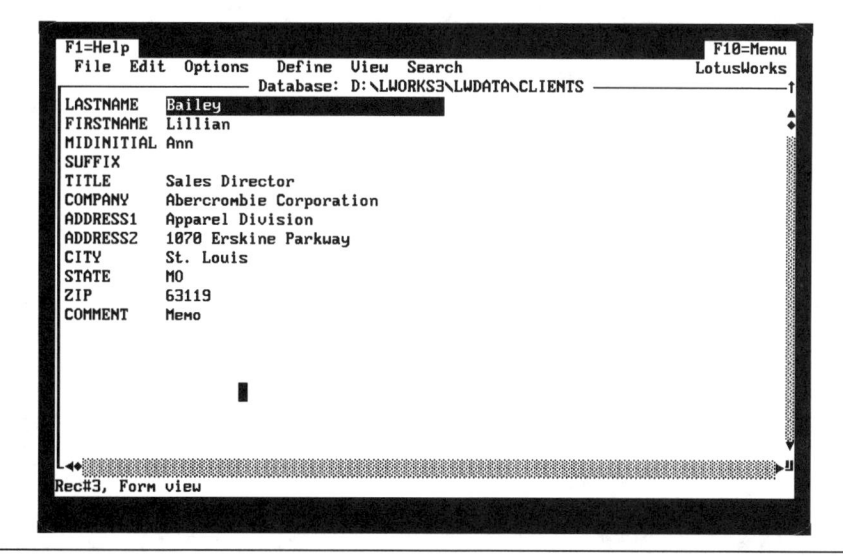

```
F1=Help                                                    F10=Menu
    File  Edit  Options  Define  View  Search              LotusWorks
                    Database: D:\LWORKS3\LWDATA\CLIENTS
    LASTNAME   Bailey
    FIRSTNAME  Lillian
    MIDINITIAL Ann
    SUFFIX
    TITLE      Sales Director
    COMPANY    Abercrombie Corporation
    ADDRESS1   Apparel Division
    ADDRESS2   1070 Erskine Parkway
    CITY       St. Louis
    STATE      MO
    ZIP        63119
    COMMENT    Memo




Rec#3, Form view
```

**FIGURE 4.9:** Form view displays data for a single record at a time; the default form assigns one field to each line.

By creating an alternative form, you could display the same data like this:

```
F1=Help                                                    F10=Menu
   File  Edit  Options  Define  View  Search              LotusWorks
                    Database: D:\LWORKS3\LWDATA\CLIENTS
                              CLIENT


Michael                         Muller                    CPA
Principal
Muller and Associates
250 Washington Street

Boston             MA 02111
Comment ▓▓▓▓▓▓▓




Rec#5, Form view
```

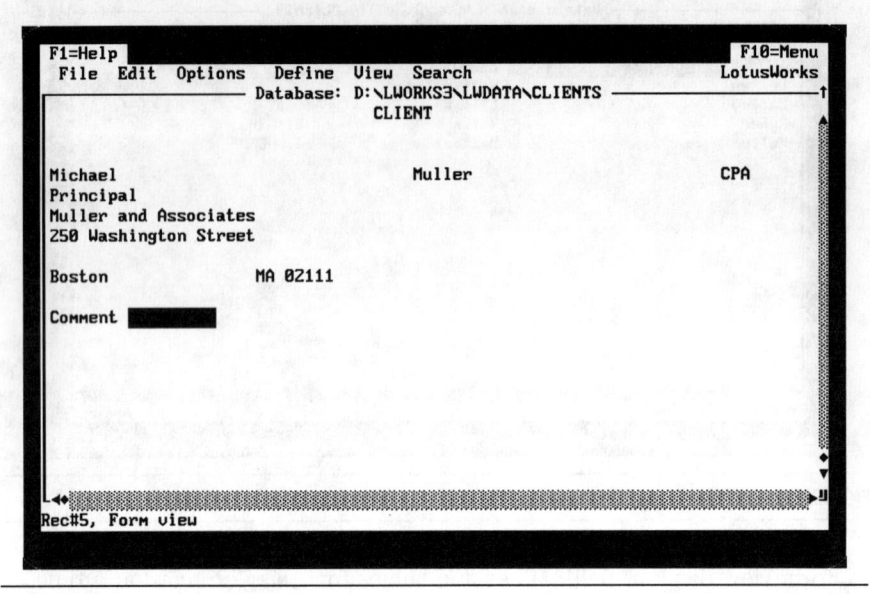

**FIGURE 4.10:** An alternative form to display the same data

Or you could display it like this:

```
F1=Help                                                    F10=Menu
   File  Edit  Options  Define  View  Search              LotusWorks
                    Database: D:\LWORKS3\LWDATA\CLIENTS
                              CLIENT

          FIRST NAME    Michael
         MIDDLE NAME
           LAST NAME    Muller
              SUFFIX    CPA
               TITLE    Principal
             COMPANY    Muller and Associates
            ADDRESS1    250 Washington Street
            ADDRESS2
                CITY    Boston
               STATE    MA
                 ZIP    02111
             COMMENT        ▓▓▓▓▓▓



Rec#5, Form view                                          Caps
```

**FIGURE 4.11:** Another form to display the same data

Note that Table view and Form view do not affect the fields in the actual database; they simply alter the way fields are displayed on the screen and on the printed page.

## Viewing Data in Tables

To use Table view, you must do three things:

1. Create a table (or use the default table). For information on creating tables, see "Creating Custom Tables" later in this chapter.
2. Save it. (Once you save a table, you can use it over and over.)
3. Retrieve the table if it is not already active. (When you create a table, it becomes active.)

Once a table is active, you can shift into table view by pressing Alt+V or by selecting View Change Table on the Menu line.

## Viewing Data in Forms

Form view enables you to view the data for each record laid out in a form instead of in the sequence of fields that appears in the database. You can view all or selected fields, and you can position the fields in whatever order and wherever on the screen you like. You can dress up the form and make it more readable by adding titles, field labels, instructions, lines, boxes, borders, and shading to the display, as in a printed form.

To use form view, you must do three things:

1. Create a form (or use the default form). For information on creating forms, see "Creating Custom Forms" later in this chapter.
2. Save it. (Once you save a form, you can use it over and over.)
3. Retrieve the form if it is not already active. (When you create a form, it becomes active.)

Once a form is active, you can shift into table view by pressing Alt+V or by selecting View Change Form on the Menu line.

## Finding the Records You Want

One of the most useful powers of the Database service is the ability to find and rearrange the records as you want them. LotusWorks is a great file clerk! You can tell it to select all the records that meet a certain set of conditions, and it will filter them out of the database almost instantly. You can display, print, or perform other operations on the active subset of records, and when you are finished, restore the subset back to the full database.

To get LotusWorks to find records, you must specify the conditions you want the records to meet. These are called search criteria. The most common methods of finding records are to specify a range of record numbers or to specify values in one or more fields that distinguish the desired records from the others. For instance, to find the records of all your customers in the state of New York, you could enter the search expression STATE = "NY". To find all the customers who owe more than $100, you could search with the expression BALANCE > 100. To find all the customers who live in New York and owe more than $100, you could search with the expression STATE = "NY" .AND. BALANCE > 100.

## Conducting a Search

The general process for conducting a search is to specify the search criteria for the records you want or to select a previously saved file of search criteria and then to execute the search. LotusWorks finds the records that meet the search conditions and displays them on the screen. These become the active records, and all other records in the current database become temporarily inactive. Any further commands apply only to the active records until you restore the inactive records.

> NOTE: Once you create the criteria for a search, the set of criteria is automatically saved, and you can use it over and over without creating the criteria anew every time.

The specific steps in conducting a search are as follows:

1. Select Search Criteria. The following dialog box appears:

Managing Your Necessary Data **135**

[screenshot of Search Criteria dialog box]

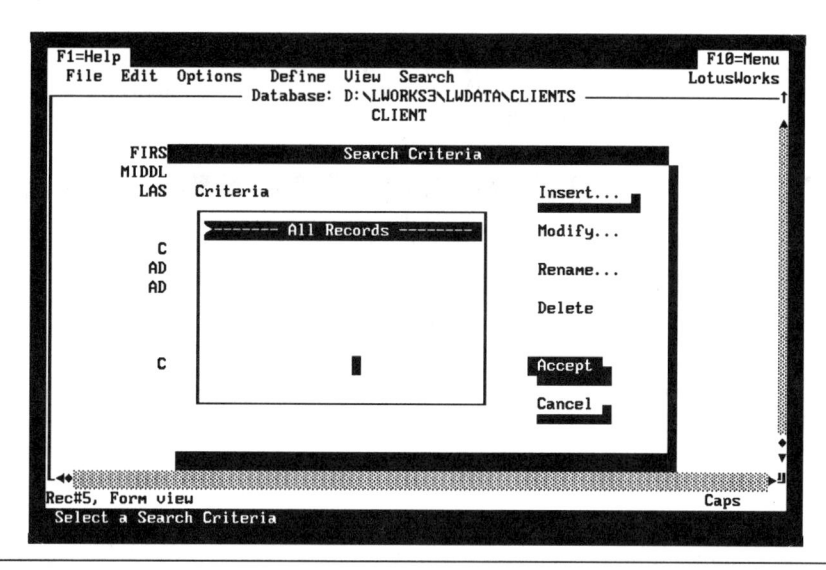

**FIGURE 4.12:** Use the Search Criteria dialog box to select the criteria you want to use in the search or to specify new criteria.

2. If the search criteria you want to use have already been defined and given a name, move the cursor to the desired name in the Criteria box, press Enter or select Accept to initiate the search, and skip to step 3 below.

   If the criteria you want to use have not been defined and saved, you need to specify them. Press the Tab key to move the cursor to the Insert option, and press Enter or select Accept. The following dialog box appears:

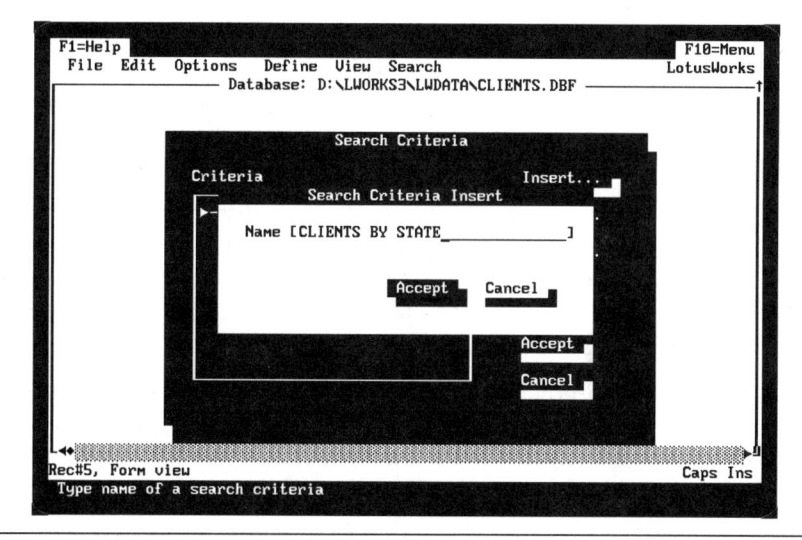

[screenshot of Search Criteria Insert dialog box with Name [CLIENTS BY STATE]]

**FIGURE 4.13:** Enter a descriptive name for the criteria to be used in the search and select Accept.

a. Enter a descriptive name for the search criteria you want to use (for example, TEXAS CUSTOMERS or 1992 ORDERS) and press Enter or select Accept. The following dialog box appears:

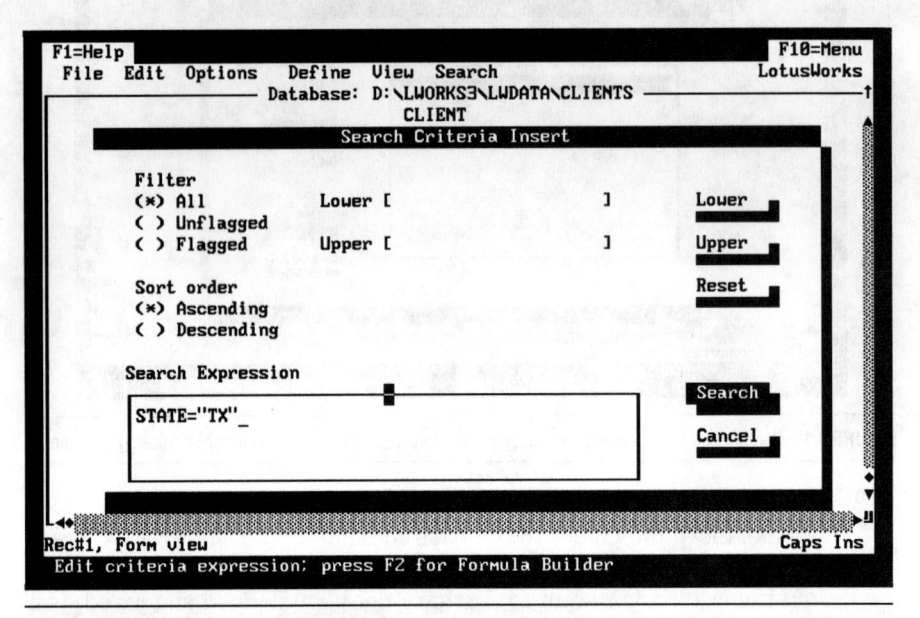

**FIGURE 4.14:** Specify the type of search to perform.

This screen enables you to specify the search conditions. At the Filter option check the button labeled All if you want to search all records, check Unflagged if you want the search to include unflagged records only, or check Flagged if you want the search to include flagged records only. (For an explanation of flagged and unflagged records, see the sections titled "Deleting Records" and "Clearing Flagged Records" later in this chapter.)

b. If you want the records to appear in a particular order, specify the sort order (Ascending or Descending) in which you want them to appear. (For an explanation of sort orders, see the section titled "Specifying a Sort Order" later in this chapter.)

c. Specify the criteria for the search. LotusWorks gives you two ways to specify search criteria. One is to identify a group of consecutive records by specifying a lower limit and/or an upper limit for records to be included in the selected group. The other way is to enter a mathematical search expression and have LotusWorks select the records that meet the conditions of the search expression. (For instructions, see "Writing Search Expressions.")

To specify a search expression, tab to the Search Expression box, type the search expression, and select Accept. To set a lower and/or upper record limit, tab to the Lower and/or Upper option. When you select either of these options, LotusWorks moves you to the current database view and lets you page through the records until you designate one record to be the relevant limit. To designate the record, press Enter when the cursor is on the record. When you finish setting the limits, select Accept. LotusWorks returns you to the first Search Criteria dialog box.

d. At the first Search Criteria dialog box, select Accept to initiate the search. LotusWorks automatically saves the search criteria under the name that you entered.

3. LotusWorks finds all the records that match the specified criteria and displays them in the order specified. These become the active records; the remainder of the database is rendered inactive until you restore the active subset to the full database. If you are in Form view, LotusWorks displays one record at a time. If you are in Table view, it displays a screenful of records at a time. If you print from the database or perform other database operations at this point, LotusWorks acts only on the active records and does so until you restore the subset of active records to the full database.

If you wish to conduct a further search within the subset of active records previously found, simply repeat the search procedure using new search criteria. LotusWorks searches for the records within the active subset that meet the new search criteria. The records turned up by the new search become the new active subset, and all other records are rendered inactive until you restore the full database.

## Writing Search Expressions

To specify the criteria for a search, you write a search statement composed of one or more expressions. Each expression has three parts:

1. A field name that is in the current database (such as STATE)

2. A logical operator (such as the equal sign = or the greater-than symbol >)

3. A number or set of characters (such as 100 or "NY") that can be found in the named field

> IMPORTANT: To specify character data in a search expression, always put double quotation marks around the desired characters. To specify numeric values in a search expression, enter the desired values without quotation marks.

You may have up to 254 characters in a search expression. You may write search expressions in all uppercase letters, all lowercase, or a combination of uppercase and lowercase. You may insert blank spaces between the parts of expressions, as done here for clarity, or omit blank spaces entirely. If you are writing a highly complex search expression, you may need to omit the blank spaces in order to have enough room for the entire expression.

## Compound Search Expressions

You can use the operators .AND. and .OR. to combine expressions to express more complex search conditions. For example:

STATE = "NY" .AND. BALANCE > 100 means "find the records of all customers who are located in New York state AND have a balance greater than $100."

STATE = "NY" .OR. BALANCE > 100 means "find the records of all customers who either are located in New York state OR have a balance greater than $100."

STATE = "NY".OR.STATE ="CA" .AND. BALANCE > 100 means "find the records of all customers who are located in either New York or California AND have a balance greater than $100."

CAUTION: Each expression in a compound statement must be complete. If you try to enter the statement STATE="NY".OR."CA", LotusWorks will reject it. You must write STATE = "NY".OR. STATE ="CA".

> IMPORTANT: There must be a period immediately before and after the .AND., .OR., and .NOT. operators. The operators may be written in uppercase letters, lowercase letters, or a combination.

## Operators

You can use the same operators in LotusWorks search expressions as in rule expressions. (For a list of the operators, see "Writing Rule Expressions" earlier in this chapter.)

Please note that you may use logical operators with numeric data and character data. For example:

Balance>500 finds all the records with a balance greater than $500.

Lastname>"Martin" finds all the records with last names that come after "Martin" in the alphabet.

## Searching for Strings of Characters

### Searching Within a Field

You can search for a sequence of characters (a string) within a specified field by using a special operator called the string operator ($) in a search expression. For example, the statement

"National"$COMPANY

finds all the records that have the word "National" in the COMPANY field. The statement

"Assoc"$COMPANY.OR."Nat"$COMPANY

finds all the records that have the characters Assoc (as in Association or Associations) OR Nat (as in National) in the COMPANY field.

### Searching Anywhere Within a Record or Sort Order

You can use the Search Find command to search for a text string anywhere within a record or a sort order. Press F7 or select Search Find, enter the string of characters you wish to find, and check the check box to indicate whether to conduct a global search (search all fields) or to search according to a sort order (see "Creating a Sort Order" later in this chapter). The string does not have to be a complete word, and it can contain more than one word. You can also use wildcard characters in Find statements.

For example, to find all the records containing the string "national", press F7 or select Search Find, enter "national" in the text box that appears, and select Find. The statement Assoc* finds all the records that have the characters Assoc (such as Association, Associates) in any field. The statement N* finds all the record containing a word that begins with N.

## Searching for Dates

LotusWorks does not let you write dates directly into search expressions because if it did, there would be no way it could distinguish between date numbers and dates intended as character data (text). There is a special function (DTOC), however, that makes it possible to search for values in date fields. DTOC stands for "Date to Character." This function converts values in date fields to character data (text).

To convert dates to text, type DTOC() and type the name of the date field within the parentheses. For example, the statement

DTOC(Duedate)>="01/01/92" finds all the records with due dates on or after January 1, 1992.

To find all records with a date of March 30, 1992 in a field named DUEDATE, you could use the statement:

DTOC(DUEDATE)="03/30/1992"

Another way to find the same records would be to use this statement:

"03/30/1992"$DTOC(DUEDATE)

## Saving, Retrieving, and Deleting Search Criteria

Once you create the criteria for a search, LotusWorks automatically saves the criteria under the name you entered. The name remains active for future retrieval until you delete it.

To retrieve a set of search criteria that you have previously created, select Search Criteria, move the cursor to highlight the desired name in the Criteria box and select Accept. This initiates the search, using the criteria you have highlighted.

To delete a set of search criteria permanently, select Search Criteria, move the cursor to highlight the name in the Criteria box that you wish to delete and click on the Delete option or Tab to the Delete option and press Enter. LotusWorks immediately deletes the specified criteria.

## Restoring Inactive Records

To restore all inactive records to the full database, select Search Criteria, move the cursor to highlight the All Records option, and select Accept. LotusWorks restores the database to its original order and set of records.

## Deleting Records

When you conduct a *search* operation, LotusWorks singles out the records that match your search criteria for further action. You can always return the records to the full database.

When you *delete* records, however, LotusWorks removes them from the database entirely and destroys the data they contained.

Deleting records is a two-step process: first you *flag* the records to be deleted, then you *delete* them.

### Deleting Records Manually

To delete a record manually, follow these steps:

1. Move the cursor to the record to be deleted.
2. Press Alt+F or select Edit Flag.
3. When the dialog box appears, select Current record.
4. Select Set flag. LotusWorks flags the record and displays an asterisk alongside the record number at the bottom of the screen to indicate that the record is flagged.
5. Repeat steps 1 through 4 for each record to be deleted.
6. When all the desired files have been flagged, Select File Pack. LotusWorks prompts you to be sure you want to delete the record(s).

*If you accidentally flag a record that you don't want to delete, you can remove the flag by moving the cursor to the flagged record, selecting Edit Flag, selecting Current record, and selecting Clear flag.*

> CAUTION: Be careful with the Pack command. Once you delete a record, the data cannot be recovered!

7. Be sure you have selected the correct record(s) then select Continue to confirm that you wish to delete the record(s).

## Automatically Selecting Records for Deletion

You can automatically select records for deletion by performing a search and then deleting all the active records. The steps are as follows:

1. Perform a search to filter out the records for deletion. (See "Finding the Records You Want" earlier in this chapter.)

2. Press Alt+F or Select Edit Flag.

3. Select All records.

4. Select Set flag. LotusWorks flags all the active records.

5. Select File Pack. LotusWorks prompts you to be sure you want to continue.

6. Be sure that you want to delete all the active records, then select Continue to confirm your choice. LotusWorks deletes the active records.

7. Restore the inactive records. (See "Restoring Inactive Records" earlier in this chapter.)

## Deleting Duplicate Records

If you think you may have entered duplicate records into a database by mistake or by transferring records from another database, you can use the following technique to have LotusWorks find and delete any duplicates:

1. Move the cursor to the first record in the database.

2. Press Alt+F or Select Edit Flag.

3. Select Duplicate records.

4. Select Set flag. LotusWorks flags all the duplicate records.

5. Select File Pack.

6. Select Continue to confirm that you wish to delete all the duplicate records.

## Clearing Flagged Records

To clear a flag from a record, move the cursor to the record in either Table View or Form View and press Alt+F or select Edit Flag. When the Edit Flag dialog box appears, select Current record and Clear flag.

If all active records have been flagged, you can remove all the flags at once by selecting the All records option and Clear flag. If all duplicate records have been flagged, you can remove all the flags at once by selecting the Duplicate records option and Clear flag.

# Creating a Sort Order

Usually it is useful to have records appear in a particular order when you display them on the screen or print them in tables and forms. A nice thing about a database is that you don't have to worry about the actual order in which records are stored because you can always view or print them in the order you want, including different orders for different purposes. For instance, if you are preparing mailing labels, you might want them to appear in ZIP code or carrier-route order. For a customer list, you might want the records to appear in alphabetical order by company name and/or client name. For an employee roster, you might want them to appear in alphabetical order by last name then first name, within departments.

You can output records from a database in the order you want by creating a sort order based on the data in one or more fields. The sort order does not physically rearrange the records stored in the database; it merely indexes them to be displayed in a particular order. The default sort order is record-number order.

## Sort Expressions

Each sort order must have a sort expression that specifies the order of the sort. The sort expression must contain the name of at least one field whose values form the basis for the sorting. For example, the simple expression LASTNAME would sort records in a name-and-address database into alphabetical order by last names. The expression COMPANY would sort the records into alphabetical order by company names.

You can perform more complicated sorts by writing more complex sort expressions. They can specify conditional rules and/or sequences of sorts on multiple fields. For example, suppose you want to sort the records in a database into alphabetical order by state. The sort expression would be simply:

STATE

If you want to sort into reverse alphabetical order by state, the sort expression is:

INVERT(STATE)

The INVERT function tells LotusWorks to sort the salaries into descending order.

> For a more complete explanation of Database functions, see "Database Functions" later in this chapter. A complete list of LotusWorks Database functions can be found in Appendix B.

Suppose you want to display a table showing accounts receivable ranged from high to low. You need to sort the records from high to low according to the amounts in the BALANCE field. The sort expression is:

INVERT(BALANCE)

Suppose you want to sort the records into alphabetical order by last name and within each last name by first name as in a telephone directory. The following sort statement does the trick:

LOWER(LASTNAME+FIRSTNAME)

This sorts the records into last-name order and into first-name order within last names, without regard to the case of names. The + operator tells LotusWorks to sort first on the FIRSTNAME field and then on the LASTNAME field to produce the desired result. The LOWER function converts all characters to lowercase for the sort, thus eliminating any distinction between uppercase and lowercase letters.

Here are some other examples of sort expressions:

IF (COMPANY = "",LOWER(LASTNAME+FIRSTNAME),COMPANY)

This sort statement orders records into alphabetical order by company; however, if a record has the company name blank, it uses the last name plus first name instead. The IF statement tells LotusWorks, "if the company field is blank, use LASTNAME+FIRSTNAME, otherwise use the COMPANY field for the sort."

$$DEPARTMENT+STR(SALARY,-10)$$

This statement orders records by department and within departments by salary. Because a single sort cannot handle both character and numeric data at the same time, the numeric SALARY values have to be converted to character data. The STR (for string) function makes this conversion. The minus sign in the STR function causes the character salary string to be aligned to the right, which is necessary to sort the string into the correct numeric order.

$$DEPARTMENT+STR(INVERT(SALARY),-10)$$

This statement is similar to the previous one but orders the salaries from high to low instead of low to high.

## Creating a New Sort Order

To create a new sort order, follow these steps:

1. Press Alt+O or select Search Sort Order. The following dialog box appears:

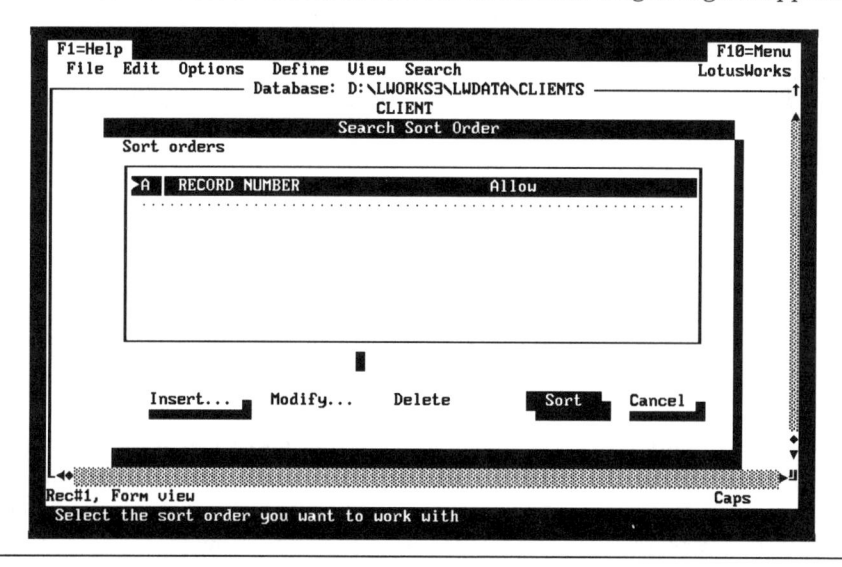

**FIGURE 4.15:** To create a new sort order, move the cursor to the dotted line and select Insert.

2. Move the cursor to the dotted line and select Insert. The following dialog box appears:

```
F1=Help                                                      F10=Menu
 File   Edit   Options   Define   View   Search              LotusWorks
                    Database: D:\LWORKS3\LWDATA\CLIENTS
                                 CLIENT
                           Search Sort Order
        Sort orders
                        Search Sort Order Insert

        File [STALPHA__]                    Duplicate records
                                            (*) Allow
        Name [ALPHA ORDER BY STATE_____]   ( ) Warn
                                            ( ) Prevent

        Expression
        ┌─────────────────────────────────┐
        │ STATE_                          │
        │                                 │  Accept
        │                                 │
        │                                 │  Cancel
        └─────────────────────────────────┘


Rec#1, Form view                                           Caps Ins
 Edit search order expression; press F2 for Formula Builder
```

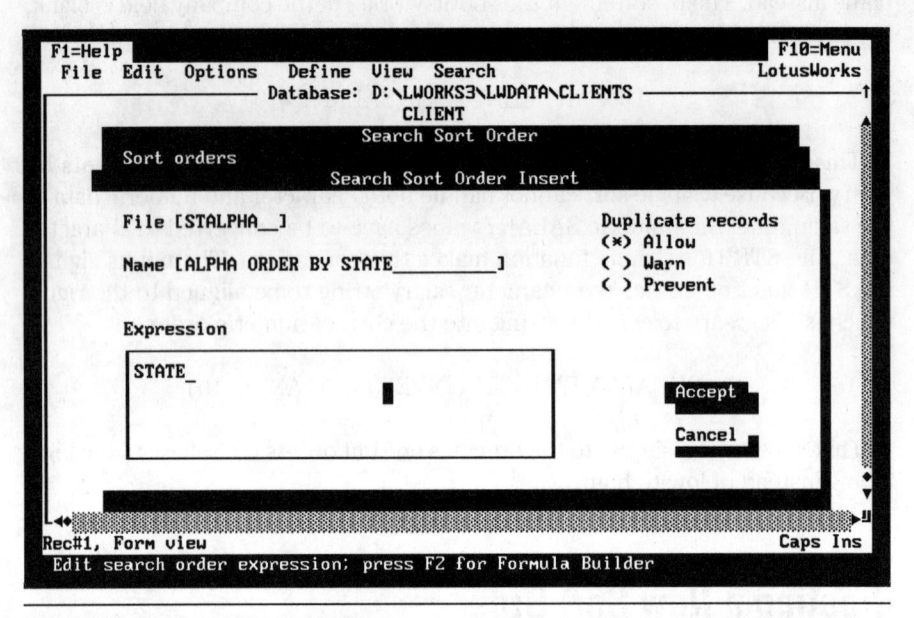

**FIGURE 4.16:** The sort-order expression builder

3. In the File text box, type a descriptive name of up to eight characters for the file to hold the sort order. Don't enter a file name extension; Lotus-Works does that for you.

4. Tab to the Name text box and type a descriptive name (such as "Alpha by State") for the Sort order. LotusWorks will display this name in a list box, so you can use a longer and more descriptive name than the file name.

5. Tab to the Expression box and type a sort statement specifying the order in which you want the records to appear.

6. Check whether to allow duplicate records, to warn of duplicate records, or to forbid duplicate records.

7. Select Sort.

*It's a good idea always to inspect the sorted records as soon as you create a new sort order to be sure the sort turns out as you intended. You can see the order most easily in Table view.*

LotusWorks sorts the active records into the order specified and saves the sort order under the name that you entered. The records appear in the current sort order in both Form view and Table view, but the order is easiest to see in Table view. Press Alt+V if you want to change to Table view.

## Saving and Retrieving a Sort Order

LotusWorks automatically saves each sort order with the database to which it applies. To retrieve an existing sort order, press Alt+O or select Search Sort order. The following dialog box appears:

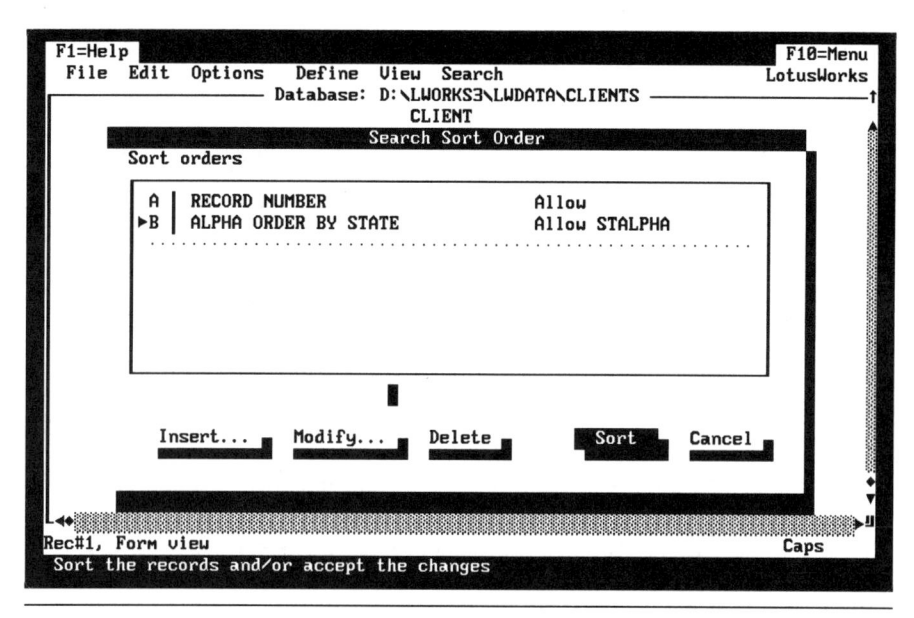

**FIGURE 4.17:** The Search Sort order dialog box

Move the pointer to highlight the name of the desired sort order and select Sort. LotusWorks immediately displays the active records in the selected sort order. LotusWorks continues to sort records according to the current sort order until you select another sort order.

## Modifying a Sort Order

If you don't get a sort order right the first time, you can modify it at any time. Press Alt+O or select Search Sort order, move the cursor to highlight the name of the desired sort order, and select the Modify option. The following dialog box appears:

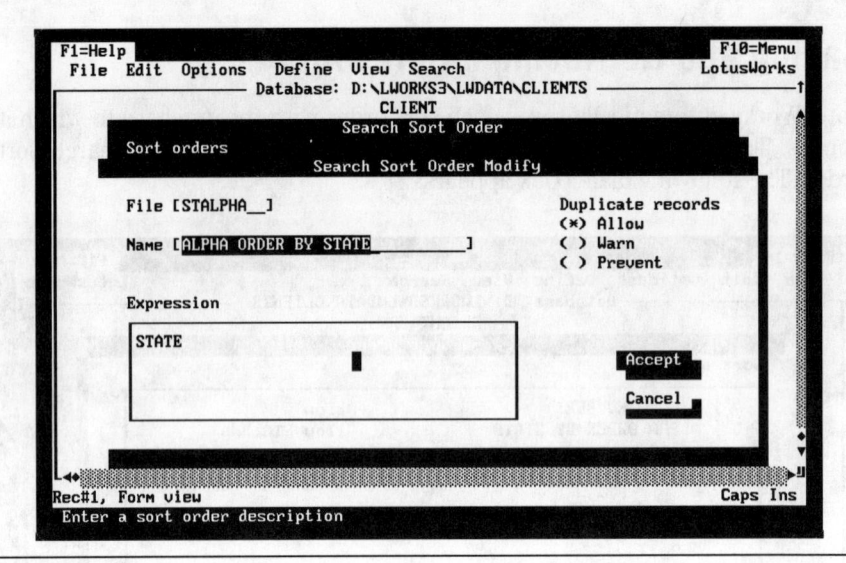

**FIGURE 4.18:** The Search Sort Order Modify dialog box lets you change the name, sort expression, and/or duplicate records setting of an existing sort order.

You can change anything about a search order except the name of the file where it is stored. Enter any changes you wish to make in the name, sort expression, or duplicate records setting and select Accept. LotusWorks returns you to the Search Sort Order dialog box. To initiate the sort and save the revised sort order, select Sort.

## Deleting a Sort Order

Once created, a sort order is saved with its database and may be retrieved and used until it is deleted. To delete a sort order, press Alt+O or select Search Sort order, tab to the Delete option, and press Enter. LotusWorks removes the sort order name from the list box, but the deletion does not take effect at that point. To accept the deletion, select Sort. If you make a mistake and wish to cancel the deletion, select Cancel.

## Creating Custom Tables

LotusWorks automatically creates a default table format for each database. The default table shows all the fields in the order in which they appear in the database. Although this format is useful for many purposes, there are times when other table formats are better. Almost any database, for example, contains too much information to display on a single page or screen. With a custom table you can select the fields for display and arrange them in whatever order you like. For instance, if you wish to view two fields that are widely separated in a database—such as a name field and a phone number field—you can locate them side-by-side in a custom table. You can create several tables for different purposes from the same database. You can arrange the records to appear in different orders for different tables, and you can create special report tables that group records in meaningful ways and calculate total and subtotal values for the groups. You can name and save the tables and retrieve them whenever you want to use them again. Creating a custom table does not affect the underlying database.

## Creating the Table

Here are the steps for creating a custom table:

1. Retrieve the desired database.
2. Shift into Table view: press Alt+V or select View Change Table view.
3. Select View Table setup. The following dialog box appears:

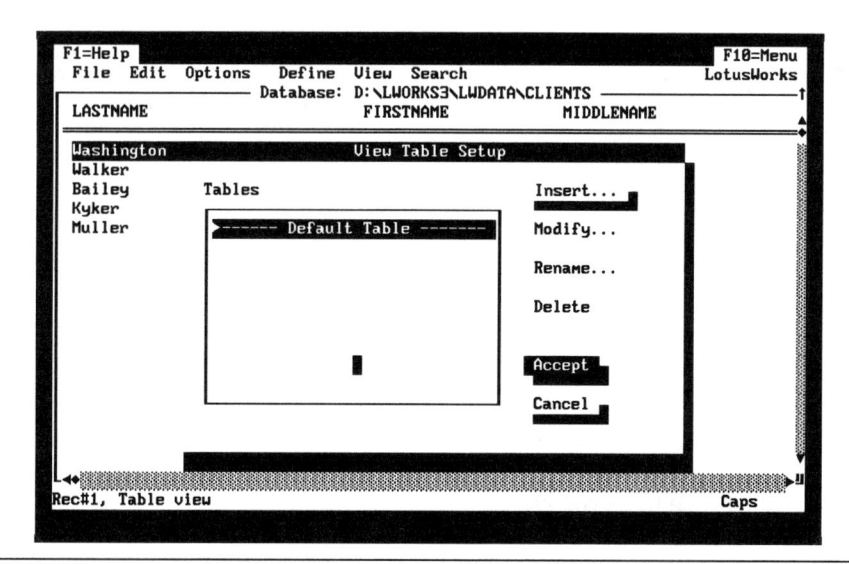

**FIGURE 4.19:** The View Table setup dialog box

4. Select Insert. The following dialog box appears:

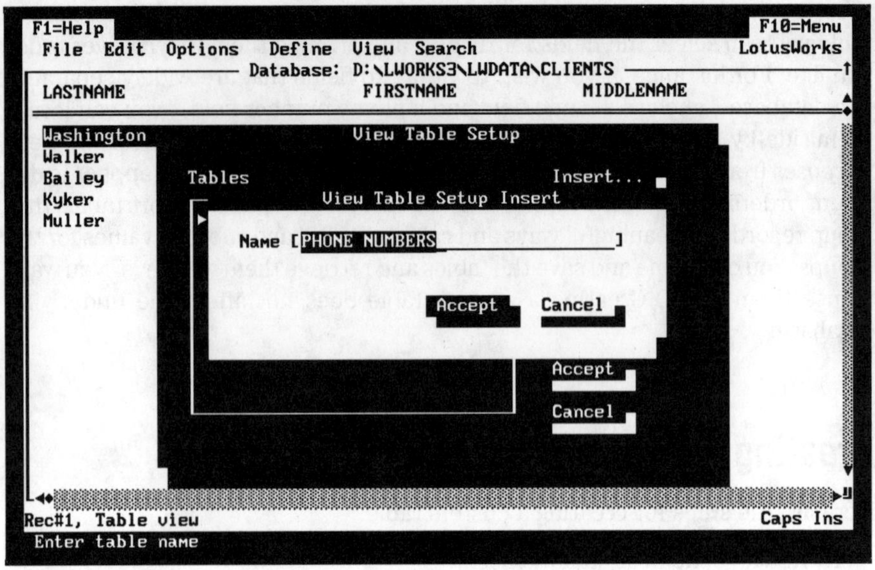

**FIGURE 4.20:** Enter a name for the custom table in the View Table Setup Insert dialog box and select Accept.

Type a descriptive name for the custom table in the text box. The name can have more than one word, as long as it fits within the text box. When you have entered the name, select Accept. The View Table Setup Insert dialog box appears. It displays all the fields in the database.

Use this dialog box to design the custom table. Delete the fields that you do not want to appear in the table by highlighting each field and selecting Delete. (This will not affect the underlying database.)

Arrange the fields into the order you want. If necessary, you can delete a field from its current position. To insert a field between two fields already in the table, highlight the lower of the two fields and select Insert. LotusWorks displays a list of all the fields in the database for you to choose from. Highlight the field you want and select Accept to insert it.

*If you have a mouse, use it to insert and delete the fields in the setup box. It's quicker and easier than using the keyboard.*

5. When all the fields you want for the table are listed in the order in which you want them to appear, select Accept to accept the changes. LotusWorks returns you to the View Table Setup dialog box and displays the name of the table you are creating.

Managing Your Necessary Data **151**

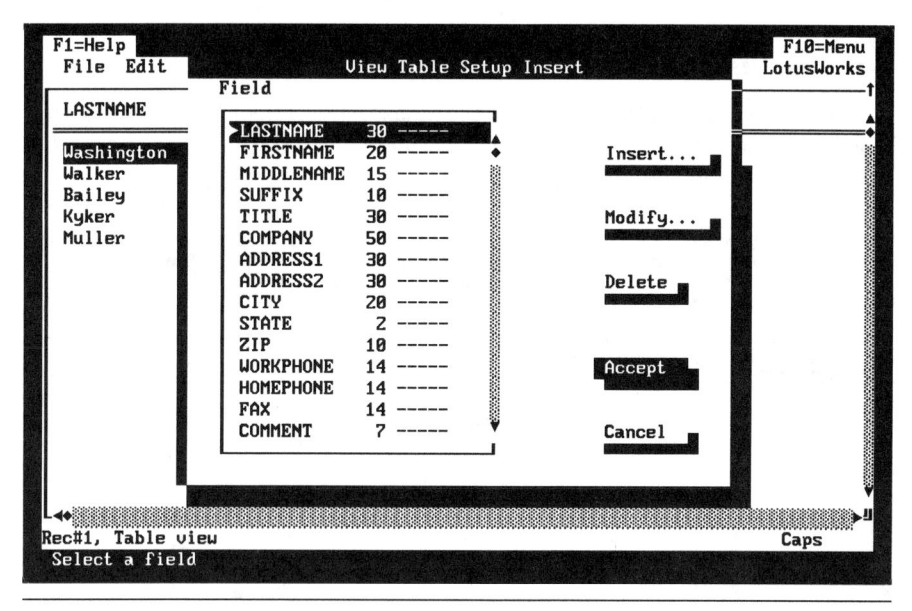

**FIGURE 4.21:** Use the View Table Setup Insert dialog box to select the fields for the custom table and put them into the desired order.

6. If you want to modify, rename, or delete the table at this point, select one of those options. Otherwise, select Accept to activate the new table setup. LotusWorks automatically saves the new table setup with the database.

LotusWorks displays the active records on the screen in the new table format until you select or create another table setup.

## Retrieving a Custom Table

To retrieve the table in the future, first retrieve the database to which it belongs (select File Retrieve, move the cursor to the name of the database, and select Retrieve); then select View Table setup, move the cursor to the table name, and select Accept. LotusWorks activates the table and displays the records in the new table setup. To see the table, switch into Table view (press Alt+V or select View Change Table view).

## Modifying a Custom Table

To change a custom table, retrieve its database, then select View Table setup. When the View Table Setup dialog box appears, highlight the name of the table to be modified and select Modify. The following dialog box appears:

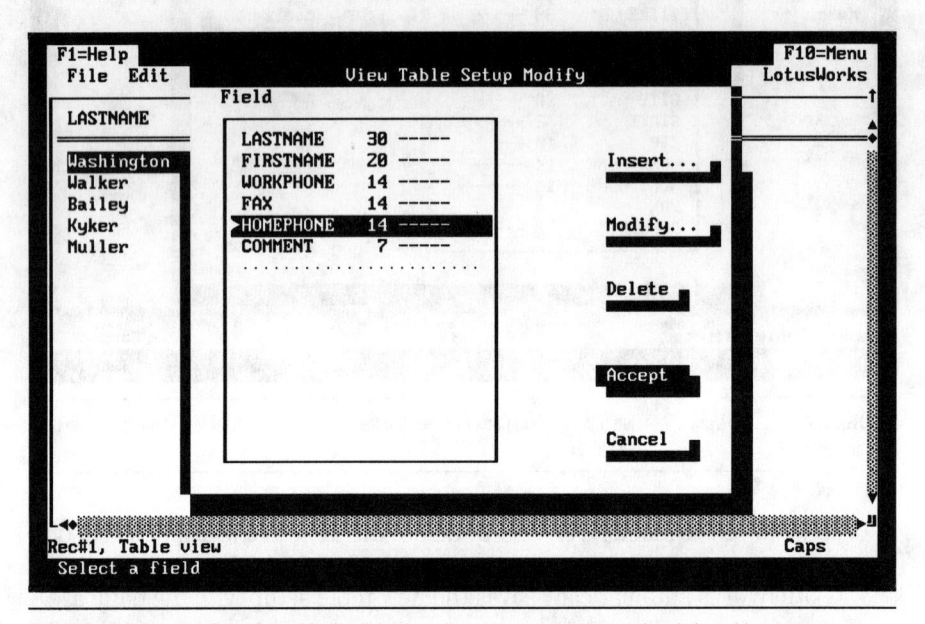

```
F1=Help                                                    F10=Menu
   File  Edit              View Table Setup Modify         LotusWorks
                  Field
   LASTNAME
                  LASTNAME      30  -----
   Washington     FIRSTNAME     20  -----
   Walker         WORKPHONE     14  -----      Insert...
   Bailey         FAX           14  -----
   Kyker         ►HOMEPHONE     14  -----      Modify...
   Muller         COMMENT        7  -----
                                               Delete

                                               Accept

                                               Cancel


   Rec#1, Table view                                       Caps
   Select a field
```

**FIGURE 4.22:** The View Table Setup Modify dialog box allows you to make changes in existing table setups.

This dialog box enables you to modify and delete existing fields in the table and to insert new ones. To use it, highlight the field you want to modify or delete or the position where you want to insert a new field and select the appropriate option—Insert, Modify, or Delete. If you select Modify, another dialog box pops up, allowing you to change the widths of the field displays in the form and allowing you to define or modify a summary field. (For information about summary fields, see "Creating a Summary Report Table" later in this chapter.)

## Deleting a Custom Table

To delete a custom table that you no longer need, retrieve the table's database and select View Table setup. When the View Table setup dialog box appears, move the cursor to highlight the name of the table to delete and select Delete. LotusWorks immediately erases the table name from the screen. At this point, you can cancel the deletion by selecting Cancel or pressing Esc. To accept the deletion, select Accept. LotusWorks permanently deletes the table and returns you to the database screen.

## Creating a Print Layout for a Table

LotusWorks enables you to set and save a number of printing specifications in a print layout for each table. They include the page length, margins, page numbers, and, if necessary, a setup string for your printer. LotusWorks also lets you specify a header and footer for each table. Once you create a print layout for a table, LotusWorks saves it with the table and activates it whenever you retrieve the table.

The steps for creating a print layout for a table are as follows:

1. Select the database for the table.
2. Go into Table view and select the table you wish to print. (This step is important; you must be in Table view to print a table.)
3. Select File Print Layout. The following dialog box appears:

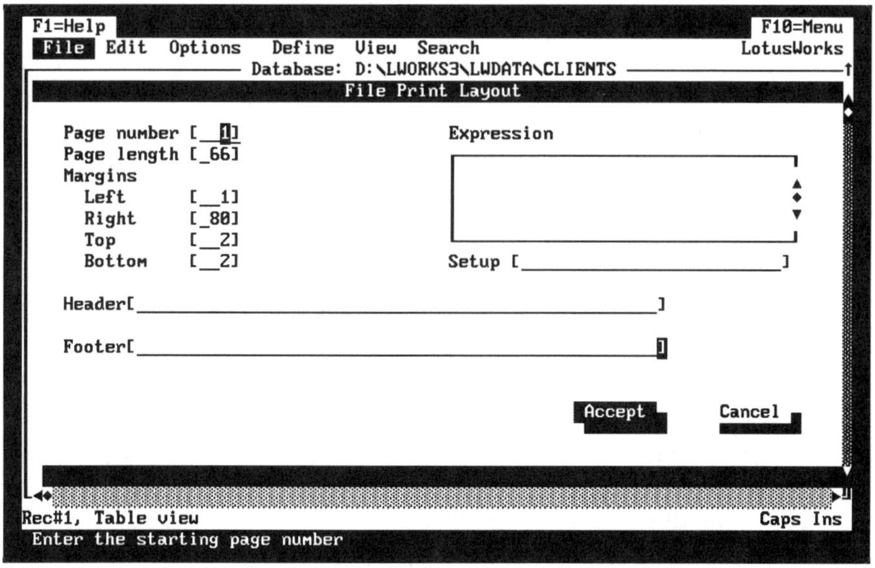

**FIGURE 4.23:** The File Print Layout dialog box in Table view

4. Select and enter the layout options you desire for the table. The options are:

   a. **Page number.** If you want a page number to print automatically in a header or footer and you want to start with a number other than 1, enter the starting number in the Page number box.

   b. **Page length.** Enter the number of lines to be printed on each page. The number depends on the printer, the page orientation (portrait or landscape), and the size of paper. A standard U.S. letter-size page (8½" × 11") in portrait orientation normally has 66 lines, which is the default value. Some laser printers, however, print a maximum of 60 lines on an 11-inch page. If you are using paper of a different size, printing in landscape orientation, or printing something other than six vertical lines to the inch, you may need to try a few settings with your printer to find the right number to enter in this box.

   > IMPORTANT: Ordinarily, the Database service prints in portrait orientation. However, you can print in landscape orientaton on most printers by entering an appropriate printer setup string in the Setup text box in the File Print Layout dialog box. See you printer manual fort the correct setup string to use.

   c. **Margins (left, right, top, and bottom).** Enter the number of columns you want for the left and right margins and the number of rows you want for the top and bottom margins of the table. The left and right margins are measured in columns from the left edge of the paper (1 column = 1 character), starting with 0 at the left edge, with a maximum of 254 columns. The top and bottom margins settings indicate the number of rows between the edge of the page and the first or last row of text.

   > NOTE: Be aware that headers and footers print in the top and bottom margins. Be sure to make your margins big enough to hold them.

   d. **Expression.** This box lets you enter a break expression to create a summary report table. Enter an appropriate break expression if you are printing a summary table. See "Creating a Summary Table Report" later in this chapter for instructions.

   e. **Setup.** This box lets you enter a string of setup characters for your printer, if needed. Many printers accept setup strings to change type styles, type sizes, type attributes, and the print orientation. If your printer needs a print string for the table you are laying out, enter the string here. See your printer manual for instructions.

   f. **Header.** This box lets you enter a one-line header to appear at the top of each printed page. In addition to regular text, you may use the special character # to enter an automatic page number, @ to enter an automatic date, and the vertical bar (|) to align text to the left, center, or right, as in word processing headers. See "Creating Headers and Footers" in Chapter 3 for more information on using these symbols.

   g. **Footer.** This box lets you enter a one-line footer to appear at the bottom of each printed page. As with the header line, you may use the #, @, and | characters to set up automatic page numbering, enter the date automatically, and align the text to the left, center, or right.

5. When all of the options have been set, select Accept. LotusWorks saves the print layout with the table and returns you to the File Print menu.

Any time you retrieve the table in the future, the print layout automatically becomes current.

To use the print layout and print the table, please see "Printing Tables" later in this chapter.

## Creating a Summary Report Table

One of the handiest features of the LotusWorks Database service is the ability to generate reports with summary statistics for groups of records within a database. For instance, you can generate sales reports with subtotals for each sales person and a total for the company, or a quarterly report with totals for each month and quarter. You can generate reports that show the high, low, total, and average values for groups of records, and the number of records in each group. And you can generate all of these without difficult programming.

A summary report table is simply a special type of custom table. It has summary information printed for certain specially designated fields. To create a summary report table, you first create a custom table in the regular manner and then modify it to specify the fields for which you want summary information. The summary information does not appear on the screen, but it is printed when you print the table. To print the table, you sort the records into an order that makes sense for the particular summary breakdown and then use a print layout that has breaks in the appropriate places for the summary information.

```
                         CLIENT SUMMARY REPORT

CLIENT                   SERVICE         DATE       RATE  HOURS   FEE
===========================================================================
ABC Corporation          Consultation    03/13/1992   75   1.50   112.50
ABC Corporation          Plan Update     03/23/1992   50   8.00   400.00
----section total--------------------------------------------------------
                                                          9.50   512.50

Antic Corporation        Handbook Revisi 04/20/1992   45   4.00   180.00
Antic Corporation        Staff Handbook  03/23/1992   45   6.50   292.50
Antic Corporation        Staff Handbook  03/24/1992   45   3.00   135.00
----section total--------------------------------------------------------
                                                         13.50   607.50

Friendly Service Co.     Business Plan   03/18/1992   75   6.50   487.50
Friendly Service Co.     Business Plan   03/19/1992   75   4.25   318.75
Friendly Service Co.     Business Plan   03/20/1992   75   7.00   525.00
Friendly Service Co.     Plan Revision   04/20/1992   75   4.00   300.00
----section total--------------------------------------------------------
                                                         21.75  1631.25

Kyker and Company        Crisis Mgt Stud 04/15/1992   75   8.00   600.00
Kyker and Company        Crisis Mgt Stud 04/16/1992   75   8.00   600.00
Kyker and Company        Crisis Mgt Stud 04/17/1992   75   8.00   600.00
----section total--------------------------------------------------------
                                                         24.00  1800.00

----report total--------------------------------------------------------
                                                         68.75  4551.25
```

**FIGURE 4.24:** A summary report table

Three elements are required to produce a summary report table: the summary table, the print layout, and an appropriate sort order. Here is how to create them.

## Creating the Summary Table

1. Retrieve the database for the report.

2. Create a table containing all the fields that you want to appear in the report. See "Creating a Custom Table" earlier in this chapter for details.

3. Modify the table to specify the fields for which you want summary information:

    a. Select View Table setup, highlight the table to be modified, and select Modify. The following dialog box opens:

Managing Your Necessary Data **157**

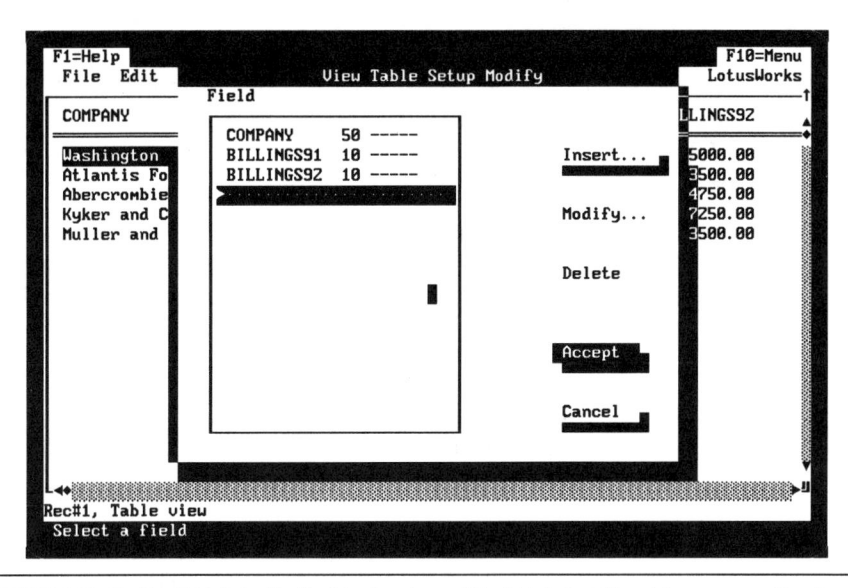

**FIGURE 4.25:** The View Table Setup Modify dialog box shows all the fields in the table and the summary settings for each.

b. Highlight a field that you want to summarize, and select Modify. Another dialog box opens:

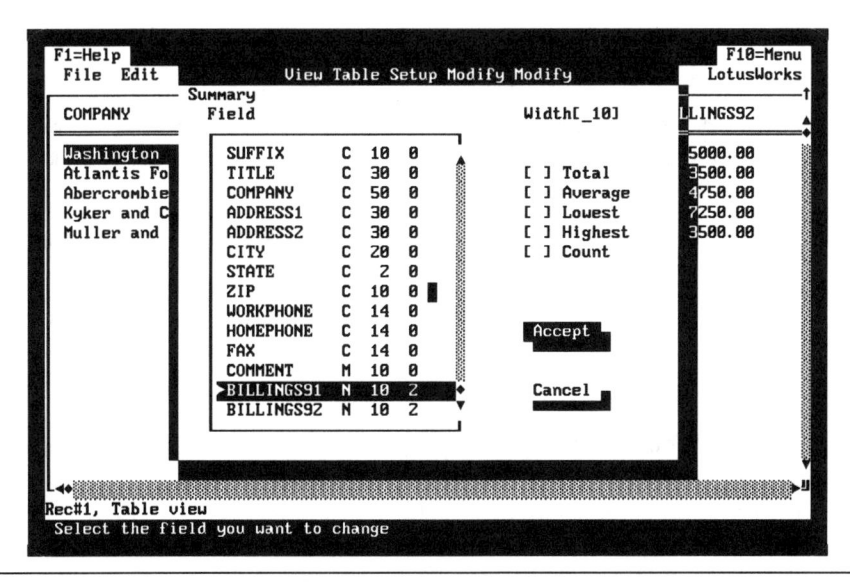

**FIGURE 4.26:** The View Table Setup Modify Modify dialog box allows you to specify a summary field and the type of summary information to report.

This dialog box displays the name, field width, type of data, and number of decimal places for each field in the current table. It also allows you to select a field to be a summary field, to vary the width of the field in the report, and to specify the type of summary information to print.

c. Highlight the field to be summarized, change the width setting if you wish, and check each type of summary information that you want to appear in the report. You may check one or more of the following options for the appropriate types of fields:

| Use This Option | In This Type of Field | To Do This |
| --- | --- | --- |
| Total | Numeric only | Total the contents of the field |
| Average | Numeric only | Compute the average (mean) value of a field. The average is the Total divided by the number of records in the group or report, including blank records and records containing zero |
| Highest | Numeric and Date | Report the highest value in a field |
| Lowest | Numeric and Date | Report the lowest value in a field |
| Count | Any type | Count the number of records (including blank records and records containing zeros) |

d. Select Accept. LotusWorks returns you to the View Table Setup Modify dialog box and displays an initial letter beside the highlighted field for each of the summary options you selected.

e. Repeat steps 3.b, 3.c, and 3.d for each field for which you want a summary in the report.

4. When all the summary fields have been selected, select Accept. LotusWorks returns you to the View Table Setup dialog box.

5. Select Accept. LotusWorks returns you to the database screen.

The summary information does not appear on the screen, but it will appear when you print the report table.

## Creating the Sort Order

The records in a summary report must be sorted into an order that is consistent with the summary breakdown (see "Creating the Summary Table" above), or else the the breaks will occur in the wrong places and the report will not make sense. If the report is to break and print summary information after each state, for example, the records must be grouped into order by state. If the report is to break after each client, the records must be grouped by client. And so on.

The sort expression for a summary table is written like the sort expression for any other table (see "Creating a Sort Order" earlier in this chapter), but it must include the field on which you want summary breaks to be based. It should sort the records into the exact order in which you want them to appear in the final report. For example, suppose you want a report of client billings to break down the billings by client, and within that by type of service provided, and within that by date of service. And suppose you want to print summary information for each client, like this:

```
                             SUMMARY OF CLIENT FEES

ABC Corporation         Consultation    03/13/1992    75    1.50     112.50
----section total----------------------------------------------------------
                                                            1.50     112.50
---------------------------------------------------------------------------
Friendly Service Co.    Business Plan   03/18/1992    75    6.50     487.50
Friendly Service Co.    Business Plan   03/19/1992    75    4.25     318.75
Friendly Service Co.    Business Plan   03/20/1992    75    7.00     525.00
----section total----------------------------------------------------------
                                                           17.75    1331.25
---------------------------------------------------------------------------
ABC Corporation         Plan Update     03/23/1992    50    8.00     400.00
----section total----------------------------------------------------------
                                                            8.00     400.00
---------------------------------------------------------------------------
Antic Corporation       Staff Handbook  03/23/1992    45    6.50     292.50
Antic Corporation       Staff Handbook  03/24/1992    45    3.00     135.00
----section total----------------------------------------------------------
                                                            9.50     427.50
---------------------------------------------------------------------------
----report total-----------------------------------------------------------
                                                           36.75    2271.25
---------------------------------------------------------------------------
```

**FIGURE 4.27:** A summary table of client billings

The sort expression for the summary table should look like this:

CLIENT+SERVICE+DTOC(DATE)

*To make it easy to keep track of which sort order goes with which summary table, give the sort order the same name as the summary table.*

The sort expression says "sort by client, and within that by service, and within that by date." The expression is appropriate for a summary table because it contains the field on which the summary break is based (CLIENT) as well as the other fields needed to put the records into the desired order. (Note that in this case the DTOC function must be used to convert a date field to text characters because a single sort expression cannot have more than one type of data.)

For more information about sort expressions, see "Creating a Sort Order" earlier in this chapter.

## Creating the Print Layout

The summary report needs to have a break in the printing after each group of records to display summary information for the group. You create such a break by entering a break expression in the Print Layout dialog box. The break expression specifies the field or condition on which report breaks are to be based. LotusWorks creates a break after each change of values in the specified field.

Break expressions have the same syntax as sort expressions. You may use LotusWorks database functions in both types of expression. The following are examples of break expressions:

STATE

Inserts a break and prints summary information after the last record for each entry in the STATE field.

CLIENT

Inserts the break and summary information after the last record for each name in the CLIENT field.

MONTH(DUEDATE)

Inserts the break and summary information after the last record for each month in which the values in the DUEDATE field fall.

IF((NOW−DUEDATE)>30,"OVERDUE","CURRENT")

Divides accounts into two categories, Overdue and Current, based on the values in the DUEDATE field and inserts the break and summary information after the last record in each category. The IF statement says, "If an account is more than 30 days overdue ((NOW−DUEDATE) >30), label it OVERDUE; otherwise label it CURRENT."

Here are the steps to create the print layout.

1. If the database you want is not already current, retrieve the database for the summary report.

2. If the table you want is not already current, retrieve the table for the summary report.

3. If you are not already in Table view, press Alt+V to switch into Table view.

4. Select File Print Layout. The following dialog box appears:

```
F1=Help                                                      F10=Menu
 File  Edit  Options  Define  View  Search           LotusWorks
 ─────────────── Database: D:\LWORKS3\LWDATA\CLIENTS.DBF ───────────
                          File Print Layout

     Page number  [__1]            Expression
     Page length  [_66]
     Margins                       ┌────────────────────────┐
        Left     [__3]             │ CLIENT                 │
        Right    [_80]             │                        │
        Top      [__6]             │                        │
        Bottom   [__6]             └────────────────────────┘
                                   Setup [_____]

     Header[|SUMMARY OF CLIENT FEES_____]

     Footer[|- # -_____]


                                        Accept        Cancel



Rec#1, Table view
Accept the settings as displayed
```

**FIGURE 4.28:** Enter a break expression in the Expression box.

5. Check the settings for Page number, Page length, and the Margins and change them if necessary.

6. Enter a break expression for the report in the Expression text box using the syntax described above.

7. Enter a header and/or footer for the summary report as you wish.

8. Select Accept. LotusWorks saves the print layout with the summary table and returns you to the File Print menu.

## Printing the Table

Once you have set up a summary report table, its print layout, and its sort order, it is easy to print the table. You simply make the table current and print it as you would any other table. Here are the steps:

1. Retrieve the database, if it is not already current.

2. Retrieve the table, if it is not already current.

3. Select the sort order that matches the summary table.

4. Select File Print Print and check the print settings. See "Printing Tables" later in this chapter.

5. If all the print settings are correct select Print.

# Creating Custom Forms

As with custom tables, LotusWorks creates a default form for each database, showing all the fields and their field names in the order in which they were created. You can create custom forms, however, to view or enter data in formats that are more convenient than the default format. Custom forms can display as many or as few fields as you like, along with titles, text instructions, and custom field labels in place of field names. You can position the fields anywhere on the form. You can also create lines and shading to make forms easier to read and use.

For example, you can create a form that looks like this:

Managing Your Necessary Data **163**

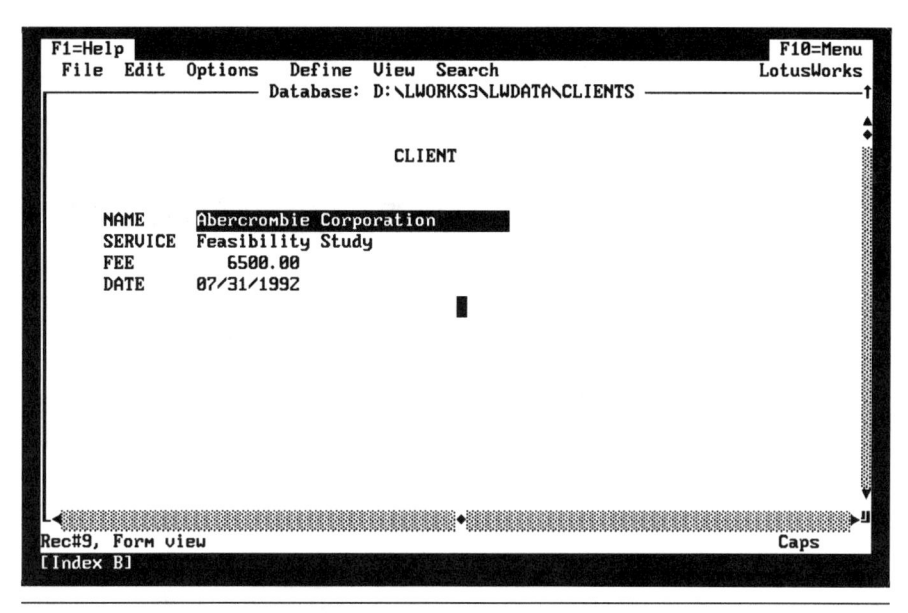

```
F1=Help                                                    F10=Menu
   File  Edit  Options   Define   View   Search           LotusWorks
                    Database:  D:\LWORKS3\LWDATA\CLIENTS


                             CLIENT


       NAME      Abercrombie Corporation
       SERVICE   Feasibility Study
       FEE          6500.00
       DATE      07/31/1992










Rec#9, Form view                                          Caps
[Index B]
```

**FIGURE 4.29:** A custom-designed data entry form

Here is another example:

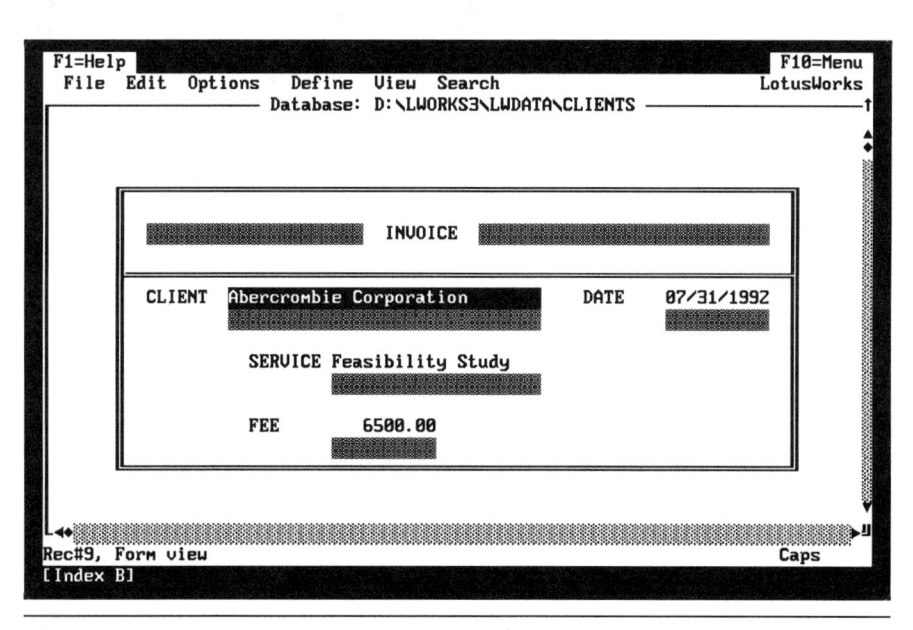

```
F1=Help                                                    F10=Menu
   File  Edit  Options   Define   View   Search           LotusWorks
                    Database:  D:\LWORKS3\LWDATA\CLIENTS



                         ▓▓▓▓▓▓ INVOICE ▓▓▓▓▓▓


           CLIENT   Abercrombie Corporation     DATE   07/31/1992


                    SERVICE  Feasibility Study


                       FEE      6500.00




Rec#9, Form view                                          Caps
[Index B]
```

**FIGURE 4.30:** A custom-designed form with lines and shading

Here are the steps to create a form:

1. Retrieve the database to be used for the form.
2. Select View Form setup. The following dialog box appears:

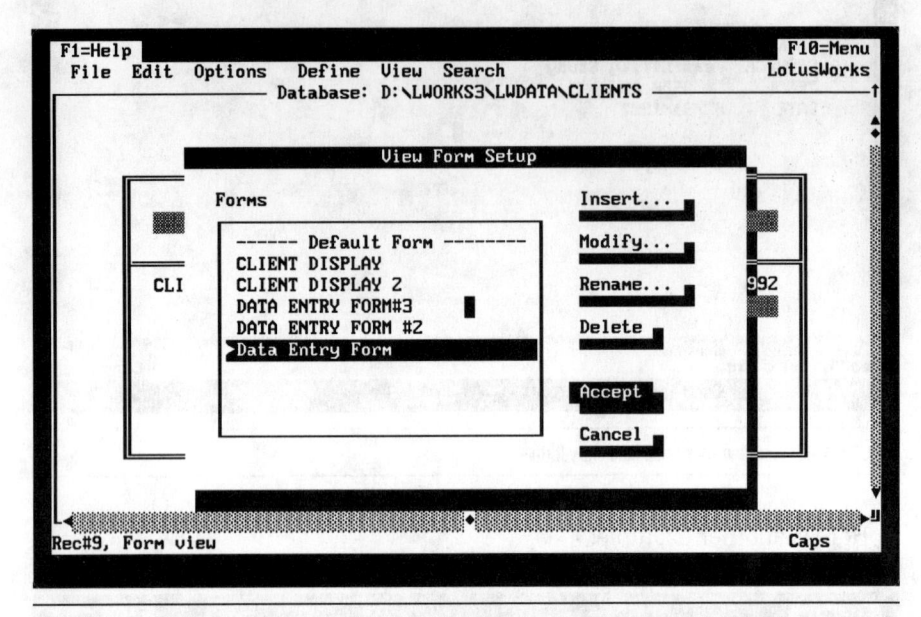

```
F1=Help                                                      F10=Menu
 File  Edit  Options  Define  View  Search           LotusWorks
                  Database: D:\LWORKS3\LWDATA\CLIENTS

                         View Form Setup

          Forms                          Insert...

                ------ Default Form ------
                CLIENT DISPLAY            Modify...
   CLI          CLIENT DISPLAY 2
                DATA ENTRY FORM#3         Rename...         992
                DATA ENTRY FORM #2
                >Data Entry Form          Delete

                                          Accept

                                          Cancel


Rec#9, Form view                                             Caps
```

**FIGURE 4.31:** The View Form Setup dialog box lists the forms you have created, as well as the Default Form.

3. Select Insert, to indicate that you want to start a new form. The View Form Setup Insert dialog box appears:

Managing Your Necessary Data **165**

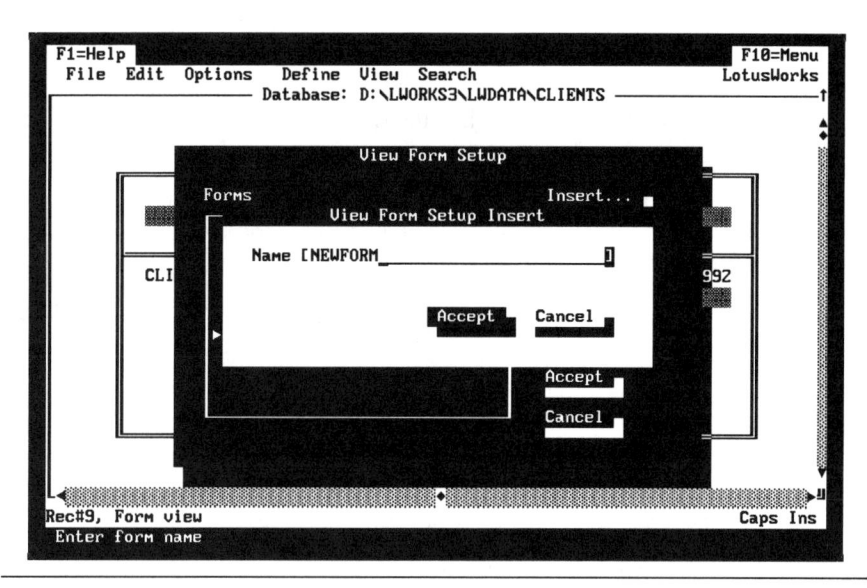

**FIGURE 4.32:** Enter a name for the new form and select Accept.

4. Type a descriptive name for the new form in the Name text box. The name can be as long as the text box and may contain more than one word, if you wish. When you are finished, select Accept. The Forms Editor screen opens:

**FIGURE 4.33:** The Forms Editor screen

*Make a sketch first. Before you begin to create a form on the screen, make a pencil sketch of the form showing the locations of fields, titles, labels, and borders. It will help you visualize the form and save you keystrokes when you lay out the form on the screen.*

5. Use the Forms Editor to lay out the form. The general tasks are as follows. For the specifics on how to use the Forms Editor, see "Using the Forms Editor" immediately following this section.

   a. Unless you want to use all or nearly all the fields in the database, select Edit Reset Clear to erase all the fields from the screen and start with a blank form. This way you can select fields for the form one by one and move them around without without interfering clutter.

   b. Insert the fields that you want to appear on the form and move them into position.

   c. Type title lines and labels for the fields

   d. Add lines, boxes, and borders to the form, if you wish.

   e. Format the number fields. For each field that contains numbers, you can select an appropriate format for the display.

6. When all the desired fields, lines, and number formats have been specified, press Alt+Q or select File Quit to exit the Forms Editor screen and return to the View Form setup dialog box. Notice that the new form name appears in the text box.

7. Select Accept. LotusWorks saves the new form and returns you to the database screen. The form is now saved and active.

## Using the Forms Editor

You use the Forms Editor to create a new form or to modify an existing one. It contains the tools to select fields from the database, position fields on the form, create text titles and instructions, create labels for fields, draw lines, format numbers, and rearrange the elements to get the form to your liking. Here is how it works.

### Getting to the Forms Editor

To get to the Forms Editor:

1. Select View Form setup. The View Form setup dialog box appears.

2. If you are creating a new form, select Insert; when the View Forms Setup Insert dialog box appears, enter a name for the form and select Accept. If you are modifying an existing form, highlight the form to modify and then select Modify.

## Inserting a Field

To insert a new field into a form:

1. Go into the Forms Editor.
2. Move the cursor to the position on the screen where you want the new field to appear.
3. Select Edit Insert field. The following dialog box appears:

*To save time, select Edit Reset, Clear all the fields from the screen, then insert only the fields you want to appear on the form.*

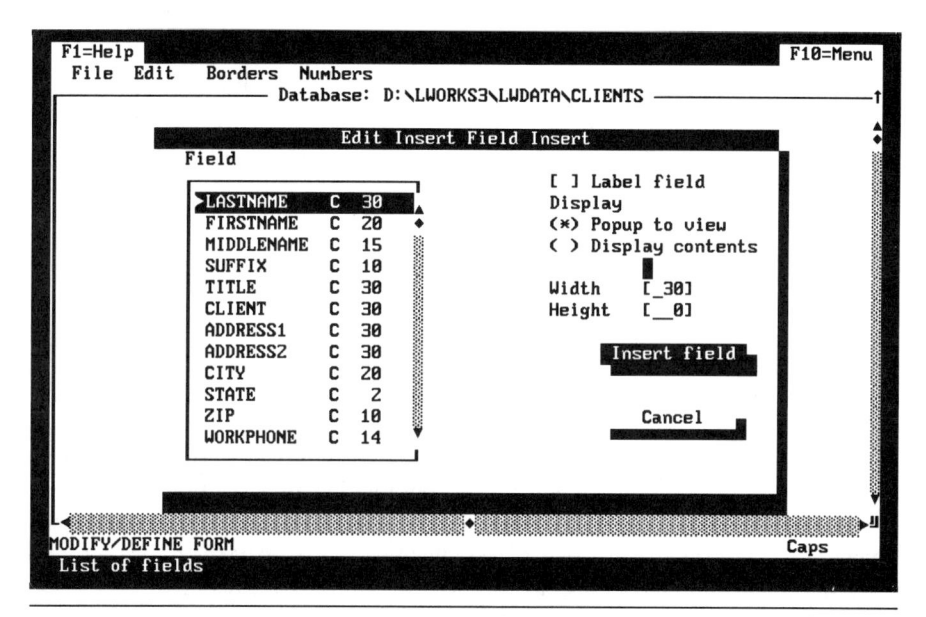

```
F1=Help                                                        F10=Menu
   File  Edit   Borders  Numbers
                     Database: D:\LWORKS3\LWDATA\CLIENTS
                        Edit Insert Field Insert
             Field
                                              [ ] Label field
             ▶LASTNAME     C  30               Display
              FIRSTNAME    C  20               (*) Popup to view
              MIDDLENAME   C  15               ( ) Display contents
              SUFFIX       C  10
              TITLE        C  30               Width   [_30]
              CLIENT       C  30               Height  [__0]
              ADDRESS1     C  30
              ADDRESS2     C  30                  Insert field
              CITY         C  20
              STATE        C   2
              ZIP          C  10                     Cancel
              WORKPHONE    C  14


MODIFY/DEFINE FORM                                              Caps
List of fields
```

**FIGURE 4.34:** The Edit Insert Field Insert dialog box.

The Edit Insert Field Insert dialog box lists all the fields in the current database. You may insert as many or as few fields as fit your purpose (and fit the available space in the form!).

4. Use the mouse or arrow keys to highlight the first field to be inserted into the form, and press Tab to move the cursor to the Label field option.

5. If you want to use the database field name as the label for the field on the form, press the Spacebar to put an X in the Label field check box. If you want to enter a more descriptive label for the field on the form instead, leave this option blank (press the Spacebar if necessary to remove the X from the Label field check box). Press Tab to move the cursor to the next field.

6. If you have selected a memo field to edit, the cursor moves to the Display option; otherwise it skips directly to the Width option. If you are editing a memo field, select the Popup to view option if you want the form to display the memo field on command, or select Display contents if you want the form to display the contents of the memo field automatically. After making your selection, press the Tab key to move to the Width option.

7. With the cursor on the Width text box, enter the number of characters to display for the field. You may display the entire field or, if you wish, just a portion of it. When you have entered the number, press Tab to move to the next field.

8. If you have selected a memo field to edit, the cursor moves to the Height option. Enter a number indicating the number of lines of text to display for the memo field. When you have entered the number, press Tab to move to the next field.

9. Select Insert field to complete the insertion.

Repeat steps 1 through 9 for each new field until all the desired new fields have been inserted.

## Editing an Area of the Form

You can edit an area of the form by using the Move block, Copy block, and Delete block options. These options work on a rectangular area (or block) that you specify. A block can contain any combination of adjacent text, fields, and blank spaces and can be as small as part of a single line or as large as the entire screen. You start each command by specifying the command and then indicating a block on which the command is to act.

**Moving the Contents of an Area to a New Position.** To specify a block and move its contents to a new position:

1. Move the cursor to the point on the screen where you want the top-left corner of the block to begin.

2. Select Edit Move block.

3. Press the arrow keys to extend the block to the right and down until the block covers the desired area and press Enter or drag the mouse to highlight the desired block. LotusWorks shades the area within the block.

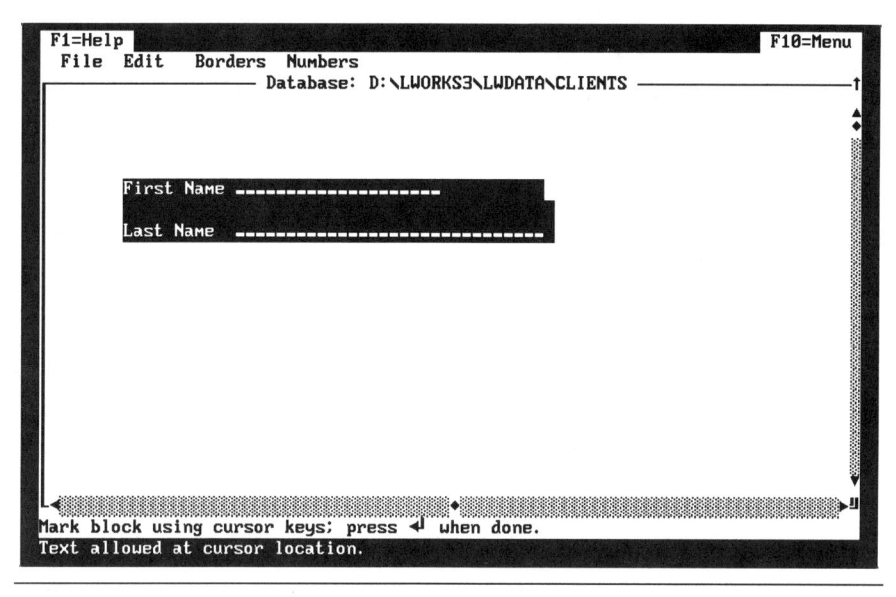

**FIGURE 4.35:** LotusWorks shades the area within the block.

4. Move the block with the arrow keys to the desired new position on the screen and press Enter to deposit the block, or use the mouse to drag the block to the new position and release the mouse button to deposit the block.

LotusWorks moves the block from its former position to the new position, writing over anything that exists in the new position.

**Copying the Contents of an Area to a New Position.** To copy a block to a new position:

1. Move the cursor to the top-left corner of the area to be copied.
2. Select Edit Copy block.
3. Press the arrow keys to extend the block to the right and down until the block covers the desired area and press Enter, or drag the mouse to highlight the desired block. LotusWorks shades the area within the block.
4. Move the copy of the block with the arrow keys to the desired new position and press Enter to deposit the copy, or use the mouse to drag the block to the new position and release the mouse button to deposit the copy.

LotusWorks leaves the original block intact and puts a copy of the block in the new position, writing over anything that exists in the new position.

*If you simply want to reposition a field or text horizontally on the same line, you can position the cursor on the line and use the Spacebar, Delete, and Backspace keys to reposition the field or text, as you would with the word processor. If you want to reposition elements vertically, however, you must use the Move block procedure.*

**Deleting the Contents from an Area.** To delete a block:

1. Move the cursor to the top-left corner of the area where the contents are to be deleted.
2. Select Edit Delete block.
3. Press the arrow keys to extend the block to the right and down until the block covers the desired area.
4. Press Enter to delete the contents of the block.

LotusWorks erases everything within the block. You may enter or move new items into the resulting space or leave it blank.

## Maintaining Spacing—The Float Option

Sometimes it is desirable to have a field always print in the same fixed position, regardless of the effects of trimming trailing blank spaces and suppressing blank lines. (For information about suppressing trailing blank spaces and blank lines, see "Creating a Print Layout for a Form" later in this chapter.) This may be the case for fields such as ZIP codes in mailing labels or phone numbers in a card file. For example, when you set a form print layout to trim trailing blank spaces and suppress blank lines (as you would for address labels), LotusWorks normally closes the gaps and prints each field adjacent to the previous one. If you want to exempt a field from these effects and have it be printed in a fixed position every time, however, you can make it into a floating field. The Edit Float option prints a field exactly in the position where it appears on the screen.

To create a floating field, move the field to the desired position on the screen, position the cursor at the beginning of the field, and select Edit Float. Lotus-Works displays a small, hollow triangle on the screen to indicate a floating field. The triangle does not appear when the field is printed.

## Formatting Number Fields

You can add formats to number fields to make them more descriptive. To specify a format for a number field:

1. Enter the Forms Editor.
2. Move the cursor to the desired number field and select Numbers.

3. Select the appropriate number format for the field. The options are:

    Normal      Displays numbers and decimals.
    Blank 0     Displays a blank space if the field value is zero.
    Currency    Displays numbers as currency.
    Percent     Displays numbers as percentages.

You can have a combination of Blank 0 and other formats, such as Normal and Blank 0 or Currency and Blank 0. To change from one setting to another, first select Normal, then select the new setting or settings. When you exit the Forms Editor, the numbers will be displayed with the specified format.

> NOTE: Specifying a number format in a form affects that form only. It has no effect on the underlying database or on any other forms or tables based on the database.

4. Press Enter.

## Drawing Lines

You can add lines, boxes, and borders to make forms more attractive and easier to read. To do so, follow these steps:

1. Enter the Forms Editor.

2. (Important!) Move the cursor to the point on the form where you want to start a line. Be sure to position the cursor before taking the next step.

3. Select Borders and select a line or shading option. You have the option of drawing a single line, double line, a lightly shaded border, a medium-shaded border, or a heavily shaded border. You can have more than one type of line on a single form.

    Even though the heading says Border, you can use Light, Medium, and Heavy borders to create shading for emphasis just about anywhere on a form except over a field. Beware, however, that if you put shading over text, the shading writes over the text and deletes it.

4. Use the arrow keys to draw a line, box, or border. Use the Delete and Backspace keys to erase any mistakes. (You may have to practice with this a bit at first to get the feel of it.)

5. Press Enter when you're finished with each line, box, or border. This stops the drawing, like lifting a pen from the paper.

6. Repeat the process until you have drawn all the desired elements.

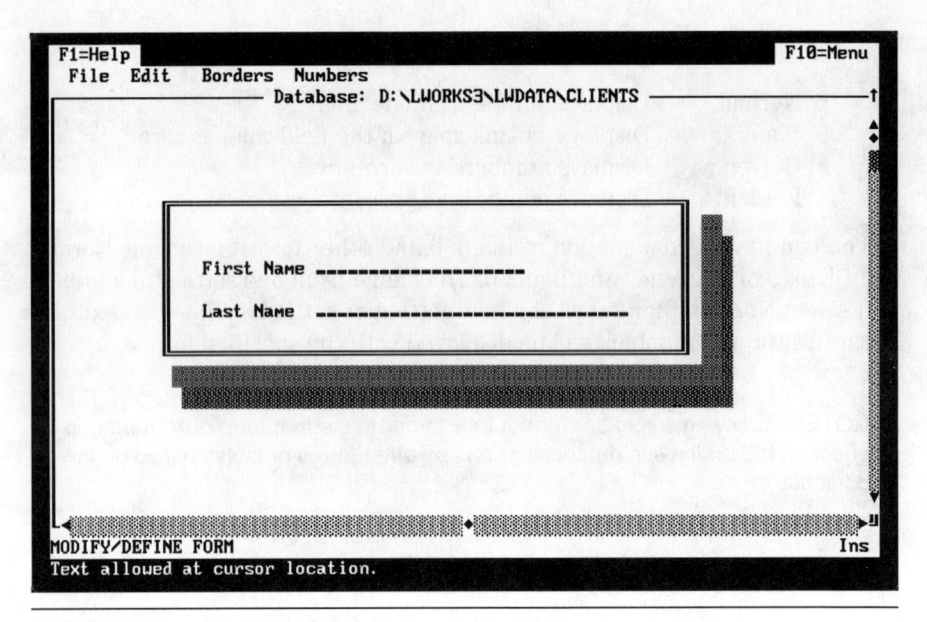

**FIGURE 4.36:** You can put a border anywhere on a form except on a field.

## Exiting the Forms Editor

When you have finished laying out or modifying a form, press Alt+Q (or select File Quit) to leave the Forms Editor. LotusWorks returns you to the View Form setup dialog box. Select Accept to save your work. LotusWorks returns you to Form View and displays the changes you have just made.

## Retrieving a Form

To retrieve the form in the future, first retrieve the database to which it belongs, then retrieve the form (select View Form setup, move the cursor to the name of the form, and select Accept).

## Creating a Print Layout for a Form

LotusWorks enables you to set and save printing specifications for forms just as you do for tables. The specifications are saved in a print layout for each form.

The specifications are similar to the ones for tables, but there are some options that are particular to printing forms. LotusWorks gives you the option of printing multiple forms and records on each page. This is especially useful for creating mailing labels. Once you create a print layout for a form, LotusWorks saves it with the form and activates it whenever you retrieve the form.

The steps for creating a print layout for a form are as follows:

1. Select the database for the form.

2. Select the form you wish to print.

3. Select File Print Layout. The following dialog box appears:

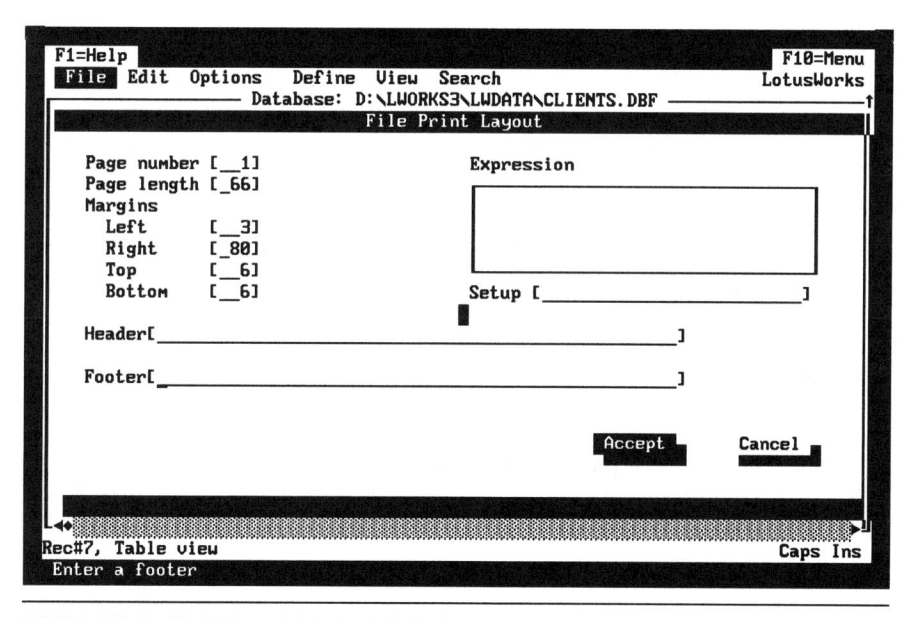

**FIGURE 4.37:** The File Print Layout dialog box in Table view

4. Select and enter the layout options you desire for the form. The options are:

   a. **Page number.** If you want a page number to print automatically in a header or footer and you want to start with a number other than 1, enter the starting number in the Page number box.

   b. **Page length.** Enter the number of lines to be printed on each page. The number depends on the printer, the page orientation, and the size of paper. A standard U.S. letter-size page (8½" × 11") in portrait orientation normally has 66 lines, which is the default value. Some laser printers, however, print a maximum of 60 lines on an 11" page. If you are using paper of a different size, printing in landscape orientation, or printing something other than six vertical lines to the inch, you may need to try a few settings with your printer to find the right number to enter in this box.

> IMPORTANT: Ordinarily, the Database service prints in portrait orientation. However, you can print in landscape orientation on most printers by entering an appropriate printer setup string in the Setup text box in the File Print Layout dialog box. See your printer manual for the correct setup string to use.

c. **Margins (left, right, top, and bottom).** Enter the number of columns you want for the left and right margins and the number of rows you want for the top and bottom margins of the form. The left and right margins are measured in columns (1 column = 1 character) from the left edge of the paper, starting with 0 at the left edge, with a maximum of 254 columns. The top and bottom margins settings indicate the number of rows between the edge of the page and the first or last row of text.

> NOTE: Be aware that headers and footers print in the top and bottom margins. Be sure to make your margins big enough to hold them.

d. **Forms across and Forms down.** Leave these options blank unless you are laying out labels. See "Printing Labels" later in this chapter for instructions on labels.

e. **Trim spaces.** When selected, this option eliminates any trailing blank spaces from character data, so that adjacent fields print without leaving a gap. For example, it prints the contents of a first name field and a last name as John Smith instead of John      Smith.

f. **Suppress blanks.** When selected, this option prevents a blank line from appearing when a data field is empty. This is useful in addresses, for example, if some records have entries for a company name or a second address line and other records do not.

g. **Setup.** This box lets you enter a string of setup characters for your printer, if needed. Many printers accept setup strings to change type styles, type sizes, type attributes, and the print orientation. If your printer needs a print string for the form you are laying out, enter the string here. See your printer's manual for instructions.

h. **Header.** This box lets you enter a one-line header to appear at the top of each printed page. In addition to regular text, you may use the special character # to enter an automatic page number, @ to enter an automatic date, and the vertical bar (|) to align text to the left, center, or right, as in word processing headers. See "Creating Headers and Footers" in Chapter 3 for more information on using these symbols.

i. **Footer.** This box lets you enter a one-line footer to appear at the bottom of each printed page. As with the header line, you may use the #, @, and | characters to set up automatic page numbering, enter the date automatically, and align the text to the left, center, or right.

5. When all of the options have been set, select Accept. LotusWorks saves the print layout with the form and returns you to the File Print dialog box.
   Any time you retrieve the form in the future, the print layout automatically becomes current.

To use the print layout and print the form, please see "Printing Tables" next.

# Printing from Databases

The Database service not only enables you to select, manipulate, and display data, it also enables you to print the results in a variety of useful ways. You can format and print forms, tables, and labels without ever leaving the Database service, and you can mail-merge information from databases into word documents in the Word Processing service.

## Printing Tables

Tables print one record on each line, with as many lines as each page will hold. You can use tables to print client lists, employee directories, inventories, class and team rosters, work logs, and just about any other kind of list that requires only one line for each record and does not require any mathematical calculations by columns or fields. (Use the Spreadsheet service for any tables requiring calculations by columns.)

Here are the steps for printing a table:

1. Be sure that your printer is turned on and properly connected to the computer.

2. If the database for the table is not current, retrieve it.

3. If you are not already in Table view, press Alt+V or select View Change Table view to switch to it.

4. Select the table to print: select View Table setup, highlight the name of the table to print, and select Accept.

5. If you want to print a selection of records rather than the entire database, perform a search to make the desired records active. See "Finding the Records You Want" earlier in this chapter for directions.

6. If you want the records to appear in a particular order perform a sort on the currently selected records. See "Creating a Sort Order" earlier in this chapter for directions.

7. Select File Print Layout and check the layout for printing. See "Creating a Print File Layout for a Table" earlier in this chapter.

8. Select Print (File Print Print). The following dialog box appears:

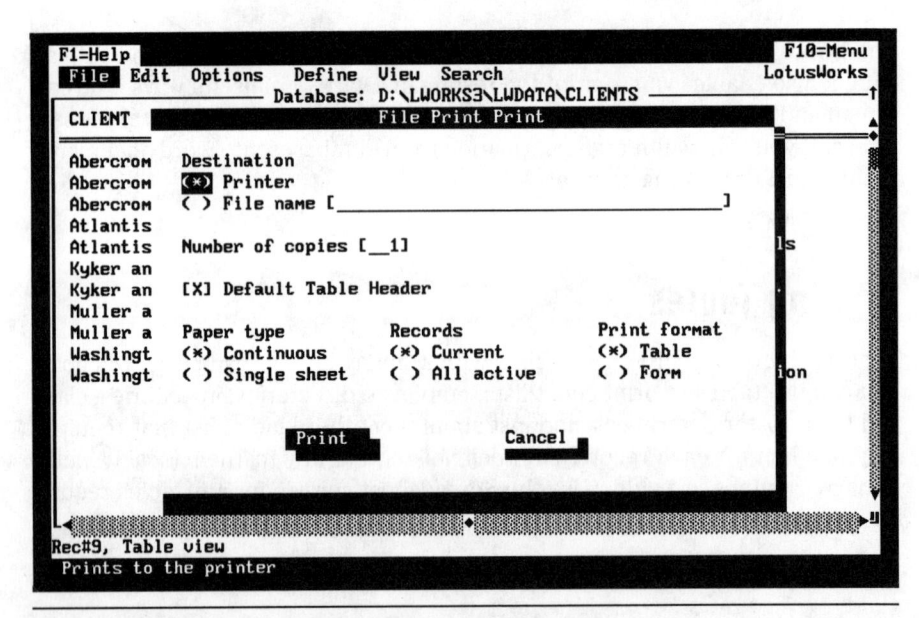

```
F1=Help                                                          F10=Menu
 File  Edit  Options  Define  View  Search                      LotusWorks
                    Database: D:\LWORKS3\LWDATA\CLIENTS
 CLIENT                       File Print Print

 Abercrom    Destination
 Abercrom    (*) Printer
 Abercrom    ( ) File name [_____]
 Atlantis
 Atlantis    Number of copies [__1]                              s
 Kyker an
 Kyker an    [X] Default Table Header
 Muller a
 Muller a    Paper type          Records            Print format
 Washingt    (*) Continuous      (*) Current        (*) Table
 Washingt    ( ) Single sheet    ( ) All active     ( ) Form     ion


                         Print              Cancel


Rec#9, Table view
Prints to the printer
```

**FIGURE 4.38:** Check the print settings each time before before you print a table.

9. Check the print settings each time before you print, and set the options in the dialog box as appropriate. Once these options are set, they will remain until you change them. The options are:

    a. **Destination.** Check a button to indicate whether to send the table to the printer or to a file for printing later.

    b. **Number of copies.** Enter the number of copies of the table to print.

    c. **Default Table Header.** The default table header consists of the column labels and the double line that you see at the top of the database screen in Table view. If you check this box, LotusWorks prints the column labels and double line at the top of each page. If you leave the box blank, LotusWorks prints the table without the column labels.

    d. **Paper type.** Select the appropriate type (continuous or single-sheet) for your printer. If you use a laser printer, check continuous rather than single-sheet.

    e. **Records.** Check whether to include only the currently selected record (1 record) or all the active records in the printout. Normally you will want to print all active records.

    f. **Print format.** Be sure that the Table option is selected.

10. When all the options have been set, select Print to begin printing.

*Make it a habit to check the print options each time before you print.*

> **NOTE:** If the table extends beyond the width of the page you are printing, LotusWorks prints the rest of the table on another page. It's best to keep your tables to the width of one page. If you need to display additional fields, create a second table with enough information from the first table to identify each record.

# Printing Forms

You have seen that LotusWorks enables you to create an almost endless variety of forms. You can also use LotusWorks to print them. Generally, LotusWorks forms print one record to each page, however, for labels and other special forms, you may print multiple records on each page. The fields are printed on the page as they appear on the screen. You can print invoices, statements of account, insurance forms, customer and client records, name-and-address cards, bibliographic notes, files of recipes, and just about any other database document where you need to print information about each record on a label or a separate page.

Except for a few steps, the process for printing a form is similar to the process for printing a table:

1. Be sure that your printer is turned on and properly connected to the computer.

2. If the desired database is not current, retrieve it.

3. Switch into Form view if you are not already in it: press Alt+V or select View Change Form view.

4. Select the form to print: select View Form setup, highlight the name of the form to print, and select Accept.

5. If you wish to print a selection of records, perform a search to make the desired records active. (See "Finding the Records You Want" in Chapter 3.)

6. If you want the forms to print in a particular order, perform a sort on the currently selected records. (See "Creating a Sort Order" earlier in this chapter.)

7. Select File Print Layout and check the layout for printing. (See "Creating a Print Layout for a Form" earlier in this chapter.)

8. Select File Print Print. The same dialog box appears as when you are printing a table:

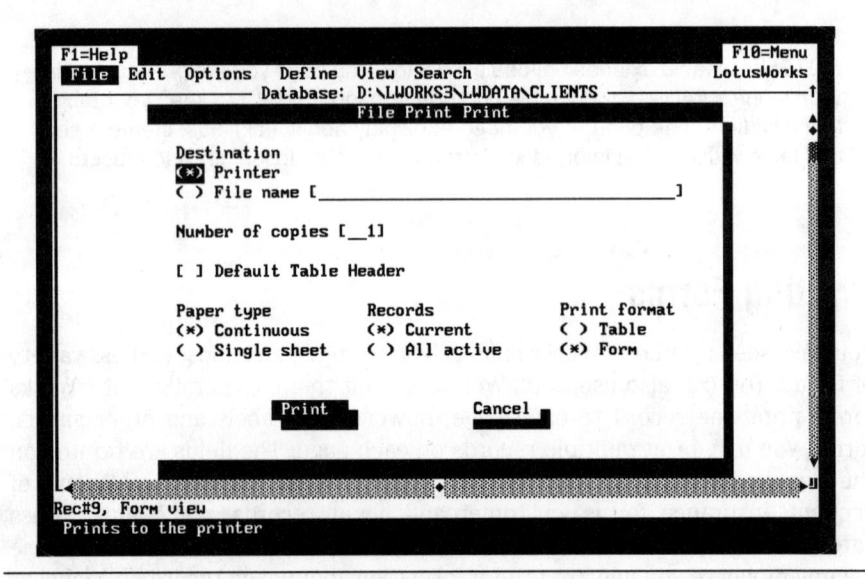

```
F1=Help                                                          F10=Menu
 File  Edit  Options   Define   View  Search                    LotusWorks
                     Database: D:\LWORKS3\LWDATA\CLIENTS
                              File Print Print

       Destination
       (*) Printer
       ( ) File name [_____]

       Number of copies [__1]

       [ ] Default Table Header

       Paper type            Records              Print format
       (*) Continuous        (*) Current          ( ) Table
       ( ) Single sheet      ( ) All active       (*) Form

                      Print                Cancel


Rec#9, Form view
 Prints to the printer
```

**FIGURE 4.39:** Check the print settings each time before before you print a form.

9. Set the options in the dialog box as appropriate. Once these options are set, they will remain until you change them. The options are:

   a. **Destination.** Check a button to indicate whether to send the table to the printer or to a file for printing later.

   b. **Number of copies.** Enter the number of copies of the form to print.

   c. **Paper type.** Select the appropriate type (continuous or single-sheet) for your printer. If you use a laser printer, check continuous rather than single-sheet.

   d. **Records.** Check whether to include only the currently selected record (1 record) or all the active (unflagged) records in the printout.

   e. **Print format.** Be sure that the Form option is selected.

10. When all the options have been set, select Print to begin printing.

## Printing Labels

Printing labels in LotusWorks 3.0 is a variation of printing forms. The first step is to create a form. Give the form a distinctive name, such as "MAILABLS." Arrange the fields of the form to fit the space on the labels. If you are creating mailing labels, the form might look like this:

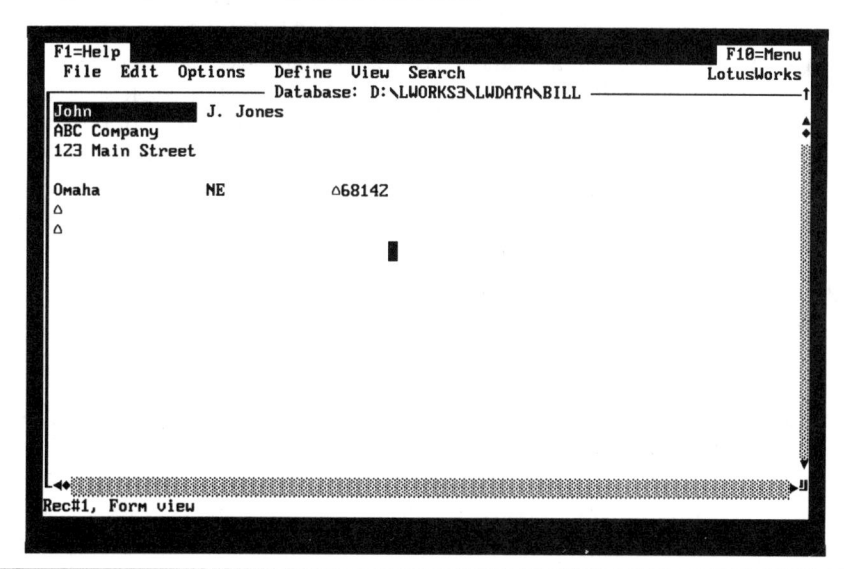

```
F1=Help                                                       F10=Menu
    File  Edit  Options   Define  View  Search              LotusWorks
                          Database: D:\LWORKS3\LWDATA\BILL
John              J. Jones
ABC Company
123 Main Street

Omaha             NE           ₀68142
₀
₀




Rec#1, Form view
```

**FIGURE 4.40:** A field arrangement for a mailing label form

The second step is to create the print layout for the labels. Do this as you would for any other form (see "Creating a Print Layout for a Form" earlier in this chapter), but when you get to the File Print Layout dialog box, be sure to enter a number in the Forms across option for the number of labels you want to print across each page and a number in the Forms down option for the number of labels you want to print down each page. LotusWorks figures out the width, depth, and spacing for you automatically.

In most cases, the left margin should be set to 0 and the right margin to the width of the paper on which you are printing (80, for a typical 8½-inch wide page). If necessary, you can change the left margin to make the printing line up where you want it on the page.

If you are printing labels with a dot-matrix printer, you should set the page length to the length of the label and, in most cases, set the top and bottom margins to zero. Generally, printers print six vertical lines to the inch, so for a label one inch deep the page length is 6, and for a label two inches deep the page length is 12. If necessary, you can add a blank line or two at the top of the label form to adjust the vertical spacing and make the addresses print in the center of the labels.

*Once you find the correct combination of layout settings for your printer and the labels you are printing, make a note of them for future reference whenever you are laying out labels again. If necessary, you can always return to the File Print Layout dialog box for the labels form to see how you did it the first time.*

If you are printing labels with a laser printer, you should set the page length to the setting your printer requires for an 11-inch page (66 rows). For some printers the setting will be 66 and for some it will be less. Because laser printers do not print to the very edge of the page, labels for laser printers typically have about a half-inch of blank space at the top and bottom of each sheet. Try setting the top and bottom margins to 3 rows. You may have to vary the settings for individual printers. If the addresses print too close together on successive labels whenever blank lines are suppressed, insert a Float symbol on one or more lines beneath the last line of the form to maintain vertical spacing so that the addresses print evenly down the sheet.

If you are printing mailing labels or other forms with names and parts of addresses in different fields, be sure to check the Trim spaces and Suppress blanks boxes. See "Suppressing Unneeded Spaces" earlier in this chapter.

You can skip the Header and Footer boxes when you're laying out labels. For other types of forms, you may or may not wish to fill in these options, depending on the form.

To print the labels, follow the same steps as for printing any other form:

1. Retrieve the database.
2. Select the labels form that you designed.
3. Perform a search to make the desired records active.
4. Select a sort order (such as ZIP Code order or Alphabetic by Last Name) if you want the labels to be printed in a particular order.
5. Select File Print Print and check the print settings.
6. Select Print.

LotusWorks prints the number of labels or forms you have specified across and down the page, each form containing the data from one record. It prints as many pages as necessary to print the records you have selected.

## Merge Printing (Mail-merge)

Merge printing is the same thing as mail-merging. It requires two documents: a database containing the variable data to be inserted and a master document containing the fixed text. You can use any database with appropriate fields for merge printing. Unlike previous versions of LotusWorks, LotusWorks 3.0 launches mail merging from the Word Processing service rather than the Database service. See Chapter 3 for instructions on preparing master documents and preforming mail-merges.

# Copying Data from One Database to Another

There are a number of occasions when you may need to to copy data from one database to another. For example, suppose you need to create a merge document containing information from two different databases. Or suppose a master database grows so large that you need to divide it into two smaller ones. Or suppose you need to copy some records from one database (such as a prospect list) to another (such as a customer list). LotusWorks has three features to enable you to perform these operations: the File Transfer Append option, the File Export Extract option, and the LOOKUP function. Here is how they work.

## Appending Records from Another Database

The Append option copies all the records from another database and adds them to the end of the database in the active window. LotusWorks copies the data from all the fields that match those in the active window. Because the procedure merely copies records, it has no effect on the original database.

To use this option, retrieve the database that you want to be the receiving database and select File Transfer Append. A list box of database files appears. Select or enter the path and file name of the database from which to copy. LotusWorks automatically copies the records and adds them to the end of the database in the active window.

## Extracting Records to a New Database

The Extract option copies all the active *records* from one database to a new database. You may extract all the fields or only the ones that appear in the current table view. The records in the original database are not affected.

To use this option, follow these steps:

1. Retrieve the database from which you wish to extract records.

2. Go into Table view.

3. If you want to extract only some of the *records*, perform a search to make the desired records active. If you want to extract all the records, skip this step.

4. If you want to extract only some of the *fields* (as you would to split the database or to create a special subset of a large database), select the fields to extract or, if necessary, create a table containing only the fields to be extracted. If you want to extract all the fields, skip this step.

5. Select File Transfer Extract. A dialog box appears.

6. Type a file name for the new database file. If you want to save the file in a directory other than the current one, include the path with the file name. LotusWorks automatically creates the correct file extension.

7. At the Fields option, select All if you want to extract all the fields, or Table view only if you want to extract only the fields that appear in the current table.

8. Select Extract. LotusWorks creates the new file under the path and filename you specified and extracts the data for all active records and the fields you specified. The procedure does not affect the original database. LotusWorks leaves it intact and displays it in the current window.

9. To see the new database, open a new window and retrieve the database. For more information on opening a new window, see "Working with Multiple Task Windows" in Chapter 2.

Once you see that the new database is correctly built, you can consider whether to delete any fields from the original database. It is best to leave the original intact to use as a backup if needed.

*Always play it safe with your valuable data! If you are splitting an original database, it is best to copy some of the fields to one new database and the rest of the fields to another new database, rather than destroy any of the original data. That way, you can always keep the original data on a floppy disk for backup, if necessary.*

## Using Data from External Databases

It's a good idea to keep names, addresses, and phone numbers in a single database. That way, whenever any of this information changes, there is only one file to update and there is no danger of getting different information for the same record into different files.

For some purposes, however, you may need to draw data from more than one database for a specific task. For example, suppose you are mail-merging a collection letter and you need to use names and addresses from one database and account balance information from another. Or suppose you are creating an invoice form and you want to draw customer name and address information from your master address list but draw the other information from an order database.

You can solve these problems and avoid having duplicate data files or having to enter or update data more than once by using the LOOKUP function in conjunction with Lookup data fields. Here is how.

1. If it is not already current, retrieve the database to which you wish to bring data.

2. If the current database does not already have them, create a new character or numeric field for each field to be drawn from an external database. (The LOOKUP function cannot be used with Date, Logical, or Memo fields). These "lookup fields" may draw from more than one database, if necessary. For more information on creating fields, see "Designing Databases" earlier in this chapter.

3. Create a lookup rule for each lookup field. The rule tells LotusWorks to read the value for the field from an external database rather than from the current one. You create the lookup rule by selecting Define Rules Modify Insert, selecting the Lookup Rule type, highlighting the desired field, and entering a lookup expression.

The lookup expression takes the following form:

LOOKUP(keyfield,"returnfield","lookupdatabase"[,"sortorder"])

The elements of the lookup expression are as follows:

Keyfield
: A field that is common to the current database and the external "lookup" database. The field can be a record number, an account number, or any other character or numerical data field, as long as it meets two conditions: (1) each record must have a unique value in the key field, and (2) the same key field must appear in both the current and the external database.

Returnfield
: The field in the lookup database from which data will be read. It can be any character or numeric field in the lookup database.

Lookupdatabase
: Any external database that has at least one field in common with the current database.

Sortorder
: An optional expression. If it is used, LotusWorks searches the records in the order specified by the sort order. If it is not used, LotusWorks searches the active records in their current order.

> **NOTE:** In the Lookup expression the name of the keyfield is written without quotation marks and the names of the returnfield and lookupdatabase must be surrounded by double quotation marks. The double quotation marks tell LotusWorks that the returnfield and lookupdatabase are external to the current database.

The Lookup expression tells LotusWorks to find the record in the lookup database whose value in the key field matches the value in the key field of the current database, then look up the return field for that record, and return the value in that field to the lookup field of the current database.

Suppose, for example, that you keep customers' names and addresses in a database named "Customer," and you keep account balance information in a database named "Accounts." Suppose each customer has a customer identification number that appears in both databases. You could bring information on each customer's balance into a field in the Customer database with the following lookup formula:

LOOKUP(CUSTID,"BALANCE","ACCOUNTS")

This lookup expression says, "Look up the customer i.d. number for the current record, find the matching number in the CUSTID field of the ACCOUNTS database, and return the value in the BALANCE field for that record.

3. Select Accept, and when the Define Rules Modify dialog box appears, select Accept again. LotusWorks displays the information from the lookup database on the screen. When you perform a mail-merge operation from the Word Processing service, LotusWorks prints the data from the lookup expression as it it were in the current database.

# Using Macros with Databases

A macro, you may recall, is a stored sequence of keystrokes that LotusWorks plays back automatically when you press the appropriate Ctrl+key combination. In the Database service, as in any other service, you can use a macro to automate any sequence of keystrokes.

There are many ways you can use macros to save work with databases. For example:

- **Launch a database.** If you have a database that you use regularly, such as a database for telephone dialing and logging telephone calls, you can create a macro to retrieve it automatically with just a couple of keystrokes.
- **Execute a search.** If you have a standard search that you frequently perform, such as a search for accounts past due over a certain number of days, you can use a macro to save the search and automatically execute it.
- **Execute a sort order.** Just as you can launch a search with a macro, you can also launch a sort order.

- **Select and print a form or table.** If you have defined and saved a form or table, you can use a macro to retrieve it quickly and print it.
- **Execute a combination of a database, search, sort order, and form or table with a single key combination.**

No doubt, you will think of additional ways to automate routine tasks in your own work with the LotusWorks macro feature.

To create a macro, select Options Macros Learn. The following dialog box appears showing the 26 possible Ctrl+key combinations:

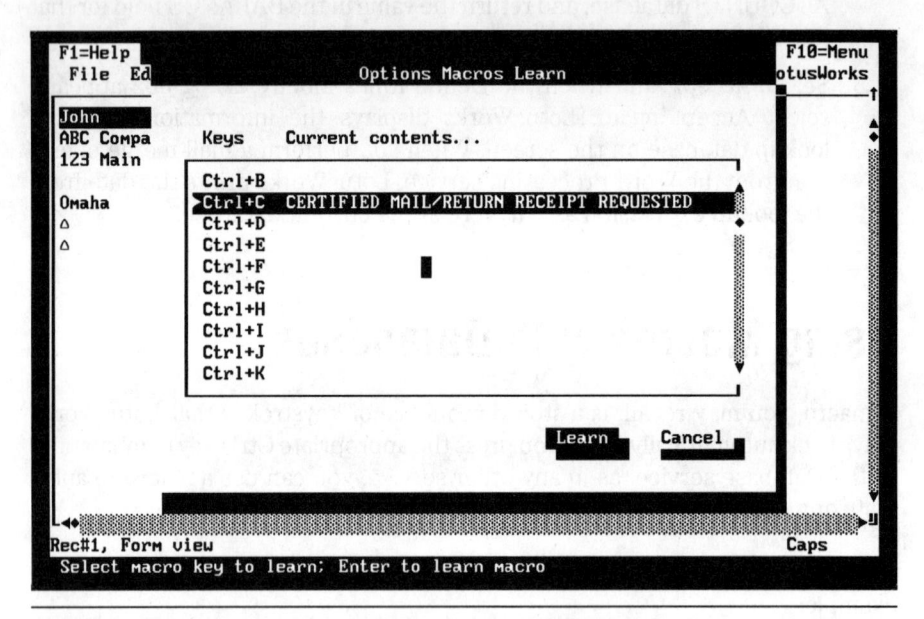

```
F1=Help                                                      F10=Menu
 File  Ed              Options Macros Learn                 otusWorks
┌─────────┐
│ John    │
│ ABC Compa│   Keys     Current contents...
│ 123 Main │
│          │   Ctrl+B
│ Omaha    │  ►Ctrl+C   CERTIFIED MAIL/RETURN RECEIPT REQUESTED
│ Δ        │   Ctrl+D
│ Δ        │   Ctrl+E
│          │   Ctrl+F
│          │   Ctrl+G
│          │   Ctrl+H
│          │   Ctrl+I
│          │   Ctrl+J
│          │   Ctrl+K
│
│                                          Learn    Cancel
│
Rec#1, Form view                                              Caps
Select macro key to learn; Enter to learn macro
```

**FIGURE 4.41:** Select one of the 26 Ctrl+key combinations to use to trigger the macro.

There are 26 letter Ctrl+key combinations (Ctrl+A through Ctrl+Z) for each LotusWorks service. Thus you can have up to 26 service-specific macros in each service.

Move the cursor to the Ctrl+key combination (for example, Ctrl+C) that you want to trigger the macro and select Learn. This starts the recording of the macro. Enter the keystrokes that you want to be recorded, in the order you want them to be performed. When you are finished, press the Ctrl+key combination (for example, Ctrl+C) to stop the recording. *Remember, LotusWorks records every keystroke you make until you press the Ctrl+key combination for the macro to stop the recording.*

To play back a macro that you have recorded, you can select Options, Macros, Run and select the macro from the list box. *The quickest way, however, is simply to press the Ctrl+key combination associated with the desired macro.*

To launch a database automatically from any LotusWorks service, record the following sequence of keystrokes:

| | |
|---|---|
| Ctrl+F6, D | To go to the Database service |
| F10,F,R | To tell LotusWorks to retrieve a file |
| Tab | To move the cursor to the File text box |
| [Path and Filename] | To specify the database to be retrieved |
| Enter | To retrieve the database |

To run the macro, press Ctrl + the letter key that you assigned to the macro.

To record over an existing macro, simply record the new macro as if there were no existing macro.

If you make a mistake in a macro, there are two ways to correct it. The easiest way is simply to record the correct macro over the old macro. You may also edit the macro by selecting Options, Macro, Edit. This is also the only way to put certain keystrokes (such as Esc) into a macro. For a complete list of keynames, see Appendix D. For more information on editing macros, see your LotusWorks User's Guide.

# Dialing and Logging Telephone Calls from a Database

If you have a modem connected to your computer, a great way to work smarter is to use LotusWorks and a database to dial telephone calls automatically and to log notes on calls that you make and receive. You simply include one or more fields in the database for telephone numbers and a memo field for notes on phone calls. When you want to make a call, move the cursor to the desired telephone number and press Alt+D or select Options Dial.

Although you can create a separate database for this purpose, there is no need to. It is more efficient simply to include the appropriate fields in your business contacts database and to define a table for telephone use.

To dial from a database,

1. Be sure the modem is properly connected and turned on. (Most modems provide for a telephone set to be connected to the modem while the modem is connected to the telephone line. Connect the modem this way.)

2. Move the cursor to the desired record and highlight the desired telephone number. (Table view is best for this purpose.)

3. Press Alt+D or select Options Dial. LotusWorks dials the phone number.

4. When the telephone starts ringing, pick up the telephone receiver and use it in the normal manner. When you are finished talking, hang up the receiver. This automatically terminates the call.

*When you set up your telephone dialing table, put the telephone number at or near the left margin, to save time in selecting the telephone number.*

You can log notes on telephone calls that you receive as well as calls that you originate. To log notes into a memo field:

1. Dial the call (or answer the phone if you are receiving the call).

2. Move the cursor to the memo field of the person with whom you are talking.

3. Press F2 twice, or select Edit Select and press F2 to open the Memo editor. (It's quickest to press F2 twice.)

4. Move the cursor below any previous entries and enter the date and time of the call and any free-form notes you wish to make.

5. When the call is over, press Enter to exit the memo editor.

## Modifying the Address Example Database

A good way to get your feet wet with database operations is to examine the example databases included with LotusWorks 3.0 and modify them for your own use. Here is a look at the Address database and some things you can do to modify it.

> NOTE: If you want to restore any of the example databases after you finish modifying them, you can do so by running the install program and reinstalling the examples from your backup copy of the original LotusWorks disks.

## Accessing the Q_ADDR Database

You can access the Address database by opening the Database service, selecting File Retrieve, and selecting the file named Q_ADDRS.DBF. (If you have not installed the example files onto the current drive, you may have to specify the drive path and file name, then select Retrieve. For example, A:Q_ADDRS.DBF.)

In Form view, the first record of the database looks like this:

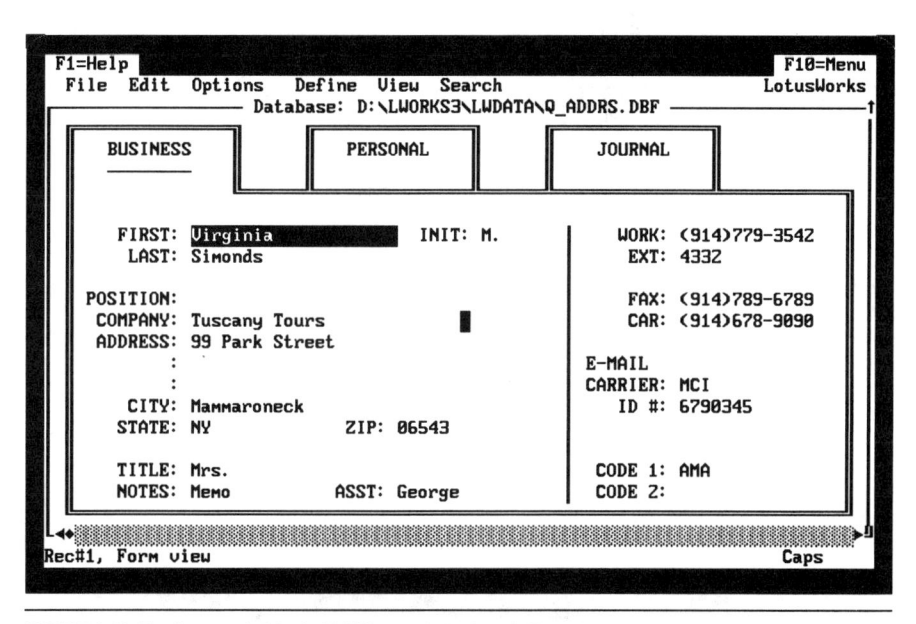

```
F1=Help                                                          F10=Menu
   File  Edit  Options   Define  View  Search                  LotusWorks
                   Database: D:\LWORKS3\LWDATA\Q_ADDRS.DBF

     BUSINESS              PERSONAL               JOURNAL


       FIRST: Virginia              INIT: M.       WORK: (914)779-3542
       LAST: Simonds                                EXT: 4332

    POSITION:                                       FAX: (914)789-6789
     COMPANY: Tuscany Tours                         CAR: (914)678-9090
     ADDRESS: 99 Park Street
            :                                     E-MAIL
            :                                    CARRIER: MCI
        CITY: Mammaroneck                           ID #: 6790345
       STATE: NY              ZIP: 06543

       TITLE: Mrs.                                CODE 1: AMA
       NOTES: Memo            ASST: George        CODE 2:


Rec#1, Form view                                                    Caps
```

**FIGURE 4.42:** The first record of the Q_ADDRS example database in Form view

## Adding a Field

Suppose you want to add a field named SUFFIX between the B_LAST field and the B_WORK field to hold name suffixes. Suffixes are those things that come after the last name, such as Jr., III, Ph.D., USN-Ret. Here is how you can do it:

> NOTE: This procedure adds a field to the Q_ADDRS database but not to the current form. After you add the field to the database, you can add it to the current form by selecting View Form Setup and modifying the current form. See "Creating Custom Forms" earlier in this chapter.

1. Select Define Fields Modify. The following dialog box appears:

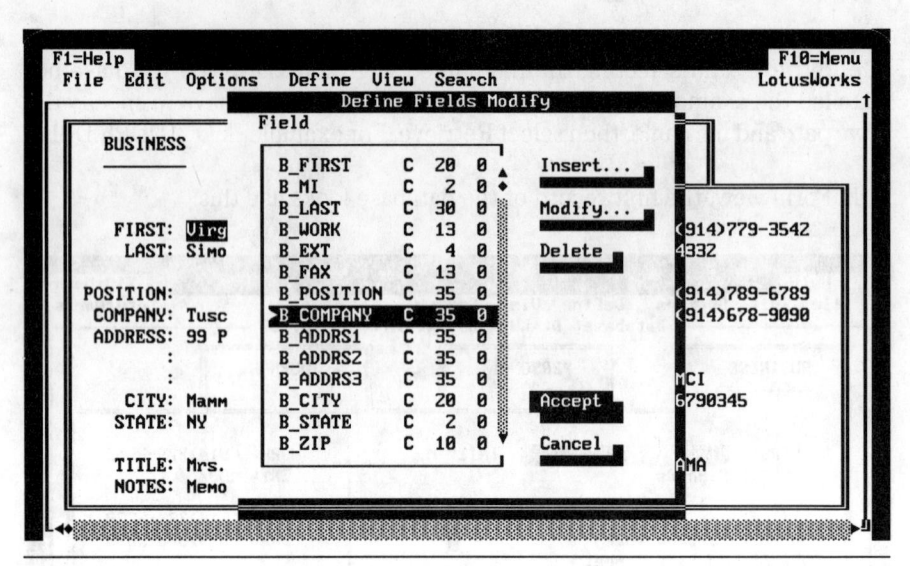

**FIGURE 4.43:** The Define Fields Modify dialog box of the Q_ADDRS database

2. Move the cursor to the B_WORK field and press Tab to highlight the Insert option.

3. Select Insert. The following dialog box appears:

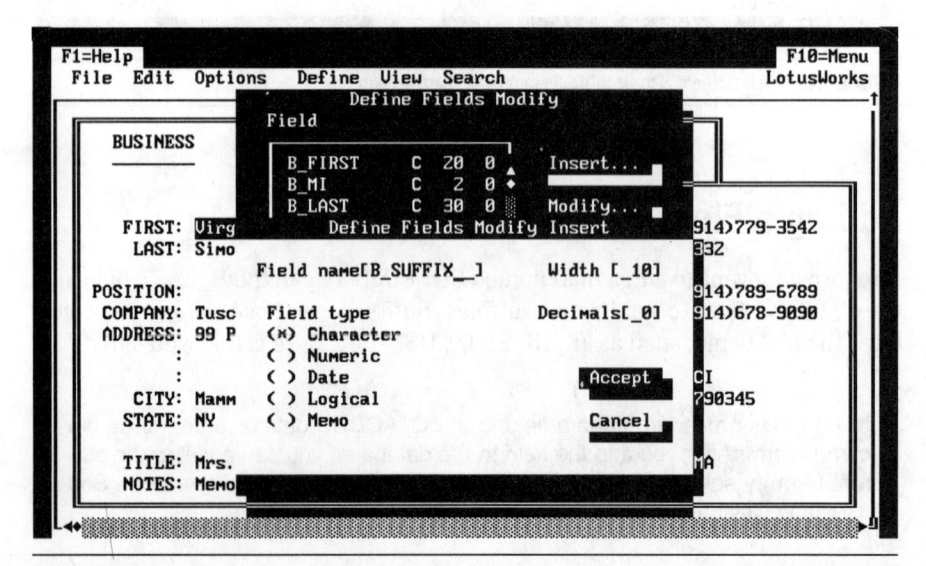

**FIGURE 4.44:** The second Define Fields Modify dialog box

4. Enter the name of the new field, B_SUFFIX, into the text box.
5. Specify field type: CHARACTER.
6. Tab to the Width option and enter 10.
7. Select Accept to complete the insertion and exit the second dialog box.
8. Check the first dialog box to be sure the new field is in the correct position, is spelled correctly, and has the correct width specified.
9. Select Accept to accept the changes as displayed and return to the database. LotusWorks displays the new field in the position where you inserted it.

## Deleting a Field

To delete the field you just added:

1. Select Define Fields Modify. The following dialog box appears:

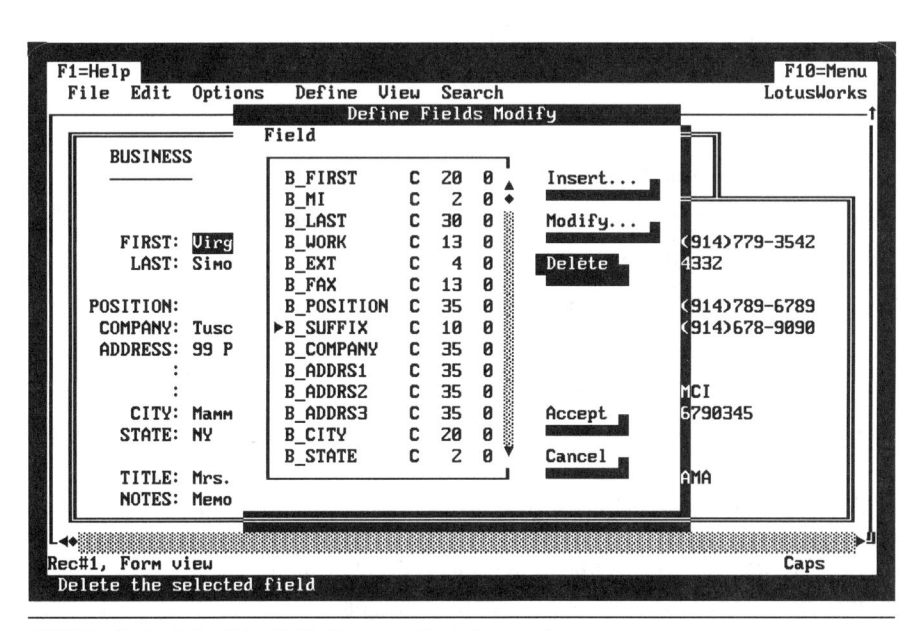

**FIGURE 4.45:** The Define Fields Modify dialog box of the Address database

2. Move the cursor to the B_SUFFIX field and press Tab to highlight the Delete option.

3. Select Delete.

4. Select Accept to complete the deletion and return to the database. LotusWorks deletes the B_SUFFIX field from the screen.

## Creating a Telephone Log Table

Now suppose you want to use the Q_ADDRS database as a telephone dialing directory and phone call log. The best way is to create a special table for this purpose and include a memo field for the log. There are two tasks: (1) add the memo field to the new database and (2) create a table with the desired fields in the desired order to be retrieved and used in the future. Here is how:

First, add the memo field to the database:

1. Select Define Fields Modify.

2. Move the cursor to the blank line and press Tab to highlight the Insert option.

3. Select Insert.

4. Enter the name of the new field, PHONELOG, into the text box.

5. Tab to the Field Type column and press the Down Arrow to highlight the Memo field type.

6. Select Accept to complete the insertion and exit the second dialog box.

7. Check the first dialog box to be sure the new field is displayed, is spelled correctly, and is of the correct type (Memo).

8. Select Accept to accept the changes as displayed and return to the database.

Second, create the table. For purposes of this illustration, the table needs to have six fields: B_WORK (which holds a business phone number for each record), B_EXT (which holds an extension number, if any), PHONELOG (the memo field for notes on phone conversations), B_LAST, B_FIRST, and B_COMPANY. (Later, you can set up the table with as many or as few fields as you like.) To create the table, you need to copy some fields to different positions in the table and delete other fields. Here are the steps:

1. Select View Table setup. Move the cursor to the last table name and select Insert.

2. Enter a name for the table (in this case, call it "Phonelog") and press Enter.

3. When the dialog box appears, move the cursor to the B_WORK field and select the Insert option.

4. When the dialog box appears, move the cursor to the B_FIRST field and select Accept. LotusWorks inserts the B_FIRST field between the B_LAST and B_WORK fields.

5. Move the cursor to highlight the B_WORK field and select Insert.

6. When the dialog box appears, move the cursor to the PHONELOG field and select Accept. LotusWorks inserts the PHONELOG field just ahead of the B_LAST field.

7. Move the cursor to highlight the PHONELOG field and select Insert.

8. When the dialog box appears, move the cursor to the B_WORK field and select Accept. LotusWorks inserts the B_WORK field just ahead of the PHONELOG field.

9. Now you are ready to delete all the unneeded fields. Move the cursor to highlight the B_MI field and select Delete. LotusWorks removes the B_MI field name from the screen.

10. Repeat step 9 for the B_POSITION field and all the other unneeded fields until the list of fields looks like this:

    B_WORK
    B_EXT
    PHONELOG
    B_LAST
    B_FIRST
    B_COMPANY

11. When the list of fields is complete, select Accept. LotusWorks temporarily inserts the new table name (PHONELOG) into the list of tables. To complete the setup and save the table, select Accept. LotusWorks returns you to the database screen.

12. Press Alt+V to display the new table, if it is not already displayed.

To use the phone dialer, be sure that there is a phone number in the current record and that your modem is switched on. Move the cursor to highlight the phone number, press Alt+D to dial, and when the phone starts ringing, pick up the receiver. To record notes in the memo field, move the cursor to the field and press F2 twice. To terminate the phone call, simply hang up the phone.

## Composing with Database Functions

Earlier in this chapter you encountered a LotusWorks function—the LOOKUP function. A database function is a small prerecorded program that performs an operation on data when you enter the name of the function into a database expression. By combining functions, operators, and values into formulas or expressions, you can perform complex and powerful operations on data.

LotusWorks 3.0 has a large number of special functions that you can use to compose expressions. There are functions to perform operations on character strings, such as testing for types of characters, generating and altering character strings, specifying substrings within character strings, transforming characters to upper- or lowercase, and trimming blanks from character strings. Some functions perform data conversions, for example, from character to ASCII code number, ASCII code number to character, character to date, date to character, character to numeric, numeric to character, and to invert data. Some functions move the record pointer to the beginning or end of the file. Others supply information about databases: the status of records, database and field names, and the structure of databases. And some functions report the time and date from the computer system or perform date operations, logical tests, or mathematical operations.

Functions can be combined in an almost infinite variety of combinations to tell LotusWorks what you want it to do.

## Syntax

The syntax is the set of grammatical rules that LotusWorks uses to interpret functions and expressions. Each function must be written in a particular syntax. Generally the function name must be followed by one or more parameters separated by commas and enclosed within parentheses. Parameters can be field names, values, functions, or expressions composed of these elements joined by operators.

You may write functions in all uppercase characters (as shown here), all lowercase, or a mixture of cases.

To make the order of operations clear, you can put parentheses around functions or parameters within functions, just as you would in an algebraic expression. You can also write functions within functions. Just remember to keep the parentheses straight. Each function must have an opening and closing parenthesis around its parameters, and for each opening parenthesis there must be a closing parenthesis in the same expression.

## The IF Function

One function is so useful and versatile that it deserves special attention. The IF function performs logical tests. It takes the form, "if a specified condition exists, perform a specified action; otherwise perform another specified action." This simple structure can be used as a building block to give a wide variety of instructions to LotusWorks for an almost limitless variety of conditions and situations.

The syntax of the function is IF(logical condition, expression1, expression2). This means "if the logical condition exists, perform expression1, otherwise perform expression2." Notice that there are parentheses around the three parameters, and the parameters are separated by commas.

To see how this works, consider the expression IF(ORDER=>100, ORDER*0.95, ORDER). This expression says "if the order is equal to or greater than $100, calculate a 5% discount on the total bill; otherwise, bill the full amount of the order." You can accomplish the same result in this case by omitting the final parameter: IF(ORDER=>100,ORDER*0.95).

You can also nest IF functions within each other to express more complicated conditions. For example, the expression IF(ORDER=>100.AND.ORDER < 200,ORDER*0.95,IF(ORDER=>200, ORDER*0.90) says "if the order is equal to or greater than $100 and less than $200, calculate a 5% discount, and if the order is equal to or greater than $200, calculate a 10% discount."

The IF function is just one of many LotusWorks 3.0 database functions. A complete list of the database functions appears in Appendix B.

## A Final Word About Databases

As we said at the beginning of this chapter, there is no single best way to use databases. How you use them depends on the nature of your business, your personal thinking style, and your own ingenuity. Once you try identifying your necessary data and managing it with databases, however, you probably will find big payoffs right away. And in time you will probably invent applications and variations that are uniquely your own.

# 5

# Saving Work with Numbers

Computerized spreadsheets are marvelous tools for working with numbers. They can execute prewritten financial and statistical formulas, perform meticulous math operations, and help you enter data, all flawlessly and almost instantly. You can even use them to keep track of text data, such as your personal calendar and daily to-do list.

Computerized spreadsheets get their name from the familiar row-and-column ledger sheets long used in financial analysis, but unlike pencil-and-paper spreadsheets, the computer versions can do the math for you. If you change one value or formula in a spreadsheet, LotusWorks automatically recalculates all the other numbers in the spreadsheet that are affected by it.

The LotusWorks Spreadsheet service can help you analyze almost any kind of information that can be expressed in numerical terms. It can also import data from Lotus 1-2-3 spreadsheets and export data to them. This chapter shows you how.

*In this chapter, you'll learn how to:*
- *Work smart with spreadsheets*
- *Know when to use spreadsheets*
- *Design spreadsheets*
- *Set up and save spreadsheets*
- *Write spreadsheet formulas*
- *Use spreadsheet @functions to automate complex calculations*
- *Use lookup tables to save work*
- *Tailor the appearance of spreadsheets*
- *Print single and multiple reports from spreadsheets*
- *Create and use spreadsheets within spreadsheets*

## Working Smart with Spreadsheets

The key to working smart with spreadsheets, as with other LotusWorks services, is to let LotusWorks do as much of your work as possible. This means using some of the same work-saving features as with other services, such as drawing on stored data whenever possible, using macros to automate operations, and saving spreadsheet setups to reuse in the future. It also means using the LotusWorks spreadsheet functions to help you automate calculations.

A spreadsheet @function is a small prerecorded program that performs a complex mathematical formula on spreadsheet data when you enter the name of the function into a spreadsheet and order LotusWorks to recalculate the spreadsheet. Spreadsheet @functions require only that you provide the data and, in some cases, that you specify parameters telling how the formulas are to be applied. The LotusWorks spreadsheet @functions can automate a wide range of mathematical tasks, such as:

**Date and Time Calculations.** The date and time @functions can enter the current date and time, calculate the time between specified dates and/or times, and perform date and time projections.

**Financial Calculations.** The financial @functions can automate many common financial calculations, including three forms of depreciation, internal rate of return for a series of cash flows, net present value of a series of future cash flows, future value of a series of equal payments, the amount of the periodic payment needed to pay off a loan, present value of a series of equal payments, the number of payment periods of an investment, the number of compounding periods necessary for an investment to grow to a specified future value, and the interest rate necessary for an investment to grow to a specified future value.

**Logical Calculations.** The logical @functions evaluate conditions in data as either true or false. This is useful for performing conditional operations. For example, you can tell LotusWorks to perform an operation if specified data meets a particular stated condition but to perform a different operation or not perform an operation at all if the data does not meet the stated condition.

**Mathematical Calculations.** Mathematical @functions tell LotusWorks to perform mathematical and trigonometric operations, such as calculating the sum, average (mean), square root, or variance of a set of numbers.

**Special @Functions.** Special @functions enable you to look up numbers and strings of characters in spreadsheets and to obtain information about spreadsheets, such as the contents of a cell, the number of columns or rows in a range, and whether the value in a particular cell is missing or matches a specified condition.

**Statistical @Functions.** The LotusWorks statistical @functions tell Lotus-Works to perform statistical operations on a set of numbers, such as calculating the average (mean), square root, or variance.

**String @Functions.** String @functions perform operations on and provide information about strings of text in cells of spreadsheets. The string @functions can tell you if one string of characters is an exact match for another string of characters, can find one string of characters within another string, and can tell you the number of characters in a string. They can also convert character data to all uppercase or all lowercase; convert the first character of each word in a string to uppercase; remove leading or trailing spaces from a string of characters; replace characters in one string with characters in another; and perform other operations on strings.

## When to Use a Spreadsheet

When you are working with numbers, the question arises whether to use the Spreadsheet or Database service. You can store data and perform certain kinds of math operations with either service. Generally the Database service is best if you can perform math operations on all records (rows) in a field at the same time or if you need to merge print numeric data interspersed with text. The Spreadsheet service is best if you need to perform math operations on individual cells (the intersections of columns and rows), create a graph, or use one of the special spreadsheet @functions.

Specifically, use a spreadsheet if:

- You need to address math calculations to individual cells or a group of cells within a row or column

- You need to perform math calculations in both horizontal and vertical directions

- You need to use one of the special spreadsheet @functions

- You need to create a graph

- You do not need to merge print the numeric data

## Spreadsheet Terms

Before you begin using the Spreadsheet service, it is helpful to know a few special spreadsheet terms.

**Spreadsheet.** Each LotusWorks spreadsheet is organized into columns and rows. You can have up to 256 columns or 8,192 rows in each spreadsheet. Each column is identified by a letter (A, B, C, . . . Z, AA, AB, AC, . . . AZ, BA, BB, BC. . . BZ, and so on up to columns IT, IU, and IV). Each row is identified by a number from 1 to 8192. Thus, a LotusWorks spreadsheet is huge, and you can see only a small part of it on the computer screen at any one time.

**Cell.** At the intersection of each column and row is a cell. Cells hold the data, labels, and formulas for spreadsheets. Each cell can hold a single number, label, or formula.

**Cell Address.** Each cell is identified by a unique cell address made up of the column identifier and row identifier where the cell is located. Thus, cell A1 is located at the intersection of column A and row 1; cell B3 is located at the intersection of column B and row 3; and cell AA123 is located at the intersection of column AA and row 123. Theoretically, it is possible (although not practical) to have data in over 2 million cells in a spreadsheet.

**Range.** A range is a rectangular block of one or more adjoining cells identified for subsequent action. The action can be to format, copy, or move the cells, incorporate them into a formula, recalculate them, print them in a report, incorporate them into a graph, or perform some other activity.

Each range is identified by a *range address*. The range address is made up of the cell address of the top-left cell in the rectangle followed by two periods and the cell address of the bottom-right cell. For example, the range address A1..C3 includes all the cells from A1 at the top left to C3 at the bottom right.

Once you have designated a range on which to perform actions, you can give the range a name (for example, *Totals* or *Graph1*). Naming ranges provides an easy way to refer to them in commands and formulas and to keep track of special-purpose ranges within large spreadsheets.

You may designate numerous ranges within a single spreadsheet if it suits your purpose. For example, you could have certain ranges that print as tables, some that generate graphs, and some that are used for holding data and interim calculations that do not appear in reports at all.

**Cell Pointer.** The cell pointer in the Spreadsheet service is similar to the screen cursor in other LotusWorks services. When you move the pointer to a cell in a spreadsheet, LotusWorks highlights the entire cell. You may then enter data, a label, or a formula into the cell. When you move into Edit mode, the cell pointer changes into a blinking cursor and moves up to the edit line immediately below the menu bar. Thus, the cell pointer shows the data entry point in cells, and the cursor shows the data entry position on the edit line.

**Label.** A label is a string of text entered into a cell. Labels are used to identify columns and rows, create titles, and provide explanation in spreadsheets.

**Formula.** A spreadsheet formula is a mathematical expression that calculates a data value for a cell. (Databases may also have formulas.) Spreadsheet formulas may be up to 254 characters long and may contain data values, cell addresses, range addresses, range names, @functions, and operators.

Three types of formula are possible in LotusWorks spreadsheets:

- **Numeric.** A numeric formula calculates a numeric cell value using numbers (or cells containing numbers) and arithmetic operators. For example, the formula +C2+2 is a numeric formula when the data in cell C2 is numeric. It adds 2 to the value in cell C2. The formula +C2*2 multiplies the value in cell C2 by 2, and the formula +C2/2 divides the value in cell C2 by 2. Numeric formulas are the most common formulas in business spreadsheets.

- **String.** A string formula is a formula that connects (concatenates) one string of text to another. It calculates a text cell value using spreadsheet labels or text enclosed within " " (double quotation marks) and the concatenation operator (&). For example, the formula +"Your account is "&C2 adds the text data in cell C2 to the phrase "Your account is." If the text in cell C2 is the word "current," the resulting sentence is **Your account is current.** If the text in cell C2 is the word "overdue," the resulting sentence is **Your account is overdue.** String formulas are not as common as numeric formulas, but they are extremely useful in appropriate situations.

- **Logical.** A logical formula evaluates a mathematical statement and decides whether the statement is true or false. If the statement is true, LotusWorks produces a value of 1 in the cell; if the statement is false, LotusWorks produces a value of 0 in the cell. For example, the formula +C2 >=100 results in 1 (true) if the value in cell C2 is greater than or equal to 100; otherwise the formula results in 0 (false). The formula

+ORDERS<1000 results in 1 (true) if the value in the range named ORDERS is less than 1,000; otherwise it results in 0 (false).

Logical formulas are most useful for testing whether data values in a spreadsheet meet specified conditions. Logical formulas must include at least one logical operator and may include text data, numbers, cell or range addresses, cell or range names, @functions, and other formulas.

**Operator.** An operator is a symbol used between values in a formula that tells LotusWorks what mathematical operation to perform on the values. Three types of operators are possible in LotusWorks spreadsheets:

- **Arithmetic.** Arithmetic operators tell LotusWorks to perform an arithmetic operation on numeric data. Examples are + (add), – (subtract), * (multiply), and \ (divide).

- **String.** There is one string operator: & (concatenate). It joins two cell labels or text strings.

- **Logical.** Logical operators tell LotusWorks to compare two numbers or text strings and return a logical result. Examples are = (equals), <> (not equal to), > (greater than), < (less than), >= (greater than or equal to), <= (less than or equal to), #AND#, #OR#, and #NOT#.

For a more complete explanation of spreadsheet operators, see "Operators" later in this chapter.

**@Function.** An @function (pronounced "at-function") is a small built-in LotusWorks program that automatically performs a particular type of calculation when included in a formula. There are 75 spreadsheet @functions in LotusWorks. An @-sign must always precede the function name. Most @functions also require you to specify one or more parameters that tell the @function what data to include in the calculation. For example, the expression @sum(C2..C10) calculates the sum of the values in cells C2 through C10. The expression @avg(C2..C10) calculates the average (mean) of the values in cells C2 through C10.

**Current Spreadsheet.** The current spreadsheet is the spreadsheet that is currently visible on the screen, as contrasted with other spreadsheets that may be visible in other windows or may be stored on disk.

**Window.** A window is the portion of a spreadsheet that can be viewed on the screen. You can split the screen window vertically or horizontally to view two portions of the same spreadsheet and scroll them separately or together.

# Designing Spreadsheets

Although you can always revise a spreadsheet after it has been created, you save time in the long run by planning the design of your spreadsheet before you start entering data. In the beginning, you may find it helpful to sketch the spreadsheet grid on a sheet of paper before you start building the spreadsheet on the computer. Be sure to sketch in the titles, column and row labels, and spacing among elements you want to use.

In most cases you should allow three or four rows at the top of the spreadsheet for a title and column labels and allow at least one column at the left for row labels.

You should also give some thought to what the rows and columns should represent. Although you can assign data either way, it is customary (and therefore clearer to your readers) to have the columns represent the subjects being studied, and the columns represent the characteristics about the subjects that are being analyzed. For instance, if you are analyzing time-series data, the columns

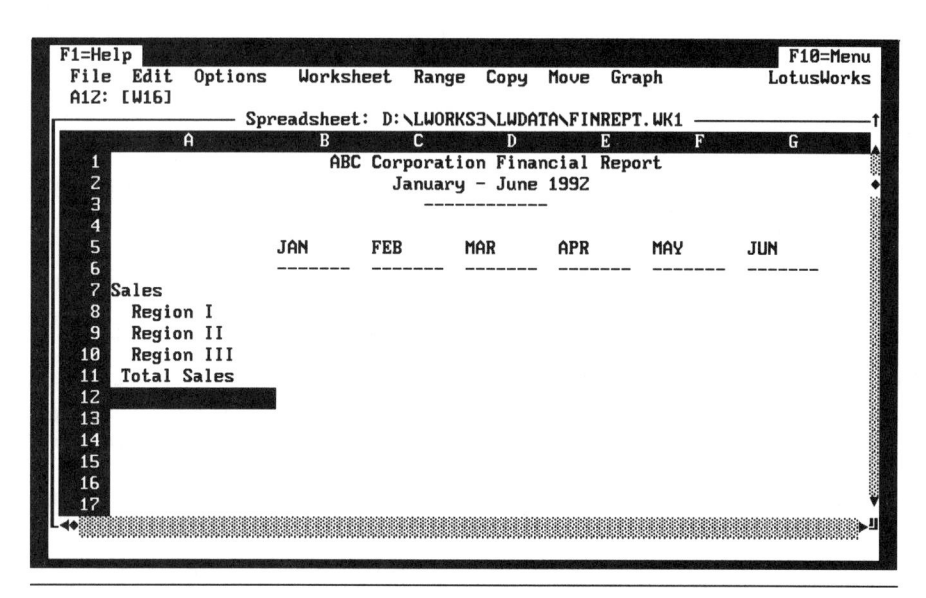

**FIGURE 5.1:** Allow space in your spreadsheet for titles, column and row labels, and spacing.

should represent the time periods (years, quarters, months, etc.), and the rows should represent the observations (respondents, subjects, accounts, etc.).

Another design decision is whether to have one or several grids of data on the same spreadsheet. Most spreadsheets contain a single grid of data, but it is possible to have multiple grids separated from each other on the same large spreadsheet. It makes sense to do so if the grids share common elements with each other, if they are mathematically linked, if they depend on each other in a logical way, or if they need to be printed together. When LotusWorks recalculates the large spreadsheet, it recalculates all the data within it. Even if you have several small spreadsheet grids, it is possible to print each separately by defining a group of cells (a "range") containing the spreadsheet and then printing the range. (See the previous section for a definition of a range.)

## Setting Up and Saving Spreadsheets

Spreadsheets can be simple or complex. You'll probably do best to build relatively simple spreadsheets for your first few efforts, then add refinements as you gain proficiency. You'll get the hang of simple spreadsheets right away.

The following are general steps in building a finished spreadsheet:

1. Open the Spreadsheet service to a blank spreadsheet. Save the spreadsheet after each of the following steps.
2. Create a title.
3. Create headings (labels) for the spreadsheet columns and rows.
4. Enter data into cells.
5. Create formulas for the appropriate cells. Manually check the results of each formula for accuracy as you create it and revise the formula if necessary.
6. Adjust the column widths and number formats, if necessary.
7. Define and name groups of cells (ranges) that are to be printed as reports or graphs.
8. Test print the spreadsheet, check the appearance and math, and revise if necessary.
9. Save the finished spreadsheet.

As you gain proficiency in building spreadsheets for your own particular needs, you may prefer to build some spreadsheets in sections or in different orders, but this is a good way to proceed while you're getting started.

## Building a Practice Spreadsheet

Here is a spreadsheet you can build quickly to get some practice. The finished spreadsheet looks like this:

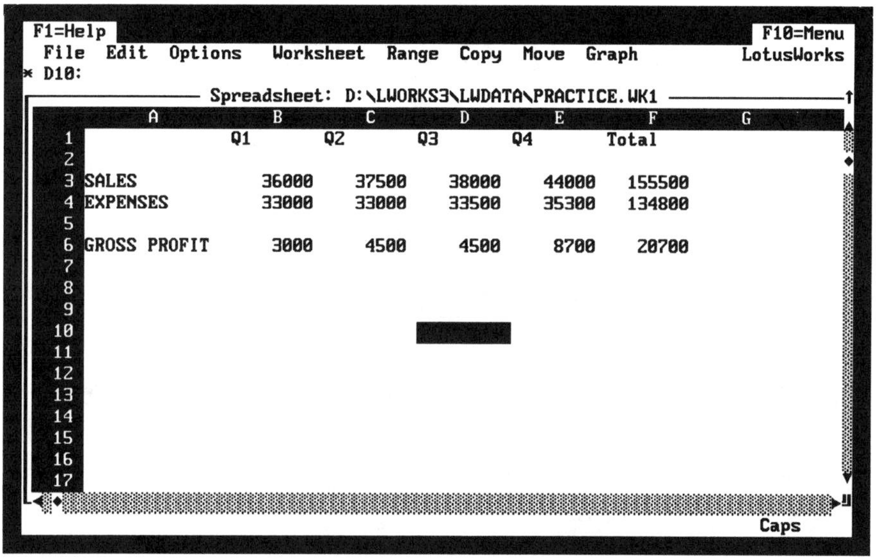

**FIGURE 5.2:** A practice spreadsheet

Select the Spreadsheet service and, when the blank, untitled spreadsheet appears on the screen, follow these steps:

1. Enter the labels for the columns. Move the cell pointer to cell B1, type *Q1*, press the Right Arrow key, type *Q2*, press the Right Arrow key, type *Q3*, press the Right Arrow key, type *Q4*, press the Right Arrow key, type *Total* and press Enter.

2. Enter the labels for the rows. Move the cell pointer to cell A3, type *SALES*, press the Down Arrow key, type *EXPENSES*, press the Down Arrow key twice, type *GROSS PROFIT*, and press Enter.

3. Widen column A to 14 spaces, so that the label GROSS PROFIT fits without running over into the next column. Press Alt+W, press Tab, press the Right Arrow key five times or type *14*, press Tab, and press Enter.

4. Enter a formula to subtract EXPENSES from SALES to get GROSS PROFIT in column B. Move the cell pointer to cell B6, type *+B3–B4* and press Enter.

5. Copy the formula from cell B6 to the range of cells C6..E6. Press F10, C, Tab; enter *c6..e6*; press Tab, and press Enter. When you copy the formula, it automatically adjusts to the relative position of each new cell in the range.

6. Enter a formula to sum the sales to get a total for row 3. Move the cell pointer to cell F3, type *@SUM(B3..E3)* and press Enter.

7. Copy the formula from cell F3 to cells F4 and F6. Press F4, press Alt+C, move the cell pointer to cell F4 and press Alt+P. Move the cell pointer to cell F6 and press Alt+P again.

At this point, the spreadsheet is ready for some data. It looks like this:

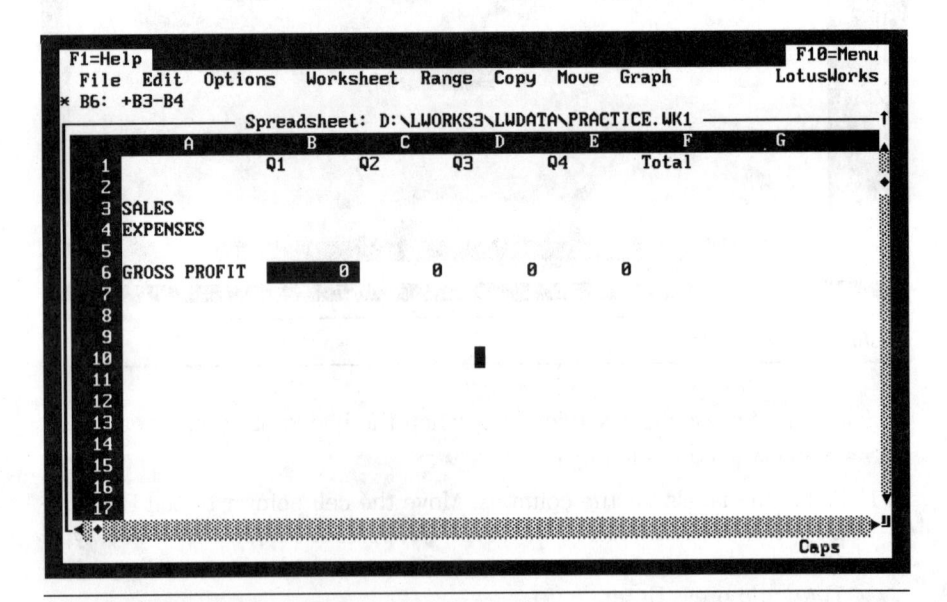

**FIGURE 5.3:** The practice spreadsheet with labels and formulas entered

If you enter data into cells B3..E4, the spreadsheet automatically calculates the GROSS PROFIT for each quarter. Try entering different data values in cells B3..E4 and see what happens.

To save the practice spreadsheet to disk, press Alt+S; when the File Save dialog box appears, type *PRACTICE* in the File text box and select Save. LotusWorks saves the spreadsheet to disk with the name PRACTICE.WK1. To confirm this, you can select File Retrieve and press the Down Arrow key to locate the spreadsheet in alphabetical order.

## Entering Text and Numbers into Cells

Each cell in a spreadsheet can hold one entry: a text label, number, or formula. A text label usually contains one or more words but can also contain numbers and other symbols. To enter data into a cell, move the cell pointer to highlight the desired cell, then type the data and press Enter.

The first character you enter tells LotusWorks the type of data. Entering a numeral or one of the symbols + − ( @ signals a number or formula. Entering any other character signals a text label.

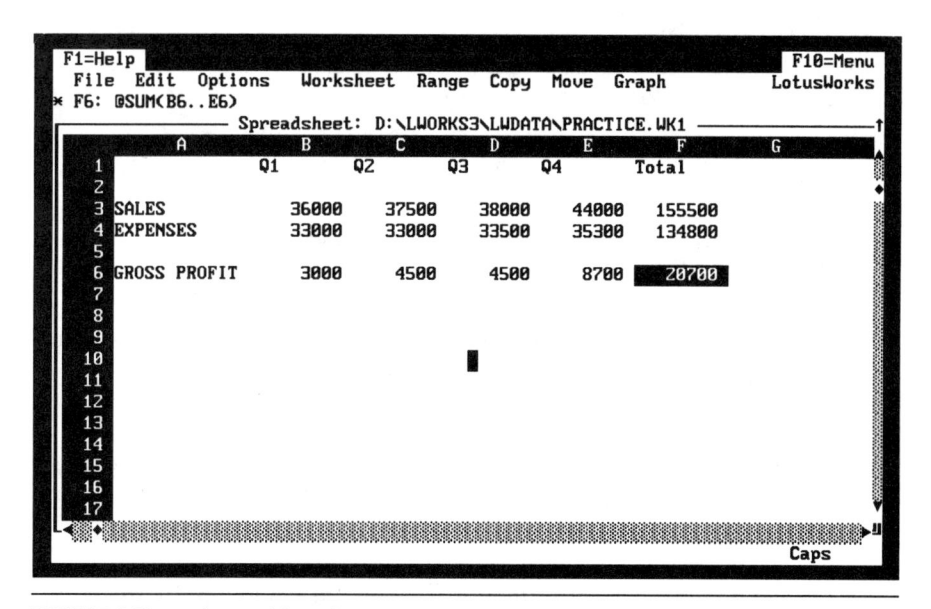

**FIGURE 5.4:** The practice spreadsheet with sample data entered

When you enter numbers, enter the decimal points (if any) but do not enter any commas. LotusWorks inserts the commas automatically when you select an appropriate number format.

When the first character signals a text label, LotusWorks automatically treats the data as text and inserts an apostrophe before the first character. This is the default label-prefix; it aligns the label to the left side of the cell. If you prefer to align the label to the right, enter a double quotation mark (") before you begin entering the label. If you prefer to align the label to the center of the cell, enter a circumflex (^) before you begin entering the label.

If you wish to begin a label with a numeral (such as 1992) or one of the other characters that otherwise signals a number or formula (such as +, −, (, or @), you have to tell LotusWorks to treat the characters as a text label rather than a number or formula. To do so, simply enter an apostrophe, double quotation mark, or circumflex before you begin entering the label.

There is a special procedure for entering dates and times that are to be used in calculations. For instructions, see "Entering Dates and Times" later in this chapter.

> NOTE: If a row of asterisks appears in a cell, the cell is too narrow for the number of digits. To display the digits, adjust the column width to accommodate the entire data value. See "Adjusting Column Widths" later in this chapter for instructions.

## Selecting Cells and Ranges for Further Action

Many operations in the Spreadsheet service use the same basic, two-step procedure: first, you specify a target cell or range of cells, and then you select a command to act on the target range. You will use this simple two-step procedure over and over.

To select a single target cell for further action, click the mouse on the cell or move the cell pointer to the cell and press F4. LotusWorks highlights the cell. The next command you select is applied to the selected cell.

To select a target range with a mouse, click on the top-left cell of the range, hold down the mouse button, and drag the mouse down and to the right until the entire range is highlighted, then release the mouse button. The range remains highlighted. To select a target range with the keyboard, move the cursor to the top-left cell of the range, press F4, and then use the Right and Down Arrow keys to move the cell pointer down and to the right until the entire range is highlighted. The next command you select is applied to the selected range.

## Editing Data

Everybody makes data entry mistakes. Sooner or later you will, too. When you need to correct or change the data in a cell, there are three ways to do it.

### To edit as you enter data:

Simply press the Backspace key to erase back to the point where you want to change the data, then enter the replacement data and press Enter.

### To replace data already in a cell:

Move the cell pointer to the cell containing the data to be replaced, then simply type the replacement data and press Enter. LotusWorks erases the previous entry and retains the replacement entry.

### To edit data already in a cell:

1. Select the cell containing the data to be replaced.
2. Turn on EDIT mode (press F2 or double-click the mouse on the cell).
3. Move the cursor to the point on the edit line where you want to change the data. (Press the arrow keys.)
4. Press Delete or Backspace to delete the text to be changed, if appropriate.
5. Enter the replacement text, if appropriate.
6. Press Enter to store the edited data and exit from Edit mode.

## Erasing the Contents of a Cell or Range

Just as you may need to edit data from time to time, you may also need to erase the entire contents of a cell or range. The simplest way to do this is first to select the cell or range (see the previous section) and then press Alt+B. The following dialog box appears:

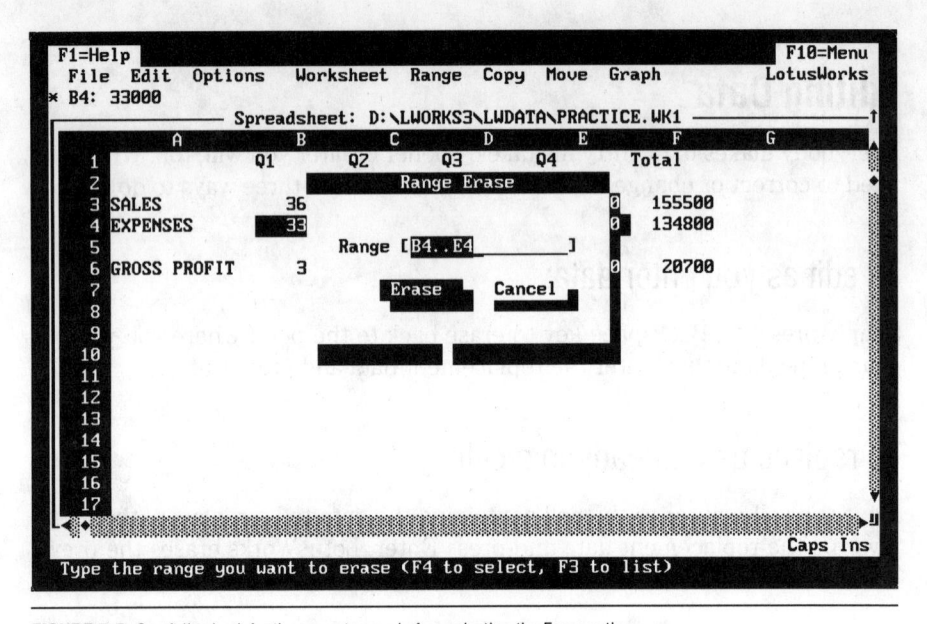

**FIGURE 5.5:** Carefully check for the correct range before selecting the Erase option.

Carefully check for the correct range setting and then select Erase. If you prefer to use the menu, select the cell or range, then select Range Erase.

Either way you initiate it, this procedure completely erases the cell's contents, whether the cell contains a number, label, or formula.

> CAUTION: Be careful when you erase data from a cell or range! Once data is erased from a spreadsheet, it is destroyed and cannot be recovered.

## Creating, Viewing, and Deleting Range Names

For a lot of reasons, it's a good idea to give names to ranges that are used in formulas. It not only provides an easy way to refer to ranges in commands and formulas, it's an accurate way. If you add columns or rows to a spreadsheet, LotusWorks automatically adjusts the range within each range name to accommodate the changes. Descriptive range names make it is easier to identify and remember special-purpose ranges than if you simply use the cell references. And typing mistakes are easier to detect in range names than in ranges identified by cell references.

To give a name to a range of cells, first use the mouse or F4 key and arrow keys to select the desired range. Next, select Range Name Create. The following dialog box appears:

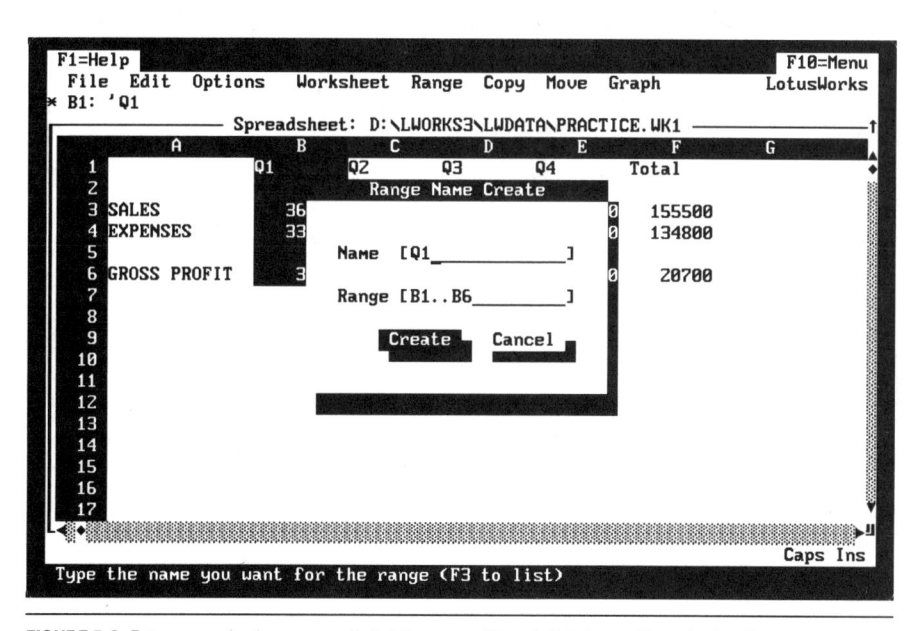

**FIGURE 5.6:** Enter a name for the range, verify that the range address is listed correctly, and select Create.

Enter a name for the range, check to be sure that the range address is listed correctly, and select Create.

To view the range names for a spreadsheet from anywhere in the spreadsheet select Range Name Create and press the F3 key. A dialog box appears listing the names and addresses of all ranges that have been declared for the spreadsheet.

To delete a range name, select Range Name Delete. The following dialog box appears:

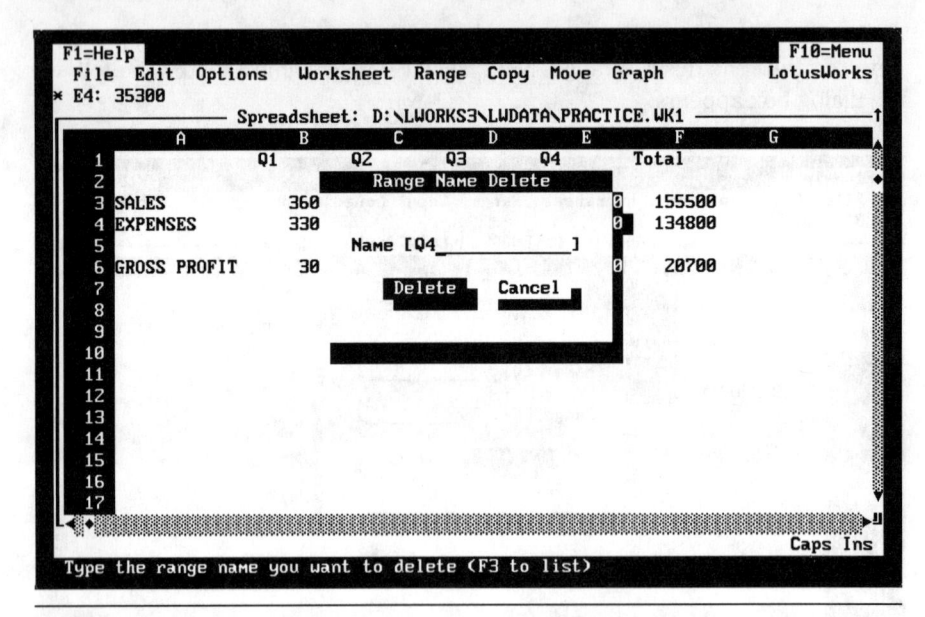

**FIGURE 5.7:** Enter or select the range name to be deleted and select Delete.

You may enter the range name to be deleted (or press F3 and select it from a list box) and select Delete. LotusWorks deletes the range name immediately, without any further instructions. If you accidentally delete a range name by mistake, you can undo the mistake by simply recreating the range name.

## Changing Number Formats

Often it is desirable to display numbers in a different format from the general format that is the LotusWorks default. For instance, you may need to change the number of decimal places displayed, show a dollar sign or other currency symbol, display a date, or display numbers expressed in percentages or scientific (E) notation. LotusWorks allows you to display numbers in the following formats:

### LotusWorks Number Formats

NOTE: Some LotusWorks formats require you to specify the number of decimal places to be displayed. In the following table, these formats are followed by the numeral two in brackets [2], to show how the format would appear if 2 decimal places were specified.

| Format | Displays 1234.567 as | Displays −1234.567 as |
| --- | --- | --- |
| Fixed, [2] | 1234.57 | −1234.57 |
| Scientific | 1.23E+03 | −1.23E+03 |
| Currency,[2] | $1234.57 | ($1234.57) |
| , (comma),[2] | 1,234.57 | (1,234.57) |
| Percent,[2] | 123456.70% | −123456.70% |
| Date/Time | 18-May-03 (or other format) | N./A. |
| General [2] | 1234.57 | −1234.57 |
| +/− | ++++++++++++++++++++ | ------------------------- |
| Hidden | | |
| Text (displays the underlying formula, if any) | +C3−C2 | +C3−C2 |

When you change a number format, only the appearance of the number changes; the underlying numerical value of the data stored in the spreadsheet does not change. (LotusWorks stores numbers and performs numerical calculations to 15 significant figures.)

The *Fixed* format displays numbers without thousands separators and allows you to specify up to 15 decimal places. It displays a minus sign for negative values and a leading zero for decimal values.

The *Scientific* format displays numbers in E notation (numbers in powers of 10), with an exponent from −99 to +99 and up to 15 decimal places. When the number of digits to the right of the decimal point exceeds the column width, LotusWorks rounds the number.

The *Currency* format displays numbers with a currency sign and thousands separators and allows you to specify up to 15 decimal places. It displays parentheses or a minus sign for negative numbers and a leading zero for decimal values. (See the note at the end of this section on changing the default currency symbol.)

The , *(comma)* format displays numbers with thousands separators, parentheses for negative values, and a leading zero for decimal values. It allows you to specify up to 15 decimal places. (See the note at the end of this section on changing the default style of numerical punctuation.)

The *Percent* format displays numbers multiplied by 100, with a percent sign, up to 15 decimal places, and a leading zero for decimal percentages.

The *Date/Time* format option displays a popup box from which you can select from several date and time formats.

> **IMPORTANT:** To use the date and time formats, you must enter dates and times with @functions rather than as text. Dates must be entered using the @DATE() or a related @function, and times must be entered using the @TIME() or a related @function. (See "Entering Dates and Times" later in this chapter.)

The date and time formats are as follows:

| Format | Example |
|---|---|
| DD-MMM-YY | 01-Aug-92 |
| DD-MMM | 01-Aug |
| MMM-YY | Aug-92 |
| Long Int'l Date* | 08/01/92 |
| Short Int'l Date* | 08/01 |
| HH:MM:SS (AM/PM) | 11:35:43 PM |
| HH:MM (AM/PM) | 11:35 PM |
| Long Int'l Time* | 23:35:43 |
| Short Int'l Time* | 23:35 |

*See the note at the end of this section on changing the default formats for International dates and times.

The *General* format displays numbers with no thousands separators and no trailing zeros to the right of the decimal point. When the number of digits to the right of the decimal point exceeds the column width, LotusWorks truncates the number.

The *+/−* format displays numbers as a series of plus or minus signs or a period. The number of signs displayed equals the entry's value truncated to the nearest whole number (for instance, 5.75 appears as five plus signs; −5.75 appears as five minus signs). Numbers between −1 and +1 appear as a single decimal point or period.

The *Hidden* format turns off the display of numbers. Although the hidden numbers do not appear on the screen or in printed reports, the data remains in the spreadsheet and apperars on the edit line. The data is still used in any formulas based on the hidden cells, and the display can be restored ("unhidden") if you wish. This format is useful for sensitive information, such as salaries, that is needed for calculations but that you may not want to have appear in printed reports.

The *Text* format displays a cell's formula, if there is one, or the number or label, if there is no formula.

To change a number format, follow these steps:

1. Select a cell or range of cells to receive the new format.
2. Select Range Format. The following dialog box appears:

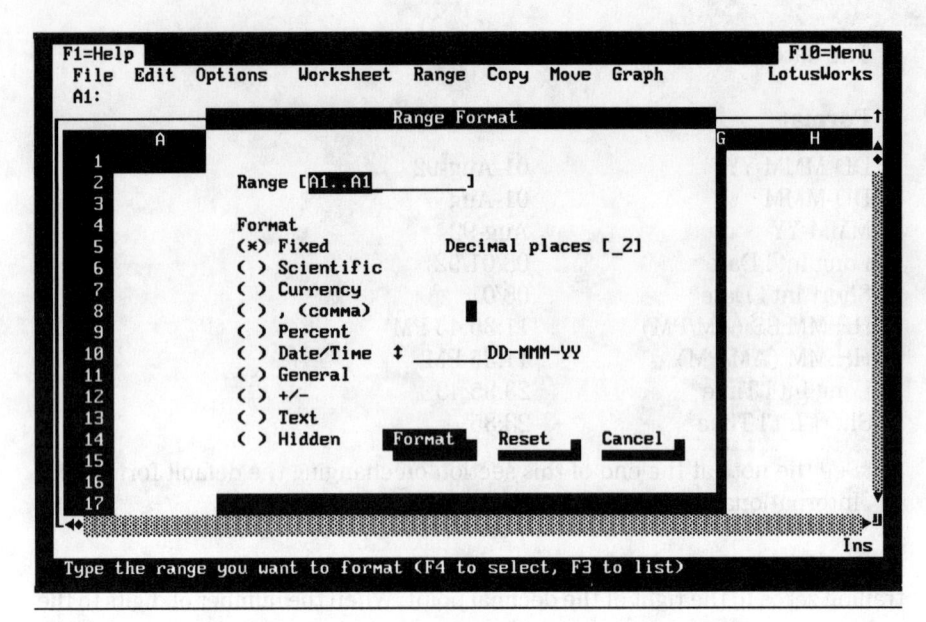

```
F1=Help                                                              F10=Menu
 File  Edit  Options    Worksheet   Range  Copy  Move  Graph         LotusWorks
 A1:
                                Range Format
            A                                                    G          H
 1
 2          Range [A1..A1        ]
 3
 4          Format
 5          (*) Fixed              Decimal places [_2]
 6          ( ) Scientific
 7          ( ) Currency
 8          ( ) , (comma)
 9          ( ) Percent
10          ( ) Date/Time  ‡         DD-MMM-YY
11          ( ) General
12          ( ) +/-
13          ( ) Text
14          ( ) Hidden      Format    Reset    Cancel
15
16
17
                                                                            Ins
 Type the range you want to format (F4 to select, F3 to list)
```

**FIGURE 5.8:** Select the desired format and enter the number of desired decimal places, if appropriate.

3. Select the desired number format. If you select Fixed, Currency, Comma, Percent, or General, you must also enter the number of decimal places to display.

   If you select Date/Time, a popup box appears, and you must also select a specific format within that category.

4. Select Accept.

> NOTE: You can change the default currency symbol, style of numerical punctuation, and formats for International dates and times by using the Worksheet Global Default command. See Chapter 15 of the LotusWorks User's Guide for details.

## Adjusting Column Widths

If a row of asterisks appears in a cell, it means that the column is too narrow to display all the digits in the cell's data value. To see the data, you must widen the column. Conversely, if you need to fit more columns on a printed page, it may be necessary to make all the columns as narrow as possible.

To change the width of one or more adjacent columns:

1. Select the desired range that includes at least one cell in each of the columns you wish to change.

2. Press Alt+W or select Worksheet Column Width. The following dialog box appears:

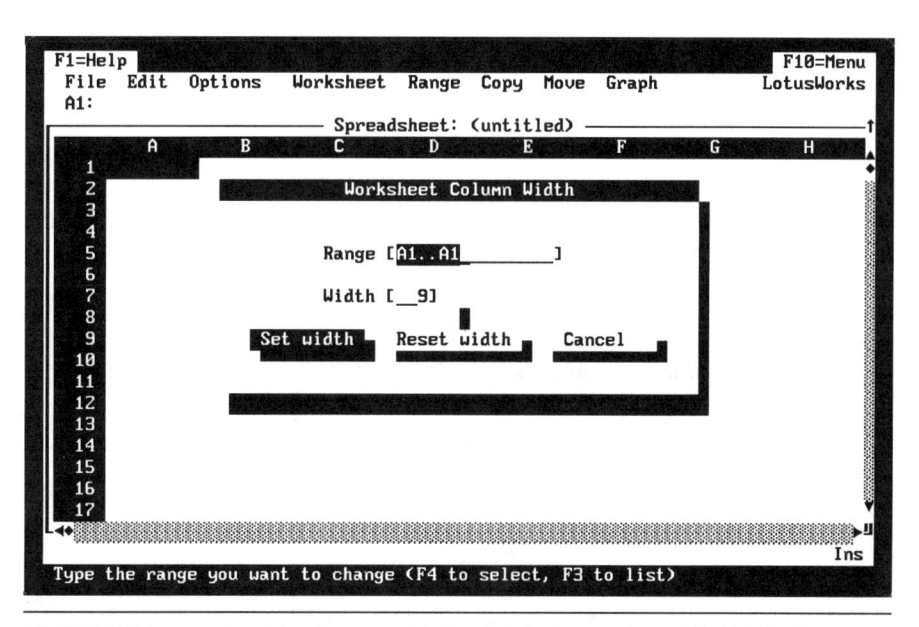

**FIGURE 5.9:** Enter the number of characters you want for the selected column or columns in the Width text box or press the Left and Right Arrow keys to get the desired width.

3. Enter the number of characters you want for the selected column or columns in the Width text box. Alternatively, you may press Tab and then use the Right and Left Arrow keys to adjust the selected columns to the desired width.

4. Select Accept. LotusWorks changes the column width to the number of characters you specified.

NOTE: If you want to adjust all remaining columns in a spreadsheet to the same width, select Worksheet Global Column width and use the Right and Left Arrow keys to set the desired width. LotusWorks adjusts all the columns to the specified setting except those previously set with Worksheet Column width.

## Inserting Rows and Columns

As you build spreadsheets, it is sometime useful to add one or more new columns or rows between existing ones. When you do so, LotusWorks moves the existing data to make room for the new columns or rows.

To insert columns or rows:

1. Move the cell pointer to a cell where you want to insert rows or columns.
2. Press Alt+I or select Worksheet Insert. The following dialog box appears:

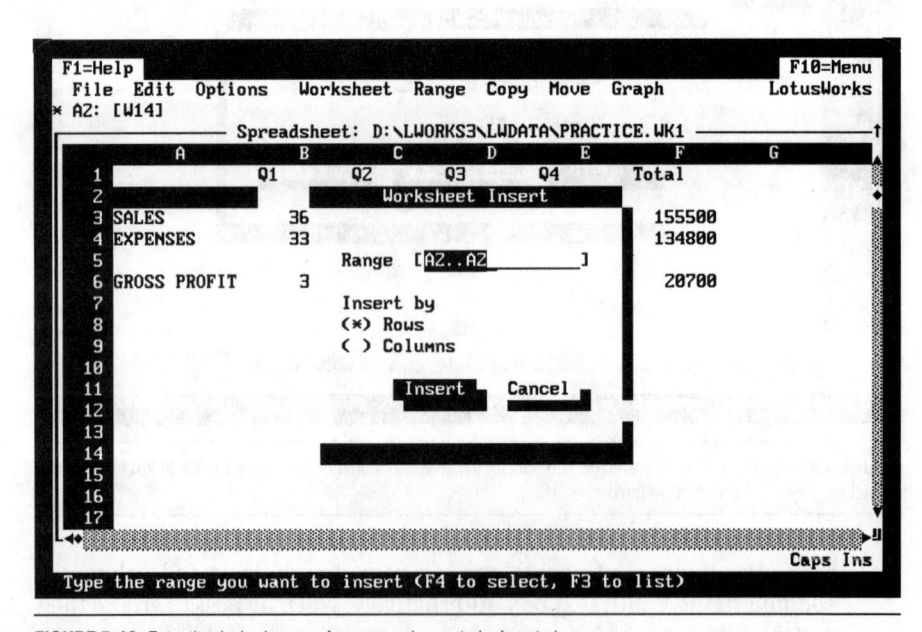

**FIGURE 5.10:** Enter the desired range of rows or columns to be inserted.

Saving Work with Numbers **219**

3. Enter the desired range of rows or columns to be inserted. For example, if you wish to add three rows at cell C3, enter C3..C5. If you wish to add three columns at cell C3, enter C3..E3. If you wish to add one row or column, simply enter the cell address where you want the row or column to be inserted.
4. Select either Rows or Columns to indicate which you wish to insert.
5. Select Insert. LotusWorks inserts the new, empty rows or columns at the first cell address and moves all the other rows down and columns to the right to make room for the new ones.

## Deleting Rows and Columns

Just as you sometimes need to insert blank rows or columns in spreadsheets, sometimes you need to delete one or more rows or columns. Here are the steps:

1. Select a range containing one or more cells in each row or column that you wish to delete.
2. Select Worksheet Delete. The following dialog box appears:

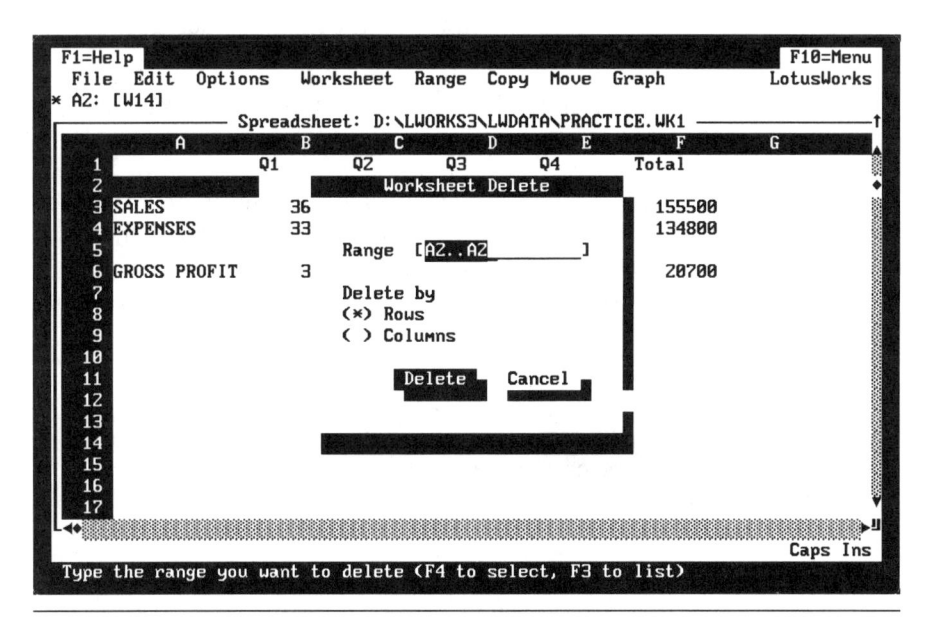

**FIGURE 5.11:** The range you have selected appears in the text box.

3. Select either Rows or Columns.

4. Select Delete. LotusWorks deletes the specified rows or columns (including any data they contain) and moves the rows below or the columns to the right to take their place.

## Copying Data

The copy feature is one of the most important capabilities of LotusWorks spreadsheets. Not only can you use it to copy data, labels, and formulas from cell to cell and range to range, but when LotusWorks copies a formula, it automatically adjusts the cell addresses in the formula to reflect the formula's new location. You do not have to rewrite the formula. As you will see, this can save a tremendous amount of work in setting up spreadsheets.

There are two ways to copy with LotusWorks:

1. The Copy option copies data directly from one location to another in the same spreadsheet.

2. The Edit Copy option copies data to the Clipboard, from which it can be pasted over and over to other locations in the same spreadsheet or a different one.

Ordinarily the Edit Copy option is quicker, easier, and more versatile, but you should know how to use both procedures.

With either procedure, if you tell LotusWorks to copy the contents of a cell to a range of cells, LotusWorks copies the contents into *every* cell in the destination range. If you tell LotusWorks to copy the contents of a range to a single cell, LotusWorks copies the contents into the destination cell plus enough adjoining cells to complete the range.

> CAUTION: If any cells in the destination range contain data, the data will be destroyed! The Copy and Edit Copy commands write the copied data over any preexisting data in the destination range.

## The Copy Option

To use the Copy option:

1. Select the cell or range whose contents you want to copy. See "Selecting Cells and Ranges for Further Action" earlier in this chapter.

2. Select Copy. The following dialog box appears:

```
F1=Help                                                         F10=Menu
  File  Edit  Options   Worksheet   Range  Copy  Move  Graph    LotusWorks
* F3: [W9] @SUM(B3..E3)
────────────── Spreadsheet: D:\LWORKS3\LWDATA\PRACTICE.WK1 ──────────────
          A          B          C          D         E        F         G
   1                 Q1         Q2         Q3        Q4       Total
   2                          Copy
   3  SALES                                                   155500
   4  EXPENSES                                                134800
   5
   6  GROSS PROFIT         From range [F3..F3         ]        20700
   7
   8                       To range   [F6             ]
   9
  10                           Copy      Cancel
  11
  12
  13
  14
  15
  16
  17
                                                              Caps Ins
Type the range you want to copy to (F4 to select, F3 to list)
```

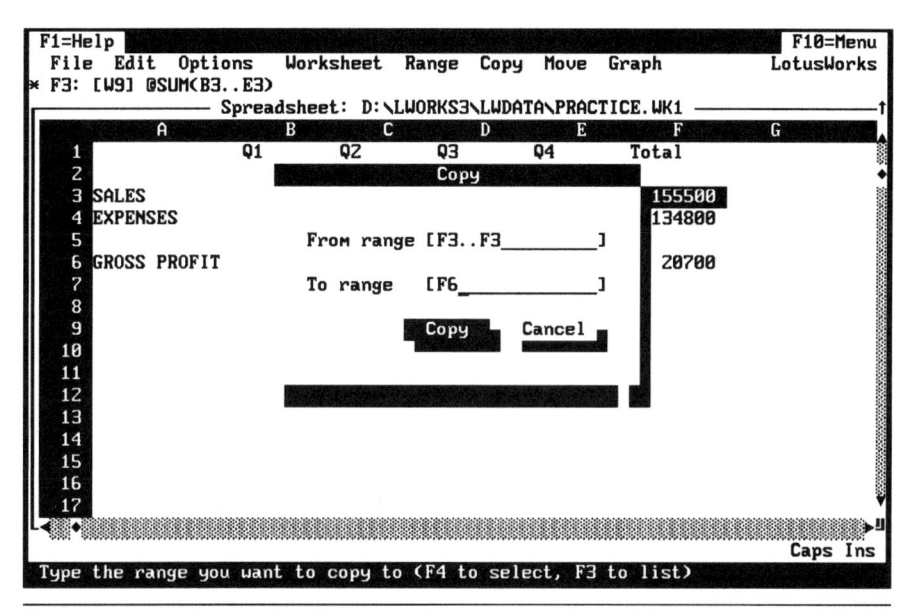

**FIGURE 5.12:** Specify the destination for the copied data in the To range text box.

3. The *From* range text box contains the address of the cell or range you selected. If necessary, you may specify a different cell or range address.

> **NOTE:** To select a different range, press F4 to return to the spreadsheet, use the arrow keys to highlight the desired range, and then press Enter to return to the dialog box. LotusWorks displays the range you selected.

4. Enter the address of the destination cell or range in the *To* range text box.

5. Select Copy. LotusWorks copies the data in the *From* range to the *To* range.

### The Edit Copy Option

To use the Edit Copy option:

1. Select the cell or range whose contents you want to copy.
2. Press Alt+C or select Edit Copy. (No dialog box appears.)
3. Move the cell pointer to the top left corner of the desired destination range.
4. Press Alt+P or select Edit Paste to deposit the copied text in the destination range.

## Moving Data

Moving data is similar to copying it, except that the data is actually moved from one location to another in the spreadsheet.

As in copying data, there are two ways to move data:

- The Move option moves data directly from one location to another in the same spreadsheet.
- The Edit Cut option cuts data to the Clipboard and deletes it from the original location. From the Clipboard, the data can be pasted to other locations in the same spreadsheet or to a different spreadsheet.

If you tell LotusWorks to move the contents of a cell or range to another cell or range, LotusWorks moves the contents into the destination cell or range and deletes the data from the original cell or range. If you tell LotusWorks to move the contents of a range to single cell, LotusWorks moves the contents into the destination cell plus enough adjoining cells to complete the range.

### The Move Option

To use the Move option:

1. Select the cell or range whose contents you want to move. See "Selecting Cells and Ranges for Further Action" earlier in this chapter.
2. Select Move. The following dialog box appears:

Saving Work with Numbers **223**

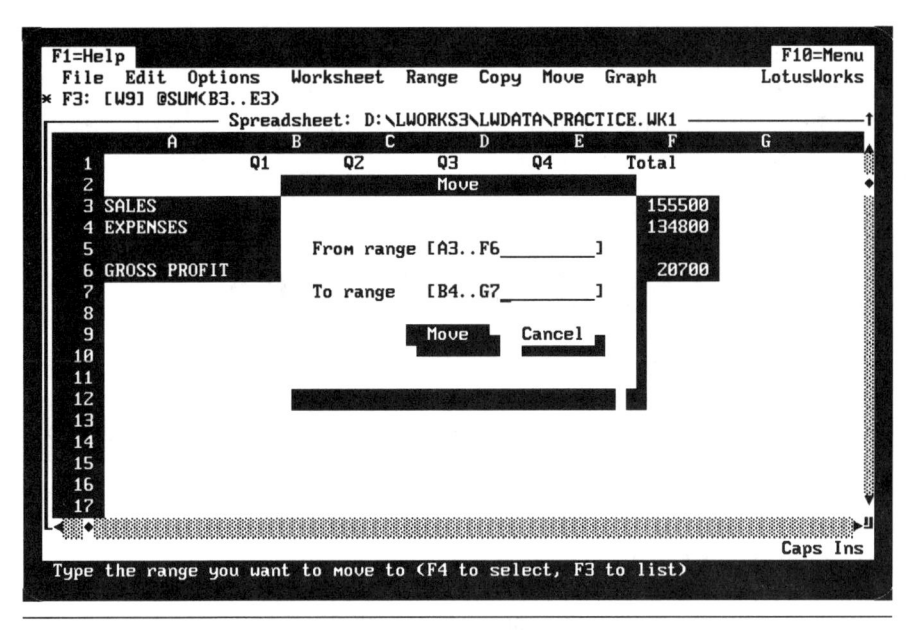

**FIGURE 5.13:** Specify the destination for the moved data in the To range text box.

3. The *From* range text box contains the address of the cell or range you selected. You may specify a different cell or range address if necessary.

NOTE: To select a different range, press F4 to return to the spreadsheet, use the arrow keys to highlight the desired range, and then press Enter to return to the dialog box. LotusWorks displays the range you selected.

4. Enter the address of the destination cell or range in the *To* range text box.
5. Select Move. LotusWorks moves the data in the *From* range to the *To* range.

## The Edit Cut Option

To use the Edit Cut option:

1. Select the cell or range whose contents you want to copy. (Press F4 or drag the mouse.)
2. Press Alt+X or select Edit Cut. LotusWorks removes the selected data from the screen.

3. Move the cell pointer to the top-left corner of the desired destination range.

4. Press Alt+P or select Edit Paste to deposit the cut text in the destination range.

## Creating Spreadsheet Formulas

Formulas are the means of getting LotusWorks to do mathematical calculations for you. Instead of entering a number or text label into a spreadsheet cell, you can enter a formula into the cell and have LotusWorks calculate and display a data value for the cell. For example, the formula +B2–C2 means "subtract the data value in cell C2 from the data value in cell B2 and enter the result in this cell." The formula (B2+C2)/100 means "add the value in cell B2 to the value in cell C2, divide the sum by 100, and enter the result in this cell."

Formulas are the real workhorses of spreadsheets. The sooner you learn to write spreadsheet formulas, the sooner you can get LotusWorks to do serious spreadsheet work for you.

### Writing Spreadsheet Formulas

A spreadsheet formula is a mathematical expression. It is can contain data values, range addresses, range names, operators, and @functions. You write spreadsheet formulas much as you write formulas in algebra, except that in some cases a symbol must appear before the rest of the formula to tell Lotus-Works to treat the expression as a formula, and some of the spreadsheet operators are different from algebraic operators.

To enable LotusWorks to distinguish a formula from a data value or label, you must follow certain conventions when entering the formula into a cell:

- The first character must clearly indicate a formula. If a formula begins with a number, an @function, or one of the symbols + – ( LotusWorks always treats it as a formula.

- Use a plus sign (+) at the beginning of a formula to indicate a positive value; use a minus sign (–) to indicate a negative value.

- When the first element is a cell address or range name, use +, –, or ( to begin the formula.
- Do not include spaces in a formula, except in text strings that are enclosed within quotation marks.

The following are some examples of LotusWorks spreadsheet formulas:

| Formula | Meaning |
| --- | --- |
| 7+C2 | Add 7 to the contents of cell C2. |
| +C2*12 | Multiply the contents of C2 by 12. |
| +C2+C3 | Add the contents of cells C2 and C3. |
| –C2+C3 or +C3–C2 | Subtract the contents of cell C2 from the contents of cell C3. |
| (C2–C3)/3 | Subtract the contents of cell C3 from the contents of cell C2 and divide the difference by three. |
| @AVG(F3..F15) | Average the values in the range F3..F15. |
| @SUM(PAYMENTS) | Sum the values in the range named PAYMENTS. |
| @IF(PAID, "Thank you.", "Please pay balance due.") | If the content of the cell named PAID is 1 (True), print the words "Thank you." Otherwise print "Please pay balance due." |
| @IF(TODAY >= DUEDATE+30),"Overdue") | If today is 30 or more days after the account's due date, print the word "Overdue." |

Examples of Spreadsheet Formulas

## Entering Formulas

To enter a formula into a cell, enter a symbol indicating a formula (+ – ( @), and then type the formula. The plus sign or other symbol tells LotusWorks that the entry is a formula rather than a text label or number. Here are the steps:

1. Move the cell pointer to the desired cell.
2. Press the plus key (+) or other symbol indicating a formula.
3. Type the formula.
4. Press Enter.

## Using Cell Pointing

You can get LotusWorks to write cell addresses in formulas for you, and at the same time guard against mistakes, by using "cell pointing." Cell pointing is a technique of selecting cells rather than typing cell addresses as you write formulas. When you use cell pointing, LotusWorks writes the cell addresses for you. For example, to write the formula +B2–C2, move the cell pointer to the cell that you want to hold the formula, type +, move the cell pointer to cell B2, press –, move the cell pointer to cell C2, and press Enter. Notice that the correct cell addresses appear in the formula on the edit line and that the answer appears in the cell.

## Operators

Operators are symbols placed between values in formulas to tell LotusWorks what mathematical operations to perform on the values. The following operators can be used to create LotusWorks spreadsheet formulas:

### Spreadsheet Operators

**Numeric Operators**

| Operator | Operation | Example | Result |
|---|---|---|---|
| + | Addition | +C2+C3 | Adds the values of cells C2 and C3 |
| – | Subtraction | +C2–C3 | Subtracts the value in C3 from that in C2 |
| * | Multiplication | +C2*C3 | Multiplies the value in C2 by the one in C3 |
| / | Division | +C2/C3 | Divides the value in C2 by the one in C3 |
| ^ | Exponentiation | +C2^3 | Raises the value in C2 to the third power |

**String Operators**

| Operator | Operation | Example | Result |
|---|---|---|---|
| & | Concatenation | +C2&C3 | Joins the string in cell C3 to the string in C2. |

## Logical Operators

| Operator | Meaning | Example | Result |
|---|---|---|---|
| < | Less than | +C2<C3 | Returns True (1) if value of cell C2 is less than the value of cell C3; otherwise False (0). |
| <= | Less than or equal to | +C2<=C3 | Returns True (1) if value of C2 is less than or equal to the value of C3; otherwise False (0). |
| > | Greater than | +C2>C3 | Returns True (1) if value of C2 is greater than the value of C3; otherwise False (0). |
| >= | Greater than or equal to | +C2>=C3 | Returns True (1) if value of C2 is greater than or equal to value of C3; otherwise False (0). |
| + | Equals | +C2=C3 | Returns True (1) if value of C2 is equal to the value of C3; otherwise False (0). |
| <> | Not equal to | +C2<>C3 | Returns True (1) if value of C2 is not equal to the value of C3; otherwise False (0). |
| #AND# | Logical AND | +C2>0#AND#C3<>0 | Returns True (1) only if the logical expressions on both sides of the #AND# are true; otherwise False (0). |
| #OR# | Logical OR | +C2>0#AND#C3<>0 | Returns True (1) if either one of the logical expressions on each side of the #OR# is true; otherwise False (0). |
| #NOT# | Logical NOT (Reverses the logical state of a single expression.) | +#AND#C2=C3 | Returns True (1) if the logically reversed value of C2 ("not C2") equals the logical value of C3; otherwise False (0). |

## Order of Precedence in Spreadsheet Formula Calculations

LotusWorks does not necessarily calculate spreadsheet formula expressions in the order they are written. Rather, the order of calculation is determined by rules of precedence based on the type of mathematical operation. LotusWorks performs exponentiation operations before multiplication and division operations and multiplication and division operations before addition and subtraction operations. Multiplication and division have the same precedence, and addition and subtraction have the same precedence.

### Order of Precedence in Spreadsheet Calculations

| Operator | Operation | Order of Precedence |
|---|---|---|
| ^ | Exponentiation | 1 |
| − (before a value) | Negative value | 2 |
| + (before a value) | Positive value | 2 |
| * | Multiplication | 3 |
| \ | Division | 3 |
| + (between values) | Addition | 4 |
| − (between values) | Subtraction | 4 |
| = | Equal | 5 |
| <> | Not Equal | 5 |
| < | Less Than | 5 |
| > | Greater Than | 5 |
| <= | Less Than or Equal To | 5 |
| >= | Greater Than or Equal To | 5 |
| #NOT# | Logical NOT | 6 |
| #AND# | Logical AND | 7 |
| #OR# | Logical OR | 7 |
| & | Concatenation (joining strings) | 7 |

For example, for the formula 5+3*6/2, LotusWorks multiplies 3 by 6 and divides the result by 2, then adds 5 to the result for a total of 14.

> If you want LotusWorks to perform an operation of lower precedence before an operation of higher precedence, enclose that operation within parentheses. LotusWorks performs expressions within parentheses before expressions outside the parentheses.

## Copying and Moving Formulas

Copying and moving formulas is similar to copying and moving data, with one important difference. If you are copying a formula, the result depends on whether the formula contains absolute or relative cell references. If the formula contains *absolute* cell references or no cell references at all, LotusWorks copies it without change. If the formula contains *relative* cell reference, the cell references change in direct relation to the distance bewen the new location and the original one.

## Saving Work with Relative, Absolute, and Mixed Cell References

LotusWorks lets you write formulas with three kinds of cell references: relative, absolute, and mixed. By using these carefully, you can write a formula once and copy it to other cells instead of having to write the formula from scratch in every single cell.

### Relative Cell References

Whenever you copy a formula containing a *relative* cell reference, the cell reference in the formula changes in relation to the new location of the formula. Thus, you can copy a cell containing relative cell references, and LotusWorks automatically adjusts the formula to have the same relative effect in the new location. For example, if the formula +B3+2 is copied one cell to the right, the formula becomes +C3+2; if it is copied one cell to the left, the formula becomes +A3+2. If the formula is copied down one cell, it becomes +B4+2; if it is copied up one cell, it becomes +B2+2.

> IMPORTANT: Only copied formulas adjust to their new location. Moved formulas remain the same.

## Absolute Cell References

In contrast, whenever you copy a formula containing an *absolute* cell reference, the cell reference remains the same regardless of the new location of the formula. Absolute cell references are indicated by a dollar sign ($) immediately before each part of the cell reference. For example, the cell reference $B$3 always refers to cell B3, even if the formula is moved or copied to another cell.

## Mixed Cell References

Formulas can also contain mixed cell references: one part of the reference can be absolute and one part can be relative. For example, the cell reference $B3 always refers to column B (the absolute reference), but the row number (3) is relative, so it changes in relation to the new location of the formula. If you copy the formula right one column and down one row, it changes to $B4. The cell reference B$3 has the opposite effect: the reference always refers to row 3 (the absolute reference), but the column letter changes in relation to the new location of the formula. So if you copy it right one column and down one row, it changes to C$3.

## Using Relative, Absolute, and Mixed Cell References

*To save time in writing the same formula in multiple cells, write the formula in one cell using relative and/or absolute cell references as appropriate, then copy it to the remaining cells or ranges.*

You can use absolute, relative, and mixed cell references to save time in writing similar formulas to multiple cells. The trick is to write the formula in one cell using relative and/or absolute cell references, then copy the formula to different cells. For example, suppose you need to write similar formulas across a range of cells (such as a row of totals at the bottom of a spreadsheet or a column of row totals at the right edge of the spreadsheet). You can simply write the formula in the first cell of the range using relative cell references and then copy the formula to the other cells in the range. The cell references adjust automatically to each cell location.

As another example, suppose you need to have a formula appear exactly the same way in several places within a spreadsheet. If you write the formula using absolute cell references, you can then copy the formula to the new cell locations, and each location will contain the identical formula.

## Converting Formulas to Values

LotusWorks makes it possible to copy a range and, in the process, copy the results of the cell formulas rather than the formulas themselves. This is useful, for example, if you want the current values in a range to be fixed while leaving the formulas in the original range intact so that their values can be updated in the future.

To copy a range and convert its formulas to values, select the range to be copied, then select Range Value. The following dialog box appears:

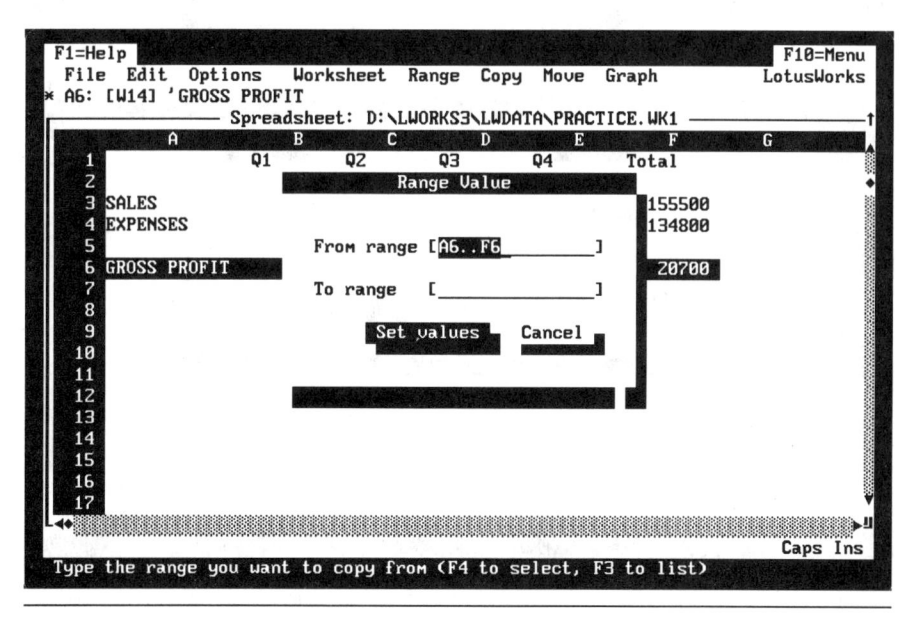

**FIGURE 5.14:** Enter the range from which to copy values and the range to receive the values.

Check to be sure that the range specified in the From range box is correct, enter the range to receive the data in the To range box, and select Set values. LotusWorks copies the values but not the formulas to the To range.

## Finding Cells by Value or Formula

When you are editing a spreadsheet, it is often extremely useful to be able to find all the cells that contain a particular character string, number, @function, or formula without having to examine every single cell. This is especially the case if you are dealing with a large spreadsheet with widely scattered formulas. You can do this with the Worksheet Search option.

To find cells by value or formula, press F7 or Alt+F (or if you prefer to use a menu, select Worksheet Search). The following dialog box appears:

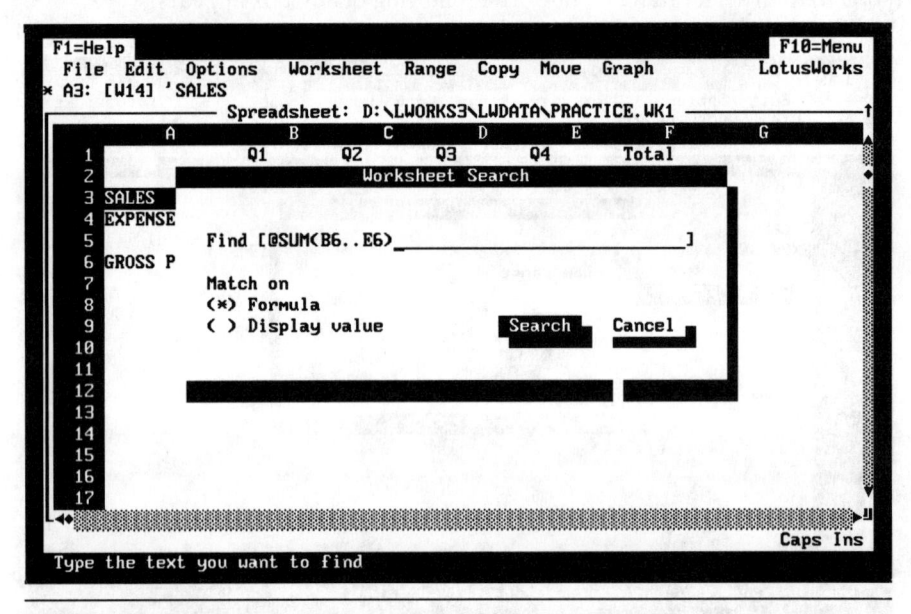

```
F1=Help                                                          F10=Menu
   File  Edit  Options  Worksheet  Range  Copy  Move  Graph      LotusWorks
 A3: [W14] 'SALES
              ──── Spreadsheet: D:\LWORKS3\LWDATA\PRACTICE.WK1 ────
           A         B         C         D         E         F         G
   1                 Q1        Q2        Q3        Q4        Total
   2  ┌──────────────────── Worksheet Search ────────────────────┐
   3  │SALES                                                      │
   4  │EXPENSE                                                    │
   5  │         Find [@SUM(B6..E6)                              ] │
   6  │GROSS P                                                    │
   7  │         Match on                                          │
   8  │         (*) Formula                                       │
   9  │         ( ) Display value         Search    Cancel        │
  10  │                                                           │
  11  │                                                           │
  12  └───────────────────────────────────────────────────────────┘
  13
  14
  15
  16
  17
                                                              Caps Ins
Type the text you want to find
```

**FIGURE 5.15**: To find a cell by its value or formula, enter the character string, number, or formula you want to find, select Formula or Display value, and select Search.

Enter the value or formula you want to find, specify whether to match on the Formula or Display value, and then select Search. LotusWorks searches to the right and then down the spreadsheet and highlights the first cell that contains the formula or value that you have specified.

To find the next occurrence of the specified formula or value, press F7 or Alt+F again and then simply press Enter. LotusWorks repeats the search each time you issue the command until it reaches the end of the spreadsheet or until you change the entry in the Find text box.

# Recalculating Spreadsheets

There are several options that govern the way LotusWorks calculates and recalculates spreadsheets. You can set it to recalculate the spreadsheet automatically or manually, and in "natural" order, row-wise order, or column-wise order.

## Automatic and Manual Recalculation

The default method of recalculating LotusWorks spreadsheets is automatic. This means that LotusWorks automatically recalculates all cells in the spreadsheet each time you make a change in a cell's contents. This setting works well for most purposes, but automatically recalculating the entire spreadsheet can be slow if you are building a large spreadsheet and are entering data into a large number of cells. In that case you should use the manual setting. It does not recalculate the spreadsheet until you give the command to do so.

To change the method of recalculation, select Worksheet Global Recalculation. The following dialog box appears:

*Changing the setting from automatic to manual recalculation can speed your data entry when you are entering numerous items in large spreadsheets.*

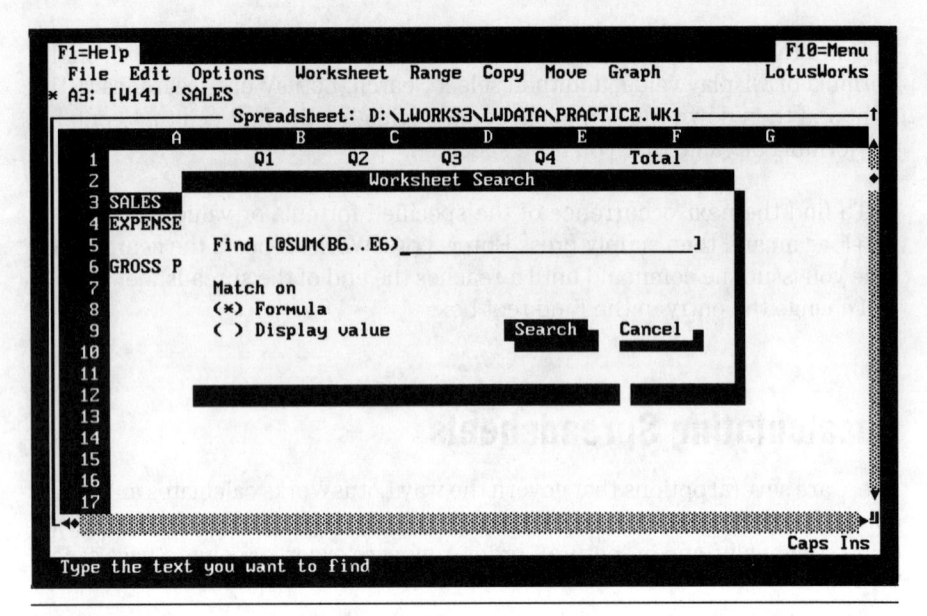

```
F1=Help                                                           F10=Menu
  File  Edit  Options    Worksheet  Range  Copy  Move  Graph       LotusWorks
* A3: [W14] 'SALES
─────────────── Spreadsheet: D:\LWORKS3\LWDATA\PRACTICE.WK1 ───────────────
          A         B         C         D         E         F         G
   1                Q1        Q2        Q3        Q4        Total
   2                        Worksheet Search
   3  SALES
   4  EXPENSE
   5             Find [@SUM(B6..E6)                    ]
   6  GROSS P
   7             Match on
   8             (*) Formula
   9             ( ) Display value          Search    Cancel
  10
  11
  12
  13
  14
  15
  16
  17
                                                               Caps  Ins
Type the text you want to find
```

**FIGURE 5.16:** For recalculations, you may set the automatic or manual method and natural, column-wise, or row-wise order.

To change the method of recalculation, select Worksheet Global Recalculation. The following dialog box appears:

> CAUTION: If you have the recalculation method set to Manual, be sure to recalculate the spreadsheet when you have finished entering data. To be safe, it's best to change the setting back to automatic once you have finished entering data.

Select either Automatic or Manual, and then select Accept. LotusWorks sets the method you specified.

## The Calc Command (F9)

You can command LotusWorks to recalculate a spreadsheet at any time, regardless of which method is set in the Worksheet Global Recalculation dialog box. To issue the command, simply press F9 from anyplace within the spreadsheet. If you prefer to use a menu, select Options Calc.

## Order of Calculation

The default order of calculation is "Natural." This means that LotusWorks recalculates all values on which a formula depends before recalculating the formula. For instance, if a formula in one cell contains a reference to a value in another cell, LotusWorks calculates the value in the second cell before calculating the formula. Unless there is a particular reason to recalculate the spreadsheet column-by-column or row-by-row, it is best to leave the recalculation order set to Natural.

In some cases the logical relationships among spreadsheet cells require recalculating a spreadsheet in column-by-column or row-by-row order to produce an accurate result. For instance, you might want business results for a series of years to be calculated year-by-year, even if some formulas reference values from later years. In the Worksheet Global Recalculation dialog box, the Columnwise option recalculates spreadsheets in column order (A1, A2, A3, B1, B2, B3, etc.), and the Rowwise option recalculates them in row order (A1, B1, C1, A2, B2, C2, etc.).

## Iterations

The Iterations option lets you set a limit on the number of times (up to 99) that LotusWorks recalculates the spreadsheet for each recalculation. This enables you to limit runaway recalculations in case you inadvertently create a formula with a circular reference (that is, a formula in which the value of a cell is affected by the value of another cell whose value is affected by the value of the first cell). Unless you have a formula that requires multiple iterations, it is best to leave the Iterations option set to 1, the default.

*Unless you have a formula that requires multiple iterations, it is best to leave the Iterations option set to 1, to guard against accidental runaway recalculations.*

# Using Spreadsheet @Functions

You can use LotusWorks @functions for a wide variety of complex calculations, from adding a column or row of numbers or calculating the payment on a loan to looking up numbers in a table. For example, to add a column or row of numbers, you can use the @sum function: to add the values in the range B15..G15, the formula would be @SUM(B15..G15). To calculate the monthly payment on a loan, you can use the @PMT function: for a loan of $10,000 for 48 months at 10 percent interest, the formula would be @pmt(10000,10/12,48). To look up values in a table, you can use the @HLOOKUP or @VLOOKUP function.

Most @functions have three parts:

- The @ (at sign), which always is the first character
- The name of the function
- One or more arguments enclosed in parentheses

An argument specifies the data on which the function works. Depending on the @function, the data may be one or a combination of numbers, cells, ranges, formulas, and other @functions.

To enter an @function:

1. Select the cell where you want the @function to appear.
2. Type @, the @function name, and (.
3. Type or select the first argument. See "Selecting Cells and Ranges for Further Action" earlier in this chapter.
4. If there is another argument, type a comma.
5. Type or select the next argument (if any).
6. Repeat steps 4 and 5 until you have specified all the arguments.
7. Type ) to complete the @function.
8. Press Enter to store the @function in the cell.

For a complete list of the 75 @functions in LotusWorks 3.0, see Appendix C.

## The @IF Function

There is one @function that you should learn to use early on: the @IF function. The @IF function performs logical tests. It takes the form, "if a specified condition exists, perform a specified action, otherwise perform another specified action." This simple structure can be used as a building block in spreadsheet formulas to give a wide variety of instructions to LotusWorks for an almost limitless variety of conditions and situations.

The syntax of the @IF function is @IF(*logical condition,expression1, expression2*). This means "if the specified logical condition exists, perform expression1, otherwise perform expression2." Notice that the three arguments are enclosed within parentheses, the arguments are separated by commas, and there are no spaces between the arguments.

To see how this works, consider the formula @IF(C3>=100,C3*0.95,C3). This formula says "if the value in cell C3 is $100 or more, calculate a 5% discount; otherwise, use the value in C3."

If you gave the name ORDER to cell C3, you could write the same formula as follows: @IF(ORDER>=100,ORDER*0.95, ORDER).

You can also nest @IF functions within each other to express more complicated conditions. For example, the formula

@IF(ORDER>=200,ORDER*0.90,@IF(ORDER>=100,ORDER*0.95,ORDER))

says "If the order is $200 or more, calculate a 10% discount; and if the order is $100 or more (but less than $200), calculate a 5% discount; otherwise, do not calculate a discount." Notice that both @IF functions must be complete—that is, each @IF function must have a complete set of parentheses.

*If LotusWorks rejects one of your formulas when you press Enter, check the formula carefully to see if any terms are misspelled or if the formula violates any syntactical rules.*

> NOTE: When you nest @IF statements, they must be nested in an order that makes logical sense. Write the most inclusive condition first, then the less inclusive conditions in order of inclusiveness. In the case above, the condition of ORDER>=200 comes in the most inclusive @IF statement, and the condition ORDER>=100 comes in an @IF statement nested within the first one.

You can achieve the same result using the #AND# operator with the following formula:

@IF(ORDER>=100#AND#ORDER<200,ORDER*0.95,@IF(ORDER>=200, ORDER*0.90, ORDER)).

## Entering Dates and Times

You can enter a date or time as text if you do not need to perform any calculations on it. Simply enter it as a label: type an apostrophe ('), caret (^), or quotation mark (") to specify the position within the cell and then type the date or time in any format you wish—for example, '1/1/92, ^1 JAN 1992, "1 JAN 1992, '1 January 1992, '1:00 p.m., '13:00, or '1300.

If you want to use a date or time in math calculations, however, you must enter it using an @function and one of the date or time formats.

To enter a date, use the function @DATE(*YY,MM,DD*), where *YY* is the last two digits of the year, *MM* is a one- or two-digit number for the month, and *DD* is a one- or two-digit number for the day. For instance, to enter January 31, 1992, you enter @DATE(92,1,31).

To display the date correctly, you must select a date/time format for the cell. To do this, select Range Format. The following dialog box appears:

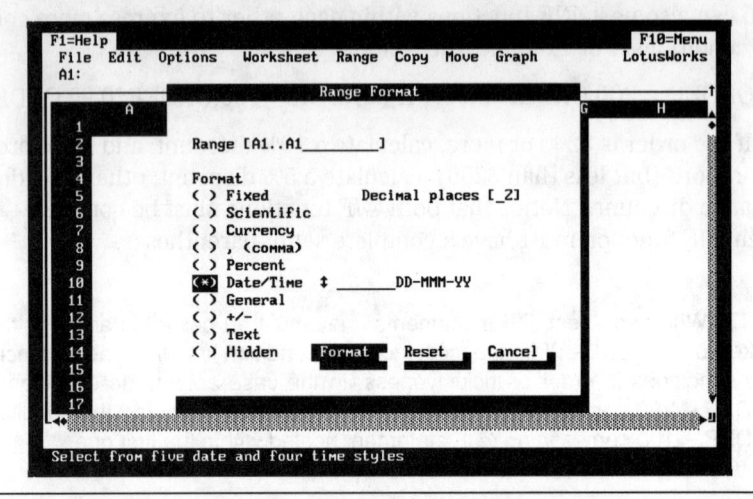

```
F1=Help                                                           F10=Menu
 File  Edit  Options  Worksheet  Range  Copy  Move  Graph       LotusWorks
A1:
                              Range Format
        A                                                   G         H
 1
 2
 3        Range [A1..A1_____]
 4
 5        Format
 6        ( ) Fixed            Decimal places [_2]
 7        ( ) Scientific
 8        ( ) Currency
 9        ( ) , (comma)
10        ( ) Percent
11        (*) Date/Time  ‡  _____DD-MMM-YY
12        ( ) General
13        ( ) +/-
14        ( ) Text
15        ( ) Hidden       Format   Reset   Cancel
16
17
Select from five date and four time styles
```

**FIGURE 5.17:** To display dates and time correctly, select Range Format Date/Time, and the specific format you want.

When you select the Date/Time option and press Tab, another dialog box pops up:

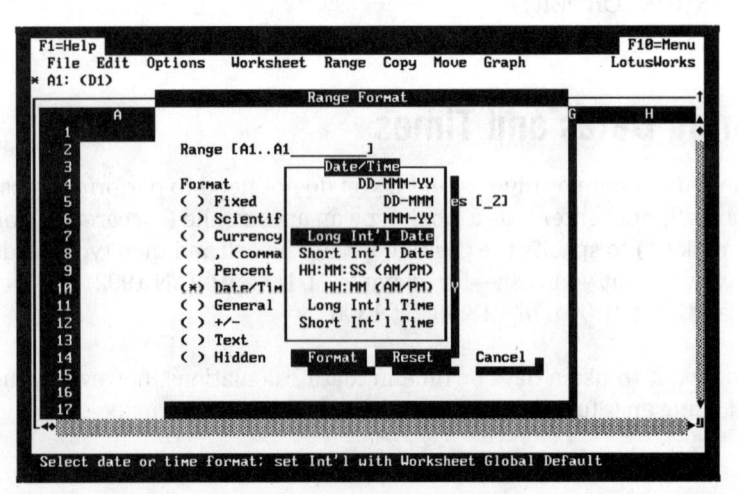

```
F1=Help                                                           F10=Menu
 File  Edit  Options  Worksheet  Range  Copy  Move  Graph       LotusWorks
* A1: (D1)
                              Range Format
        A                                                   G         H
 1
 2
 3        Range [A1..A1_____]
                               Date/Time
 4        Format              DD-MMM-YY
 5        ( ) Fixed           DD-MMM              es [_2]
 6        ( ) Scientif        MMM-YY
 7        ( ) Currency   Long Int'l Date
 8        ( ) , (comma   Short Int'l Date
 9        ( ) Percent   HH:MM:SS (AM/PM)
10        (*) Date/Tim  HH:MM (AM/PM)
11        ( ) General   Long Int'l Time
12        ( ) +/-       Short Int'l Time
13        ( ) Text
14        ( ) Hidden       Format   Reset   Cancel
15
16
17
Select date or time format; set Int'l with Worksheet Global Default
```

**FIGURE 5.18:** Select the specific format you want from the Date/Time popup dialog box.

Select the specific date or time format you want and select Format to exit the dialog box.

To enter a time, use the function @TIME(*HH,MM,SS*), where *HH* is a two-digit number for the hour (based on the 24-hour clock), *MM* is a one- or two-digit number for the minutes, and *SS* is a one- or two-digit number for the seconds. For instance, to enter 12:01 A.M. (one minute past midnight), you would enter @TIME(0,1,0). To enter 1:01 P.M., you would enter @TIME(13,1,0).

As with dates, to display times properly you must select Range Format Date/Time, and the desired time format. For examples of the date and time formats, see "Changing Number Formats" earlier in this chapter.

## Performing Date and Time Math

You can use the @DATE and @TIME functions to perform date and time calculations, such as adding a number of days to a date or determining the difference between two dates or two times. Simply use the @DATE or @TIME function as you would a number or cell reference in a formula. Be sure that the cell containing the formula is formatted appropriately for the answer. The following are some examples:

| To determine this: | Use this formula: | Result: | Format: |
| --- | --- | --- | --- |
| 60 days after March 15, 1992 | @DATE(92,3,15)+60 | 05/14/92 | Long Int'l Date |
| 118 days before June 30, 1992 | @DATE(92,6,30)–118 | 03/0/492 | Long Int'l Date |
| Number of days between 1/1/91 and 9/15/92 | @DATE(92,9,15) –@DATE(91,1,1) | 623 | General Numeric |
| Number of hours between 9:15 A.M. and 7.30 P.M. | @TIME(19,30,0) –@TIME(9,15,0) | 10:15 | Short Int'l Time |
| Number of hours between 1/1/92 at 12:30 P.M. and 3/15/92 at 3:30 A.M. | (@DATE(92,3,15)+ @TIME(3,30,0)– (@DATE(92,1,1)+ @TIME(12,30,0))*24 | 1767 | General Numeric |
| Number of days between the date in cell C3 and the date in cell C2 | +C3–C2 | (an integer) | General Numeric |

Examples of Date and Time Math

# Tailoring the Appearance of Spreadsheets

*To center the title of your spreadsheet, put the cellpointer on cell A1, press the Spacebar several times, and type the title. To adjust the spacing, place the cell pointer on cell A1, press F2, and move the cursor with the arrow keys; use the spacebar to insert blank spaces; use the Del or Backspace keys to remove blank spaces.*

Once a spreadsheet is calculating properly, you must examine its appearance and legibility—especially if it is to be printed. The following are some techniques you can use to improve the appearance of spreadsheets.

## Setting Titles

Ordinarily, when you scroll large spreadsheets to see cells that are off the screen, the top rows scroll off the screen as you move down, and the left-most columns scroll off as you move to the right, making it difficult to identify the cells that come into view. Fortunately, there's a way to cure the problem. LotusWorks lets you "freeze" one or more rows at the top and/or one or more columns at the left edge of a spreadsheet for a title area. Once the title area is set, the cell pointer will not move into the area, and the area remains in view on the screen at all times, even if you move the cell pointer to a different part of the spreadsheet. In this way, when you scroll the spreadsheet, the column and row labels you have set remain visible on the screen.

To set a title area (assuming you have already entered the labels you want), use the arrow keys or mouse to move the cell pointer to the cell immediately below and/or to the right of the desired title area and select Worksheet Titles. The following submenu appears:

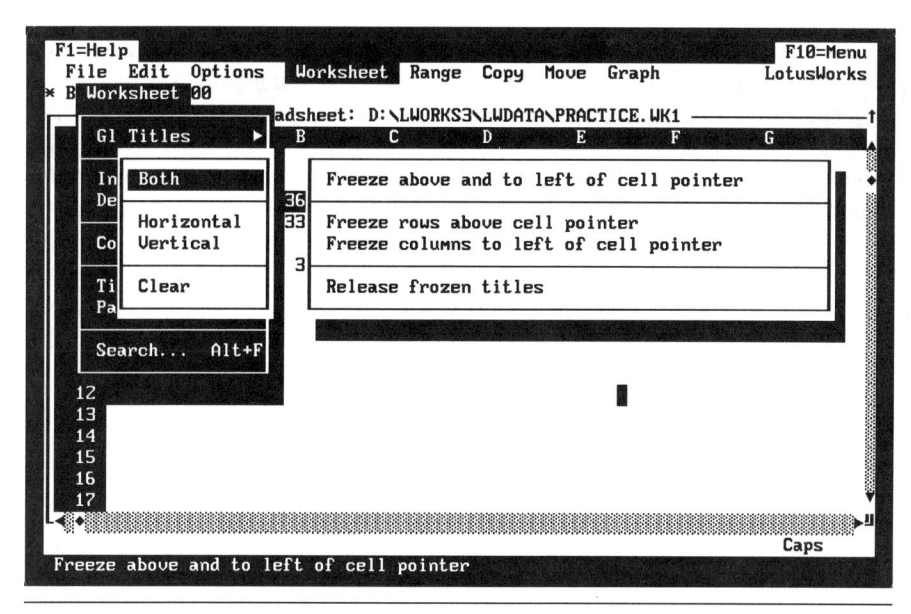

**FIGURE 5.19:** The Worksheet Titles menu lets you freeze all cells above and/or to the left of the cell pointer.

The Both option freezes all rows above and all columns to the left of the cell pointer. The Horizontal option freezes all rows above the cell pointer (but not columns). The Vertical option freezes all columns to the left of the cell pointer (but not rows). Once a title area has been set, you cannot move the cell pointer into the area until you release the setting by selecting the Worksheet Titles Clear option.

## Hiding and Unhiding Columns and Cells

Sometimes it is desirable to blank out sensitive information from a spreadsheet presentation without removing the data from the spreadsheet. LotusWorks gives two ways to do this.

To hide a range of one or more columns so that neither the data nor labels show, first select the column or range of columns to hide. (You need select only one row in each column.) Next, select Worksheet Column Hide, check to see that the correct range is listed, and select Hide. The data, formulas, and labels in the hidden range remain active in the spreadsheet calculations but do not appear on the screen or in printed reports. To redisplay a hidden range, select Worksheet Column Display.

You can also hide the contents of a range of cells within one or more columns without hiding the entire columns. For instance, in publishing a directory of project account codes from a spreadsheet, you could hide the account codes of projects not meant for general distribution. To do this, select the cell or range to be hidden, then select Range Format (or press Alt+N) and select the Hidden format type. The data and formulas in the cells with the Hidden format remain active in the spreadsheet but do not appear on the screen or in printed reports; the column labels and the data and formulas in all other cells remain both active and visible. To "unhide" the data and formula for a cell, press ALT+N and select any format type other than Hidden.

## Aligning Labels within Columns

In the default mode, LotusWorks aligns labels to the left edge of columns and numbers to the right edge. In some cases, the appearance of a spreadsheet can be improved by aligning some or all labels to the right edge or to center them within columns.

To change the label alignment of a cell or range of cells, first select the desired cell or range, then select Range Label (or press Alt+L), check to be sure the correct range is specified, select the desired label alignment (Left, Right, or Center), and select Label. This changes the alignment prefix (', ", or ^) in the label of each selected cell, just as if you had entered each symbol individually.

To change the label alignment for an entire spreadsheet at one time, select Worksheet Global Labels, select the desired alignment (Left, Right or Center), and select Label. This command does not change the alignment of existing labels, but all subsequently entered labels will have the new alignment.

## Creating a Line in a Cell or Row

Usually it helps the legibility of spreadsheets to insert lines at strategic points. For example, it helps to have lines to separate column headers from the first row of data and to separate the last row of data from any rows that carry totals, averages, or other statistical measures. If a spreadsheet covers more than one topic, it often helps to demarcate the topics with a line or a few blank rows.

An easy way to create a line across a cell is to select the cell and enter \- (backslash and hyphen). To create a double line, enter \= (backslash and equal sign). To create a dashed line, enter \-# (backslash, hyphen, and space). To create a line across an entire row, create the line in one cell and then copy it to the remaining cells in the row.

You can use the backslash key to repeat any character or combination of characters (including blank spaces) across a cell. For example: # # # #, ******, and ========.

## Sorting Rows Based on Data

You may find it useful to arrange the rows of a spreadsheet into different orders for different presentations. For instance, you might want to print a sales staff roster with the names in alphabetical order but print a sales report from the same spreadsheet with the salespersons listed in order from high to low sales volume.

LotusWorks enables you to sort the rows of a range based on the values appearing in one or two columns of the spreadsheet. You can sort them into ascending alphabetical order (A,B,C...), descending alphabetical order (Z,Y,X...), ascending numerical order (1,2,3...), or descending numerical order (100,99,98...).

To sort a range, first select the range to be included in the sort, then select Range Sort. The following dialog box appears:

**244**   The Lotus Guide to LotusWorks

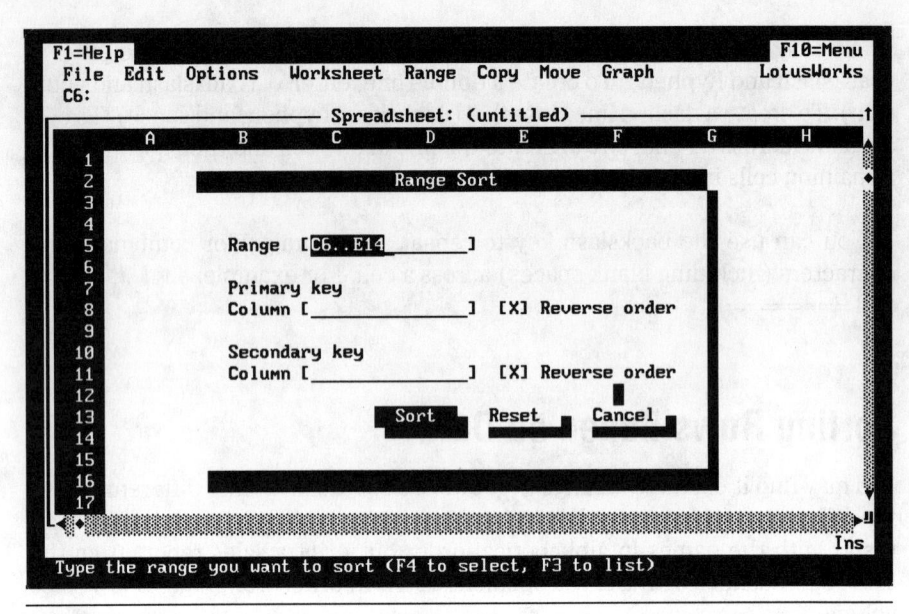

```
F1=Help                                                    F10=Menu
  File   Edit   Options   Worksheet   Range   Copy   Move   Graph        LotusWorks
C6:
─────────────────── Spreadsheet: (untitled) ───────────────────┐
         A         B         C         D         E         F         G         H
   1
   2                     ┌─────────────── Range Sort ───────────────┐
   3                     │                                          │
   4                     │                                          │
   5                     │   Range  [C6..E14      ]                 │
   6                     │                                          │
   7                     │   Primary key                            │
   8                     │   Column [              ]  [X] Reverse order │
   9                     │                                          │
  10                     │   Secondary key                          │
  11                     │   Column [              ]  [X] Reverse order │
  12                     │                                          │
  13                     │          Sort      Reset     Cancel      │
  14                     │                                          │
  15                     │                                          │
  16                     └──────────────────────────────────────────┘
  17
                                                                     Ins
Type the range you want to sort (F4 to select, F3 to list)
```

**FIGURE 5.20:** To sort a range, specify a column for the primary key, a column for the secondary key (if desired) and the sort order.

Check to be sure that the range is correctly specified. Next, in the text box labeled Primary Key Column, enter the *address* or *name* of a cell located in the column that you want to be the primary sort key—that is, a cell from the column on which the primary (main) sort is to be based. If you want to sort in ascending alphabetical or numerical order, leave the Reverse order option blank; if you want to sort in descending alphabetical or numerical order, select the Reverse order option.

You may also specify a secondary sort key, if you wish. The secondary key sorts any rows that have the same primary sort key values. For instance, to alphabetize a roster, you can set the last-name column as the primary sort key and the first-name column as the secondary sort key; if any rows have the same last name, the secondary key sorts them by first name. If you want to use a secondary sort key, enter a cell address or cell name from the column that you want to be the secondary sort key, and select the sort order you desire (blank or Reverse) for the secondary sort.

The final step is to select Sort.

**FIGURE 5.21:** Range A3..CII sorted into ascending order, with cell C3 as the only sort key.

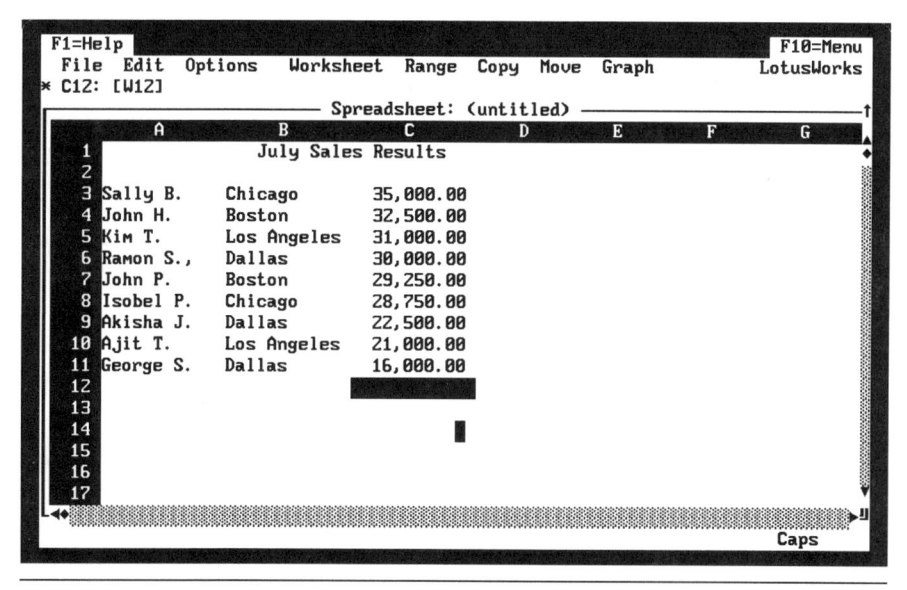

**FIGURE 5.22:** Range A3..CII sorted into descending order, with cell C3 as the only sort key.

```
F1=Help                                                    F10=Menu
  File  Edit  Options   Worksheet  Range  Copy  Move  Graph   LotusWorks
» C12: [W12]
                     ─── Spreadsheet: (untitled) ───
         A           B           C           D      E      F      G
   1              July Sales Results
   2
   3  John P.    Boston      29,250.00
   4  John H.    Boston      32,500.00
   5  Isobel P.  Chicago     28,750.00
   6  Sally B.   Chicago     35,000.00
   7  George S.  Dallas      16,000.00
   8  Akisha J.  Dallas      22,500.00
   9  Ramon S.,  Dallas      30,000.00
  10  Ajit T.    Los Angeles 21,000.00
  11  Kim T.     Los Angeles 31,000.00
  12
  13
  14
  15
  16
  17
                                                              Caps
```

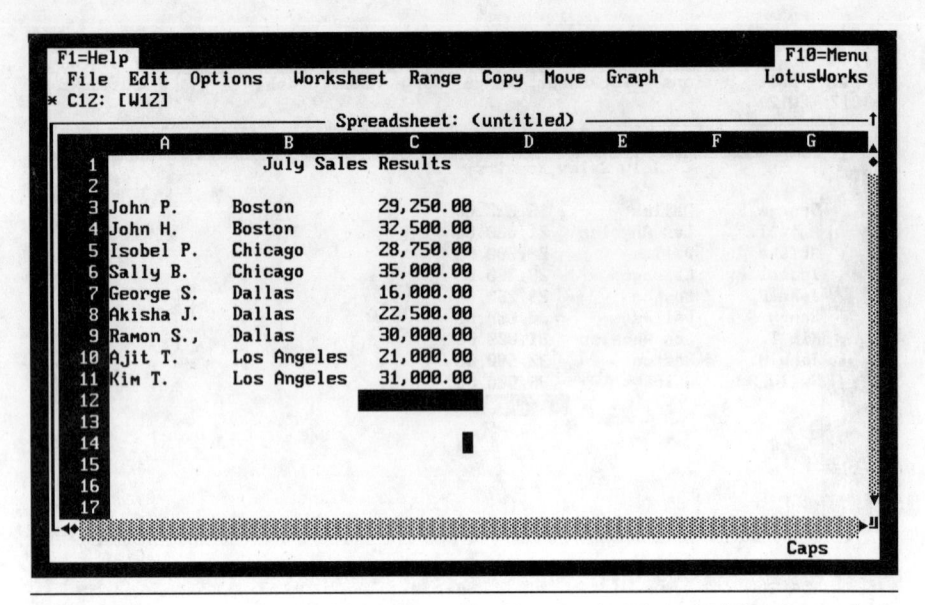

**FIGURE 5.23:** Range A3..C11 sorted into ascending order with cell B3 as the primary key and cell C3 as the secondary key.

# Protecting and Unprotecting Cells and Spreadsheets

Once you have completed a spreadsheet, it's a good idea to protect it. LotusWorks enables you to protect the contents of selected cells or the entire spreadsheet from change. This is especially useful for guarding cell formulas from accidental changes.

To protect a cell or range of cells, first select the cell or range to be protected, then select Range Protect, check to be sure the correct range is listed, and select Protect. The formulas in the cells continue to function, but no one can change the formulas or data in protected cells until you remove the protection. To remove protection from a cell or range, first select the desired cell or range, then select Range Unprotect, check the range listing, and select Unprotect.

To protect an entire spreadsheet, select Worksheet Global Protection, select the Enable option, and select Accept. This prevents changes to any cell of the current spreadsheet but allows formulas and data in the cells to function. To undo global protection, select Worksheet Global Protection, select the Disable option, and select Accept.

## Printing Reports from Spreadsheets

There are many more possibilities in printing from spreadsheets than simply to print a spreadsheet in its entirety. You can think of a spreadsheet as your calculation tool and printed reports (along with graphs) as your presentation tools. The spreadsheet may be large, but the reports don't necessarily have to be large. You can print more than one report from each spreadsheet. This capability is especially important for large spreadsheets that model complex or multi-dimensional phenomena. For instance, you can select ranges that show particular data relationships within a spreadsheet and print one or more reports and graphs for each range. If you were preparing a balance sheet for a business, for example, you could print one report showing assets, one showing liabilities, and one showing the total balance sheet. You can also have one or more graphs for each print range. In preparing to print from spreadsheets, do give some thought in advance to the audiences for your reports and how best to convey and focus attention on the various subsets of important information within each spreadsheet.

Printing from spreadsheets generally involves four steps: selecting the range of cells to print, naming the range, setting the layout for the printed report, and issuing the print order to the printer. Here is how to do it.

1. Select the range of cells to print. Use the mouse or the F4 and arrow keys to select the entire range of cells that you want to print, even if the range is too large for one page.

2. Name the range. Select Range Name Create, enter the name of your choice, check to be sure the correct range is listed, then select Create. It's a good idea to give the print range a name related to the report. That way, you don't have to try to remember or keep track of the exact print range address for every report. Be aware, also, that you can have more than one print range from the same spreadsheet.

3. Set the layout. Select File Print Layout. The following dialog box appears:

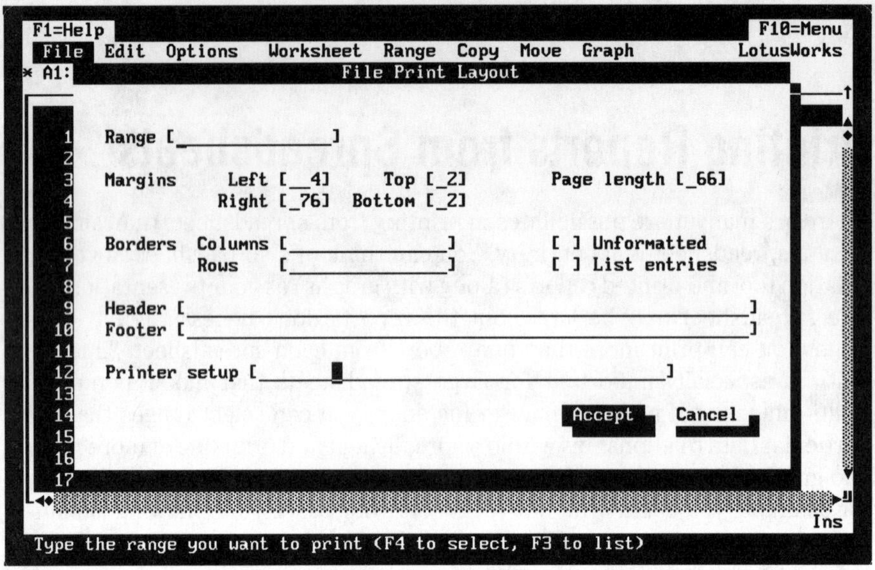

```
F1=Help                                                          F10=Menu
 File  Edit  Options  Worksheet  Range  Copy  Move  Graph      LotusWorks
* A1:                        File Print Layout

   1
   2    Range [_____]
   3    Margins    Left [__4]   Top [_2]    Page length [_66]
   4               Right [_76]  Bottom [_2]
   5
   6    Borders  Columns [_____]   [ ] Unformatted
   7             Rows    [_____]   [ ] List entries
   8
   9    Header [_____]
  10    Footer [_____]
  11
  12    Printer setup [_____█_____]
  13
  14                                        Accept   Cancel
  15
  16
  17
                                                                    Ins
Type the range you want to print (F4 to select, F3 to list)
```

**FIGURE 5.24:** To set the print layout, enter the print range, border ranges, and header and footer information, and select Accept.

- First, check the **Range** listing and if it is not correct, enter the name or address of the range you want to print. Next, check the settings for margins and paper length. Try the default settings the first time, then adjust them if necessary. Once you get a group of settings that you like, you will probably tend to leave them in place unless you have to change them to squeeze a large spreadsheet onto the page.

- The **Borders** entries refer to the columns and rows that you want to print on every page. For instance, if the print range extends beyond the bottom of the first page and you want the column labels to print on every page, enter the range of the column labels. If your print range extends off the page to the right and you want row labels to print alongside their associated data on every page, enter the range of the row labels.

- The **Header and Footer** text boxes enable you to enter information to be printed as a header or footer on every page of the report. You can have one line in each header and footer. You can have all or part of the header and footer text align to the left, center, or right and have headers and footers print page numbers and the current date.

As in the Word Processing service, to position all or part of a header or footer on the left, center, or right side of the page, insert one or more vertical bars (|). Text entered without a vertical bar is aligned to the left margin. Text entered after one vertical bar is centered. Text entered after two vertical bars is positioned on the right side of the page. Enter a number symbol (#) to print a page number. Enter @ to print the current date.

| Enter this text | To print this line in the header or footer |   |   |
|---|---|---|---|
| Sales Report | Sales Report | | |
| \|Sales Report | | Sales Report | |
| \|\|Sales Report | | | Sales Report |
| @ | January 31, 1992 | | |
| Page # | Page 1 | | |
| @\|Draft 1\|Page # | January 31, 1992 | Draft 1 | Page 1 |
| @\|\|# | | | 1 |
| \|- #- | January 31, 1992 | -1- | |

Positioning Text in a Header or Footer

- The **Printer setup** text box enables you to enter a printer startup string, if appropriate. If you want to print in compressed type or landscape mode or both, many printers require you to enter a startup string to switch to these modes. See your printer instructions for the startup string to enter.

  When all the layout options are set to your liking, select Accept.

4. Issue the order to print. Select File Print Print. The following dialog box appears:

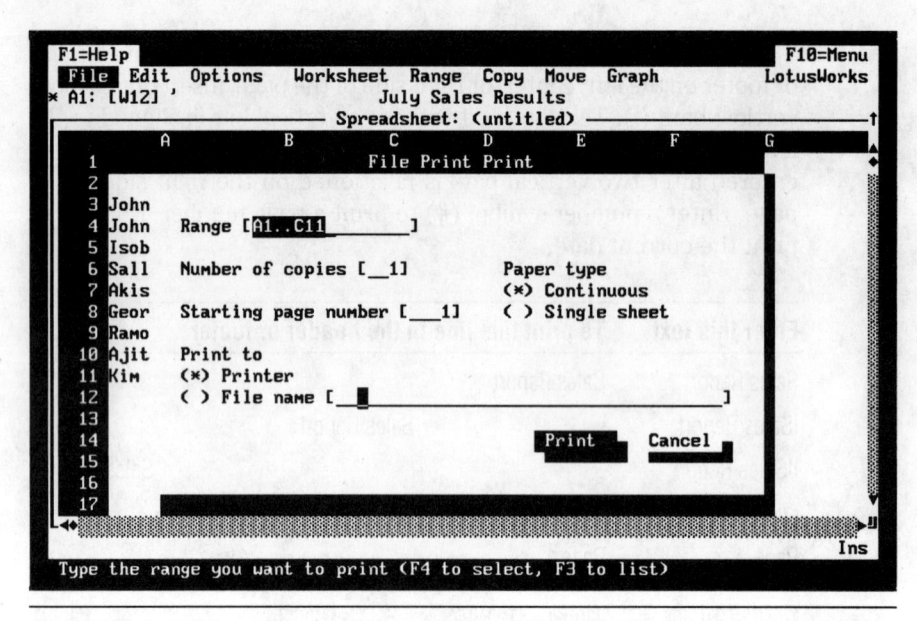

```
F1=Help                                                           F10=Menu
 File  Edit  Options   Worksheet  Range  Copy  Move  Graph        LotusWorks
* A1: [W12] '                    July Sales Results
───────────────────── Spreadsheet: (untitled) ─────────────────────┬
         A         B         C         D         E         F         G
  1                              File Print Print
  2
  3 John
  4 John      Range [A1..C11        ]
  5 Isob
  6 Sall      Number of copies [_1]           Paper type
  7 Akis                                      (*) Continuous
  8 Geor      Starting page number [___1]     ( ) Single sheet
  9 Ramo
 10 Ajit      Print to
 11 Kim       (*) Printer
 12           ( ) File name [_                                    ]
 13
 14                                            Print      Cancel
 15
 16
 17
                                                                   Ins
Type the range you want to print (F4 to select, F3 to list)
```

**FIGURE 5.25:** To print the report, check the print range, number of copies, and starting page number, then select Print.

Check the range listing and correct it if necessary. Change the Number of copies setting if you want to print more than one copy. Change the Starting page number setting if you are using page numbering and want it to start on a number other than one.

The Paper type setting refers to the type of paper feed: continuous (fanfold) or individual sheets. The Individual sheets option causes the printer to pause between pages. If you have a laser printer, select the Continuous option. Once you set this for your printer, it will tend to remain the same.

The Print to option lets you specify sending the report to your printer for printing or to a file on a disk for storage. If you choose to send it to a file on a disk, be sure to specify a complete path and file name for the print file.

When all the settings are to your liking, select Print.

If the range you selected is too large to fit on one page, LotusWorks prints the extra columns on additional pages at the end of the spreadsheet.

# Using Multiple Ranges within a Spreadsheet

Just as you can have multiple print ranges within a spreadsheet, you can have multiple calculation ranges. By creating multiple ranges within a spreadsheet, you can create several "small spreadsheets" within the large spreadsheet. You need to do this if you want one spreadsheet to be able to access and retrieve information from another spreadsheet. For example, you can create a range to hold a table of data such as product descriptions or prices and then access the table from another range in the spreadsheet. Because there is no need to display the table of data, you can locate it in an out-of-the-way region of the spreadsheet and print only the range that draws data from the table.

Multiple ranges are also a means to keep related spreadsheets together, even if they do not depend on each other mathematically. For instance, if you produce reports each quarter on topics such as sales, hours billed to each client, and employee absences, you could keep three separate spreadsheets within one large spreadsheet. Keep in mind, however, that if you create several small spreadsheets within a large one, all of the small spreadsheets are recalculated each time you recalculate any one of them. Unless the spreadsheets are quite small, it's probably best to keep them separate.

When you have more than one small spreadsheet within a large one, it's a good idea to create a range name for each one. That makes it easier to refer to the spreadsheets in formulas and makes it easier to find them when you have not used them for a while.

*If you have several ranges within one spreadsheet, you can view the range names by selecting Range Name Create and pressing F3.*

# Viewing Through Window Panes

A good way to view multiple ranges of a spreadsheet is with window "panes." LotusWorks lets you split the screen window into two panes to get two views of the same spreadsheet. The two panes can be set up to split the screen vertically or horizontally and to scroll in unison or separately. In this way, you can view two widely separated parts of a spreadsheet at the same time. For example, if two columns of a spreadsheet are too widely separated to fit on the screen at the same time, you can locate each in a vertical pane and view them side-by-side on the screen. If you have a lookup table (see below) or multiple ranges defined in the same spreadsheet, you can use panes to view two or more ranges at the same time.

To set up panes, move the cell pointer to the cell in the spreadsheet where you want the split to occur and select Worksheet Panes. When the Panes submenu appears, select Horizontal to split the screen window horizontally or Vertical to split it vertically. LotusWorks splits the screen at the cell pointer location and displays the column letters and row numbers in each pane. You can press the Tab key to move the cell pointer back and forth between panes.

To move the cell pointer back and forth between panes, press the Tab key. To view two different regions of the spreadsheet, be sure that scrolling synchronization is switched off (select Worksheet Panes Unsync), tab to the desired pane, and scroll to the desired region of the spreadsheet. To turn scrolling synchronization back on, select Worksheet Panes Sync.

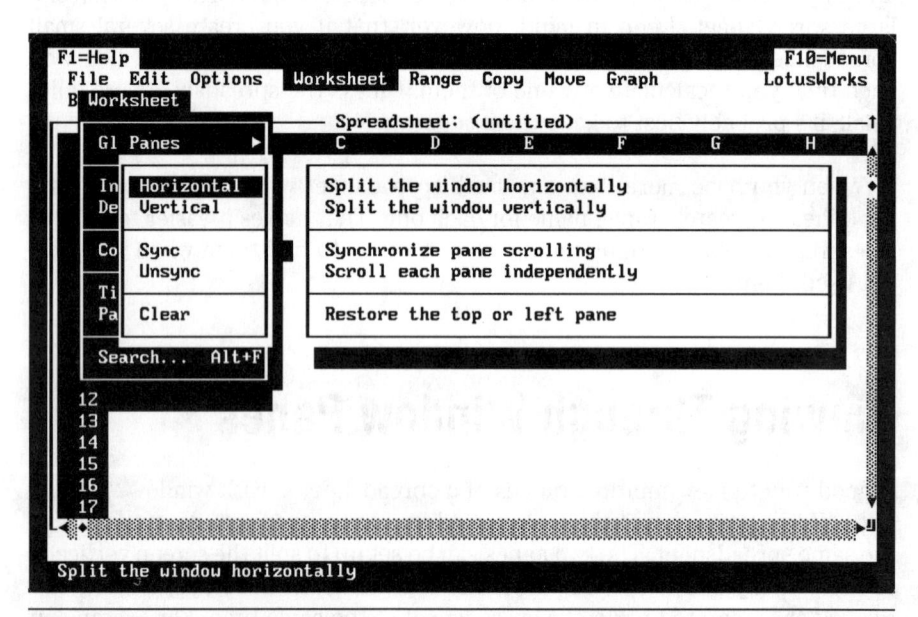

**FIGURE 5.26:** The Worksheet Panes submenu

To clear the screen window of panes, select Worksheet Panes Clear. LotusWorks restores the display to show the top-left pane full-screen.

# Using Lookup Tables

Lookup tables are ranges containing data that is "looked up" and retrieved by other ranges. If you have data that is used in multiple formulas and that changes from time to time, you can save yourself work and headaches by putting the data into a lookup table and having the formulas retrieve the data from the table. That way, when you update data values, you have to update only one set of values, and you can be sure that all instances of the values throughout the spreadsheet are updated accurately, with no accidental omissions. You can also use a lookup table to save work in typing text strings into cells by entering a short code into each cell with a formula to retrieve the full text string from a table. Examples of data that are good candidates for lookup tables are prices, product descriptions, and standard descriptions of services performed for clients. Any time you have data that is used in more than one formula and that must be updated from time to time, try to put it into a lookup table.

LotusWorks provides two @functions for table lookups: @HLOOKUP and @VLOOKUP. The functions perform, respectively, "horizontal" lookups and "vertical" lookups. Here is how they work.

The @HLOOKUP function returns the contents of a cell in a specified row of a horizontal lookup table. A horizontal lookup table is one that has numbers in ascending order across the cells in the top row. The syntax of the function is @HLOOKUP(*x, range, row-offset*). LotusWorks compares the number *x* to each cell in the top row of the range specified by *range*. When it finds a cell that contains the number closest to but not exceeding *x*, it moves down that column the number of rows specified by *row-offset* and returns the contents of the cell.

For example, you could build a horizontal lookup table of employee billing rates for different of tasks as follows:

```
F1=Help                                                              F10=Menu
 File  Edit  Options   Worksheet  Range  Copy  Move  Graph           LotusWorks
* A10: [W10]
                    ─── Spreadsheet: (untitled) ───
         A           B           C       D        E        F        G
   1  RATES       Tasks          1       2        3        4
   2
   3  Emp #       Name
   4   101        Sam Abraham    100     100      150      175
   5   102        Maria Garcia    75      75      100      125
   6   103        Rene Prudhomme  75      75      100      125
   7   104        Jeffrey Brown   40      50       60       85
   8   105        Mary Ostrum     40      50       60       85
   9
  10
  11
  12
  13
  14
  15
  16
  17
```

**FIGURE 5.27:** Example of a horizontal lookup table

In this case, the formula @HLOOKUP(2,RATES,6) returns the billing rate of $50.00 per hour for task 2 for employee #104 (Jeffrey Brown) from the Rates range (A1..F8).

The @VLOOKUP function returns the contents of a cell in a specified row of a vertical lookup table. A vertical lookup table is one that has numbers in ascending order down the cells of the first column. The syntax of the function is @VLOOKUP($x$, range, column-offset). LotusWorks compares the number $x$ to each cell in the first column of the range specified by *range*. When it finds a cell that contains the number closest to but not exceeding $x$, it moves across the row the number of columns specified by *column-offset* and returns the contents of the cell.

The table in Figure 5-27 can also be treated as a vertical lookup table because it contains ascending numbers in the first column. If it is treated as a vertical lookup table, the formula @VLOOKUP(102,RATES,4) returns the billing rate of $100.00 per hour from the RATES range (A4..F8) for employee #102 (Maria Garcia) for task 3 (located in the fourth column over from the first one).

```
F1=Help                                                              F10=Menu
   File  Edit  Options  Worksheet  Range  Copy  Move  Graph          LotusWorks
 * A10: [W10]
                        ─── Spreadsheet: (untitled) ───
        A           B            C       D       E       F       G
   1  RATES       Tasks          1       2       3       4
   2
   3  Emp #       Name
   4   101        Sam Abraham    100     100     150     175
   5   102        Maria Garcia   75      75      100     125
   6   103        Rene Prudhomme 75      75      100     125
   7   104        Jeffrey Brown  40      50      60      85
   8   105        Mary Ostrum    40      50      60      85
   9
  10
  11
  ...
```

**FIGURE 5.28:** The table in Figure 5-27 treated as a vertical lookup table

# Combining Data from Other Spreadsheets

You can't directly link two separate spreadsheet files (that is, have formulas in one LotusWorks spreadsheet file directly access cells in another), but you can combine two spreadsheet files into one or copy the contents of selected ranges from one spreadsheet to another. These capabilities are useful, of course, for building new spreadsheets based on previous ones and for copying formulas and data from one spreadsheet to another, but they also are useful for creating specialized spreadsheets for special purposes—such as graphs and multi-part tables drawn from more than one spreadsheet.

**Combining spreadsheets.** To combine two spreadsheets, first retrieve the spreadsheet file that you want to be the receiving spreadsheet and make that spreadsheet current. Move the cell pointer to the point in the spreadsheet where you want the first cell of the second spreadsheet to appear. Bear in mind that in combining spreadsheets, LotusWorks writes over and destroys the contents of any cells located in the receiving range. Next, select File Transfer Combine, select the desired spreadsheet from the list that appears or specify the path, and select Combine. LotusWorks inserts the second spreadsheet starting at the cell pointer location and writing over any data in the range covered by the second spreadsheet.

*To view both spreadsheets simultaneously when you are combining spreadsheets, retrieve one spreadsheet into one window, open a second window, retrieve the second spreadsheet into it, then resize and drag the windows so that you can view both simultaneously. You can see the combined result directly on the screen.*

**256** The Lotus Guide to LotusWorks

*If you want to combine a spreadsheet into the middle of another one, first move the contents of enough cells in the receiving spreadsheet to make room for the new spreadsheet.*

**Extracting selected cell contents.** To transfer a range of data and spreadsheet settings from the current spreadsheet to a new file on disk, first select the range of cells whose contents you want to copy to the new spreadsheet. Next, select File Transfer Extract. The following dialog box appears:

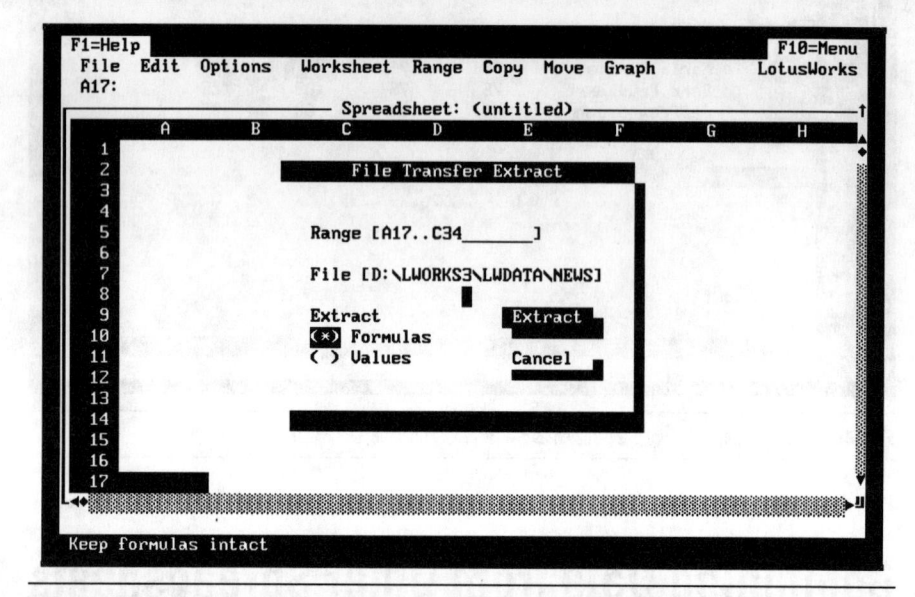

```
F1=Help                                                              F10=Menu
  File  Edit  Options  Worksheet  Range  Copy  Move  Graph      LotusWorks
  A17:
                         ─── Spreadsheet: (untitled) ───
       A       B       C       D       E       F       G       H
  1
  2                    File Transfer Extract
  3
  4
  5              Range [A17..C34_____]
  6
  7              File [D:\LWORKS3\LWDATA\NEWS]
  8
  9              Extract                    Extract
 10              (*) Formulas
 11              ( ) Values                 Cancel
 12
 13
 14
 15
 16
 17
Keep formulas intact
```

**FIGURE 5.29:** Enter the path and file name of a new spreadsheet file to receive the extract.

Check to be sure the range is specified correctly in the Range field and then move to the File text box and enter the path and file name of a new spreadsheet file to receive the extracted data. (You can extract data into an existing file, but the process erases all existing data in the file. It's always safer to use a new one.) LotusWorks copies the data into the new spreadsheet file, starting at cell A1 and writing over all existing contents in the receiving spreadsheet file.

> CAUTION: Be aware that if a receiving spreadsheet already contains *any* data or formulas, the Extract procedure destroys the *entire* existing contents.

When you have entered the new file name, select either Formulas or Values (depending on whether you want to extract formulas intact or extract only the products of the formulas) and select Extract. LotusWorks copies the selected range into the specified spreadsheet.

# Using Macros with Spreadsheets

There are many ways to use macros to save keystrokes in spreadsheets. You can use them to automate virtually any spreadsheet operation that you perform repeatedly. For instance, you can create a macro to retrieve a spreadsheet file that you use frequently. Each time you need to retrieve the spreadsheet, you can simply open a new spreadsheet file and execute the file-retrieval macro. Another use is to record formulas that you write frequently. For example, if you often need to copy the same range of data from one spreadsheet to another or from one part of a spreadsheet to another part of the same spreadsheet, you can automate the process by recording the required keystrokes in a macro. Another use for macros is to automate a standard spreadsheet setup that you use frequently. For instance, you can use a macro to generate the labels and formulas for an expense report form or a periodic financial report.

## Creating and Running Spreadsheet Macros

Macros work the same way in the Spreadsheet services as in other services. To create a spreadsheet macro, you select Options Macros Learn; select one of the Ctrl+key combinations to hold the macro; type the keystrokes to be recorded; then press the Ctrl+key combination to end recording. As with other services, macros created in the spreadsheet service are specific to the Spreadsheet service. To play back a macro, you simply press the macro's Ctrl+key combination. If you don't remember the Ctrl+key combination, you can select Options Macros Run and select the desired macro from the listing in the macro-viewer dialog box.

Here are three sample spreadsheet macros. If you wish, you can record these macros yourself, performing the keystrokes indicated, to gain practice in creating macros. When you finish recording them, be sure to try them out by pressing the appropriate Ctrl+key combination.

### 1. Retrieve a Spreadsheet

**Ctrl+R**  This macro retrieves a spreadsheet file Named REPORT.WK1 into the current window. The keystrokes are as follows:

{F10}fr{Tab}report{Tab}{Enter}

Here is what the keystrokes mean:

| | |
|---|---|
| {F10} | Press F10 to go to the Menu line. |
| f | Press F to select the File menu. |
| r | Press R to select File Retrieve |
| {Tab} | Press Tab to move the cursor to the box. |
| report | Type the name of the spreadsheet file (report). |
| {Tab} | Press Tab to move the cursor to the Retrieve action button. |
| {Enter} | Press Enter to execute the Retrieve command. |

## 2. Write a Formula

**Ctrl+A**  This macro creates a formula to add the values in the three cells immediately above the cell containing the formula:

@sum ({Up} {Up} {Up}.{Down} {Down} {Enter} {Right}){Enter}

Here is what the keystrokes mean:

| | |
|---|---|
| @sum( | Start the formula with the @sum function. |
| {Up} {Up} {Up} | Press the Up Arrow key three times to move the pointer up three cells. |
| . | Type a period to begin cursor pointing. |
| {Down} {Down} | Move the pointer down two cells. |
| {Enter} | Press Enter to end cursor pointing with three cells selected. |
| {Right} | Press the Right Arrow key to move the cursor one place to the right. |
| ) | Type a closing parenthesis to end the formula. |
| {Enter} | Press Enter to enter the formula. |

## 3. Create Labels and Formulas for a Spreadsheet

**Ctrl+S** This macro creates the labels and formulas for the spreadsheet below. First, it enters the labels for the first row and the first column; then it widens the first column to 14 spaces; then it enters the formula +B3–B4 and copies it into the range C6..E6. The illustration shows how the spreadsheet looks with data entered in the range B3..E4.

{Home}{Right}'1ST QTR{Right}'2ND QTR{Right}'3RD QTR{Right}'4TH QTR{Enter}

{Home}{Down}{Down}SALES{Down}EXPENSES{Down}{Down}GROSS PROFIT{Enter}

{Alt+W}{Tab}14{Tab}{Enter}{Right}+B3–B4{Enter}{F10}c{Tab}c6..e6{Tab}{Enter}

Here is a breakdown of the keystrokes:

| | |
|---|---|
| {Home} | Move the pointer to cell A1. |
| {Right} | Move the pointer one cell to the right. |
| '1st Qtr | Type a column label. (Note: The label must begin with an apostrophe because the label begins with a numeral.) |
| {Right} | Move the pointer one cell to the right. |
| '2nd QTR | Type the second column label. |
| {Right} | Move the pointer one cell to the right. |
| '3rd QTR | Type the third column label. |
| {Right} | Move the pointer one cell to the right. |
| '4th QTR | Type the fourth column label. |
| {Enter} | Press Enter to complete the label. |
| {Home} | Move the pointer to cell A1. |
| {Down}{Down} | Move the pointer down two cells. |
| SALES | Type a row label. |
| {Down} | Move the pointer down one cell. |
| EXPENSES | Type the second row label. |
| {Down}{Down} | Move the pointer dwon one cell. |
| GROSS PROFIT | Type the third row label. |

| | |
|---|---|
| {Enter} | Complete the last row label. |
| {Alt+W} | Press Alt+W to widen the column. |
| {Tab} | Press Tab to move the cursor to the text box. |
| 14 | Type 14 to set the column width to 14 spaces. |
| {Tab} | Press Tab to move to the Set width action button. |
| {Enter} | Press Enter to select Set width. |
| {Right} | Move the pointer one cell to the right. |
| +B3–B4 | Type the formula +B3–B4. |
| {Enter} | Press Enter to complete the formula. |
| {F10} | Press F10 to move to the Menu line. |
| c | Type c to select the Copy menu. |
| {Tab} | Press Tab to move to the To range text box. |
| c6..e6 | Type the destination range c6..e6 |
| {Tab} | Press Tab to move the cursor to the Copy action button. |
| {Enter} | Press Enter to execute the Copy command. |

*To create a macro of a spreadsheet setup, first set up the spreadsheet manually to get it the way you want. Then, using the setup as a guide, reenter the labels and formulas as you record the macro.*

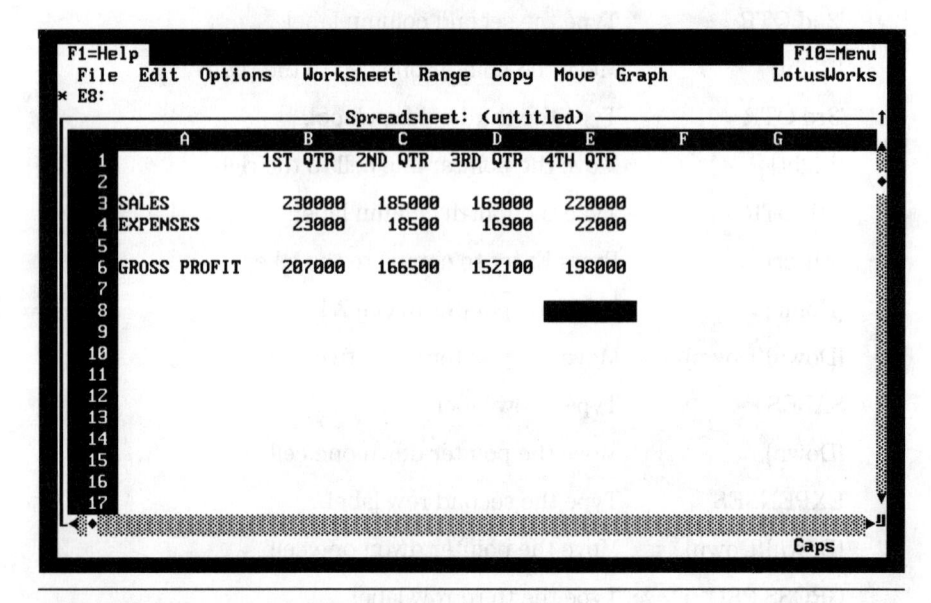

**FIGURE 5.30:** The finished spreadsheet with data entered

## Editing Spreadsheet Macros

If you miskey while recording a macro, you can always go back and rerecord the macro, using the same Ctrl+key combination. If the macro is long, however, you may prefer to edit it to correct the mistake. Simply select Options Macros Edit. When the macro-viewer dialog box appears, select the macro to be edited and then select Edit. The complete macro appears in the Macro definitions dialog box. You can edit the macro string just as you would edit text in the word processing service.

Notice that the names of named keys and function keys appear within curly brackets—for example, {F10}, {Tab}, {Alt+W}, {Up}, {Down}, {Right}, {Left}, and {Enter}. The letter, number, and symbol keys (such as A, 2, @, +, –, /, \, ?, .) appear just as they are typed.

A complete list of the LotusWorks key names appears in Appendix D.

# Importing and Exporting Spreadsheet Data

If you ever need to swap data with another spreadsheet system, LotusWorks enables you to add spreadsheet data from a DIF or ASCII file to the current spreadsheet and to copy data from the current spreadsheet to a DIF file. (Most spreadsheet systems can read and write to the DIF format and save printer output to an ASCII file.) ASCII files should be in table format, with one or more spaces separating the columns and a carriage return and line feed terminating each row. If you want to import a phrase that contains spaces and have it appear within a single cell, use " (double quotation marks) to enclose the phrase.

*If you have an ASCII file that is not quite in the correct table format for the Spreadsheet service, you may be able to use it by importing the file into the LotusWorks Word Processing service, editing it with the Word Processor to get it into the proper format for the Spreadsheet service, exporting it as an ASCII file, and then importing it into the Spreadsheet service.*

## Importing Spreadsheet Data

To import data from a DIF or ASCII file, first move the cell pointer to the point in the current spreadsheet where you want the imported data to appear. (Bear in mind that if you import a file to a location that already contains data, Lotus-Works writes over the existing data with the new data.) Select File Transfer Import. The following dialog box appears:

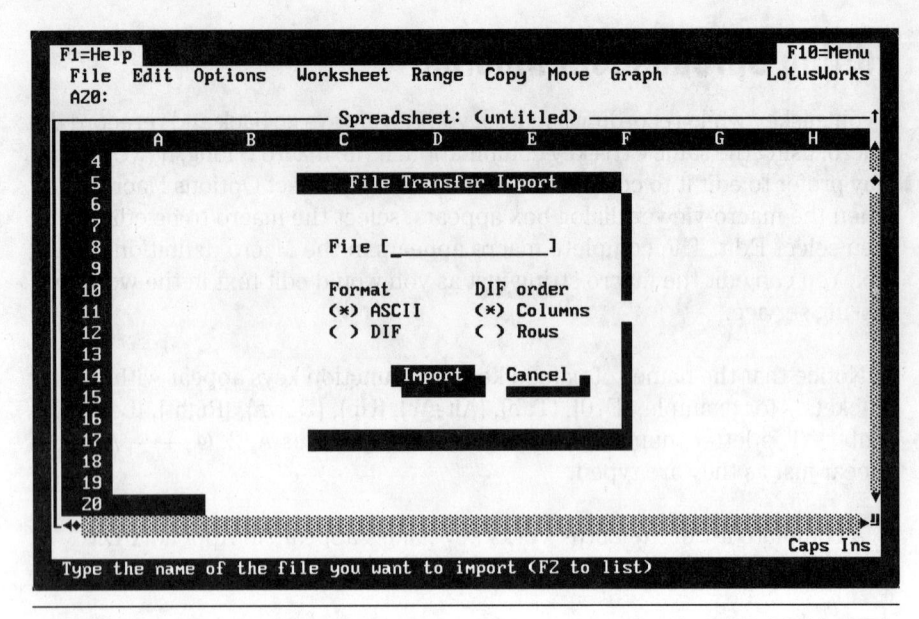

```
F1=Help                                                        F10=Menu
  File  Edit  Options   Worksheet  Range  Copy  Move  Graph      LotusWorks
  A20:
                         ─── Spreadsheet: (untitled) ───
         A       B        C       D       E       F       G       H
    4
    5
    6                       ┌─── File Transfer Import ───┐
    7                       │                            │
    8                       │    File [            ]     │
    9                       │                            │
   10                       │  Format         DIF order  │
   11                       │  (*) ASCII      (*) Columns│
   12                       │  ( ) DIF        ( ) Rows   │
   13                       │                            │
   14                       │      Import     Cancel     │
   15                       │                            │
   16                       └────────────────────────────┘
   17
   18
   19
   20
                                                              Caps  Ins
  Type the name of the file you want to import (F2 to list)
```

**FIGURE 5.31:** Enter the path and name of the file to be imported, the format, the order of the data (if a DIF file), and select Import.

Enter the path and name of the ASCII or DIF file to be imported; select ASCII or DIF format; if it is a DIF file, select Columns or Rows to specify order of the data; and select Import. LotusWorks copies all the data from the file into the current spreadsheet starting at the cell pointer location. If there are not enough columns or rows left in the worksheet, LotusWorks imports as much data as will fit.

## Exporting Spreadsheet Data to a DIF File

To save data from the current spreadsheet to a DIF file, first select the range of data to be exported, select File Transfer Export. The following dialog box appears:

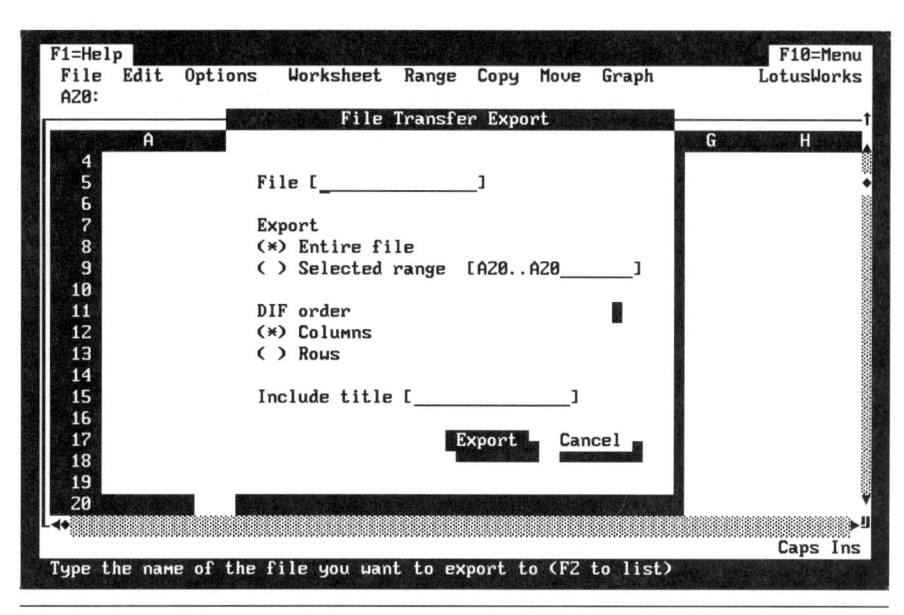

**FIGURE 5.32:** Enter a path and name for the export file; specify whether the entire file or a range is to be exported, and select the DIF order.

Enter a path and name for the export file; specify whether the entire file or a range of data is to be exported; specify whether the DIF order is by columns or rows; enter a title for the spreadsheet, if you wish; then select Export.

# Copying Data To and From the Word Processing Service

You can copy data from a spreadsheet into a word processing document with the Edit Copy and Edit Paste options. (You cannot use the copy command to copy spreadsheet data to a word processing document.) For instance, you can copy spreadsheet data into a word processing document to create a table in a report. Once the data is pasted into the word document, of course, it becomes ordinary text and ceases being a spreadsheet that can perform math. Formulas do not transfer to word documents.

*If you want to convert a character label composed of numbers to numeric format, move the cell pointer to the label, press F2, delete the apostrophe from in front of the numbers, and press Enter. LotusWorks changes the numbers from character (text) to numeric data.*

To copy spreadsheet data to a word document:

1. Select the range you want to copy from the current spreadsheet.
2. Press Alt+C.
3. Press Ctrl+F6 to return to the LotusWorks screen.
4. Open the Word Processing service.
5. Retrieve the desired word document or create a new one.
6. Move the cell pointer to the point in the document where you want the spreadsheet data to appear.
7. Press Alt+P to paste the data.

You can also copy text from a word document into a spreadsheet. Simply reverse the process above:

1. Select the text to be copied.
2. Press Alt+C.
3. Retrieve the spreadsheet (or shift to it if you have it current in another window).
4. Move the cell pointer to the cell where you want to insert the text.
5. Press Alt+P to paste the text.

If you paste numbers from a word document in this manner, LotusWorks treats them as a label.

## Modifying the LotusWorks Quickstart Spreadsheets

A good way to get familiar with spreadsheet design is to retrieve and modify some of the Quickstart spreadsheets that are bundled with LotusWorks. Simply select File Retrieve from the Spreadsheet service and select any of the files that appear in the list box. If you plan to modify the spreadsheet, it's a good idea to save it under a different file name before you begin modifying it. That way you won't accidentally corrupt the original example. (If you do accidentally change the original spreadsheet by mistake, you can restore it by copying the original spreadsheet file from your backup LotusWorks disks to your hard disk.)

Once the spreadsheet is current, move the cell pointer to the area you want to modify. (You may have to search in some cases to find the spreadsheet within the larger spreadsheet file.) Move the cell pointer from cell to cell and observe the text, numbers, and formulas that appear on the status line.

Because the example spreadsheets have protection turned on, you won't be able to modify a spreadsheet until you turn its protection off. To do this, select Worksheet Global Protection and then select the Disable option.

## Example Spreadsheets

Here are three additional spreadsheets that illustrate some of the main Lotus-Works spreadsheet procedures and features.

### A Daily Appointment Schedule and To-Do List

This spreadsheet enables you to enter, view, and print your daily appointments and items to do. The spreadsheet is composed entirely of text and performs no calculations. The finished spreadsheet looks like this:

```
DATE :
DAY  :
----------------------------------------------------------------
|TO DO                         |
|------------------------------|--------------------------------
|Pri- |                        |        | 8:00AM|
|ority|TASK                    |Done?   |    15 |
|-----|                        |--------|    30 |
|     |                        |        |    45 |
|     |                        |        |-------|----------------
|     |                        |        | 9:00  |
|     |                        |        |    15 |
|     |                        |        |    30 |
|     |                        |        |    45 |
|     |                        |        |-------|----------------
|     |                        |        |10:00  |
|     |                        |        |    15 |
|     |                        |        |    30 |
|     |                        |        |    45 |
|     |                        |        |-------|----------------
|     |                        |        |11:00  |
|     |                        |        |    15 |
|     |                        |        |    30 |
|     |                        |        |    45 |
|     |                        |        |-------|----------------
|     |                        |        |12:00  |
|     |                        |        |    15 |
|     |                        |        |    30 |
|     |                        |        |    45 |
|     |                        |        |-------|----------------
|     |                        |        | 1:00PM|
|     |                        |        |    15 |
|     |                        |        |    30 |
|     |                        |        |    45 |
|     |                        |        |-------|----------------
|     |                        |        | 2:00  |
|     |                        |        |    15 |
|     |                        |        |    30 |
|     |                        |        |    45 |
|     |                        |        |-------|----------------
|     |                        |        | 3:00  |
|     |                        |        |    15 |
|     |                        |        |    30 |
|     |                        |        |    45 |
|     |                        |        |-------|----------------
|     |                        |        | 4:00  |
|     |                        |        |    15 |
|     |                        |        |    30 |
|     |                        |        |    45 |
|     |                        |        |-------|----------------
|     |                        |        | 5:00  |
|     |                        |        |    15 |
|     |                        |        |    30 |
|     |                        |        |    45 |
|     |                        |        |-------|----------------
|     |                        |        | 6:00+ |
|     |                        |        |       |
|     |                        |        |       |
----------------------------------------------------------------
```

**FIGURE 5.33:** The finished Daily Appointment Schedule and To-Do List

To use the Appointment Schedule and To-Do List, retrieve the spreadsheet, enter appointments and to-do items as labels in the areas provided, then save the spreadsheet under a separate file name that identifies the date, such as JUN1392 or JUN1492.

If you want to be able to retrieve the spreadsheet quickly, you can create a macro to retrieve the file for any particular day. Simply record these keystrokes:

{F10}   Move to the Menu line.

f       Select the File menu.

r       Select File Retrieve

{Tab}   Tab to the text box.

When you run the macro, enter the file name for the day you want and press Enter.

To build the spreadsheet, follow these steps:

---

### Building the Appointment Schedule and To-Do List Spreadsheet

**Columns**
Set columns A through K to the following widths (see "Adjusting Column Widths" earlier in this chapter):

| | |
|---|---|
| A, C, E, G, I, K | 1 space |
| B, F | 5 spaces |
| D, J | 25 spaces |
| H | 7 spaces |

**Labels**
Enter the following labels into the cells and ranges indicated. To save time entering data into ranges, enter the data into the first cell, then copy the contents to the rest of the range.

| | |
|---|---|
| A3..K3 | \- |
| A4..A59 | \| (vertical bar) |
| B1 | DATE |
| B2 | DAY |
| B4 | TO DO |
| B5..J5 | \- |
| B6 | Pri- |
| B7 | ority |
| B8..F8 | \- |
| B50..K60 | \- |

| | |
|---|---|
| C1..C2 | : (colon) |
| C6..C7; C9..C59 | \| |
| D7 | Task |
| E6..E7; E9..E59 | \| |
| F7 | Done? |
| G4; G6..G59 | \| |
| H6 | (space)8:00AM |
| H11 | (space)9:00 |
| H16 | 10:00 |
| H21 | 11:00 |
| H26 | 12:00 |
| H31 | (space)1:00PM |
| H36 | (space)2:00 |
| H41 | (space)3:00 |
| H46 | (space)4:00 |
| H51 | (space)5:00 |
| H56 | (space)6:00+ |
| H7..H9 | (3 spaces)15 |
| | (3 spaces)30 |
| | (3 spaces)45 |

(Copy and paste range H7..H9 into ranges H12..H14; H17..H19; H22..H24; H27..H29; H32..H34; H37..H39; H42..H44; H47..H49; H52..H54.)

| | |
|---|---|
| H10..J10 | \- |

(Copy and paste range H10..J10 into ranges H15..J15; H20..J20; H25..J25; H30..J30; H35..J35; H40..J40; H45..J45; H50..J50; H55..J55.)

| | |
|---|---|
| I6..I9 | \| |

Copy range I6..I9 into ranges I11..I14; I16..I19; I21..I24; I26..I29; I31..I34; I36..I39; I41..I44; I46..I49; I51..I54; I56..I59;.)

| | |
|---|---|
| K4..K59 | \| |

**Testing and Printing the Speadsheet**
The best way to test this spreadsheet is to view it on the screen and then print it. To print it, select and name A1..K60 as a print range. Try setting the File Print Layout margins to Left 4, Right 85, Top 0, and Bottom 0. (You may have to adjust these for your printer.)

**Protecting and Saving the Spreadsheet**
It's a good idea to protect the labels and column boundaries in the spreadsheet to guard against accidentally writing over or erasing them. Select each of the following ranges, then select Range Protect Protect.

A1..G3; A4..A58; C4..E58; G4..G58; A59..G59

The final step is to save the spreadsheet. Pick a name that you can remember, such as APPTMNT or TO_DO.

# A Loan Amortization Schedule

This spreadsheet calculates the amount of the periodic payment for a loan when you specify the loan amount, annual interest rate, term of the loan, the number of payment periods per year, and the year and month of the first payment. For each payment, the spreadsheet automatically calculates and displays the payment number, date, beginning loan balance, interest portion of the payment, principal portion of the payment, ending loan balance, and cumulative interest of the loan.

This spreadsheet makes use of the @DATE, @YEAR, and @MONTH functions to create dates and the @PMT function to calculate the monthly payment. It also uses a lookup table to calculate the month and year for each loan payment.

Notice that some formulas use absolute cell references (for example, $E$6), some use relative cell references (for example, +F18), and some use both (for example, $E$12–D18).

Some of the formulas may appear complicated at first, but if you look closely at the constituent parts of each @function, you can probably figure them out.

To use the Loan Amortization Schedule, simply enter data for the six items in cells E3..E9 at the top of the spreadsheet. Notice that to enter an interest rate, you must enter the decimal fraction for the percentage rate (for example, 0.115 for 11.5%). LotusWorks performs the rest of the calculations for you.

The finished spreadsheet (with data for a $10,000 loan for 36 months at 11.5% annual interest) looks like this:

```
LOAN AMORTIZATION SCHEDULE
-----------------------------------------------------------------------
     Loan Principal                    $10,000.00
     Annual Interest Rate                   0.115

     Starting Month (MM)                       3
     Starting Year (YY)                       92
     Term (Years)                              3
     Payment Periods per Year                 12
     --------
     Start Date                         03/01/92
     Monthly Payment                      $329.76
     Number of Payments                       36
=======================================================================
PMT.  PMT.    BEGINNING    INTEREST   PRINCIPAL   ENDING      CUMULATIVE
NO.   DATE    BALANCE      PORTION    PORTION     BALANCE     INTEREST
=======================================================================
  1   Mar-92  10,000.00     95.83      233.93    9,766.07        95.83
  2   Apr-92   9,766.07     93.59      236.17    9,529.90       189.42
  3   May-92   9,529.90     91.33      238.43    9,291.47       280.75
  4   Jun-92   9,291.47     89.04      240.72    9,050.76       369.80
  5   Jul-92   9,050.76     86.74      243.02    8,807.73       456.53
  6   Aug-92   8,807.73     84.41      245.35    8,562.38       540.94
  7   Sep-92   8,562.38     82.06      247.70    8,314.68       623.00
  8   Oct-92   8,314.68     79.68      250.08    8,064.60       702.68
  9   Nov-92   8,064.60     77.29      252.47    7,812.12       779.96
 10   Dec-92   7,812.12     74.87      254.89    7,557.23       854.83
 11   Jan-93   7,557.23     72.42      257.34    7,299.89       927.25
 12   Feb-93   7,299.89     69.96      259.80    7,040.09       997.21
 13   Mar-93   7,040.09     67.47      262.29    6,777.80     1,064.68
 14   Apr-93   6,777.80     64.95      264.81    6,512.99     1,129.63
 15   May-93   6,512.99     62.42      267.34    6,245.65     1,192.05
 16   Jun-93   6,245.65     59.85      269.91    5,975.74     1,251.90
 17   Jul-93   5,975.74     57.27      272.49    5,703.25     1,309.17
 18   Aug-93   5,703.25     54.66      275.10    5,428.15     1,363.83
 19   Sep-93   5,428.15     52.02      277.74    5,150.41     1,415.85
 20   Oct-93   5,150.41     49.36      280.40    4,870.00     1,465.20
 21   Nov-93   4,870.00     46.67      283.09    4,586.91     1,511.88
 22   Dec-93   4,586.91     43.96      285.80    4,301.11     1,555.83
 23   Jan-94   4,301.11     41.22      288.54    4,012.57     1,597.05
 24   Feb-94   4,012.57     38.45      291.31    3,721.26     1,635.51
 25   Mar-94   3,721.26     35.66      294.10    3,427.17     1,671.17
 26   Apr-94   3,427.17     32.84      296.92    3,130.25     1,704.01
 27   May-94   3,130.25     30.00      299.76    2,830.49     1,734.00
 28   Jun-94   2,830.49     27.13      302.63    2,527.85     1,761.14
 29   Jul-94   2,527.85     24.23      305.53    2,222.32     1,785.36
 30   Aug-94   2,222.32     21.30      308.46    1,913.86     1,806.66
 31   Sep-94   1,913.86     18.34      311.42    1,602.44     1,825.00
 32   Oct-94   1,602.44     15.36      314.40    1,288.03     1,840.36
 33   Nov-94   1,288.03     12.34      317.42      970.62     1,852.70
 34   Dec-94     970.62      9.30      320.46      650.16     1,862.00
 35   Jan-95     650.16      6.23      323.53      326.63     1,868.23
 36   Feb-95     326.63      3.13      326.63       (0.00)    1,871.36
```

**FIGURE 5.34:** The Loan Amortization Schedule spreadsheet

To build the Loan Amortization Schedule Spreadsheet, follow these steps. Save the spreadsheet to an appropriate file name (such as LOANCALC) as you go along.

# Building the Loan Amortization Schedule Spreadsheet

**Columns**
Set columns A-G to the following widths:
- A     5 spaces
- B     8 spaces
- C     13 spaces
- D     10 spaces
- E,F,G     12 spaces

**Labels**
Enter the following labels into the cells and ranges indicated. To save time entering data into ranges, enter the data into the first cell, then copy the contents to the rest of the range.

| Cell | Label |
|---|---|
| A1 | LOAN AMORTIZATION SCHEDULE |
| A2..G2 | \- |
| B3 | Loan Principal |
| B4 | Annual Interest Rate |
| B6 | Starting Month (MM) |
| B7 | Starting Year (YY) |
| B8 | Term (Years) |
| B9 | Payment Periods per Year |
| B10 | \- |
| B11 | Start Date |
| B12 | Monthly Payment |
| B13 | Number of Payments |
| A14..G14 | \= |
| A15..B15 | PMT. |
| C15 | BEGINNING |
| D15 | INTEREST |
| E15 | PRINCIPAL |
| F15 | ENDING |
| G15 | CUMULATIVE |
| A16 | NO. |
| B16 | DATE |
| C16 | BALANCE |
| D16..E16 | PORTION |
| F16 | BALANCE |
| G16 | INTEREST |
| A17..G17 | \= |

**The Lookup Table**
To create the lookup table, enter the following data and formulas into the range J3..L14:

| Cell | Value |
|---|---|
| J3 | 1 |
| J4..J14 | +J3+1 (Enter +J3+1 into cell J4 and copy into range J5..J14.) |

| | |
|---|---|
| K3..K13 | 0 |
| K14 | 1 |
| L3 | 2 |
| L4..K13 | +L3+1 (Enter +L3+1 into cell L4 and copy into range L5..L13.) |
| L14 | 1 |

**Formulas and Data**

Enter the following formulas and data into the indicated cells:

| | |
|---|---|
| E11 | @DATE(E7,E6,1) |
| E12 | @PMT($E$3,$E$4/12,$E$8*$E$9) |
| E13 | +$E$8*$E$9 |
| A18 | 1 |
| B18 | @DATE($E$7,$E$6,1) |
| C18 | +$E$3 |
| D18..D19 | +$E$4/$E$9*C18 (Write the formula into cell D18 and copy into cell D19.) |
| E18..E19 | @if(C18>0.1,$E$12–D18,@CHAR(32)) (Write the formula into cell E18 and copy into cell E19.) |
| F18..F19 | +C18–E18 (Write the formula into cell F18 and copy into cell F19.) |
| G18 | +D18 |
| A19 | +A18+1 |
| B19 | @DATE(@YEAR(B18)+@VLOOKUP(@MONTH(B18),$I$3..$K$14,1),@VLOOKUP(@MONTH(B18),$I$3..$K$14,2),1) |
| | (This long formula says, "Write a date consisting of (1) the year that is in cell B18 plus any additional years indicated by looking up the previous month in the lookup table, (2) the month indicated by looking up the previous month in the lookup table, and (3) day 1.") |
| C19 | +F18 |
| G19 | +G18+D19 |

Now, the enjoyable (and time-saving) part! Copy range A19..G19 into range A20..G53. In one step, this transfers all the necessary formulas for 36 payments. If you want the spreadsheet to handle more payments, copy the range A19..G19 into additional rows at the bottom of the spreadsheet.

**Number Formats**

The last stage in building the spreadsheet is to format the number columns. Press Alt+N and select the following formats for the various ranges:

| | |
|---|---|
| E3 | Currency,2 (Currency, 2 decimal places) |
| E11 | Date (Long Int'l Date) |
| E12 | Currency,2 |
| A18..A53 | General |
| B18..B53 | Date 3  (*MMM-YY*) |
| C18..G53 | ,2(Comma, 2 decimal places.) |

That's it. Try out the spreadsheet with various numbers entered into cells E3 through E9. Check the results to be sure that the formulas are referencing the correct cells and calculating as they should. If you want to try a loan larger than $1 million widen columns C, F, and G.

To print the report, select cells A1..G53 for a print range.

# A Calculator for Business Financial Ratios

This spreadsheet calculates a variety of standard financial ratios used to evaluate the solvency, liquidity, funds management, and profitability of businesses. When you enter data about a business's assets, liabilities, and monthly income and expenses, the spreadsheet automatically calculates total assets, total liabilities and equity, earnings, and seventeen key ratio indicators.

The spreadsheet has four parts. One part calculates total assets and the percentage each element is of the total. The second part calculates total liabilities and equity and the percentage each element is of the total. The third part calculates earnings and the percentage of total sales eaten up by each category of expense. The fourth part calculates 17 indicators of financial performance.

Although this spreadsheet is longer than the Amortization Schedule example, its formulas are simpler. Most are simply ratios or sums. Many can be merely copied from other cells. As you can see, spreadsheets do not necessarily have to have complicated programming to be extremely useful.

Note that certain cells that appear in several formulas are given range names (for example, *TA* for Total Assets, *CA* for Current Assets, *EAT* for Earnings After Taxes, *SALES* for Sales, etc.). This is optional, but it is a good practice. It makes it easy to document formulas and to keep track of absolute cell references when you have numerous formulas in a long spreadsheet. If you ever have to go back and decipher a long spreadsheet when the formulas are no longer in mind, you'll appreciate the cues provided by the range names.

The calculator can be used for large or small firms. The sample data data shown here are for a small firm.

The finished spreadsheet looks like this:

BUSINESS FINANCIAL RATIOS CALCULATOR

```
===============================================================
ASSETS
===============================================================
                                          31-Dec-91  RATIOS
                                          ---------  -------
Current Assets
  Cash                                      $10,000      2%
  Marketable Securities                      10,000      2%
  Accounts Receivable              65,000               13%
  Less: Allowance for Doubtful Accounts    15,000        3%
                                          ---------  -------
  Net Accounts Receivable                   50,000     10%
  Inventory                                 30,000      6%
  Prepaid Expenses                          15,000      3%
  Other                                          0      0%
                                          ---------  -------
Total Current Assets                       115,000     22%

Noncurrent Assets
  Property, Plant and Equipment   500,000              97%
  Less: Accumulated Depreciation  100,000              19%
                                          ---------  -------
  Net Property, Plant, and Equipment       400,000     78%
  Investment in Subsidiaries                     0      0%
                                          ---------  -------
Total Noncurrent Assets                    400,000     78%

Total Assets                              $515,000    100%
                                          =========  =======


===============================================================
LIABILITIES
===============================================================
                                          31-Dec-91  Ratios
                                          ---------  -------
Current Liabilities
  Notes Payable                            $50,000     10%
  Accounts Payable                           8,500      2%
  Accrued Expenses                           4,500      1%
  Other Current Liabilities                      0      0%
                                          ---------  -------
Total Current Liabilities                   63,000     12%

Long-Term Debt                             150,000     29%

Stockholders' Equity
  Common Stock                               5,000      1%
  Retained Earnings                        297,000     58%
                                          ---------  -------
Total Stockholders' Equity                 302,000     59%
                                          ---------  -------
Total Liabilities and Equity              $515,000    100%
                                          =========  =======
```

**FIGURE 5.35:** The Business Financial Ratios Calculator

```
===============================================================================
INCOME STATEMENT
===============================================================================
                                                       Monthly
                                          31-Dec-91    Ratios
                                          ---------    -------
Gross Sales                                $900,000     100%
Cost of Goods Sold                          250,000      28%
                                           --------    ----
Gross Margin                                650,000      72%

Operating Expenses              550,000                  61%
Depreciation                     15,000                   2%
                                           --------    ----
                                            565,000      63%
                                           --------    ----
Earnings before Interest and Taxes           85,000       9%
Interest Expense                             18,000       2%
                                           --------    ----
Earnings before Taxes                        67,000       7%
Income Taxes                                 15,000       2%
                                           --------    ----
Earnings after Taxes                         52,000       6%
Cash Dividends                                    0       0%
                                           --------    ----
Earnings after Dividends                    $52,000       6%
                                           ========    ====


===============================================================================
RATIOS
===============================================================================

                                                        -------

SOLVENCY
  Debt/Equity Ratio                                         71%
  Times Interest Earned                                      5

LIQUIDITY
  Net Working Capital                                    52,000
  Net Working Capital/Assets                                10%
  Current Ratio                                            183%
  Quick Ratio                                              111%
  Cash Ratio                                                32%

FUNDS MANAGEMENT
  Receivables/Sales (Annualized)                             0%
  Days Sales in Receivables                                  2
  Payables/Cost of Goods Sold (Annualized)                   0%
  Days Cost of Goods Sold in Payables                        1
  Inventory Turnover (Annualized)                        10000%
  Days Cost of Goods Sold in Inventory                       4
  Sales/Fixed Assets (Annualized)                        36000%

PROFITABILITY
  Return on Sales (Annualized)                               6%
  Return on Total Assets                                   121%
  Return on Stockholders' Equity                           207%
```

**FIGURE 5.35 (continued):** The Business Financial Ratios Calculator

To build the spreadsheet, follow these steps. Be sure to save the spreadsheet to an appropriate file name (such as RATIOS) as you go along.

## Building the Business Financial Ratios Calculator

**Columns**
Set columns A–D to the following widths:

| | |
|---|---|
| A | 40 spaces |
| B | 9 spaces |
| C, D | 10 spaces |

**Labels**
Enter the following labels in the cells and ranges indicated:

| | | |
|---|---|---|
| A1 | ' | BUSINESS FINANCIAL RATIOS CALCULATOR |
| A4 | \= | (Copy into range B4..D4. Copy range A4..D4 and paste into ranges A6..D6, A34..D34, A36..D36, A59..D59, A61..D61, A90..D90, A92..D92.) |
| A5 | ASSETS | |
| D7 | RATIOS | |
| C8, D8 | '---------(9 Hyphens) | (Paste into cells B14, C14, D14, C19, D19, C25, D25, C28, D28, C38, D38, C44, D44, C52, D52, C54, D54, C64, D64, C67, D67, C72, D72, C74, D74, C77, D77, C80, D80, C83, D83, D95) |
| A9 | Current Assets | |
| A10 | Cash | (Note: Indent labels in A10..A18 one space) |
| A11 | Marketable Securities | |
| A12 | Accounts Receivable | |
| A13 | Less: Allowance for Doubtful Accounts | |
| A15 | Net Accounts Receivable | |
| A16 | Inventory | |
| A17 | Prepaid Expenses | |
| A18 | Other | |
| A20 | Total Current Assets | |
| A22 | Noncurrent Assets | |
| A23 | Property, Plant, and Equipment | (Indent labels in A23..A27 one space) |
| A24 | Less: Accumulated Depreciation | |
| A26 | Net Property, Plant, and Equipment | |
| A27 | Investment in Subsidiaries | |
| A29 | Total Noncurrent Assets | |
| A31 | Total Assets | |
| C32, D32 | \= | (Paste into cells C56, D56, C85, D85) |
| C35 | LIABILITIES | |
| D37 | Ratios | |

| | | |
|---|---|---|
| A39 | Current Liabilities | |
| A40 | Notes Payable | (Indent labels in A40..A43 one space) |
| A42 | Accrued Expenses | |
| A43 | Other Current Liabilities | |
| A45 | Total Current Liabilities | |
| A47 | Long-Term Debt | |
| A49 | Stockholders' Equity | |
| A50 | Common Stock | (Indent labels in A50..A51 one space) |
| A51 | Retained Earnings | |
| A53 | Total Stockholders' Equity | |
| A55 | Total Liabilities and Equity | |
| A60 | INCOME STATEMENT | |
| D62 | Monthly | |
| D63 | Ratios | |
| A65 | Gross Sales | |
| A66 | Cost of Goods Sold | |
| A68 | Gross Margin | |
| A70 | Operating Expenses | |
| A71 | Depreciation | |
| A75 | Earnings before Interest and Taxes | |
| A76 | Interest Expense | |
| A78 | Earnings before Taxes | |
| A79 | Income Taxes | |
| A81 | Earnings after Taxes | |
| A82 | Cash Dividends | |
| A84 | Earnings after Dividends | |
| A91 | RATIOS | |
| A96 | SOLVENCY | |
| A97 | Debt/Equity Ratio | (Indent labels in A97..A98 one space) |
| A98 | Times Interest Earned | |
| A100 | LIQUIDITY | |
| A101 | Net Working Capital | (Indent labels in A101..A105 one space) |
| A102 | Net Working Capital/Assets | |
| A103 | Current Ratio | |
| A104 | Quick Ratio | |
| A105 | Cash Ratio | |
| A107 | FUNDS MANAGEMENT | |
| A108 | Receivables/Sales (Annualized) | (Indent labels in A108..A114 one space) |
| A109 | Days Sales in Receivables | |
| A110 | Payables/Cost of Goods Sold (Annualized) | |
| A111 | Days Cost of Goods Sold in Payables | |
| A112 | Inventory Turnover (Annualized) | |
| A113 | Days Cost of Goods Sold in Inventory | |
| A114 | Sales/Fixed Assets (Annualized) | |

A116          PROFITABILITY  
A117          Return on Sales (Annualized)          (Indent labels in A117..A119 one space)  
A118          Return on Total Assets  
A119          Return on Stockholders' Equity

**Range Names**
Enter the following range names for the cells indicated. The range names will be used in formulas for the key ratios. See "Creating, Viewing, and Deleting Range Names" in this chapter.

C20 *CA*          (Total Current Assets)  
C31 *TA*          (Total Assets)  
C45 *CL*          (Current Liabilities)  
C47 *LTD*         (Long-term Debt)  
C53 *EQUITY*    (Stockholders' Equity)  
C55 *TL*          (Total Liabilities)  
C65 *SALES*      (Gross Sales)  
C66 *COGS*       (Cost of Goods Sold)  
C75 *EBIT*        (Earnings Before Interest and Taxes)  
C81 *EAT*         (Earnings After Taxes)  
C84 *EAD*        (Earnings After Dividends)

**Number Formats**
Set the following number formats for the cells and ranges indicated:

**Format Cells and Ranges**
Date, 1      C7, C37                                   (*DD-MMM-YY*)  
Date, 3      C63                                          (*MMM-YY*)  
Currency, 0   C10, C31, C40, C55, C65, C84, D101   (Currency, 0 decimal places)  
Comma, 0     B11..B12, C11..C29, C40..C53, C66..C81   (Comma, 0 decimal places)  
Percent, 0     D10..D100, D102..D119                (Percent, 0 decimal places)

**Formulas**
Enter the following formulas into the cells indicated. As you finish entering each formula, enable Protection for the cell (select Range Protect Protect).

C7, C37, C64     @DATE(91,12,31)  
C15                +B12−B13  
C20                @SUM(C10..C18)  
C26                +B23−B24  
C29                +C26+C27  
C31                +CA+C29  
C45                @SUM(C40..C43)  
C53                +C50+C51  
C55                +CL+LTD+EQUITY  
C68                +SALES−COGS  
C73                +B70+B71  
C75                +C68−C73  
C78                +EBIT−C76

| | | |
|---|---|---|
| C81 | +C78–C79 | |
| C84 | +EAT–C82 | |
| D10 | +C10/$TA | Paste into D11, D15..D18, D20, D26..D27, D29, D31 |
| D12 | +B12/$TA | Paste into D13, D23..D24 |
| D40 | +C40/$TL | Paste into D41..D43, D45, D47, D50..D51, D53, D55 |
| D65 | +SALES/$SALES | Paste into D66, D68, D73, D75..D76, D78..D79, D81..D82, D84 |
| D70 | +B70/$SALES | Paste into D71 |
| D97 | +(CL+LTD)/EQUITY | |
| D98 | +EBIT/C76 | |
| D101 | +CA–CL | |
| D102 | +D101/TA | |
| D103 | +CA/CL | |
| D104 | +(C10+C11+C15)/CL | |
| D105 | +(C10+C11)/CL | |
| D108 | +C15/(SALES*12) | |
| D109 | +D108*365 | |
| D110 | +C41/(COGS*12) | |
| D111 | +D110*365 | |
| D112 | +COGS*12/C16 | |
| D113 | +365/D112 | |
| D114 | +(SALES*12)/C16 | |
| D117 | +EAT/SALES | |
| D118 | +(EAT/ASSETS)*12 | |
| D119 | +(EAT/EQUITY)*12 | |

## Testing the Spreadsheet

When you finish building the spreadsheet, enter some data and observe the calculations that result. Then enter the data displayed in Figure 5-35. Carefully check each formula to be sure that it is drawing from the correct cells and calculating correctly. When you are satisfied that the spreadsheet is okay, try it out with real data.

*Protect all cells containing formulas to guard against accidental erasures when you're entering data.*

## Creating a Table of Historical Data

The financial ratios produced by the calculator give you a snapshot of your business. To get a better picture of the trends over time, you may wish to copy key elements of the spreadsheet each month to a table of historical data. For most businesses, the key elements for such a table are the Date, Total Assets, Current Assets, Net Working Capital, Monthly Gross Sales, Monthly Earnings After

Taxes, the Current Ratio, Days Sales in Receivables, Days Cost of Goods Sold in Payables, Debt/Equity Ratio, and Annualized Return on Equity. If other indicators are important to your business, you may prefer to include other indicators in the table. As described below, you can even use a macro to automate the copy process.

To create the table, set columns F–P to the following widths:

| | |
|---|---|
| F | 7 spaces |
| G, H, I, J, K, M, P | 11 spaces |
| L, O | 8 spaces |
| N | 10 spaces |

Set the following number formats for the columns in the table (make the columns 36 rows long):

| | |
|---|---|
| F | Date, 3 |
| G, H, I, J, K | Currency, 0 |
| L, O, P | Fixed, 2 |
| M, N | Fixed, 0 |

Enter Labels for the column headings as in the following illustration:

```
                              NET      MONTHLY  MONTHLY            DAYS      DAYS     DEBT/    ANNUALIZED
            TOTAL    CURRENT  WORKING  GROSS    EARNINGS  CURRENT  SALES IN  COGS IN  EQUITY   RETURN
DATE        ASSETS   ASSETS   CAPITAL  SALES    AFTER TAXES RATIO  REC'VBLES REC'VBLES RATIO   ON EQUITY
```

**FIGURE 5.36:** Column headings for the Historical Data range

The following macro copies the appropriate data each month. To use the macro, position the cell pointer in the first blank row of column F and press Ctrl+H (or whatever key combination you have assigned to the macro).

+C7{Right}+TA{Right}+CA{Right}+D101{Right}+SALES{Right}+EAT{Right}
+D103{Right}+D109{Right}+D111{Right}+D117{Right}+D119

## An Interactive Financial Statement

This spreadsheet is composed of six small spreadsheets. It is interactive in that the values in some spreadsheets are drawn from values in others. The spreadsheet reports the financial results of a company (Ajax Properties) with three profit centers (divisions). It breaks down each division's results by quarter and consolidates the annual totals into a company-wide summary report. It also calculates return on sales by quarter and by division.

Because three of the spreadsheets have identical structures and formulas, it is possible to build one and then simply copy and relabel it to create the other two. It is also possible to copy some elements from the first spreadsheet to save work in creating the remaining three. Be sure to save the master spreadsheet to a file after you create each new part.

## Spreadsheet #1

### Columns
Set columns A–F to the following widths:

| | |
|---|---|
| A | 25 spaces |
| B–E | 9 spaces |
| F | 10 spaces |

### Labels
Enter the following labels into the cells indicated:

| | |
|---|---|
| A1 | ' AJAX MANAGEMENT COMPANY (Add blank spaces after the apostrophe to center the title on the page.) |
| A2 | ' 1992 Financial Performance |
| A4 | Residential Division |
| B4 | Qtr1 |
| C4 | Qtr2 |
| D4 | Qtr3 |
| E4 | Qtr4 |
| F4 | TOTAL |
| A5 | '------------------------ (24 hyphens) |
| B5..F5 | '-------- (8 hyphens) |
| A6 | Sales |
| A7 | Less: Cost of Sales |
| A8..F8 | (Copy lines from A5..F5) |
| A9 | Gross Profit |
| A11 | EXPENSES |
| A12 | Rent |
| A13 | Utilities |
| A14 | Salaries & Wages |
| A15 | Other Expenses |
| A16 | (Copy lines from A5..F5) |
| A17 | Total Expenses |
| B18..F18 | '======== (8 equal signs; enter into cell B18 and copy into C18..F18) |
| B19 | Profit Before Tax |
| B21 | Return on Sales |

With the labels entered, the first spreadsheet looks like this:

```
                       AJAX MANAGEMENT COMPANY
                       1992 Financial Performance

Residential Division      Qtr1       Qtr2       Qtr3       Qtr4      TOTAL
------------------------  --------   --------   --------   --------  --------
Sales
Less: Cost of Sales
------------------------  --------   --------   --------   --------  --------
Gross Profit

EXPENSES
Rent
Utilities
Salaries & Wages
Other Expenses
------------------------  --------   --------   --------   --------  --------
Total Expenses
                          ========   ========   ========   ========  ========
Profit Before Tax

Return on Sales
```

**FIGURE 5.37:** Label structure for the profit center spreadsheets

## Formulas

Enter the following formulas into the cells indicated:

| | | |
|---|---|---|
| F6  | @SUM(B6..E6)  | Copy into cell F7 and range F12..F15 |
| B9  | +B6–B7        | Copy into range C9..F9 |
| B17 | @sum(B12..B15)| Copy into range C17..F17 |
| B19 | +B9–B17       | Copy into range C19..F19 |
| B21 | +B19/B6       | Copy into range C21..F21 |

## Number Formats

Assign the following number formats to the ranges indicated:

| | | |
|---|---|---|
| B6..F19  | , 0        | (Comma, no decimal places) |
| B21..F21 | Percent, 2 | Percent, 2 decimal places) |

## Data

To make the spreadsheet match this example, enter the following numbers into the cells indicated:

| | |
|---|---|
| B6 | 500000 |
| C6 | 525000 |
| D6 | 495000 |
| E6 | 560000 |
| B7 | 350000 |
| C7 | 345000 |
| D7 | 360000 |

| | |
|---|---|
| E7 | 370000 |
| B12..E12 | 15000 |
| B13..E13 | 30000 |
| B14..E14 | 12000 |
| B15..E15 | 5000 |

That completes the first spreadsheet. Before copying it, you should check to see if the formulas calculate correctly. The recalculated spreadsheet looks like this:

```
                    AJAX MANAGEMENT COMPANY
                    1992 Financial Performance

Residential Division     Qtr1      Qtr2      Qtr3      Qtr4     TOTAL
------------------------ --------  --------  --------  -------- --------
Sales                    500,000   525,000   495,000   560,000 2,080,000
Less: Cost of Sales      350,000   345,000   360,000   370,000 1,425,000
------------------------ --------  --------  --------  -------- --------
Gross Profit             150,000   180,000   135,000   190,000   655,000

EXPENSES
Rent                      15,000    15,000    15,000    15,000    60,000
Utilities                  3,000     3,000     3,000     3,000    12,000
Salaries & Wages          12,000    12,000    12,000    12,000    48,000
Other Expenses             5,000     5,000     5,000     5,000    20,000
------------------------ --------  --------  --------  -------- --------
Total Expenses            35,000    35,000    35,000    35,000   140,000
                        ========  ========  ========  ======== ========
Profit Before Tax        115,000   145,000   100,000   155,000   515,000

Return on Sales           23.00%    27.62%    20.20%    27.68%    24.76%
```

**FIGURE 5.38:** The Residential Division spreadsheet

## Spreadsheet #2

To create the second spreadsheet, copy range A4..F21 to range A23..F40. Change the label in cell A23 to Commercial Division, and enter the following numbers into the cells indicated:

| | |
|---|---|
| B25 | 250000 |
| C25 | 240000 |
| D25 | 245000 |
| E25 | 250000 |
| B26 | 125000 |
| C26 | 125000 |
| D26 | 130000 |
| E26 | 135000 |
| B31..E31 | 12000 |
| B32..E32 | 12000 |
| B33..E33 | 17500 |
| B34..E34 | 3500 |

The completed spreadsheet #2 looks like this:

```
Commercial Division      Qtr1      Qtr2      Qtr3      Qtr4     TOTAL
-----------------------  --------  --------  --------  --------  --------
Sales                    250,000   240,000   245,000   250,000   985,000
Less: Cost of Sales      125,000   125,000   130,000   135,000   515,000
-----------------------  --------  --------  --------  --------  --------
Gross Profit             125,000   115,000   115,000   115,000   470,000

EXPENSES
Rent                      12,000    12,000    12,000    12,000    48,000
Utilities                 12,000    12,000    12,000    12,000    48,000
Salaries & Wages          17,500    17,500    17,500    17,500    70,000
Other Expenses             3,500     3,500     3,500     3,500    14,000
-----------------------  --------  --------  --------  --------  --------
Total Expenses            45,000    45,000    45,000    45,000   180,000
                        ========  ========  ========  ========  ========
Profit Before Tax         80,000    70,000    70,000    70,000   290,000

Return on Sales           32.00%    29.17%    28.57%    28.00%    29.44%
```

**FIGURE 5.39:** The Commercial Division spreadsheet

## Spreadsheet #3

To create the third spreadsheet, copy the range A4..F21 to range A42..F59. Change the label in cell A42 to Land Division, and enter the following numbers into the cells indicated:

| | |
|---|---|
| B44..E44 | 50000 |
| B45..E45 | 45000 |
| B50..E50 | 3000 |
| B51..E51 | 0 |
| B52..E52 | 1500 |
| B53..E53 | 0 |

The completed #3 three looks like this:

```
Land Division             A1        Q2        Q3        Q4       TOTAL
-----------------------  --------  --------  --------  --------  --------
Sales                     50,000    50,000    50,000    50,000   200,000
Less: Cost of Sales       45,000    45,000    45,000    45,000   180,000
-----------------------  --------  --------  --------  --------  --------
Gross Profit               5,000     5,000     5,000     5,000    20,000

EXPENSES
Rent                       3,000     3,000     3,000     3,000    12,000
Utilities                      0         0         0         0         0
Salaries & Wages           1,500     1,500     1,500     1,500     6,000
Other Expenses                 0         0         0         0         0
-----------------------  --------  --------  --------  --------  --------
Total Expenses             4,500     4,500     4,500     4,500    18,000
                         ========  ========  ========  ========  ========
Profit Before Tax            500       500       500       500     2,000

Return on Sales            1.00%     1.00%     1.00%     1.00%     1.00%
```

**FIGURE 5.40:** The Land Division spreadsheet

## Spreadsheet #4

The fourth spreadsheet reports company-wide results by quarter. The finished spreadsheet looks like this:

```
AJAX QUARTERS             Qtr1      Qtr2      Qtr3      Qtr4      TOTAL
-----------------------  --------  --------  --------  --------  --------
Sales                    800,000   815,000   790,000   860,000  3,265,000
Profit Before Tax        195,500   215,500   170,500   225,500    807,000
-----------------------  --------  --------  --------  --------  --------
Return on Sales           24.44%    26.44%    21.58%    26.22%    24.72%
```

**FIGURE 5.41:** The finished AJAX QUARTERS spreadsheet

To build the spreadsheet, first copy the contents of range A4..F9 into range A65..F70, then make the following changes:

**Format**

Enter the following format changes:

    B70..F70    Percent, 2

**Labels**

Enter the following labels into the cells indicated. Leave the other labels unchanged.

    A67    Sales
    A68    Profit Before Tax
    A70    Return on Sales

## Formulas

Enter the following formulas into the cells indicated:

| | | |
|---|---|---|
| B67 | +B6+B25+B44 | Copy into range C67..E67 |
| B68 | +B19+B38+B57 | Copy into range C68..E68 |
| F67 | @sum(B67..E67) | (This formula should already be in the cell.) |
| F68 | @sum(B68..E68) | (This formula shold already be in the cell.) |
| B70 | +B68/B67 | Copy into range C70..F70 |

## Spreadsheet #5

The fifth spreadsheet reports return on sales by quarter and division. The completed spreadsheet looks like this:

```
Ajax Return on Sales       Qtr1      Qtr2      Qtr3      Qtr4     TOTAL
-----------------------   -------   -------   -------   -------   -------
Residential Division      23.00%    27.62%    20.20%    27.68%    24.76%
Commercial Division       32.00%    29.17%    28.57%    28.00%    29.44%
Land Division              1.00%     1.00%     1.00%     1.00%     1.00%
-----------------------   -------   -------   -------   -------   -------
Return on Sales           24.44%    26.44%    21.58%    26.22%    24.72%
```

**FIGURE 5.42:** The Ajax Return on Sales spreadsheet

To build the spreadsheet, first copy the contents of range A4..F9 into range A75..A80. Next, move the cell pointer to any cell on row 77 and insert a new row. Press Alt+I, check to be sure that the Range box lists a one-row range and the Insert by Rows is selected, then select Insert.

### Format

Change the number format as follows:

    B77..F81    Percent, 2

### Labels

Enter the following labels into the cells indicated. Leave the other labels intact.

| | |
|---|---|
| A75 | Ajax Return on Sales |
| A77 | Residential Division |
| A78 | Commercial Division |
| A79 | Land Division |
| A81 | Return on Sales |

### Formulas

Enter the following formulas into the cells indicated:

| | | |
|---|---|---|
| B77 | +B21 | Copy into C77..F77 |
| B78 | +B40 | Copy into C78..F78 |
| B79 | +B59 | Copy into C79..F79 |
| B81 | +B70 | Copy into C81..F81 |

## Spreadsheet #6

The final spreadsheet reports yearly totals by division. It draws its data from the first three spreadsheets. The finished spreadsheet looks like this:

```
                     AJAX MANAGEMENT COMPANY
                     1992 Financial Performance

AJAX COMPANY SUMMARY  Residential  Commercial    Land         TOTAL
--------------------  -----------  -----------  -----------  -----------
Sales                   2,080,000      985,000      200,000    3,265,000
Less: Cost of Sales     1,425,000      515,000      180,000    2,120,000
--------------------  -----------  -----------  -----------  -----------
Gross Profit              655,000      470,000       20,000    1,145,000

EXPENSES
Rent                       60,000       48,000       12,000      120,000
Utilities                  12,000       48,000            0       60,000
Salaries & Wages           48,000       70,000        6,000      124,000
Other Expenses             20,000       14,000            0       34,000
--------------------  -----------  -----------  -----------  -----------
Total Expenses            140,000      180,000       18,000      338,000
                      ===========  ===========  ===========  ===========
Profit Before Tax         515,000      290,000        2,000      807,000

Return on Sales             24.76%       29.44%       1.00%       24.72%
```

**FIGURE 5.43:** The Ajax Company Summary spreadsheet

To build the spreadsheet, first copy range A1..F21 to range H1..M21. Next, delete column K. Move the cell pointer to any cell in column K, select Worksheet Delete, check to see that the Range box lists a cell in column K, then select Delete by Columns and select Delete.

### Columns
Make the following changes in column widths:
| | |
|---|---|
| H4 | 21 spaces |
| I4..L4 | 12 spaces |

### Labels
Adjust the dashed line in cell I5 to fit the new column width and copy it into ranges J5..L5, I8..L8, and I16..L16. Adjust the double dashed line in cell I18 to fit the new column width and copy it into range J18..L18.

Enter the following labels into the cells indicated. Leave the other labels unchanged.

    H4    AJAX COMPANY SUMMARY
    I4    Residential
    J4    Commercial
    K4    Land
    L4    TOTAL (It should already say this.)

**Formulas**

Enter the following formulas into the cells indicated:

    I6    +F6
    J6    +F25
    K6    +F44
    L6    @SUM(I6..K6)    Copy into cell L7 and range L12..L15.
    L9    +L6–L7
    L17    @SUM(L12..L15)    (This formula should already exist.)
    L19    +L9–L17    (This formula should already exist.)
    L21    +L19/L6    (This formula should already exist.)

Copy the contents of range I6..K6 into the following ranges:

    I7..K7
    I9..K9
    I12..K15
    I17..K17
    I19..K19
    I21..K21

**Number Formats**

Assign the following number formats to the ranges indicated:

    I6..L19    , 0    (Comma, 0 decimal places)
    I21..L21    Percent, 2    (Percent, 2 decimal places)

**Testing the Spreadsheets**

Inspect the spreadsheets to see that the formulas access the correct cells and calculate properly.

# Spreadsheet Ideas

The uses of spreadsheets are almost limitless. Here are some possibilities you might like to consider for your own use.

- **On-line documentation for office procedures.** You can write a series of instructions within a spreadsheet and, using the Go to option (F5), create a menu so that users can call up the desired instructions. Press Home to return to the menu.

- **Create a menu to identify and retrieve spreadsheets that you use frequently.** By creating a macro to retrieve each spreadsheet and listing all the macros on a spreadsheet named Menu, you can keep track of the macros and spreadsheets. The procedure is explained in Chapter 8.

- **Automate your expense reports.** Put your expense report form into a spreadsheet and have it do the math for you. Save time and avoid math errors.

- **Create billing rate tables.** Put your employees' i.d. numbers and billing rates into a lookup table, then use @HLOOKUP or @VLOOKUP to retrieve the appropriate rate into a spreadsheet when you are preparing time sheets for client billing.

- **Do financial projections.** Build formulas that calculate financial results for past time periods, then copy the formulas into additional cells to project financial results for future time period based on previous performance.

- **Automate your estimating procedures.** If your business requires estimating costs for jobs, put all the fixed and variable cost factors into a spreadsheet that will do the math for you when you enter the combination of variables to be used.

- **Track inventories.** List your inventory of parts or supplies in a spreadsheet and use @IF logic to signal time to order more when the count of an item reaches a specified minimum level.

- **Plan and track progress of projects.** List projects, tasks, employees assigned, starting dates, due dates, milestones, time on task, and estimated time to complete in a spreadsheet. You can use a spreadsheet to produce a Gantt chart to make the timelines visible.

- **Build models for "What If" analyses.** Build spreadsheets based on past performance data, then change the values of key variables or assumptions to see what would happen under other conditions. One example is "break-even" analysis: build a spreadsheet showing the fixed and variable costs of producing a product, then vary the price and volume of sales to see what combinations of price and volume are necessary to pay for costs and begin making a profit. (See the next chapter for an example.)
- **Combine spreadsheets with graphs to provide vivid visual presentations of data.** The next chapter tells how.

## An Additional Word About Spreadsheets

Spreadsheets are some of the most generally useful tools available on personal computers. Their use is limited only by your own imagination. Don't hesitate to try designing spreadsheets of your own for your own particular needs. Once you have tried a few, you will probably be surprised and pleased with the new ones you can invent.

# 6

# Making Numbers Graphic

The graphics capability of LotusWorks is an adjunct to the Spreadsheet service, but it is really a major tool in itself. Graphs are excellent devices for viewing and showing relationships among numbers. Numerical patterns that are difficult to detect in a spreadsheet or table—and statistical relationships that are meaningless to statistical novices—pop up clearly and vividly in appropriate graphs. This makes graphs valuable for analyzing data and unequaled for drawing attention to and communicating numerical relationships.

LotusWorks enables you to generate five types of graphs from spreadsheet data. Once you have a spreadsheet containing the data to portray, the procedure of producing a graph is almost automatic. You simply select the type of graph, select the data ranges to portray, and if you wish, enter text for titles, labels, and legends; LotusWorks automatically selects an appropriate scale and draws the graph.

A graph remains linked to the spreadsheet from which it is generated, so you can retrieve it in the future. If you change the data in a spreadsheet, LotusWorks automatically updates any graphs drawn from the spreadsheet. This makes it easy to update spreadsheets and graphs for reports.

The Graph module is a valuable tool for your data analysis and presentations. This chapter tells you how to use it.

*In this chapter, you'll learn how to:*
- *Say it with graphs*
- *Choose the right graph*
- *Add titles, labels, and legends*
- *Adjust the scale*
- *Name and save graphs*
- *Print graphs*
- *Print single and multiple graphs from the same spreadsheet*

# Saying It with Graphs

Graphs are unsurpassed for communicating most kinds of numerical information to most audiences. If you doubt it, just look at the number of newspapers, magazines, and television programs that are turning to "info-graphics" to communicate complicated information quickly, clearly, and easily. People get ideas quicker and understand them better from the pictorial representations of graphs than they do from conventional tabular presentations of numbers. This goes for trained analysts and managers as well as for untrained audiences. When you can, say it with graphs. It is an excellent way to analyze and communicate.

There are three important keys to graphs that work:

- Choosing an appropriate graph type.
- Providing clear titles and labels.
- Keeping the appearance simple but accurate.

LotusWorks gives you good tools for all three.

The importance of providing clear titles and labels can hardly be emphasized too much. Omitting reference points, sources, and data identifications from a graph is like leaving words out of a sentence. At best, it's confusing to the viewers; at worst, it gives the impression you're trying to mislead them.

Creating a simple but accurate appearance is to some extent a matter of judgment. Fortunately, LotusWorks does almost all the designing for you. In general, it's a good idea to focus on one idea at a time from a spreadsheet and design a graph to present the idea clearly. Nevertheless, the purpose of a graph should be to reveal, not obscure. It's important not to obscure other relationships that may be in the data, or to leave any relationships unreported. Because you can have many graphs from the same spreadsheet, LotusWorks gives you the opportunity to zero in and create as many graphs as you need to communicate all the information in a spreadsheet.

Keep in mind that the spreadsheet does not always have to come first. Graphs can help convey ideas even when you lack firm data. In such cases, you may conceive the graph idea first and then build a spreadsheet that will generate the graph.

Perhaps the most important tip for saying it with graphs is to "think pictorially" when you are planning a written or spoken presentation. Think about how the information you want to convey will appear to the viewers, listeners, or readers. Present one idea or item of information at a time, and present it in an order that the intended audience can easily take in. Actively look for situations where graphs can help convey the ideas and information. When you find these situations, LotusWorks can help you produce the graphs with little effort.

## Choosing the Right Graph

The type of graph to use depends on the type of data you have and the relationships you wish to display. LotusWorks gives you the choice of using line graphs, bar graphs, stacked bar graphs, XY graphs, and pie charts. Each type is appropriate for some purposes but not others.

**Line Graphs.** Line graphs illustrate the magnitude of one or more data variables over time. LotusWorks plots time periods on the x-axis, the values of the variable or variables on the y-axis, and draws a straight line between each pair of data points. The resulting line makes it easy to see changes in data values over time. You can have up to six variables plotted on a LotusWorks line graph. A line graph looks like this:

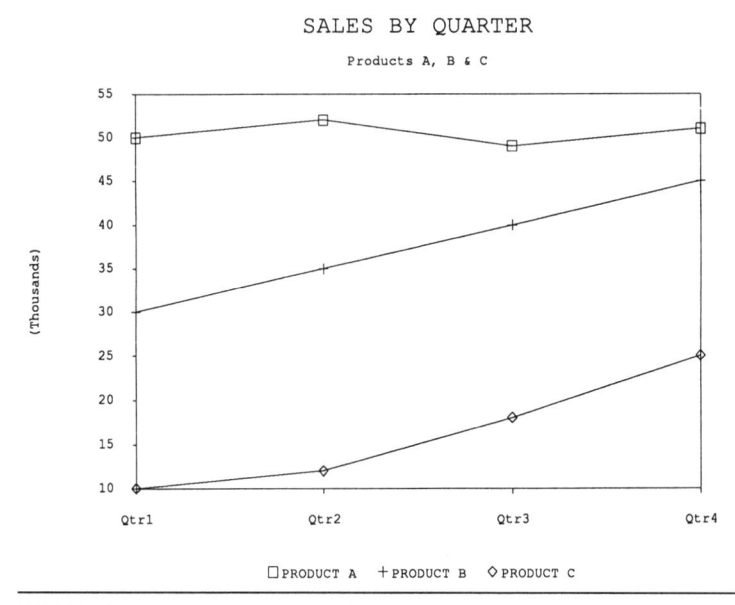

**FIGURE 6.1:** Line graph with three variables (data ranges)

The spreadsheet from which the line graph was drawn looks like this:

```
F1=Help                                                            F10=Menu
   File  Edit  Options  Worksheet  Range  Copy  Move  Graph        LotusWorks
 * D8:
                  Spreadsheet:  D:\LWORKS3\LWDATA\SS6B.WK1
            A          B         C         D         E         F        G
  1                   Qtr1      Qtr2      Qtr3      Qtr4      TOTAL
  2                 --------  --------  --------  --------  --------
  3    PRODUCT A    50,000    52,000    49,000    51,000    202,000
  4    PRODUCT B    30,000    35,000    40,000    45,000    150,000
  5    PRODUCT C    10,000    12,000    18,000    25,000     65,000
  6                 --------  --------  --------  --------  --------
  7    TOTAL        90,000    99,000   107,000   121,000    417,000
  8
  9
 10
 11
 12
 13
 14
 15
 16
 17
```

**FIGURE 6.2:** Spreadsheet from which the line graph was drawn

**Bar Graphs.** Bar graphs illustrate time-series data or separate variables at the same point in time. They portray variables as bars or rectangles, with the length of each bar representing the magnitude of a data variable. They make it easy to compare individual variables. If a graph has multiple variables, it displays the bars for each time period side-by-side. The data shown in Figure 6.2 looks like this in a bar graph:

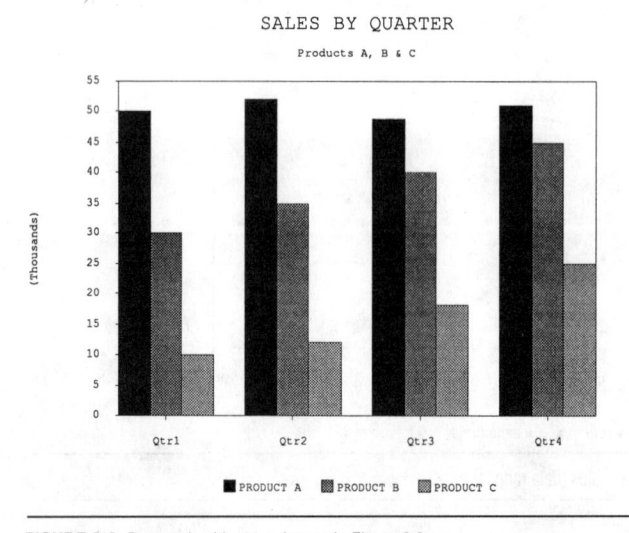

**FIGURE 6.3:** Bar graph with same data as in Figure 6.2

> NOTE: LotusWorks adds shading to the bars if you specify black and white in the Graph Type dialog box. Otherwise, it generates the bars with distinctive colors.

**Stacked Bar Graphs.** Stacked bar graphs illustrate the magnitudes of variables and of the parts that make up the whole variables. For instance, a stacked bar graph can be used to show annual sales over time and sales by quarter or sales by product within each year. Stacked bar graphs portray variables as bars or rectangles, with the constituent parts "stacked" atop each other (instead of side-by-side as in a multi-variable bar graph). The height of each bar indicates the magnitude of the variable. Stacked bar graphs can be used to show the same type of data as bar graphs, provided the variables have constituent parts. Stacked bar graphs look like this:

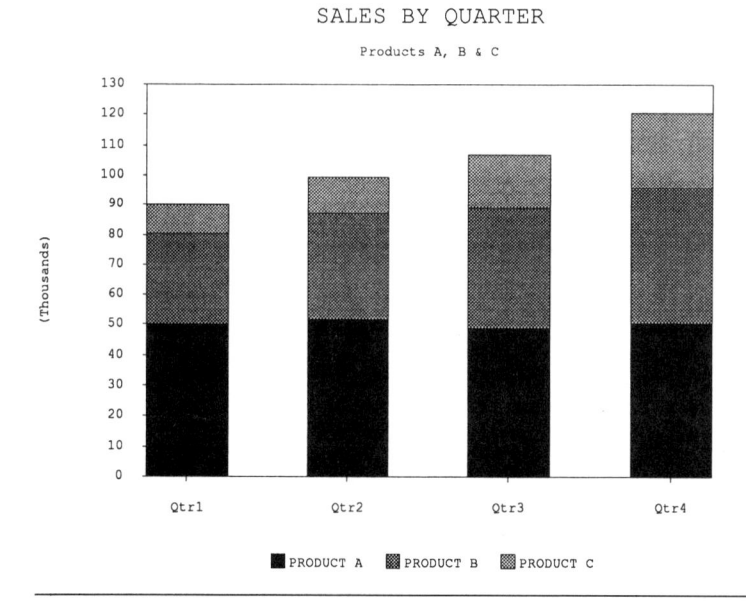

**FIGURE 6.4:** Stacked bar graph showing annual sales by quarter

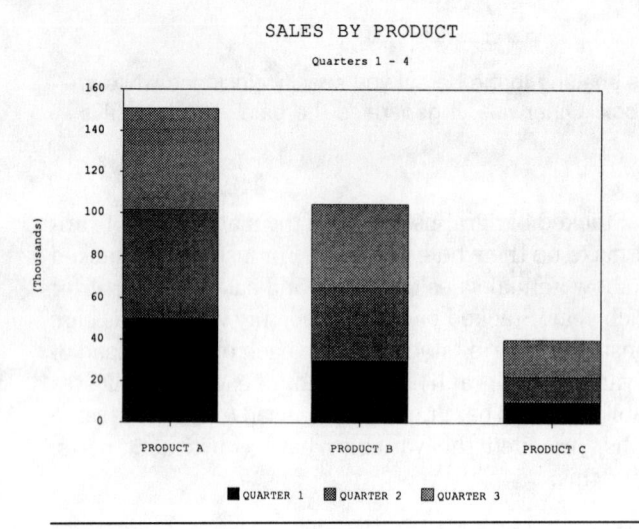

```
                    SALES BY PRODUCT
                      Quarters 1 - 4
     160

     140

     120

     100
(Thousands)
      80

      60

      40

      20

       0
           PRODUCT A      PRODUCT B      PRODUCT C

           ■ QUARTER 1   ▨ QUARTER 2   ▨ QUARTER 3
```

**FIGURE 6.5:** Stacked bar graph showing annual sales by product

**XY Graphs.** XY graphs illustrate the relationship between paired variables, such as sale price and sale volume, or vehicle weight and miles-per-gallon. The graph plots one variable along the x-axis and one along the y-axis to produce a single point where the two values intersect. Each pair is represented by a single point on the graph. If only a few pairs are plotted, an XY graph is like a line graph without the lines drawn between points. If there are a lot of pairs, an XY graph can be called a scatter plot.

XY graphs are useful to see how one variable affects another and to see if there is correlation among different pairs of variables. Here are two examples of XY graphs:

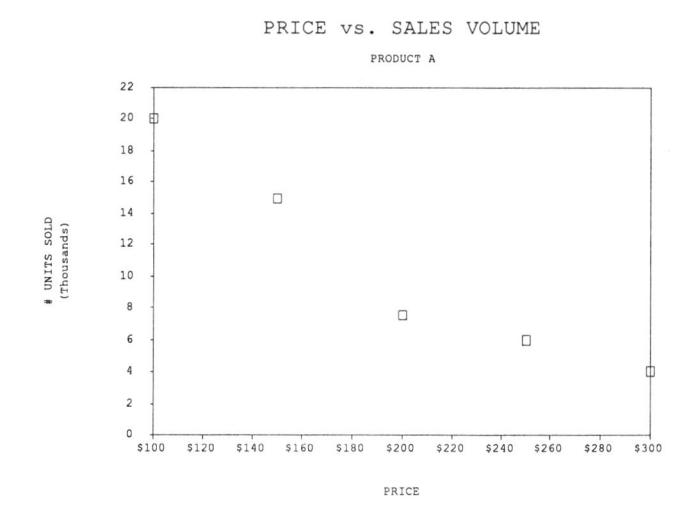

**FIGURE 6.6:** XY graph showing the relationship between price and sales volume for a product

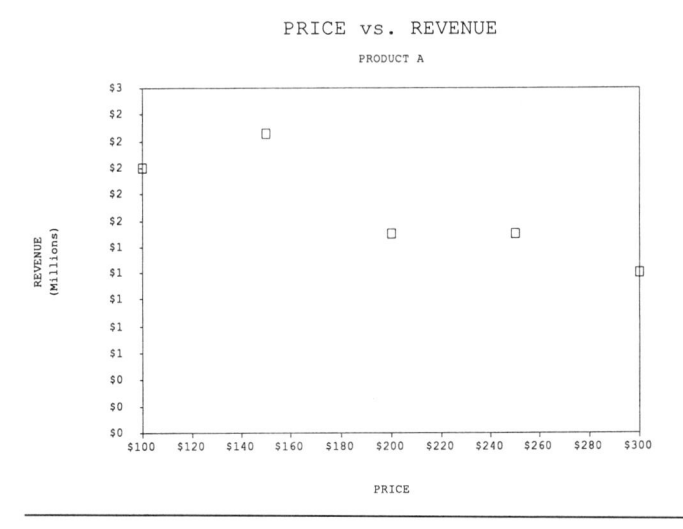

**FIGURE 6.7:** XY graph showing the relationship between price and revenue for the same product

**Pie Graphs.** Pie graphs (or pie charts) portray the parts of a whole as slices of a circular "pie." The size of each slice indicates the variable's percentage of the total. For example, pie graphs can show the relative size of each source of revenue or each category of expenditure for a company. Pie graphs label each part as a percentage of the whole; the sum of the parts is always 100 percent.

LotusWorks lets you fill the slices of pie graphs with color or distinctive patterns of hatching for clarity. It also lets you separate ("explode") one or more slices slightly from the others for emphasis or to draw attention to a particular variable.

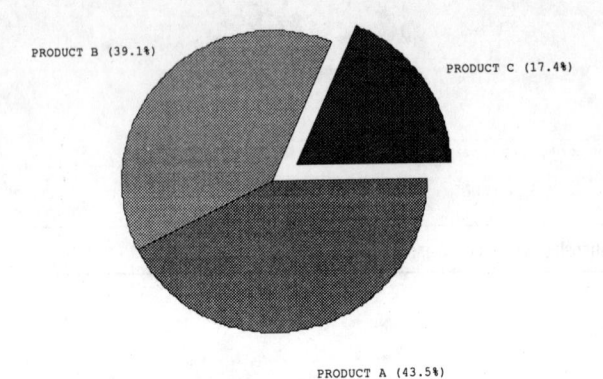

**FIGURE 6.8:** Pie graph with one slice exploded

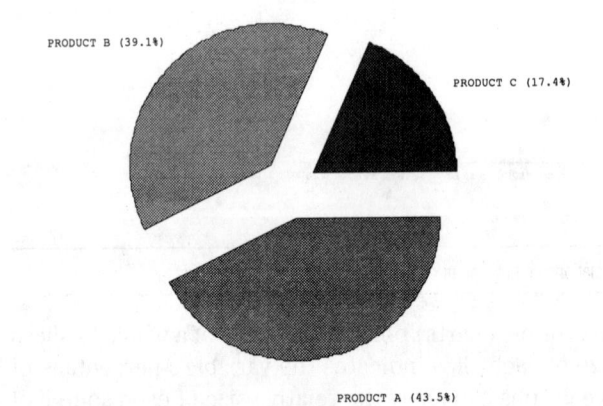

**FIGURE 6.9:** The same pie graph with all slices exploded

# Data Ranges for Graphs

The data for a graph come from ranges that you specify in the graph's spreadsheet. LotusWorks enables you to specify up to six data ranges (labeled A through F) for inclusion in each graph. One data range, called the "X-range," always holds the labels for the X-axis of the graph. If you don't specify otherwise, LotusWorks uses the contents of the A-range of the spreadsheet as the X-range. However, if you wish, you can specify different labels for a graph from the ones you use for the spreadsheet. To have different X-axis labels, include them in a separate row or column of the spreadsheet and then specify that range as the X-range for the graph.

Data ranges for graphs can be of any length, but each data range must come from only one row or one column of the spreadsheet, and all the ranges in any one graph must be the same length (contain the same number of cells).

## Line, Bar, and Stacked Bar Graphs

LotusWorks allows you to specify from one to six ranges of data for each line graph, bar graph, or stacked bar graph. If you specify one range of data, there will be one line or set of bars in the graph; if you specify more than one range, there will be multiple lines or sets of bars in the graph.

You may specify that data ranges appear in the graph in the order in which they appear in the spreadsheet or in a different order. For example, you can specify that data in rows 3, 4, and 5 of a spreadsheet appear in data ranges C, A, B of the graph, if it makes sense to do so.

## XY Graphs

XY graphs require two data ranges (besides the X-range)—one in the A-range and one in the B-range. The data ranges must be located alongside each other in the spreadsheet and must be of the same length. Each pair of cells in the data ranges becomes one point on the XY graph.

## Pie Charts

Pie graphs require (in addition to the X-range) one range for data and one range to specify three attributes of the pie chart: colors, hatching patterns, and whether or not to "explode" individual slices. The spreadsheet data to be graphed always goes into the A-range. Each column in the spreadsheet becomes one slice in the pie chart.

The B-range is reserved for data specifying attributes of the pie chart. If you do not include an entry in the B-range, LotusWorks automatically assigns colors (or hatching, if you specify black and white in the Graph Type dialog box) and does not explode any slices. If you wish to specify any of these attributes, add a range to the spreadsheet somewhere parallel to the range used for data and then specify this range as the B-range. To explode a slice or specify a special treatment of color or color and hatching, enter a number from the following table into the desired cell in the range:

### Specifying Pie Chart Attributes

To specify a color, enter a value of 1-16 into the B-range cell. To specify a combination of color and hatching, enter a value of 17-80.

To specify an exploded slice, add 100 to the color/hatching number. For example, 1 = Green, 101 = Green, Exploded; 7 = Bright Blue, 107 = Bright Blue, Exploded; 71 = Bright Blue Coarse Hatch, 171 = Bright Blue Coarse Hatch Exploded.

| Colors | Light Hatch | Medium Hatch | Coarse Hatch |
|---|---|---|---|
| 1 = Green | 17 | 33 | 65 |
| 2 = Cyan | 18 | 34 | 66 |
| 3 = Red | 19 | 35 | 67 |
| 4 = Magenta | 20 | 36 | 68 |
| 5 = Yellow | 21 | 37 | 69 |
| 6 = Dark Gray | 22 | 38 | 70 |
| 7 = Bright Blue | 23 | 39 | 71 |
| 8 = Bright Green | 24 | 40 | 72 |
| 9 = Bright Cyan | 25 | 41 | 73 |
| 10 = Bright Red | 26 | 42 | 74 |
| 11 = Bright Magenta | 27 | 43 | 75 |
| 12 = Bright Yellow | 28 | 44 | 76 |
| 13 = Gray | 29 | 45 | 77 |
| 14 = White | 30 | 46 | 78 |
| 15 = Black | 31 | 47 | 79 |
| 16 = Blue | 32 | 48 | 80 |

## Generating Graphs

Although the details vary with the types of graphs you choose and the features you add to them, the general steps for generating a graph are the same for all graphs. They are:

1. Get a spreadsheet: create or retrieve a spreadsheet that contains the data to be graphed.
2. Specify the type of graph.
3. Specify the data ranges to be included in the graph.
4. Preview the graph to see if the data ranges are correct and if any titles and adjustments to the scale are needed.
5. Add a legend, titles, and data labels, and/or adjust the scale, if you wish.
6. Do a final preview to be sure the graph appears as you want it.
7. Name the graph.
8. Save the spreadsheet.

## Specifying the Graph Type

To specify a graph type, select Graph Type. The following dialog box appears:

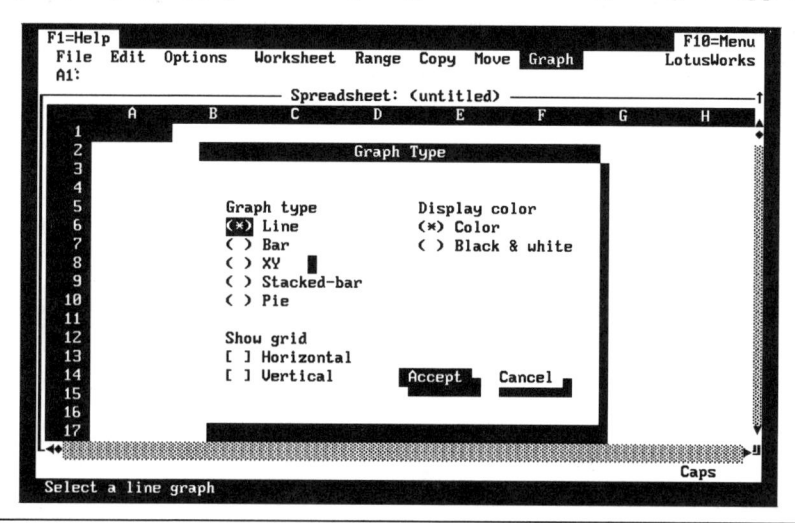

**FIGURE 6.10:** The Graph Type dialog box

*In the Graphics module, if you are using the keyboard to select options, you do not have to cycle through all the options in each dialog box. Simply set the ones that apply to your graphs and press Enter.*

Select the desired graph type, according to the guidelines in the previous section. Check the Color or Black and white option, as appropriate for your computer monitor. If you want horizontal and/or vertical grid lines to appear on the graph, check either or both of the Horizontal and Vertical options.

When all the options are set to your liking, select Accept. LotusWorks returns you to the Graph menu.

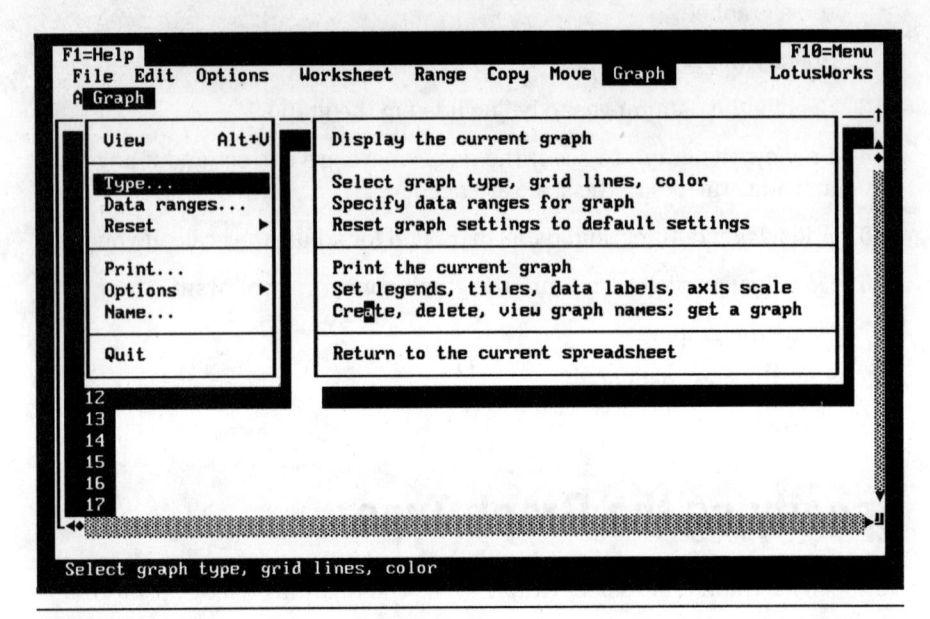

**FIGURE 6.11:** The Graph menu lets you specify the graph type, data ranges, titles, legends, scales, and other attributes for graphs.

Making Numbers Graphic **303**

# Specifying the Data Ranges

Select Data Ranges. The following dialog box opens:

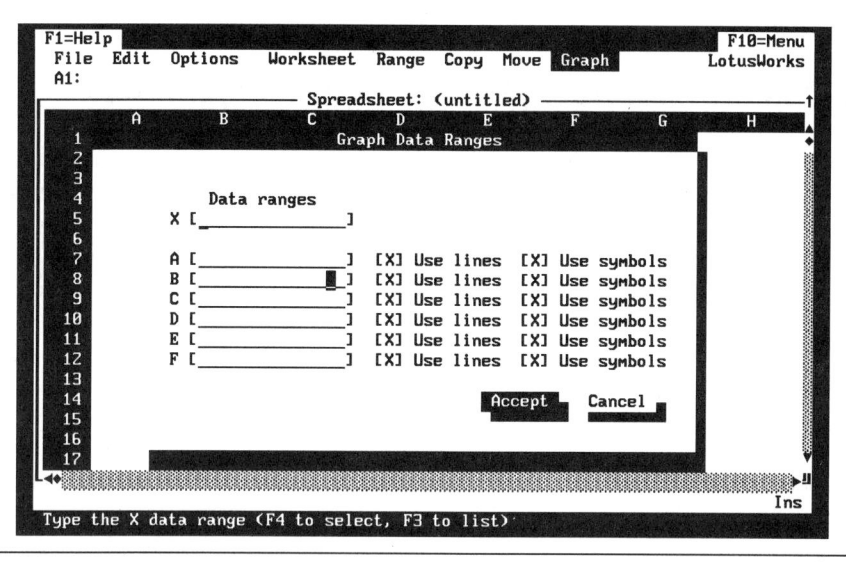

**FIGURE 6.12:** The Data Ranges dialog box

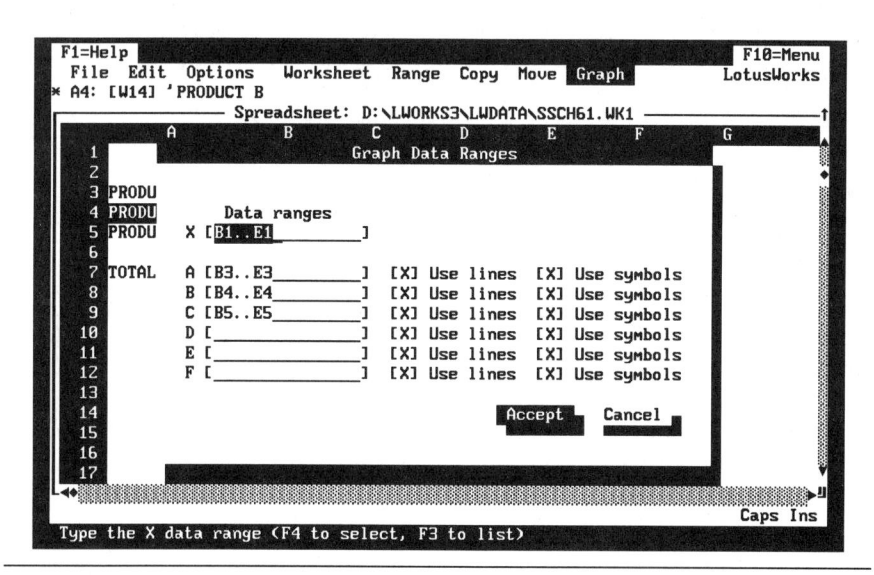

**FIGURE 6.13:** The data ranges for the graph shown in Figure 6.4

Enter one or more data ranges to be included in the graph. The X-range is reserved for the spreadsheet range that contains the labels for the X-axis. (Refer to the section "Data Ranges for Graphs" earlier in this chapter for information on specifying data ranges for the different types of graph.)

## Selecting and Deselecting Symbols and Lines

LotusWorks ordinarily plots line graphs and XY graphs with symbols placed at each data point and lines connecting the data points. Each data range has a unique identifying symbol. In some cases, however, you may wish to eliminate either the symbols or the lines to enhance the graph's appearance. (Don't eliminate both—the graph won't appear at all!) Also, in some cases it may not be appropriate to connect data points with lines: for instance, in a scatter plot, or when the data does not represent a time series, or when there can be more than one value on the Y-axis for each value on the X-axis.

To suppress either symbols or lines on a graph, deselect either the Use lines or Use symbols check box beside each data range on the Graph Data Ranges dialog box.

When all the ranges have been specified, select Accept. LotusWorks selects a scale that encompasses all the specified data within the graph window and creates the graph you have specified. LotusWorks returns you to the Graph menu.

## Previewing the Basic Graph

It's a good idea to check the graph at this point to be sure that the correct data ranges have been specified. Press V from the Graph menu or select Graph View to view the graph. Press Alt+V repeatedly to toggle back and forth between Graph View and the Spreadsheet.

That's all you have to do to generate a basic graph. In some cases that may be enough. In most cases, however, you will want to add titles, a legend, and other attributes to dress up the basic graph. The next section tells how.

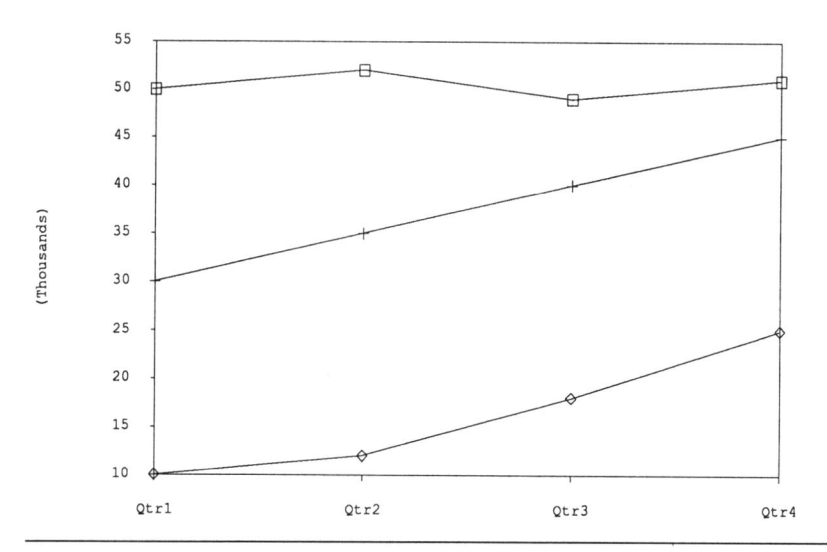

**FIGURE 6.14:** A basic graph as automatically generated by LotusWorks 3.0

# Adding Titles, Data Labels, Legends, and Grids

If you plan to present a graph to others—or even if you only intend to save it for yourself—you should always label it clearly. You can easily add one or two title lines, titles for the X- and Y-axes, data labels and/or a legend to a Lotus-Works graph. You can also adjust the scale and add grid lines (on all but pie graphs) to make the graph easier to read.

You add all of these attributes except grids from the Graph Options submenu. It's best to add one attribute at a time and to check the appearance by viewing the graph before proceeding to the next attribute.

## Legends

A legend is one means of labeling the data ranges of a graph. The legend (if used) appears below the graph and displays a text label for each data range in the graph alongside the symbol or a small rectangle displaying the color and/or hatching pattern used for the data range.

To create a legend, select Graph Options Legend. The following dialog box appears:

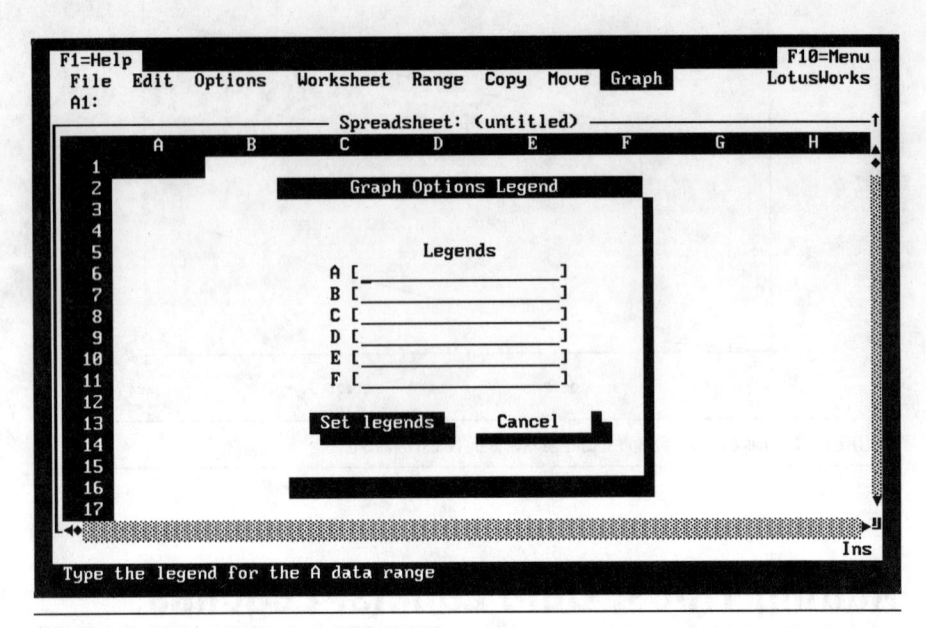

```
F1=Help                                                          F10=Menu
 File   Edit   Options   Worksheet   Range   Copy   Move   Graph   LotusWorks
 A1:
                        ── Spreadsheet: (untitled) ──
         A        B        C        D        E        F        G        H
  1
  2              ┌─────── Graph Options Legend ───────┐
  3              │                                    │
  4              │              Legends               │
  5              │         A [            ]           │
  6              │         B [            ]           │
  7              │         C [            ]           │
  8              │         D [            ]           │
  9              │         E [            ]           │
 10              │         F [            ]           │
 11              │                                    │
 12              │                                    │
 13              │      Set legends     Cancel        │
 14              │                                    │
 15              └────────────────────────────────────┘
 16
 17
                                                                     Ins
 Type the legend for the A data range
```

**FIGURE 6.15:** The Graph Options Legend dialog box

Enter a text label for each data range to be included in the graph. When you have entered all the labels, select Set legends. LotusWorks sets the legend and returns you to the Graph Options submenu.

## Titles

*Press V from the Graph menu or select Graph View to check the appearance of the graph after you add each attribute.*

LotusWorks allows you to specify an overall title for each graph, a subtitle for the graph, and a "title" or label for each axis. LotusWorks automatically centers graph titles on the first one or two lines at the top of the graph. It centers the X-axis title and the legend at the bottom of the graph. It places the Y-axis title alongside the Y-axis. (There are no X- or Y-axis titles on pie graphs.)

Making Numbers Graphic **307**

To create a title, select Graph Options Titles. The following dialog box appears:

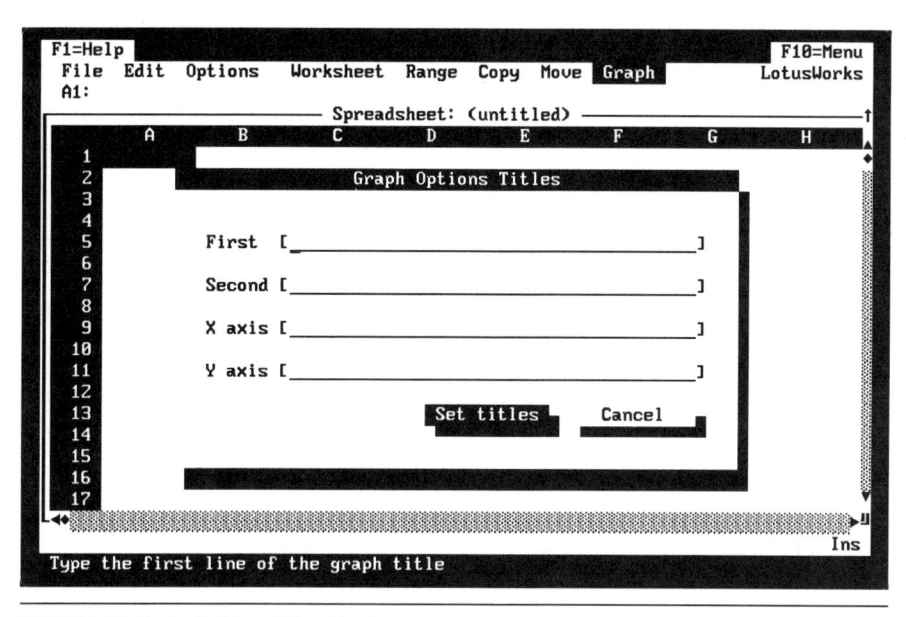

```
F1=Help                                                    F10=Menu
 File  Edit  Options  Worksheet  Range  Copy  Move  Graph   LotusWorks
 A1:
                     ───── Spreadsheet: (untitled) ─────
        A      B      C      D      E      F      G      H
  1
  2              ┌──────── Graph Options Titles ────────┐
  3              │                                      │
  4              │                                      │
  5              │   First  [_____]│
  6              │                                      │
  7              │   Second [_____]│
  8              │                                      │
  9              │   X axis [_____]│
 10              │                                      │
 11              │   Y axis [_____]│
 12              │                                      │
 13              │           [ Set titles ]  [ Cancel ] │
 14              │                                      │
 15              └──────────────────────────────────────┘
 16
 17
                                                          Ins
 Type the first line of the graph title
```

**FIGURE 6.16:** The Graph Options Titles dialog box

Enter text for titles into as many of the text boxes as you like and select Set titles. LotusWorks returns you to the Graph Options submenu.

# Data Labels

The Data labels option enables you to label each data point or bar on a graph, if you wish. You use the contents of one or more ranges to create the labels. The label ranges can contain numbers, formulas, or text. For example, if you specify the same ranges for both a graph's data and its data labels, LotusWorks displays the numerical data value for each data point or bar. If you put text labels into a different range of the spreadsheet and then specify that range for data labels, LotusWorks displays one of these labels for each data point or bar. If you specify ranges containing formulas, LotusWorks uses the results of the formulas as the data labels.

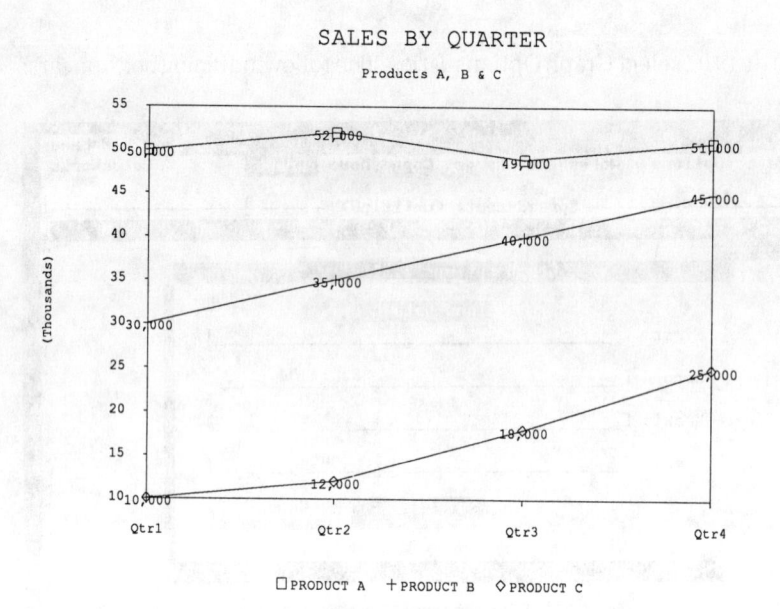

**FIGURE 6.17:** A line graph with data labels drawn from the same ranges as the graph's data

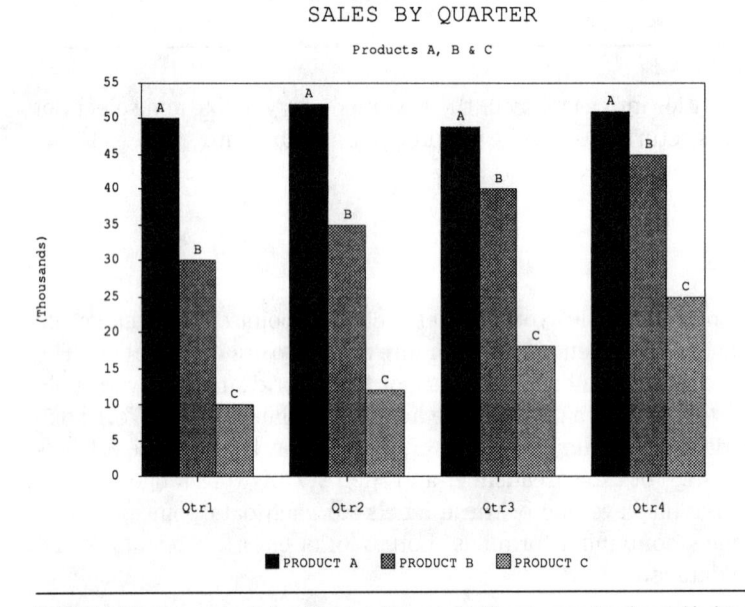

**FIGURE 6.18:** A bar graph with text data labels (drawn from different ranges than the graph's data ranges)

To create data labels, select Graph Options Data labels. The following dialog box appears:

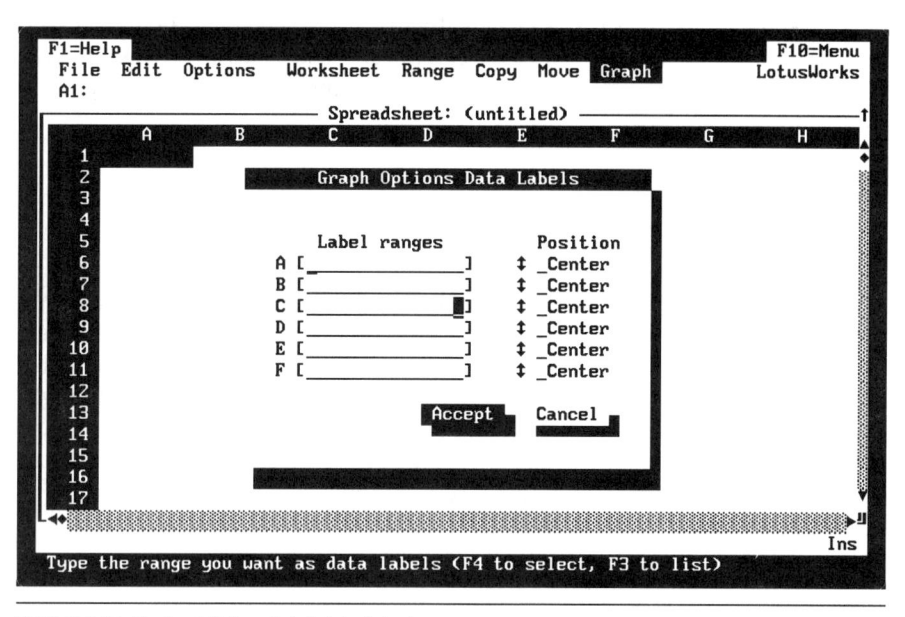

```
F1=Help                                                           F10=Menu
  File  Edit  Options   Worksheet  Range  Copy  Move  Graph       LotusWorks
  A1:
                         Spreadsheet: (untitled)
         A      B        C        D        E        F        G        H
    1
    2                       Graph Options Data Labels
    3
    4
    5                    Label ranges              Position
    6                 A [_____]          ‡ _Center
    7                 B [_____]          ‡ _Center
    8                 C [_____]          ‡ _Center
    9                 D [_____]          ‡ _Center
   10                 E [_____]          ‡ _Center
   11                 F [_____]          ‡ _Center
   12
   13                         Accept      Cancel
   14
   15
   16
   17
                                                                      Ins
  Type the range you want as data labels (F4 to select, F3 to list)
```

**FIGURE 6.19:** The Graph Options Data Labels dialog box

Enter a label range for each data range in your graph. The label range can be the same as the data range, or it can be a different range in the spreadsheet, but there must be as many cells in each label range as in the corresponding data range.

When you enter each label range and press Tab, a popup box opens to display options for positioning the data label. The choices are Center, Left, Above, Right, and Below. If you do not specify a choice, the position defaults to Center. You may need to experiment with the positions of data labels to find the combination that looks best on any given graph.

When you have entered all the data labels and positions, select Accept. LotusWorks returns you to the Graph Options submenu.

## Scale

Most graphs are perfectly adequate with the scale and scale indicators that LotusWorks automatically selects. For special cases, however, LotusWorks allows you to modify several scale attributes manually to get the graph you want.

## Adjusting the Scale

LotusWorks automatically selects a scale for the X- and Y-axis of each graph based on the largest and smallest data values on the axis. There may be times, however, when it makes sense to change the scale. For instance, if the automatic scaling does not include the zero point on one or both axes, you might want to change the scale to include the zero point to provide a visual reference for the magnitude of data values. Or, if you want to compare a graph with an existing graph, you might need to adjust the minimum and maximum values to make the scales of the two graphs comparable.

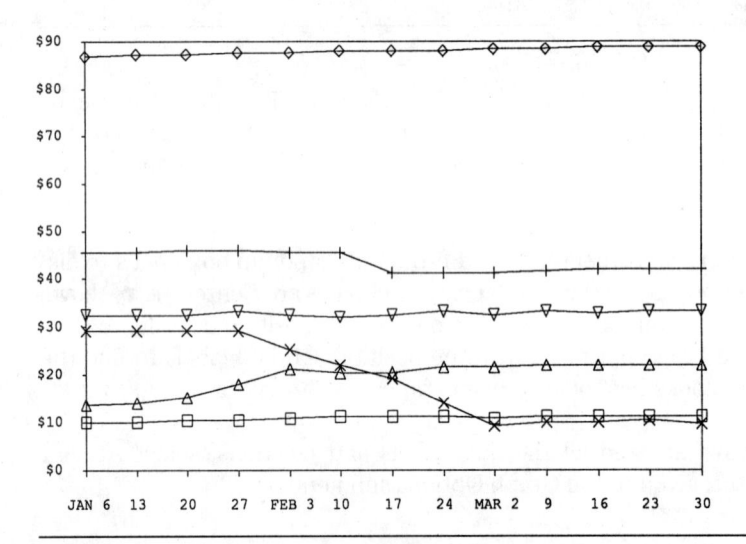

**FIGURE 6.20:** A graph of daily stock prices with the scale set automatically

STOCK PRICES

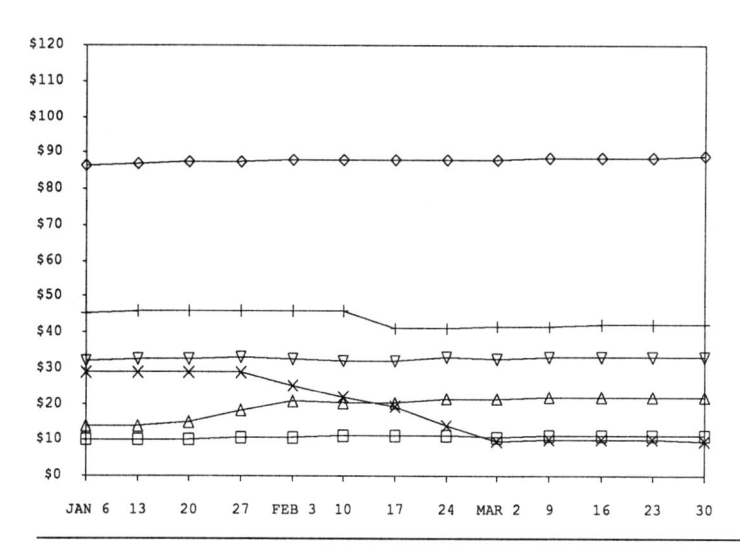

**FIGURE 6.21:** A graph of daily stock prices with the scale set manually

To adjust the scale select Graph Options Scale. Tab to the scale you want to change (Y or X) and press the Spacebar to cancel the Automatic option. Enter the minimum value you want to be displayed into the Lower text box and the maximum value into the Upper text box. Repeat for the other axis, if you wish. When you finish, check the settings of the Show Units option and the Skip option (see below).

## Suppressing the Scale Unit Indicator

LotusWorks often displays an indicator of the scale units (such as "Thousands") alongside each axis. If you want this indicator not to appear, simply deselect the Show units option in the Graph Options Scale dialog box for the Y-axis, X-axis, or both.

## Using a Skip Factor to Reduce Crowding on the X-Axis

If the X-axis for a graph is overcrowded with data points, you can specify a "skip factor" to reduce the number of data points that LotusWorks plots. A skip factor of $n$ means that LotusWorks displays every $nth$ data point on the X-axis. Thus, if you specify a skip factor of 2, LotusWorks displays every other data point; if you specify a skip factor of 10, LotusWorks displays every 10th data point.

To specify a skip factor, tab to the Skip box in the Graph Options Scale dialog box and enter the skip factor you desire. You may need to experiment with different skip factors to find one that produces the best result for any given graph.

## Formatting Numbers on the X- and Y-Axes

You can tailor the format of numbers that are displayed on the X-axis or Y-axis of a graph to any of the number formats (such as Currency or Percent) that are used in spreadsheets. You can even use Date and Time formats. To change a number format, select Graph Options Scale. The following dialog box appears:

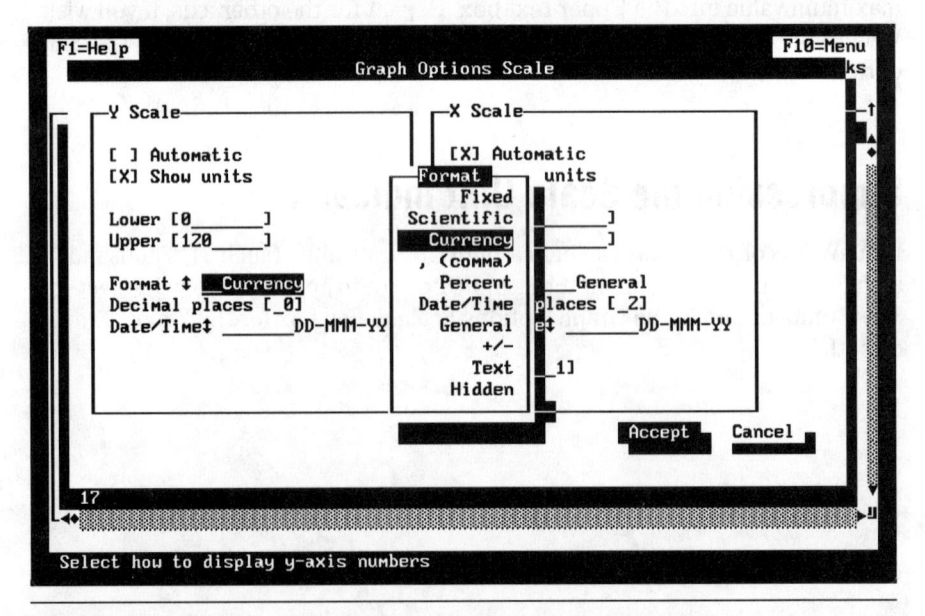

**FIGURE 6.22:** Select Format to change the format of numbers displayed on the X-axis or Y-axis of a graph.

Select Format, and a list of the spreadsheet number formats pops up. Complete any selections you may wish to make for the X-axis, Y-axis, or both, and select Accept. LotusWorks changes the number formats to the one(s) you selected and returns you to the Graph Options Scale dialog box.

When you have finished setting all the Scale options you care to, select Accept. LotusWorks returns you to the Graph Options submenu.

## Quitting the Graph Options Submenu and Reviewing Your Work

When you have set all the options to your liking, select Quit to exit the Graph Options submenu. LotusWorks returns you to the Graph menu.

At this point, it's a good idea to check your graph one last time, to be sure that all the attributes appear as you want them before you name and save the graph. To view the graph from the Graph menu, press V or select Graph View.

# Grid Lines

LotusWorks lets you add horizontal grid lines, vertical grid lines, or both to all but pie graphs. These can provide reference points for comparisons and thereby make some graphs easier to read and interpret but they can also add unnecessary clutter. LotusWorks makes it easy to try out graphs with and without grid lines.

To have grid lines appear you must indicate the type of lines when you select the graph type. Select Graph Type; select the graph type you want; and select either the Horizontal or Vertical option (or both) under the Show grid label. When you finish selecting the grid options, select Accept. You may wish to view the graph with and without grid lines to see which version communicates most clearly.

## Naming and Saving Graphs

When all the graph attributes have been specified and you are satisfied with the graph's appearance, the final steps are to name the graph and save it. If you have only one graph for a spreadsheet, the graph's settings are automatically saved with the spreadsheet, whether you name the graph or not. If you want to save more than one graph with a spreadsheet, however, you must name each graph. It's a good practice, anyway. Naming a graph saves its settings within the spreadsheet. When you save the spreadsheet, it automatically saves any graphs that are based on it.

To name a graph, select Graph Name. The following dialog box appears:

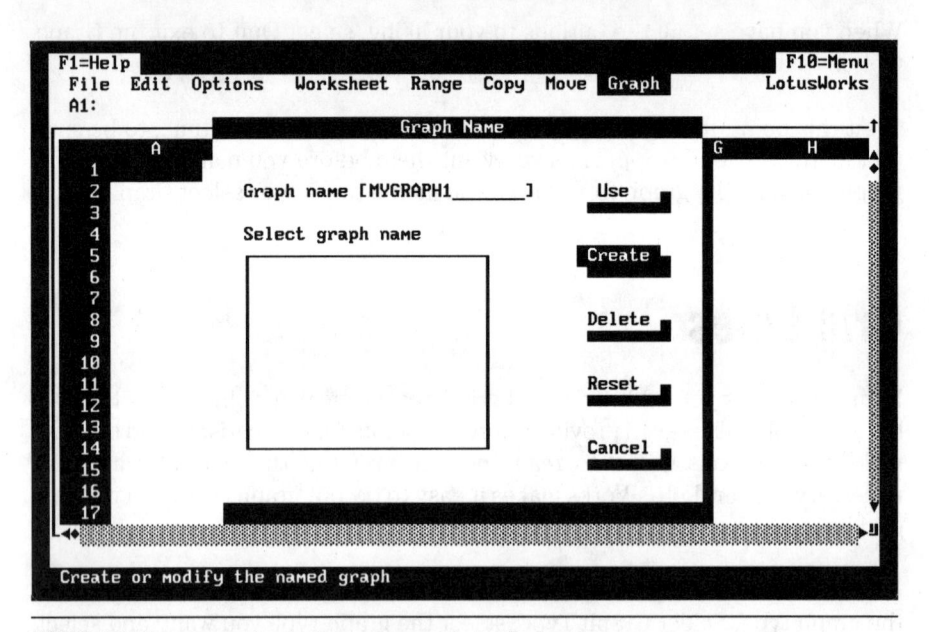

**FIGURE 6.23:** To name a graph, enter the graph name and select Create.

Enter a name for the graph in the Graph name text box and select Create. LotusWorks puts a copy of the graph name in the Select graph name list box. Select Use or press Esc to exit the dialog box, select Quit to exit the Graph menu, and press Alt+S to save the spreadsheet.

Once a graph has been named, it is automatically saved whenever you save the spreadsheet on which it is based.

## Retrieving Graphs

To retrieve a graph that has been saved, first retrieve its spreadsheet. Then, select Graph Name, enter the desired graph name or select it from the Select graph name list box, and select Use. LotusWorks returns you to the Graph menu. When you press V or select View, LotusWorks displays the graph.

## Printing Graphs

It is almost as easy to print a graph as it is to view it on the screen. Once you have a graph created or retrieved, select Graph Print. The following dialog box appears:

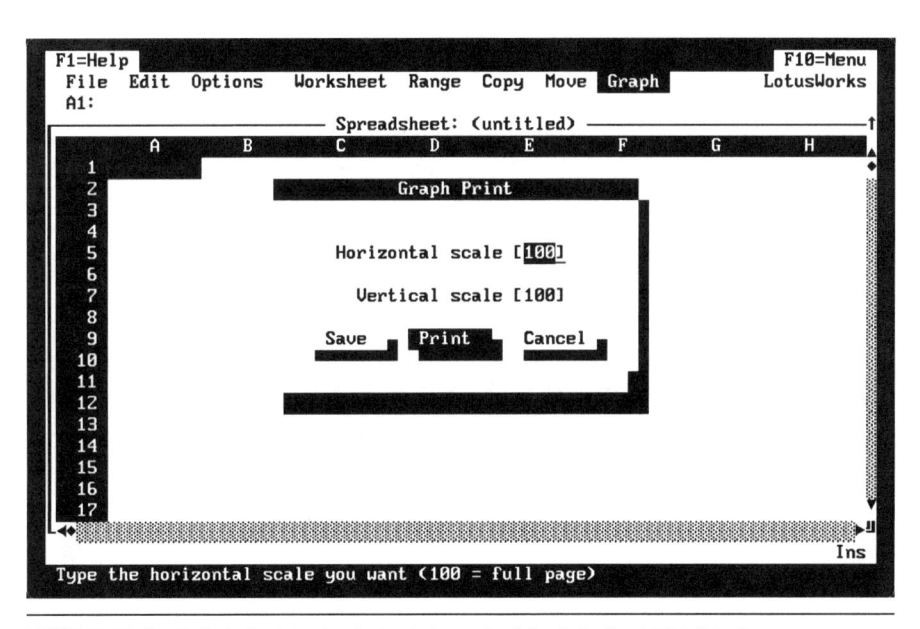

**FIGURE 6.24:** Specify the horizontal and vertical scale for graph printing in the Graph Print dialog box.

    LotusWorks normally prints graphs at 100 percent of the horizontal and vertical scales. If you would like reduce either print dimension (for example, to fit the space on a page), enter a number between 1 and 100 into the Horizontal scale and/or Vertical scale text boxes to indicate the percentage (1–100%) at which to print the graph. Keep in mind, however, that if you reduce one dimension substantially more than the other, you may produce an image that distorts, exaggerates or diminishes the true relationships among the data.

*To print two graphs on the same page, use the Word Processing service's Include feature and include both graphs on an otherwise blank page, then print from the Word Processing service with the File Print Print command.*

If you wish to save the print dimensions with the graph, select Save.

When you have specified and saved the print dimensions you want, select Print.

> NOTE: To print graphs, your printer must have graphics capability, and you must have the appropriate print driver installed. If you have difficulty printing graphs, check to see if the correct printer was specified in the Install program.

## Bringing Graphs into Word Processing Documents

LotusWorks enable you to print graphs directly at desired points within reports and other word processing documents—with proper headers, footers, and page numbering—instead of having to print them on separate pages. To print an existing graph within a word processing document, you must, of course, be in the Word Processing service. Move the cursor to the point in the word processing document where you want the graph to appear and select Edit Include Graph. The following dialog box appears:

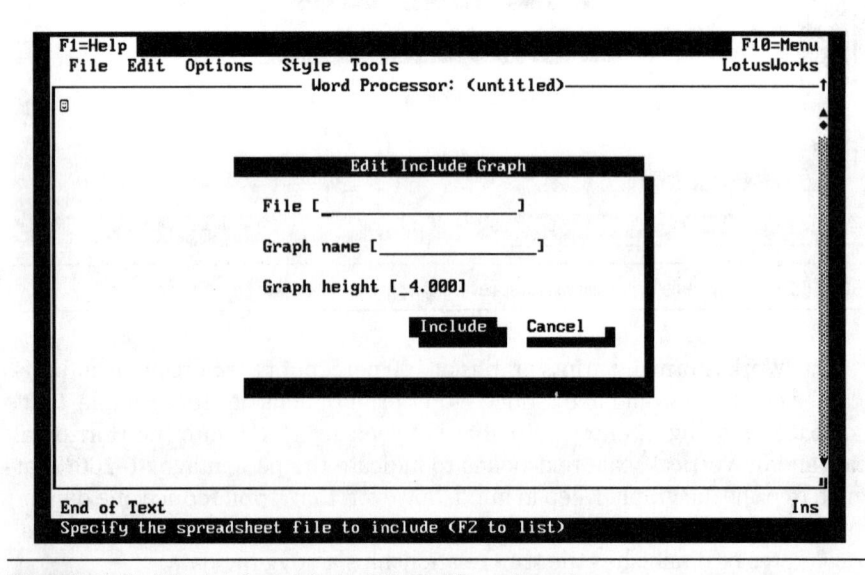

**FIGURE 6.25:** The Edit Include Graph dialog box in the Word Processing service

Enter the file name of the spreadsheet and the graph name of the graph you want to print. Enter the left and right margins you want for the graph (if they are different from the ones already displayed in the Left and Right text boxes) and enter a setting in inches for the height of the graph.

> IMPORTANT: You can print multiple graphs arranged vertically on a page, but you cannot print graphs side-by-side on the same page. Neither can you print text next to a graph.

When all the dimensions for the graph are specified, select Include. Lotus-Works returns you to the Word Processing screen and inserts the word "Graph" and the path and name of the spreadsheet and graph sourrounded by double angle brackets (« ») at the cursor. The graph itself does not appear on the word processing screen, but it will appear at the point you have specified when the document is printed.

# Examples

Here are two somewhat dissimilar graph examples. One shows how to build and save two pie charts of the sort that might be used in a written report or a live presentation. The other shows how to build a reusable calculation tool for performing break-even analysis. These do not by any means exhaust the possibilities for creating graphs with LotusWorks, but they do illustrate the main techniques used in building most graphs.

## Where Our $$ Come From, Where Our $$ Go

Here are two simple but effective pie charts that you can easily build. One shows revenue by source ("Where Our $$ Come From") and one shows expenditures by category ("Where Our $$ Go").

The finished pie graphs look like this:

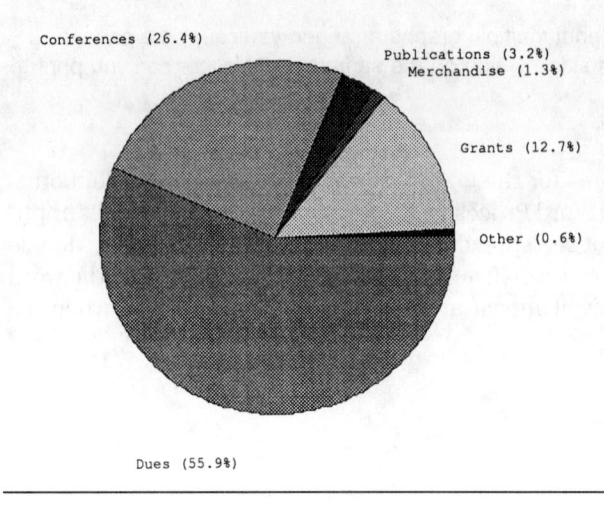

WHERE OUR $$ COME FROM

Conferences (26.4%)
Publications (3.2%)
Merchandise (1.3%)
Grants (12.7%)
Other (0.6%)
Dues (55.9%)

**FIGURE 6.26:** A pie graph to show revenue by source

WHERE OUR $$ GO

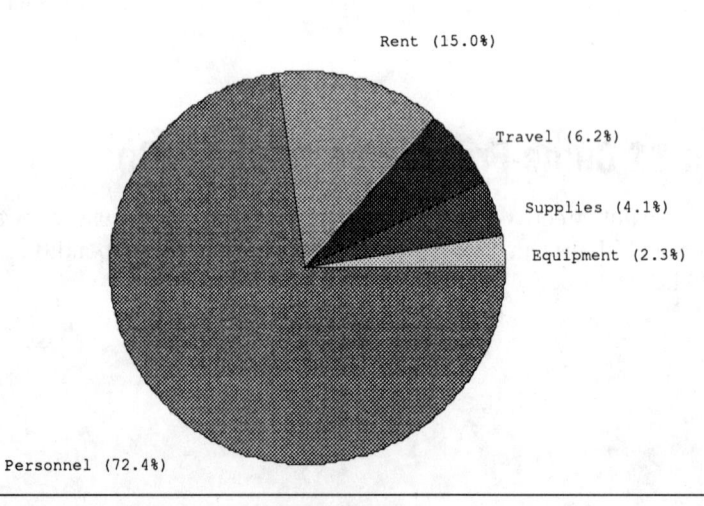

Rent (15.0%)
Travel (6.2%)
Supplies (4.1%)
Equipment (2.3%)
Personnel (72.4%)

**FIGURE 6.27:** A pie graph to show expenditures by category

To build the pie graph, follow these steps:

## Building the Pie Graphs

### Columns
Set the widths of columns A through G to 13 spaces.

### Labels
Enter the following labels into the cells indicated:

| | | | |
|---|---|---|---|
| A1 | Revenue | A4 | Expenditures |
| B1 | Dues | B4 | Personnel |
| C1 | Conferences | C4 | Rent |
| D1 | Publications | D4 | Travel |
| E1 | Merchandise | E4 | Supplies |
| F1 | Grants | F4 | Equipment |
| G1 | Other | G4 | Other |

### Data
Enter the following data into the cells indicated:

| | | | |
|---|---|---|---|
| B2 | 365000 | B5 | 410000 |
| C2 | 125000 | C5 | 85000 |
| D2 | 8500 | D5 | 35000 |
| E2 | 6000 | E5 | 23000 |
| F2 | 60000 | F5 | 13000 |
| G2 | 3000 | G5 | 25000 |

### Graph 1

| | |
|---|---|
| Type | Pie |
| Data Ranges | X-Range = B1..G1 |
| | A-Range = B2..G2 |
| Title | WHERE OUR $$ COME FROM |
| Name | REVENUE |

(Save Graph 1 under the graph name REVENUE before you start building Graph 2.)

### Graph 2

| | |
|---|---|
| Type | Pie |
| Data Ranges | X-Range = B4..F4 |
| | A-Range = B5..F5 |
| Title | WHERE OUR $$ GO |
| Name | EXPENDITURES |

(Save Graph 2 under the graph name EXPENDITURES so that the settings will not be lost or confused with those of Graph 1.)

When you finish building the graphs, save the entire spreadsheet. Check the data for errors, and if you find any, correct them and save the spreadsheet again. To view the first graph, you need to retrieve it: select Graph Name, enter REVENUE or select the graph name from the list box, select USE, and select View from the Graph menu (or press Alt+V from the spreadsheet) to view the graph. To view the second graph, follow the same procedure, but select the graph name EXPENDITURES.

To print either of the pie graphs, retrieve the graph, select Graph Print, modify the Horizontal and Vertical scales if desired, and select Print.

## Break-Even Calculator

Here is a spreadsheet-and-graph combination in which the graph plays an integral and vital role.

In break-even analysis, the object typically is to determine how many units of a particular product must be sold in order to pay back the start-up costs and start making a profit. In this reusable calculator, you can vary the amount of start-up investment, the required rate of return, the fixed cost, the variable cost per unit, the selling price per unit, and the sales volume. A line graph displays one line for the required dollar return and one for the profit at different levels of sales. The point where the lines intersect is the break-even point. Usually the break-even point can only be estimated from the spreadsheet, but it shows very clearly in the graph.

Making Numbers Graphic  **321**

The finished Break-Even calculator looks like this:

```
F1=Help                                                         F10=Menu
 File  Edit  Options  Worksheet  Range  Copy  Move  Graph       LotusWorks
A17: [W40]
                 Spreadsheet: D:\LWORKS3\LWDATA\BREAKEVN.WK1
                         A                              B              C
 1  BREAK-EVEN CALCULATOR
 2
 3  =====================================================
 4  Investment                               $250,000
 5  Required % Return on Investment               15%
 6  Required $ Return                         $37,500
 7
 8  Fixed Cost                                $25,000
 9  Variable Cost/Unit                          $3.12
10  Selling Price/Unit                          $5.00
11  Marginal Gross Profit/Unit                  $1.88
12
13  Lower Limit of Sales Volume (1,000s)           10
14  Increment of Sales (1,000s)                    10
15
16
17
```

**FIGURE 6.28:** The spreadsheet for the Break-Even Calculator (Part A)

```
F1=Help                                                         F10=Menu
 File  Edit  Options  Worksheet  Range  Copy  Move  Graph       LotusWorks
I17: [W11]
                 Spreadsheet: D:\LWORKS3\LWDATA\BREAKEVN.WK1
          D              E          F          G          H          I
 1  Sales Volume         10         20         30         40         50
 2  =========================================================================
 3  Required Return  $37,500    $37,500    $37,500    $37,500    $37,500
 4  Profit           ($6,200)   $12,600    $31,400    $50,200    $69,000
 5
 6
 7
 8
 9
10
11
12
13
14
15
16
17
```

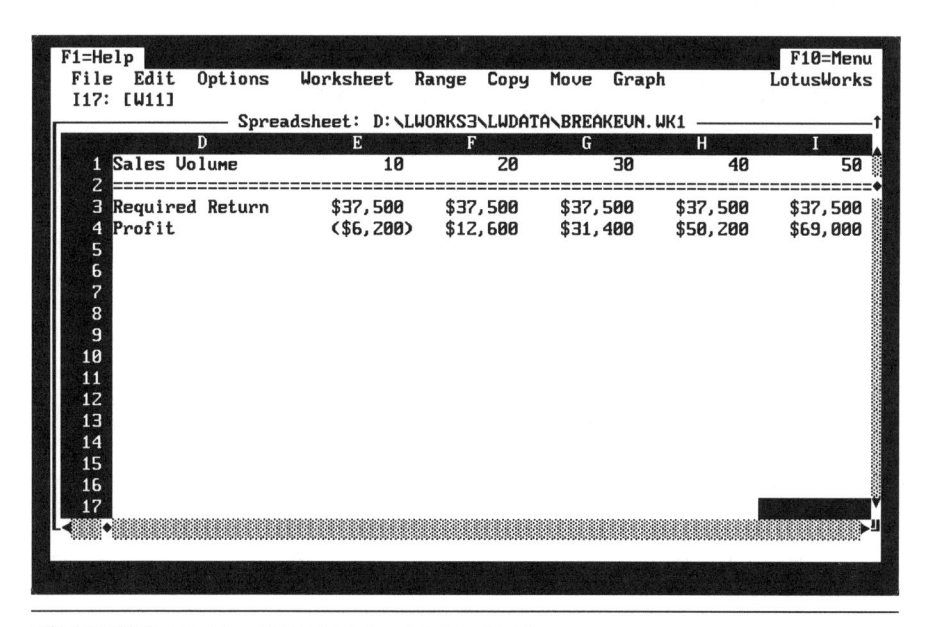

**FIGURE 6.29:** The spreadsheet for the Break-Even Calculator (Part B)

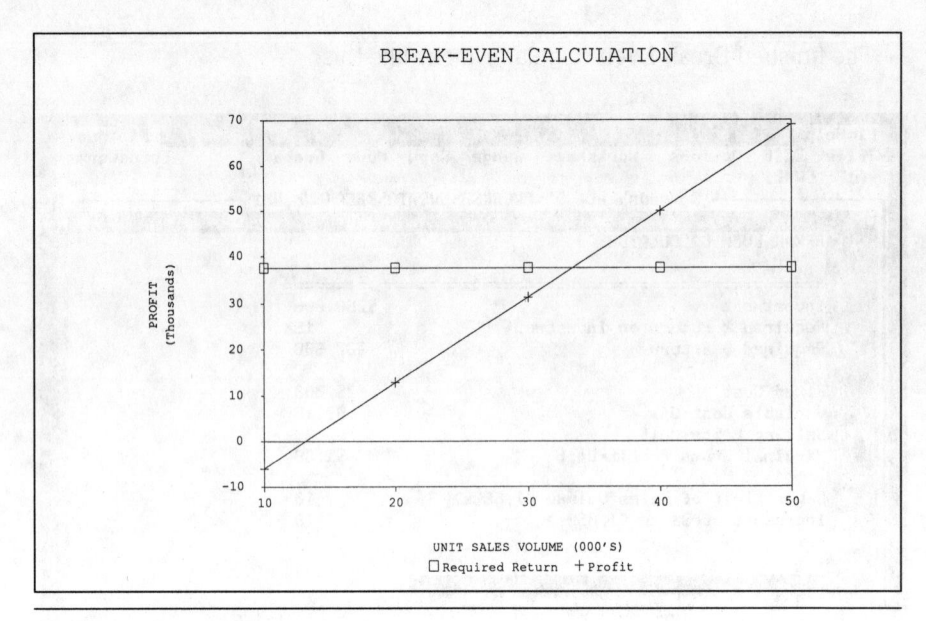

```
                    BREAK-EVEN CALCULATION

         70

         60

         50

         40
PROFIT
(Thousands)
         30

         20

         10

          0

        -10
           10        20        30        40        50
                  UNIT SALES VOLUME (000'S)
                  □ Required Return  + Profit
```

**FIGURE 6.30:** The graph for the Break-Even Calculator

To build the Break-Even Calculator, follow these steps. Save the spreadsheet periodically under an appropriate name, such as BREAKEVN.

## Building the Break-Even Calculator

### Columns
Set the following column widths:

| | |
|---|---|
| A | 40 spaces |
| B | 12 spaces |
| C | 9 spaces |
| D | 18 spaces |
| E..I | 11 spaces |

### Labels
Enter the following labels into the cells and ranges indicated:

| | |
|---|---|
| A1 | BREAK-EVEN CALCULATOR |
| A3..B3, D2..I2 | \= |
| A4 | Investment |
| A5 | Required % Return on Investment |
| A6 | Required $ Return |
| A8 | Fixed Cost |

## Building the Break-Even Calculator *(continued)*

| | |
|---|---|
| A9 | Variable Cost/Unit |
| A10 | Selling Price/Unit |
| A11 | Marginal Gross Profit/Unit |
| A13 | Lower Limit of Sales Volume (1,000s) |
| A14 | Increment of Sales (1,000s) |
| D1 | Sales Volume |
| D3 | Required Return |
| D4 | Profit |

**Number Formats**

Set the following number formats for the cells and ranges indicated (see "Changing Number Formats" in Chapter 5):

**Format Cells and Ranges**

| | |
|---|---|
| Currency, 0 | B4, B6, B8, E3..I4 |
| Percent, 0 | B5 |
| Currency, 2 | B9..B11 |
| General | B13..B14 |

**Formulas**

Enter the following formulas into the cells indicated and enable Protection for the cells:

| | | |
|---|---|---|
| B6 | +B4*B5 | |
| B11 | +B10−B9 | |
| E1 | +B13 | |
| F1 | +E1+$B$14 | Copy into range G1..I1 |
| E3 | +$B$6 | Copy into range F3..I3 |
| E4 | +(E1*$B$11*1000)−$B$8 | Copy into range F4..I4 |

**Graph**

| | | |
|---|---|---|
| Type | Line | |
| Data Ranges | X-Range | = E1..I1 |
| | A-Range | = E3..I3 |
| | B-Range | = E4..I4 |
| Legend | A-Range | Required Return |
| | B-Range | Profit |
| Titles | First | BREAK-EVEN CALCULATION |
| | X-axis | UNIT SALES VOLUME (000'S) |
| | Y-axis | PROFIT |

To test the spreadsheet and graph, enter the following data in the cells indicated and see if the results match those in Figures 6.28 and 6.29. If they don't match, check to be sure your formulas are correct. When you are satisfied that the spreadsheet is correct, press Alt+V and check the graph.

        B4      250000
        B5      0.15
        B8      25000
        B9      3.12
        B10     5.00
        B13     10
        B14     10

When the spreadsheet and graph are correct, try entering different values in the cells above and observe the differences they make in the spreadsheet and graph.

## Graphic Ideas

The uses of graphs are almost as limitless as the uses of spreadsheets. Here are some possibilities.

- **Cover Illustration.** Use a graph to decorate the cover of a report—and emphasize a major point at the same time. Use the Word Processing service to create the cover text and use the Include feature to include the graph at print time.

- **Periodic Performance Reports.** Include graphs in periodic reports on sales, production, expenditures, work completed, etc. Once you have the spreadsheets and graphs set up, you can simply update the spreadsheets for each reporting period, and the graphs automatically follow. You can update the text in the Word Processing service.

- **Cost Control.** To help you keep an eye on the trend of your expenditures, record your monthly expenses for travel, office, telephone, sales, or other purposes in a spreadsheet, adding a new column to the spreadsheet each month. Attach a line or bar graph, and each month when you update the spreadsheet you get a vivid, instant picture of the trend of your expenditures over time.

- **Communicating Data Patterns.** If you want student or company performance results to have an impact, put the information into a line or bar graph and show the trend over time. It gets the message across.

- **Communicating Statistical Relationships.** If you need to convey statistical information to a lay audience, use a graph to display the data pictorially instead of (or in addition to) reporting abstract descriptive statistics. (This is a good tactic for communicating to statistically sophisticated audiences, as well.) For instance, to show the shape of a data distribution, use a line or bar graph. To show the degree of association (correlation) between two variables, use an XY graph.

- **Macro-Retrieve.** If you have a graph (and spreadsheet) that you update frequently, you can save time and keystrokes by creating a macro to retrieve the spreadsheet and graph automatically.

# A Final Word About Graphs

Graphs are unsurpassed for communicating most kinds of numerical information to most audiences. The pictorial representation of information has more impact with audiences, and it reinforces what the numbers say. Nevertheless, most people fail to use graphs as much as they could in presentations and written documents—probably because it's difficult and time-consuming to draw graphs by hand. LotusWorks frees you of these limitations. It enables you to produce accurate and attractive graphs in scarcely any time at all. Take advantage of this capability and experiment freely with graphs. It's a windfall that can put you ahead of nearly everyone else.

# 7

# Telecommunicating

Many people overlook PC communications when they think of saving work with a PC. This is unfortunate because nearly all offices can use PC communications to advantage in some way. For small firms, with limited personnel and money, PC communications can often bring substantial competitive advantage. LotusWorks makes it easy to find out if you can use telecommunications to your advantage.

## Using PC Communications to Work Smart

There are two aspects to working smart with PC communication: finding useful resources and making good use of PC communications techniques to access them.

### Resources

If you have not used PC communications before, you may be surprised at the number of resources available via telephone and the ways these resources can be used. They can be grouped into six basic categories:

**On-Line Information Services.** The array of information available on-line is enormous and is growing day by day. It ranges from quickly changing data, such as stock price quotes and economic projections, to more stable information, such as corporate descriptions, census data, law services, newsletters, articles from magazines, journals, and newspapers, and specialized databases on almost every industry and discipline. Many

---

*In this chapter, you'll learn how to:*

- *Use PC Communications to work smart*
- *Set up to telecommunicate*
- *Get connected*
- *Automate dialups and logins*
- *Conduct PC to PC communications*
- *Automate data and file transfers*
- *Trouble-shoot data communications*

*If you are a CompuServe member, the LotusWorks Forum is a good source of ideas and help from other Lotus-Works users and from Lotus Development Corporation. To reach the Lotus-Works Forum, first dial Compu-Serve and log in. When the ! prompt appears, enter GO LOTUSB. When the menu appears, select option 1, and then select the LotusWorks option.*

on-line services, such as CompuServe, Prodigy, and Dialog, also offer bulletin boards and forums where you can leave messages for other users. CompuServe even provides forums for questions and answers about Lotus products, including LotusWorks.

Many small businesses use on-line information services as a tool for competitive advantage. On-line services can enable even the smallest firms to keep up with market trends, do research on companies and markets, consult with experts, and make contact with potential suppliers and clients locally, nationally, and internationally.

The price of on-line information services varies from a few dollars an hour during non-business hours for message forums and data in the public domain to well over a hundred dollars an hour for some proprietary publications and databases. The investment can be well worth it, however, where the information is needed quickly, you do not have the time or perhaps the local resources to obtain it through conventional library research, or the information simply is not available by other means. The key to controlling the cost is to map out an information search strategy in advance, so that you can log on, conduct an efficient search, download the information you need, upload any messages to others, and log off promptly. You can then use the information off-line.

---

### Tips for Using On-Line Information Services

- Read the documentation and rate structure for the service carefully in advance. Pay particular attention to techniques for narrowing searches to get the specific information you need.

- Take advantage of non-prime-time rates whenever you can.

- Always have a specific goal in mind when you use the service.

- Plan each search as much as possible before you log on.

- If you are looking for articles, use abstracts to help you find the right ones.

- When you are leaving messages for others, compose the messages off-line, then upload them in a bunch.

- If you intend to use a source regularly, record a login script (macro) to automate and speed up the dial-up, login, and as much of the search and download procedures as possible. (Login scripts are described later in this chapter.)

**E-Mail Services.** Electronic mail (or "E-mail") service is offered by long-distance telephone companies, such as MCI Mail, Sprint Mail, and AT&T Mail, as well as by on-line information services such as CompuServe, Genie, and America Online. With E-mail, you can send a message to one or more addressees almost anywhere in the world, and it is held in each addressee's "mailbox" until the addressee logs in by telephone and reads the message. You get notification when the addressee reads the message, whether or not there is an immediate reply. Messages you receive work the same way: you can read them, send replies if you like, and save, print, or discard each message as appropriate.

If you have a personal office or small business, you can use E-mail to advantage in a variety of ways. With E-mail, a small business can put on a big-business front. You can receive orders and messages even if you're out of the office or busy doing other things. You can communicate easily with associates, customers, and suppliers in other time zones and overseas. You can send messages from one type of computer to another. You can use E-mail to send and receive messages from your computer to telex and facsimile machines. You can use it to keep in touch with others when you are traveling. You can even send files to one computer system at home from a different computer system at work.

Many public relations firms use E-mail to broadcast a single news release to an entire list of newspapers, trade publications, and trade associations. You can use the same technique to announce new products to clients and customers.

In most E-mail services, you can send a binary computer file (such as a file generated by LotusWorks) along with your text message. In this way, you can send active word processing, spreadsheet, graph and database files back and forth to employees and business associates in other locations across the country or around the world. If they have LotusWorks, they can edit and print the files just as you do.

Most E-mail services also offer gateways to other E-mail networks. This makes it possible to send and receive computer-generated messages to individuals and companies even if they do not subscribe to the same service that you do. Some also link to the Internet network that links many universities, government agencies, and research centers.

E-mail rates are quite inexpensive, especially if you can dial into a service with a local call. Sometimes it is less costly to FAX to the United States from overseas via an on-line information service or a U.S. domestic telephone carrier than it is via the regular overseas telephone company. E-mail carriers do not all charge the same rates or calculate usage charges the same way, however, so in

*To give your E-mail a business-like appearance, create a standard "letterhead" in the Word Processing service and save it in a macro or boilerplate format. For more information, see "Creating and Using Boilerplate" in Chapter 3.*

considering an E-mail service, check to see which ones offer the services you need, and then see which rating structure best fits your pattern of usage.

**Mainframe Computer Systems.** The terminal emulation capability of LotusWorks makes it possible to use your PC as a terminal and dial into mainframe and minicomputer systems that can communicate with ANSI, VT100, VT52, or TTY terminals over asynchronous modems. You can't download data to the PC this way, but you can perform mainframe operations just as if you had a mainframe terminal. The only cost is for the telephone time.

**Other PCs.** More and more small businesses are finding it useful for some purposes to communicate directly from PC to PC. Many printers and typesetters, for example, use PC-to-PC file transfers to receive copy from customers, either for manual data entry or for entering files directly into desktop publishing systems. Writers and ad agencies can send drafts back and forth for approval and editing the same way. Businesses and institutions with multiple locations find that they can send reports and move draft documents quickly and easily from office to office by having one PC call another. The only cost is for the telephone service.

*To find out the telephone numbers of private bulletin boards in your area, contact the nearest PC club or PC dealer. Once you dial into one board, you can usually find a list of U.S. bulletin boards for downloading.*

**Private Bulletin Boards.** A source often overlooked by small businesses is private PC bulletin boards. These are operated by private individuals and businesses. There are now thousands covering all sorts of topics and located in almost every community in the United States and Canada. Individuals can use them to advertise services and products, post questions and get answers about technical and business problems, and make contact with potential customers, suppliers, and partners, just as on some of the large national information services. In most cases there is little or no charge for using the bulletin board—in fact, many board operators are pleased to have you participate as long as you contribute to the conversations. Private bulletin boards tend to be come and go rather frequently, but many stay in operation year after year and attract hundreds of users. They can be an excellent way to contact customers.

**Direct Connection to Other PCs.** One means of PC-to-PC communications does not involve the telephone at all. You can connect two PCs directly via a modem eliminator (or "null modem") cable and transfer files between machines at astonishing rates. This can be useful for transferring large amounts of data or transferring data between PCs (such as a laptop and a desktop machine) which do not have matching floppy disk drives. All it takes is LotusWorks loaded on both machines (or LotusWorks on one and another telecommunications software system on the other) and a null modem cable connecting the serial ports on the two machines.

## Accessing the Resources

Accessing the information resources above requires three things: a modem connected to your PC and one connected to the computer with which you plan to communicate; communications software in operation at each end of the telephone connection; and agreement between the two parties on which communications parameters and file transfer protocols to use. With LotusWorks, you already have the communications software you need at your end of the line. The rest of this chapter describes how to make the communications links to access the resources.

## A Brief Introduction to Data Communications

Data communications has its own jargon. If you are new to data communications, knowing the following few terms and concepts will make the process less mysterious.

**Digital and Analog Communications.** Telephones and computers communicate in fundamentally different ways. Telephones convert the sound waves of the human voice into electrical waves, transmit them along the telephone line, and then convert them back to sound waves in the receiver. Thus, voice telephones are called analog communications. Computers, on the other hand, communicate digitally. Instead of transmitting continuous electrical waves, computers send on-off electrical impulses. Each "on" or "off" signal makes up one "bit" of information, and seven or eight bits make up one "byte" or roughly one character of information. To send computer communications over telephone lines, it is necessary to convert the computer's bits and bytes into analog electrical waves and back again.

**Modem.** The name modem comes from the terms "modulate-demodulate." The modem is the device that converts digital signals into analog electrical waves for the telephone line and converts them back again when they are received. The task is formidable, because the modem and serial port have to convert the data bits traveling from the PC eight abreast into a single-file stream of data, transmit the data over the telephone line, then convert the received data from single file back into eight abreast—and do all this 1200, 2400, 9600, or 19,200 times per second.

**Baud Rate.** Baud is a measure of the speed with which bytes of data are transmitted and received. Most PC modems transmit and receive at 1200, 2400, 4800, 9600, or 19,200 baud over ordinary telephone lines.

**Xon/Xoff.** Xon/Xoff is a method of coordinating the flow of data between two computers. It enables each computer to signal when it is ready to send or receive more data, so that the data does not flow faster than it can accept it. Flow control is useful when electrical interference or "noise" on the telephone line slows communications and gets the computers out of synchronization (indicated by strange "garbage" characters on the screen). Communication is surer—but slower—when Xon/Xoff flow control is switched on. When telephone connections are good and comparable modems are used, it usually is not necessary.

**Full-Duplex and Half-Duplex ("echo typed") modes.** The communications mode (full-duplex or half-duplex) refers to the data path over the telephone line. Half-duplex is like a single lane road: one end can't transmit until the other end stops. Full-duplex is like a two-lane highway: both ends can send and receive at the same time. In half-duplex mode, the local computer must echo-type on its screen every character that is sent. In full-duplex mode, the receiving computer echoes each character back to the screen of the sending computer. Most PC communications are conducted in full-duplex mode.

**Parity.** Parity refers to a method of error checking by which numbers indicating the number of data packets are sent to help ensure that no data bits were accidentally lost along the way. Both computers have to use the same parity settings for parity to work. The options are typically called even parity, odd parity, and no parity (None).

**Data Bits.** In PC communications, each byte or digital "word" is composed of either seven or eight bits of data. For text communications (where a reader can usually tell if a transmission error occurred), seven data bits are often used. For binary file transfers, however, the computers must perform their own error checking, and eight data bits are normally used. As with parity, both computers have to be set for the same number of data bits.

**Stop Bits.** In PC communications, the end of each packet of data is marked by either one or two "stop" bits. Both computers must be set for the same number of stop bits (usually one) for successful data communications to occur.

**File-Transfer Protocols.** In contrast to text communications, where humans can proofread the result, binary file transfers require careful error checking by the computers to ensure that no transmission errors accidentally corrupt the files. Several file-transfer protocols have been developed that automatically check for errors. If the receiving computer detects an error in an incoming packet of data, it tells the sending computer to resend the packet. LotusWorks supports the Xmodem, CRC-Xmodem, 1K-CRC-Xmodem, and Kermit file-transfer protocols. In addition, LotusWorks has a Text option that sends ASCII text and displays it on the screen without error checking.

**Terminal Emulation.** Whenever LotusWorks communicates, it emulates a computer terminal. Terminal emulation simply means that the PC acts like a computer terminal. This requires software to translate the keystrokes of the PC keyboard into the appropriate signals for the terminal being emulated. LotusWorks can emulate ANSI, DEC VT100, DEC VT52, as well as TTY terminals.

# Setting Up To Telecommunicate

LotusWorks has two mechanisms for setting up telecommunications: the Setup *program* (accessed from the LotusWorks Screen) and the Setup *command* (accessed from the Communications service). You use the Setup program when you first install LotusWorks or when you install new equipment to tell LotusWorks about your telephone and modem installations. Later, you use the Setup command in the Communications service to specify and save communications settings for each new remote computer with which you communicate.

The first step in setting up to telecommunicate is to connect an internal or external Hayes or Hayes-compatible modem to your computer and to a telephone line. See the instructions for your modem for the correct way to connect the modem.

> CAUTION: LotusWorks can be used only with Hayes modems and modems that are 100-percent Hayes-compatible.

The next step is to run the Setup program on the LotusWorks Screen to tell LotusWorks about your telephone and modem installation. Go to the LotusWorks screen and select Setup Modem. The following dialog box appears:

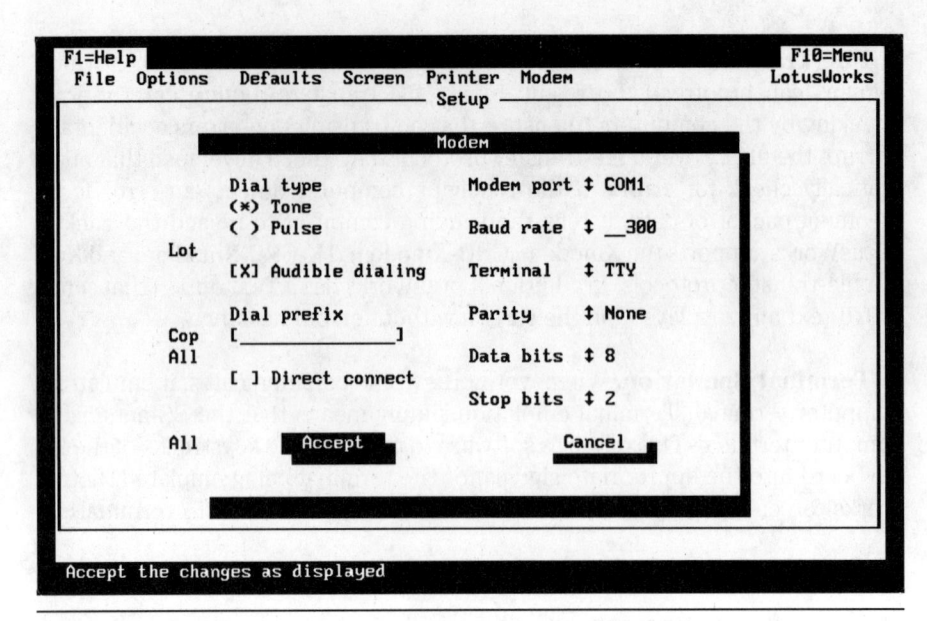

```
F1=Help                                                          F10=Menu
   File  Options   Defaults   Screen   Printer   Modem        LotusWorks
                              ─ Setup ─
                               ┌ Modem ┐

              Dial type           Modem port  ‡ COM1
              (*) Tone
              ( ) Pulse           Baud rate   ‡ __300
        Lot
              [X] Audible dialing Terminal    ‡ TTY

              Dial prefix         Parity      ‡ None
        Cop   [_____]
        All                       Data bits   ‡ 8
              [ ] Direct connect
                                  Stop bits   ‡ 2

        All        Accept                Cancel

Accept the changes as displayed
```

**FIGURE 7.1:** Use the Setup program to tell LotusWorks about your telephone and modem.

Set the **Dial type** option for the type of telephone you are using (Tone for touch-tone phones, Pulse for rotary dial phones).

Check the **Audible dialing** box to indicate whether you want to be able to hear the modem dialing or not. (Audible dialing usually helps when you are first seting up your modem and want to be sure it's dialing).

Use the **Dialing prefix** box to specify any numbers that need to be dialed before dialing a telephone number. If you need to dial "9" and/or an authorization code to reach an outside line, for example, enter those numbers in the Dialing prefix box. If you need the computer to pause for a second after dialing a number, insert a comma after the number. If you need it to pause longer, insert more commas until the pause is the right length.

Check the **Direct connect** box only if your computer is connected directly to another computer via a null modem. If you are communicating through a modem, leave this box blank.

Select the **Modem port** setting that indicates the computer port where your modem or null modem is connected (COM1 or COM2). If your computer has more than two serial ports, be sure to connect the modem to either COM1 or COM2.

Select the highest **Baud rate** that your modem can handle. If you are communicating with another computer that can handle only a lower baud rate, the modem will automatically adjust downward to match the rate.

Select the **Terminal** option that matches the type of communication you do most frequently. If most of your data communications are with on-line information services, E-mail services, or other PCs, select the TTY terminal type. If most of your other communications are with a mainframe or minicomputer that require an ANSI, VT52, or VT100 terminal, select one of these options. You can always change this setting in the Communications service to communicate with particular computers.

Select the **Data bits, Parity,** and **Stop bit** options that fit the type of communication you do most frequently. In most cases this will be a combination of either 7 data bits–even parity–1 stop bit or 8 data bits–no parity–1 stop bit. If you are unsure about which combination to use, select 7 data bits–even parity–1 stop bit. That is the most common combination. You can always change these settings in the Communications service to communicate with particular computers.

When you have finished specifying the modem and dialing settings, select Accept.

Once you have set up the LotusWorks defaults for telecommunications, you probably will not have to change them unless you change modems, change to or from a null modem, or change your type of telephone service.

For information on using the Setup command in the communications service, see "Setting and Saving the Communications Parameters" later in this chapter.

# Getting Connected

## Before You Begin . . .

Before you begin data communications for the first time, it is important to recognize that for successful data communications to occur, quite a few things have to be in order. Several pieces of equipment must be connected correctly (two computers, two modems, a telephone line, and their connecting cables), and a number of software settings (communications parameters and file-transfer protocols) must be coordinated exactly. If your data communications are not successful on the first try, don't despair! It is not unusual for something to go wrong the first time. (In fact, it probably is exceptional for something *not* to go wrong on the first try!) Once your computer and connected equipment are set up correctly, data communications usually proceeds quickly and easily thereafter.

It's a good idea the first time to try communicating with an on-line service, a bulletin board system, or a remote PC (with an experienced operator) that you know is functioning correctly, rather than to try to link up with another untried PC.

If the first try is unsuccessful, be patient and systematically check all of the switches, connections, and software settings on your computer, modem, and telephone. Loose cables are a no-no, as are disconnected telephone handsets, cables plugged into the wrong connectors, and power switches turned off. If you have trouble, consult the Trouble-Shooting Data Communications table at the end of this chapter.

## Preparing to Communicate

In order to communicate, you must have some information from the remote computer: its phone number, a user name or account number and password to use in the login if required, and the communications parameters to set. If you are preparing to communicate with another PC, you should agree with the other computer operator on a time to begin the first communication.

## Setting and Saving the Communications Parameters

*Most on-line services use seven data bits, even parity, and one stop bit, but check each service's instructions to be sure.*

You set the communications parameters for each remote computer with the Setup command in the Communications service. (Don't confuse the Setup command with the Setup program, which is accessed from the LotusWorks menu.) Once the telecommunications parameters for a session have been set, they can be saved in a file for future use.

Even though there are hundreds of possible combinations of baud rate, parity, data bits, and stop bits, in practice most PC communications use only four: either 1200 or 2400 baud, and either seven data bits-even parity-and-one stop bit, or eight data bits-no parity-and one stop bit. Just be sure you know what parameters the other computer is using. If you are setting up PC-to-PC communications, be sure to get agreement in advance on the parameters to use.

To set the communications parameters, select Setup from the Communications service. The following dialog box appears:

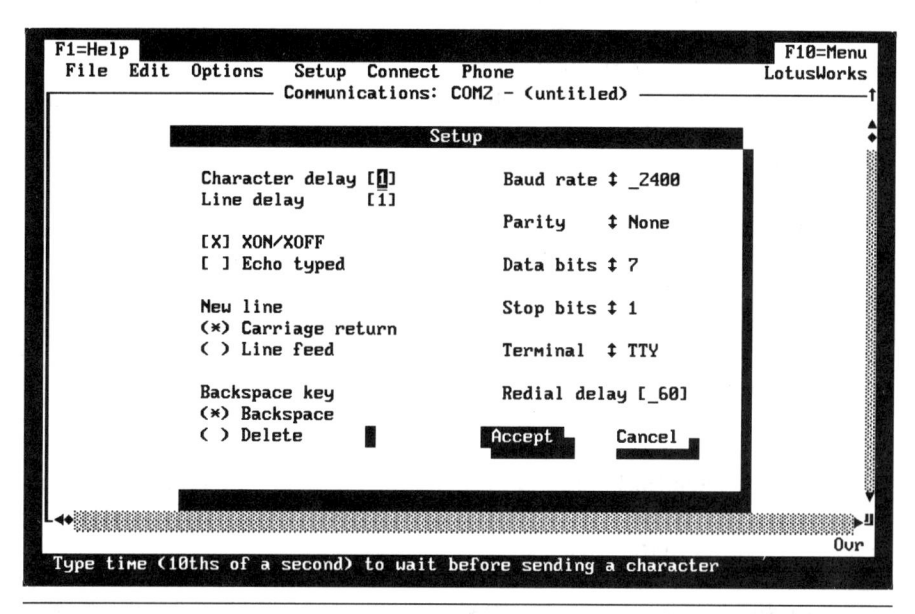

```
F1=Help                                                         F10=Menu
   File  Edit  Options   Setup  Connect  Phone                 LotusWorks
                     Communications: COM2 - (untitled)
   ┌────────────────────────── Setup ──────────────────────────┐
   │                                                           │
   │     Character delay [0]      Baud rate ‡ _2400            │
   │     Line delay     [1]                                    │
   │                              Parity    ‡ None             │
   │    [X] XON/XOFF                                           │
   │    [ ] Echo typed            Data bits ‡ 7                │
   │                                                           │
   │    New line                  Stop bits ‡ 1                │
   │    (*) Carriage return                                    │
   │    ( ) Line feed             Terminal  ‡ TTY              │
   │                                                           │
   │    Backspace key             Redial delay [_60]           │
   │    (*) Backspace                                          │
   │    ( ) Delete                 Accept      Cancel          │
   │                                                           │
   └───────────────────────────────────────────────────────────┘
                                                                Ovr
   Type time (10ths of a second) to wait before sending a character
```

**FIGURE 7.2:** Use the Setup command in the Communications service to set the communication parameters for each remote computer.

The **Character delay** and **Line delay** options enable you to set the waiting times before sending each character and line of a login script. The default settings are the fastest. Normally you do not have to change them, but if the remote computer misses part of the data you send during login, try increasing the Character delay and Line delay values.

The **XON/XOFF** option sets this type of flow control either on or off. Use it with the Text protocol, but only if your modem sends data too fast for the other modem (or vice versa) and the other modem has the Xon/Xoff feature. Usually you can leave it switched off.

The **Echo typed** option should be switched on only for half-duplex operation. For normal PC communications, leave it switched off.

The **New line** option tells LotusWorks to start a new line after receiving each carriage return character or after each line-feed character. Which option you should select depends upon how the other computer is sending data. If each line of text you receive prints over the previous line on the screen, set the option to Line feed. (This inserts a line-feed after each line.) If you get double-spacing between each line of characters, set the option to Carriage return (to omit the extra line-feed at the end of each line).

Set the **Baud rate** to the highest rate that both modems can handle. If you set the rate too high, or if a noisy phone line forces a lower transmission rate, most modems adjust downward automatically to match the other modem and the line conditions.

Set the **Parity** option to match that of the other computer—usually even parity or no parity.

Set the **Data bits** to 7 or 8, to match the setting of the other computer.

Set the **Stop bits** to 1 or 2—usually 1—to match the setting of the other computer.

Change the **Terminal** option only if you intend to operate in terminal emulation mode. Otherwise, leave it at the default setting of TTY. See "Terminal Emulation" earlier in this chapter.

The **Redial delay** option tells LotusWorks how many seconds to wait before automatically redialing, in case of a busy signal. Set this to whatever interval you wish.

When all of the options have been set, select Accept. This sets the communications parameters for the current session but it does not save them.

To save the current communications parameters for future use, press Alt+S or select File Save, enter a descriptive file name and path for the settings, and select Save. Once you have saved the settings this way, you can retrieve them in the future by selecting File Retrieve, entering the name and path of the file, and selecting Retrieve.

## Dialing

There are three ways to dial a remote computer to initiate data communications:

- If you have a telephone handset and modem on the same telephone line, you can manually dial a regular voice phone call and then switch to data communications.

- You can type a phone number in LotusWorks and have the modem dial.
- You can create a login script to have LotusWorks and the modem dial automatically.

The first method is handy for setting up communications with another PC, and the second method is useful if you're making only one or two calls to another computer. For data calls that you make repeatedly, however, the login script is by far the quickest and handiest method. The first two methods are described below, and the third method is described under "Automating Dialups and Logins" later in this chapter.

## Manually Dialing a Voice Call and Switching to Data

To make a voice call and switch to data communications, you and the party you are calling must each have a telephone handset as well as a PC connected to a modem. The other party must also have a copy of LotusWorks or some other communications software package. Either party can initiate the voice call by dialing in the normal manner. You make the switch to data communications by each entering a Hayes modem command from the keyboard into an active Communications screen.

Turn on your computer and modem, and select the Communications service before you dial. Dial the call and establish communications with the user at the remote computer. A voice call is a good way to coordinate the communication parameters with the other party and plan the data session. While the voice call is underway, no data communications can take place.

When you are ready to switch to data communications, follow these steps:

1. Select Phone Modem. LotusWorks displays a message box.

2. Tell the other user to type *ATA* (using all capital letters) and press Enter. (If the other user has LotusWorks 3.0, the user can simply press Alt+A, instead.)

3. Select Continue to close the message box on your screen.

4. When you and the remote user hear a high-pitched modem tone, both of you should hang up your handsets. To test the data connection, type a few short messages to each other. You should be able to see each other's typing on the screen. While a data connection is underway, no voice communications can take place.

If you want to switch back from a data connection to a voice connection, both parties should pick up their telephone receiver (the modem tone still sounds), and do *one* of the following:

- Press Alt+H
- Type *ATH* and press Enter
- Select Phone Hangup

You can then resume your voice call.

## Modem Dialing

To have the modem dial, you do not need to have a telephone handset connected to the modem (but you and the other party do need to have the same communications parameters set). Turn on your modem, select the Communications service, and when the initials OK appear on the screen, press Alt+D or select Phone Dial. The following dialog box appears:

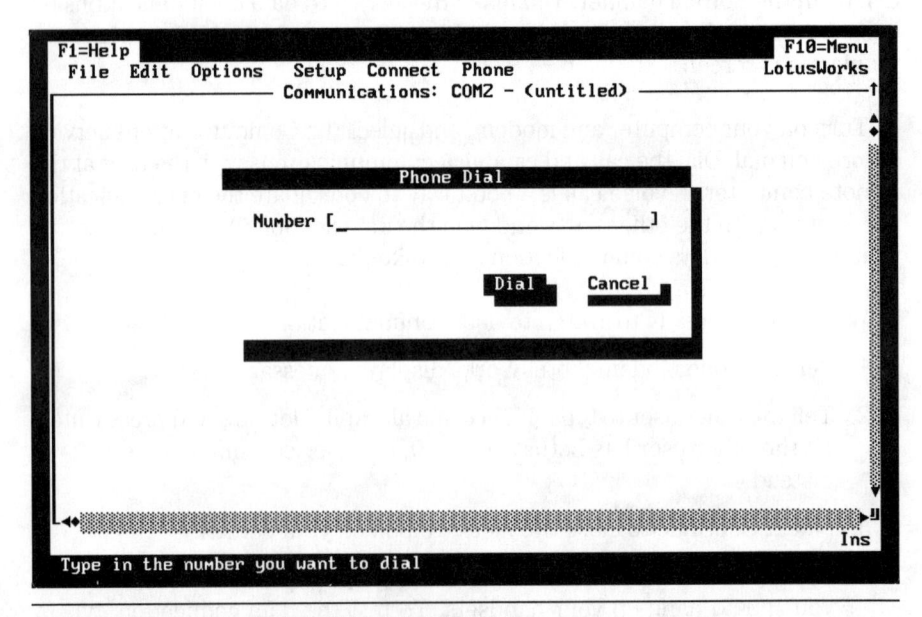

**FIGURE 7.3:** Enter the phone number to dial and select Dial.

Enter the phone number to dial, including area code, if necessary. You may type the number either with or without spaces and punctuation—for example, (302) 555-1234 or 3025551234. If you are making a long distance call, enter the digits necessary to reach the desired long distance service (for example, 0, 1, or 011). If you need to dial 9, and/or any other digits to reach an outside line, enter those digits first, but do *not* enter any digits that you have already entered in the Dialing prefix box on the LotusWorks Setup Modem Defaults screen. When you have finished entering the telephone number, select Dial.

LotusWorks tests your modem and prints characters on the screen as it dials the number and receives responses from the other computer. If your modem has a speaker and you have Audible dialing turned on in the LotusWorks Setup Modem screen, you can hear the modem dial and the phone ring, and when the other modem answers, you can hear the high-pitched carrier tone from the modem.

When a connection has been made, you receive a message such as "Connect" or "Connect at 2400 baud" in the LotusWorks Communications window. (The exact message depends on your modem and the way you have its message options set.) You are then ready to conduct the data session.

*If it is necessary to dial certain digits every time you dial, it is best to put those digits into the Dialing prefix box on the LotusWorks Setup Modem screen. You can save the rest of each phone number in a separate communications login script file. If you have to dial different digits for different calls, it's best to save each entire phone number in a separate login script file.*

## Answering

You can have your PC answer automatically when other computers call by making the Communications window active and setting your modem to Auto-answer. See your modem manual for instructions. No special setting in Lotus-Works is required.

You can also manually direct your PC to answer calls. When you hear the telephone ring, simply press Alt+A when the Communications window is active, or select Phone Answer from the menus.

## Disconnecting

To end a data session and terminate the telephone call, press Alt+H or select Phone Hangup. LotusWorks sends a hangup command to the modem and echoes the status on the screen when the call terminates.

> IMPORTANT: If you disconnect from an on-line information service without first logging off the service, the remote computer may think you are still connected and continue to charge your account!

## Interrupting a Data Transfer

Sometimes when you are transferring a data file via modem, you may wish to interrupt the data transfer without terminating the phone call (for instance, if you discover that you are sending the wrong file by mistake).

If you need to interrupt a data transfer, press Alt+B or select Phone Break. This causes LotusWorks to send a break signal, which halts the data flow but leaves the data session and phone call connected. You can then resume data communications with a new command, or press Alt+H to terminate the session and hang up the phone.

## Viewing and Capturing the Communications Dialog

Once you are connected to another computer, any information you type on your keyboard is sent to the other computer, and vice versa. The dialog between the two computers is displayed on the screen in the Communications window as communications take place.

### Viewing the Communications History On-Screen

When the screen fills up, the oldest lines scroll off the top of the screen, but they are kept temporarily in memory (until that, too, fills up). You can review the lines that are still in memory by selecting Options History and then pressing PgUp or the Up Arrow key repeatedly. To return to the active communications window and resume the session, press Esc.

> CAUTION: When you review the dialog, LotusWorks temporarily suspends communications until you press Esc. Therefore, you should wait until a pause in the incoming screen data to review the previous dialog. Otherwise, you might miss important new dialog while you are reviewing the old dialog.

## Capturing the Communications History in a File

You can also capture the screen dialog in a file and save it. You should use this approach when you want to be sure to save *all* the dialog in a session. Later you can review the dialog or screen or print it by retrieving the file in the Word Processing service.

To capture the screen dialog to a file, press Alt+T or select File Capture before initiating data communications or while the computers are connected. The following dialog box appears:

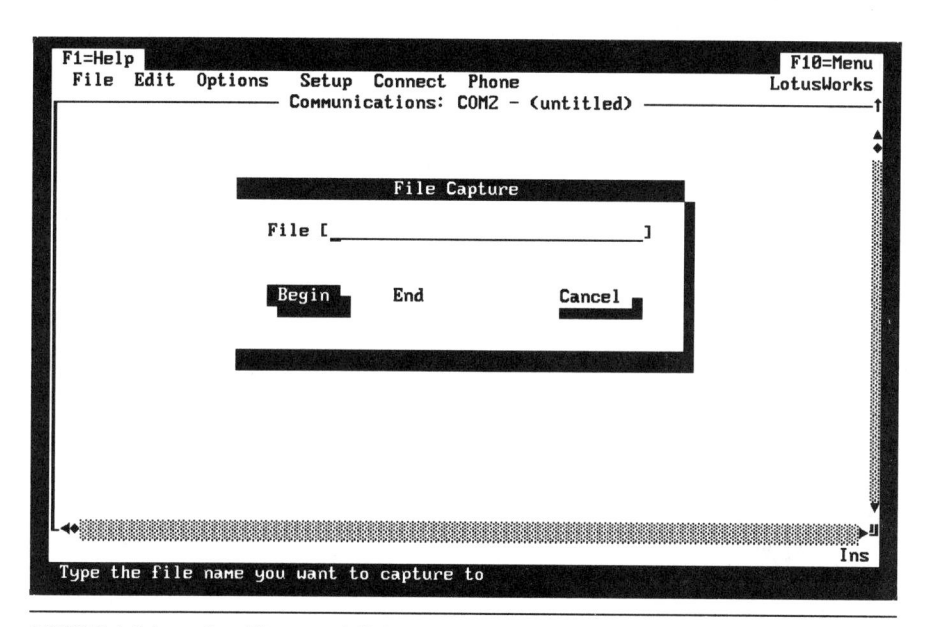

**FIGURE 7.4:** Enter a path and file name to hold the communications dialog to be captured and select Begin.

Enter a path and file name in the text box to hold the communications dialog to be captured, then select Begin. All subsequent dialog is captured in ASCII format in the file you named until you end File Capture.

To end File Capture, press Alt+T or select File Capture again and select End.

### Viewing Communications Full-Screen

To see more of the communications dialog at a time, select Options Full Screen. This causes the menus and scroll bars to disappear and the communications window to be blown up to full-screen. To return from Full Screen, press F10.

## Sending and Receiving Data Files

Once you are connected to another computer, you can send ("upload") and receive ("download") text and data files using one of the file-transfer protocols that LotusWorks supports. Both computers must use the same protocol.

### Which Protocol Should You Choose?

| Use this protocol: | To send: | Considerations in choosing: |
| --- | --- | --- |
| Text | Text (ASCII) files, such as files created with File Transfer Upload or File Capture. | Use only if accuracy is not a concern. Is fast but provides **no error checking**. Displays the text on the screen as file is sent and received. |
| Text (with Wait for Echo on) | Text files. | Provides error checking but is very slow. |
| Xmodem | Text or binary files. Binary files include word processing, spreadsheet, and database files produced by LotusWorks and other programs. | Provides less error checking than CRC-Xmodem or 1K CRC-Xmodem but is more widely available than these two. |
| CRC-Xmodem | Text or binary files. | Provides better error checking than Xmodem. Use this if the remote computer supports it and does not support 1K CRC-Xmodem or Kermit. |
| 1K CRC-Xmodem | Text or binary files. | Provides better error checking than Xmodem and is faster than Xmodem or CRC-Xmodem. |
| Kermit | Text or binary files. | Provides error checking and is fastest of all; transfers files without changing the file size or file date, and lets you use wildcards in a file name to send a batch of files with one command. **Use Kermit if the other computer supports it.** |

## Sending

To send a file, first coordinate with the remote computer on a file-transfer protocol to use, then press Alt+U or select File Transfer Upload. The following dialog box appears:

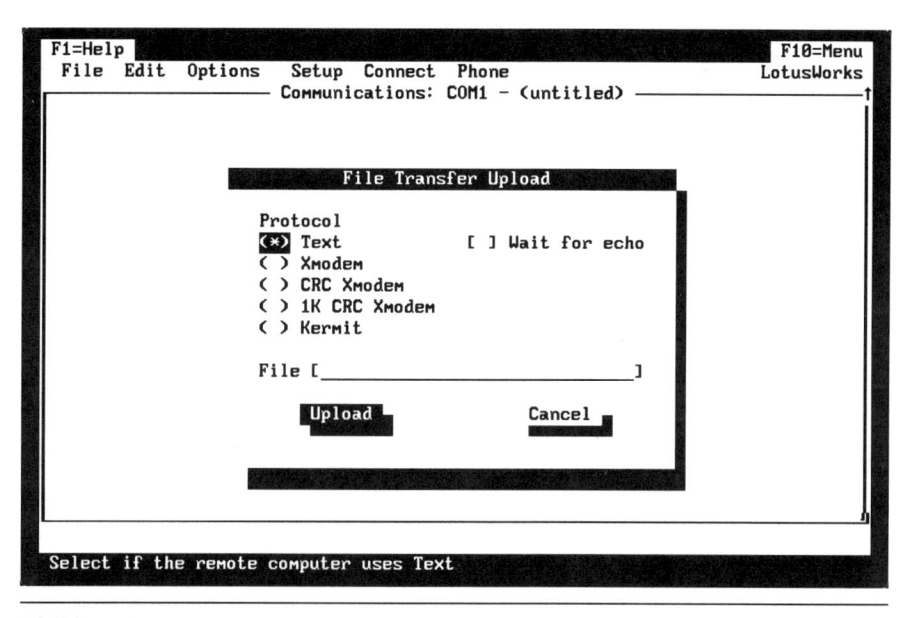

**FIGURE 7.5:** To send a file, enter the path and name of the file, select a protocol to use, and select Upload.

Enter the path and name of the file you wish to send, select the agreed-upon file-transfer protocol, and press Upload. The computer should begin transferring the file immediately. If you are using the Text protocol, the text appears on the screen as it is being transferred. If you are using one of the other protocols, a dot appears at the bottom of the screen for each packet of data transferred.

> **NOTE:** If transmission does not begin within one minute, cancel the upload and check to be sure that both computers are using the same file-transfer protocol.

To cancel a file upload, press Alt+U or select File Transfer Upload, and select Cancel.

## Receiving

To receive a file from a remote computer, first coordinate with the remote computer operator on a file-transfer protocol to use, then press Alt+R or select File Transfer Download. The following dialog box appears:

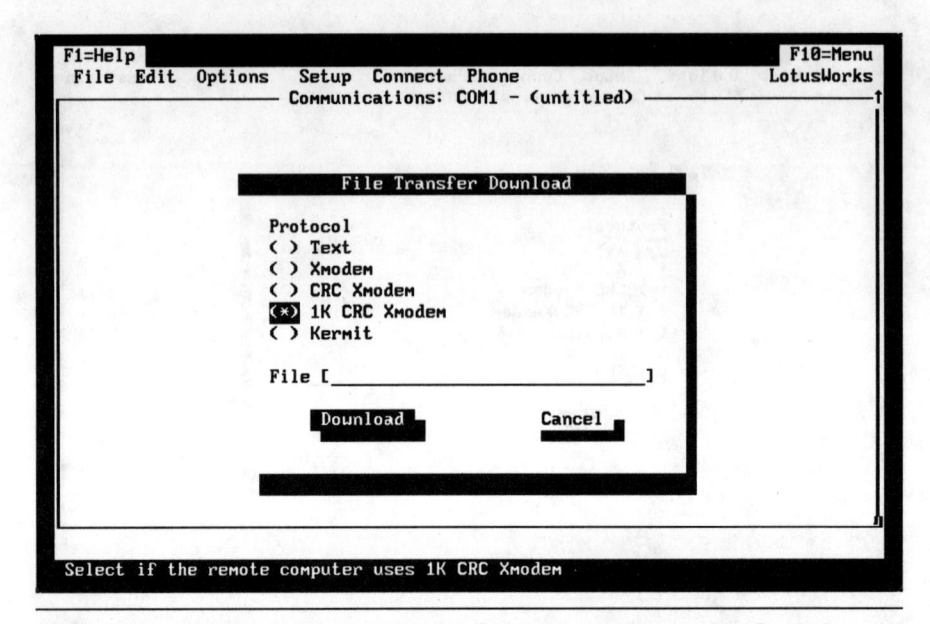

```
F1=Help                                                    F10=Menu
   File  Edit  Options   Setup  Connect  Phone             LotusWorks
                   Communications: COM1 - (untitled)

                        File Transfer Download

                    Protocol
                    ( ) Text
                    ( ) Xmodem
                    ( ) CRC Xmodem
                    (*) 1K CRC Xmodem
                    ( ) Kermit

                    File [_____]

                        Download            Cancel


Select if the remote computer uses 1K CRC Xmodem
```

**FIGURE 7.6:** To receive a file, enter a path and name for the file, select a protocol to use, and select Download.

Enter a path and name for the file to be received (it does not have to be the same file name that the remote computer uses), select the agreed-upon file-transfer protocol, and select Download. The computer should begin transferring the file immediately. As in sending a file, if you are using the Text protocol, the text appears on the screen as it is being transferred, and if you are using one of the other protocols, a dot appears at the bottom of the screen for each packet of data transferred.

To cancel a file download in progress, press Alt+R or select File Transfer Download, and select Cancel.

## A Note About Using Binary Protocols . . .

All the communications protocols except the Text protocol are binary protocols. When you are sending or receiving files with a binary protocol, you may occasionally see an E in place of a dot at the bottom of the screen when you are uploading or an R in place of a dot when you are downloading. An E means that an error has been detected in uploading; an R means that a packet has been retransmitted. Usually, errors are caused by electrical interference on the telephone line. If the dots continue following the letter, it means that the retransmission was successful. If a large number of errors occur, however, you should go to the Setup screen and try a lower baud rate and/or increase the character delay and line delay settings. If you still get a large percentage of errors, try disconnecting and redialing the call to see if you can get a better telephone line connection.

# Using Accelerator Keys in Communications

Accelerator keys can save you time in any LotusWorks service, but they are especially important in telecommunications, where extra time can cost you extra money. The following is a list of accelerator keys that are especially useful to speed telecommunications operations.

### Accelerator Keys for Communications

| Accelerator Key | Function | Menu Equivalent |
| --- | --- | --- |
| Alt+A | Answer the phone. | Phone Answer |
| Alt+B | Send an interrupt signal. | Phone Break |
| Alt+C | Copy text to the clipboard. | Edit Copy |
| Alt+D | Dial a phone number. | Phone Dial |
| Alt+H | Hang up (disconnect) the phone. | Phone Hangup |
| Alt+P | Send the contents of the clipboard to the modem. | Edit Paste |
| Alt+Q | Close the Communications window. | File Quit |
| Alt+R | Receive (download) a file from a remote computer. | File Transfer Download |
| Alt+S | Save communications settings, phone number, and login script in a file. | File Save |
| Alt+T | Save the communications dialog in an ASCII capture file. | File Capture |
| Alt+U | Send (upload) a file to a remote computer. | File Transfer Upload |
| Alt+Z | Switch between full-screen and a sized window. | Options Window Zoom |
| F1 | Display a help screen. | |
| F2 | In a dialog box, display the file viewer. | |
| F4 | Select text. | Edit Select |
| F6 | Move to the last active window. | Options Window Swap |
| Alt+F6 | Move to the next active window. | Options Window Next |
| Ctrl+F6 | Switch to the LotusWorks screen. | LotusWorks |
| F9 | Stop recording a login script. | |
| F10 | Activate the Communications menu. | |
| Alt+F10 | Alternate between displaying menus with descriptive text or not. | |

## PC-to-PC Telecommunications

Communicating with another PC works like communicating with any other computer, but there are a few preparations you need to make beforehand. The first is to find out whether the remote modem is in auto-answer or manual mode. If it is in manual mode, then of course you need to coordinate with the remote operator on which of you will initiate the call and at what time.

> NOTE: The remote PC does not have to be running LotusWorks, but it must have data communications software as well as a modem, and the remote operator must be present to communicate with you.

Second, agree on the communications parameters and file transfer protocols to use. Carefully coordinate the baud rate, parity, number of data bits, number of stop bits, and whether or not to use Xon/Xoff. If the remote PC is using a communications package other than LotusWorks, some of the remote operator's terminology may be slightly different. Be sure that the remote communications package supports at least one of the file transfer protocols that LotusWorks supports.

Third, see if you need to use a password to get into the remote computer. (Some PC communications programs can be set up to require a caller to enter a password before data communications can proceed.)

If you plan to download a file from the remote computer, you need to press Alt+R (or select File Transfer Download) and enter a file name before the remote operator sends the file. Tell the remote operator to give you a few seconds to get set up. If you plan to upload a file to the remote PC, be sure to give the remote operator time to set up a file to receive the file you plan to send before you send it.

Once you are connected, you and the remote operator can type messages back and forth to each other. If the other operator is present, this is a good time to clarify communications parameters, file names, protocols, and what you intend to do.

# Composing and Sending E-Mail

You can save money on E-mail connect-time charges by composing messages in the Word Processing service before you begin communications. When you are ready to communicate, copy a message to the Clipboard, switch to the Communications service, and dial the E-mail service. When you have a data connection and are ready to send the message, press Alt+P to "paste" the contents of the Clipboard to the modem.

*To save E-mail connect-time charges, compose messages offline in the Word Processing service, copy a message to the Clipboard, then switch to the Communications service and send the message by "pasting" it to the modem.*

If you need to send another message, press F6 to switch back to the Word Processing service, copy the next message to the Clipboard, press F6 again to switch back to the Communications service, and when you are ready to send the message, press Alt+P again. You can repeat this process until all the messages have been sent.

## Automating Dialups and Logins

You can save a lot of time and protect against dialing errors in any calls that you make frequently by creating login scripts to dial the calls automatically. A login script is simply a file that contains the communications parameters, phone the number, and (if appropriate) the login sequence for a call. When you initiate a call using a login script, LotusWorks automatically sets the communications parameters, dials the call, and logs in to the remote computer, using the information recorded in the login script. That might sound complicated to create, but it's really quite easy.

### Recording a Login Script

To create a login script, follow these steps:

1. Make the call and data connection manually a few times, to familiarize yourself with the communications parameters, phone number, and login procedure. It's a good idea to write down these procedures for reference when you are recording the login script.

2. Select Setup and set the communications parameters for the call.

3. Select Connect Learn. The following dialog box appears:

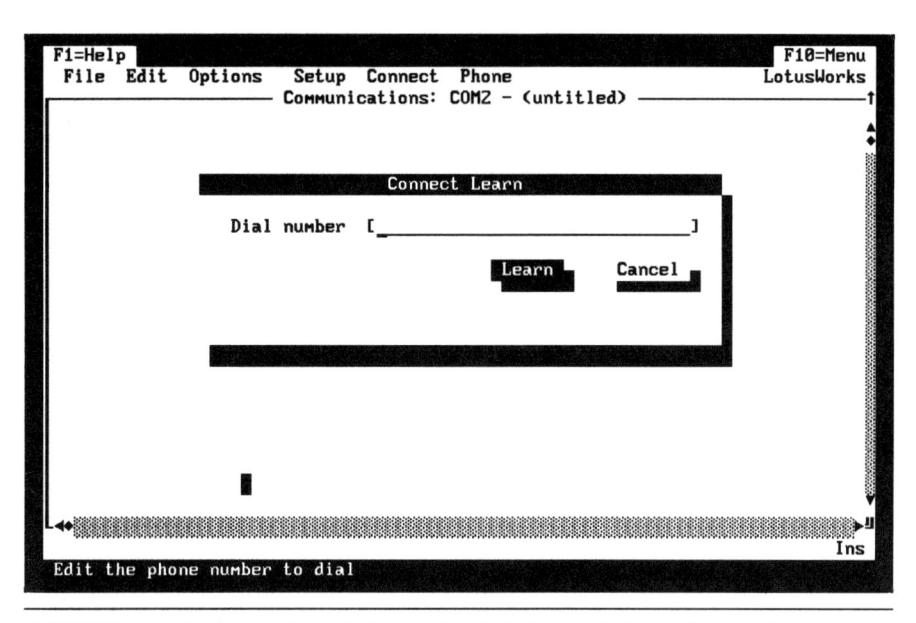

**FIGURE 7.7:** Enter a telephone number for the login script, and select Learn to begin recording keystrokes.

Enter the telephone number for the computer you want to dial, and select Learn. LotusWorks dials the telephone number and begins recording your keystrokes and the data coming from the other computer.

4. When the call is connected, go through your regular login procedure. To ensure that the keystroke sequence is recorded correctly, wait for each response from the remote computer before you type the next command. Record keystrokes up to the point where you can no longer make the same keystrokes for every call.

5. Press F9 to stop recording. You may save the login script at any time without interfering with the telephone connection. Conduct the rest of your data session as you normally would, and then log off the remote computer and disconnect the phone call.

6. Save the login script: Press Alt+S or select File Save, enter a descriptive file name for the login script, change the path if necessary, and select Save.

*To save time with standard communications setups, record them in login scripts without telephone numbers and then retrieve one when you want to use a particular setup.*

**NOTE:** Be sure to use File Save to save each login script before you leave the communications window or record another. Otherwise you'll lose your handiwork.

> CAUTION: Be aware that if you record a password in a login script, anyone who can use your computer can use your password! This not only weakens your security, it threatens the security of the remote computer. You may want to record passwords to on-line information services and private bulletin boards as a convenience, but be prepared for the risk that someone else could use your accounts without your knowledge. *Never* record the password of a remote mainframe or PC that does not belong to you!

## Using a Login Script

To use a login script, follow these steps:

1. Retrieve the login script: select File Retrieve, select or enter the file name of the desired login script, and select Retrieve.
2. Select Connect Run. LotusWorks runs the script and dials the telephone call automatically.

That's all there is to it.

## Editing a Login Script

If you make a mistake in recording a login script, or if there is a change in a telephone number, user-identification code, or password, you can always edit the script to make the change. Simply retrieve the script and select Connect Edit. The following dialog box appears:

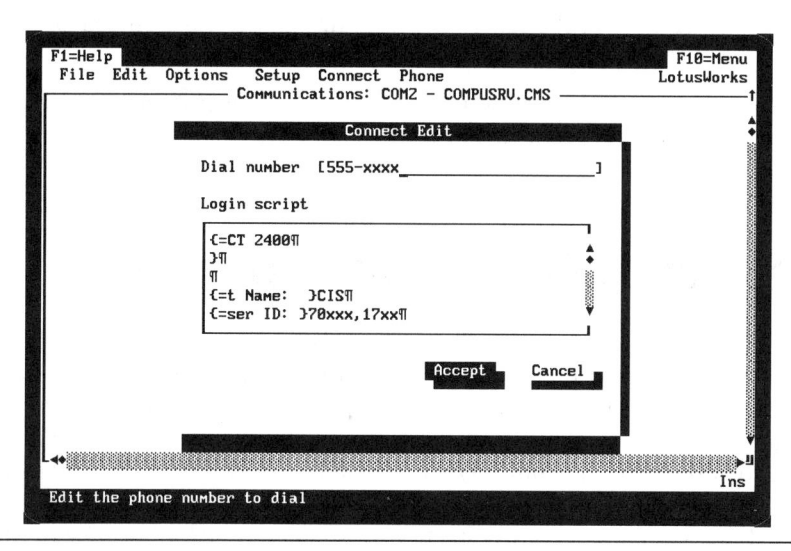

```
F1=Help                                                    F10=Menu
    File Edit Options  Setup Connect Phone               LotusWorks
                   ──── Communications: COM2 - COMPUSRV.CMS ────
                        ┌──────── Connect Edit ────────┐
                        │  Dial number [555-xxxx_____]│
                        │                              │
                        │  Login script                │
                        │  ┌─────────────────────────┐ │
                        │  │ {=CT 2400¶             │ │
                        │  │ }¶                     │ │
                        │  │ ¶                      │ │
                        │  │ {=t Name:  }CIS¶       │ │
                        │  │ {=ser ID: }70xxx,17xx¶ │ │
                        │  └─────────────────────────┘ │
                        │                              │
                        │            Accept   Cancel   │
                        └──────────────────────────────┘

    Edit the phone number to dial                         Ins
```

**FIGURE 7.8:** Enter a new telephone number, user-id, password, or other change for the login script, and select Accept.

Even if some of the other symbols are cryptic, you can easily identify the telephone number, user-id, and password information. You can edit any of these just as you would in a Word Processing document. When you have made all the desired changes, select Accept to return to the Communications window. To finish the edit, be sure to save the edited login script (press Alt+S or select File Save).

## Launching the Login Script with a Macro

For the ultimate in automating a login script, you can create a macro to retrieve and launch it. Then, with a single keystroke, you can set the communications parameters, dial the telephone, log in, and conduct as much of the communications session as you have recorded in the script! Here is how.

After you have created and saved the login script, create the macro:

1. Select Options Macros Learn.

2. Select a Ctrl+key combination for the macro and select Learn.

3. Select File Retrieve, enter the name of the login script, and select Retrieve to retrieve the login script.

4. Select Options Macros Run to launch the script.

5. Immediately end the macro by pressing the Ctrl+key combination you selected for the macro.

Thereafter, whenever you want to run the login script, simply press the Ctrl+key combination for the script macro.

## Automating File and Text Transfers

There are a couple of ways to automate at least some of the process of transferring files. One is to create a login script for the entire transfer process and a macro to retrieve and launch it, as described earlier in this chapter. This works well for situations such as sending reports or downloading stock quotes, in which you dial, log in, and upload/or download a file with the same name every time. By keeping Connect Learn switched on as you go through an entire communications session from beginning to end, you can create a "login" script that automatically dials, logs in, performs the file transfer or transfers, and logs off, all unassisted. (If you upload and download files with different names, you can automate most of the process by creating a login script of all the steps up to the point where you enter the file name.)

Another way to automate file and data transfers is with a macro alone. This is the best approach if you are communicating with another PC, if you transfer files with different file names, if you need to enter information from the keyboard, or if you otherwise cannot script the entire data communications session.

In this case, the macro should begin at the point after a data communications session is underway when you are ready to begin the file transfer. The macro can automate at least the keystrokes to select File Transfer Upload or Download and the protocol to use, leaving the dialog box open and ready for you to enter a file name.

# Using Your PC as a Terminal

You can use LotusWorks to have your PC emulate an ANSI, VT52, or VT100 terminal when communicating with a mini- or mainframe computer. When you do, LotusWorks re-maps the PC keyboard slightly to make it more like the terminal it is emulating.

### Terminal Key Differences

| VT52 or VT100 Key | LotusWorks Key |
|---|---|
| PF1 | Ctrl+F1 |
| PF2 | Ctrl+F2 |
| PF3 | Ctrl+F3 |
| PF4 | Ctrl+F4 |
| Numeric Keypad – (Minus sign) | Numeric Keypad * (Asterisk) |
| Numeric Keypad , (Comma) | Numeric Keypad – (Minus sign) |
| Numeric Keypad Enter | Numeric Keypad + (Plus sign) |

To use the PC in terminal mode, follow these steps:

1. Select Setup, set up the communications parameters, and select the terminal you want the PC to emulate.

2. Dial the telephone and establish data the data connection in the usual manner. Just remember that as you key in data, some keys work in a slightly different manner from the normal PC keyboard. Also, you'll notice that the characters you type are not sent to the remote computer until you press Enter, and data comes from the remote computer one screenful at a time.

3. When you are ready to end the communications session, log off the remote computer, then press Alt+H or select Phone Hangup to disconnect the telephone.

> NOTE: When the PC is communicating in terminal mode, be sure to log off the remote computer before issuing the command to disconnect the telephone call (hangup).

# Examples

Here are two examples of automated telecommunications: a login script to establish data communications with another PC and a macro to launch a script to dial CompuServe, log in, and navigate to the LotusWorks forum, and a script to launch communications with another PC. As you will see, login scripts are not difficult to record. The secret is to give some thought in advance to what you want the script to do and then break down the script into parts and build one part at a time.

## A Login Script for PC-to-PC Communications

Unlike communicating with an on-line information service or a bulletin board, when you communicate with another PC, there are normally no login procedures. This simple login script sets the communication parameters, automatically dials the remote PC, and, when the modems establish the connection, automatically sends a message identifying the caller.

For this script, assume that your modem communicates at 2400 baud and that you and the remote PC operator have agreed to use no parity, eight data bits, and one stop bit.

The first task is to set the communications parameters. Select Setup and select the following settings:

| | |
|---|---|
| XON/XOFF | Unselected |
| Baud rate | 2400 |
| Parity | None |
| Data bits | 8 |
| Stop bits | 1 |

The rest of the settings should be the default values. When you have finished selecting the settings, select Accept.

The next task is to record the login script. Select Connect Learn and enter a name by which to identify the script file. (You'll probably want to enter some version of the name of the remote PC owner.) When you finish typing the file name, press Tab, and select Learn to begin recording. The functions and keystrokes are as follows:

| Function | Keystrokes |
|---|---|
| Issue the Dial command. | Alt+D |
| Enter the telephone number of the remote PC and select the Dial action button. | XXX-XXXX<br>Tab<br>Enter |
| When you get the message that the modems are connected, issue a greeting message. | This is Bill's PC calling. Ready to proceed? |
| Stop the recording | F9 |

To view the login script, select Connect Edit. The following dialog box appears:

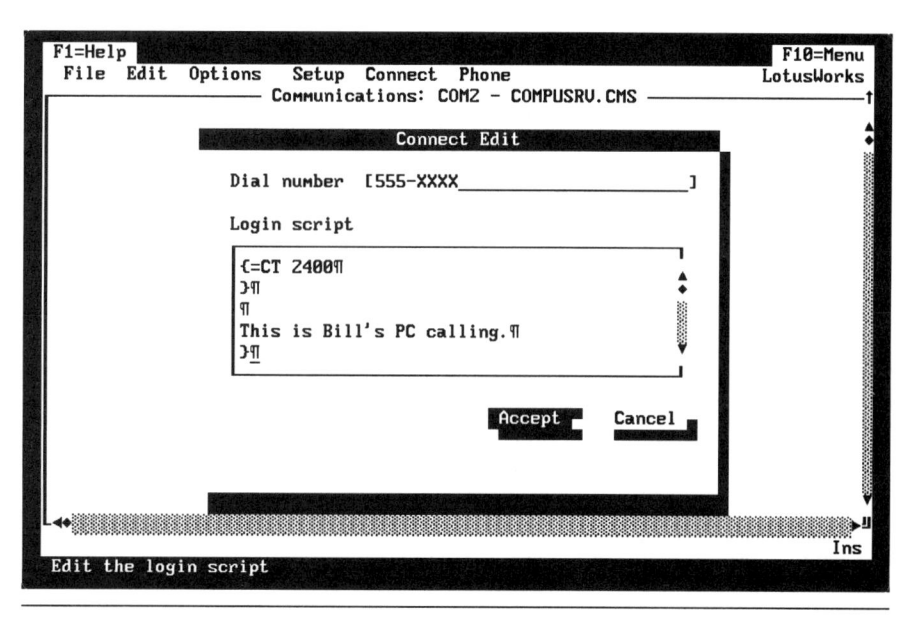

**FIGURE 7.9:** The Connect Edit dialog box with the PC-to-PC login script

To test the login script, select File Retrieve and retrieve the login file (if it is not already active). Then select Connect Run.

You do not have to save the login script separately. When you enter the file name for the script, LotusWorks saves the file automatically.

## A Login Script and Launching Macro

The second login script is more complicated than the first one, but only slightly so. For purposes of this example, assume that you have a 2400-baud modem.

There are three steps in building the login script and macro: (1) set up and save the communications parameters, (2) record and save the login script, and (3) record and save the launching macro. Here are the steps in more detail:

1. Set up and save the communications parameters. Select Setup, switch XON/XOFF off, and set the other parameters to 2400 Baud, no parity, 7 data bits, and 1 stop bit. When you have finished, select Accept. To save the settings, press Alt+S (or select File Save), enter COMPUSRV for the file name, and select Save.

2. Record the login script. With the communications parameters still set, select Connect Learn, enter COMPUSRV for the login file name, select Learn, and begin typing the keystrokes to dial CompuServe and log in. The functions and keystrokes are:

| Function | Keystrokes |
| --- | --- |
| Issue the Dial command. | Alt+D |
| Enter a phone number for CompuServe and dial the phone. | XXX-XXXX<br>Tab<br>Enter |
| When the remote computer prompts for the service, enter CIS. | CIS |
| When the remote computer prompts for your User ID, type XXXXX,XXXX and press Enter. (Use your actual User ID, if you have one.) | XXXX,XXXX |
| When the remote computer prompts for your password, type XXXX/XXXXX and press Enter. (Use your actual password if you have one.) | XXXX/XXXXXX<br>Enter |
| When the ! prompt appears, enter GO LOTUSB and press Enter. | GO LOTUSB<br>Enter |
| When the ! prompt appears again, press Enter. | Enter |
| When the ! prompt appears again, press 2 Enter, to select the Messages option. | 2<br>Enter |
| When the ! prompt appears again, press 1 Enter, to select by section and subject. | 1<br>Enter |
| When the ! prompt appears again, press 9 Enter, to select the LotusWorks section. | 9<br>Enter |
| Press F9 to end recording. | F9 |

To view the login script, select Connect Edit. A dialog box opens showing the script characters.

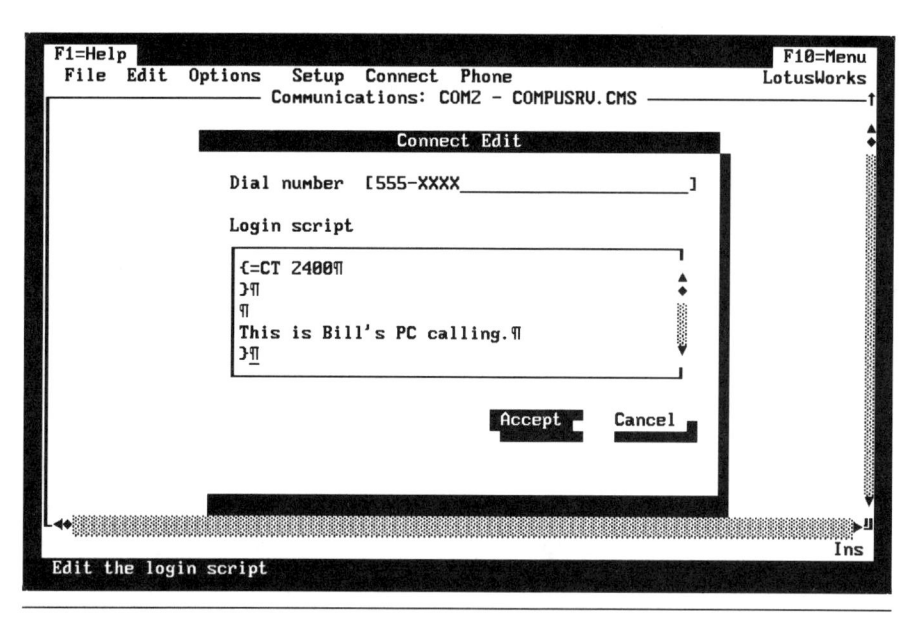

**FIGURE 7.10:** The Connect Edit dialog box showing the first five lines of the login script

Press Tab to move the cursor inside the box, and scroll through the script to see how the script is constructed. Notice that the script shows the last 10 characters of each prompt displayed by the remote computer and the keystrokes (including Enter) that you typed in response.

3. Create the launching macro. The macro performs two functions: it retrieves the login script and then runs the script. To create the launching macro, select Options Macros Learn; select an unused macro Ctrl+key (such as Ctrl+L) select Learn; and record the macro. The complete macro looks like this:

{F10}FR{Tab}{COMPUSRV.CMS}{Tab}{Enter}{F10}CR

The breakdown of keystrokes is as follows:

**Retrieve the Login Script**

| | |
|---|---|
| Activate the Menu line. | [F10] |
| Activate the File menu. | F |
| Select the Retrieve option. | R |
| Move to the File text box. | {Tab} |
| Enter the name of the script file. | {COMPUSRV.CMS} |
| Move to the Retrieve action button. | {Tab} |
| Execute the Retrieve command. | {Enter} |

**Run the Login Script**

| | |
|---|---|
| Move to the Menu line. | {F10} |
| Select the Connect menu. | C |
| Select the Run command. | R |

To use the script, simply open the Communications service and press the Ctrl+key that you selected for the launching macro.

## Ideas for Telecommunications

Here are some more ideas for using telecommunications.

- **Send files to your commercial printer.** More and more printing companies are accepting copy via modem for typesetting and printing. Having the copy in machine form saves you money on data entry, and sending it via modem saves time and money over hand delivery of a diskette or hard copy.

- **Send files to a colleague or contractor.** When you need to share a spreadsheet with a colleague or have a contractor edit a document for you, you can save time by sending the files via telephone.

- **Send files to yourself.** When your office and home PCs do not have compatible floppy disk drives, you can work on both machines and transmit files back and forth via modem.

- **Keep in touch on the road and with distant colleagues.** If you're traveling with a laptop computer, you can keep in touch with employees and colleagues through E-mail. It's especially handy for overseas travel, when there are large differences in time zones. Using E-mail is also a good way to save money on communications in many countries with high long distance telephone rates. You can also send draft documents back to your home office for printing and production.

- **Consult with experts.** When you need to get specialized expertise—whether on the best equipment to buy or who knows about doing business in another country—you can nearly always find what you need by leaving a message on one of the specialized bulletin boards or forums operated by government agencies, on-line information services, and private individuals. At the least, you can save valuable time researching whom to contact, and often you can get valuable answers to your questions for free.

- **Research business opportunities.** You can use on-line information services to search for information in a wealth of specialized publications and databases and to make contact with potential customers, suppliers, and partners through the forums and bulletin boards.

## Trouble-Shooting Data Communications

| Symptom | Possible Cause | What to Do |
| --- | --- | --- |
| Modem does not dial | Modem is not plugged in and turned on. | Check modem plug and switch. |
| | Wrong modem port selected on Setup program screen. | Connect modem to Com1 o Com2 port and select the port on the Setup program screen. |
| | Telephone or modem cable not secure. | Check all cable connections. |
| | Dialing prefix to get outside line not set up. | Enter dialing prefix in the Setup Defaults dialog box. |
| | Telephone number not entered in Dial box. | Enter a telephone number in the Phone Dial text box. |
| Weird characters ("garbage") appear randomly on the screen. | Static or electrical interference on the telephone line. | Redial the call. |
| Incoming characters are garbled. | Mismatched communications parameters. | Select Setup and be sure the baud rate, parity, data bits, and stop bits settings match those on the remote computer. |
| Characters you type do not appear on the screen. | Remote computer is communicating in half-duplex mode. | Select Setup and turn on the Echo typed setting. |
| Each character appears twice on the screen. | Echo typed setting is on while communicating in full duplex mode. | Select Setup and turn off the Echo typed setting. |
| File upload or download does not work. | Computers not using the same protocol. | Check to be sure the protocol matches that of the remote computer. |
| Incoming information writes over existing information. | PC is not receiving a line-feed at end of each line. | Select Setup and change the New Line setting from Carriage return to Line feed. |
| Incoming information is double-spaced. | PC is receiving two line-feeds at end of each line. | Select Setup and change the New Line setting from Line feed to Carriage return. |

# A Final Word About Telecommunications

Computer telecommunications is a powerful tool that can perform a variety of services which are useful for offices and small businesses. It's there if you need it, and the LotusWorks Communications service makes the tool easily accessible. Like any other tool, however, PC communications is really only what each user makes of it.

# 8

# Building Applications

Once you know how to use the various LotusWorks services, you have the tools to create custom "applications" of your own. Custom applications are simply word processing documents, spreadsheet and database setups, login scripts, and combinations of these that you put together and launch with a single keystroke. You may be surprised at the number of sophisticated applications you can create from combinations of simple building blocks. The master tool that makes this possible is the macro.

## Using Macros to Assemble Your Own Applications

The purpose of assembling your own applications is to save yourself time and work. The basic technique is to construct a word processing, spreadsheet, database, graph, or communications setup—or some combination of these—that you can use over and over, and create one or more macros to stick them together and launch them. A couple of general examples are illustrated in this chapter. As you get familiar with LotusWorks, you probably can conceive much better applications to help in your own work.

## Building a Custom Desktop Environment

If there are particular document formats, spreadsheets, databases, or login scripts that you use frequently, you can install them in a

*In this chapter, you'll learn how to:*

- Use macros to assemble your own applications
- Build a custom desktop environment
- Build an automated telephone dialer and log
- Get ideas for other custom applications

**365**

menu on the desktop to create a custom PC environment tailored to your work. The menu you create does not interfere with the normal use of LotusWorks; it simply makes it easier to keep track of and select the special formats and setups you have created. This can be especially valuable in an office where more than one person needs to use the standard tools that you have created.

There are four general steps in building the custom environment:

1. Create and save the documents, setups, and login scripts that you want to appear on the menu. In this example, there is a memo format, a business letter format, a financial spreadsheet, a client database, and a login script to "call the bank."
2. Create a macro to launch each menu item. The macros are created in the Word Processing service, but they can reach out to launch files in any of the services.
3. Create the menu "screen" in the Word Processing service.
4. Create a Ctrl+M macro that retrieves the menu whenever you like.

Here are the steps in more detail:

1. Create and save the documents, setups, and login scripts that are to appear on the menu. For sake of illustration, assume there are five such items that have been saved in the following files:

   MEMOFRMT.LWD

   LTRFRMT.LWD

   SS.WK1

   CLIENTS.DBF

   BANK.CMS

2. Go to the Word Processing Service, select Options Macro Learn, and record five macros—one to launch each file from the Word Processing service. In each case, press Ctrl+F6 to move directly to the LotusWorks screen, type the first letter of the desired service, press PgDn to move the cursor directly to the (new file) option (regardless of the number of files open), press Enter to open the service, and then use File Retrieve to retrieve the specified file. The keystrokes for each macro are as follows:

| Macro | Keystrokes |
|---|---|
| Ctrl+A | {Ctrl+F6}w{PgDn}{Enter}{F10}FR{Tab}MEMOFRMT{Tab}{Enter} |
| Ctrl+B | {Ctrl+F6}w(PgDn){Enter}{F10}FR{Tab}LTRFRMT{Tab}{Enter} |
| Ctrl+C | {Ctrl+F6}s{PgDn}{Enter}{F10}FR{Tab}SS{Tab}{Enter} |
| Ctrl+D | {Ctrl+F6}d{PgDn}{Enter}{F10}FR{Tab}CLIENTS{Tab}{Enter} |
| Ctrl+E | {Ctrl+F6}c{PgDn}{Enter}{F10}FR{Tab}BANK{Tab}{Enter} |

The breakdown of functions and keystrokes is as follows:

| Macro | Function | Keystrokes |
|---|---|---|
| Ctrl+A | Go to the Lotus Works Screen. | {Ctrl+F6} |
|  | Select a new file in the Word Processing service. | W |
|  |  | {PgDn} |
|  |  | {Enter} |
|  | Activate the Menu line. | {F10} |
|  | Select the File menu. | F |
|  | Select the Retrieve command. | R |
|  | Move to the File text box. | {Tab} |
|  | Enter the name of the file. | MEMOFRMT |
|  | Move to the Retrieve action button. | {Tab} |
|  | Execute the Retrieve command. | {Enter} |
| Ctrl+B | Go to the LotusWorks Screen. | {Ctrl+F6} |
|  | Select a new file in the Word Processing service. | W |
|  |  | {PgDn} |
|  |  | {Enter} |
|  | Activate the Menu line. | {F10} |
|  | Select the File menu. | F |
|  | Select the Retrieve command. | R |
|  | Move to the File text box. | {Tab} |
|  | Enter the name of the file. | LTRFRMT |
|  | Move to the Retrieve action button. | {Tab} |
|  | Execute the Retrieve command. | {Enter} |

| Macro | Function | Keystrokes |
|---|---|---|
| Ctrl+C | Go to the LotusWorks Screen. | {Ctrl+F6} |
| | Select a new file in the Spreadsheet service. | S |
| | | {PgDn} |
| | | {Enter} |
| | Activate the Menu line. | {F10} |
| | Select the File menu. | F |
| | Select the Retrieve command. | R |
| | Move to the File text box. | {Tab} |
| | Enter the name of the file. | SS |
| | Move to the Retrieve action button. | {Tab} |
| | Execute the Retrieve command. | {Enter} |
| Ctrl+D | Go to the LotusWorks Screen. | {Ctrl+F6} |
| | Select a new file in the Database service. | D |
| | | {PgDn} |
| | | {Enter} |
| | Activate the Menu line. | {F10} |
| | Select the File menu. | F |
| | Select the Retrieve command. | R |
| | Move to the File text box. | {Tab} |
| | Enter the name of the file. | CLIENTS |
| | Move to the Retrieve action button. | {Tab} |
| | Execute the Retrieve command. | {Enter} |
| Ctrl+E | Go to the LotusWorks Screen. | {Ctrl+F6} |
| | Select the Communications service. | C |
| | | {PgDn} |
| | | {Enter} |
| | Activate the Menu line. | {F10} |
| | Select the File menu. | F |
| | Select the Retrieve command. | R |
| | Move to the File text box. | {Tab} |
| | Enter the name of the file. | CLIENTS |
| | Move to the Retrieve action button. | {Tab} |
| | Execute the Retrieve command. | {Enter} |

When you have finished creating the five macros, it's a good idea to exit LotusWorks temporarily so that the macros are saved before proceeding with the next step.

3. Create the menu screen. Go to the word processing service, open a new file, and enter the following information into the document:

**MENU**

Press the Ctrl+key of your choice:

| Ctrl+A | = | Memo Format |
| Ctrl+B | = | Business Letter Format |
| Ctrl+C | = | Financial Spreadsheet |
| Ctrl+D | = | Client Database |
| Ctrl+E | = | Call the Bank |

The menu document looks like this:

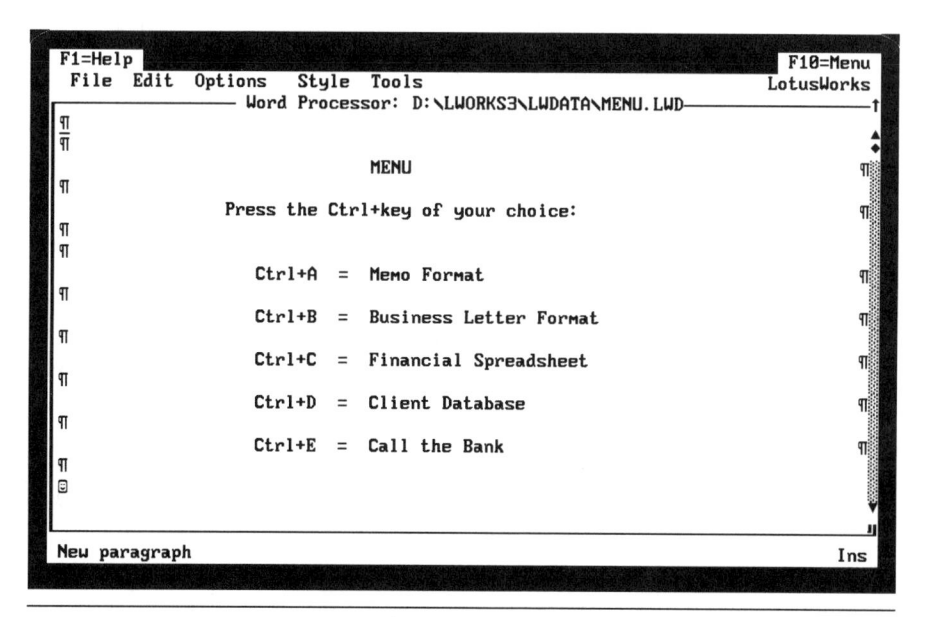

**FIGURE 8.1:** The menu screen for the custom desktop environment.

When you have finished creating the menu document, save it under the name MENU.LWD.

4. Select Options Macro Learn and record the Ctrl+M macro to launch the menu from the Word Processing service. The keystrokes are:

{Ctrl+F6}w{PgDn}{Enter}{F10}FR{Tab}MENU{Tab}{Enter}

The breakdown of functions and keystrokes is:

| Macro | Function | Keystrokes |
| --- | --- | --- |
| Ctrl+M | Go to the LotusWorks Screen. | {Ctrl+F6} |
| | Select a new file in the Word Processing service. | W |
| | | {PgDn} |
| | | {Enter} |
| | Activate the Menu line. | {F10} |
| | Select the File menu. | F |
| | Select the Retrieve command. | R |
| | Move to the File text box. | {Tab} |
| | Enter the name of the file. | MENU |
| | Move to the Retrieve action button. | {Tab} |
| | Execute the Retrieve command. | {Enter} |

*If you want to be able to retrieve the menu directly from any service, record the Ctrl+M macro in each service. You can use the same keystrokes in all four services.*

That's all there is to it. The environment is really just a series of macros with one screen to remind you which macro is which. To test the environment, go to the Word Processing service and press Ctrl+M. You should be able see the menu screen you created. To test the various launch macros, create dummy documents for each of the menu item files (MEMOFRMT.LWD, LTRFRMT.LWD, SS.WK1, CLIENTS.DBF, and BANK.CMS) and try out each macro in turn.

Once you get the hang of creating macro menus, you'll probably want to add variations of your own. You may even wish to create a menu for each Lotus-Works service.

# Building an Automated Telephone Dialer and Log

One option in the Database service automatically dials a telephone call through a modem if you highlight a phone number in a database and select the option. If you can dial a phone number with one keystroke, however, why not use a macro and perform several other functions as well? That's the basis of the automated telephone dialer and log.

This example shows how a useful application can be built from simple parts. The Dialer/Log is composed of a simple database and two macros. The database holds names, addresses, and phone numbers. One macro dials the phone from the database, switches to voice communications, opens a word processing document for you to use as the telephone log, and moves the cursor to a new line in the log. You can use the application to dial numbers and then jot down notes while the phone call is in progress or as soon as it's finished. The second macro makes it possible to use the log for incoming telephone calls, as well.

You can build the Dialer/Log as follows:

1. Create the database. For dialing purposes, it need hold only names and phone numbers. However, you can include addresses and other information if you like. For the sake of illustration, this example uses the Q_ADDRS.DBF file that comes with LotusWorks. Be sure that the file is stored in Table view.

2. Create the Log. Go to the Word Processing service and save a blank document in a file named LOG.LWD.

3. Create the dialing macro. Go to the Database service, select Options Macros Learn, select an unused macro Ctrl+key (such as Ctrl+D), select Learn, pick up the telephone receiver, and type the following keystrokes:

    Alt+D ,,,, Ctrl+F6 w PgDn Enter F10 f r Tab L O G Tab Enter , Ctrl+End Enter Enter.

    When you are finished, press Ctrl+D (or the Ctrl+key you picked for the macro) to stop recording. The complete macro looks like this:

    {Alt+D},,,,{Ctrl+F6}w{PgDn}{Enter}{F10}fr{Tab}LOG{Tab}{Enter}, {Ctrl+End}{Enter}{Enter}

    The breakdown of functions and keystrokes is:

*If you are creating a table for automatic phone dialing, it will save you time in dialing and looking up numbers if you put the phone number in the first or second field and put the last name and first name in fields immediately alongside the phone number.*

| Function | Keystrokes |
| --- | --- |
| Dial the phone | {Alt+D} |
| Pause while the modem dials | ,,,, |
| Open the LOG file | {Ctrl+F6}w{Enter}{F10}fr{Tab}LOG{Tab}{Enter} |
| Pause while the LOG file opens | |
| Move the cursor to the end of the file, skip a line, and start a new line | {Ctrl+End}{Enter}{Enter} |

> The commas cause the macro to pause briefly. You can record them as you would any other keystroke.

4. Create the incoming macro. Select Options, Macros, Learn; select an appropriate Ctrl+key; record the macro. The complete macro looks like this:

> {Ctrl+F6}w[PgDn}{Enter}{F10}fr{Tab}LOG{Tab}{Enter},
> {Ctrl+End}{Enter}{Enter}

The breakdown of functions and keystrokes is:

| Function | Keystrokes |
| --- | --- |
| Open the LOG file | {Ctrl+F6}w[PgDn}{Enter}{F10}fr{Tab}LOG{Tab}{Enter} |
| Pause while the LOG file opens | |
| Move the cursor to the end of the file, skip a line, and start a new line | {Ctrl+End}{Enter}{Enter} |

The application is now complete. To use it for dialing, be sure that your modem is connected and turned on. Open the Database service, retrieve the Q_ADDR.DBF file, move the cursor to highlight a phone number to dial, pick up the telephone receiver, and press Ctrl+D (or whatever Ctrl+key you have selected for the dialing macro). You can enter notes into the log at any time you like by typing on the keyboard.

To use the Dialer/Log for incoming calls, simply answer the phone and press the Ctrl+key you selected for the incoming macro.

# Ideas for Other Custom Applications

Here are some more ideas for custom applications:

- **Menu for Document Formats.** In the Word Processing service, you can create a separate menu for all of your standard document formats, with a macro to launch each format. You can do the same thing for spreadsheet setups, database setups, and login scripts.

- **Boilerplate Organizer.** In the Word Processing service, you can put each bit of boilerplate into a macro and list the macros in a separate menu within the general word processing menu.

- **Printer Macros.** Because each printer setup tends to be unique, you can create a macro for each style layout you use frequently, including typeface, type size, and page orientation. In spreadsheets, printer macros can specify the ranges and graphs to print for multi-range reports.

- **Search Macros.** In the Database service, you can put complex search statements into macros that can be run repeatedly when you are defining search criteria.

- **E-Mail Launcher.** To save on-line connect time when sending E-mail, you can create a macro that automatically returns you to the Word Processing service each time you want to copy a message to the Clipboard and one that returns you to Communications to paste it to the modem.

- **Automatic Date and Time Stamper.** If you like to have the date or the date and time appear on some documents, you can create a macro that creates a footer in word processing documents and "stamps" one or both in the footer and then formats it. (These are four separate menu options on the Edit and Style menus.) The date and time do not appear on the screen, but they appear when you print the document.

# A Final Word About Custom Applications

As you can see, a custom application does not have to be very complicated or sophisticated to be effective in saving you time and work. As you go about your business with LotusWorks, keep your mind open for operations that can be automated with the LotusWorks tools. As you get in the habit of seeking ways to save work, you'll come up with more ideas. The best tool for expanding LotusWorks is your imagination.

# A

# Upgrading to LotusWorks 3.0

The spreadsheet files (those with the file name extension .WK1) from previous versions of LotusWorks are fully compatible with LotusWorks 3.0. LotusWorks 3.0 can use the .WK1 files produced by LotusWorks 1.0, and LotusWorks 1.0 can use .WK1 files produced by LotusWorks 3.0.

LotusWorks 3.0 can also use communications files (those with the .CMS file name extension) produced by previous versions, but earlier versions cannot use the .CMS files produced by LotusWorks 3.0.

Word processing files (those with the .DOC extension) and database files (those with the .DBF extension) produced by earlier versions of LotusWorks must be converted before they can be used by LotusWorks 3.0. Word processing and database files produced by LotusWorks 3.0 cannot be used by previous versions of LotusWorks.

## Upgrading Word Processing Files

When you convert a LotusWorks 1.0 word processing file, the Upgrade program leaves the original LotusWorks 1.0 file intact. It gives the new file the same name as the old one but changes the file name extension from .DOC to .LWD. It converts most of the formats and embedded commands, but some that are not compatible with LotusWorks 3.0 are not included in the new version of the document. Generally, the Upgrade program converts text attributes (such as bold, underline, subscript, and superscript), tabs (but not the location of the tab stops), text alignment settings, headers, footers, embedded date commands, embedded merge commands, and default page margins and paragraph spacing. It does not convert user-defined type styles or tab settings.

> NOTE: You should examine upgraded mail-merge documents carefully. LotusWorks 3.0 initiates mail merging from the Word Processing service, whereas previous versions initiated it from the Database service. The Upgrade program inserts the new document's name as the database file name in the embedded mail merge command. You may need to change the name of the database LotusWorks 3.0 is to use when printing the mail-merge document.

To convert a word processing file, follow these steps:

1. Exit LotusWorks (if you are in it) to return to DOS.

2. Make the directory that contains LotusWorks 3.0 the current directory. (For example, if you have LotusWorks in the C:\LWORKS3 directory, make that directory current.) See your DOS manual if you need help changing directories.

3. Type the following command:

   upgrade [drive]:\[directory]\[oldfilename]

   where:

   [drive] is the letter of the drive where the old file is located

   [directory] is the name of the directory where the old file is located

   [oldfilename] is the name of the old file (You can omit the .DOC file name extension.)

   For example: upgrade C:\LWORKS3\LWDATA\[old filename]

   If you want to convert more than one file at once, you can use the * and ? wildcard characters in place of some or all of the old file names. For example, the command upgrade [drive]:\[directory]\*.DOC will convert all the .DOC files in the specified directory.

4. Press Enter. The Upgrade program converts all the files you have specified, places the new files in the current directory, and leaves the old files intact in the old directory.

Once you have converted a file, retrieve it into LotusWorks 3.0, examine it carefully (print it, if necessary), and be sure you are satisfied with it before you destroy the old file.

# Upgrading Database Files

The naming conventions for database form, table, and search files are different in LotusWorks 3.0 from those in LotusWorks 1.0. In LotusWorks 1.0, the form, table, and search files associated with a given database can have file names distinct from the database file name. In LotusWorks 3.0, all form, table, and search files carry the same name as their database, but with unique file name extensions. (Files with the .NDX file name extension do not have to be converted to be used with dBASE III PLUS.)

To convert the LotusWorks 1.0 form, table, and search files for LotusWorks 3.0, you simply copy the files into the \LWORKS3\LWDATA subdirectory and rename them to give them LotusWorks 3.0 file names. The steps are as follows.

1. Go into LotusWorks 1.0, retrieve a database to be converted, and attach all the index files you want to the database file, using the F5 Index Attach command in LotusWorks 1.0. In most cases, the index files will already be attached to the database.

2. Exit LotusWorks 1.0.

3. Copy up to seven Form files into the \LWORKS3\LWDATA subdirectory and change their names to LotusWorks 3.0 names. The new names should have the extension .F00, .F01, .F02, .F03, .F04, .F05, and .F06. The COPY command is as follows:

   COPY [drive]:\[directory]\[oldfilename] [newdrive]:\[lworks3\lwdata\[databasename].F0[#]

   where:

   [drive] is the letter of the drive where the old file is located

   [directory] is the name of the directory where the old file is located

   [oldfilename] is the name of the old file

   [newdrive] is the letter of the drive where LotusWorks 3.0 is located

   [databasename] is the name of the database

   F0[#] is the new file name extension (.F00, .F01, .F02, etc.)

> NOTE: While it is possible simply to rename the old files and then move them into the \LWDATA subdirectory, the procedure outlined here is safer. With this procedure, the old files are retained and can still be used in LotusWorks 1.0, if there should be any reason to do so.

4. Use the DOS COPY command to copy up to seven Table files into the \LWORKS3\LWDATA subdirectory and change their names to LotusWorks 3.0 names. The new names should have the extension .T00, .T01, .T02, .T03, .T04, .T05, and .T06. The COPY command should be as follows:

COPY [drive]:\[directory]\[oldfilename] [newdrive][lworks3\lwdata\[databasename].T0[#]

5. Copy up to seven Search files into the \LWORKS3\LWDATA subdirectory and change their names to LotusWorks 3.0 names. The new names should have the extension .S00, .S01, .S02, .S03, .S04, .S05, and .S06. The COPY command is as follows:

COPY [drive]:\[directory]\[oldfilename] [newdrive]:\[lworks3\lwdata\[databasename].S0[#]

6. Copy the database file itself into the \LWORKS3\LWDATA subdirectory. The COPY command is:

COPY [drive]:\[directory]\[databasename].DBF [newdrive]:\[lworks3\lwdata\[databasename].DBF

That is all it takes to upgrade to LotusWorks 3.0. When you no longer need to use LotusWorks 1.0 or any of its files, you can delete the program and associated data files.

# B

# Database Functions

A database function is a built-in program that performs a particular action in a database. By putting the function into a field rule, you can have LotusWorks perform the action automatically. LotusWorks has 72 predefined database functions that you can use singly and in combination to create formulas for database field rules. (See Chapter 4 for information on writing database formulas.)

The syntax for database functions consists of a function name and (usually) one or more arguments enclosed within parentheses. The function name specifies the action to be performed. The arguments specify the data to be acted upon. You write the argument immediately following the function name. In most cases the argument consists of one or more values, field names, or logical expressions.

> IMPORTANT: Text strings in arguments always must be enclosed within double quotation marks. If you get an expression error message when you write a field rule, check to be sure you have put a quotation mark (") at the beginning and end of any text data in the rule.

The database functions fall into seven categories, as described in the following tables. A detailed description of each function, in alphabetical order by function name, follows the tables.

## Type of Database Function

| Type of Function | Description |
| --- | --- |
| Database information | Provides information about the current database |
| Data conversion | Converts values from one type of data to another |
| Date | Performs calculations with dates and times |
| Logical | Evaluates whether specified conditions are true or false |

| | |
|---|---|
| Lookup | Finds and enters data from another database or a pop-up box in the current database |
| Mathematical | Calculates with numbers |
| String | Manipulates or provides information about character strings |

## Database Information Functions

There are eight functions that provide information about the current database:

| Function | Action |
|---|---|
| BOF (Beginning of File) | Returns true if the cursor is at the first record of a database, false if it is not |
| DELETED | Returns true if a record is flagged, false if it is not |
| DBF | Returns the name of the current database |
| EOF (End of File) | Returns true if the cursor is at the last record of a database, false if it is not |
| FIELD | Returns the field name for a specified offset number |
| RECCOUNT | Calculates the number of fields in a database |
| RECNO | Returns the record number of the current record |
| RECSIZE | Calculates the number of characters reserved for each record |

## Data Conversion Functions

There are nine functions that convert values from one data type to another:

| Function | Action |
|---|---|
| ASC | Returns the ASCII coded number that corresponds to the first character in a text string |
| CDATE | Converts a date expressed as date data into a text string of the form "YYMMDD" |
| CHR | Returns the character that an ASCII code number represents |
| CTOD (Character to Date) | Converts a date expressed as a text (character) string to date data |
| DTOC (Date to Character) | Converts a date expressed as date data into a text (character) string with the form MM/DD/YYYY |

| | |
|---|---|
| INVERT | Returns the complement of a number, string, or date |
| STR | Converts a number to a text string with a specified length and number of decimal places |
| VAL | Converts a number expressed as text (character data) to numeric data |
| Z_BLANK | Converts a number to a text (character) string and zeros to blanks |

## Date Functions

There are eight functions that perform calculations with dates:

| **Function** | **Action** |
|---|---|
| CDOW (Character Day of Week) | Returns the day of the week in character format for a specified date |
| CMONTH (Character Month) | Returns the name of the month in a specified date |
| DAY | Returns the day of the month in a specified date |
| DATE | Returns the current system date (as set in the computer) |
| DOW (Day of Week) | Returns the number of the day of the week (1-7) in a specified date |
| MONTH | Returns the number of the month (1-12) in a specified date |
| TIME | Returns the current system time (as set in the computer) |
| YEAR | Returns the year in a specified date |

## Logical Functions

There are nine logical database functions that evaluate whether specified conditions are true or false:

| **Function** | **Action** |
|---|---|
| EXIST | Returns true if a value is in a sort order, false if it is not |
| FOR | Executes an argument if another argument, entered as a formula, results in true |
| IF, IIF | Executes one argument if a specified condition is true, another if it is false (IF and IIF produce the same result in LotusWorks, but formulas that use the IIF form can be used with dBASE III and dBASE III PLUS.) |

| | |
|---|---|
| ISALPHA | Returns true if the first character in a string is a letter, false if it is not |
| ISBLANK | Returns true if a field is blank, false if it is not |
| ISLOWER | Returns true if the first character in a string is lowercase, false if it is not |
| ISUPPER | Returns true if the first character in a string is uppercase, false if it is not |
| PATTERN | Searches for a specified substring in a string and returns true if the substring is in the current field, false if it is not |

## Lookup Functions

There are four functions that find values in other databases and enter them into the current one:

| Function | Action |
|---|---|
| CLOOKUP | Finds the record in another database that is closest to a specified value in a sort order without exceeding the value, and returns the value from a specified field |
| DLIST | Displays a list of values from a sort order in a pop-up box and enters the one you select into the current field |
| LIST | Displays a list of specified values in a pop-up box and enters the one you select into the current field |
| LOOKUP | Finds the record (if any) in another database that exactly matches a specified value in a sort order, and returns the value from a specified field |

## Mathematical Functions

There are ten functions that simplify mathematical calculations:

| Function | Action |
|---|---|
| ABS | Calculates the absolute value of a number |
| EXP | Calculates the number e, raised to a specified power |
| INT | Returns the integer portion of a number, without rounding the value |
| LOG | Calculates the natural logarithm (base e) of a number |
| MAX | Selects the larger of two values |
| MIN | Selects the smaller of two values |
| MOD | Returns the remainder (modulus) of a division operation |

| | |
|---|---|
| RAND | Returns a random value from 0 to 1 |
| ROUND | Rounds a number to a specified number of places |
| SQRT | Calculates the positive square root of a number |

## String Functions

There are 17 string functions in all. Ten functions return information about or perform operations on strings of text:

| Function | Action |
|---|---|
| AT | Calculates the beginning position of a substring within a string of text |
| LEFT | Returns a specified number of characters from the beginning of a string of text |
| LEN | Counts the characters in a string of text |
| REPLICATE | Duplicates a string of text a specified number of times |
| RIGHT | Returns a substring of a specified length from the end of a string of text |
| SOUNDEX | Returns a four-character string that is phonetically equivalent to another string |
| SPACE | Returns a string composed of a specified number of spaces |
| STUFF | Replaces characters in one string with characters from a different string |
| SUBSTR | Returns a substring of text, beginning at a specified character in a string |
| WORD | Returns a word from a specified position in a string of text |

There are seven functions that manipulate strings of text:

| Function | Action |
|---|---|
| F_UPPER | Converts the first letter in a string of text to uppercase |
| LOWER | Converts the uppercase letters in a string of text to lowercase |
| LTRIM | Removes blank spaces from the beginning of a string of text |
| RTRIM | Removes blank spaces from the end of a string of text |
| TRIM | Removes blank spaces from the end of a string of text |
| UPPER | Converts the lowercase letters in a string of text to uppercase |
| W_UPPER | Converts the first letter of each word in a string to uppercase; converts the other letters to lowercase |

# Function Descriptions

The detailed descriptions of functions that follow use these conventions:

- Function names and field names appear in uppercase. Example: ABS

- Argument names appear in lowercase italics. Example: AT(*substring, string*) Actual arguments used in the examples are not enclosed in italics.

- Optional arguments are enclosed in square brackets [ ]. Example: DLIST(*sort-order,[database,][field1,][field2,]...[fieldn]*). When you use an optional argument, do not enter the brackets.

| Function Syntax | Action |
|---|---|
| ABS(*x*) | Calculates the absolute value of *x*. *X* can be a number or the name of a numeric field. |
| | Use ABS when a number (such as a percentage difference) needs to be positive. Use –ABS to force a number to be negative. Use SQRT(ABS(*x*)) to find the square root of a negative number. |
| | Examples: |
| | ABS(–1000)=1000 |
| | SQRT(ABS(–4))=2 |
| ASC(*string*) | Returns the ASCII code number of the first character in *string*. *String* can be a text string enclosed within quotation marks or the name of a character field. |
| | Examples: |
| | ASC("LotusWorks")=76 |
| | ASC(TITLE)=76 if the TITLE field contains the text "LotusWorks" for the current record |
| AT(*substring,string*) | Looks for an occurrence of *substring* in *string* and, if it finds one, returns the number of the starting position of *substring*; otherwise, it returns 0. *Substring* and *string* each can be a text string enclosed within quotation marks or the name of a character field. |
| | Examples: |
| | AT("d",NAME)=4 if NAME contains "Fred Smith" |
| | AT("Avenue",ADDRESS)=0 if the current record has "115 Main Street" in the ADDRESS field |

| | |
|---|---|
| BOF( ) | Returns true if the cursor is at the first record of the database, and returns false if the cursor is at any other record. |
| CDATE(*date-number*) | Converts *date-number* to a text string in the form "YYYYMMDD." *Date-number* can be a date in the form MM/DD/YYYY or the name of a date field. |

You can use the CDATE function in search criteria to search on date fields, as in the following examples.

Examples:

Conversion:

CDATE(CTOD("06/28/65"))="19650628"

CDATE(BIRTHDATE)="19650628" if the *Birthdate* field contains 06/28/1965 for the current record

CDATE(DATE( ))=the current date in text form

Search criteria:

CDATE(BIRTHDATE)="19650628" searches the *Birthdate* field for the date June 28, 1965

CDATE(DOB)="19510112" searches the *DOB* field for the date January 12, 1951

**Note:** The CDATE and DTOC functions produce similar results, however, sort orders containing the CDATE function order dates chronologically, whereas those containing the DTOC function order dates by month, day, and year. See DTOC.

| | |
|---|---|
| CDOW(*date-number*) | Returns the day of the week for *date-number*. *Date-number* can be a date number or the name of a date field. (A date number cannot be written directly into a formula. It must be produced indirectly by another function, such as DATE ( ) or CTOD ( ).) |

Examples:

CDOW(CTOD("06/28/65"))="Monday"

CDOW(BIRTHDATE)="Monday" if the date in the *Birthdate* field is June 28, 1965

CDOW(DATE())="Saturday" if the current date is 02/29/92

| | |
|---|---|
| CHR(*x*) | Returns the ASCII character that corresponds to ASCII code number *x*. *X* can be a number between 0 and 255 or the name of a numeric field. |

You can use CHR to enter printable characters that do not appear on the keyboard, such as foreign language characters and math symbols.

Examples:

CHR(157)=¥

CHR(CURRENCY)=¥ if the *Currency* field contains 157 for the current record

CHR(172)=¼

CHR(241)=±

CLOOKUP(*key-field*,"*return-field*","*database*")

Finds the record in *database* whose value in *key-field* matches (or exceeds most closely) the value in the current field and returns the value in that record's *return-field*. *Database* is the name of a different database from the current one. *Key-field* is the name of a field that is common to both the current database and *database*. *Return-field* is the name of the field in *database* from which you want LotusWorks to return a value.

**Note:** The names of the *return-field* and *database* must be enclosed within double quotation marks.

You can use a sort-order stored in an .NDX file in place of the database name in the CLOOKUP function.

CLOOKUP works like LOOKUP, except that LOOKUP returns a blank value if it does not find an exact match for the key value, whereas CLOOKUP moves to the next higher value in the key field if it does not find an exact match.

CLOOKUP is useful for many situations where you need a lookup table based on ranges of key values. Typical cases are price and discount schedules, where prices or discounts vary with the volume of products ordered, and loan schedules, where interest rates vary with the term of a loan. For example, suppose you wanted to compose a lookup rule for the following loan schedule in a database named LOAN.DBF:

| Term | Rate |
|---|---|
| 3 | 17 |
| 6 | 14 |
| 12 | 11 |
| 36 | 10.5 |
| 60 | 10 |
| 120 | 9.75 |

Database Functions **387**

Now suppose you created a form with a field labeled *Term of Loan in Months.* You could use the following lookup rule for the field to find the appropriate interest rate:

CLOOKUP(TERM,"RATE","LOAN")

When you enter a number in the *Term of Loan in Months* field, LotusWorks returns the appropriate rate from the LOAN.DBF database. For instance, if you enter a number that appears in the Term column (such as 12), LotusWorks returns the corresponding number from the Rate column. If you enter a number that lies between two numbers in the Term column (such as 42), LotusWorks moves to the next longest term (60) and returns the rate for that term.

**Tip:** You can use the LIST or DLIST functions to have LotusWorks display a list of valid values when you enter a value that does not appear in the key-field. Use the functions with a *verify* rule to have the list appear automatically whenever an incorrect value is entered. Use the function with a *manual* rule to enable the user to display the list on demand by pressing F9.

**Tip:** To speed database operations, use a Lookup field rule with the CLOOKUP function rather than a Verify or Calculate field rule. With the Lookup type of field rule, LotusWorks performs the lookup only when you enter a new value into the field containing the CLOOKUP rule, whereas with Verify and Calculate rules, LotusWorks repeats the lookup every time any field in a form is recalculated.

CMONTH(*date-number*)  Returns the name of the month in *date-number.* Date-number can be either a date or the name of a date field. (A date number cannot be written directly into a formula. It must be produced indirectly by another function, such as DATE() or CTOD.)

**Note:** The CMONTH function returns a text string. It must be used in a character field.

Examples:

CMONTH(DATE())=the current month (in text data)

CMONTH(CTOD("03/03/1993"))="March"

CMONTH(BIRTHDATE)="March" if the *Birthdate* field contains 03/03/1993, or 03/03/93, or any other March date for the current record

**CTOD(*string*)** — Converts a text date to a date number. *String* can be a text string that expresses a date in the form MM/DD/YY or MM/DD/YYYY, or the name of a character field containing such a text string.

You can use CTOD to convert dates expressed as text into date numbers that can be used in searches or date calculations.

**Important:** LotusWorks does not allow calculations directly on dates in rule or search expressions because it would not know whether to interpret the characters as dates, numeric expressions, or text. If you want an expression to perform calculations on a date, use the CTOD function to express the date. For example, CTOD("12/03/93") expresses December 3, 1993 as a date-number. DATE( )-CTOD("12/03/93") calculates the number of days between the system date and December 3, 1993.

Examples:

CTOD("03/03/1993")=03/03/1993 (date)

CTOD(TEXTDATE)=03/03/93 if the character field *Textdate* for the current record contains the text "03/03/93".

CTOD(TEXTDATE)+30=04/12/93 if the *Textdate* field contains "03/03/93" for the current record.

**DATE()** — Returns the current system date set in the computer. DATE() does not take an argument, but you must include the parentheses.

Because DATE() returns a date-number, it can be used in date calculations.

Examples:

DATE()=the current date

DATE()-(INVOICEDATE+30)=the number of days an invoice is more than 30 days overdue, if INVOICEDATE is a date field containing the date of the invoice

**DAY(*date-number*)** — Returns the day of the month (1 to 31) in *date-number*. Date-number can be a date-number or the name of a date field. (A date number cannot be written directly into a formula. It must be produced indirectly by another function, such as DATE() or CTOD.)

**Note:** The DAY() function returns a number. It must be used in a number field unless converted to text.

You can use the DAY() function to supply the day argument to other date or time functions.

Examples:

DAY(DATE())=the current day

DAY(CTOD("06/28/1965"))=28

DAY(BIRTHDATE)=28 if the date field *Birthdate* contains the date 06/28/1965 or any other date with the 28th day of the month in it

DBF()

Returns the name of the current database. DBF() does not take an argument, but you must include the parentheses.

Example:

DBF()="CLIENTS" if the name of the current database is "CLIENTS.DBF"

DELETED()

Returns true if the current record is flagged, false if it is not flagged. DELETED does not take an argument, but you must include the parentheses.

You can use DELETED() in a search statement to restrict the active database to those records that have been flagged.

Example:

DELETED() .AND. BALANCE>500 This search statement returns all the records that have been flagged and have a balance of more than $500.

DLIST(*sort-order [,database][,field1][,field2][,...fieldn]*)

Displays a pop-up box listing values from a specified sort order and, optionally, from one or more fields in another database that you specify, and enters into the current form the value(s) that you select from the pop-up box.

You can enter only the data in the sort-order field entered into the current database; the other (optional) fields are displayed to help you choose the right data.

You can use DLIST with manual and verify rules to display the options available for a field. With manual rules, the list appears when you press F9. With verify rules, the list appears automatically if you enter data into a field that does not meet the verification conditions defined in the rule for the field.

DOW(*date-number*)

Returns the number of the day of the week that *date-number* represents. (Sunday is 1, Monday is 2, Tuesday is 3, etc.). Date-number can be a date or the name of a date field.

Examples:

DOW(CTOD("06/28/65"))=2

DOW(BIRTHDATE)=2 if *Birthdate* is a date field containing the date 06/28/65 or any other date that represents a Monday.

DTOC(*date-number*)   Converts *date-number* into a character string with the form MM/DD/YYYY. *Date-number* can be a date expressed in the form MM/DD/YYYY or the name of a date field.

When used in a sort-order formula, DTOC sorts by month rather than in chronological sequence.

**Note:** The CDATE and DTOC functions produce similar results, however, sort orders containing the CDATE function order dates chronologically, whereas those containing the DTOC function order dates by month, day, and year. See CDATE.

Examples:

Conversion:

DTOC(CTOD("06/28/65"))="06/28/1965"

DTOC(BIRTHDATE)="06/28/1965" if the *Birthdate* field is a date field and contains 06/28/1965 for the current record

DTOC(DATE())=the current date in text form

Search criteria:

DTOC(BIRTHDATE)="06/28/1965" searches the BIRTHDATE field for the date June 28, 1965

DTOC(DOB)="01/12/1951" searches the DOB field for the date January 12, 1951

EOF()   Returns true if the cursor is at the last record of the database, and returns false if the cursor is at any other record. EOF() does not take an argument, but you must include the parentheses.

EXIST(*key,sort-order*)   Returns true if a key value is found in a sort order and false if it is not. *Key* is a text string or number that you enter into a form. *Sort-order* is the name of a sort order associated with a database.

Examples:

Suppose you have a sort order named CLIENTS and a key field named *Custno*. You can use EXIST to create a verify rule as follows:

EXIST(CUSTNO,"CLIENTS")! Invalid customer number. Try again.

If the value you enter in the *Custno* field is not found in the sort order CLIENTS, LotusWorks displays the error message "Invalid customer number. Try again."

In the following example, if the entry in the *Custno* field is found in the CLIENTS sort order, it is used; if it is not found, the DLIST function causes a popup box to appear listing all the valid values in CLIENTS.

IF(EXIST(CUSTNO,"CLIENTS"),CUSTNO,DLIST("CLIENTS"))

EXP(*x*)  Calculates the value of the constant *e* (approximately 2.718282) raised to the power *x* (the natural logarithm of *x*). *X* can be a number not greater than 709 or the name of a numeric field containing such a number. (If a number larger than 709 is used for *x*, the result is too large for LotusWorks to store. If *x* is larger than 230, LotusWorks can calculate and store but cannot display the resulting number in e notation. If *x* is less than -709, EXP returns 0.

Examples

EXP(-1.33)=0.2644772613

EXP(ENUMBER)=0.2644772613 if ENUMBER is a number field containing the value -1.33.

FIELD(*offset*)  Returns the name of the field located in the position indicated by *offset*. *Offset* is a number that represents the position of the field. The first field has the offset number 0, the second field has the offset number 1, and so on.

Examples:

FIELD(5)="LASTNAME" if the fifth field in the current database is named *Lastname*.

FIELD(7)="BALANCE" if the seventh field in the current database is named *Balance*.

FOR(*search-criteria,sort-order*)  Returns the records that meet the *search-criteria* in the specified *sort-order*. *Search-criteria* is a search formula that evaluates to true or false. *Sort-order* is a sort formula that evaluates to a string, number, or date value.

You can use FOR to select specific records in a database and order them all at once. Only those records for which the *search-criteria* are true appear in the sort order.

Examples:

FOR(HIREDATE<01/01/85,LASTNAME) This sort-order formula sorts the records by the field *Lastname* and displays the records of only the employees hired before January 1, 1985.

FOR(STATE="CA",CITY) This sort-order formula sorts the records by the field *City* and displays the records of only the cases located in California.

**F_UPPER(*string*)**  Capitalizes the first letter in *string*. *String* can be a text string or the name of a character field.

Examples:

F_UPPER(smith)=Smith

F_UPPER(LOWER(LASTNAME)) This formula converts the text string in the *Lastname* field to lower case, then converts the first letter to uppercase.

**IF(*condition,x,y*)**  Evaluates *condition* and returns *x* if condition is true, *y* if *condition* is false. *Condition* can be a logical formula or the name of a logical field. *X* and *y* can be character, date, or numeric values, the names of fields that contain such values, or expressions containing such values and/or field names. However, *x* and *y* must be the same type of data and must match field's data type.

You can nest IF functions within IF functions to create more complex conditions.

Examples:

IF(QUANTITY>=25,.1,0) This statement calculates a value for a *Discount* field: if the quantity purchased is 25 or more, the discount is 10% (.1); if the quantity is less than 25, the discount is 0.

IF(PERFORMNCE>=90,SALARY+BONUS,SALARY)

This statement says, "If an employee's performance is 90 or more, give the employee his or her salary plus bonus; otherwise, give only the salary."

IF(SALES>=1000000,10000,IF(SALES>=500000,5000, IF(SALES>10000,1000,0)))

This statement uses nested IF functions to calculate a sales bonus. It says, "If SALES are $1,000,000 or more, the bonus is $10,000; if SALES are $500,000 or more but less than $1,000,000, the bonus is $5,000; if SALES are $100,000 or more but less than $500,000, the bonus is $1,000; otherwise, the bonus is 0."

IF(BALANCE>=0,STR(BALANCE),"OVERDRAWN")

This statement calculates the entry for a character field. It says, If BALANCE is 0 or more, print the balance; if BALANCE is less than 0, print the word OVERDRAWN. Because BALANCE is a numeric field and we want to print the balance amount in a character field, it is necessary to use the STR function to convert the value in BALANCE to a text string.

**Note:** To create a formula that you can export to dBASE III Plus, use the special function IIF instead of IF.

IIF(*condition,x,y*)

Performs exactly the same function as IF, but can be used in dBASE III Plus databases.

INT(*x*)

Returns the integer part of *x*, without rounding. *X* can be a number or the name of a numeric field.

Examples:

INT(3.3333)=3

INT(LOANAMT/36)=972 if *Loanamt* is a numeric field containing the value 35000.

INVERT(*expression*)

Returns the complement of *expression*. *Expression* can be a character, numeric, or date field name.

You can use INVERT in a sort-order formula to sort a field into inverse order-that is, from high to low or in reverse alphabetical order.

Examples:

INVERT(SALARY) sorts database records into descending order according to the values in the SALARY field.

DEPARTMENT+INVERT(HIREYEAR)+NAME sorts database records into departments in alphabetical order, and within each department by inverse date of hire (most recent year first), and within each year by name in alphabetical order.

ISALPHA(*string*)

Returns true if the first character in *string* is a letter and false if it is not. *String* can be a number, text string, field name, or conditional expression.

| | |
|---|---|
| ISBLANK(*x*) | Returns true if *x* is blank and false if it is not. *X* can be a text, numeric, date, logical, or blank value, or the name of a field. |
| | You can use ISBLANK to identify records that have blank entries in a particular field. |
| | Examples: |
| | ISBLANK(" ")=True |
| | ISBLANK(LASTNAME)= False if the *Lastname* field contains data for the current record |
| ISLOWER(*string*) | Returns true if the first character in *string* is lowercase, false if it is not. *String* can be a text string or the name of a character field. |
| | Examples: |
| | ISLOWER("Smith")=False |
| | ISLOWER(LASTNAME)=True if the *Lastname* field for the current record contains de Santos or any other entry starting with a lowercase letter |
| ISUPPER(*string*) | Returns true if the first character in *string* is uppercase, false if it is not. *String* can be a text string or the name of a character field. |
| | Examples: |
| | ISUPPER("smith")=False |
| | ISUPPER(LASTNAME)=True if the *Lastname* field for the current record contains Smith or any other entry starting with an uppercase letter. |
| LEFT(*string,x*) | Returns the first *x* characters in *string*. *String* can be a text string or the name of a character field. *X* can be a positive integer or the name of a field that contains a positive integer. If *x* is 0, LotusWorks returns an empty string. If *x* is larger than the length of *string,* LotusWorks returns the entire string. LotusWorks counts each punctuation mark and blank space as a character. |
| | Examples: |
| | LEFT("Los Angeles",7)="Los Ang" |
| | LEFT(COMPANY,8) returns the first eight characters of the name the *Company* field for each record |

LEN(*string*)  Returns the number of characters in *string*. *String* can be a text string or the name of a character field. LotusWorks counts punctuation marks and blank spaces within the string as part of the string.

Examples:

LEN("")=0

LEN("de los Angeles")=14

LEN(LASTNAME)=25 if the *Lastname* field has been defined as 25 characters long

**Important:** If a character field name is specified, the LEN function by itself returns the defined length of the entire field. To get the length of a text string without counting leading or trailing blank spaces, use LTRIM or RTRIM with the LEN function.

For example, consider a record with the entry "●●●de los Angeles" in the *Lastname* field, where each bullet is a leading blank:

LEN(LASTNAME)=25 if the *Lastname* field has been defined as 25 characters long

LEN(RTRIM(LASTNAME))=17 This expression trims the trailing blanks but not the three leading blanks and counts the resulting string.

LEN(LTRIM(RTRIM(LASTNAME)))=14 This expression trims both the leading and trailing blanks and counts the character string.

LIST(*string1,string2...stringn*)  Displays a pop-up box containing up to specified 12 strings and enters the string selected by the user from the pop-up box into the field for the current record. *String1, string2...stringn* must be text strings.

**Note:** You must enclose each string within double quotation marks.

You can use LIST with manual and verify rules to display the options available for entries into a text field. When you select an option, LotusWorks enters the string into the field for you.

When you create a verify rule using LIST, LotusWorks displays the pop-up box automatically if data entered into a field does not meet the specified condition for that field. If you create a manual rule using LIST, LotusWorks displays the pop-up box whenever you press F9 when the pointer is on the field containing the manual rule.

**Examples:**

LIST("30 Days","60 Days","90 Days") If put into a manual rule, this statement displays the three options (30 Days, 60 Days and 90 Days) in a popup box whenever you press F9. If put into a verify rule, it displays the three options if you try to enter anything other than one of the three options into the field.

IF(GRADE="", LIST("A","B","C","D","F","I"),GRADE) This statement displays the available grade options (A,B,C,D,F, and I) if you leave the *Grade* field blank.

LOG(*x*)   Calculates the common logarithm (base 10) of *x*. *X* can be a number or the name of a numeric field.

**Examples:**

LOG(6)=1.791759

LOG(NUM)=1.791759 if the *Num* field contains the number 6 for the current record

LOOKUP(*key-field*,"*return-field*","*database*")
Finds the record in *database* whose value in *key-field* exactly matches the value in the current field and returns the value in that record's *return-field*. *Database* is the name of a different database from the current one. *Key-field* is the name of a field that is common to both the current database and *database*. *Return-field* is the name of the field in *database* from which you want LotusWorks to return a value.

**Note:** The names of the *return-field* and *database* must be enclosed within double quotation marks.

You can use a sort-order stored in an .NDX file in place of the database name in the LOOKUP function.

LOOKUP works like CLOOKUP, except that LOOKUP returns a blank value if it does not find an exact match for the key value, whereas CLOOKUP moves to the next higher value in the key field if it does not find an exact match.

LOOKUP is useful for many situations where you need a lookup table based on specific discreet key values. Typical cases are parts and customer lists, where a number is a key to other descriptive information.

Examples:

| PARTNO | DESCRPTN | PRICE |
|--------|----------|-------|
| 101 | Sales Kit | $35.00 |
| 102 | Brochures (500) | $25.00 |
| 103 | Banner, 3' × 5' | $120.00 |
| 104 | Presentation Folders (25) | $50.00 |

Suppose you wanted to have an invoice form automatically display the description and price when you enter a part number. You could use the following rule formulas with a database named PARTS.DBF:

LOOKUP(PARTNO,"DESCRPTN","PARTS")

With this rule, when you enter a number in the field containing the rule, LotusWorks looks for a matching number in the PARTNO field of the PARTS.DBF database. If it finds one, it returns the corresponding description from the DESCRPTN field in the PARTS.DBF database. If LotusWorks does not find a match, it returns a blank value.

LOOKUP(PARTNO,"PRICE","PARTS")

With this rule, when you enter a number in the field containing the rule, LotusWorks looks for the matching number in the PARTNO field of the PARTS.DBF database and, if it finds a match, returns the corresponding price from the PRICE field in the PARTS.DBF database. Of course, if you enter a number that does not appear in the PARTNO field, LotusWorks returns a blank value.

**Tip:** You can use the LIST or DLIST functions to have LotusWorks display a list of valid values when you enter a value that does not appear in the key-field. Use the functions with a *verify* rule to have the list appear automatically whenever an incorrect value is entered. Use the function with a *manual* rule to display the list when you press F9.

**Tip:** To speed database operations, use a Lookup field rule with the LOOKUP function rather than a Verify or Calculate field rule. With the Lookup type of field rule, LotusWorks performs the lookup only when you enter a new value into the field containing the LOOKUP rule, whereas with Verify and Calculate rules, LotusWorks repeats the lookup every time any field in a form is recalculated.

| | |
|---|---|
| LOWER(*string*) | Converts the uppercase letters in *string* to lowercase. *String* can be a text string or the name of a character field. |
| | Examples: |
| | LOWER("LotusWorks")=lotusworks |
| | LOWER(LASTNAME)=washington, if the character field *Lastname* contains "Washington" |
| LTRIM(*string*) | Removes any blank spaces that come before the text (leading blanks) in *string*. *String* can be a text string or the name of a character field. |
| | Examples: |
| | LTRIM( "•••1450")=1450, where each bullet (•) represents a blank space |
| | LTRIM(ACCOUNTNO)=1450 if the account number for the current record is "•••1450" |
| MAX(*x,y*) | Returns the larger number, *x* or *y*. *X* and *y* can be numbers or the names of numeric fields. |
| | Example: |
| | MAX(SCORE1,SCORE2)=100 if SCORE1 contains 90 and SCORE2 contains 100 |
| MIN(*x,y*) | Returns the smaller number, *x* or *y*. *X* and *y* can be numbers or the names of numeric fields. |
| | Example: |
| | MIN(SCORE1,SCORE2)=90 if SCORE1 contains 90 and SCORE2 contains 100 |
| MOD(*x,y*) | Calculates the remainder (modulus) of *x/y*. *X* and *y* can be numbers or the names of numeric fields. |
| | **Note:** The sign of the dividend (*x*) determines the sign of the result. If *x* is 0, MOD returns 0 (that is, zero divided by any number is zero). If *y* is 0, MOD returns ERR (that is, ERROR, because a number cannot be divided by 0). |
| | Examples: |
| | MOD(17,3)=2 |
| | MOD(−17,3)=−2 |
| | MOD(17,0)=ERR |

## Database Functions

MONTH(*date-number*)

Returns the number of the month (1 to 12) in *date-number*. *Date-number* can be a date number or the name of a date field. (A date number cannot be written directly into a formula. It must be produced indirectly by another function, such as DATE() or CTOD.)

**Note:** The MONTH function returns a number. It must be used in a number field unless converted to text.

You can use the MONTH function to supply the month argument to other date or time functions.

MONTH(BIRTHDATE)=12 if the *Birthdate* field contains a date in the month of December for the current record

MONTH(DATE())=the current month

MONTH(CTOD("07/04/1992"))=7

IF(MONTH(BIRTHDATE)<=6,STARTMONTH="September", STARTMONTH="January") This formula states that if the month in the *Birthdate* field is June or earlier, the starting month is September; otherwise, the starting month is January.

PATTERN(*substring,string*)

Returns true if *string* contains *substring*, false if it does not. *String* can be a string or the name of a character field. *Substring* can be a string or the name of a character field.

**Note:** The PATTERN function performs a case-sensitive search for *substring*. You can use the wildcard characters * and ? with the PATTERN function.

Examples:

PATTERN(LASTNAME,COMPANY)=True if the entry in the *Lastname* field for the current record is "brook" and the entry in the *Company* field is Stonebrook Farms for the same record.

PATTERN(LASTNAME,COMPANY)=False if the entry in the *Lastname* field for the current record is "Brook" and the entry in the *Company* field is "Stonebrook Farms" for the same record. (The result is false because PATTERN performs a case-sensitive search.)

RAND()

Generates a random number between 0 and 1. RAND() does not take an argument, but you must include the parentheses.

**Note:** The sequence of random numbers is the same for each session. Each time you use update rules to update the database, RAND generates a new random number.

To generate random numbers in different intervals, mutiply RAND() by the size of the desired interval. You can then use the ROUND() and INT() functions with RAND() to create random whole numbers.

Examples:

RAND()=0.123456, or any number between 0 and 1

INT(RAND()*100)+1=13, or any random whole number between 0 and 100

RECCOUNT()   Returns the number of records in the current database. RECCOUNT does not take an argument, but you must include the parentheses.

RECNO()   Returns the record number of the current record. RECNO does not take an argument, but you must include the parentheses.

RECSIZE()   Returns the number of characters reserved for each record (that is, the sum of the sizes of all defined fields). RECSIZE () does not take an argument, but you must include the parentheses.

REPLICATE(*string,x*)   Duplicates *string* *x* times. The resulting string must be less than 255 characters long. *String* can be a text string or the name of a character field. *X* can be a positive integer or the name of a numeric field that contains a positive integer.

Examples:

REPLICATE("*",15)=***************

REPLICATE("SALE ",6)=SALE SALE SALE SALE SALE SALE

RIGHT(*string,x*)   Returns the last *x* characters in string. *String* can be a text string or the name of a character field. *X* can be a number or the name of a numeric field. If *x* is 0, the result is an empty string. If *x* is larger than the length of string, RIGHT returns the entire string. LotusWorks counts each punctuation mark and blank space as a character.

Examples:

RIGHT("Los Angeles",7)="Angeles"

RIGHT(COMPANY),8) =" " if the last eight characters in the *Company* field are blank spaces

RIGHT(TRIM(LASTNAME,5))="Smith" if the LASTNAME field contains "Gomez-Smith" for the current record

**ROUND(x,y)**   Rounds the number *x* to *y* places. *X* can be a number or the name of a numeric field. *Y* can be a number from −100 to 100, or the name of a field that contains such a number.

If *y* is positive, LotusWorks rounds to the number of decimal places indicated by *y*. If *y* is negative, LotusWorks discards any decimal portion, moves *y* places to the left and rounds to the nearest number. For instance, −2 rounds to the nearest hundred, -3 rounds to the nearest thousand, −4 rounds to the nearest ten thousand, and so on.

If *y* is 0, LotusWorks rounds to the nearest integer.

Examples:

ROUND(1234.56789,2)=1234.57

Suppose a field named *Amount* contains the number 1234.56789. ROUND() produces the following results in the formulas indicated:

ROUND(AMOUNT,2)=1234.57

ROUND(AMOUNT,0)=1235

ROUND(AMOUNT,−2)=1200

**RTRIM(*string*)**   Removes any blank spaces that come after the text (trailing blanks) in *string*. *String* can be a text string or the name of a character field.

**Note:** The TRIM and RTRIM functions produce exactly the same results. You can use the RTRIM function to remove trailing blanks before joining one string to another with the + (plus) operator.

Examples:

RTRIM( "Brown•••••••••")=Brown, where each bullet (•) represents a blank space

RTRIM(LASTNAME)=Brown if the *Lastname* field contains "Brown•••••••••" for the current record

RTRIM(FIRSTNAME)+" "LASTNAME="Sally Siegel" if the *Firstname* field contains "Sally" and the *Lastname* field contains "Siegel" for the current record

**SOUNDEX(*string*)**   Returns a four-character text string that has the same phonetic sound as the first few characters in *string*. *String* can be a text string or the name of a character field.

SOUNDEX is useful for looking up names that can be spelled various ways.

Example:

To find all the persons named Smith or Smyth in a database, enter the following formula for the search criteria:

SOUNDEX(LASTNAME)=SOUNDEX(Smith)

**SPACE($x$)**    Returns a string consisting of $x$ spaces. $X$ can be a positive integer or the name of a numeric field containing such a number.

You can use the SPACE function to specify blank spaces when joining strings.

Example:

TRIM(FIRSTNAME)+SPACE(1)+LASTNAME=James Jones if the FIRSTNAME field contains "James" and the *Lastname* field contains "Jones"

**SQRT($x$)**    Returns the square root of $x$. $X$ can be a non-negative number or the name of a field containing such a number.

**Note:** If $x$ is a negative number, LotusWorks returns ERR (error).

Examples:

SQRT(25)=5

SQRT(−25)=ERR

**STR($x$[,$y$][,$n$])**    Converts the number $x$ to a text string with length $y$ and $n$ decimal places. $X$ can be a number or the name of a numeric field. The optional parameter $y$ can be a positive integer or the name of a field containing a positive integer. The optional parameter $n$ can be a positive integer from 0 to 15 or the name of a numeric field containing such an integer.

**Note:** If you do not specify $y$, STR produces a default field width of 10. You must allow one space for the decimal point, and one space for a minus sign if $x$ is a negative number. If you do not specify $n$, STR rounds $x$ and the resulting string to the nearest whole number.

Examples:

STR(AMOUNT,10,0)="●●●●●●1234", if AMOUNT contains the number 1234 (Each bullet represents a blank space.)

STR(AMOUNT)="●●●●●●1234" if AMOUNT contains the number 1234

STR(AMOUNT,8,2)="1234.00o", if AMOUNT contains the number 1234

STR(AMOUNT,8,2)="-1234.00", if AMOUNT contains the number –1234

STUFF(*original-string,start-number,x,new-string*)

Replaces *x* characters in *original-string* with *new-string* beginning at *start-number*. *Original-string* and *new-string* can be text strings or the names of character fields. *Start-number* and *x* can be any non-negative integers or the names of numeric fields that contain such integers. If *start-number* is greater than the length of *original-string*, STUFF appends *new-string* to *original-string*. If *x* is 0, STUFF inserts *new-string* at the beginning of *original-string*.

**Note:** STUFF counts punctuation marks and blank spaces as characters.

You can use STUFF to replace one set of characters with another (for example, to change a department name wherever it appears throughout a company directory or to change Blvd. to Boulevard wherever it appears in a name-and-address database).

Examples:

STUFF("Personnel Department",1,20,"Human Resources Division") This statement changes the name Personnel Department to Human Resources Division.

IF(ZIP="44444",STUFF(ZIP,6,5,"-1234"),ZIP) This statement says, if the mailing code in the *ZIP* field is 44444, add the additional mailing code "-1234" to the end of the mailing code.

**Note:** The *ZIP* field must be a character field at least 10 characters wide in order to use this statement.

SUBSTR(*string,start-number,x*)

Returns *x* characters from *string*, beginning with the character at *start-number*. *X* and *start-number* can be positive integers or the names of numeric fields containing such numbers. *String* can be a text string or the name of a character field.

SUBSTR is useful for copying part of a text string that is not located at the beginning or end of a field.

**Note:** If *x* is 0, SUBSTR returns an empty string. If *x* is larger than the length of *string*, LotusWorks returns the characters from *start-number* to the end of *string*. If you do not know the length of *string*, use a large number for *x*; LotusWorks ignores the extra length.

Examples:

SUBSTR(COMPANY,1,3)="ABC" if the *Company* field contains "ABC Service Corporation"

SUBSTR(COMPANY,5,7)="Service" if the *Company* field contains "ABC Service Corporation"

To search the *Phone* field of a database for telephone numbers beginning with the area code 305, you can use the following formula for the search criteria:

SUBSTR(PHONE,1,3)="305"

**Tip:** You can search for a substring without specifying a starting point by using the $ operator in a search formula. For example, the formula "Comp" $ COMPANY finds all the records that have the substring "Comp" anywhere in the *Company* field.

TIME()

Returns the current time from the computer's system clock in text form. The format is "HH:MM:SS." TIME() does not take an argument, but you must include the parentheses.

**Important:** LotusWorks recalculates the TIME() function each time you use update rules to update a database.

**Note:** You cannot perform time arithmetic with LotusWorks database functions.

Example:

TIME()="14:00:00" if the time on the system clock is two P.M.

TRIM(*string*)

Removes any blank spaces that come after the text (trailing blanks) in *string*. *String* can be a text *string* or the name of a character field.

**Note:** The TRIM and RTRIM functions produce exactly the same results.

You can use the TRIM function to remove trailing blanks before joining one string to another with the + (plus) operator.

Examples:

TRIM( "Brown•••••••")=Brown, where each bullet (•) represents a blank space

TRIM(LASTNAME)=Brown if the *Lastname* field contains "Brown•••••••" for the current record

TRIM(FIRSTNAME)+" "+LASTNAME="Sally Siegel" if the *Firstname* field contains "Sally" and the *Lastname* field contains "Siegel" for the current record

| | |
|---|---|
| UPPER(*string*) | Converts the lowercase letters in *string* to uppercase. *String* can be a text string or the name of a character field.

**Note:** UPPER capitalizes all the letters in *string*. W_UPPER capitalizes the first letter of each word in *string* and converts all other letters to lowercase. LOWER converts all letters in *string* to lowercase.

Examples:

UPPER(LASTNAME)="SIEGEL" if the LASTNAME field contains "Siegel"

UPPER(ADDRESS)="110 PARK STREET, APT. 3" if the ADDRESS field contains "110 Park Street, Apt. 3" |
| VAL(*string*) | Converts a number entered as a text string into its corresponding numeric form. *String* can be a text string or the name of a character field containing a number. If the first character in *string* is not a number, VAL returns 0.

You can use the VAL function when you want to perform math calculations with numbers entered as text.

Examples:

VAL("110.75")=110.75

VAL("$110.75")=0

VAL("110.75")*.10=11.08

VAL(IDNO)=12345 if the IDNO field contains "12345" for the current record

VAL(SUBSTR(TAGNO,4,3)>500 find the records with values in the TAGNO field greater than 500, ignoring the first three characters in the field |
| WORD(*string,x*) | Returns the *x*th word in string. *String* can be a text string or the name of a character field. *X* can be a number or the name of a numeric field.

Examples:

WORD("Four score and seven years ago",4)="seven"

WORD(COMPANY,1)="ABC" if the COMPANY field contains "ABC Service Company, Inc." for the current record |

W_UPPER(*string*) — Converts the first letter of each word in *string* to uppercase and all other letters to lowercase. *String* can be a text string or the name of a character field.

**Note:** W_UPPER capitalizes the first letter of each word in *string*. UPPER capitalizes all the letters in *string*. LOWER converts all letters in *string* to lowercase.

Examples:

W_UPPER(LASTNAME)="Siegel" if the *Lastname* field contains "SIEGEL"

UPPER(ADDRESS)="110 Park Street, Apt. 3" if the *Address* field contains "110 park street, apt. 3"

YEAR(*date-number*) — Returns the year from *date-number*. *Date-number* can be a date-number or the name of a field containing a date number. (A date number cannot be written directly into a formula. It must be produced indirectly by another function, such as DATE() or CTOD.)

**Note:** The YEAR function returns a number. It must be used in a number field, unless it is converted to text.

You can use the YEAR function to supply the year argument to other date or time functions.

Examples:

YEAR(DATE())=the current year

YEAR(CTOD("12/31/1992"))=1992

YEAR(BIRTHDATE)=1965 if the *Birthdate* field contains any date in the year 1965 for the current record

YEAR(BIRTHDATE)+65=2030 if the *Birthdate* field contains any date in the year 1965 for the current record

ZBLANK(x) — Converts *x* to a string. If *x* is zero, ZBLANK returns an empty string. *X* can be a number or the name of a numeric field.

If you want to suppress printing of a field if it contains a value of zero (such as unneeded item numbers on an order form), you can create a form for the order and use ZBLANK in a calculated field rule for each field in the form that you want to leave blank when the value is zero. For example, you can use ZBLANK(ITEM2), ZBLANK(QTY2), ZBLANK(PRICE2), ZBLANK(ITEM3), ZBLANK(QTY3), ZBLANK(PRICE3), and so on. If you use ZBLANK in the form, the original values in the database remain unchanged.

Examples:

ZBLANK(30000)="30000"

ZBLANK(BONUS)="5000" if BONUS is a numeric field containing 5000 for the current record

ZBLANK(BONUS)="" if BONUS is a numeric field containing 0 for the current record

# Spreadsheet @Functions

A spreadsheet @function is a built-in program that performs a particular action in a spreadsheet. It is called an "@function" (pronounced "at-function") because all spreadsheet function names begin with an @ sign. By putting an @function into a formula, you can have LotusWorks perform the calculation automatically. You can use a spreadsheet @function by itself in a formula, combine it with other @functions and formulas, or use it in a macro. LotusWorks has 80 predefined spreadsheet @functions. (See Chapter 5 for information on writing spreadsheet formulas.)

Each @function has a specific structure, which takes one of the following forms:

@FUNCTION

or

@FUNCTION(*argument1,argument2,...,argumentn*)

@FUNCTION is the name of the @function. It tells LotusWorks what action to perform. The @ sign tells LotusWorks that the entry is an @function rather than a label.

(*Argument1,argument2,...,argumentn*) are the arguments for the @function. Arguments specify information needed to complete the action or calculation indicated by the @function name. In most cases arguments can consist of one or more data values, cell addresses, ranges, or expressions. Arguments can express logical conditions, text or numeric data, and the locations of text and numeric data.

The spreadsheet @functions fall into seven categories, as described in the following tables. A detailed description of each @function, in alphabetical order, follows the tables.

# Type of Spreadsheet Function

| Type of @Function | Description |
|---|---|
| Date and Time | Calculates with numbers that represent dates and times |
| Financial | Performs calculations commonly used in financial analyses, such as for loans, annuities, cash flows, and depreciation |
| Logical | Calculates based on whether specified conditions are either true or false |
| Mathematical | Calculates with numbers |
| Special | Provides information about special situations in spreadsheets |
| Statistical | Performs calculations commonly used in statistical analyses, such as averages, standard deviations, and variances |
| String | Searches for and changes text data (labels) in spreadsheets |

## Date and Time @Functions

There are 11 date and time @functions. Five @functions calculate with dates:

| Function | Action |
|---|---|
| @DATE | Calculates the date number for the specified year, month, and day |
| @DATEVALUE | Converts a string date into its equivalent date number |
| @DAY | Calculates the day of the month in a date number |
| @MONTH | Calculates the number of the month in a date number |
| @YEAR | Returns the number of the year in a date number |

Five @functions calculate with times:

| Function | Action |
|---|---|
| @HOUR | Returns the hour in a time number |
| @MINUTE | Returns the minutes in a time number |
| @SECOND | Returns the seconds in a time number |
| @TIME | Produces the time number for a specified hour, minute, and second |
| @TIMEVALUE | Converts a date expressed as a text string into its equivalent time number |

One @function produces the current date and time number:

| Function | Action |
|---|---|
| @NOW | Produces the date and time number for the current date and time |

## Financial @Functions

There are 11 @functions that perform special financial calculations. Three @functions calculate depreciation:

| @Function | Action |
|---|---|
| @DDB | Calculates the double-declining balance depreciation allowance of an asset for one period |
| @SLN | Calculates the straight-line depreciation allowance of an asset for one period |
| @SYD | Calculates the sum-of-the-year's-digits depreciation allowance of an asset for one period |

Two @functions can be used for capital budgeting:

| @Function | Action |
|---|---|
| @IRR | Calculates the internal rate of return for a series of cash flows |
| @NPV | Calculates the net present value of a series of future cash flows |

Four @functions calculate annuities:

| @Function | Action |
|---|---|
| @FV | Calculates the future value of a series of equal payments |
| @PMT | Calculates the amount of the periodic payment required to pay off a loan |
| @PV | Calculates the present value of a series of equal payments |
| @TERM | Calculates the number of payment periods of an investment |

Two @functions calculate single-sum compounding:

| @Function | Action |
|---|---|
| @CTERM | Calculates the number of compounding periods necessary for an investment to grow to a given future value |
| @RATE | Calculates the periodic interest rate necessary for an investment to grow to a given future value |

## Logical @Functions

Logical @functions evaluate whether logical condition expressions are true or false. Most return 1 if a condition is true and 0 if it is false. One @function (@IF) performs an action that you specify if the condition is true and another specified action if the condition is false. There are seven logical @functions:

| @Function | Action |
| --- | --- |
| @FALSE | Returns the logical value 0 (false) |
| @IF | Performs one specified action if the specified condition is true, and another action if the condition is false |
| @ISERR | Returns 1 (true) if an expression is in error (ERR) and 0 (false) if it is not |
| @ISNA | Returns 1 (true) if an expression produces NA ("Not Available") and 0 (false) if it does not |
| @ISNUMBER | Returns 1 (true) if a value is a number, NA, ERR, or blank, and 0 (false) if it is a label or text string |
| @ISSTRING | Returns 1 (true) if a value is a label or a text string and 0 (false) if it is a number, NA, ERR, or blank |
| @TRUE | Returns the logical value 1 (true) |

## Mathematical @Functions

There are 17 @functions that perform special mathematical and trigonometric calculations. Ten @functions perform mathematical calculations:

| @Function | Action |
| --- | --- |
| @ABS | Calculates the absolute (positive) value of a number |
| @EXP | Calculates the number e raised to a specified power |
| @INT | Returns the integer portion of a number, without rounding the number |
| @LN | Calculates the natural logarithm (base e) of a number |
| @LOG | Calculates the common logarithm (base 10) of a number |
| @MOD | Calculates the remainder (modulus) of a division operation |
| @PI | Returns the number Pi (calculated at 3.1415926536) |
| @RAND | Returns a random number from 0 to 1 |
| @ROUND | Rounds a number to a specified number of decimal places |
| @SQRT | Calculates the positive square root of a number |

There are seven @functions that calculate trigonometric functions:

| @Function | Action |
|---|---|
| @ACOS | Calculates the arc cosine of a number |
| @ASIN | Calculates the arc sine of a number |
| @ATAN | Calculates the arc tangent of a number |
| @ATAN2 | Calculates the four-quadrant arc tangent of a number |
| @COS | Calculates the cosine of an angle |
| @SIN | Calculates the sine of an angle |
| @TAN | Calculates the tangent of an angle |

## Special @Functions

There are nine @functions that provide information about spreadsheets in special situations. Three @functions provide information about cells and ranges:

| @Function | Action |
|---|---|
| @@ | Returns the contents of a cell referred to by a formula in another cell |
| @COLS | Returns the number of columns in a specified range |
| @ROWS | Returns the number of rows in a specified range |

Two @functions perform error trapping:

| @Function | Action |
|---|---|
| @ERR | Returns the value ERR (error) |
| @NA | Returns the value NA (not available) |

Four @functions perform lookup calculations:

| @Function | Action |
|---|---|
| @CHOOSE | Finds a specified number or text string in a list of numbers and/or strings |
| @HLOOKUP | Finds the contents of a cell in a specified row in a range |
| @INDEX | Finds the contents of a cell in a row and column in a range |
| @VLOOKUP | Finds the contents of a cell in a specified column in a range |

## Statistical @Functions

Statistical @functions perform calculations on a list of numbers. You must observe the following rules when using statistical @functions:

- Statistical @functions perform calculations on the values specified by the argument *list*. Each entry in *list* can be a number, a formula, or the name or address of a range that contains one or more numbers or formulas.

- Statistical @functions ignore blank cells in their calculations. For example, the formula @AVG(C2..C10) calculates the average of the values in cells C2 through C10; if one of the cells is blank, LotusWorks ignores the blank cell and divides the sum of the values by eight rather than by nine to compute the average.

- Statistical @functions assign the value 0 (rather than blank) to all cell labels that are included in a range or list used as the argument and includes these cells in calculations. If you include a cell containing a label in a list for an @AVG calculation, LotusWorks considers the label cell to have a value when it calculates the average.

- Statistical @functions (except @COUNT) return ERR or NA if any cell in a range or list used as the argument contains an ERR or NA message.

There are seven statistical @functions:

| @Function | Action |
| --- | --- |
| @AVG | Computes the average (mean) of a list of numbers |
| @COUNT | Returns the number of non-blank cells in a range or list of ranges |
| @MAX | Finds the largest number in a list of numbers |
| @MIN | Find the smallest number in a list of numbers |
| @STD | Calculates the population standard deviation of the numbers in a list |
| @SUM | Calculates the sum of the numbers in a list |
| @VAR | Calculates the population variance of the numbers in a list |

# String @Functions

There are 18 string @functions in all. Five @functions return information about strings of text:

| @Function | Action |
|---|---|
| @CHAR | Returns the text character that corresponds to a specified ASCII code number |
| @CODE | Returns the ASCII code number that corresponds to the first character in a specified text string |
| @EXACT | Returns 1 (true) if two text strings are exactly the same, and 0 (false) if the strings are different |
| @FIND | Returns the position of the first character of one text string within another string |
| @LENGTH | Returns the number of characters in a text string |

Thirteen string @functions manipulate text strings:

| @Function | Action |
|---|---|
| @LEFT | Returns the specified number of characters from the beginning of a text string |
| @LOWER | Converts the uppercase letters in a text string to lowercase |
| @MID | Returns a specified number of characters from a text string, starting at a specified character |
| @N | Returns the number in the first cell in a range or 0 if the first cell contains a label |
| @PROPER | Converts the first letter of each word in a text string to uppercase and the rest to lowercase |
| @REPEAT | Duplicates a text string a specified number of times |
| @REPLACE | Replaces characters in one text string with characters from a different string |
| @RIGHT | Returns the specified number of characters from the end of a string |
| @S | Returns the string in the first cell of a range |
| @STRING | Converts a number into a label with a specified number of decimal places |
| @TRIM | Removes leading, trailing, or consecutive blank spaces from a text string |
| @UPPER | Converts the lowercase letters in a string to uppercase |
| @VALUE | Converts a number expressed as text data into numeric data |

## @Function Descriptions

The detailed descriptions of @functions that follow use these conventions:

- @Function names and range names appear in uppercase. Example: @ABS
- Argument names appear in lowercase italics. Example: @CHOOSE(*x,list*) You must substitue the type of information required by the argument. Actual arguments used in the examples are not enclosed in italics.
- Optional arguments are enclosed in square brackets [ ]. When you use an optional argument, do not enter the brackets.

| Function Syntax | Action |
|---|---|
| @@(*location*) | Returns the contents of the cell specified in *location*. *Location* can be a cell address or cell name. @@ displays the contents of *location* in the cell that contains @@. |

Examples:

@@(B25) displays the contents of cell B25 in the cell that contains the @@ function.

@@(TOTAL) displays the contents of the cell named TOTAL in the cell that contains the @@ function.

@ABS(*x*)     Calculates the absolute value of *x*. *X* can be a number, the address or name of a cell that contains a number, or a formula that returns a number.

Use @ABS when a number (such as a percentage difference) needs to be positive. Use −@ABS to force a number to be negative. Use @SQRT(@ABS(*x*)) to find the square root of a negative number.

Examples:

@ABS(−1000)=1000

@SQRT(@ABS(−4))=2

@ACOS(*x*)     Calculates the arc cosine (inverse cosine) of *x*, which is to say, the angle measured in radians whose cosine is *x*. The result of @ACOS is a number from 0 to Pi. *X* represents the cosine of an angle and can be a number, the address or name of a cell that contains a number, or a formula that returns a number from −1 to 1.

Use @ACOS to find the size of an angle when you know its cosine.

To convert radians to degrees, multiply by 180/@PI.

Examples:

@ACOS(0.33)=1.234492 radians

@ACOS(0.33)*180/@PI=70.73122 degrees

@ASIN(x)  Calculates the arc sine (inverse sine) of x, which is to say, the angle measured in radians whose sine is x. The result of @ASIN is a number from −Pi/2 to Pi/2. X represents the sine of an angle and can be a number, the address or name of a cell that contains a number, or a formula that returns a number.

Use @ASIN to find the size of an angle when you know its sine.

To convert radians to degrees, multiply by 180/@PI.

Examples:

@ASIN(0.33)=0.336303 radians

@ASIN(0.33)*180/@PI=19.26877 degrees

@ATAN(x)  Calculates the arc tangent (inverse tangent) of x, which is to say, the angle measured in radians whose tangent is x. The result of @ATAN is a number from −Pi/2 to Pi/2, which expresses the size of the angle in radians. X represents the tangent of an angle and can be a number, the address or name of a cell that contains a number, or a formula that returns a number.

Use @ATAN to find the size of an angle when you know its tangent.

To convert radians to degrees, multiply by 180/@PI.

Examples:

@ATAN(0.33)=0.318747 radians

@ATAN(0.33)*180/@PI=18.26288 degrees

@ATAN2(x,y)  Calculates the four-quadrant arc tangent of y/x (that is, the angle whose tangent is y/x). The result of @ATAN2 is a number from −Pi to Pi, which expresses the size of the angle in radians. X and y each can be any numeric value, expressed as a number, the address or name of a cell that contains a number, or a formula that returns a number.

If y is 0, @ATAN2 returns 0; if both x and y are 0, @ATAN2 returns ERR.

Examples:

@ATAN2(3,1)=0.321750 radians

@ATAN2(3,1)*180/@PI=18.43494 degrees

@ATAN2(0,0)=ERR

**@AVG(*list*)**

Calculates the average (mean) of the numbers in *list*. *List* can be a series of numbers, cell or range addresses, formulas that return numbers, or a combination of these, separated by commas or other argument separators. Empty cells are disregarded in the calculation. Cells containing labels or blank spaces count as zero.

**Caution:** Be careful with cells that appear to be empty but actually contain blank spaces or the prefixes of labels. Rather than disregard them in @AVG calculations, LotusWorks counts these as containing the value zero, which can greatly affect the average.

Examples:

@AVG(2,4,6,8)=5

@AVG(B2..B4)=10 if the values in cells B2 through B4 are 5, 10, and 15, respectively

@AVG(B2..B4)=10 if the value in cell B2 is 5, the value in cell B4 is 15, and cell B3 is empty

@AVG(B2..B4)=6.66667 if the value in cell B2 is 5, the value in cell B4 is 15, and cell B3 contains a label prefix (')

**@CHAR(*x*)**

Returns the ASCII text character that corresponds to ASCII code number *x*. *X* can be an integer between 1 and 255, the name or address of a cell that contains such an integer, or a formula that returns such an integer. If *x* is not an integer, @CHAR truncates it to an integer. If *x* is not between 0 and 255, @CHAR returns ERR.

Examples:

@CHAR(156)=£

@CHAR(C3)=÷ if the value in cell C3 is 246

**@CHOOSE(*x,list*)**

Returns the *x*th number or label from *list*. *X* can be a positive integer that is equal to or less than the number of items in *list*, it can be the name or address of a cell that contains such an integer, or it can be a formula that returns such an integer. *List* represents a series of numbers or labels, or the names and/or addresses of cells containing numbers or labels, separated by commas or other argument separators.

**Note:** The first item in the list is considered 0, the second is considered 1, and so on. Strings must be enclosed within double quotation marks.

Examples:

@CHOOSE(2,"Sam","Mary","Sally","Joe","Kelly")="Sally"

@CHOOSE(B3, 10,9,8,7,6,5,4,3)=6 if cell B3 contains a formula resulting in the value 4

@CHOOSE(2,MONTHS)="March" if MONTHS is the name of a range of cells containing the months of the year

@CODE(*string*)
Returns the ASCII code number of the first character in *string*. *String* can be a string, the name or address of a cell containing a label, or a formula or @functions the results in a string.

Examples:

@CODE("Branscomb")=66, the ASCII value for B

@CODE(C13)=66 if cell C13 contains the label "Branscomb"

@COLS(*range*)
Returns the number of columns in *range*. *Range* can be the name or address of a range of cells.

You can use @COLS to determine the number of columns in a range in order to perform other tasks based on the size of the range.

Examples:

@COLS(M4..AU19)=35 because the range contains columns M through AU (35 columns)

@COLS(GRADES)=13 if Grades is the name of the range B3..N38

@COUNT(*list*)
Counts the number of nonblank cells in *list*. *List* can be a series of names or addresses of cells and/or ranges of cells, separated by commas or other argument separators.

@COUNT counts every cell in *list* that contains an entry of any kind—including a number, a label, a label prefix, or one of the values ERR or NA. @COUNT does not count blank cells if they occur in a range; however, @COUNT counts blank cells if you specify them individually in *list*.

Examples:

@COUNT(C2..C10)=9 if none of the cells is blank

@COUNT(C2..C10)=7 if both cells C2 and C10 are blank

@COUNT(C2..C10,C11)=1 if cells C2..C10 are blank (because cell C11 is specified individually, it is counted whether it is blank or not)

@CTERM(*interest,future-value,present-value*)
Returns the number of periods required for an investment (*present-value*) to grow to a *future-value*, earning a fixed interest rate. *Interest* can be a number that represents a periodic interest rate or the name or address of a cell containing such a number. The interest rate must be expressed as a decimal fraction (such as 0.1). The period can be monthly, annual, or any other appropriate

period, but the interest rate must be expressed in terms appropriate for the period. *Future-value* and *present-value* can be numbers or the names or addresses of cells that contain numbers. Both arguments must be either positive or negative.

@CTERM calculates according to the following formula:

> ln(*fv/pv*)/ln(1+*int*) where *fv* is the future value, *pv* is the present value, *int* is the interest rate, and *ln* is the natural logarithm.

Examples:

@CTERM(0.10,15000,10000)=4.254163 years, if the annual interest rate is 10%

@CTERM(0.06,10000,5000)=11.89566 years if the annual interest rate is 6%

@CTERM(0.015,1000,500)=46.55552 months if the monthly interest rate is 1.5%

### Using Compound Interest Rates

The examples above show the results of simple interest rates. To calculate the results of compound interest rates, divide both the interest rate and the result of @CTERM by the number of compounding periods within the interest period. The formula is:

> @CTERM(*interest/# compounding periods*),*future-value*, *present-value*)/# *compounding-periods*

Examples:

@CTERM(0.10/12,15000,10000)/12 =4.071522 years (This shows that 4.07 years are required for $10,000 to grow to $15,000 at 10% if interest is compounded monthly.)

@CTERM(0.06/365,10000,5000)/365=11.55340 (This shows that 11.55 years are required for $5,000 to grow to $10,000 at 6% interest if interest is compounded daily.)

@DATE(*year,month,day*)   Returns the the date-number for the specified date. *Year* can be a two-digit or three-digit number between 00 and 199 or the name or address of a cell containing such a number. *Month* can be a two-digit number between 1 and 12 or the name or address of a cell containing such a number. *Day* can be a two-digit number between 1 and 31 or the name or address of a cell containing such a number.

**Note:** To calculate the year value for dates in the 20th century, enter the last 2 digits of the year. Example: 92=1992. To calculate the year value for dates in the 21st century, add 100 to the last 2 digits of the year. Example: 192=2092.

Spreadsheet @Functions **421**

Because @DATE returns a date-number, it can be used in date calculations. Dates entered with @DATE or @DATEVALUE are the only ones that can be used for operations that require chronological calculation of dates.

To have the results of an @DATE calculation appear in date format rather than as a number, format the cell that contains the @DATE function using one of the date formats with the Range Format or Worksheet Global Format menu options.

Examples:

@DATE(92,12,31)=31-DEC-92 in a cell formatted as DD-MMM-YY

@DATE(192,12,31)=31-DEC-2092 in a cell formated as DD-MMM-YY (LotusWorks displays four digits for years in the twenty-first century.)

@DATEVALUE(*string*)  Calculates the number of days since January 1, 1900 for *string*. The result is a date number that can be formatted as a date. *String* can be a text string in date format, a formula that evaluates to a text string in date format, or the address or name of a cell that contains a string in date format. If *string* is not in date format, LotusWorks returns ERR. You must enclose *string* in double quotation marks.

You can use @DATEVALUE to convert text dates to date numbers for arithmetic calculations.

Examples:

@DATEVALUE("18-JAN-65")=23760

@DATEVALUE(BIRTHDATE)=33969 if the cell named *Birthdate* contains "31-DEC-92"

@DAY(*date-number*)  Returns a number between 1 and 31 representing the day of the month in *date-number*. *Date-number* can be a date number, the name or address of a cell that contains a date number, a formula that returns a date number, or an @function that returns a date number.

Examples:

@DAY(@NOW)=today

@DAY(@DATEVALUE("07/04/92"))=4

@IF(@DAY(G7)<=5,"Weekday","Weekend")

This formula states that if the day in cell G7 is Friday or earlier, print Weekday; otherwise, print Weekend.

@DDB(*cost,salvage, life, period*)

Calculates the depreciation allowance of an asset with an initial value of *cost*, an expected useful *life*, and a final *salvage* value for a specified *period* of time, using the double-declining balance method.

*Cost* is the amount paid for the asset and must be a number greater than or equal to *salvage*. *Salvage* is the estimated value of the asset at the end of its useful life. *Life* is the number of periods that the asset takes to depreciate to its salvage value and must be a number greater than *period*. *Period* is the number of the time period for which the depreciation is being calculated.

@DDB uses the following formula to calculate the double-declining balance depreciation for any period:

($bv$*2)/$n$ where $bv$ is the book value in the period being calculated and $n$ is the life of the asset.

**Note:** The function @SLN calculates the straight-line method of depreciation and the function @SYD calculates the sum-of-the-year's-digits method of depreciation.

Examples:

@DDB(5000,500,4,3)=$625 This calculates the double-declining balance depreciation for the third year of an asset that cost $5,000 and has a salvage value after four years of $500.

@DDB($B$2,$B$4,$B$3,D4)=$625 if $B$2 contains the cost of $5000, cell $B$4 contains the salvage value of $500, cell $B$3 contains the useful life of 4 years, and cell D4 contains the period 3

@ERR

Returns the value ERR to indicate an error. @ERR does not take an argument.

You can use @ERR with the @IF function to identify error conditions. All cells that depend on a cell containing ERR also display ERR.

Examples:

@IF(COST>0,@ERR,COST)=ERR if a negative number is entered in the cell named *Cost*

@IF(C5<1 OR C5>12,@ERR,C5)=ERR if a number less than 1 or greater than 12 is entered into cell C5.

@EXACT(*string1,string2*)

Compares *string1* to *string2* and returns true (1) if the strings match exactly and false (0) if they do not. *String1* and *string2* can be text strings, formulas that return text strings, or the names or addresses of cells that contain labels or string formulas. You must enclose the text strings within double quotation marks.

@EXACT is more precise than the equal operator (=) in formulas because unlike =, @EXACT distinguishes between uppercase and lowercase letters and between letters with and without accent marks.

Examples:

@EXACT(LASTNAME,"de los Angeles")=1 (true) if the cell named *Lastname* contains the text string "de los Angeles"

@EXACT(BIRTHDATE,"01/01/65")=0 (false) if the cell named *Birthdate* does not contain the text string "01/01/65"

@EXP(*x*)     Returns the value of the constant *e* (approximately 2.718282) raised to the power of *x* (the natural logarithm of *x*. *X* can be a number less than or equal to 709, a formula that evaluates to such a number, or the name or address of a cell that contains a such number or formula. (If a number larger than 709 is used for *x*, the result is too large for LotusWorks to store. If *x* is larger than 230, LotusWorks can calculate and store but cannot display the resulting number in E notation. If *x* is less than −709, EXP returns 0.)

Examples:

@EXP(1)=2.718282

@EXP(C10)=0.286505 if cell C10 contains the value −1.25 or a formula that evaluates to −1.25

**Note:** @LN is the inverse of @EXP.

@FALSE     Returns the logical value 0. @FALSE does not take an argument.

Using @FALSE in formulas that evaluate logical conditions is the same as using the value 0, but @FALSE makes the formula easier to understand.

Examples:

@IF(C10=>21,@TRUE,@FALSE)=0 if the value in cell C10 is less than 21

@IF(B3>49999,@TRUE,@FALSE)=0 if the value in cell B3 is 49999 or less

@FIND(*search-string,string,start-number*)

Calculates the position in *string* at which LotusWorks finds the first occurrence of *search-string*, starting with the character indicated by *start-number*. *Search-string* and *string* are text strings, formulas that return text strings, or the names or addresses of cells that contain labels or string formulas. *Start-number* is a positive integer or zero.

**Note:** The comparison is case-sensitive. LotusWorks counts the first character as 0, the second character is 1, and so on.

If LotusWorks does not find *search-string* in *string*, @FIND returns ERR. @FIND also returns ERR if *start-number* is greater than the number of characters in *string*, or if *start-number* is negative.

You can use @FIND to determine the position of a particular character or set of characters within a text string.

Examples:

@FIND("s","ABC Business Services",0)=6

@FIND("v","COMPANY,0)=16 if the cell named COMPANY contains "ABC Business Services"

@FV(*payments,interest,term*)

Calculates the future value of an investment, based on a series of equal *payments*, earning a periodic *interest* rate, over the number of payment periods in *term*. *Payments*, *interest*, and *term* can be numbers or the names or addresses of cells that contain numbers.

**Note:** *Interest* must be expressed as a decimal fraction in the same units as *term*. If *term* is expressed in years, the interest rate must be an annual rate. If *term* is expressed in months, the interest rate must be a monthly rate. To change an annual interest rate to a monthly interest rate, divide the rate by 12.

You can use @FV to determine if an investment will produce the results you want at the end of *term*.

@FV uses the following formula to calculate future value:

$pmt*\{(1+int)^n-1\}/int$ where pmt is the periodic payment, *int* is the periodic interest rate, and *n* is the number of periods

Examples:

@FV(1000,0.065,15)=24182.16 This formula calculates the future value of 15 annual payments of $1,000 each, at an annual interest rate of 6.5%.

@FV(500,0.1/12,12)=6282.78 This formula calculates the future value at the end of 12 monthly payments of $500 each, at an annual interest rate of 10% (0.1/12).

@FV(250,0.109/12,48)=14957.83 This formula calculates the future value at the end of 48 payments of $250 each, at an annual interest rate of 10.9% (0.109/12).

@HLOOKUP(*x,range,row-offset*)

Returns the contents of a cell located in a specified row and column of a horizontal lookup table.

A horizontal lookup table is a table in which the cells in the top row contain numbers in ascending order from left to right. @HLOOKUP compares the value *x* to the contents of each cell in the top row of the table specified by range, starting at the leftmost cell and moving to the right. When it finds the cell that contains *x* or the number closest to but not exceeding *x*, it moves down that column the number of rows specified by *row-offset* and returns the contents of the cell at that location.

*X* can be an integer or the name or address of a cell that contains an integer. *Range* can be the name or address of the range that contains the horizontal lookup table. *Row-offset* can be an integer or the name or address of a cell containing an integer between 0 and 8191.

You can use @HLOOKUP to find values when a table is organized with a key variable arranged in ascending order in the top row.

**Note:** For tables organized with a key variable arranged in ascending order in the leftmost column, use the @VLOOKUP function. For tables in which you know the column and row in which a lookup value is located, use the @INDEX function.

Example:

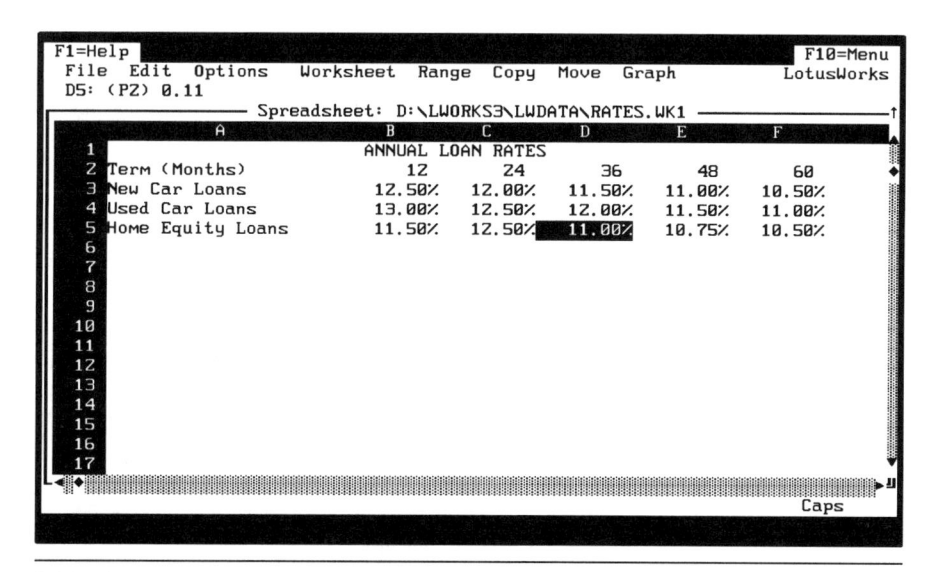

```
F1=Help                                                          F10=Menu
 File   Edit    Options    Worksheet   Range   Copy   Move   Graph        LotusWorks
 D5: (P2) 0.11
 ─────────────── Spreadsheet: D:\LWORKS3\LWDATA\RATES.WK1 ───────────────
          A              B         C         D         E         F
   1                  ANNUAL LOAN RATES
   2  Term (Months)       12        24        36        48        60
   3  New Car Loans    12.50%    12.00%    11.50%    11.00%    10.50%
   4  Used Car Loans   13.00%    12.50%    12.00%    11.50%    11.00%
   5  Home Equity Loans 11.50%   12.50%    11.00%    10.75%    10.50%
   6
   7
   8
   9
  10
  11
  12
  13
  14
  15
  16
  17
                                                                    Caps
```

**FIGURE C.1:** A horizontal lookup table.

**@HLOOKUP(36,B2..F5,3)=11%** This formula tells LotusWorks to search the top row for the value 36, then move down three rows and return the value in the cell at that location (11%).

**@HOUR(*time-number*)**

Returns the hour from *time-number*. The hour will be a number from 0 (midnight) to 23 (11:00 P.M.) inclusive. *Time-number* can be a time number or the name or address of a cell containing a time number.

You can use @HOUR to extract the hour portion of time numbers created with the @NOW, @TIME, and @TIMEVALUE functions for use in time calculations that involve whole hours, such as hourly wages or time stamps on spreadsheets.

Examples:

@HOUR(@NOW)=11 if the current time is 11:15:00.

@HOUR(@TIMEVALUE("13:35"))=13

**@IF(*condition, x,y*)**

Evaluates *condition* and returns *x* if *condition* is true, *y* if *condition* is false. *Condition* can be a logical formula or the name or address of a cell containing a logical formula. *X* and *y* can be character, date, or numeric values, the names or addresses of cells that contain such values, or formulas that result in such values. However, *x* and *y* must be the same type of data.

**Note:** You can nest @IF functions within @IF functions to create more complex conditions.

Examples:

@IF(QUANTITY>=25,.1,0)

This statement calculates a value for a discount: if the value in the cell named *Quantity* is 25 or more, the discount is 10% (.1); if the value in *Quantity* is less than 25, the discount is 0.

@IF(PERFORMANCE>=90,SALARY+BONUS,SALARY)

This statement says, "If an employee's performance is 90 or more, give the employee his or her salary plus bonus; otherwise, give only the salary."

@IF(SALES>=1000000,10000,@IF(SALES>=500000,5000, @IF(SALES>10000,1000,0)))

This statement uses nested @IF functions to calculate a sales bonus. It says, "If SALES are $1,000,000 or more, the bonus is $10,000; if SALES are $500,000 but less than $1,000,000, the bonus is $5,000; if SALES are $100,000 but less than $500,000, the bonus is $1,000; otherwise, the bonus is 0."

@IF(BALANCE>=0,BALANCE,"OVERDRAWN")

This statement says, "If the value in the cell named *Balance* is 0 or more, print the value; if the value in *Balance* is less than 0, print the word 'OVERDRAWN'."

@INDEX(*range,column,row*)

Returns the contents of the cell in *range*, located at the intersection of *column* and *row*. *Range* is a table, *column* is the offset number of the desired column, and *row* is the offset number of the desired row.

*Range* can be the name or address of the range that contains the table. *Column* and *row* can be integers or the names or addresses of cells that contain integers. If either *column* or *row* is outside of range, LotusWorks returns ERR.

**Note:** LotusWorks counts the top row of the table as row 0, the next row as row 1, and so on. It counts the leftmost column as column 0, the next column as column 1, and so on.

Use @INDEX to look up values when you know the number of rows and/or columns where the desired data value is located, as in a table of data organized by months or years.

**Note:** You can use @HLOOKUP to return values from a horizontal lookup table and @VLOOKUP to return values from a vertical lookup table. See these @functions for definitions of horizontal and vertical lookup tables.

Example:

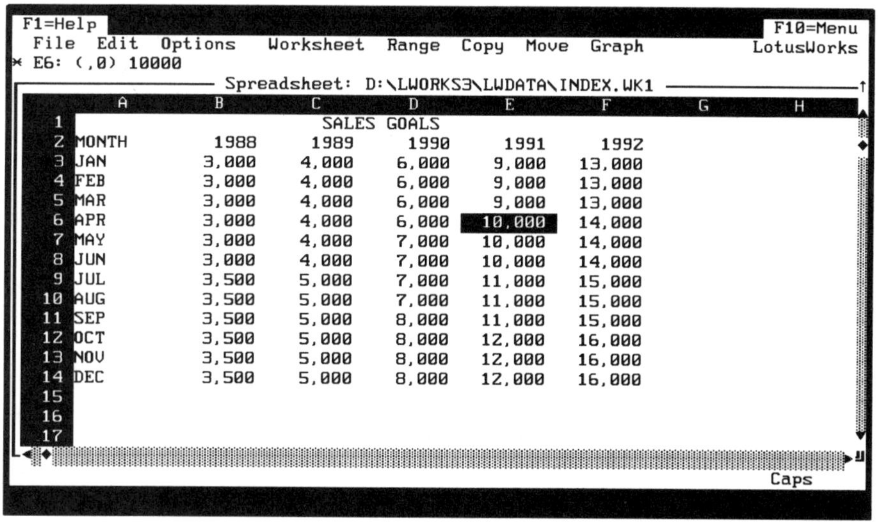

**FIGURE C.2:** An @INDEX lookup table

@INDEX(B2..F14,3,4)=10000 This formula tells LotusWorks to start at cell B2, move three columns to the right, then move down four rows and return the value in the cell at that location (10000).

@INT(*x*)

Returns the integer part of *x*, without rounding. *X* can be a number or the name or address of a cell containing a number.

Examples:

@INT(3.3333)=3

@INT(LOANAMT/36)=972 if LOANAMT is a cell containing the value 35000

@IRR(*guess,range*)

Calculates the internal rate of return (profit) for a series of cash flows generated by an investment. *Guess* represents your estimate of the internal rate of return and can be a decimal percentage or the name or address of a cell containing a decimal percentage. The internal rate of return equates the present value of an expected future series of cash flows to the initial investment. In most cases, *guess* should be a percentage between 0 and 1 (100%).

*Range* is the name or address of a single-row or single-column range of cells that contain the cash flows. LotusWorks considers negative numbers as cash outflows and positive numbers as cash inflows. Normally, the first cash-flow amount in the range represents the investment. @IRR ignores empty cells and cells that contain labels.

**Note:** LotusWorks assumes that the cash flows are received at regular, equal intervals of time.

@IRR uses a series of approximations, starting with *guess*, to calculate the internal rate of return. If @IRR can't approximate the result to within 0.0000001 after 30 iterations, it returns ERR.

**Tip:** If @IRR continues to return ERR, use @NPV to determine a better number for *guess*.

Examples:

@IRR(0.12,B3..B15)=10.45% if the range B3..B15 contains a series of cash flows whose internal rate of return is 10.45%

@IRR(0.20,PROFIT)=18.5% if *Profit* is a range containing a series of cash flows whose internal rate of return is 18.5%.

@ISERR(*x*)

Tests *x* for the value ERR and returns 1 (true) if *x* is ERR and 0 (false) if *x* is not ERR. *X* can be any value, location, text string, or condition.

The value ERR in a cell causes all formulas that refer to that cell to evaluate to ERR. You can use @ISERR with @IF in formulas to stop this effect. You can also use it to guard against errors caused by dividing by a cell whose value is zero.

Examples:

@IF(@ISERR(B10),0,B10) This formula returns 0 if the value in cell B10 is ERR; otherwise, it returns the value in B10.

@IF(@ISERR(C14/C15),0,C14/C15) This formula returns 0 if the result of C14/C15 is ERR; otherwise, it returns the result of C14/C15.

@ISNA(x)  Tests $x$ for the value NA and returns 1 (true) if $x$ is NA and 0 (false) if $x$ is not NA. $X$ can be any value, location, text string, or condition.

The value NA in a cell causes all formulas that refer to that cell to evaluate to NA. You can use @ISNA with @IF in formulas to stop this effect.

Examples:

@IF(@ISNA(B10),0,B10) This formula returns 0 if the value in cell B10 is NA; otherwise, it returns the value in B10.

@IF(@ISNA(C14/C15),0,C14/C15) This formula returns 0 if the result of C14/C15 is NA; otherwise, it returns the result of C14/C15.

@ISNUMBER(x)  Tests $x$ for the type of data and returns 1 (true) if $x$ is a number, NA, ERR, or blank; returns 0 (false) if $x$ is a text string or range. $X$ can be any value, location, text string, or condition.

You can use @ISNUMBER to print error messages for cells intended to hold numbers.

Examples:

@IF(@ISNUMBER(D7),"","ERROR—Entry must be a number") This formula returns a blank cell if a number is entered into cell D7 and returns the message "ERROR—Entry must be a number" if a label is entered.

@IF(@ISNUMBER(G21),"NUMBER","LABEL") This formula prints "NUMBER" if cell G21 contains a number and "LABEL" if it contains a label.

@ISSTRING(x)  Tests $x$ for the type of data and returns 1 (true) if $x$ is a text string or a label; returns 0 (false) if $x$ is a number, NA, ERR, or blank. $X$ can be any value, location, text string, or condition.

You can use @ISSTRING to print error messages for cells intended to hold labels.

Examples:

@IF(@ISSTRING(D7),"","ERROR—Entry must be a label") This formula returns a blank cell if a label is entered into cell D7 and returns the message "ERROR—Entry must be a label" if a number is entered.

@IF(@ISSTRING(G21),"LABEL","NUMBER") This formula prints "LABEL" if cell G21 contains a label and "NUMBER" if it contains a number.

@LEFT(*string,x*)    Returns the first *x* characters in *string*. *String* can be a text string, a string formula, or the name or address of cell containing a label or string formula. *X* can be a positive integer or the name or address of a cell that contains a positive integer. If *x* is 0, LotusWorks returns an empty string. If *x* is larger than the length of *string*, LotusWorks returns the entire string. LotusWorks counts each punctuation mark and blank space as a character.

Examples:

@LEFT("Los Angeles",7)="Los Ang"

@LEFT(COMPANY,8) returns the first eight characters in the cell named *Company*

@LENGTH(*string*)    Returns the number of characters in *string*. *String* can be a text string, a string formula, or the name or address of a cell containing a label or string formula. LotusWorks counts punctuation marks and blank spaces within the string as part of the string.

You can use @LENGTH with @TRIM to find the length of a text string without any leading, trailing, or consecutive blank spaces.

Examples:

@LENGTH("")=0

@LENGTH("de los Angeles")=14

@LENGTH(@TRIM(LASTNAME))=25 if the cell named LASTNAME contains a text entry 25 characters long exclusive of trailing blank spaces

@LN(*x*)    Calculates the natural logarithm (base e) of *x*. (A natural logarithm uses the number e, which is approximately 2.718282, as the base.) *X* can be a number greater than 0, the name or address of a cell that contains such a number, or a formula that returns such a number.

Examples:

@LN(5)=1.609437

@LN(C7)=1.609437 if cell C7 contains the number 5.

@LOG(*x*)   Calculates the common logarithm (base 10) of *x*. *X* can be a number greater than 0, the name or address of a cell that contains such a number, or a formula that returns such a number.

@LOG(5)=0.698970

@LOG(C7)=0.698970 if cell C7 contains the number 5.

@LOWER(*string*)   Converts the uppercase letters in *string* to lowercase. *String* can be a text string, a string formula, or the name or address of a cell that contains a label or string formula.

Examples:

@LOWER("LotusWorks")=lotusworks

@LOWER(LASTNAME)=washington, if the cell named *Lastname* contains "Washington"

@MAX(*list*)   Returns the largest number in *list*. *List* can be a series of numbers or the names or addresses of cells that contain numbers, separated by commas or other argument separators.

**Note:** @MAX treats blank cells and labels as 0.

Example:

@MAX(25,30,35,40,45,37,16)=45

@MAX(B3..G3)=45 if the largest value in the range B3..G3 is 45

@MID(*string,start-position,x*)

Returns a text string *x* characters long from within *string*, starting at *start-position*. *String* can be a text string, the name or address of a cell that contains a label, or a formula or @function that evaluates to a text string. *X* can be a positive integer or 0. If *x* is 0, @MID returns an empty string. *Start-position* can be a positive integer or the name or address of a cell containing such an integer. If *start-position* is greater than the length of *string* minus 1, @MID returns an empty string.

**Note:** @MID counts punctuation marks and blank spaces as characters. @MID counts the first character as 0, the second character as 1, and so on.

You can use @MID when you need to extract a part of a label that is not located at the beginning or end of the label. If you need to extract a part of a label but don't know its start position, use @MID with @FIND.

Examples:

@MID("ABC Service Company",4,7)=Service

@MID(TITLE,@FIND("S",TITLE,1),7)=Service if *Title* is the name of a cell containing the label ABC Service Company.

This formula tells @MID to find the first S in TITLE and use it as the start-position for the @MID function.

@MIN(*list*)    Returns the smallest number in *list*. *List* can be a series of numbers or the names or addresses of cells that contain numbers, separated by commas or other argument separators.

**Note:** @MIN treats blank cells and labels as 0.

Example:

@MIN(25,30,35,40,45,37,16)=25

@MIN(B3..G3)=25 if the smallest value in the range B3..G3 is 25

@MINUTE(*time-number*)    Returns the number of minutes from *time-number*. *Time-number* can be a number in time format or the name or address of a cell containing such a number.

You can use @MINUTE to extract the minutes portion of time numbers created with @NOW, @TIME, or @TIMEVALUE for use in calculations such as elapsed time.

**Tip:** You can use the @TIME function to return the time number for a time that you specify.

Examples:

@MINUTE(@NOW)=29 if the current time is 9:29:00 A.M. or 29 minutes past any other hour

@MINUTE(@TIME(13,29,30))=29

@MOD(*x,y*)    Calculates the remainder (modulus) of $x/y$. $X$ and $y$ can be numbers or the names or addresses of cells containing numbers or formulas that return numbers.

**Note:** The sign of the dividend ($x$) determines the sign of the result. If $x$ is 0, @MOD returns 0 (that is, zero divided by any number is zero). If $y$ is 0, @MOD returns ERR (that is, ERROR, because a number cannot be divided by 0).

Examples:

@MOD(17,3)=2

@MOD(–17,3)=–2

@MOD(17,0)=ERR

## Spreadsheet @Functions 433

@MONTH(*date-number*)  Returns the number of the month (1 to 12) in *date-number*. *Date-number* can be a date number or the name or address of a cell that contains a date number or a formula that evaluates to a date number.

You can use the @MONTH function to supply the month argument to other date or time functions.

**Tip:** You can use @DATEVALUE to supply the date number for a date that you specify in text form.

@MONTH(@NOW)=the number of the current month

@MONTH(@DATEVALUE("07/04/92"))=7

@IF(@MONTH(BIRTHDATE)<=6,First,Second)

This formula states that if the month in the *Birthdate* cell is June or earlier, print First; otherwise, print Second.

@N(*range*)  Returns the entry in the first cell of *range* as a number. If the cell contains a label, @N returns 0. *Range* is the name or address of a range of cells.

Examples:

@N(C3..J3)=135 if cell C3 contains the number 135

@N(B3)+@N(C3)=135 if cell B3 contains a label and cell C3 contains the number 135

@NA  Returns the value NA (not available). @NA does not take an argument.

NA is a special value that indicates a number which is needed to complete a formula is not available. Any formula that refers to a cell that contains NA results in NA, unless the cell contains @ERR.

You can use @NA to flag cells where data is to be entered; formulas that refer to those cells result in the value NA until the correct data is entered.

Examples:

+C3+5=NA if cell C3 contains @NA

IF(C3<10,@NA,C3)=NA if the number in cell C3 is less than 10; otherwise it equals the number in cell C3

@NOW  Returns a number for the current date and time composed of a date number (the integer portion) and a time number (the decimal portion). The date number and time number can be used in calculations. @NOW does not take an argument.

When @NOW is used as the argument for a date function (@DATE, @MONTH, @DAY, or @YEAR), the decimal portion of @NOW is ignored. When @NOW is used as the argument for a time function (@HOUR, @MINUTE, or @SECOND), the integer part of @NOW is ignored.

LotusWorks recalculates @NOW each time you recalculate the spreadsheet. If Worksheet, Global Recalculation is set to Automatic, LotusWorks recalculates @NOW whenever it recalculates another number.

@NOW=33603.93 if it is 10:30 P.M. on December 31, 1991

@MONTH(@NOW)=12 if the current date is in the month of December

@HOUR(@NOW)=15 if the current time is between 3:00 and 3:59 P.M.

@NPV(*interest,range*)  Calculates the net present value of a series of future cash flows (*range*), discounted at a fixed periodic *interest* rate. @NPV calculates the initial investment necessary to achieve a specified cash outflow at a specified interest rate. *Interest* is a percentage expressed as a decimal fraction or the name or address of a cell containing such a decimal fraction. *Range* is a single-row or single-column range of cells that contain numbers.

@NPV assumes that the cash outflows occur at equal time intervals, that the first cash outflow occurs at the end of the first period, and that subsequent cash flows occur at the end of subsequent periods.

You can use @NPV to evaluate an investment or compare one investment with others.

Examples:

@NPV(0.1,B2..M2)=10220.53

This formula calculates the initial investment necessary (net present value) to yield 12 payments of $1,500 each (recorded in cells B2..M2) earning 10% interest.

@NPV(C2,C3..C8)=10425.73

This formula calculates the net present value necessary to yield 6 payments of $2,500 each, earning 11.5% interest, where the payments are recorded in cells C3..C8 and the interest rate (11.5%) is recorded in cell C2.

@PI                     Returns the number Pi (3.14159265636), which is the ratio of the circumference of a circle to its diameter. @PI does not take an argument.

Example:

@PI=3.1415926536

@PMT(*principal,interest,term*)

Calculates the payment on a loan at a specified interest rate for a specified number of payment periods. *Principal* is the amount loaned. *Interest* is the periodic interest rate, expressed as a decimal percentage. *Term* is the number of payment periods and must be a positive integer greater than 0. *Principal*, *interest*, and *term* can be numbers, formulas that return numbers, or the names or addresses of cells containing numbers or formulas that evaluate to numbers.

**Note:** *Interest* must be expressed in units that are appropriate for *term*. If the payment periods are years, the interest rate must be an annual rate. If the payment periods are months, the interest rate must be a monthly rate. To convert an annual rate to a monthly rate, divide it by 12.

@PMT assumes that payments occur at the end of each payment period (an ordinary annuity). To calculate the amount for periodic payments made at the beginning of each period (an annuity due), use this formula:

@PMT(*principal,interest,term*)/1+*interest*

You can use @PMT to determine the monthly payment required for a specified loan amount. To determine the converse, how large a loan you can take out for a specified monthly payment, use @PV.

Examples:

@PMT(10000,0.115,4)=3257.74 This formula calculates the annual payments for a $10,000 loan at 11.5% annual interest for four years.

@PMT(10000,0.115/12,48)=260.89 This formula calculates the monthly payments for a $10,000 loan at 11.5% annual interest for 48 months, if payments are made at the end of each month.

@PMT(10000,0.115/12,48)/(1+(0.115/12))=258.41 This formula calculates the monthly payments for an annuity-due loan (payments made at the beginning of each month) of $10,000 at 11.5% annual interest for 48 months.

@PROPER(*string*) — Converts the first letter of each word in *string* to uppercase and all other letters to lowercase. *String* can be a text string, a formula that returns a string, or the name or address of a cell that contains a label or string formula.

**Note:** If *string* is a blank cell, @PROPER returns ERR.

Examples:

@PROPER(B10)="Siegel" if cell B10 contains "SIEGEL"

@PROPER(ADDRESS)="110 Park Street, Apt. 3" if the cell named *Address* contains 110 PARK STREETt, APT. 3.

@PV(*payments,interest,term*) — Calculates the present value of an investment, based on a series of equal *payments* discounted at a periodic *interest* rate over the number of periods in *term*. *Payments* is the amount of each periodic payment. *Interest* is the periodic interest rate, expressed as a decimal percentage. *Term* is the number of payment periods and must be a positive integer greater than 0. *Payments*, *interest*, and *term* can be numbers, formulas that return numbers, or the names or addresses of cells containing numbers or formulas that evaluate to numbers.

**Note:** *Interest* must be expressed in units that are appropriate for *term*. If the payment periods are years, the interest rate must be an annual rate. If the payment periods are months, the interest rate must be a monthly rate. To convert an annual rate to a monthly rate, divide it by 12.

@PV assumes that payments occur at the end of each payment period (an ordinary annuity). To calculate the amount for periodic payments made at the beginning of each period (an annuity due), use this formula:

@PV(*payments,interest,term*)/1+interest

You can use @PV to determine how large a loan you can take out for a specified monthly payment. To determine the converse, the monthly payment required for a specified loan amount, use @PMT.

Examples:

@PV(250,0.115/12,48)=9582.58 This formula calculates the amount that can be financed (present value) at 11.5% annual interest with a monthly payment of $250 for 48 months, paid at the end of each month.

@PV(250,0.115/12,48)/(1+(0.115/12))=9491.62 This formula calculates the amount that can be financed (present value) at 11.5% annual interest with a monthly payment of $250 for 48 months, paid at the beginning of each month.

| | |
|---|---|
| @RAND | Generates a random number between 0 and 1. RAND does not take an argument.

**Note:** The sequence of random numbers is the same for each open spreadsheet. Each time you recalculate the spreadsheet, RAND generates a new random number.

To generate random numbers in different intervals, multiply @RAND by the size of the desired interval. You can then use the @ROUND and @INT functions with @RAND to create random whole numbers.

Examples:

@RAND=0.123456, or any number between 0 and 1

@INT(@RAND*100)+1=13, or any random whole number between 0 and 100 |
| @RATE(*future-value,present-value,term*) | Returns the periodic interest rate necessary for an investment (*present-value*) to grow to a *future-value* over the number of compounding periods in *term*. *Future-value*, *present-value*, and *term* can be numbers or the names or addresses of cells that contain numbers.

You can use @RATE to determine the compound rate of return of an investment (such as a stock) when you know the initial value, the final value, and the elapsed time between the two.

Examples:

@RATE(65,58.75,9)=0.011296 This formula produces the compound monthly interest rate earned on a stock purchased for $58.75 and sold nine months later for $65.

@RATE(C3,B3,D3)=0.011714 if cell C3 contains 11500, cell B3 contains 10000, and cell D3 contains 12. |
| @REPEAT(*string,x*) | Duplicates *string x* times. *String* can be a text string, a string formula, or the name or address of a cell that contains a text string or string formula. *X* can be a positive integer, a formula that evaluates to a positive integer, or the name or address of a cell that contains a positive integer or formula that evaluates to a positive integer.

You can use @REPEAT to repeat any printable character, including mathematical, graphics, and foreign language symbols.

**Note:** @REPEAT duplicates the string as many times as you specify; it is not limited by the current column width. This differs from the repeating label prefix character \ (backslash), which repeats a label only until the current column is filled. |

Examples:

@REPEAT("*",15)=***************

@REPEAT("SALE",6)=SALE SALE SALE SALE SALE SALE

@REPLACE(*original-string,start-number,x,new-string*)
Replaces *x* characters in *original-string* with *new-string*, beginning at *start-number*. *Original-string* and *new-string* each can be a text string, string formula, or the name or address of a cell that contains a label or string formula. *Start-number* and *x* each can be any positive integer, a formula that returns a positive integer, or the name or address of a cell that contains a positive integer or formula that returns a positive integer.

@REPLACE counts punctuation marks and blank spaces as characters.

**Note:** If *x* is 0, @REPLACE appends *new-string* to the end of *original string.*

Examples:

@REPLACE("213",0,3,"310") This formula replaces Area code "213" with "310"

@REPLACE(D10,@FIND("s",D10,0),1,"S") This formula replaces the first "s" in cell D10 with "S".

@RIGHT(*string,x*)
Returns the last *x* characters in string. *String* can be a text string, a string formula, or the name or address of a cell that contains a text string or string formula. *X* can be a number, a formula that returns a number, or the name or address of a cell that contains a number or a formula that returns a number. If *x* is 0, @RIGHT returns an empty string. If *x* is larger than the length of string, @RIGHT returns the entire string. LotusWorks counts each punctuation mark and blank space as a character.

@RIGHT counts punctuation marks and blank spaces as characters.

Examples:

@RIGHT("Los Angeles",7)="Angeles"

@RIGHT(@TRIM(B4,5))="Smith" if cell B4 contains "Gomez-Smith"

@ROUND(*x,y*)
Rounds the number *x* to y places. *X* can be a number, a formula that returns a number, or the name or address of a cell that contains a number or formula that returns a number. *Y* can be a number from –100 to 100, a formula that returns such a number, or the name or address of a cell that contains such a number or a formula that returns such a number.

If *y* is positive, LotusWorks rounds to the number of decimal places indicated by *y*. If *y* is negative, LotusWorks discards any decimal portion, moves y places to the left and rounds to the nearest number. For instance, –2 rounds to the nearest hundred, -3 rounds to the nearest thousand, –4 rounds to the nearest ten thousand, and so on.

If *y* is 0, LotusWorks rounds to the nearest integer.

You can use @ROUND in situations where calculating with rounded numbers is appropriate. If you wish to calculate with full precision, however, do not use @ROUND. Use Range Format or Worksheet Global Format and select FIXED to display numbers with a specified number of decimal places.

Examples:

@ROUND(1234.56789,2)=1234.57 Suppose cell C4 contains the number 1234.56789. @ROUND produces the following results in the formulas indicated:

@ROUND(C4,2)=1234.57

@ROUND(C4,0)=1235

@ROUND(C4,–2)=1200

@ROWS(*range*)  Returns the number of rows in *range*. *Range* can be the name or address of a range of cells.

Examples:

@ROWS(B3..G12)=10 (the number of rows from 3 to 12)

@ROWS(TABLE)=36 if TABLE is the name of a range containing 36 rows.

@S(*range*)  Returns the entry in the first cell in *range* as a label, if the cell contains a label, and returns an empty string if the cell is blank or contains a number. *Range* can be the name or address of a cell or a range of cells.

Examples:

@S(B1..B7)=SALES if the entry in cell B1 is SALES

@S(B1..B7)=an empty string if cell B1 is blank or contains a number

@SECOND(*time-number*)  Returns the number of seconds in *time-number*. *Time-number* can be a time number, a formula that returns a time number, or the name or address of a cell that contains a time number or formula that returns a time number.

Examples:

@SECOND(F3)=18 if cell F3 contains a time number with 18 seconds

@SECOND(F3+F4)=31 if cells F3 and F4 contain time numbers with seconds that add to 31

@SIN(*x*)  Calculates the sine of angle *x*. *X* is an angle measured in radians and can be expressed as a value, a formula that returns a value, or the name or address of a cell that contains a value or formula that returns a value.

You must express the angle *x* in radians. To convert degrees to radians, multiply degrees by @PI/180.

**Note:** You can use the following formula to calculate the cosecant, or reciprocal of @SIN:

1/@SIN(*x*)

Examples:

@SIN(1.5)=0.997494

@SIN(60*@PI/180)=0.866025

This formula calculates the sine of a 60-degree angle.

@SLN(*cost,salvage,life*)  Calculates the straight-line depreciation allowance of an asset with an initial value of *cost*, an expected useful *life*, and a final value of *salvage*, for one period. *Cost* is the amount paid for the asset and must be greater than or equal to *salvage*. *Salvage* is the estimated value of the asset at the end of its life. *Life* is the number of periods that the asset takes to depreciate to its salvage value. *Cost*, *salvage*, and *life* can be numbers or the names or addresses of cells that contain numbers.

Straight-line depreciation divides the depreciable cost of an asset (the initial value minus the salvage value) equally into each period of the asset's useful life.

You can use @SLN to calculate depreciation when the situation does not require calculating accelerated depreciation. @DDB calculates depreciation by the double-declining balance method, and @SYD calculates it by the sum-of-the-year's-digits method.

Examples:

@SLN(5000,500,5)=900

@SLN(C2,C3,C4)=1285.714 if cell C2 contains an original cost of $10,000, cell C4 contains a useful life of 7 years, and cell C3 contains a salvage value of $1,000

@SQRT(*x*)   Returns the square root of *x*. *X* can be a non-negative number, a formula that returns such a number, or the name or address of a cell containing such a number or a formula that returns such a number.

**Note:** If *x* is a negative number, @SQRT returns ERR.

Examples:

@SQRT(25)=5

@SQRT(–25)=ERR

@STD(*list*)   Calculates the population standard deviation of the numbers in *list*. *List* can be a series of numbers, formulas that return numbers, or names or addresses of cells that contain numbers or formulas that return numbers, separated by commas or other argument separators.

The standard deviation indicates the extent to which the individual numbers in a list vary from the mean of all numbers in the list. A standard deviation of 0 indicates that all number in the list are equal. The standard deviation is the square root of the variance (@VAR).

Examples:

@STD(11,13,33,25,41,22)=3.75

@STD(B2..B7)=3.75 if range B2..B7 contains the numbers 11, 13, 33, 25, 41, 22

@STRING(*x,n*)   Converts the number *x* to a label with *n* decimal places. *X* can be a number, a formula that returns a number, or the name or address of a cell that contains a number or formula that returns a number. *N* can be a positive integer from 0 to 15, a formula that returns such an integer, or the name or address of a cell that contains such an integer or a formula that returns such an integer.

Examples:

@STRING(1234,2)=the string 1234.00

@STRING(E4,3)=the string 1234.000 if cell E4 contains 1234

@SUM(*list*)   Sums the numbers in *list*. *List* can be a series of numbers, formulas that return numbers, or names or addresses of cells that contain numbers or formulas that return numbers, separated by commas or other argument separators.

You can use @SUM to sum the contents of cells in a range without having to reference every single cell in a formula.

Examples:

@SUM(100,150,200,250,300)=1000

@SUM(B2..F2)=1000 if range B2..F2 contains the numbers 100, 150, 200, 250, 300

@SYD(*cost,salvage,life,period*)

Calculates the sum-of-the-year's-digits depreciation allowance of an asset with an initial value of *cost*, an expected useful *life*, and a final value of *salvage*, for one period. *Cost* is the amount paid for the asset and must be greater than or equal to *salvage*. *Salvage* is the estimated value of the asset at the end of its life. *Life* is the number of periods that the asset takes to depreciate to its salvage value. *Period* is the particular time interval for which you wish to find the depreciation. *Cost*, *salvage*, *life*, and *period* can be numbers or the names or addresses of cells that contain numbers.

Sum-of-the-year's-digits depreciation accelerates the rate of depreciation so that more depreciation expense occurs in earlier periods than in later ones (but not so much as with @DDB).

You can use @SYD to calculate depreciation when the situation requires accelerated depreciation, such as computing a tax return. @DDB calculates depreciation by the double-declining balance method, and @SNL calculates it by the straight-line method.

Examples:

@SYD(5000,500,5,2)=1200

This formula calculates the depreciation allowance for the second year of an asset's 5-year-useful life if the initial cost was $5,000 and the salvage value is $500

@SYD(C2,C3,C4,C5)=964.2857 if cell C2 contains an original cost of $10,000, cell C3 contains a salvage value of $1,000, cell C4 contains a useful life of 7 years, and cell C5 contains 5 (indicating the 5th year).

@TAN(*x*)

Calculates the tangent of angle *x*. *X* is an angle measured in radians and can be expressed as a value, a formula that returns a value, or the name or address of a cell that contains a value or formula that returns a value.

You must express the angle *x* in radians. To convert degrees to radians, multiply degrees by @PI/180.

**Note:** You can use the following formula to calculate the cotangent, or reciprocal of @TAN:

1/@TAN(x)

Examples:

@TAN(1.5)=14.10141

@TAN(60*@PI/180)=1.732050

This formula calculates the tangent of a 60-degree angle.

@TERM(*payments,interest,future-value*)

Calculates the number of specified equal *payments* required for an investment to accumulate a specified *future-value* at a specified periodic *interest* rate. *Payments* is the amount you specify for each equal investment. *Interest* is the periodic interest rate, expressed as a decimal fraction. *Future-value* is the amount that you want to accumulate.

*Payments*, *interest*, and *future-value* can be numbers, formulas that return numbers, or the names or addresses of cells containing numbers or formulas that evaluate to numbers.

**Note:** *Interest* must be expressed in units that are appropriate for *term*. If the payment periods are to be years, the interest rate must be an annual rate. If the payment periods are to be months, the interest rate must be a monthly rate. To convert an annual rate to a monthly rate, divide it by 12.

@TERM assumes that payments occur at the end of each payment period (an ordinary annuity). To calculate the term for periodic payments made at the beginning of each period (an annuity due), use this formula:

@TERM(*payments,interest,future-value*)/1+*interest*.

You can use @TERM to determine the number of equal deposits or payments required to attain a specific amount at a specified interest rate.

Examples:

@TERM(250,0.115/12,10000)=34.02244

This formula calculates the number of payments required to produce a future value of $10,000 at 11.5% annual interest with a monthly payment of $250 paid at the end of each month.

@TERM(250,0.115/12,10000)/(1+(0.115/12))=33.69949

This formula calculates the number of payments required to produce a future value of $10,000 at 11.5% annual interest with a monthly payment of $250 paid at the beginning of each month.

@TIME(*hour,minutes,seconds*)

Calculates the time number for the specified *hour*, *minutes*, and *seconds*. *Hour*, *minutes*, and *seconds* can be numbers, formulas that return numbers, or the names or addresses of cells that contain numbers or formulas that return numbers. *Hour* must be from 0 (midnight) to 23. *Minutes* and *seconds* each must be from 0 to 59.

To make the time number appear as the time it represents, use Range Format or Worksheet Global Format to format the cell that contains the time number.

Example:

@TIME(14,15,30)=0.594097

@TIME(B2,C2,D2)=0.594097 if the values in cells B2..D2 are 14, 15, and 30, respectively

@TIMEVALUE(*string*)

Returns the time number for the time specified in *string*. *String* must be a time expressed as a string in the form "HH:MM:SS". *String* can be a text string, a string formula, or the name or address of a cell containing a text string or string formula.

To make the time number appear as the time it represents, use Range Format or Worksheet Global Format to format the cell that contains the time number.

You can use @TIMEVALUE to convert times expressed as labels into time numbers that can be used in calculations.

Examples:

@TIMEVALUE("14:15:30")=0.594097

@TIMEVALUE(C17)=0.594097 if the value in cell C17 is "14:15:30"

@TRIM(*string*)

Removes any blank spaces that come before the text (leading blanks) or after the text (trailing blanks), and any consecutive blank spaces in *string*. *String* can be a text string, a string formula, or the name or address of a cell containing a text string or string formula.

Examples:

@TRIM( "Brown•••••••••")=Brown, where each bullet (•) represents a blank space

@TRIM(C5)=Brown if cell C5 contains "Brown•••••••••"

FIRSTNAME+LASTNAME= "Sally     Siegel" if the cell named FIRSTNAME contains "Sally     " and the cell named *Lastname* contains "Siegel".

@TRIM(FIRSTNAME)+" "+LASTNAME="Sally Siegel"

| | |
|---|---|
| @TRUE | Returns the logical value 1 (true). @TRUE does not take an argument. |
| | You can use @TRUE with @IF and @CHOOSE to display 1 (true) if a specified condition is met. |
| | Examples: |
| | @TRUE=1 |
| | @IF(B10>25,@TRUE,@FALSE)=1 (true) if the contents of cell B10 are larger than 25 |
| @UPPER(*string*) | Converts the lowercase letters in *string* to uppercase. *String* can be a text string, a string formula, or the name or address of a cell containing a text string or text formula. |
| | **Note:** @UPPER capitalizes all the letters in *string*. @PROPER capitalizes the first letter of each word in *string* and converts all other letters to lowercase. @LOWER converts all letters in *string* to lowercase. |
| | Examples: |
| | @UPPER(D4)="SIEGEL" if cell D4 contains "Siegel" |
| | @UPPER(LASTNAME)="SIEGEL" if the cell named *Lastname* contains "Siegel" |
| | @UPPER(E5)="110 PARK STREET, APT. 3" if cell E5 contains "110 Park Street, Apt. 3" |
| @VALUE(*string*) | Converts a number entered as a text string into its corresponding numeric form. *String* can be a text string, string formula, or the name or address of a cell containing a text string or string formula. *String* must contain only numbers, but they can be in the form of a standard number (1234.457), a number in scientific (E) notation (1.234E+2), or a number in any other format. |
| | **Note:** @VALUE returns ERR if *string* is a blank cell or empty string, or if it contains non-numeric characters. @VALUE ignores leading and trailing blank spaces but returns ERR if *string* contains blank spaces that separate symbols from the numbers, such as $ 1234.56. |
| | You can use @VALUE when you want to perform math calculations with numbers entered as text. |
| | **Tip:** Use @VALUE to convert strings or labels to numbers. Use @STRING to convert numbers to labels. |
| | Examples: |
| | @VALUE("110.75")=110.75 |

@VALUE("$110.75")=110.75

@VALUE("$ 110.75")=ERR

@VALUE(F3)=12345 if cell F3 contains "12345"

@VAR(*list*)  Calculates the population variance of the numbers in *list*. *List* can be a series of numbers, formulas that return numbers, or names or addresses of cells that contain numbers or formulas that return numbers, separated by commas or other argument separators.

The variance indicates the extent to which the individual numbers in a list vary from the mean of all numbers in the list. A variance of 0 indicates that all number in the list are equal.

Examples:

@VAR(11,13,33,25,41,22)=2.9E+36

@VAR(B2..B7)=2.9E+36 if range B2..B7 contains the numbers 11,13,33,25,41,22

@VLOOKUP(*x,range,column-offset*)

Returns the contents of a cell located in a specified row and column of a vertical lookup table.

A vertical lookup table is a table in which the cells in the first (leftmost) column contain numbers in ascending order from top to bottom. @VLOOKUP compares the value *x* to contents of each cell in the first column of the table specified by *range*, starting at the top cell and moving downward. When it finds the cell that contains *x* or the number closest to but not exceeding *x*, it moves along that row to the right the number of columns specified by *column-offset* and returns the contents of the cell at that location.

*X* can be an integer or the name or address of a cell that contains an integer. *Range* can be the name or address of the range that comprises the vertical lookup table. *Row-offset* can be an integer or the name or address of a cell containing an integer between 0 and 8191.

You can use @VLOOKUP to find values when a table is organized with a key variable arranged in ascending order in the leftmost column.

**Note:** For tables organized with a key variable arranged in ascending order in the top row, use the @HLOOKUP function. For tables in which you know the column and row in which a lookup value is located, use the @INDEX function.

Example:

```
F1=Help                                                          F10=Menu
  File   Edit   Options    Worksheet   Range   Copy   Move   Graph      LotusWorks
» D5: (P2) [W11] 0.11
 ─────────────────── Spreadsheet: D:\LWORKS3\LWDATA\VRATES.WK1 ───────────────┐
          A        B          C         D         E       F       G       H
   1             ANNUAL LOAN RATES
   2    Term  New Car   Used Car  Home Equity
   3     12    12.50%    12.50%    11.50%
   4     24    12.00%    12.00%    11.25%
   5     36    11.50%    11.50%    11.00%
   6     48    11.00%    11.00%    10.75%
   7     60    10.50%    11.00%    10.50%
   8
   9
  10
  11
  12
  13
  14
  15
  16
  17
                                                                     Caps
```

**FIGURE C.3:** A vertical lookup table

@VLOOKUP(36,A3..D7,3)=11% This formula tells LotusWorks to search the first column for the value 36, then move to the right three columns and return the value in the cell at that location (11%).

@YEAR(*date-number*)  Returns the number of the year in *date-number*. *Date-number* can be a date number or the name or address of a cell that contains a date number or a formula that evaluates to a date number.

You can use the @YEAR function to supply the year argument to other date or time functions.

**Tip:** You can use @DATEVALUE to supply the date number for a date that you specify in text form.

@YEAR(@NOW)=the current year

@YEAR(@DATEVALUE("07/04/1992"))=1992

@IF(@YEAR(BIRTHDATE)<=93,"September","January")

This formula states that if the year in the BIRTHDATE cell is 1993 or earlier, print September; otherwise, print January.

# D

# Macro Keynames

When you record a macro using the Options Macro Learn command, LotusWorks writes the keynames into the macro for you. When you edit a macro, however, you must write the keynames yourself. In some cases, the keyname must be enclosed within curly brackets. The following is a complete list of LotusWorks keynames for macros:

| Key | Macro Keyname |
| --- | --- |
| Letter Keys | A, B, c, etc. (Type the actual letter in either uppercase or lowercase. Macros do not distinguish between uppercase and lowercase letters.) |
| Number Keys | 1, 2, 3, etc. (Type the actual numeral.) |
| Punctuation Keys | +, –, *, /, =, !, @, #, $, ?, etc. (Type the actual punctuation mark.) |
| Spacebar | (No name. Simply press the spacebar to type a space in a macro.) |
| Function Keys | {F1}, {F2}, {F3}, etc. |
| Control+Key Combinations | {Ctrl+A}, {Ctrl+B}, {Ctrl+c}, etc. |
| Alt+Key Combinations | {Alt+A}, {Alt+B}, {Alt+c}, etc. |
| Enter | {Enter} |
| Backspace | {Backspace} |
| Tab | {Tab} |
| Right Arrow | {Right} |
| Left Arrow | {Left} |
| Up Arrow | {Up} |
| Down Arrow | {Down} |
| Page Up | {PgUp} |
| Page Down | {PgDn} |
| Home | {Home} |
| End | {End} |

| | |
|---|---|
| Insert | {Ins} |
| Delete | {Del} |
| Esc | {Esc} |

# Index

Note: the main heading "@functions" is alphabetized as it is pronounced ("at-functions"). Specific @functions are alphabetized under the term following "@" (e.g. @DATE can be found under DATE)

## A

ABS database function, 384
@ABS function, 416
absolute cell references, 230
accelerator keys
    in communications, 347-48
    cues for, 36
@ACOS function, 416-17
action buttons in dialog boxes, 34
Address example database, 188-94
    accessing the Q-ADDR database, 189
    adding a field, 189-91
    creating a telephone log table in, 192-93
    deleting a field, 191
alignment
    of headers and footers, 77
    of labels within columns, 242
    of text, 62
        word documents, 70
AlphaWorks, 5
Alt+key combinations, 26, 30. See also accelerator keys
analog communications, 331
AND operator, 138
applications, custom, 365-73
    automated telephone dialer and log, 371-72
    desktop environment, 365-70
        ideas for, 373
    macros for, 365
arithmetic operators, 202
arrow keys, scrolling with, 40
ASC database function, 384
ASCII files, importing into spreadsheets, 261-62 @ASIN function, 417
asterisks, in spreadsheet cells, 208
@ATAN function, 417
@ATAN2 function, 417
@@ function, 416
AT database function, 384
@functions, 235-39, 409-47. *See also specific functions*
    date and time, 198, 410-11
    definition of, 202

    financial, 198, 411
    logical, 198, 412
    mathematical, 198, 412-13
    special, 198, 413
    statistical, 199, 414
    string, 199, 415
    types of, 198-99, 410
Audible dialing option, 334
@AVG function, 418

## B

Backspace key, 38
backup copies
    of files
        database files, 54
        on floppy disks, 54
    of hard disk, 54
    of word documents, 63
bar graphs, 294, 299
    stacked, 295, 299
baud rate, 332, 335-36, 338
beeping, on errors, 52
binary protocols, 347
BOF database function, 385
boilerplate, 8, 58, 60, 373
    creating and using, 100-101
    in macros, 100-101
bold, 75-76
borders
    in forms, 171
    printing from spreadsheets and, 248
boxes, in forms, 171
Break-Even calculator, 320-24
bulletin boards, private, 330
business contacts, 110
Business Financial Ratios Calculator, 273-80

## C

Calc command (F9), 234-35
Calculator for Business Financial Ratios, 273-80 Cancel button, 36
CDATE database function, 385
CDOW database function, 385
cell addresses, definition of, 200
cell pointer, definition of, 201
cell references
    absolute cell references, 230

451

mixed, 230
  relative, 229-30
cells, definition of, 200
centering, text, 62
central processing units (CPUs), 18
Character delay option, 337
character fields, 114
  entering data in, 119
  maximum width of, 118
@CHAR function, 418
check boxes in dialog boxes, 34
@CHOOSE function, 418
CHR database function, 385-86
clearing flagged records, 143
click-and-drag, 26
clicking the mouse (or other pointing device), 26
Clipboard, deleted text in, 74
CLOOKUP database function, 386-87
CMONTH database function, 387
@CODE function, 419
color monitors, 19
  default settings for, 52-53
@COLS function, 419
columns, spreadsheet, 200
  adjusting widths of, 217-18
  deleting, 219-20
  hiding and unhiding columns and cells, 241-42
  inserting, 218-19
combination keys, 26
commands
  entering, 2
  issuing, 27-37
    with accelerator keys, 30
    in dialog boxes, 31-35
    dimmed menu items and, 30-31
    selecting menu and submenu items, 29-30
    sequences of commands, 37
Comma number format, 214
communications, 327-63
  automated telephone dialer and log, 371-72
  automating file and text transfers, 354
  data file transfers, 344-47
    file-transfer protocols, 344
    receiving, 346
    sending, 345
  disconnecting, 341
  E-mail, 349-50
  ideas for, 360-61
  interrupting a data transfer, 342
  login scripts for automating, 350-54, 356-60
    editing a login script, 352-53
    macro for launching a login script, 353-54, 358-60
    PC-to-PC telecommunications, login script for, 356-57
    recording a login script, 350-51
    using a login script, 352
  making the connection, 335-41
    answering, 341

dialing, 338-41
setting up and saving communications parameters, 336-38
PC-to-PC, 348-49
resources available via telephone, 327-30
setting up for, 333-35
terminal emulation, 330, 333, 338, 355
trouble-shooting, 362
viewing and capturing the communications dialog
  in a file, 343
  full-screen, 344
  on-screen, 342
CompuServe, 328
Computed rule, 125
copying
  an area of a form, 169
  database files, 54
  between databases, 181-85
    appending records from another database, 182
    extracting records to a new database, 182-83
    using data from external databases, 183-85
  formulas, 229-30
  spreadsheet data, 220-22
  text, 58
    in Word Processing service, 74
    to and from the Word Processing service, 263-64
@COUNT function, 419
counting words, 58
CRC-Xmodem file transfer protocol, 344
@CTERM function, 419-20
CTOD database function, 388
Ctrl key combinations, 26
Currency format, 214-16
custom applications, 365-73
  automated telephone dialer and log, 371-72
  desktop environment, 365-70
  ideas for, 373
  macros for, 365
customer database, fields in, 115
cutting and pasting, text, 58, 74

D

Daily Appointment Schedule and To-Do List, 265-68
database files
  adding, 122
  creating, 116-17
  deleting, 122-23
  modifying, 121-22
  renaming, 122
  upgrading to LotusWorks 3.0, 377-78
database functions, 144, 194-95. See also specific functions
  database information functions, 380
  data conversion functions, 380-81
  date functions, 381
  detailed descriptions of, 384-407

## Index

logical functions, 381-82 l
ookup functions, 382
mathematical functions, 382-83
string functions, 383
syntax of, 194-95
types of, 379-80
database information functions, 380
databases, 109-96
   Address example database, 188-94
      accessing the Q-ADDR database, 189
      adding a field, 189-91
      deleting a field, 191
   backing up, 54
   building applications based on, 112
   copying between, 181-85
   definition of, 109
   designing, 112-16
   efficient use of data in, 111-12
   entering data in, 119-21, 123-30. *See also forms below*
      character fields, 119
      date fields, 120
      forms for, 129-30
      logical fields, 120
      memo fields, 120-21
      numeric fields, 119
      rules feature, 123-29
   example, 188
   fields in. *See* fields
   finding records in, 134-43
      clearing flagged records, 143
      coumpund search expressions, 138
      dates, searching for, 140
      deleting records, 141-42 inactive records, 141
      saving, retrieving, and deleting search criteria, 140-41
      steps in conducting a search, 134-37
      strings of characters, searching for, 139-40
      writing search expressions, 137-38
   forms for, 110, 112, 162-75
      copying a block to a new position, 169
      default, 162
      deleting the contents from an area, 170
      drawing lines, 171
      editing an area of the form, 168-70
      exiting the Forms Editor, 172
      floating fields, 170
      formatting numeric fields in, 170-71
      Forms Editor, 166-68
      inserting a field, 167-68
      printing, 177-79
      print layout for, 172-75
      retrieving, 172
      steps for creating, 164-66
   functions. *See* database functions
   identifying your necessary, 111
   macros with, 185-87
   printing from, 175-81
      forms, 177-79
      merge printing (mail-merge), 179-81
      tables, 175-77
   setting up and testing, 116-23
      creating the database file and fields, 116-19
   sort order for, 143-48
      creating a new, 145-46
      deleting a, 148
      modifying a, 147-48
      saving and retrieving a, 147
      sort expressions for creating a, 143-45
      summary report tables, 159-60
   storing data for word documents in, 60-61
   tables, database, 110, 112, 148-62
      default format for, 148-49
      deleting, 152-53
      modifying, 152
      printing, 175-77
      print layout for, 153-55, 160-62
      retrieving, 151
      selecting and arranging fields, 150
      steps for creating, 149-51
      summary report tables, 155-62
   testing, 121
   uses of, 110-11
   viewing data in, 130-33
   when to use, 112-13
Database service
   File menu in, 49
   saving your work in, 38
data bits, 332, 335-36, 338
data compression, 20
data conversion functions, 380-81
data entry. *See* entering data
data fields
   creating, 116-19
   length of, 118
   maximum widths of, 118-19
   types of, 114-16
data labels, 307-8
data ranges, for graphs, 299-300, 303-4
date and/or time
   automatically printing, 78-79
   embedded, 79
   entering, in spreadsheets, 237-39
   in headers and footers, 77-78
   inserting, 58
   in word document formats, 70
date and time database functions, 381
date and time formats, 214-16
date and time @functions, 198, 410-11
date and time stamper, automatic, 373
DATE database function, 388
date fields, 114
   entering data in, 120
@DATE function, 239, 420-21

dates, searching databases for, 140
@DATEVALUE function, 421
DAY database function, 388-89
@DAY function, 421
DBF database function, 389
@DDB function, 422
default settings, changing, 51-53
Defaults item, in Setup option, 52
DELETED database function, 389
deleting
    an area of a form, 170
    fields, 191-92
    headers and footers, 78
    range names, 212-13
    records, 141-42
    search criteria, 141
    a sort order, 148
    spreadsheet rows and columns, 219-20
    a table in a database, 152-53
    text, 74-75
        restoring text deletions, 75
    typing mistakes, 38
desktop environment, custom, 365-70
dialing, 338-41
    from a database, 187-88
    modem, 340-41
    a voice call manually and switching to data, 339-40
Dialing prefix option, 334
dialog boxes, 29, 31-35
    command devices in, 31-34
    definition of, 31
    exiting, 36
    navigating in, 35
Dial type option, 334
DIF files
    exporting spreadsheet data to, 262-63
    importing, into spreadsheets, 261-62
digital communications, 331
dimmed menu items, 30-31
Direct connect option, 334
directories, 9. *See also* subdirectories
    Working, default setting for, 52
directory path, saving your work and, 39
disk storage, 18
DLIST database function, 389
document formats, 61-62
    consistent, 60
    designing and launching, 58
    launching with macros, 107
    setting up and saving, 67-71
DOS commands, 9
DOS (Disk Operating System), accessing, 47
dot-matrix printers, 19
double-clicking, 26
DOW database function, 389-90
dragging the mouse (or other pointing device), 26
DTOC database function, 390

DTOC function, 140
duplicate records, deleting, 142

E

Echo typed option, 332, 337
economical writing, 59-62
editing
    forms, 166-68
        an area of the form, 168-70
    headers and footers, 78
    "intelligent," 82
    spreadsheet data, 209
    spreadsheet macros, 261
    your writing, 61
Edit Line, 25
Edit menu, 49
E-mail (electronic mail), 329-30, 349-50, 373
EMS (expanded memory), 52
entering data, 37-38
    in databases. *See* databases, entering data in in spreadsheets, 207-8
entering formulas, 225
envelopes, printing, 99-100
EOF database function, 390
equipment options, 17-21
erasing
    typing mistakes, 38
@ERR function, 422
errors, beeping on, 52
Esc key, 36
@EXACT function, 422-23
EXIST database function, 390-91
exiting
    from DOS Access feature, 47
    from LotusWorks, 54-55
    from Setup screen, 53
expanded memory (EMS), 52
EXP database function, 391
@EXP function, 423
extended memory (XMS), 52

F

@FALSE function, 423
FIELD database function, 391
fields
    character, 114
        entering data in, 119
        maximum width of, 118
    data
        creating, 116-19
        length of, 118
        maximum widths of, 118-19

Index **455**

    types of, 114-16
  date, 114
    entering data in, 120
  deleting, 191-92
  floating, 170
  inserting, 189-91
  logical, 114-15
    entering data in, 120
    length of, 118
  memo, 115-16
    entering data in, 120
    size of, 119
  numeric, 114
    entering data in, 119
    formatting, 170-71
    maximum width of, 118
figures, automatic numbering of, 79-80
File menu, 49-50
filename extensions, 38
  for database files, 54
  for word documents, 66
  file names, 12
    for word documents, 63
File Print Screen preview option, 73
File Retrieve command, 39
files, organizing your, 8-14
File Save command, 38
File Transfer Combine command, 89-90
file-transfer protocols, 333, 344
financial @functions, 198, 411
financial projections, 289
financial ratios, calculator for, 273-80
financial reports, 8
financial statement, interactive, 280-88
@FIND function, 423-24
Fixed number format, 214
flagging records, for deletion, 141-43
fonts. *See* typefaces
footers. *See* headers and footers
FOR database function, 391-92
formats, of word processing documents
form letters, 8
forms, database, 129-30, 162-75
  copying a block to a new position, 169
  deleting the contents from an area, 170
  drawing lines in, 171
  editing an area of, 168-70
  exiting the Forms Editor, 172
  floating fields in, 170
  formatting numeric fields in, 170-71
  Forms Editor for creating or modifying, 166-68
  inserting a field, 167-68
  printing, 177-79
  print layout for, 172-75
  retrieving, 172
  steps for creating, 164-66
Forms Editor, 166-68

  drawing lines in, 171
  exiting, 172
Formula rule, 124
formulas
  cell pointing and, 226
  converting formulas to values, 231-32
  copying and moving formulas, 229
  entering, 225
  examples of, 225
  finding cells by, 232-33
  logical, 201-2
  numeric, 201
  operators in, 226-27
  order of precedence of operators in, 228-29
  relative, absolute and mixed cell references in, 229-31 string, 201
  types of, 201-2
  writing, 224-25
    macros for, 258-59
Form view, 131-33
full-duplex, 332
function keys, 26
F-UPPER database function, 392
@FV function, 424

### G

General number format, 215
graphical user interface (GUI), 19, 24
Graphics mode, as option in Screen item, 53
graphs, 291-325
  bar, 294, 299
    stacked, 295, 299
  data ranges for, 299-300, 303-4
  examples of
    Break-Even calculator, 320-24
    Where Our $$ Come From, Where Our $$ Go, 317-20
  generating, 301
  ideas for, 324-25
  labels, 307-8
  legends, 305-6
  line, 293, 299
  naming and saving, 314
  pie, 300
  previewing, 304
  printing, 315-16
  retrieving, 315
  saying it with, 292-93
  scale of, 310-15
    adjusting, 310-11
    formatting numbers on the X- and Y-axes, 312-13
    grid lines, 313
    quitting the Graph Options submenu and reviewing your work, 313

skip factor, 312
suppressing the scale unit indicator, 311
selecting and deselecting symbols and lines on, 304
specifying type of, 301-2
titles, 306-7
types of, 293-98
in word documents, 91-92, 316-17
XY, 296, 299
grid lines, on graphs, 313

## H

half-duplex, 332
hard disks, 18
backing up, 54
headers and footers
automatic numbering of pages, figures and tables in, 79-80
creating, 76-79
of database tables, 154-55
deleting, 78
editing, 78
entering, 76-78
in forms, 174-75
printing from spreadsheets and, 248-49
for second and subsequent pages of letters, 103-4
starting page for, 78
in word document formats, 70
in word documents, 62
help
contextual, 45
on-screen, 45-46
Hidden number format, 215
@HLOOKUP function, 253-55, 425-26
Horizontal Scroll Bar, 25
@HOUR function, 426
hyphenating, 81

## I

IF database function, 392-93
@IF function, 195, 236-37, 426-27
IIF database function, 393
Increment rule, 127
indents, for word document formats, 69
@INDEX function, 427-28
information boxes in dialog boxes, 34
information services, on-line, 327-28
Initialize rule, 125
Initial Numbers setting, 80
installing LotusWorks 3.0, 21-24
Install program, 22
INT database function, 393
Interactive Financial Statement, 280-88

@INT function, 428
inventory, tracking, 289
INVERT database function, 393
@IRR function, 428
ISALPHA database function, 393
ISBLANK database function, 394
@ISERR function, 428-29
ISLOWER database function, 394
@ISNA function, 429
@ISNUMBER function, 429
@ISSTRING function, 429-30
ISUPPER database function, 394
italic, 75-76
Iterations option, recalculating spreadsheets and, 235

## K

Kermit file transfer protocol, 344
keyboard, 20
scrolling from the, 40-41
selecting menu and submenu items with the, 30
using dialog boxes with the, 35
key combinations, 26
keyfield, in Lookup expressions, 184
keynames, macro, 449-50

## L

labels
graph, 307-8
printing, 177-81
in spreadsheets
aligning within columns, 242
definition of, 201
entering, 207-8
landscape orientation, 93
LANs (local area networks), 21
laser printers, 19
LEFT database function, 394
@LEFT function, 430
legends, graph, 305-6
LEN database function, 395
@LENGTH function, 430
letters
form, 8
sample, 103-4
Line delay option, 337
line graphs, 293, 299
lines, in forms, 171
list boxes in dialog boxes, 34
LIST database function, 395-96
lists, 8, 110
@LN function, 430-31
Loan Amortization Schedule, 269-73

Index **457**

local area networks (LANs), 21
LOG database function, 396
@LOG function, 431
logging telephone calls
    in Address example database, 192-93
    from a database, 187-88
logical database functions, 381-82
logical fields, 114-15
    entering data in, 120
    length of, 118
logical formulas, 201
logical @functions, 198, 412
logical operators, 202, 227
login scripts
    editing, 352-53
    macro for launching, 353-54, 358-60
    for PC-to-PC telecommunications, 356-57
    recording, 350-51
    using, 352
LOOKUP database function, 183-85, 382, 396-97
lookup database functions, 382
@LOOKUP function, 253-55
Lookup rule, 126
lookup tables, in spreadsheets, 253-55
Lotus 1-2-3, 4-5
LotusWorks 3.0
    exiting from, 54-55
    first-time computer users and, 2
    installing, 21-22
    limits of, 4-5
    maximizing your productivity with. *See* productivity, maximizing your
    moving around in, 27
    starting, 23
    upgrading from previous versions of, 5
    upgrading to, 375-78
    uses of, 2-3
LotusWorks menu item, 48
LotusWorks Screen, 23-25
    LotusWorks menu item for accessing, 48
    opening a service from, 37
LOWER database function, 398
@LOWER function, 431
LTRIM database function, 398
LWDATA subdirectory, 52
LWD file name extension, 66

## M

macros
    boilerplate in, 100-101
    for custom applications, 365
    with databases, 185-87
    ideas for, 373
    keynames in, 449-50

launching document formats with, 107
    spreadsheet, 257-61
        for creating labels and formulas, 259-60
        editing, 261
        for retrieving a spreadsheet, 257-58
        for writing a formula, 258-59
    stored data for word documents in, 60
mailing labels, printing, 100
mail-merge. *See* merge printing mainframe computer systems, 330
Manual rule, 127
margins
    of database tables, 154
    of forms, 174
    for headers and footers, 77
    for word document formats, 68
mathematical database functions, 382-83
mathematical @functions, 198, 412-13
MAX database function, 398
@MAX function, 431
memo, sample, 102-3
Memo Editor, 120
memo fields, 115-16
    entering data in, 120
    size of, 119
memory, 4, 18
Menu Line, 24
menu prompts, 52
menus, 28, 48-51
    common, 49-50
    LotusWorks menu item, 48
    selecting items from, 29-30
    service-specific, 51
merge printing (mail-merge), 57-58, 95-99
    databases for, 110, 112, 181
@MID function, 431-32
Midnight color setup, 53
MIN database function, 398
@MIN function, 432
@MINUTE function, 432
mixed cell references, 230
MOD database function, 398
modem, 331
Modem item, in Setup option, 53
Modem port option, 334
modems, 20-21
@MOD function, 432
modifying, a table in a database, 152 monitors, 19
MONTH database function, 399
@MONTH function, 433
mouse, 20
    procedures for using the, 26
    scrolling with a, 41-42
    selecting menu and submenu items with a, 30
        switching among windows with a, 43
    using dialog boxes with a, 35
Mouse option, Setup option's Defaults item, 52

mouse procedures, for moving around in LotusWorks, 27
moving
    formulas, 229
    spreadsheet data, 222-24
    text, 58
    windows, 43-44
MS-DOS directories and commands, 9

## N

@NA function, 433
navigating, 27
Neon color setup, 53
New line option, 337-38
@N function, 433
NOT operator, 138
@NOW function, 433-34
@NPV function, 434
null modem cable, 330
number formats, 213-16
    in forms, 171
    on X- and Y-axes, 312-13
numbering
    figures or tables, 58
        automatically, 62, 79-80
        setting initial numbers, 80-81
    pages, 58
        automatically, 62, 79-80, 154, 173
        of database tables, 154
        setting initial numbers, 80-81
numeric fields, 114
    entering data in, 119
    formatting, 170-71
    maximum width of, 118
numeric formulas, 201
numeric operators, 226
    in rule expressions, 128

## O

1K CRC-Xmodem file transfer protocol, 344
on-line information services, 327-28
operators
    in formulas, 202
    logical, 227
    numeric, 226
    order or precedence of, 228-29
    in rule expressions, 128
    in search expressions, 139
    string, 226
Options menu, 50
Options Windows Placement command, 44
Options Window Zoom command, 44
OR operator, 138
outlining, writing and, 59

## P

page breaks, in word documents, 82
page length
    of database tables, 154
    of forms, 173-74
page numbers, 62. *See also* numbering, pages
in headers and footers, 77
panes, viewing spreadsheets through, 251-53
parity, 332, 335-36, 338
pasting. *See* cutting and pasting
path, saving your work and, 39
PATTERN database function, 399
PC-to-PC telecommunications, 330, 348-49
Percent, 214
pie charts, 300
@PI function, 435
+/- format, 215
@PMT function, 435
pointing devices, 19-20
    procedures for using, 26
pop-up boxes in dialog boxes, 34
portrait orientation, 93
previewing
    graphs, 304
    word documents, 72-73
Printer item, in Setup option, 53
printers, 19
    default settings for, 53
    macros for, 373
    startup strings for, printing from spreadsheets and, 249
printing
    from databases, 175-81
        forms, 177-79
        merge printing (mail-merge), 179-81
        tables, 175-77
    envelopes, 99-100
    graphs, 315-16
    mailing labels, 100
    merge, 57-58, 95-99
        databases for, 110, 112, 181
    merge documents, 97-99
    from spreadsheets, 247-50
    summary report tables, 162
    word documents, 92-94
print layout
    for forms, 172-75
    for a table, 153-55
        summary report tables, 160-62
productivity, maximizing your, 6-14
    analyzing y paperwork, 7-8
    automating everything, 13
    creating your own tools and menus, 14
    file and directory management, 8-12

## Index 459

integrating LotusWorks as your silent partner, 7
keeping everything clear and simple, 14
saving your setups, 12
taking it easy, 14
using the same data over and over, 12
work-saving as a goal, 6-7
project management, using spreadsheets for, 289
Prompt line, 24, 25
proofreading, 63
@PROPER function, 436
protecting, spreadsheets and cells, 246-47
pull-down menus. *See* menus @PV function, 436

### Q

Q-ADDRS.DBF, 189
Quickstart spreadsheets, modifying, 264-65
quotation marks
 in rule expressions, 129
 in search expressions, 138

### R

radio buttons in dialog boxes, 34
RAND database function, 399-400
@RAND function, 437
Random Access Memory (RAM), 18
range addresses, 200
range names
 creating, 211-12
 deleting, 212-13
 printing from spreadsheets and, 247
 viewing, 212
Range Protect command, 54
ranges
 definition of, 200
 multiple, 251
 printing from spreadsheets and, 247-48
Range Unprotect command, 54
@RATE function, 437
recalculating spreadsheets, 233-35
RECCOUNT database function, 400
RECNO database function, 400
records, 183-85. *See also* databases
RECSIZE database function, 400
Redial delay option, 338
relative cell references, 229-31
renaming, fields, 122
@REPEAT function, 437-38
@REPLACE function, 438
REPLICATE database function, 400
reports
 printing, for spreadsheets, 247-50
 sample, 104-6
Resize button, 44

restoring, text deletions, 75
retrieving
 graphs, 315
 a saved file, 39
 search criteria, 140
 a sort order, 147
 a spreadsheet, macro for, 257-58
 a table in a database, 151
revising your writing, 61, 74-75
RIGHT database function, 400
@RIGHT function, 438
ROUND database function, 401
@ROUND function, 438-39
rows, spreadsheet, 200
 deleting, 219-20
 inserting, 218-19
@ROWS function, 439
RTRIM database function, 401
rule expressions, writing, 127-29
Rules feature, in databases, 123-29
 Computed rule, 125
 Formula rule, 124
 Increment rule, 127
 Initialize rule, 125
 Lookup rule, 126
 Manual rule, 127
 Skip rule, 126
 Update rule, 126
 Verify rule, 125
 writing rule expressions, 127-29

### S

safeguarding your data, 53-54
saving, 38-39
 frequency of, 53
 graphs, 314
 search criteria, 140
 a sort order, 147
 word document formats, 71
 word documents, 66, 71-72
scale of graphs. *See* graphs, scale of
Scientific number format, 214
screen
 LotusWorks (main menu), 23-25
 Start-up screen, 23
screen display, default settings for, 52-53
Screen item, in Setup option, 52-53
scrolling, 40-42
search criteria, 134-41
 saving, retrieving, and deleting, 140-41
search expressions, writing, 137-38
searching and replacing text in word documents, 87-88
searching databases. *See* databases, finding records in
@SECOND function, 439-40

selecting
    cells and ranges, 208-9
    definition of, 35
    menu and submenu items, 29-30
    symbols and lines on graphs, 304
    text blocks, 73
services, opening, 37
Setup option, in LotusWorks Screen, 51-53
    Defaults item in, 52
    exiting, 53
    Modem item in, 53
    Printer item in, 53
    Screen item in, 52-53
Setup program, 51
setups
    saving your, 13
    subdirectory structure and, 9
setup string for printers, 53
@S function, 439
@SIN function, 440
sizing windows, 43-44
skip factor, 312
Skip rule, 126
@SLN function, 440
Snowfall color setup, 53
sorting, spreadsheet rows based on data, 243-46
sort order of databases, 143-48
    creating a new, 145-46
    deleting a, 148
    modifying a, 147-48
    saving and retrieving a, 147
    sort expressions for creating a, 143-45
    summary report tables, 159-60
SOUNDEX database function, 401-2
SPACE database function, 402
spacing, in word document formats, 69
special @functions, 198, 413
spell checking, 58, 82-85
    adding words to the dictionary, 85
    all words, 84-85
    a single word, 83-84
spreadsheets, 197-290. *See also* graphs
    appearance of, 240-47
        aligning labels within columns, 242
        creating a line in a cell or row, 242-43
        hiding and unhiding columns and cells, 241-42
        protecting and unprotecting cells and spreadsheets, 246-47
        sorting rows based on data, 243-46
        titles, 240-41
    combining data from other, 255-56
    copying data to and from the Word Processing service, 263-64
    current, definition of, 202
    definition of, 200
    designing, 202-3
    example, 265-88
    Calculator for Business Financial Ratios, 273-80
    Daily Appointment Schedule and To-Do List, 265-68
    Interactive Financial Statement, 280-88
    Loan Amortization Schedule, 269-73
    exporting data from, 262-63
    extracting selected cell contents from, 256
    formulas in, 224-39
        cell pointing, 226
        converting formulas to values, 231-32
        copying and moving formulas, 229
        @DATE and @TIME functions, 239
        dates and times, entering, 237-39
        entering, 225
        examples of, 225
        finding cells by value or formula, 232-33
        @functions, 235-36
        IF function, 236-37
        operators, 226-27
        order or precedence of operators, 228-29
        recalculating spreadsheets, 233-35
        relative, absolute and mixed cell references, 229-31
        writing, 224-25
    ideas for, 289-90
    importing data into, 261-62
    including data from, in word documents, 90-92
    labels in
        aligning within columns, 242
        definition of, 201
        entering, 207-8
    lookup tables in, 253-55
    macros for, 257-61
        for creating labels and formulas, 259-60
        editing, 261
        for retrieving a spreadsheet, 257-58
        for writing a formula, 258
    multiple ranges within, 251
    with multiple versus single grids of data, 204
    printing rps from, 247-50
    Quickstart, modifying, 264-65
    setting up and saving, 204-24
        cell or range contents, 210
        column widths, 217-18
        deleting rows and columns, 219-20
        editing data, 209
        entering text and numbers into cells, 207-8
        inserting rows and columns, 218
        moving data, 222-24
        number formats, changing, 213-16
        practice spreadsheet, building a, 205-7
        range names: creating, viewing and deleting, 211
        selecting and cells and ranges for further action, 208-9
        steps in building a spreadsheet, 204-4
    terms used in, 200-202
    viewing through window panes, 251-53
    when to use, 199

Index **461**

working smart with, 197-99
SQRT database function, 402
@SQRT function, 441
stacked bar graphs, 295, 299
starting LotusWorks, 23
statistical @functions, 199, 414
Status Line, 25
@STD function, 441
stop bits, 332, 335-36, 338
stored data, for word documents, 60-61
STR database function, 402-3
string database functions, 383
string formulas, 201
@STRING function, 441
string @functions, 199, 415
string operators, 128-29, 202, 226
STUFF database function, 403
Style menu, in Word Processing service, 67-68
styles, for word documents, 101-2
subdirectories, managing your, 9-12
submenus, 28
    exiting, 36
    selecting items from, 29-30
SUBSTR database function, 403-4
@SUM function, 441-42
summary report tables, 155-62
    creating, 156-58
    printing, 162
    print layout for, 160-62
    sort order for, 159-60
@SYD function, 442
synonyms, finding, 85-86

### T

Tab key, navigating in dialog boxes with, 35
table lookups, in spreadsheets, 253-55
tables
    automatic numbering of, 79-80
    database, 110, 112, 148-62
        default format for, 148-49
        deleting, 152-53
        modifying, 152
        printing, 175-77
        print layout for, 153-55, 160-62
        retrieving, 151
        selecting and arranging fields, 150
        steps for creating, 149-51
        summary report tables, 155-62
Table view, 130, 133
tab settings, for word document formats, 68
@TAN function, 442-43
task windows. *See* windows, LotusWorks
telecommunications. *See* communications
telephone calls, dialing and logging from a database, 187-88
telephone log table, creating a, in Address example database, 192-93
@TERM function, 443
terminal emulation, 330, 333, 338, 355
Terminal option, 335
text. *See* word documents
text blocks, 73-75
    in word documents, 73-75
text boxes in dialog boxes, 34
Text file transfer protocol, 344
Text format, 215
text labels. *See* labels
Text mode, as option in Screen item, 53
thesaurus, 58, 85-86
time. *See* date and/or time
TIME database function, 404
@TIME function, 239, 444
time @functions. *See* date and time @functions
@TIMEVALUE function, 444
Title Line, 25
titles
    graph, 306-7
    spreadsheet, 240-41
Top Line, 24
trackball, 20
TRIM database function, 404
@TRIM function, 444
@TRUE function, 445
tutorial, 46
type attributes
    assigning, 75-76
    for word document formats, 68
typefaces (fonts), 61
    document formats, 67-68
typing, entering distinguished from, 38

### U

underlining, 75-76
Update rule, 126
Upgrade program, 5
UPPER database function, 405
@UPPER function, 445
Use DOS option, 47, 52

### V

VAL database function, 405
@VALUE function, 445-46
@VAR function, 446
Verify rule, 125
Vertical Scroll Bar, 25
viewing, range names, 212
@VLOOKUP function, 446-47

## W

"What If" analyses, 290
window panes, viewing spreadsheets through, 251-53
  windows, spreadsheet, definition of, 202
windows, LotusWorks
  common features of, 24-25
  design of, 24
  multiple, 42-45
    closing, 45
    for drafting and editing word documents, 102
    opening, 43
    sizing and moving, 43-44
    switching among, 43
  scrolling contents of, 40-42
WORD database function, 405
  word documents, 57-107. *See also* document formats
  combining, 89-90
  date and/or time in
    automatic printing of 78-79
    headers and footers, 77-78
  drafts of, 61, 63
  economical writing techniques, 59-62
  editing and revising, 61
  examples of, 102-6
  filename extensions for, 66
  formats of, 7, 9
  graphs and spreadsheet data in, 90-92
  graphs in, 316-17
  headers and footers in, 76-79
  hyphenating words in, 81
  multiple windows for drafting and editing, 102
  numbering of pages, figures and tables in, 79-80
  page breaks in, 82
  previewing, 72-73
  printing, 92-94
    merge documents, 97-99
  revising, 74
  saving, 66, 71-72
  searching and replacing text in, 87-88
  sharing the workload of creating, 62-63
    spell checking, 82-85
    starting, 64-67
    steps in creating and printing, 64
    styles for, 101-2
    text blocks in, 73
    type attributes of, 75-76
word-matching feature, 58
word processing files
  maximum size of, 4
  upgrading from previous versions of, 5
  upgrading to LotusWorks 3.0, 375-76
Word Processing service, 57-107. *Seealso* word documents
  automating tasks in, 57-58
  copying data between spreadsheets and, 263-64
  correcting typing mistakes in, 38
  entering data in, 37

exiting without saving, 67
merge printing in, 95-99
Working Directory default setting, 52
work-saving as a goal, 6-7
Work Space, 25
writing. *See also* word documents; Word Processing service
  consistent formats and, 60
  economical, 59-62
  planning your, 59
  stored data and, 60
W-UPPER database function, 406

## X

Xmodem file transfer protocol, 344
XMS (extended memory), 52
Xon/Xoff, 332, 337
XY graphs, 296, 299

## Y

YEAR database function, 406
@YEAR function, 447

## Z

ZBLANK database function, 406-7